This book belongs
to Terence Winnie
return to Dr. Dunkles'
off.

GERMANY
2000 YEARS

GERMANY
2000 YEARS

KURT F. REINHARDT
Professor of Germanic Languages
Stanford University

REVISED EDITION

VOLUME I

The Rise and Fall of the "Holy Empire"

FREDERICK UNGAR PUBLISHING CO.
New York

EIGHTH PRINTING, 1972
REVISED EDITION

ISBN 0-8044-6691-2 set
ISBN 0-8044-6692-0 vol. I
ISBN 0-8044-6693-9 vol. II

Library of Congress Catalog Card No. 60-53139

Printed in the United States of America

TO MY WIFE

PREFACE TO
THE SECOND EDITION

More than ten years have passed since this book was first published. Although this new edition appears with only minor changes, a few qualifying remarks seem to be in order. While it has been found necessary to revise and supplement the bibliography, both external and personal circumstances make it inadvisable at this time to append another section covering the political and cultural history of Germany during the rise and fall of the Nazi Empire and during and following World War II. This addition is planned, however, for the not too distant future. Moreover, what the author stated in the Preface to the edition of 1949, is still essentially valid: (1) "There is no lack of able (though at times one-sided) presentations of the rise and fall of Germany under National Socialism." (2) "The author is convinced that the most recent phase of German history is [still] too close to the historian's field of vision to allow for a perspective that is duly proportioned and therefore objectively reliable. The author has therefore confined himself to making visible and intelligible certain trends in recent German history which eventually converged in the rise of National Socialism."

It remains equally true that even after the passage of more than a decade there is to this date "lacking a comprehensive survey presenting the history of Germany in its entirety, *in both its political and cultural aspects and implications.*" And the author feels as strongly as he did in 1949 that "the attempt to write such a history single-handed is such a formidable undertaking that it might almost appear presumptuous." He has embarked on this venture "fully conscious of the necessarily fragmentary nature of a work of this scope and of certain almost inevitable weaknesses in the intended synthesis. He has approached his task guided by the conviction that political and cultural history are actually inseparable, mutually mirroring and illuminating each other, so that the one cannot really be comprehended and appreciated apart from the other. In trying to integrate both, the author has scrupulously endeavored to avoid shallow popularization on the one hand and the technical intricacies of detailed specialized research on the other."

Each section dealing with a particular period in German history opens with a chronological table and a cursory account of the main political currents and events. This is followed by a discussion of the major cultural trends and movements in the several fields of human endeavor and accomplishment: in state and society; in political, economic, and social theory and practice; in literature, the plastic arts, and in music; in science and technology; in education, philosophy, and religion.

The entire history of Germany is viewed as embedded in the larger frame and context of European history and thus as an integral part of the "Western Tradition" of thought and culture. If there is any lesson to be learned from two thousand years of German history, it is the realization that Germany has always been most substantially herself when and as long as she remained conscious of her European heritage, anchorage, and responsibility, and that a temporary loss of this "European consciousness" always signified a betrayal inviting disaster and exacting retribution. As a bridge—politically and culturally—between eastern and western Europe, Germany has fulfilled in the past an important and vital function, and she may—despite the tragedy of the present partition—be destined to fulfill a similar function in the future.

Many things, of course, have changed in the two Germanies which emerged from the ruins and ashes of World War II. And while it has become customary in the West to view "the Germany that Adenauer built" with sanguine admiration and excessive expectations, some cautioning against overconfidence might aid in keeping our perspective duly balanced. History judges nations not so much by "economic miracles"—impressive though they may be—but rather by the less spectacular yet more enduring miracles of the mind and the spirit. And in this respect even Western Germany presents a picture that is not altogether inspiring.

The words which Karl Jaspers wrote in 1949 (in *The Question of War Guilt*), have today a prophetic ring: "There exists something in our national tradition, something mighty and threatening, which has become our moral ruin. . . . But what erupted in Germany has been on its way in the entire Western World as a spiritual crisis, *a crisis of faith*. This fact does not diminish our guilt. . . . But the consciousness of *the common human crisis* liberates us from the feeling of absolute isolation. And, as it concerns every human being, it may teach others a lesson. . . . If the chain of evil is not radically broken, the victors may eventually find themselves in the same situation in which we found ourselves, and with them all mankind."

Two things should be clearly and unflinchingly observed: the first is the fact that the twelve years of the Hitler tyranny have inflicted such deep wounds on the German spirit (in East and West) that the healing process will take many decades and several generations. Referring to the ravages wrought by these terrible years, Walter Muschg, a prominent Swiss literary critic and a keen observer of German intellectual affairs, entitled one of his most widely read books, "The Destruction of German Literature."*[1] The destruction of which Muschg speaks extends of course far beyond the spheres of literature and the arts: it is in its consequences almost all-pervasive. This state of affairs should not be obscured by the "miracles" of economic and political recovery in Western Germany.

---

* Walter Muschg, *Die Zerstörung der deutschen Literatur* (Bern: A. Francke Verlag, 3rd edition, 1958), cf. especially pp. 7-56.

The second observation—to which both Karl Jaspers and Walter Muschg call attention—relates to the *universal range* of certain corrosive and destructive tendencies of the present age and thus to the "common human crisis." The German philosopher Martin Heidegger, in a speech delivered in 1955, in the small southern German town of Messkirch (Heidegger's birth place), in commemoration of the nineteenth century composer Konradin Kreutzer, distinguishes between two essentially different types of "thinking": the one technical, calculating, statistically-oriented, and ultimately reducible to the "will-to-power" or a basically nihilistic "will to will"; the other reflective, meditative, contemplative and profoundly individualistic—both equally legitimate and, in a manner of speaking, "successful" in their own proper spheres and limits. But the gravest danger arises—and herein lies for Heidegger the most ominous threat of the "atomic age"—when the technological and basically impersonal and collectivist type of thinking invades and eventually drowns out completely the philosophic-meditative-individualistic processes of thought. What then follows is, according to Walter Muschg, "the power-lessness of the spirit," "the open rebellion against the intellect. . . . The great personalities, who *in solitude* create the extraordinary, are then no longer either possible or desirable. . . . And collectivism exerts its iron rule with devastating and all-destructive force even in the so-called 'free' nations": in the ghostly unreality and superficiality of the mass media of communication which, in Jeremias Gotthelf's telling phrase, "whirl about millions of human beings like so many specks of dust in the streets." It is this tyrannical rule of the mass media and their proponents—the "organization-men"—which facilitates the cultivation of "golden mediocrity" by killing the imaginative powers of the human person and by encouraging a soothing and comfortable kind of indolent passivity:

"And though you had a thousand words,
The Word, the Word is dead!" (Karl Wolfskehl)

It is against this dual threat—the anti-intellectual and essentially nihilistic "will-to-power" and the anti-personalist *Vermassung*—that Germany, in consonance with the "Western Tradition," will have to take her stand. She will have to do it offensively rather than merely in self-defense; and she must be armed with a faith at least as whole-hearted as are the totalitarian idolatries of several shades. There is no other way to prevail in view of the unprecedented challenges which confront mankind with the advent of the atomic age.

GERMANY: 2000 YEARS was generally well received a decade ago. After the book had been out of print for several years, the author and the new publisher finally decided to respond to the many requests they received from individuals, libraries, and especially from colleagues in departments of history and of German in United States colleges and universities, by preparing this new edition. The author wishes to express his gratitude to the original publishers of the work, the Bruce Publishing Company in Milwaukee, for generously relinquishing their publishing rights.

The author acknowledges gratefully much constructive criticism and many helpful suggestions for improvement of the text, some of which are embodied in the present edition. There were, as was to be expected, a few snipers— little totalitarians of the Right and of the Left—who were disturbed by the attempt to present the history of Germany *sine ira et studio*. Because I had stated in the original Preface that "the author has in this book no thesis to advance and no ax to grind," one critic asked caustically, "Why then did he write the book?" This question requires of course no answer and no comment. Another reviewer—a history professor in a prominent Catholic university— pointed an accusing "index"-finger at my gentle and sympathetic treatment of Kierkegaard and my ironic discussion of his profound influence on contemporary Protestant and Catholic theology. He suspected that my reason for doing this was the desire to fall in line with a fashionable fad. What Professor Shanahan did not suspect was the fact that I had been wrestling with Kierkegaard for more than four decades and was therefore not altogether unaware of what I was talking about.

As far as my hopes, desires, and ambitions with regard to this undertaking are concerned, they have remained as sober and restrained as they were when I wrote in the Preface of 1949: I hope "that to some extent at least I may have succeeded in telling (to use Leopold von Ranke's words) *"wie es eigentlich gewesen ist."*

Finally, I wish to express again my gratitude to the *Herder-Verlag* in Freiburg im Breisgau (Germany) for permission to utilize several of the excellent historical maps produced by the members of this firm's editorial staff (with whom I had the privilege of being associated from 1922–1925). I am also indebted to my colleague in the Department of Modern European Languages at Stanford University, Dr. Kurt Mueller-Vollmer, for material aid in revising and supplementing the bibliography.

Kurt F. Reinhardt

Stanford University, California
December, 1960

PREFACE

This book, the fruit of many years of teaching and study, aims at filling a real gap in the field of German historiography. There are available in the German language several comprehensive works dealing with either the political or cultural history of Germany. And there are some recent publications in the English language which in their discussion of German political history pay at least passing attention to the cultural context and background. This is true in particular of such presentations as E. F. Henderson's *A Short History of Germany* (New York: The Macmillan Co., 1916), 2 vols.; George N. Shuster's and Arnold Bergstraesser's *Germany: A Short History* (New York: W. W. Norton & Co., 1944); Prince Hubertus zu Loewenstein's *The Germans in History* (New York: Columbia University Press, 1945); and Veit Valentin's *The German People* (New York: Alfred A. Knopf, 1946). Ernst Richard's *History of German Civilization* (New York: The Macmillan Co., 1911) was at the time of its publication an interesting and praiseworthy attempt to present a condensed survey of German cultural history with occasional sidelights on political history. But to the present-day reader its perspective and scope appear as too limited. There is thus completely lacking a comprehensive and up-to-date survey presenting the history of Germany in its entirety, *in both its political and cultural aspects.*

The attempt to write such a history is, however, such a formidable undertaking that it might almost seem presumptuous. If the author of this book has nevertheless embarked upon this venture, he has done so fully conscious of the necessarily fragmentary nature of a work of this scope and of certain almost inevitable weaknesses in the intended synthesis. He has approached his task prompted and guided by the conviction that political and cultural history are historically and actually inseparable, mutually illuminating and supplementing each other, so that the one cannot really be comprehended and appreciated apart from the other. In trying to integrate both, the author has scrupulously endeavored to avoid shallow popularization on the one hand and the technical intricacies of detailed specialized knowledge on the other. To what extent he has been successful in this endeavor is for the reader to judge.

Each section dealing with a particular period in German history opens with a chronological table and a cursory account of political events. This is followed by a discussion of the major cultural trends and movements in the several fields of human endeavor and accomplishment: in the spheres of state and society; in political, economic, and social theory and practice; in literature, the plastic arts, and in music; in science and technics; in education, philosophy, and religion.

That the historical survey comes to a halt in 1933, the year of the National Socialist revolution, may at first glance seem rather arbitrary. The reason for not going beyond that date is twofold: in the first place there is no lack of able (if at times one-sided) presentations of the rise and fall of Germany under National Socialism; and, secondly, the author is convinced that this most recent phase of German history is too close to the historian's field of vision to allow for a perspective that is duly proportioned and therefore objectively valid. The author has thus confined himself to making visible and intelligible certain trends in recent German history which eventually converged in the rise of National Socialism. "There exists," writes Karl Jaspers in *Die Schuldfrage* (Heidelberg, 1946), "something in our national tradition, something mighty and threatening, which has become our moral ruin." But, he continues, "what erupted in Germany has been on its way in the entire western world as a spiritual crisis, a crisis of faith. This fact does not diminish our guilt. . . . But the consciousness of the common human crisis liberates us from the feeling of absolute isolation. And, as it concerns every human being, it may teach others a lesson. . . . If the chain of evil is not radically broken, the victors may eventually find themselves in the same situation in which we found ourselves, and with them all mankind."

The history of Germany is viewed in this book as embedded within the larger frame and context of Europe and European history and thus as an integral part of the "Western Tradition" of thought and culture. If there is any lesson to be gleaned from two thousand years of German history, it may be said to be the realization that Germany is always most substantially herself when and as long as she remains conscious of her European anchorage, inheritance, and responsibility, and that the temporary loss of this consciousness entails a betrayal that invites disaster and exacts retribution. As a bridge — politically and culturally — between eastern and western Europe, Germany has fulfilled an important function in the European past, and she may well be destined to fulfill a similar function in the future. However, the author has in this book no thesis to advance and no ax to grind. He merely hopes that to some extent, at least, he may have succeeded in telling (to use Leopold von Ranke's words) *"wie es eigentlich gewesen ist."*

Both the author and the publisher wish to express their gratitude to the *Herder Verlag* in Freiburg im Breisgau, and especially to Dr. Theophil Herder-Dorneich, the present head of the German publishing firm, for permission to utilize several of the excellent historical maps produced by the members of Herder's editorial staff (with whom the author had the privilege of being associated from 1922 to 1925) and contained in the volumes of the encyclopedia *Der Grosse Herder*. The perusal of two standard works on German cultural history, published by the *Herder Verlag* (F. Zoepfl's *Deutsche Kulturgeschichte,* 2 vols., 1929-1930, and Franz Schnabel's *Deutsche Geschichte im Neunzehnten Jahrhundert,* 4 vols., 1929 sqq.), has been an invaluable aid in preparing the manuscript for this book. The author is also greatly indebted to Dr. Bayard Quincy Morgan, professor emeritus and former executive head of the Department of Germanic Languages at Stanford University, for much pertinent advice and constructive criticism and for his assistance in reading the page proofs.

KURT F. REINHARDT

Stanford University, California
October 15, 1949

CONTENTS

VOLUME I

The Rise and Fall of the "Holy Empire"

Germans and Indo-Europeans. The Prehistoric Germanic Peoples
and Their Culture. The Germanic Peoples Enter the Historic
Stage. The Country. The People. Appearance. Domestic Living
and Community Life. Standard of Living, Manners, and Customs. Family Life. Virtues and Vices. The Tribes. State and
Society. Mythology and Religion.

Causes. Expansive Forces. Beginnings: Bastarnians, Cimbers,
and Teutons. Suevians and Cheruscans: Caesar, Ariovistus,
Arminius. New National Formations. Bishop Ulfilas and the
Visigoths. Arianism. The First Gothic Invasion and the Appear-
ance of the Huns. The End of the Western Empire. The Visi-
goths Continue Their March of Conquest. The Vandals. Attila,
Leader of the Huns. The Ostrogoths. Revival of Classical
Learning Under Theoderic. The Lombards. The Anglo-Saxons.
After the Migrations.

A. Merovingians

The Merovingian Kingdom of the Franks. The Baptism of
Clovis. Christianity and Paganism Among the Franks. Social
Conditions. Law and Legal Procedure. Currency and Trade.
Learning. Language: The High German Sound Shift. The
Influence of Latin Culture and the Roman Church. Christianity
As a State Religion. Christianity As the Heir of the Classical
Tradition. Monasticism. The Monks of the West. Anglo-Saxon

Missionaries. Wynfrith (Boniface), "The Apostle of the Germans." Irish Missionaries. Columbanus and Gallus.

B. *Carolingians*

The "Donation of Pepin." Pepin, "Patrician" of the Romans. Charlemagne and the Creation of the Carolingian Empire. The Personal Regime. Beginning Disintegration. Relapse Into Barbarism. Louis the Pious and His Sons. The Treaties of Verdun (843) and Mersen (870). Charles the Fat and the End of the Carolingian Dynasty. Charles the Great, King and Emperor. Administration Under Charles. Growing Feudalization of Society. Serfdom and Tenancy. Law and Order. Currency and Commerce. Carolingian "Renaissance." The "School of the Palace." Charles's Academy. The "Caroline Minuscule" and Miniature Painting. Architecture. Music. Carolingian Culture After Charles the Great. The Carolingian Abbey. Vernacular Literature in German Monasteries. National Diversity and Cultural Unity.

VOLUME II

The Second Empire and the Weimar Republic

LIST OF MAPS AND ILLUSTRATIONS

INTRODUCTION

The Heirs of Rome. Germany, placed by nature and historic fate in the center of Europe, is intrinsically linked up and interwoven with what is generally known as the European Tradition. For centuries she not only constituted a factor but represented a major exponent of that tradition. Europe, in turn, taken as a cultural, social, and intellectual whole, has been determined in its physiognomy to a large extent by the destinies, the character, the creative efforts, and the cultural achievements of those Germanic tribes which were the heirs of the civilization of the ancient world.

The form of the tradition of antiquity with which the Northern barbarians became acquainted was the political and social structure of the Roman Empire in the period of its decline. Roman civilization was still imbued with the splendor of a rich and mature intellectual, artistic, and civic life, and it could point to a high level of material prosperity, though it was lacking in spiritual depth and cultural initiative. The philosophic teachings of a Marcus Aurelius and similar representatives of high ethical standards had been supplanted by widespread naturalism and materialism, a cult of pleasure and success. Public opinion endorsed a philosophy of life which is thus scathingly described by St. Augustine (A.D. 354–430): "They do not trouble about the moral degradation of the Empire; all they ask is that it should be prosperous and secure. They say: What concerns us is that everyone should be able to increase his wealth so that he can afford a lavish expenditure and keep the weaker members of society in subjection. Let the laws protect the rights of property and leave man's morals alone. Let there be gorgeous palaces and sumptuous banquets, where anybody can play and drink and gorge himself and be dissipated by day or night. Let the noise of dancing be everywhere, and let the theatres resound with lewd merriment and with every kind of cruel pleasure. As for the rulers who devote themselves to giving the people a good time, let them be treated as gods and worshipped accordingly. Only let them take care that neither war nor plague nor any other calamity may interfere with this reign of prosperity."*

Naturally enough, such a civilization was in no way prepared to cope with those mighty forces which challenged the imperialism of the totalitarian Roman State: the biological vitality of the primitive Germanic warriors and

---

* Cf. *De Civitate Dei*, II, XX; *Ep.*, CXXXVIII, 3, 14.

forest dwellers of the North, and the spiritual vitality of Christianity, which had risen as a foreign element in the very heart of the Empire.

Out of these conflicting forces and tendencies, as they prevailed in an age of transition and violent change, Germany has grown as an integral part of European civilization, burdened and blessed with the heritage of the ancient world, destructively and constructively engaged in a constant interchange and interplay with the remnants of the old and the experiences and realities of the new.

If it is true that the character of an individual shapes his destiny, the same may be said of a people, a nation, a civilization. The character, however, of a civilization is an even more complex entity than the character of an individual. It can be analyzed, evaluated, and understood only as it displays itself in the process of historic evolution, thus mutually illuminating the significance of historical events on the one hand, and innate bents as well as acquired habits on the other. The present is linked to the past as much as to the future, and the story of the past will aid in the interpretation of the present and the shaping of the future.

The Scope of Cultural History. The history of civilization, whether it concerns itself with several, a few, or only one cultural unit, is always more ambitious and broader in scope than political or national history. Although it deals in part with an identical set of factual occurrences, it approaches, views, and interprets historical facts and events from altogether different angles. However, the fact that the history of civilization covers a much larger territory than does political historiography is not the decisive distinction. What gives cultural history or the history of civilization its peculiar character and flavor is its attempt to break through the surface of political events of a circumscribed extension and dimension in order to discover and comprehend the fundamental cultural and social unity that underlies a given civilization as a whole. This unity is evident wherever we deal with formations that owe their origin and evolution to a community of race, environment, occupation, and thought.*

Cultural Evolution: Necessity and Freedom. While race, environment, and occupation constitute important factors in historic and cultural evolution, it is the community of thought that is truly essential. Without it there could be no civilization properly so called. Through the elimination of thoughtfully planned and freely determined action the evolutionary process would be reduced to the growth of a biological species. Man, who is the chief actor on the historical stage, the actual center of all cultural life, would no longer be the determining but the completely determined element. Quite logically, then, all theories of historic determinism are compelled to link cultural development to a chain of biological and mechanical causation. These theories have been advanced in various forms and guises, the better

---

* Cf. Christopher Dawson, *The Age of the Gods* (London and New York: Sheed & Ward, 1933), Introduction.

known of which are those of Karl Marx (1818–1883), and Oswald Spengler (1880–1936).

According to Hegel, the "World Spirit" manifests itself in historic and cultural evolution, achieving an even higher degree of consciousness, reaching a climax in the organism of the National State. In the system of historic materialism as designed by Karl Marx, historic evolution culminates in the classless and stateless society of communism. Oswald Spengler conceives of cultural history as proceeding in monumental "cultural cycles," plantlike cultural organisms following their predestined course through the successive stages of generation, growth, maturity, and decay. The "maternal landscape" is their vital principle and life-imparting force. Alfred Rosenberg (1893–1947), who tried to formulate the philosophical convictions of National Socialism, espoused the "Myth of the Twentieth Century," the myth of blood, as the vital force that "is the most profound law of every genuine culture," "and which is to give conscious expression to the vegetative quality of a race." For both Marx and Rosenberg a dynamic cosmic energy is innate in human society and rules its destinies. In all these theories there is, of course, no room for a freely operating social and cultural activity, without which the establishment of social and cultural traditions seems inconceivable. G. W. F. Hegel, to whom the ideologies of both Marx and Rosenberg believed themselves heavily indebted, criticizes Plato's ideal Republic for having neglected "the principle of the independent personality of the individual," and considers the recognition and adoption of this principle the distinctive mark of Germanic-Christian civilization.

Human Reason and Cultural Integration. There is no doubt, then, that in all cultural growth and social transformation human reason and intelligence, planning and initiative play a most conspicuous part, providing for a continual enlargement of experiences and their integration and incorporation in the material, social and intellectual universe. Philosophical and religious thought is a great molder of the destinies of individuals and of nations. The great individuals themselves, for better or worse, are not only the exponents of definite and historically rooted concepts and modes of life and thought, but the molders as well, transformers and reformers, pioneers, prophets, and leaders. Civilization and its history are a continuous manifestation of the intelligent integration of new experiences, a documentation of man's co-operation with the forces, the laws, and the ends of nature. This co-operation begins in each cultural unit with the development of higher agriculture, the shaping of materials into adequate tools and instruments, the development of the mechanical arts and crafts, and the creation of the means of self-expression and communication in writing, measuring, and reading. Social forces grow into social institutions, into various forms of secular and religious rule within an organized society and a civil state. This is a kind of general framework within which civilizations in different

---

* Cf. Alfred Rosenberg, *Der Mythos des 20. Jahrhunderts* (1930).

climes and zones seem to erect their particular and individual structures. Within this framework there seems to be an amplitude admitting of well-nigh infinite varieties of realizations, so that no civilization is committed to a predestined course.

The human element, so strong in each civilization, is the correcting and controlling factor. Any *laissez-faire* attitude in regard to cultural evolution is oblivious of some of its most real forces. It overlooks forces which address this modern age even across the boundary lines of generations and centuries past; the cultural energies that are alive in the great personalities of the emperors and popes of the Middle Ages, in the synthetic minds of the Schoolmen, in the voices of the ages that were inspired and informed by the messages of Luther and Calvin, the genius of Leibniz and Kant, of Goethe and Schiller, the idealism of Fichte, the cultural pessimism of Schopenhauer, and the feverish and ecstatic optimism of Nietzsche.

German Idealism. The history of German civilization is not identical indeed with the history of her great creative minds. But it may be safely maintained that this history owes its particular shape and character to the cumulative intellectual incentives supplied by many generations of men and women who, in different stations of life and engaged in varying labors and occupations, constitute a community of thought as well as of life. These have jointly contributed to the major currents of cultural achievement and social tradition.

There is a certain dramatic tenseness, occasionally involving an aspect of tragic frustration, in the rugged outline of German cultural history. There are certain major incisions which mark an end as well as a beginning, which provide a scenic setting full of contrasts and seeming contradictions that set German civilization apart from the more epically composed development of many other nations and races. Perhaps more than in any other European nation the course of cultural movements and political events in Germany is inspired and directed by ideas and ideologies. The ideal and material strength of centuries was spent in the passionate and futile attempt to perpetuate the concept and force the realization of the Holy Roman Empire of the German Nation; or to maintain the claims of the "Imperium" as against the demands of the "Sacerdotium," Empire versus Papacy.

German Interiority. There is a specific brand of German inwardness or interiority (*Innerlichkeit*) that asserts itself no less in the great mystics of the thirteenth and fourteenth centuries than in Martin Luther's doctrine of salvation "by faith alone" (*sola fide*): the "fiducial faith" of "pure interiority" which he proclaimed as the sole requisite for justification (cf. p. 219). There is the same immediacy and directness of emotional appeal and inner experience in the pietistic movement (cf. p. 364 sqq.) of the pre-Classical age and the mystical or "magical" idealism of the post-Classical Romantic school (cf. p. 470 sqq.). This mystical idealism permeates German thought and German life, and a profoundly personal interiority imparts to the German language and diction its heavily laden and richly ornamented texture. The

fervent thoroughness of German idealism inspired in part the social and religious revolts and wars of the sixteenth and seventeenth centuries. But without
this generative power the material and cultural devastations of the Thirty
Years' War could never have issued in the cultural renascence that
characterized the age of German Classicism, little over a hundred years
after the Treaty of Westphalia (1648).

German Romanticism. It has been said that mystical and romantic yearning, a longing which is infinite by its very nature, is of the essence of the
German mind. It manifests itself in the concepts of German mythology
and nature philosophy in ancient and modern times; in the major themes
of German folk song and lyric poetry; in the "longing infinite" of the
Romantic painters, writers, and philosophers; and in the ecstatic frenzy of
the towering German-Gothic cathedral, which in its heavenward flight is
a mystical dream come true. Spengler has spoken of the eternal restlessness
of the "Faustian" soul, taking Goethe's greatest dramatic character as a
profound symbol of the aspirations of the Germanic race: a restless striving
which fulfills itself eternally *in statu viae,* considering the way not as a means
to an end but as the end and the goal itself.

Gotthold Ephraim Lessing (1729–1781) attributes a higher value to the
quest for truth than to the possession of truth. He, too, felt the fascination
of the *Faust*-theme, and composed a *Faust*-fragment, Thomas Mann (1875–
1955), the creator of many romantic characters, has his Savonarola in
the play *Fiorenza* confess: "Longing is a gigantic force but possession
emasculates." And yet, with all the apparent lack of a conventional formal
quality approved by the canon of classical aesthetics, it seems that the
German mind possesses and commands a form-character specifically its own,
unique and incomparable in its kind. It is when we make the acquaintance
of some of the greatest of German artists and writers, such as Dürer and
Holbein, Goethe and Schiller, that we realize that this spiritual unrest
is far from being aimless and endless. In between long stretches of seeking
there appear blessed isles of finding, islands of fulfillment and sublime
achievement, where the German mind has come to rest in happy balance
and harmony.

Methods of Approach and Critical Evaluation. Evaluations in the field
of cultural history are difficult and never infallible. Is classical form better
than romantic form? Is Gothic architecture the creation of a barbaric race,
as Goethe thought when his aesthetic judgment received its rules from the
art forms of antiquity? Or was he right when, in the prime of youth, he
stood in front of the Strasbourg Minster and was delighted and transported
beyond measure by that monumental spiritualization of matter that met
his eye in the sublime craftsmanship of Erwin von Steinbach? Was
eighteenth-century rationalism right when it looked at cultural progress as
a uniform law of nature, so that the bigger and better things would inevitably fall into the lap of an evolving civilization? Is contemporary
German art more mature or more perfect than the art of Dürer and Holbein

and Grünewald? Has modern literature improved and advanced beyond the scope and workmanship of the "Lay of the Nibelungs," Wolfram's "Parzival," Goethe's "Faust," Schiller's "Wilhelm Tell"? Is contemporary philosophy sounder or truer than the systems of Albert the Great, Leibniz, and Kant? Are the new forms of government and social organization, the administration of social and distributive justice more progressive or more humane than similar functions and institutions of the preceding centuries? The answers to all these questions depend upon the standard of measurement.

Cultural gain and loss, however, cannot be measured in the abstract. It can be measured only by taking into consideration concrete, historical situations and conditions. From Johann Gottfried Herder (1744–1803) we have learned how to understand and appreciate cultural history as a discipline dealing with individual organisms that must be interpreted and judged from their own premises. These vary according to climate, race, and place, and to their ethnological, geographical, and sociological environment. The interpretation of genetic relations within cultural organisms of a definite time and place becomes thus the foundation of methodology which does away with the one-sided views of a purely descriptive, or purely pragmatic, or purely normative approach.*

Past, Present and Future. To understand those facts, events, currents, and movements that display themselves significantly within a given historical frame of reference, in the light of particular premises and circumstances, and to refrain from simplified and single-tracked judgments, becomes singularly imperative in viewing the landscape of the Germany of today. Past and present, tradition and progress seem to meet in the form of an open challenge which has to be accepted and comprehended in the interest of the welding process of a future Germany and a future German civilization. Friedrich Nietzsche (1844–1900) has well expressed the plight and the hope of an anticipated Germany of the future: "We do not yet know the goal toward which we are being driven after having thus broken away from our ancient foundations. But it is these foundations that have implanted in us the strength which now urges us into the distant future, into adventure. . . ."

---

* Cf. H. A. Hodges, *The Philosophy of Wilhelm Dilthey* (London: Routledge & Keagan Paul, 1952).

PART I. THE GERMANIC PAST AND THE CREATION OF THE EMPIRE OF CHARLEMAGNE

A. MEROVINGIANS

440–461	Pope Leo I (the Great)
482–511	Clovis, King of the Franks
486	Clovis defeats the Romans under Syagrius at Soissons, and becomes absolute ruler of a mixed Germanic-Roman population
496	Clovis defeats the Alemans
496	Clovis is converted to Roman Catholicism
507	Clovis defeats the Visigoths
590–604	Pope Gregory (the Great)
687–714	Pepin of Heristal, Mayor of the Palace
687	Pepin of Heristal restores unity to the Frankish kingdom
715–741	Charles Martel, Mayor of the Palace
732	Charles Martel defeats the Arabs at Poitiers
741–768	Pepin the Younger (the Short) becomes king of the Franks: the first king of the Carolingian Dynasty
672–754	Boniface (Wynfrith), "Apostle of the Germans"

B. CAROLINGIANS

754–756	The "Donation of Pepin" establishes the Papal States
768–814	Charles the Great (Charlemagne, Karl der Grosse, Carolus Magnus)
772–804	Wars against the Lombards, Bavarians, Avars, and Saxons
774	Charles defeats the Lombards and becomes King of Lombardy
778	Campaign in Spain. Death of Count Hruotland at Roncesvalles
782	Execution of 4500 (?) Saxons at Verden on the Aller
787	Second Council of Nicaea
794	Council of the Western bishops at Frankfurt
800	Charles the Great receives the Imperial Crown from Pope Leo III
814–840	Louis (Ludwig) the Pious, Emperor
840–855	Lothar I, Emperor, eldest son of Louis the Pious
843	Treaty of Verdun between Louis the German, Charles the Bald, and Lothar I
843–877	Charles the Bald, Emperor (875)
855–869	Lothar II, King, son of Lothar I
876–887	Charles the Fat, youngest son of Louis the German (Emperor after 881)
870	Treaty of Mersen between Charles the Bald and Louis the German
888	Deposition of Charles the Fat
889–918	Illegitimate Carolingians and Tribal Duchies

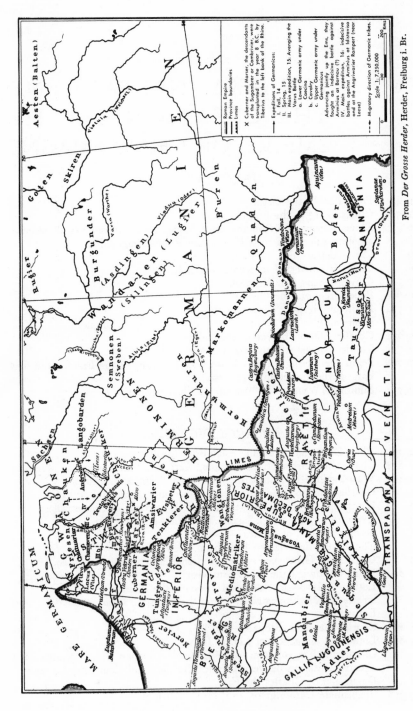

Germany at the Time of Tacitus (End of the First Century).

From *Der Grosse Herder*, Herder, Freiburg i. Br.

Chapter 1

ORIGINS

Germans and Indo-Europeans. The Germanic peoples of prehistoric and historic times represent one branch of the Indo-Germanic or Indo-European family of nations. The majority of contemporary anthropologists, ethnologists, and linguists consider the unity that existed among the Indo-Europeans as one of speech rather than of race. There is no doubt, however, that most of these peoples belonged racially to the nordic dolicocephalic (long-skulled) type. Comparative philology names as linguistic members of the Indo-European family the ancient inhabitants of India, Persia, Greece, the old Italic and modern Romanic nations, Celts, Slavs, and the various Germanic peoples. Exact knowledge as to their origins, their homes, their culture, and their migrations is lacking. No literary documents are extant to tell us of their lives and their activities; our only sources of information are a common stock of words, and a certain amount of archaeological and ethnological evidence.

It is quite possible that the unity of the Indo-Europeans came to an end with the passing of the Neolithic Age (*c.* 2000 ʙ.c.). It seems to be ascertained that the Indo-Europeans were peasants with a rather advanced agriculture, that their social life rested on patriarchal customs and institutions, their family life on monogamy. Their religion included, among a pantheon of minor deities, belief in the supreme power and majesty of the sky-god (Dyaus-Pitar, Jupiter, Zeus, Tyr, Thor, Wodan, etc.).

As to their original homes, the opinions are divided. The two major theories point to inner Asia and northern Europe, in particular to the Baltic region. This latter theory assumes that the Indo-Germanic peoples spread from northern Europe and ultimately penetrated into Turkestan and India.

The Prehistoric Germanic Peoples and Their Culture. In prehistoric times most of the territory that is today occupied by the German people was inhabited by the Celts. But even the Celts were not the original inhabitants of this region. They were preceded by three much more primitive types of Illyrian, Celtic, and Germanic culture. Ancient Thuringia, occupying a central position, must have acted as a unifying and co-ordinating focus, the

3

result being the creation of a Celtic cultural center in the southwestern part of what is today the territory of Germany.

In the second millennium B.C. these aboriginal populations were seized by a typically Indo-Germanic *wanderlust* which carried them into Russia and Greece. Bastarnians and Cimbers began to grow restless and started upon their migrations, some time during the first millennium B.C. The Slavs took possession of those districts that were vacated by the Goths, the Burgundians, the Alemans, and the Marcomans. The Thuringians were the main carriers of a steadily gaining Germanization in the North of present-day Germany. At the same time, they were an important factor in the creation of the highly developed "Lusation Culture" (*Lausitz-Kultur*) of the middle Bronze Age (*c.* 1200 B.C.), which had its center in the east and southeast.

By 500 B.C. the greater part of northern Europe was inhabited by Germanic tribes, and the aboriginal Celts found themselves hard pressed. In the southwest the Germanic advance was temporarily checked by Celtic strongholds, but during the last centuries of the pre-Christian era the Celts gradually receded toward the Alps.

Archaeological finds illustrate the successive stages of this advancing Germanic culture. Some of the tools and implements of the Stone and Bronze ages show exquisite workmanship and an 'original arrangement of ornamental and decorative design. The oldest musical instruments of Germanic culture that have been unearthed date back to *c.* 800 B.C. They are called "lurers" (from Old Norse *"ludhr"*), alphornlike, S-shaped wind instruments, from four to six feet long, made of bronze and sometimes beautifully decorated. They have been found in pairs perfectly tuned one to the other. Comprising the diatonic scale and major triad, they allow for twenty-two notes and produce musical sounds of a solemn and majestic, noble and war-

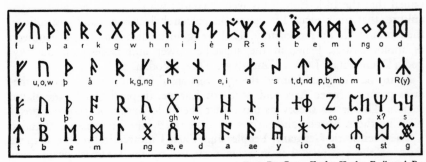

From *Der Grosse Herder*, Herder, Freiburg i. Br.

Runic Alphabets. Top Row: Old German; Second Row: Norse; Bottom Rows: Anglo-Saxon.

like character. Twenty-three "lurers" are in the possession of the National Museum in Copenhagen. Their tonal quality has been tested in several public concerts in Denmark.

An ancient Germanic script, based on an alphabet of symbolic signs which are known as "runes" (from Gothic *run*, "secret, mystery") has come down to us in the form of inscriptions on weapons and monuments. The inscriptions and symbols are of a ritualistic, magic, or oracular significance, but as they all date from the post-Roman period it is very doubtful whether they were known to the prehistoric tribes. It is much more likely that the runic symbols were derived from Italic alphabets. They occur in all Germanic regions and are characterized by their rugged, angular shape. The symbols were scratched or carved on wood, metal, or stone. Altogether nearly 3000 such inscriptions have been discovered, most of them in Scandinavia. The knowledge of runic symbols is still alive in some parts of present-day Sweden.

The existence of a primitive Germanic poetry, of religious dances and cultic ceremonies is, in the absence of documents, more or less a matter of conjecture. Certain conclusions may be drawn with a reasonable amount of probability by referring to analogical customs and habits of other primitive peoples. So it may be assumed that the various arts and crafts of the ancient Germanic peoples were organically interrelated; that there prevailed a unity of poetry, music, and the dance; that music, poetry, and dances were strongly rhythmical and constituted part of the religious cult and of all those rites and ceremonies in which the meaning of group life manifests itself.

The Germanic Peoples Enter the Historic Stage. The Germanic tribes had ceased to be full-fledged barbarians when they finally made their appearance in the history of Europe. They represented a peasant culture of at least a thousand years' duration and of a definite physiognomy in its agriculture, its craftsmanship, and its standard of living.

Pytheas of Massilia (Marseilles), a contemporary of Alexander the Great (356-323 B.C.), who traveled from Marseilles to Britain and the coast of the North Sea, was the first one to mention the early Germanic peoples of historic times. He also tells of amber fisheries that he found on the west coast of Jutland. Julius Caesar (100-44 B.C.) knew the Germanic lands and tribes from personal contact and experience, and so did Cornelius Tacitus (A.D. 54-120) whose *Germania* contains the most comprehensive and detailed information on Germanic culture as it existed at the beginning of the Christian era. As a writer of history, Tacitus was a pragmatist: in his desire to castigate the physical and moral decadence of Imperial Rome he painted the picture of the vigorous young barbarians in bright and glowing colors, putting strong emphasis on their virtues and passing mildly or silently over their vices.

The documentary evidence that is available suggests that light and shade were more evenly distributed. The same qualification applies to some of the highly idealized statues that were produced by Roman artists, although there can be no doubt that the makers of these sculptures were deeply impressed with the vigor and the noble bearing of these young Germanic giants. Vivid scenes of Germanic life are depicted on Roman triumphal arches and columns, commemorating imperial victories over the barbarians. Most illuminating of all, for prehistoric and early historic times alike, are, of course, the finds that have been unearthed in all parts of Germany, from moors and lakes, fields and forests, caves and tombs.

The Country. As early as in Caesar's time the Germanic tribes had advanced far into central and southern Germany. Germanic settlements had been established on both banks of the Rhine, in Bohemia, and along the Danube, not to speak of the Germanic population of the Scandinavian North, of England, Greenland, and Iceland. The surrounding Celtic states in the south and west had been conquered and dispersed.

According to the Romans, Germany at that time consisted mainly of impenetrable forests and impassable swamps. "Who would ever think of leaving Asia, Africa, or Italy and migrate to Germany?" asks Tacitus. "It is a wild country under an inclement sky, hard to cultivate, a gloomy sight for anyone who does not call it his home." This description applied especially to the northwestern frontier districts. There were indeed moors and swamps and huge, densely grown forests extending through a large part of the Germanic regions and, often enough, seriously impeding the advancing Roman armies. The climate was rough and damp. On the other hand, approximately one fifth of the area known to have been inhabited by Germanic tribes, and especially the plains and valleys alongside the big rivers and the coast regions, was richly populated and well cultivated.

The People. In the latter part of the first century A.D. from three to four million people were living on approximately the same territory that in modern times marked the geographical boundaries of Germany up to 1945. It is the prevailing opinion today that the Germanic variety of the Nordic and Phalic races originated in the coastal region of the Baltic as the result of a process of miscegenation. In Julius Caesar's time three major divisions, the same that characterize the Germanic nations to this day, may be distinguished: (1) the *eastern Germans,* who lived on the Oder and Vistula, comprising, among others, the Visigoths, the Ostrogoths, the Burgundians, and the Vandals; (2) the *northern Germans,* who occupied the southern part of Scandinavia, the adjacent islands, and Jutland; (3) the *western Germans,* who dwelled in the most southerly part of Jutland and in the oblong space between the Elbe, the North Sea, the Rhine, and the Main. The name *German* is probably of Gallic-Celtic origin. It has come into general usage since Caesar's time, and may imply the meaning of "neighbor" or "brother." The name *deutsch* (Old High German *diutisk,* from *Theoda,* "people, tribe") is of later origin and occurs first in its latinized form *theodiscus (lingua theodisca)* in documents of the eighth and ninth centuries.

Among the three major groups of Germanic peoples the northern Germans, due to their remoteness from the influence of the Mediterranean civilizations, have best preserved their ancient Germanic traits. The eastern Germans played a most significant part in the final destruction of the Roman Empire and the formation of the new Romanic civilizations. The descendants of the Western tribes are the present-day Germans, the French, the Dutch, the Flemings, and the Anglo-Saxons.

Appearance. Despite specific tribal characteristics the Germans appear as a unity when compared with the Italic and other Mediterranean populations. They were people of fair complexion, with reddish-blond hair, and of powerful build. Ausonius, a Roman rhetorician and poet of the fourth century A.D., has left a poetical description of one of his slaves, a girl named Bissula of the tribe of the Suevians: "Bissula, born and brought up on the Rhine, the wintry river, German her features, golden her hair, her eyes of blue color; Bissula, inimitable in wax or by the brush of the painter; adorned by nature with charms which defy all artificial tricks. Well may other maidens use powder or rouge, her face does not owe its rosiness to the deftness of her fingers. Painter, mix the whiteness of the lilies with the purple of the roses: thus you will get the proper colors for Bissula's portrait."

While the women may have refrained from using powder and rouge, Tacitus tells us that the men used artificial dyes to give their hair a color of flaming red, probably to make themselves appear more fearful to their enemies on the battlefield. Their clothing was simple, and male and female fashions were almost identical. They wore tight-fitting sleeveless undergarments of linen or wool, breeches or trousers of the same material, and a coarse woolen outer garment in form of a cloak, often adorned with fine furs and held together on the right shoulder by an artfully shaped metal pin or brooch. Shoes were made of one piece of leather and fastened with a string around the ankles. Both men and women were fond of metal adornment which they fastened to their necks, arms, ears, fingers, and feet. The women wore necklaces of metal, amber, or glass.

The characteristic weapons were: the *framea,* a short javelin that could be thrown as well as used in hand-to-hand fighting; a hatchet called the *francisca* (Frankish: *weapon*); slings; and bows and arrows. Later on, a daggerlike sword appears as distinguished from the long, double-edged sword which is infrequently found in the earlier period. The only defensive weapon was a huge wooden shield, either oval, square, or round in shape and fortified on the outside with leather or iron bands. It was painted in the different tribal colors: white with the Cimbers, red with the Saxons, brown with the Frisians. The shield was the symbol of manhood and of freedom, and its loss in battle was proof of disgraceful cowardice. The Germans frequently crossed rivers on their shields or, using them as sleighs, slid down the icy slopes of the Alps into the Italian plains.

Domestic Living and Community Life. In Tacitus' time the Germanic house had lost some of its original primitive appearance. The Germans had, however, not yet learned from the Romans how to build in stone. Most of their dwellings were simple log houses. They were either constructed of firm wooden beams or consisted of a wooden framework (*Fachwerk*), filled in with clay, rock, and brushwood. The simplest form was the round hut, made of wood and wickerwork. Most of the houses had steep roofs covered with straw or brushwood, extending almost to the ground on one side as a protection against adverse climatic influences. Ordinarily the huts had only one room, in the center of which stood the open hearth. As Chimneys were unknown, the smoke escaped either through the door or a dormer window. Tables and stools were used, and benches ran along the walls.

The Germanic and Roman villages differed in their layouts. The Roman village had a planned regularity of design, while the typical Germanic village consisted of irregularly scattered houses, fenced off from each other and from the outside world, and a wicker fence surrounding the whole group of houses. Caves were dug in the ground outside the house and covered with leaves and dung. They served as storerooms, as a protection against the severe climate or in case of danger, and, according to Pliny, as workshops for the women and maids engaged in weaving.

The fields and plowlands were owned and cultivated by the community. All the arable land of a village was divided up and apportioned to the members of the community, with lots being redistributed every year so as to give each one the same advantages and disadvantages of soil and sun. The methods of cultivation and the seeding and harvesting periods were decreed by the village community. Outside the arable area lay the pastures and woods, the *allmende* or commons, which were likewise owned by the community, and in the use of which each one shared equally. Cities were unknown to the ancient Germans, and in the beginning they even refrained from settling down in those Roman cities which they had gained by conquest.

Standard of Living, Manners and Customs. As is to be expected, the early Germans lived simply and unpretentiously. Their main subsistence consisted of bread, ·vegetables, and meats. Cattle were bred for dairy purposes, sheep for their wool. Next to pork, horse meat was the principal animal food. Westphalian ham was known and appreciated even by the Romans. The Christian Church finally succeeded in eradicating the habit of eating horse meat, which it opposed on account of its intimate connection with pagan sacrificial rites. Salt was used for seasoning in the earliest times, some of the salt mines having been inherited from the Celts and worked by Celtic slaves. It was obtained in the simplest way: the brine was poured over burning logs or glowing charcoal; the water evaporated, and the salt remained. Mead (*Met*) and various kinds of beers were extensively brewed. "As a drink the Germans consume a liquid made of barley or wheat which is adulterated into a sort of wine," says Tacitus. Some of the tribes held a strong prejudice against the importation of Roman wines as contributing to enervation and effeminacy.

The slaves worked in the fields, the women in the house, and the men attended to the hunt and the business of war. The craft that was regarded as especially honorable and the only one worthy of a freeman was the art of smithing, the manufacturing of arms and ornaments. It is also the only handicraft that stands out in the world of Germanic mythology, in the heroic sagas and epics. The work of the women included the household arts of cooking, sewing, spinning, and weaving. The garments, found in excavations in all regions of Germanic influence, are adorned with embroideries which show the interlacing band ornament so typical of all Germanic ornamentation. It is characterized by a phantastic interplay of lines: lines with apparently no beginning and no end, entirely abstract in design, but feverishly agitated and indicative of the forceful expressionism of Germanic mentality.

The freeman had much time for leisure and loafing. He was fond of outdoor life, but he felt no pangs of conscience when he lay on a bearskin for days, sleeping, dreaming, and meditating in front of his hearth fire. Periods of inertia and introspection alternated with periods of alertness and wide-awake, energetic action. The long, dark nights of the winter season encouraged the German's natural bent for meditative brooding. But the long winters also contributed to that healthy intimacy of family life which aroused the admiration of Tacitus.

Family Life. "Strictly upheld there," says the Roman historian, "is the marriage bond, and there is no aspect of their cultural life that deserves higher praise." Although marriage had passed through the usual primitive stages of rape and purchase, it was early considered as the most important civil contract. The father was the head of the family and of the household. In the earliest times he even possessed the judicial power of life and death over wife, children, and slaves.

At the time of Caesar and Tacitus monogamy was the generally prevailing practice. Juridically the women occupied an inferior position, although actually they were highly respected and even credited with an intimate relation to supernatural powers, and with the gifts of prophecy, divination, and healing. Their advice was sought and greatly esteemed, particularly in matters of vital concern for the well-being of the community. Motherhood was woman's supreme title of honor, chastity her prime virtue. Adultery on the part of a woman was cruelly punished by the outraged husband: stripped of her garments, she was whipped through the village and frequently killed during or after the ordeal. Infidelity on the part of the husband was more frequent and went unpunished. As is the case with several Indo-Germanic peoples, earlier customs had made it obligatory for the wife to follow her husband in death.

Marriage consisted of two major phases: the ceremony of betrothal, and the nuptials. Betrothal signified the transferring of the guardianship of the future wife from her family to her husband who was usually chosen by the girl's father or guardian (*Muntwalt, Vormund*). The day after the nuptials the husband presented his newly wedded wife with her dowry (*Morgen-*

gabe) which was to offer her protection and security in the case of widow-hood, desertion, or divorce.

Tacitus shows himself impressed with the large size of the Germanic family: "It is considered shameful to limit the number of children or to kill one of the offspring." Nevertheless, infanticide was not infrequent in the case of sickly or otherwise undesirable children.

Virtues and Vices. The ancient Germanic peoples possessed, as we have shown, a culture decidedly their own, but it was a culture of peasants and warriors, lacking the finish and refinements of more advanced types of civilization. They were children of nature, and there was something childlike in the mixture of violence and sentimentality, of harshness and tenderness that characterizes their lives. Their lust of adventure and love of warfare made them frequently oblivious of humane considerations and inhibitions. They tortured criminals, occasionally killed their prisoners of war, and broke solemnly sworn treaties without scruples. They indulged in immoderate drinking and gambling, a man frequently losing his property and his liberty in a game of dice. On the other hand, unswerving loyalty and unbending heroism are the two outstanding virtues of the Germanic warrior, virtues that are glorified again and again in the heroic epics and sagas. Honor and glory rank higher in the scale of values than life itself, so that even women preferred death to slavery and disgrace.

These character traits were supported and complemented by a rich and deep emotional and imaginative life (*Gemüt*) which animated tree and forest; brook, river, and lake; wind, cloud, and sky; weaving the raiment of Germanic folklore out of the threads of creative fancy.

We have here, then, a society of armed and warlike peasants whose ethics of loyalty and honor and heroic deeds is opposed to an ethics of humility, compassion, and charity as taught by some of the higher world religions, above all by Christianity. Germanic loyalty and sense of honor inspires the exaltation of vengeance. But self-respect and honor demand that the enemy be honorable and respectable.

This whole ethical code is highly personalistic: superindividual motivations, such as patriotism or religious idealism, are strangely lacking.

Tacitus devotes a special chapter to the Germanic virtue of hospitality, which was indeed practiced to the highest degree. The visitor would remain with his host as long as there was food and drink in the house, and after-wards both guest and host would go to a neighbor's house where they were received with the same generous hospitality. No distinction was made between strangers and friends, and friendships that had such a casual beginning frequently endured through generations.

The salesman was almost as graciously received as the traveler. Roman merchants sold their German customers weapons of bronze and iron and ornaments of silver, which were preferred to those of gold. All commercial intercourse was based on barter. The monetary value of Roman coins went unappreciated. They were, however, worn as ornaments or stored away in treasure chests. The word used for the measure of barter indicates that cattle provided its standard and fixed value: *pecunia* in Latin; *Faihs* in Gothic; *fihu* in Old Saxon and Old High German; *fee* in English; *Vieh* in modern German. The great highway by which Roman civilization entered Germany was the valley of the Moselle river.

The Tribes. The tribal organization of the Germanic peoples was based on the natural organism of the family. The Germanic tribes are natural units distinguished by specific hereditary character traits which are the result of a community of race, the influence of a common ethnological and geographical environment, and similar or identical social and cultural experiences. A knowledge of Germanic tribal life will aid in the understanding of the complex character of the German nation and the appreciation of its cultural achievements.

The process of the formation of the Germanic tribes continued well into the thirteenth century A.D. Three important phases may be distinguished: (1) the *High Germanic* tribes, crossing the Rhine and Danube rivers, penetrated into Gaul and the Alpine districts; (2) the *Saxons* expanded and spread into parts of present-day Franconia and Thuringia; (3) the third movement, in which all the original tribes participated, took place east of the Elbe, the Saale, and the middle Danube.

The individual tribes are marked off from one another by dialect, custom, popular traditions, racial characteristics, literary and artistic expression. Some of them have fulfilled definite functions in the formative stages of German civilization. The Franks were the most important factor in welding the political, social, and intellectual frame of the western European tradition to the foundation of the cultural heritage of pagan and Christian Rome. The Alemans were next in taking over the reins of the Empire, proving exceptionally gifted in statesmanship, and presenting Germany with a series of great dynastic leaders. The Bavarians in their Austrian branch inherited and administered the task of ruling over the destinies of the *Reich* until, with the rise of Prussia, the younger tribes (*Neustämme*) of the north and northeast began to dominate the historic scene. The Frank Charlemagne forced the Saxons into the unity of the Roman Empire of the German nation, and the Saxon emperors were soon to take a decisive hand in the political and cultural development of the realm. The Franks and Thuringians were entrusted with the great and difficult work of colonization east of the Elbe and Saale. And it was the territory of the new colonial settlements that gave birth to the idea of German national unity and to the unified New High German language.

State and Society. The tribal organization was made up of groups of related families which were united by the strong ties of blood relationship. The gradual growth of the Germanic State may serve to illustrate the fallacy of Rousseau's and Hobbes' theories of the origins of organized civil society. The ancient Germans had not yet developed the conception of the state, and when it finally came into being, it was the outgrowth of a natural expansion of the family, not the result of an artificial and arbitrary contract based on considerations of utility and expediency. The Germanic tribesman had a strong sense of the primacy of the family as an organism endowed with specific natural and inalienable rights of its own.

Sons and daughters stayed with their families until they were married, and even then the sons continued to cultivate their family bonds and traditions. The male blood relations formed the Germanic *Sippe* (*syb,* "clan"). A certain number of clans constituted what might be called the ancient Germanic State. The head of the clan enjoyed some special privileges in regard to property and authority. Verbal offenses, bodily injuries, and murder were dealt with by the clan by means of the blood feud. Usually it was not the culprit who became the object of vengeance or was bound to offer restitution or compensation, but the most prominent member of the *Sippe*. The amount of compensation (*weregild, Wergeld*) was fixed in later times by a regular tariff which is preserved in the oldest written laws. The compensation was received by the *Sippe,* and so strong was the concept of personality and personal responsibility that he who could induce the most influential freemen to vouch for him was judged right.

The larger units of the Germanic tribes and peoples grew out of the smaller units of the *Sippe*. A *Sippe* comprised from fifty to one hundred families. The annual redistribution of land was made by drawing "lots." The different lots of the fields and the homestead together formed the "hide" or *hufa* (*Hufe*). Private ownership of land makes its appearance during and after the period of migrations.

A more artificial unit than the clan was that of the "hundreds," the "Mark Community" or *Hundertschaft,* comprising from 100 to 120 households. Geographically the territory owned by a "Mark Community" was designated as a *Gau* (Latin, *pagus;* English, *shire*).

The population was divided into two classes: the freemen and the slaves. Only the freemen, that is, only those who descended from free parents, were full-fledged members of a tribe or a village community. And only the freemen shared in the common ownership of land, were permitted to take up arms in case of war, and were admitted to the popular assemblies. The most prominent members of the class of freemen were the noblemen (ethelings) who stood out by virtue of distinguished ancestry, superior capabilities, or special merits, but enjoyed no legal prerogatives. The caste of the slaves was made up chiefly of prisoners of war and their children. Members of the tribe who had gambled away their liberty were usually sold to foreign traders. The slaves were regarded as pieces of personal property or merchandise, and marriages between freemen and slaves were prohibited. Whenever such a marriage occurred, the children belonged to the class of the unfree. Otherwise, according to Tacitus, the treatment of slaves was relatively humane. Slaves who had acquired their freedom were rare exceptions, and their social position was ambiguous and indefinite, although

Tacitus claims that with tribes that were ruled by kings the freedmen sometimes rose to positions above freemen and noblemen.

The assembly of freemen expressed the sovereign power of the people in its legislative, judicial, and executive branches. These assemblies were called the *Ding* (*mahal, moot,* "thing"). Custom and tradition were important factors in their decisions, making for elasticity and flexibility of procedure. The popular assembly elected the king or *Herzog* (duke), who was given unlimited power in time of war, but who had to give up his office when peace was restored. The *Ding* also acted as a court of justice in all cases referring to public peace and order, and in grievous offenses which involved or endangered the commonweal, such as disturbances of the public peace, high treason, desertion, cowardice, moral turpitude, sacrilege. Capital punishment was imposed as a propitiatory sacrifice to the gods, and priests* were the executioners.

The *Ding,* whether convening as the representation of the Mark Community or of the whole tribal community, was called together and presided over by the "leader" or chieftain. A village community was headed by the "alderman" or "senior"; the hundreds by a distinguished member of the nobility (*Markgraf, Gaugraf*). The chiefs of the combined mark community constituted in many cases the leadership of the tribe. With some of the eastern tribes a limited monarchical rule under the leadership of a hereditary king seems to have been customary.

The followers of the chief were called the *thegans* (*Degen*) or thanes, representing in their entirety the *gasindi* (*Gesinde*) or *trustio.* "It is disgraceful for the chief," says Tacitus, "to be outdone in bravery by the thanes, disgraceful for the thanes not to equal the bravery of the chief. But it brings reproach and lifelong infamy to survive the chief after he has fallen in battle." The relationship between leader and thanes provided ample opportunity for the practice of the Germanic virtue of loyalty, the *Nibelungentreue* of the sagas and epics. The basis of this relationship is an unwritten contract of mutual service, trust, and obligation, and the thane was willing to subordinate his own judgment completely to the superior authority of the leader. However, violation of the trust on the part of the chief immediately invalidated the contract.

Civil law and criminal law in the modern sense were unknown to the Germanic tribes. Custom, however, frequently acquired the force of law, establishing definite legal traditions which were handed on by word of mouth and in symbolic language. Laws fixed in writing do not occur until after the migration period. Even in much later times Roman law has never been able to obliterate the survival of important legal elements of indigenous tribal concepts, and the reform of the German law codes under National

---

* The Germanic tribes had no special caste of priests but designated some worthy members of the community as *Ewarte* (protectors of Sacred Law).

Socialism was primarily concerned with the elimination of the so-called "alien" spirit of Roman Law.

Mythology and Religion. It is perhaps in their mythological and religious concepts that peoples are truest to themselves and most expressive of their innermost being. Early Germanic religion must not be judged according to the mature religious ideology of the North Germanic Edda, which received its shape as late as the eighth century A.D. and is partly influenced by Christianity. On the other hand, pre-Christian documents and reports on Germanic religion are completely lacking, because the written tradition begins only with the conversion of the Germanic tribes. The Roman historians, in their turn, are anything but unbiased observers, and their reports refer primarily to the southern tribes. The judgment of the early Christian missionaries is similarly colored by their uncompromising opposition to Germanic paganism. It is therefore very difficult to give an objective account of ancient Germanic religious beliefs and cultic observances. Our most reliable guides and informants are the old Icelandic sagas and the many archaeological finds of the Stone and Bronze Ages.

The gods of the genuinely Germanic religion were conceived as personal powers to which the Germanic tribesman maintained a personal relationship. They were feared and revered as superhuman guardians and protectors, of whom the worshiper expected certain favors and advantages. His relationship to his gods was very much like his relationship to his chiefs: it was based on an attitude of *"do ut des,"* of mutual service, trust, and loyalty. The god is man's *fulltrui* (the term is familiar to the Icelanders), one who can be trusted implicitly, the god-friend, and the Germanic warrior-peasant's heroic philosophy of life is projected into the skies where he visualizes the cosmic strife that rages between gods and giants, ending with the *Götter-dämmerung* (twilight of the gods) and the destruction of the gods by the giants.

Both gods and giants are "beyond good and evil." Neither are exemplary moral types to be imitated or even approximated, with the possible exception of Balder, who appears as the just and peace-loving judge. Both gods and giants are shrewd and powerful, but neither omnipotent nor eternal. Their battle is one between cosmic powers, not one between moral forces or ethical principles. Man approaches them in awe and fear, trying to propitiate their wrath and gain their favor by offering them human and other sacrifices.

There are antagonistic elements, then, in the Germanic concept of the divine, the trust-inspiring and the awe-inspiring in close proximity. Although they seem hard to reconcile, they supplement each other, and together they express the spirit of the Germanic pagan religion. Donar-Thor is the friendly, good-natured god of a peasant religion, the real *fulltrui,* while Wodan-Odin represents the mysterious and demonic elements in Germanic religion. Thor is the guardian of the pastures, the god who watches over the changing seasons and climates, the donor of rich harvests, prosperity, and honorable peace. He is the protector of married life and the guarantor of justice. But even Thor is at the same time the god of war, thus combining in himself the contrasting elements of friendly guardianship and dark and dangerous irrationality. With his hammer he smashes the enemies of men. He seems to be related to the ancient Aegaean thunder-god whose emblems were the double ax and the bull. To the Roman historians he is known as Hercules and Jupiter, and the Romans named after him the fifth day of the week (Thor's Day, Thursday, *Donnerstag*).

Ziu-Sachsnot is the war-god of the Saxons. The Romans called him Mars, naming after him the second day of the week (Ziu's Day, Tuesday, *Dienstag*). Wodan, whom the Scandinavians know as Odin, is the youngest of the Germanic sky-gods, the majestic god of death, of storm, of the battlefield, of wisdom, and of witchcraft. He is the leader of the army of disembodied souls, familiar to the Roman writers as Mercurius, and living on in the name of the third weekday (Wodan's Day, Wednesday). Even after having been raised to the position of the supreme sky-god he retained his original character of incalculable and unfathomable irrationality. He destroys heroes and protects cowards; he sows discord among friends and relations. He changes his attachments and affiliations, deserting his friends when they need him most. In his unreliability the arbitrariness of Fate appears personified and rationalized. In his capacity as the "father of all" (*Allvater*) he represents a symbolization of superindividual care and concern: he links the destinies of men with the cosmic fate of the gods and giants, gathering the proven heroes of the battlefield into *Valhalla* to save them for the final and monumental contest.

All Germanic peoples worshiped the great Mother Goddess Nerthus (*Hertha,* later *Njödr, Hödur*) whose cult has an almost exact parallel in that of Cybele, the mother of the gods, in Asia Minor. Some Germanic tribes call her *Frija* or *Frigg,* making her the patroness of love and matrimony. The Romans connected her with Venus and named after her the sixth day of the week (*Dies Veneris,* French *"Vendredi,"* Frija's Day, Friday, *Freitag*). Nerthus and her cult apparently belonged to the religion of the earth, of vegetation and sexual reproduction of the more ancient peasant culture, while the high gods or sky-gods are the creation of the more advanced warrior society which had, however, retained its peasant traditions. This dualism is even more manifest in the Old Norse mythology of early medieval times: the Scandinavians know two divine races or families, *Vanir* and *Aesir,* the former gods of the earth, the latter gods of the sky.

Heaven and earth, mountain and forest were populated by friendly and hostile spirits, elves, nymphs, dryads, dwarfs, goblins, witches, and werewolves. The spirits of the dead were believed to live on for a certain period of time in the trees and springs near the scenes of their former lives and activities.

Summarizing, it may be said that Germanic mythology and religion offer no final answer to the quest of the purpose and meaning of life. Even the best and most heroic life is ultimately lived and spent in vain. The gods, too, are subject to the decrees of Fate. And the final combat terminates the existence of the earth, of the gods, and of men. When *Ragnarök,* the fatal time, has arrived, "the sun will turn black, the earth sinks into the sea, the stars disappear from the skies, smoke and fire rage, burning flames lick the skies" (*Wöluspa*). The heroes cannot save the gods, but must perish with them, vanquished by the hostile powers. But what will happen to those hostile powers which survive the twilight of the gods, no tale will ever tell.

Thus Germanic mythology and religion dismiss us with an open question. This question was answered in the stormy centuries of the migrations with the reception of a new world religion in which the Germanic warrior-peasant rose above and beyond the stature of the gods of his cultural childhood.

Chapter 2

MIGRATIONS

Causes. The mass-movement of Germanic peoples (*Völkerwanderung*) which coincided with and in part contributed to the downfall of the Roman Empire and brought about decisive changes in the political map of Europe, appears as one of the last phases of the Indo-European migrations. The final outburst of these cataclysmic forces swept over the European continent, leaving behind ruin and destruction, to be sure, but also the seeds of a regeneration of Mediterranean culture and the formation of a Germanic and European civilization.

What was it that caused these peoples to abandon their native lands and, in many cases accompanied by their wives and children, their livestock and all their movable possessions, to look for new homes? One of the main reasons was the increase in population and the growing scarcity of habitable and arable land. The culture of the southern countries with their mild climate and their highly developed art of living exercised a strong power of attraction and fascination. Lust of adventure and the warlike spirit of ambitious leaders added a further motive. The increasing pressure of neighboring tribes, adverse social and political conditions, defeat in war, intertribal quarrels and rivalries were also back of the desire for a radical change in the form of a new start in more favorable surroundings. Finally, it may be said that the migrations were a manifestation of Germanic restlessness, a response to the romantic urge to seek out and conquer the distant unknown, the outgrowth of *"Fernweh"* and *"Wanderlust."*

Expansive Forces. The basis of the collective migratory movements was originally given in the organizations of the *Sippe* (clan) and *Stamm* (tribe). Later on, this basis grew broader, other communities and entire tribes following the lead of one group, thus giving the movement momentum and intensifying the force of its impact.

We see eastern and western Germans adopting different methods in the ways in which they migrate and settle in the newly acquired territories: while Visigoths and Ostrogoths, Vandals, Burgundians, and Langobards migrate in compact groups, carrying their movements in sweeping strides into Italy, Spain, and North Africa — Franks, Alemans, Bavarians, and Thuringians proceed more slowly and hesitatingly, maintaining close contact with their former homes. Of the northern Germans only the surplus popula-

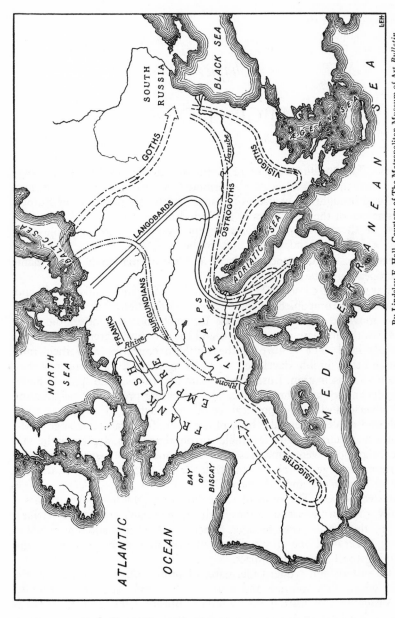

By Lindsley F. Hall, Courtesy of The Metropolitan Museum of Art *Bulletin*

Migration of European Tribes From the Second Through the Sixth Century After Christ.

tion leave their native shores on the North Sea, setting out for the conquest and settlement of Britain.

The Germanic migrations are often rather arbitrarily dated from the arrival of the Huns in Europe in A.D. 375. However, the migratory movement of the Germanic tribes had actually started long before that time. The Germanic expansion at the expense of the Celts lasted until Caesar's time. The Romans had early realized the danger which threatened from the northern barbarians. In vain they used force and cunning to break the power and spirit of their potential Germanic enemies. Roman armies marched into the Germanic lands, subjecting the conquered populations to Roman rule. They fortified the new boundaries, encouraged discord and rivalry among the different tribes, and even admitted increasing numbers of individuals and finally entire tribes into the Empire as imperial soldiers, army officers, and commanders, as semiservile agricultural workers, and as *foederati* or allies. This gradual infiltration of barbarians into the Empire acted in itself as a subversive element, and weakened further the already undermined structure of a waning civilization.

Beginnings: Bastarnians, Cimbers, and Teutons. The migrations of the Cimbers and Teutons mark the prelude of the more decisive events that were to follow. The first Germanic tribe to reach the frontiers of the Mediterranean world were the East Germanic Bastarnians who, at the beginning of the second century B.C., settled in the region between the lower Danube and the Black Sea. Toward the end of the pre-Christian era they were decisively defeated by the Romans and later mingled with the Goths and other tribes.

About 120 B.C. the Cimbers and Teutons started from their homes in Jutland and Schleswig-Holstein respectively, migrating in a southerly and southwesterly direction, finally entering Gaul and defeating several Roman armies, spreading fear and terror wherever they went (*"Terror Cimbricus," "Furor Teutonicus"*). They failed, however, to take advantage of their victory, so that the Romans were given ample time to prepare for an efficient counterattack. In two battles Teutons and Cimbers were annihilated by the Roman general Marius (156–86 B.C.), the Teutons at Aquae Sextiae (102 B.C.), the Cimbers on the Raudian Fields in the plain of Vercellae (101 B.C.), in the region of the upper Po river.

The first Germanic invasion of Italy thus ended in tragedy and defeat. As was customary in Germanic warfare, women and children, the aged and infirm, awaited the outcome of the battle barricaded behind the bulwark of wagons (*Wagenburg*), the women encouraging the warriors with singing and shouting, even repulsing with clubs and axes those who attempted to flee. After the victors had denied the women's request to permit them to enter the service of the Vestal Virgins,* so that their honor would be

---

* *Vesta* is the ancient Helic goddess of the hearth fire (Greek, *Hestia*). The "Vestal Virgins" in ancient Rome guarded the hearth fire in Vesta's Temple. They were chosen by lot and enjoyed special privileges in the city of Rome.

protected, the wives of these Germanic warriors first killed their children and then committed suicide.

The destruction of the Teutons and their subsequent disappearance from historical records proves conclusively that, aside from their being one of the Germanic tribes, there is no etymological or other connection between "German" (*deutsch*) and "Teutonic."

Suevians and Cheruscans: Caesar, Ariovistus, Arminius. About three decades after the extinction of the Cimbers and Teutons we find Ariovistus in Gaul. Ariovistus was the leader of the powerful tribe of the Suevians with whom Julius Caesar struggled for the possession of the Gallic province. He was defeated by Caesar's superior man power and strategy and had to withdraw across the Rhine, which therewith became the temporary boundary line between German and Roman territory.

The threatening neighborhood of the warlike tribes caused the emperor, Augustus (63 B.C. — A.D. 14), to occupy and fortify the Germanic lands up to the Danube, while his stepsons Drusus and Tiberius penetrated into the interior of Germany and conquered the territory between the Rhine and the Weser. Roman imperialism had already visualized an expansion of the colonial empire east to the river Elbe and south through Bohemia to Budapest, when these ambitious plans were thwarted and the Roman advance into Germanic territory halted by a major German victory.

The Roman colonial policy in Germany suffered its first severe setback at the hands of Arminius (Hermann), a Cheruscan prince who, in the famous battle in the Teutoburg Forest (A.D. 9), attacked and defeated the powerful Roman legions which were under the command of the provincial governor, Varus. At the end of the third day Varus fell upon his own sword, not daring to face his emperor after the annihilation of three legions. The battle marked a turning point in the destinies of Rome as well as of Germany, and Roman pride and prestige never quite recovered from this severe blow. Arminius, who had received his military training in the Roman armies, proved himself the docile disciple of sophisticated Roman strategies. The victory had been effected by a conspiracy of several Germanic tribes and, with the aid of cunning and deceit, resulted in the liberation of the greater part of Germany from Roman domination. Augustus' grandson, Germanicus, failed in several attempts to regain the former supremacy.

Once more the Rhine became the boundary line, until a few decades later the Romans proceeded to reoccupy some of the territory on the eastern bank of the river, concluding their colonial expansion into Germany with the construction of the *limes* or frontier wall which was begun under Emperor Claudius and completed under the emperors of the Flavian dynasty (first century B.C.). It was to facilitate the protection and supervision of the frontier districts, and extended into present-day Austria and Hungary. The *Saalburg* in the Taunus Mountains is part of the "limes," owing its restoration to Emperor William II. The fertile lands of the Rhine and Danube became the seat of a rich Roman provincial culture whose memory is still preserved in the ruins of irrigation works, aqueducts, baths, temples, and palaces, among which the *Porta Nigra* (Black Portal) in Treves (Trier) is the most monumental (first century B.C.). German cities of Roman origin, such as Strasbourg (*Argentoratum*), Mainz (*Mogontiacum*), Köln (*Colonia Agrippinensis*), Augsburg (*Augusta Vindelicum*), Regensburg (*Castra Regina*), Wien (*Vindobona*), and the net of highways linking these centers of urban life and culture, give evidence of the Romans' amazing building activity. Agricultural methods were greatly improved, and the commercial transactions of Roman merchants extended far to the north, including the rich amber trade of the Baltic.

New National Formations. For about 150 years relative peace was maintained between the Romans and the Germanic tribes. In the meantime, the beginning of the major phase of the great Germanic migrations was foreshadowed by a steady increase of the Germanic populations and a growing restlessness among the tribes. Their agricultural methods were relatively undeveloped and too inefficient to extract from the soil the necessary amount of food supplies. Their large herds of cattle made them look out for new pastures.

By the beginning of the fourth century A.D. we find that the political events of the recent past had led to the formation of several new nations. Wars, conquests, new alignments and alliances had strengthened the national consciousness, so that a number of smaller tribes joined in larger national confederations. On the eve of the second and major phase of the migrations two great East Germanic groups occupied the territory along the Rhine: the Franks were settled on the lower Rhine and the Alemans on the upper Rhine; in the northwest, along the coast of the North Sea and in the Danish peninsula, were the Saxons, Angles, and Jutes, the future conquerors of England; the Frisians, too, were located on the North Sea, the Vandals on the upper reaches of the Oder, the Langobards (Lombards) between the Oder and the Vistula, while the Burgundians drifted westward from the Vistula to the Main, and the Thuringians retained their ancient central position. Far in the southeast we find the kingdoms of the Ostrogoths (*Ostgoten*) and Visigoths (*Westgoten*), the greatest of the new Germanic nations. In the second century A.D. they had migrated from their old homes on the Baltic to southern Russia and advanced to the Black Sea.

Bishop Ulfilas and the Visigoths. The Visigoths, settled on the lower Danube in the immediate neighborhood of the Romans, were the first successful invaders of the Empire. They were the first of the Germanic peoples to accept Christianity, through their Bishop Ulfilas, who began his missionary activity among his countrymen in 341. Having been taken to Constantinople in his younger years as a hostage, he had acquired a mastery of Latin and Greek and later utilized this knowledge in his famous translation of the Bible into the Gothic tongue. He had invented for this purpose a special alphabet that followed the Greek pattern, thereby providing the most essential instrument for the creation of a written German literature.

Arianism. Ulfilas' translation of the Bible aided greatly in the spread of Christianity among the Visigoths, and through them among the Ostrogoths, Vandals, Burgundians, and other Germanic peoples. But while the Romans were adherents of the Catholic form of Christianity as embodied in the Roman Mother Church, the Visigoths, their bishop, and all those peoples that followed their example professed the creed of Arius (256–336), the founder of Arianism, who was born in Lybia and died in Constantinople. His Christology, which denied the divinity of Christ and the consubstantiality of the Father and the Son, and thereby attacked the Catholic dogma of the Trinity, was condemned as heretical by the First General Church Council of Nicaea (325).

The Arian sect gained immeasurably in power and prestige after the Vandals in North Africa, the Visigoths in southern Gaul and Spain, the Ostrogoths in Italy, and the Burgundians in southern France had succeeded in establishing powerful kingdoms, making Arianism their state religion, so that the terms "Arian" and "Germanic" were henceforth used synonymously, in polemical opposition to "Roman."

As a state religion Arianism had identified itself with these Germanic nationalities to such a degree that it did not survive their downfall and destruction. The adoption of Roman Catholicism by those nations which lived through the stormy centuries of the migrations and emerged victoriously from the disaster dealt the deathblow to the remnants of the Arian Sect. It lingered on to the seventh century and then disappeared from ecclesiastical and secular history.

The First Gothic Invasion and the Appearance of the Huns. When the Visigoths finally invaded the Roman Empire, they did so not so much of their own volition as under the pressure thrust upon them by the advancing Huns who, after having conquered the Ostrogoths in 375, threatened to overrun the territory of the Visigoths. The Huns were fierce and barbaric Mongolian or Tartaric nomads. For centuries they had been the scourge of civilized China until they were expelled by the emperors of the Han dynasty. As early as 49 B.C. they started on their westward movement, in search of new pastures.

The Gothic historian Jordanes describes them as short, broad-shouldered, and bowlegged, with hideous and beardless faces of yellow complexion, inseparable from their horses, living, fighting, eating, and sleeping on horseback.

With the appearance of the Huns in eastern Europe the prolonged border warfare between Romans and Germans enters upon a new stage. Shortly after the Mongolians had conquered the Ostrogoths and subjected them to their rule, the Visigoths, in fear and horror of the irresistibly advancing savages, asked permission of the Romans to cross the Danube and enter Roman territory. After having been admitted under humiliating terms and with much abuse and ill treatment by Roman officials, they took up arms and destroyed the imperial army, which joined battle with them at Adrianople

(378) under the personal command of the eastern Emperor Valens, who was killed in battle.

The End of the Western Empire. The battle of Adrianople marked the beginning of the end of the Roman Empire of the West. After Constantinople had been established as the second capital of the Empire by Emperor Constantine (A.D. 330), the center of gravity had shifted to the East. The growing estrangement between the eastern and western parts of the Empire was deepened by the adoption of Arianism in the East.

After the death of Emperor Theodosius (395) the Roman commonwealth was divided into the Eastern Empire under Arcadius, and the Western Empire under Honorius. While Constantinople and the Eastern Empire were spared the harassing experiences of the barbarian onslaught, and were capable of continuing the revival of the cultural traditions of classical Rome, the Western Empire was exposed to the full and brutal force of the invasions. About the middle of the fifth century West Rome found herself thrown back upon her original Italian boundaries. The East Germanic mercenary soldiers who were put in charge of Rome's defense, the Romans having grown unfit for military service, deposed Romulus Augustulus, the last emperor of the West, mockingly called "the little emperor," and proclaimed their leader Odovacar of the tribe of the Scirians as their king (476).

Thus the western Roman Empire of glorious memory came to an end, a disaster of extraordinary dimensions which shocked the pagan and Christian world alike. It seemed that the end of all things had come. In 396, when the storm was only beginning and the worst was yet to come, St. Jerome wrote: "The mind shudders when dwelling on the ruin of our day. For twenty years and more, Roman blood has been flowing ceaselessly over the broad countries between Constantinople and the Julian Alps, where the Goths, the Huns, and the Vandals spread ruin and death. Bishops live in prison, priests and clerics fall by the sword, churches are plundered, altars are turned into feeding-troughs. How many Roman nobles have been the prey of the barbarians! On every side sorrow, on every side lamentation, everywhere the image of death." And at the end of the sixth century Pope Gregory the Great, looking back from the chaotic disorder of the end phase of the migration period to the material prosperity of the early Christian centuries, repeated the words of Jerome: "Everywhere death, every- where mourning, everywhere desolation! In the age of Trajan, on the contrary, there was long life and health, material prosperity, growth of population. Yet while the world was still flourishing, in men's hearts it had already withered."

The Visigoths Continue Their March of Conquest. The battle of Adrianople in 378 was an epochal event in that it sounded the death knell for the almost legendary superiority and invincibility of Rome. Theodosius (379-395), who had succeeded the defeated Emperor Valens, permitted the Visigoths to settle in Thrace, exempting them from taxation and enrolling 40,000 of them in the Roman armies. The events that followed center in the political and military leadership of Alaric, king of the Visigoths (398–410). For a while his aggressive ambition was checked by the Roman general, Stilicho, who was himself of Germanic race. Their forces and talents were evenly matched. But after Stilicho had fallen a victim to the jealousy of Emperor Honorius, Alaric led his people down into Italy, marched three times upon Rome, and, in the year 410, entered and sacked the city. He died in the same year. His brother-in-law Ataulf married Gallia Placidia, half sister of Honorius, and obtained from the emperor the permission to settle his people in southwestern Gaul, from where they expanded into Spain, establishing there a new Visigothic kingdom which lasted in Gaul until the coming of the Franks in the sixth century, and in Spain till the Mohammedan invasion of 711.

The Vandals. The Visigoths had been preceded in the possession of Spain by the Vandals who, coming from the German East, had reached the Spanish peninsula in 406. Invited by the imperial ruler of North Africa, Count Boniface, to come to his assistance in his rebellion against Rome, they crossed the straits of Gibraltar in 429, under the inspired leadership of Gaiseric (428–477), entered Africa, and devastated the region of the North African seaboard. While they besieged the city of Hippo (430), St. Augustine, its bishop, died inside the city walls.

In 439 Gaiseric captured Carthage, the largest city and the most important harbor on the African coast, which he used as a naval base to strike at the dwindling commerce of the Empire. In 455 the Vandals sacked and pillaged Rome, sparing, however, the Christian churches, and carrying the golden roof of the temple of Jupiter back to their own capital. Their African kingdom lasted until 534, when it was destroyed by the armies of the Eastern emperor, Justinian (527–565).

That the Vandals were not the beasts of prey and wanton savages which they are frequently depicted to be — the term "vandalism" was coined by a French bishop in the eighteenth century — is suggested by the words of Salvianus, a Roman-Gallic priest who weighs the merits of Romans and barbarians against each other: "Whose wickedness," he asks, "is as great as that of the Romans? There is none of that kind found among the Vandals, none among the Goths. One thing is certain: the Vandals have been very moderate. Who can help but admire their tribes who, although entering the richest cities, concerned themselves with the pleasures of the corrupt only in so far as they scorned their moral corruption, and adopted only their good qualities? Among the Goths there are no unchaste people but Romans, and among the Vandals not even Romans; not that they alone are chaste, but, to relate something new, incredible, and almost unheard of: they have made even the Romans chaste."

And again he says: "They are growing from day to day, and we decline; they prosper, and we are humiliated; they flourish, and we wither." This may be as one-sided a statement as some of the reports of Tacitus, and it may have been prompted by the same reasons. We hold no brief for the Vandals: they were barbarians and, to a certain degree, they acted as savages, destroying, looting, marauding wherever they went. But they were not unsusceptible to higher cultural influences and impulses: they let themselves be persuaded by Pope Leo I to spare the lives of the civilian population of Rome, the churches, and some of the art treasures of the city. Only too quickly they succumbed to the sophistication, the luxuries, and the moral corruption of Mediterranean culture, paying for the surrender of their national traditions with the loss of their national existence.

Attila, Leader of the Huns. After having forced the Visigoths across the Danube into Roman territory (cf. p. 22), the Huns had organized an empire of their own north of the Black Sea and the lower Danube, thus being a constant threat to the peace and stability of the Eastern Empire. Under their great leader Attila who, as King Etzel, lives on with his people in the idealized account of the greatest of German folk epics, the Lay of the Nibelungs (*Nibelungenlied*), they crossed the southern frontier (445), and ravaged the provinces south of the Danube to the walls of Constantinople. Then they turned on the Western Empire, crossed the Rhine, and invaded Gaul.

Repulsed in 451, in the fierce but undecisive battle on the Catalaunian Fields (near Châlons-sur-Marne), by the combined efforts of Romans and barbarians, Attila returned in the following year, entered Italy, and, after sacking several cities in the north, returned to the region of the Danube and died shortly afterward. We are told that this unexpected retreat and the fact that Attila refrained from attacking and destroying Rome was due to the interference and persuasive power of Pope Leo I. Attila's empire crumbled almost immediately after his death. The Huns as a tribe disappeared from Europe and from the historic scene even more suddenly than they had originally emerged from the Asiatic steppes, although their race was partially absorbed by the Turks and Hungarians.

The Ostrogoths. After Odovacar of the tribe of the Scirians had deposed Romulus Augustulus (cf. p. 23) and subsequently taken over the government (476), he was granted the title of "Patrician" by the Eastern emperor, Zeno. This was nothing but an official acknowledgment of an actual situation, Italy having been ruled by barbarian generals for the past two decades. But in 489 Odovacar himself met the fate of the emperors whose place he had usurped. After Attila's death the Ostrogoths had freed themselves from the rule of the Huns and, under their capable leader and King, Theoderic (the Great), who is commemorated as Dietrich von Bern (Verona) in the German sagas and epics, waged war upon Odovacar. Not being able to prevail over him in battle, Theoderic resorted to trickery, invited Odovacar to negotiate a peace treaty, and assassinated him. Thereupon he conquered Italy and established his court at Ravenna.

As a ruler (489–526), Theoderic was relatively just and progressive, and is thus portrayed by Procopius, the historian of the Eastern Empire: "His manner of ruling over his subjects was worthy of a great emperor; for he maintained justice, made good laws, protected his country from invasion, and gave proof of extraordinary prudence and valor." He called philosophers and poets to his court and fostered a literary revival. Formally he recognized the superiority of the Eastern emperor Anastasius, he too holding the title of "Patrician"; actually, however, he was not only the king of the Ostrogoths but the independent ruler of Italy.

The problems of Theoderic's rule were complicated by the fact that Italy was now composed of two distinct races whose members lived side by side, preserving their own traditions, practicing their own laws, cultivating their own religion: Romans and Goths; Catholics and Arians. The military rule and caste was purely Gothic, the civil government purely Roman. And Theoderic insisted that these divisions be strictly observed and maintained. In this he succeeded to a remarkable extent, even in handling the difficult religious situation. "We cannot," he wrote, "impose religion, because no one can be compelled to believe against his will." Theoderic's death coincided with the splendid revival of the Eastern Empire under Justinian (527–565). Factional strife soon weakened the resistance of the Gothic kingdom, and made it the prey of Justinian's armies. And thus the powerful Ostrogoths, too, disappeared from the history of civilization.

Revival of Classical Learning Under Theoderic. The revival of learning and literature, which Theoderic encouraged, was to serve as an important link between the classical culture of antiquity and the Christian humanism of the early Middle Ages. Under Theoderic's rule the civil administration was in the hands of highly cultured Roman officials who carefully preserved the classical inheritance. Boethius (480–525) and Cassiodorus (490–583), scholars and educators of great distinction, were both in the service of Theoderic. Boethius has been called "the last of the classics and the first of the schoolmen." He transmitted to the medieval West the knowledge of Aristotelian logic and Greek (Euclidean) mathematics. While in prison and awaiting his execution for an alleged conspiracy against Theoderic, he composed his *Consolations of Philosophy,* a perfect blend of classical tradition and a thoroughly Christian philosophy of life.

Cassiodorus, in his position as Minister of State, tried to reconcile the Germanic and Roman types of culture. After his plan of a Christian university had failed and the outbreak of the Gothic wars began to impede his cultural activities, he founded a monastery at Vivarium, in the region of his Calabrian estates, collected a library, and drew up two programs of monastic studies ("Institute of Divine and Secular Letters"), including a compendium of the seven Liberal Arts. It was his idea to harmonize the essential features of the classical Roman curriculum with the needs and requirements of the new Christian society. Thus he made Vivarium the cradle of the Western tradition of monastic learning.

The Lombards. The last of the invaders of Italy were the West Germanic Lombards (Langobards, *longo bardi,* the long-bearded ones), who settled in the northern and central parts of Italy and whose influence extends to medieval history and civilization. They invaded northern Italy in 568, and were able to maintain their rule over the conquered territories for about two hundred years. In 774 their power was destroyed by Charlemagne, who himself assumed the title of "King of the Lombards." Racially they were absorbed by the new Romance populations, the name of the province of Lombardy being one of the few reminders of their national identity.

The Anglo-Saxons. After the Roman legions had been withdrawn from Britain at the beginning of the fifth century, to come to the rescue of the Romans in Italy and Gaul, the Jutes, Angles, and Saxons sailed from their homes on the North Sea and conquered the British Isles in the course of the two succeeding centuries. The Romanized Celtic population was destroyed or pushed back into the hill country of Wales and Cornwall. They remained apart from the race of the Germanic and pagan invaders, who developed Germanic institutions along the same lines as the Germanic peoples on the Continent.

After the Migrations. The Germanic kingdoms which originated during the centuries of the migrations were of relatively short duration, with the exception of those of the Franks and the Anglo-Saxons. The conquest of Gaul by the Frankish tribes, completed early in the sixth century, marks one of the milestones of German and European history, and transcends in scope, substance, and consequences the confines of the migration period. All the other tribes and nationalities were soon absorbed by the numerical and cultural superiority of the native Roman populations.

This process of assimilation and fusion, which ultimately issued in the formation of medieval and modern Europe, worked to the mutual advantage of the two cultures and races: the barbarians adopting the habits, attitudes, and outlook of the higher civilization, and the Romans experiencing the regenerative and purgative effects of a young and undespoiled cultural vitality. The new Romance (Latin) nations whose languages grew out of the vulgar Latin of the provincial populations of the Empire, owe their cultural and national existence to this Germanic-Roman synthesis. But while with them the Roman tradition remained the dominating element in life and thought, in art and literature, in religion and philosophy, the Franks and Anglo-Saxons instilled the vigorous individuality and originality of their own national heritage into the receptive molds of pagan and Christian Rome. The culture of the Franks, in particular, stands out as the fountainhead and pattern of a future German civilization.

It appears, then, that despite so many instances of a stupendous waste and loss of spiritual and material goods, the listless squandering of an inherited treasury of ideas and accomplishments by ruthless barbarians, the age of the migrations represents the incubation period of German culture. It ended with a considerable expansion of the habitable area of the German peoples, and it provided the natural and ideal setting for those national entities that had proven culturally most healthy, promising, and creative in the sifting process of these dark centuries.

Chapter 3

THE FRANKS AND THE
CHRISTIANIZATION OF GERMANY

A. MEROVINGIANS

The Merovingian Kingdom of the Franks. We have seen that of all those Germanic tribes who played a prominent part in the migrations, only the Franks and the Anglo-Saxons succeeded in creating civil organizations that survived the dark centuries of destruction and ruin. And among those peoples who stayed within the confines of their homelands the Franks were destined to become the founders of a civilized German state and the pioneers of the German civilization of the future.

The name "Franks" probably means "the free ones," i.e., the people on the right (east) bank of the Rhine who were nontributary to the Romans. They are first mentioned in A.D. 241, located in the region of the middle and lower Rhine, and comprising the two major groups of the Salians and Ripuarians. After A.D. 400 we find them in northern Gaul and in present-day Holland and Belgium. By virtue of a long tradition of contact and association with the Roman Empire, they formed the real bridge between the civilizations of ancient Rome and medieval Europe. In Gaul the Roman and barbarian societies met and complemented each other, providing through their fusion the basis of new social and cultural organisms.

In the year 486 Clovis (Clodovech), a Salian Frank of the family of Meroveus, became the absolute ruler of a strong Germanic kingdom of mixed Germanic-Roman population. He had cleared his way to the throne by the murder of all possible rivals and, after his accession, consolidated his rule by successive victories over the Gallo-Romans under Syagrius at Soissons (486), the Alemans (496), the Visigoths (507), and subsequently all the Frankish tribes, including the Ripuarians. Under Clovis' successors the Burgundians, Thuringians, Bavarians, Langobards, and Saxons were made tributaries of the Merovingian kingdom.

However, the remaining two and a half centuries of the Merovingian dynasty were characterized by internecine struggles among the rulers and pretenders, by crime, corruption, and degeneracy which undermined the prestige of the crown and let the actual rulership pass into the hands of the chief ministers, the "mayors of the palace," who governed the country.

In the seventh century the Frankish kingdom was split into three parts,

Frankish Kingdom in 481   Original possession of Clovis
Conquests of Clovis   Boundaries of Kingdom of Clovis
Conquests of his sons   Conquests of Pepin

From *Der Grosse Herder,* Herder, Freiburg i. Br.

Kingdom of the Franks From Clovis to Charlemagne (481–768).

known as Austrasia, Neustria, and Burgundy, each under its own king and mayor of the palace. The customary Frankish law for the inheritance of private property applied also to the order of royal succession, the Frankish king regarding his kingdom as his private domain which he divided among his sons. Thus each of the three kings of Austrasia, Neustria, and Burgundy had retained the title "Rex Francorum," King of the Franks. Neustria (New Land) included the territory north of the Loire with the principal cities of Paris, Soissons, and Orléans; Austrasia (East Land) comprised the eastern part of the Frankish kingdom, the territory of the later province of Lorraine with its capital Metz; Burgundy was located in the southern region of the Rhone, and included the cities of Lyon, Vienne, and Geneva.

Unity was restored in 687, when the ruling power was concentrated once more in the hands of Pepin of Heristal, the former mayor of Austrasia. Among his successors, Charles Martel (the "Hammer"), regent and mayor of the palace (*maior domus*), has earned the reputation of having saved Western civilization from the attack of the Mohammedan Arabs who, on their steady advance from the Arabian desert, along the northern coast of Africa, through Spain and into Gaul, were defeated by the Franks near Poitiers in 732. Upon Charles Martel's death the kingdom was again divided between his two sons, Pepin the Younger and Carloman. After Carloman had retired to a monastery, Pepin felt that his sovereign power was firmly enough established to warrant the deposition of the Merovingian puppet king and to claim the crown for himself and his family. With the moral support of Pope Zacharias he had himself crowned king of the Franks and solemnly consecrated by Boniface, the papal nuncio and primate of Germany, thereby establishing an important precedent regarding the future relations of Church and State. In thus obtaining the title of King of the Franks Pepin the Younger became the first royal member of that family of mayors of the palace who for three generations ruled the destinies of the Frankish realm, and who have come to be known as Carolingians from the greatest of their number, Charlemagne.

The Baptism of Clovis. When Clovis first took possession of the throne, there was one great remaining obstacle to prevent the union of Romans and Franks in the territory in which they lived side by side: the Franks were heathens, the Romans were Catholic Christians. Persuaded by his Burgundian wife Clotilde and prompted by political considerations, King Clovis had himself solemnly baptized, and was received into the Church at Reims on Christmas Day, 496, together with three thousand of his followers. This event marked a turning point in the history and civilization of Europe and of Germany. It inaugurated the close alliance between the Frankish kingdom and the Church, an alliance which, in turn, provides the background of Western medieval culture. As the champion of Roman Catholicism against Arianism, Clovis undertook his campaign against the Visigoths in 507, naïvely veiling his desire of conquest in the words reported by Bishop Gregory of Tours: "Verily it grieves my soul that these Arians should hold a part of Gaul; with God's help let us go and conquer them and take their territories."

Christianity and Paganism Among the Franks. That Christianity was frequently embraced reluctantly and practiced only nominally by the Franks, may well be imagined. **The** Germanic peoples in their heroic age were pagans at heart, and they remained so for some time to come, even when giving lip service to the Christian God. Pagan rites continued in the guise of Christian ceremonies and Christian forms of worship; the pagan deities lived on in the images and character traits of Christian saints; magical beliefs and practices eagerly fastened themselves on the devotion to sacred objects and places, relics and shrines. At the time of the summer solstice, burning wheels, symbolizing the sun, could still be seen rolling down the mountain slopes; pagan dances and love feasts were performed in Christian churches to honor the saints on their feast days; Christian priests moved into the places that had been vacated by the Germanic witches, sorcerers, and weathermakers.

The external routine of Roman administration was almost slavishly imitated by the barbarian king. He had his "sacred palace" with its hierarchy of officials, headed by the "mayor of the palace." The administrative unit was no longer the Germanic "hundreds" but the Roman *civitas* with its surrounding territory. The *civitas* or municipality was divided into hundreds and under the authority and jurisdiction of a count (Old English: *gerefa;* "sheriff," *Graf*) who was the king's appointee. This adaptation of Roman institutions was however outweighed by the prevalence of barbarian elements in the Merovingian State. What consolidated society was not so much the civil authority of the State, but the personal loyalty of the tribesman to his chief and his kinsfolk, of the warrior to his leader.

Social Conditions. Class distinctions, which in the earliest times seem to have been based upon the amount of freedom enjoyed, were more and more determined in Merovingian times by the possession of property, although the concept of absolute ownership was still unknown. We may roughly distinguish between freedom, semifreedom, and slavery. The large freeholders were mostly members of the aristocracy, constituting the king's mounted bodyguard, and taking the place of the old Germanic thanes. As military leaders they became more and more indispensable to the rulers. An increasing number of vassals thus received their lands as loans or fiefs (Latin: *feodum, beneficium*) from the king, the land theoretically remaining the king's property and the vassal or steward taking an oath of lifelong fidelity (fealty). The small freeholders frequently renounced their freedom and gave up their lands to some powerful secular or clerical overlord to receive it back as a "fief," in order to escape indebtedness or military service and, at the same time, to enjoy the protection of the liege lord.

As the king's vassals grew more influential they acquired important privileges, especially the so-called "immunity" which freed them from the jurisdiction of the royal courts, thus weakening the central power and authority of the State. This development marked the beginnings of "feudalism" or the "feudal" system which was to provide the political, economic, and social pattern of medieval society, and which signified the transition from the public ownership of the primitive Germanic tribes to the age of private property and the eventual rise of capitalism.

Slave trading had gained considerably, and the number of slaves increased during the migrations, because many members of the subdued populations had been reduced to the status of slaves. In Merovingian times it was still considered legal for a creditor to enslave an insolvent debtor, and enslavement was the lot of those convicted of treason, rape, and other major crimes.

Although the Church did not immediately abolish slavery — slaves were held on ecclesiastical estates to the end of the sixth century — the ecclesiastical authorities did much to ease their lot, granting them a certain amount of protection within Church territory, and gradually working toward their liberation. The institution of slavery disappeared only in proportion to the growing estimation of human life and personality.*

Law and Legal Procedure. Judicial power had passed from the tribe and the hundreds to the king. He (later on the mayor of the palace) was the supreme judge. Following the Roman model he established "the King's Court," in which the count administered justice and pronounced judgment in the local centers of the hundreds in the king's name. To determine the guilt or innocence of the accused, the old Germanic "ordeal" or appeal to "God's Judgment" (*Gottesurteil*) was still in favor. So was the duel or trial by combat, which was fought with swords, clubs, or axes. Duels between members of the opposite sexes were not uncommon, the woman as the weaker combatant being granted certain advantages. The ordeal is known in various forms, the most common being the "cauldron test" (*Kesselprobe*), in which the suspect had to take with his bare hand a stone or a ring out of a cauldron of boiling water; the "fire test" (*Feuerprobe*) which consisted in walking a certain distance, carrying red-hot irons in one's hands, or in walking barefoot over glowing plowshares; and the "water test" (*Wasserprobe*), requiring the victim to be bound and thrown into a tank. His floating upon the surface of the water was considered proof of his guilt.

The crude and barbaric administration of justice was gradually modified by the codification of Germanic law in the Latin language which followed closely upon the codification of Roman Law under Justinian I of the Eastern Empire (527–565). All the German tribes believed that every man should be judged according to the traditional legal concepts of his own people (*Volksrecht*). Thus each of the tribes had its own ancestral code. The tribal laws of the Franks, the Alemans, the Bavarians, and the Saxons were written down in Merovingian times. Even earlier the Romanized East Germanic Visigoths, Ostrogoths, and Burgundians had committed their legal concepts to writing. From the later years of Clovis' rule (508–511) dates the oldest code of German tribal law which is completely preserved: the *Lex Salica* (Salic Law), containing a detailed scale of punishments that range from simple offenses to major and capital crimes.

Currency and Trade. In Merovingian times fines and compensations were paid largely in coin, which presupposes the adoption of some system of currency, although a money economy in the medieval and modern sense was still lacking. The barter system was still commonly practiced, money being valued as a treasure rather than a means of exchange. However, the Franks were acquainted with Roman money, and Clovis introduced the

---

* During the Middle Ages the institution of slavery was gradually transformed into various forms of serfdom (*Leibeigenschaft*), which in some European countries persisted well into the eighteenth and nineteenth centuries.

gold standard of coinage as the unit of measurement (gold *solidus* or *shilling*), a shilling representing the value of approximately three dollars.

In the course of the seventh century the silver shilling replaced the gold shilling as the standard of coinage.* In order to counteract avaricious and usurious practices in commercial dealings, the first general prohibition of the taking of interest was decreed by the Church in 787, thereby opening a new field of remunerative activity to the Jews, who were outside the jurisdiction of canon law and therefore able to monopolize the money trade to the end of the Middle Ages.

Learning. In almost every department of civilization, then, we find a crossing and blend of Roman and barbarian, Christian and Germanic impulses and influences, frequently with a marked preponderance of the barbarian elements. As regards the field of education, the Romans had continued and further developed the Druidic (Celtic) schools which they had found well established in Gaul, with a curriculum that included the teaching of theology, philosophy, rhetorics, astronomy, mathematics, and law. Marseille, Toulouse, Bordeaux, Reims, Lyon, among other cities, were such Druidic and afterward Roman centers of learning.

The founding of cathedral schools and monastic schools as well as of those parish schools that were recommended by the Council of Vaison (529) contributed to the continuation and revival of learning when, toward the end of the Merovingian period, it was in danger of disintegration. Books, which had replaced the rolled manuscripts of antiquity in the fifth century A.D., were now being collected by the newly founded monasteries on German soil, and the crude script of the Merovingian age experienced a considerable refinement at the beginning of the Carolingian epoch, probably owing to the influence of the Irish missionaries (cf. p. 37 sq.).

Language: The High German Sound Shift. Roman, Germanic, and Celtic elements mingled in the linguistic expression of Merovingian times, symbolically revealing the struggle of two ages, two races, two cultures. Between 500 and 800 the speech of the Franks, the Alemans, and the Bavarians was considerably altered by the so-called Second or High German Sound Shift,** which resulted in a sharper distinction between the High (i.e., south) and the Low German (including Anglo-Saxon, Dutch, and Flemish or Walloon) languages, literatures, and cultures. This sound shift affected principally old Germanic *p, t,* and *k,* which changed their character in High German dialects, as in the following examples.

Germanic *p* became *pf* or *f* in High German (but not in Low German), for example, Gothic: *slêpan;* High German: *schlafen;* English: sleep.

---

* The following examples may give some idea on the purchasing power of the shilling: a cow cost 3 sh. or $9; an ox 2 sh. or $6; a steer 3 sh. or $9; a horse 12 sh. or $36; a serf 12 sh. or $36; a long sword (*spatha*) 3 sh. or $9; a long sword with belt 7 sh. or $21.

** The First or "Germanic Sound Shift," which created the dividing line between the Germanic and other Indo-European languages, had occurred about 500 B.C. At that time the tenues (voiceless stopped consonants), *t, p, k* were transformed into voiceless spirants (fricative consonants); the Indo-European aspirated mediae (voiced stopped consonants) *dh, bh, gh* into voiced spirants; the Indo-European mediae *d, b, g* into tenues.

Germanic *t* acquired a *ts* sound (spelled z or tz) or an *s* sound, for example, Gothic: *twai;* High German: *zwei;* English: two. Gothic: *itan;* High German: *essen;* English: eat.

Germanic *k* became *ch,* for example, Gothic: *juk;* High German: *Joch;* English: yoke. There is still no agreement among philologists as to the cause of these phonetic changes.

The Influence of Latin Culture and the Roman Church. On the whole, then, the Frankish State in Merovingian times showed relatively small evidence of the influence of Christian culture. Greed, avarice, treachery, and moral depravity was evidenced in many actions of the rulers. The dominant force was still the spirit of the primitive warrior tribe. And yet Christian impulses were strong enough to leave an enduring impress on the culture of the Frankish kingdom, and to work almost imperceptibly as a leaven to prepare the medieval synthesis of Germanic, Roman, and Christian elements.

The power that acted as the principle of integration in the new political and cultural organism of the Frankish kingdom was the Roman-Christian tradition. In the early period of the Empire Rome had been an international city, and Greek was then the language of the Roman Church. With the growing estrangement of the eastern and western parts of the Empire the Roman Church gradually became Latinized. Latin culture was henceforth embodied in Roman Catholicism, and with the conversion of the barbarians Christianity rose from its subordinate role as the religion of conquered populations to a dominating and culturally formative force in the new civilization.

Christianity As a State Religion. Christianity thus confronted the Germanic peoples, the Franks especially, as a compelling force which challenged and tested their adaptive and creative cultural capacities, causing a cultural "break," signifying the transition from primitivity to maturity. The idea of divine providence and omnipotence imparted a new meaning and value to the life and work of the Germanic warrior, whose faith in the protective power of his national deities had been shaken even before Christian missionaries cut down Donar's sacred oak trees and destroyed the heathen sanctuaries.

Since Christianity had become a State religion under Emperor Constantine (306–337) it felt, even more strongly than before, the necessity of combining its historic continuity with its universal mission. Regarding itself as a supernatural society, the Church recognized the State as a natural society. Before it had become a State religion, Christianity had shown itself radically opposed to the social and moral conditions that prevailed in the Roman Empire, and it had refused to co-operate with a society that bore the marks of corruption and decadence. The Church, with its own organization and hierarchy, its system of government and administration, its rules of membership and initiation, was an autonomous social organism whose social philosophy would never come to terms with the culture of the Empire.

Yet with all these glaring antagonisms, certain typically Roman characteristics were also embodied in the primitive Christian Church. Pope Clement I, in his Epistle to the people of Corinth (A.D. 96), insisted that that order which he calls the law of the universe should likewise be the principle of the new Christian society. He stressed moral discipline and subordination as essential virtues. Constantine himself considered a church which proclaimed such ideals the logical ally of the universal claims and traditions of the Empire.

Christianity As the Heir of the Classical Tradition. The fourth century finds the Church organized according to the model of the Empire. While the eastern churches began to look to Constantinople as their spiritual and political center, Rome, the capital of the Empire in the West, became also a center of the Church. While the East shows itself creative in the fields of philosophy and the arts, among the Christian thinkers of the West only Augustine stands out as highly original, whereas the majority are eclectics, utilizing the riches of eastern Christian wisdom, and being satisfied with the cultivation of the traditional Roman civic virtues of order and discipline. This western Roman tradition is alive in Bishop Ambrose of Milan (340–397) and, coupled with a strong moral sense and the fervor of his Christian faith, it makes him the first exponent of the ideal of a Christian state in the West. Early in the fifth century Ambrose's ingenious disciple, St. Augustine (354–430), constructed a system of thought that was to stimulate and occupy the Western mind for more than a thousand years. Later in the fifth century, Pope Leo I combined Ambrose's conviction of the providential mission of the Roman Empire with the doctrine of the primacy of the see of the bishop of Rome as the successor of Peter, the "Prince of the Apostles."

Thus the Roman Church had developed an autonomy and a social and religious authority which embodied some of the most constructive elements of Roman culture, and which enabled it to stand on its own feet when the Empire collapsed, fully equipped to become the heir of ancient Rome and to transmit its cultural assets together with Christian doctrine to the new barbarian peoples. The survival of classical literature and the rhetorical tradition, and its cultivation by the Christian theologians and poets of the "patristic age" (the age of the "Church Fathers"), prepared the way for the rise of the medieval literatures of Europe. Church doctrine and Scriptures on the one hand, Hellenistic and classical cultural traditions on the other— these heterogeneous aspects of waning and rising social orders were certainly powerful stimuli in a period of transition.

The Graeco-Roman schools of rhetorics represented, it is true, only the literary side of ancient culture, while its scientific aspects were assimilated by the Christian and Moslem East. The West was affected only by the late revival of Greek philosophy in the form of Neo-Platonism (second and third centuries A.D.) which so strongly influenced medieval thought and culture. Just as there would be no medieval philosophy without Augustine, so without Dionysius the Areopagite (fifth century A.D.) one important branch in the tradition of mystical theology and in particular the linguistic splendor and speculative depth of the German mystics of the thirteenth and fourteenth centuries would be unthinkable (cf. p. 146 sq.).

Both writers were greatly indebted to Neo-Platonism, Augustine being a professional rhetorician, and deriving from his acquaintance with the system of Plotinus (204–269) his idea of God as the source of being and intelligence, and of the soul as a spiritual substance that finds beatitude in mystical union with the Uncreated Light. Even after his conversion to Christianity, so elaborately described in his *Confessions,* he retained the Graeco-Roman and Platonic emphasis upon the elements of order and rationality in the universe, and the conviction of the metaphysical goodness and beauty of all created being as emanating from the eternal source and exemplary paradigm of all goodness and beauty. To be sure, the strict religious orthodoxy of the following centuries temporarily obscured this heritage of Christian Platonism, only to restore it to full and sovereign splendor in the thought and life of the later Middle Ages and the early Renaissance.

Monasticism. The conversion of the Franks and a number of other Germanic tribes during the Merovingian Age was chiefly due to the missionary zeal and fearless enthusiasm of Irish and Anglo-Saxon monks. It was toward the end of the migration period (*c.* A.D. 500) that the monastic movement became the leading force in the political and cultural formation of Europe. Monasticism originated in the East, where hundreds of hermits and ascetics had secluded themselves in the Egyptian and Libyan deserts, forsaking all human association and cultural attachments in order to live the pure and simple life that Christ recommended in the Evangelical Counsels (Matt. 19:12; 21:29). The ideals of poverty, chastity, and obedience thus became the foundation of monastic life. But while Eastern monasticism negated and even abhorred cultural values and felt inclined to practice an extreme asceticism as an end in itself, the West gradually developed its own conception of the monastic community, in which cultural activities received due consideration but were ordered to the supreme end of Christian life, the vision and possession of God, and the imitation of Christ as a means to that end.

The Monks of the West. When Rome had been conquered by the Germanic peoples, the time seemed to have arrived to realize the genuine Western type of monasticism. In 520 Benedict of Nursia founded the monastery of Montecassino in the hill country between Rome and Naples, completing the work that had been begun by Cassiodorus at Vivarium in Calabria (cf. p. 26). "The Patriarch of the Monks of the West," as he has been called, was a descendant of the provincial Roman nobility, endowed with the Latin genius for law and order, and possessing the gifts of a great educator and organizer. In contrast to the irregularity and eccentricity that marked the lives and habits of the ascetics and hermits of the Eastern deserts, the Benedictine order from its beginning was conceived as a co-operative and economically self-sufficient society, emphasizing the necessity of a well-organized, familylike community life. The same sense of moderation that knew how to practice true devotion without submitting to the unsound precepts of extreme asceticism, dividing monastic life between prayer, work, and recreation, is embodied in Benedict's famous "Rule," which henceforth was to shape and influence the mode and standard of life in Western monasteries.

In learning and research, in agriculture, horticulture, and the mechanical arts and crafts, Benedictine monks became the teachers of the Germanic peoples, and numerous Latin loan words in German point to the educational influence of the Benedictines in these occupations. They taught the Germans the dignity of manual labor, which even the most brilliant minds of antiquity, a Plato, an Aristotle, a Cicero, had considered a fitting occupation for slaves only. Now labor for the first time was conceived of as cooperation with the laws of nature, and as the value-creating collaboration with the designs of the Author of nature.

Anglo-Saxon Missionaries. Pope Gregory the Great (590–604), himself a Benedictine monk, scholar, and mystic, was directly responsible for the Benedictine missions in England and Germany. Roman Benedictines went forth to Britain to convert the Anglo-Saxons, and inspired their Anglo-Saxon disciples to continue their crusade and carry it back to the Continent. Providing Latin texts with vernacular glosses, the Anglo-Saxon monks in Germany aided in creating the beginnings of a vernacular German culture and literature.

Wynfrith (Boniface), "The Apostle of the Germans." Wynfrith (672–754), who received the name of Boniface when he was made a bishop in 722, is known as the great organizer of the Frankish-German Church. A native of Wessex, he united in his character and work Germanic initiative and a Roman-Benedictine sense of proportion. He carried the message of Christianity into the heart of the German lands, converted the inhabitants of Hesse and Thuringia, reorganized and revived ecclesiastical discipline in Bavaria, established abbeys and bishoprics on the sites of the Germanic folkburgs and heathen sanctuaries, and was finally slain with fifty-two of his companions by pagan Frisians to whom he was preaching the Gospel. In 732 he had been made archbishop and in 738 primate and papal nuncio of Germany. He lies buried in the crypt of the Cathedral of Fulda, where he had founded the famous abbey of the same name, and where the German bishops still meet annually in solemn convention to carry on their deliberations near the tomb of the Apostle of Germany.

Irish Missionaries. Even before the Anglo-Saxon Benedictines had organized their missionary work in Germany, monks from Ireland had come to the kingdom of the Franks to preach Christ and His kingdom. Their methods, however, were altogether different, as different as was their race, their temper, and their mentality. They were representatives of that Celtic population that even in prehistoric times had played a prominent part in the development of Western culture (cf. p. 3 sq.). We know that they had originally inhabited the greater part of Germany as well as the British Isles, that the Germanic tribes owed them their acquaintance with the cultures of the Bronze and Iron Ages. Most of the Celts were conquered by the Romans, and the Christian religion reached them simultaneously with the influence of Roman culture. Only gradually did they give way to the pressure of the expanding Germanic tribes. Ireland as such had never been conquered by the Romans, and therefore remained the actual center and focus of Celtic civilization. Christianity had penetrated into the island of Erin (British: *Iwerddon;* Latin: *Hibernia*), as Ireland was originally called, during the first half of the fifth century. It was enthusiastically received, and as early as the sixth century we witness the missionary activities of Irish monks on Frankish territory.

The monasteries of Ireland were characterized by a rigid and even cruel discipline as much as by their preoccupation with scientific and artistic problems and endeavors. The monks wrote prose and poetry, prayed and conversed in their Celtic mother tongue. They excelled in the ornamentation of biblical manuscripts, which they adorned with the symbols and major characters of the Scriptures, revealing their rich and involved imaginative life in beautifully painted initial letters and lines, interspersing the spiral movement of intertwining lineament with a phantastic imagery of stylized animal motifs.

In organization and administration the Irish monasteries differed from the Anglo-Saxon and German Benedictine abbeys in that they had no uniform monastic rule. Here, too, to be sure, the vows of poverty, chastity, and obedience were considered the basis of community life. But the life in common revealed distinctly the clannish organization of national life in Ireland. One or several monks occupied the simple and primitive wooden huts which together made up the monastic settlement. The members of the congregation were members of the same tribe or clan, and the tribal chieftain usually appointed as abbot a member of his own family. Despite such peculiarities and certain deviations from the ideal type of Western monasticism, the authority of the Roman Church was recognized in Ireland, and there was no doctrinal cleavage.

The inborn unrest of the Irish temper soon found an outlet for its suppressed energies in the missionary work among the Franks which began at the end of the sixth century.

Columbanus and Gallus.   With twelve companions, Columbanus the Younger had left his monastery at Bangor in Ulster about the year 590, and soon afterward we find him in Frankish Gaul where, according to his report, "the love of mortification was scarcely to be found even in a few places." He himself founded the monasteries of Luxeuil in the French Jura Mountains, at Fontaines, and at Anegray. The name of his disciple, Gallus, is linked with his world-renowned foundation, St. Gall in Switzerland, which for a considerable length of time was the most distinguished seat of German scholarship.

Statue of St. Boniface, Apostle of Germany, at Fulda

The Cathedral in Aachen

In contrast to the disciplinary regulations in the Benedictine abbeys, Irish monasticism shows no consideration for the inherent weakness of human nature, and breathes the spirit of harsh and unbending autocracy. This un-compromising attitude, coupled with certain defects in matters of organiza-tion, accounts for the partial failure of the Irish monks' enthusiastic and un-tiring efforts. Nevertheless, their energy was not misspent. At a time when the decadent Merovingian dynasty had handed over its power to the "mayors of the palace," the Irish and Anglo-Saxon missionaries aided the advance-ment of culture and brought about the reform and restoration of the Frankish Church. Their work was sympathetically viewed and actively supported and supplemented by Charles Martel and his successors Pepin and Carloman, and henceforth the Carolingians became the promoters and patrons of ecclesiastical reform. They utilized the forces of the Christian religion and the institution of monasticism for their work of political, social, and cultural reorganization.

B. CAROLINGIANS

The "Donation of Pepin." When Boniface in the year 752 anointed Pepin, the erstwhile Merovingian mayor of the palace, he not only gave ecclesiastical sanction to the new Carolingian dynasty, but confirmed in a symbolical act the sacerdotal mission of the Frankish monarchy. The Merovingian State had been predominantly secular and national, its church had been primarily a national church, only loosely linked with Rome and the papacy. The Carolingian State was to be universal and theocratic, resting upon the alliance between the Frankish monarchy and the papacy, the monarch acting as the recognized champion and protector of the pope.

In the very same year (751) in which Pepin had been made king of the Franks, the Lombards had destroyed the Byzantine (East Roman) province of the Exarchs of Ravenna in central Italy, thus depriving the popes of their traditional protectors. In the winter of 753–754 Pope Stephen II crossed the Alps to meet Pepin at Ponthion, near Bar-le-Duc, to implore his aid against the Lombards. In 754 and 756 Pepin defeated the Lombards, and forced them to surrender to the papacy the exarchate of Ravenna, together with the duchies of Spoleto and Benevento. The Pope conferred on Pepin the dignity of "Patrician" of the Romans, a title traditionally held by the Exarchs of Ravenna, the highest Byzantine officials in Italy.

These events marked the foundation of the Papal States (States of the Church) and the beginning of the temporal power of the papacy, which was to endure until 1870, when Rome was captured by. Italian troops, and which was restored to some small extent by Benito Mussolini in the *Lateran-Treaties* of 1929. But the "Donation of Pepin" also marks the beginning of the protectorate of the Carolingians and their successors in Italy and of their intense interest in Italian affairs. It was about the time of Pepin's rule that the bold forgery of the so-called "Donation of

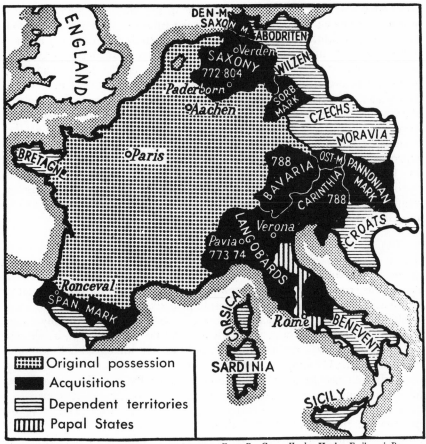

From *Der Grosse Herder*, Herder, Freiburg i. Br.

Kingdom of Charlemagne (768–814).

Constantine" made its appearance, contending that Emperor Constantine through a similar deed had willed all Italy to Pope Sylvester I (314–335).

Pepin, "Patrician" of the Romans. What had actually happened in that memorable meeting of King Pepin and Pope Stephen II was that the papacy and the Frankish kingdom had come to each other's support. For if Pepin wanted to establish his family firmly on the throne and carry through his ideas of political and social reform, he needed the moral support of the papacy. In return for his gift "to the Roman·Church, to St. Peter, and his successors the popes" he was hailed as the "New Moses" and the "New David" who had been anointed by the High Priest of the New Dispensation.

Charlemagne and the Creation of the Carolingian Empire. What had been begun by Pepin was completed by his eldest son Charles. The "Patrician" became the "Imperator." The king of the Franks accepted the universal mission of uniting all the Western nations under the dome of a Christian-Germanic civilization. For although Charles received the imperial crown from the pope, the Church in Germany retained many of its Frankish-national features, and Charles was ambitious enough to include the papacy in his far-reaching schemes. He acquired an exalted view of his authority as the divinely appointed leader of the Christian peoples, holding the two swords of spiritual and temporal power, and imposing his will on Church and State alike.

Charles earned his surname "the Great" by coping successfully with ever new and increasingly complex situations. Defeating the Lombards in 774, he redeemed Pepin's pledge to the papacy. Placing the Langobard crown on his own head, he celebrated Easter in Rome and renewed the promises of Pepin. His bitter and relentless wars with the heathen Saxons, extending over a period of more than thirty years (772–804), ended with a complete victory of Charles and the Saxons' submission to Frankish rule and to the Christian religion, which was forced upon them together with political domination. Thousands of Saxons were slaughtered at Verden on the river Aller in 782, after they had been delivered into Charles's hands by members of their native nobility. Thousands of others were deported to be employed as colonists in different parts of the Frankish kingdom. Deposing the dukes of Bavaria, Charles brought this province of southern Germany into closer union with the Frankish kingdom. He fought successfully against the Avars in the region of present-day Austria and against Slavic tribes in the eastern Alps. The famous *Chanson de Roland,* the greatest of medieval French epics, as well as the German *Rolandslied* (*c.* 1170), commemorate Charles's campaign in Saracen Spain (778). While he was on his return march through the Pyrenees, the rear guard of the Frankish army under the command of Count Hruotland (Roland) was cut off and destroyed by the Basques in the mountain pass of Roncesvalles. But Charles succeeded in getting control of a strip of land south of the Pyrenees, where he established the strongly fortified Spanish "march."

As the eighth century drew to a close, Charles's kingdom included the territories of modern France, a part of Spain, Holland, Belgium, Austria, Bohemia, Moravia, and the greater part of Italy. Since the fall of the Roman Empire the West had not seen such a vast territory under one ruler. The Frankish king was the unchallenged sovereign of Western Christendom. The pope called him the "new Constantine" and the defender of St. Peter. The princes of Scotland and Ireland paid homage to him, and the patriarch of Jerusalem offered him the keys of the Holy Sepulcher.

Thus the stage was perfectly set for the epoch-making scene that took place in Rome on Christmas Day of the year 800. After the pontifical High Mass in St. Peter's Cathedral Pope Leo III placed an imperial crown upon Charles's head, hailing and venerating him in Byzantine fashion as the august emperor of the Romans.

If we may believe Charles's biographer Einhard, Charles was in no way prepared for this honor and not only surprised but positively embarrassed. Yet he soon learned to look upon this historic hour as an event of providential significance, and he fully lived up to its vast implications and promises.

An Empire had thus been created which was Roman, Christian, and Germanic in one, and its ruler was courageous enough to visualize the creation of a league of chosen nations which would establish the kingdom of God upon earth, translating into reality the ideal state and society of Charles's favorite book, St. Augustine's *City of God*. Even if these far-reaching dreams remained largely unfulfilled, this much is true: the Western family of nations rose under Charles's leadership to an unprecedented cultural pre-eminence.

The Personal Regime. Beginning Disintegration. The Empire of Charles did not live much longer than did the genius of its founder. It lasted less than a century. Built upon the personal rule of one man who acted as the autonomous leader of his people, it was too large and unwieldy an organism to withstand for any length of time the attacks of foes from without and of disruptive forces from within. The idea of personal leadership in the Germanic past and present is based upon an unwritten sacred contract between the one who governs and those who are governed. This personal relationship, which distinguishes Germanic rule from the legalistic and abstract Roman concept of government, underlies the structure of the feudal system, and accounts for the moral greatness and the political weakness of medieval and modern Germanic State organisms. On the whole, the Empire of Charles is more noteworthy because of its historical and cultural significance than because of its material achievements. Economically and socially it never attained to that cohesion and unity that characterizes a thoroughly civilized State.

Relapse Into Barbarism. The decades that followed Charles's death witnessed the rapid disintegration of the Empire he had created. Empire and papacy alike became immersed in an abyss of anarchy and barbaric lawlessness. The governing principles of society were the law of force on the one hand and the need for protection on the other. In the course of the ninth century the State lost all contact with the urban tradition and became completely agrarian. The life of the feudal nobility was spent in warfare and private feuds. From their strongholds the feudal lords terrorized peaceful villagers and passing travelers. Bishops like other feudatories received investitures from the princes, holding their estates in return for military services, while the papacy reached the climax of depravity in the tenth century, becoming a passive tool in the hands of the Roman Consul Theophylact and the women of his house. The records of this period read like the accounts of the Germanic migrations: "The cities are depopulated, the monasteries ruined and burned, the country reduced to solitude. The strong oppress the weak, the world is full of violence against the poor. Men devour one another like the fishes in the sea" (Acts of the Synod of Troslé of the year 909).

Louis the Pious and His Sons. What had happened? Charles the Great died in 814, and was survived by only one of his sons, Louis (the "Pious"), king of Aquitaine. The year before he died Charles himself had bestowed the imperial crown upon Louis because apparently he was disinclined to surrender to the papacy the privilege of sanctioning the choice of his successor. But Louis had Pope Stephen V repeat the ceremony of coronation at Reims, three years later. Complying with the customary Frankish law of inheritance, Louis announced his plan of dividing the Empire after his death among his three sons, Lothar, Pepin, and Louis. Meanwhile Judith, Louis' second wife, was scheming to gain the greater part of the Frankish heritage for her own son Charles. The three sons of Louis' first marriage rose up in arms against their father, and when Louis the Pious died in 840, the question of the division of the Empire was still unsettled. The death of Pepin left the three brothers Lothar, Louis, and Charles as pretenders, while the functions of government were neglected and the imperial authority suffered irreparable damage. The insurgent nobility and the ambitious princes vied in their attempts to wrest as much power and prestige as possible from the central government.

The Treaties of Verdun (843) and Mersen (870). At last Louis and Charles came to an understanding, when they met at Strasbourg in 842, taking an oath of perpetual loyalty to each other. This meeting revealed the cultural cleavage that now separated the eastern and western parts of the Frankish kingdom. While the East Frankish tribes, including the Alemans, Thuringians, and Bavarians, who were united under Louis (the "German"), had preserved their old Germanic dialects, the language of the West Frankish tribes, owing to its mixture with Gallo-Latin, had developed into the Romance tongue, the ancestor of modern French. The two assembled armies no longer understood each other's language, so that the oath had to be read in German (*theodisca lingua*) and in Romanic.

The new alliance compelled Lothar to come to terms with his brothers, and in 843 the Treaty of Verdun put an end to the protracted family feud, granting Lothar the imperial title and a strip of land that ran through the center of the Empire, from the North Sea to Rome, including most of the valleys of the Rhine and Rhone. The two younger brothers retained the title of kings, Charles receiving the territories of the Romanic West, Louis those of the Germanic East. The future countries of Germany, France, and the "Lotharingian" middle kingdom were thus geographically and politically marked off. The Treaty of Mersen (870), concluded between Charles (the "Bald") and Louis (the "German") after the death of Lothar II (Lothar's son), gave Louis some additional territory in the West. After the extinction of Lothar's line Charles the Bald obtained the imperial title over the protest of Louis the German.

Charles the Fat and the End of the Carolingian Dynasty. The whole

Carolingian Empire was united once more in 884 under the rule of Charles the Fat (876–887), the son of Louis the German and the only surviving adult member of the Carolingian dynasty. Unable to cope with the ravages wrought by the invasions of Viking raiders who threatened and devastated the northern provinces of the Empire, Charles was deposed by the Frankish nobility and died shortly afterward. With his death the Carolingian Empire broke up into a disorganized mass of regional units which were badly harassed by the continued attacks of the Scandinavian Vikings of the north and the Saracens of the Mediterranean. But, strange as it seems, while this process of disintegration was going on, the idea of a united Christian-Germanic Empire of the West remained alive under the ashes of the gigantic conflagrations of the ninth century. Out of the darkness of this age the new nations of Europe were born, and the German emperors of the Saxon dynasty (919–1024) carried on the work of Charles the Great. Otto the Great (936–973), the most imposing figure among the Saxon rulers, was the great-grandchild of that Saxon etheling Widukind, at whose baptism in 785 Charles the Great, once his fiercest opponent, served as his godfather. Continuing the Carolingian tradition, Otto the Great imbued it with the tribal characteristics of the Saxons.

Charles the Great, King and Emperor. The whole epoch to which the great Charles has bequeathed his name feasted on the memory of his rule but wasted his inheritance. It was Charles who had inspired his people with new hope and confidence, showing them a definite goal to live and work for: the creation of a new and better society and civilization. In his *Life of Charles (Vita Caroli Magni)* Einhard, the royal secretary, has vividly portrayed the personality of his friend and king. There we learn that Charles was not only the greatest warrior and conqueror of his age but a farseeing statesman with definite ideals and aims which he pursued uncompromisingly.

Despite his imperial title Charles remained a Frank in word and deed, a man of simple and somewhat barbaric habits. At his request the heroic songs of his people were collected and written down, he gave German names to the four winds and the twelve months, and he even attempted to compose a grammar of the Frankish tongue, though he never succeeded in mastering the art of writing, spending many a sleepless night with honest but fruitless calligraphic exercises. Charles habitually wore Frankish dress, and only twice he acceded to the request of the Pope to appear in a large Roman tunic and shod with Roman sandals. Germanic and Frankish was his passion for hunting and swimming, not quite so thoroughly Germanic his moderation and temperance in the use of food and drink. Although a kindhearted father, he was not a model husband: his mistresses bore him a number of illegitimate children. Viewing with an open mind the cultural accomplishments of foreign nations, he preferred Frankish manners and customs to all others. On Frankish soil he wanted to be laid to his eternal rest, and workmen from all parts of the Empire co-operated in the construction of the mighty Minster at Aachen (Aix-la-Chapelle).

Administration Under Charles. The Empire of Charles was a theocratic Church-State, and the emperor exercised the functions of government as a priest-king, somewhat in the fashion of an Egyptian pharaoh, a Moslem kadi, or a Byzantine emperor. Consequently, in all his administrative institutions and political enterprises secular and religious aspects were inextricably intermingled. Thus his campaigns against the Saxons and the other Germanic tribes were political as well as religious wars, and the cross and the sword were inseparable companions. True enough, the aim of these wars was the unity and security of the Empire, but this unity was to be guaranteed and cemented by the universal acceptance of the established State religion.

The mayor of the palace and the lay referendary of Merovingian times had been supplanted by the archchaplain and the chancellor, the latter being in charge of the ministries of the interior and of finance. The organization of the chancery followed closely the Byzantine model, and included a graduated series of clerical officials. It was the emperor who laid down the rules of conduct and ritual for the clergy, who issued minute regulations for the observance of the Sunday, rules for liturgical art and music, and for monastic discipline. The emperor's emissaries (*missi dominici*) went on circuit through the counties of the Empire, two by two, a clergyman and a layman, to supervise local administration. The way in which they addressed their charges illustrates the dual secular-religious aspect of their function: "We have been sent here," we read in one of the typical exhortations, "by our Lord, the Emperor Charles, for your eternal salvation, and we charge you to live virtuously according to the law of God and justly according to the law of the world. We would have you know first of all that you must believe in one God, the Father, the Son, and the Holy Ghost." Then the king's messenger proceeds to enumerate the duties of all social classes and estates, from husbands and wives to bishops and counts, concluding as follows: "Nothing is hidden from God. Life is short, and the moment of death is unknown. Be ye therefore always prepared."

Charles regarded the Pope as his chaplain and told him that it was the emperor's duty to govern as well as defend the Church. In the famous Iconoclast Controversy that followed the Second Church Council of Nicaea (787), he went so far as to call together an anti-Council of all the Western bishops, which met at Frankfurt in 794, Charles presiding and directing the deliberations according to his superior will. The *Libri Carolini* (Carolingian Books) were prepared at his request, containing a refutation of the Greek doctrine that advocated the veneration of religious images and that had been adopted in part by the Nicaean Council. Charles's pronounced sympathy with the Oriental iconoclast movement and his refusal to recognize the authority of the Second Council of Nicaea threatened to lead to serious complications. The strain in Frankish-Roman relations was eased, however, by Pope Leo III's countermove, the coronation of Charles as Roman emperor. Thus new dignity and additional prestige was given to the Frankish king, but at the same time Charles was forced into a definite juridical relationship and close association with Rome and the papacy.

The absolutism of Charles's rule implied a paternalistic concept of government. As the father of his people the emperor felt responsible for their temporal and eternal welfare, attempting to enforce morality and religion by legislation and, if necessary, by the power of the sword. Frankish custom made him consider the Empire and its revenues as his family property. Although the general assembly of freemen, the so-called "May Field" (*Maifeld*) still met once or twice a year, it had retained only a nominal significance as far as the legislative and judicial power of the people was concerned. The agenda were carefully prepared by a special imperial synod and were then submitted to the popular assembly for formal approval. The consent of the king-emperor, however, was required to give any resolution the force of law.

These resolutions were laid down in the *Capitularies*, so called because of their being arranged according to chapters or headings. They deal with the most varied and minute matters and aspects of administration. Those that applied to public affairs concerning the whole Empire had to be published by the counts and bishops who were in charge of the local districts. Charles himself had no permanent local domicile, but traveled about among his several imperial palaces (*Pfalzen*), accompanied by the Count Palatine (*Pfalzgraf*), who represented the imperial judiciary power and was in charge of the supervision of markets and highways.

Growing Feudalization of Society. Many of the *Capitularies* deal with the economic conditions of the Empire and the management of the royal estates. We gather from these accounts that the imperial officials were not paid with money but with land that belonged either to the State or to the Church, Charles making no distinction between crown lands and Church lands, claiming title of ownership to both.

Identical obligations, including that of military service, were imposed on secular and ecclesiastical landowners alike. The imperial revenues were derived from "The King's Land," i.e., from the agricultural produce of the undistributed crown lands; from the rights of coinage; from tolls and customs duties; from the tributes paid by conquered peoples as well as by Jews and foreigners, in return for royal protection. The giving away of increasingly large territories of the royal and ecclesiastical domains to ambitious nobles in order to secure their military assistance and good will not only strengthened the power of the territorial lords at the expense of the crown, but wrought havoc in the ecclesiastical sphere by making the ruler the arbitrary dispenser of benefices and Church offices, the result being the secularization of Church institutions in addition to the secularization of Church property. The clergy had become indispensable to the emperor not only because they held the monopoly of education but because of the nonhereditary nature of their fiefs, which made them largely dependent on the royal favor and therefore much more reliable than the secular vassals.

As had been customary in Merovingian times, bishops and abbots had again become the armed leaders of their troops, thus fulfilling the obligations attached to their fiefs.

The military aristocracy, no longer controlled by the king, had the people at their mercy. Under Charles's successors the feudal lords were the only ones to whom one could turn for protection. This whole development marks the growing feudalization of the society of the ninth century. As the land grants to secular lords became increasingly hereditary, the vassals began to feel like small sovereigns, freely disposing of their land, giving away parts of their territories to their subordinate followers, so that through continuous "subinfeudation" there arose eventually a graduated system of vassalage, a symmetrical pyramid of ascending ranks, with the king at the apex. This description anticipates the structure of the fully grown feudal system of the following centuries. However, even in Charles's time the general trend and the essential features of this future development can be clearly recognized.

Serfdom and Tenancy. The economic life of the Carolingian period centers in the *Maierhof* (estate of the "mayor") or *Fronhof* (estate of the lord), and is closely linked with the institution of serfdom (*Leibeigenschaft*), which in itself admitted of different grades of social status and different degrees of income and freedom. The land was divided into estates which were self-sufficient units, administered by the king's or the lord's steward (*"maior domus," Hausmaier, Maier*). The king's seneschal or high steward was in charge of the royal estates in their entirety. In the center of each estate was located the *Maierhof,* surrounded by the huts of the peasants, each of whom had a small strip of land attached to his dwelling. Such a "village" usually also comprised a mill, a blacksmith's shop, and a church or chapel with the parish house. Part of the arable land that surrounded the village was set aside for the exclusive use of the king or lord. What remained was parceled out among the peasant tenants. The fields were divided into three parts (three-fallow system, *Dreifelderwirtschaft*), one of which was used for the planting of the summer crop, the second for the winter crop, while the third part would lie fallow. In the absence of scientific methods of fertilization this system permitted a rotating treatment of the fields, thus preventing the exhaustion of the soil. The cultivation of the fields was a communal and co-operative enterprise, although each peasant harvested the crop from his own strips of land.

The same relationship of mutual service and obligation that formed the cornerstone of the whole feudal system and that bound vassal to lord or lord to king, determined likewise the unwritten contract that tied the peasant to the lord or his steward. The lord gave the peasant protection, furnished the land, built a mill and a village church, and administered justice in the territory that he had learned to consider as his own, either by inheritance or by special grant. The peasant, in turn, enjoyed the security that went with the hereditary right to the possession of his strip of land, he took his share of the agricultural produce, and returned the privileges extended to him by making certain payments and rendering certain services to the lord, exactments whose extent and nature were determined by custom. Theoretically still a serf, the peasant of the Carolingian period had actually become a tenant, and although still unfree, this peasant tenant, being exempt from the burden of military and court service, was envied by many a small freeholder. A traditional body of legal concepts gradually developed out of the peasant-lord relationship (*Hofrechte, Weistümer,* manorial statutes), which were, however, not committed to writing until the end of the thirteenth century.

Law and Order. The administration of justice in Carolingian times was seriously handicapped by the fact that public opinion still upheld the law of the stronger or the principle that might creates right. In the almost total absence of official organs of public safety, the freeman was in duty bound to protect and defend himself, his belongings, and his family against attack and injury. Thus the peasants formed protective associations which were called "gilds" and bore close resemblance to the old Germanic "oath helpers" (*Eideshelfer, Schwurgenossen*). The members of these brotherhoods were bound by solemn oaths to assist each other in time of danger or distress, and continued to cultivate pagan rites and customs at their communal feasts and social gatherings. One of the *Capitularies* deals with these abuses, prohibiting the taking of oaths, but not interfering with the gild's aim of mutual protection. Under the influence of Christianity these "gilds" were gradually transformed into Christian brotherhoods and eventually into the vocational groups of the medieval city.

The "King's Court" concerned itself with cases of high treason and plots against the safety of the ruler and the nation. The majority of law suits fell under the jurisdiction of the "Count's Court," and the "Court of the Hundreds." Minor offenses were dealt with by the "Jurors' Court" (*Schöffengericht*), consisting of the presiding judge (*Zentner*) and usually seven jurymen (*Schöffen*).

Currency and Commerce. Some of the *Capitularies* deal with the prices of food and clothing. A decree fixes the price for the finest fur at thirty shillings, while for an ordinary one the maximal price should be ten shillings. In order to stabilize the silver denarius (*Pfennig,* penny), which had been recently devaluated by the growing scarcity and increased value of gold, its weight had been raised from 1.36 g. to 1.7 g. The value of the shilling was established as the twentieth part of a pound (*Pfund*), and new coins had been issued (twelve pence to the shilling), so that we arrive at the following currency tabulation which was to remain the same to the end of the Middle Ages: 1 pound = 20 gold shillings = 20 × 12 silver denarii (*pfennigs,* pence). With the dwindling supply of precious metals the purchasing power of money rose as compared with the Merovingian period. According to a tariff of the year 794 a bushel (*Scheffel* = fifty to sixty liters) of oats cost four to six pence; a bushel of wheat, four to six pence;

a bushel of rye, three to four pence; twelve loaves of wheat bread (of two pounds each), one penny; a chicken, half a penny; a sheep, six pence; a cow, two shillings.

Domestic and foreign trade experienced a short-lived revival under the influence of the political unification of the Frankish kingdom under Charles the Great. Commercial relations not only extended to the Germanic North, the Scandinavian countries, and England, but included even Russia and the Orient. Itinerant merchants went from Saxony to Denmark and Finland; Danes, Swedes, and Norwegians visited the markets of the Frankish kingdom. Articles of luxury, such as fancy cloths, silks, furs, rugs, jewels, and spices were imported from the Orient. Commercial activities were especially lively in the newly founded and slowly developing cities.

Following the advice of the popes, Boniface had founded most of the German bishoprics in the most thickly populated regions, in order to emphasize the significance of the episcopal sees. Thus he had considered the ancient Roman settlements on German soil as the most suitable centers of ecclesiastical life. In the period of Charles the Great we find approximately thirty bishoprics which were gradually developing into marketing and trading communities, and were endowed with special royal privileges. These Carolingian markets soon became the permanent abodes of merchants and craftsmen and present in a rudimentary form the essential features of the later medieval city. Hamburg, Bremen, Magdeburg, Erfurt, Regensburg, among others, were such marketing centers of the Carolingian period.

A regular postal service was still unknown in Charles's time. Special messengers or traveling friends served as mail carriers. The use of public highways and bridges was subject to toll. Not only the king but also the territorial lords derived part of their revenues from tolls and customs' duties, and the feudal lords made a gainful occupation of the exploitation of the itinerant merchant. Charles issued a number of decrees for the protection of trade and commerce, exempting pilgrims, courtiers, and warriors from the payment of tolls, and giving the merchants letters of safe-conduct. But despite these and other protective and preventive measures the great Charles was too much a child of his age to recognize and attack the fundamental evil of the times, which consisted in the growing accumulation of territorial possessions in the hands of secular and ecclesiastical princes and lords. The "father of the poor, of widows and orphans," as he was called after his death, was unable to defeat the forces that were to cause poverty and destitution, breeding the anarchy, lawlessness, and despair of the succeeding century.

Carolingian "Renaissance." Charles's biographer, Einhard, hails the emperor as the new Augustus, and Bishop Modoin of Auxerre speaks of the renaissance of classical antiquity. These are undoubtedly euphemistic epithets, exaggerating the scope and significance of the Carolingian revival of ancient culture. Charles was not interested in resurrecting the empires of Augustus, Constantine, or Justinian. He felt himself to be the leader of a young and vigorous nation which had conquered the Western Roman Empire and had rightfully inherited its power and tradition. As the "New David" he was the *"rex iustus"* and *"rex pacificus"* (king of justice and peace) of a new dispensation and legislation, the educator of his people, the Christian ruler of a new empire.

The "School of the Palace." The "Carolingian Renaissance," therefore, is not so much a genuine revival of antiquity as a strengthening of the continuity of the elements of ancient thought, learning, and education. Charles himself threw all his personal energy and influence into the work of restoring the time-honored principles and methods of classical learning. The educational activities had their center in the "School of the Palace," headed from 782 on by Alcuin (Alchvin, 730–804), formerly director of the famous school of York, whom Charles put in charge of three of the most prominent abbeys of the Empire. His teaching was based on the old classical curriculum of the seven liberal arts, consisting of the so-called *Trivium* (grammar, rhetorics, dialectics), and the *Quadrivium* (arithmetic, geometry, music, astronomy). Alcuin was commissioned with the revision of the Bible and the service books and thus inaugurated the Carolingian liturgical reform which provided the foundation of medieval Christian liturgy.

The "School of the Palace" set the educational standard for all the other monastic schools which were diffused throughout the Empire, such as St. Gall, Reichenau, Lorsch, Tours, Orléans, Auxerre, Pavia, and many others.

From Italy Charles had called to his court the grammarians and poets Petrus of Pisa and Paulinus of Friaul, and the Lombard Paulus Diaconus (Paul the Deacon), author of the *Historia Langobardorum* (*History of the Langobards*) and biographer of Pope Gregory the Great. From Spain came the Goth Theodulfus, a neo-classical poet and a severe critic of Germanic criminal law. And there were the Franks Angilbert, abbot of St. Riquier; Hildebold, Charles's archchaplain and later on archbishop of Cologne; and the illustrious Einhard, annalist, poet, and architect, a native of the Main district, who although a layman, was to succeed Alcuin as head of the Palace School. In his biography of Charles he shows himself influenced by the style of the classical Roman historians, especially by Suetonius. Charles made him his chief architect and put him in charge of several abbeys.

Charles's Academy. Following Oriental models Charles organized his circle of scholarly friends and advisers in the form of a court academy, in which even women, such as Charles's sister Gisela and his daughters Hruodtrut and Bertha, were received as members. Each member of the Academy was given a symbolical name, taken from the Bible or from classical literature. Charles himself was David, the poet-king of the Old Testament; Alcuin was Horatius Flaccus; Angilbert was Homer; Einhard, because of his architectural gifts, was given the name of Beseleel, the builder of the Jewish tabernacle. The entire Academy used to accompany Charles on his travels throughout the Empire. The customary readings during meals comprised poetic and prose passages from classical and patristic literature, preferably from Augustine's *De Civitate Dei*. The conversation was carried on in Latin, in which language Charles was as well versed as in his native Frankish.

The "Caroline Minuscule" and Miniature Painting. Preoccupation with classical writers in the Carolingian period led to the copying of many of the famous documents of ancient literature. We owe most of our knowledge of these masterpieces to the zeal of Carolingian copyists. Their manuscripts reveal a remarkable improvement over the crude and frequently illegible scripts of the Merovingian Age. This new style of writing, known as the "Caroline Minuscule," became the standard type for western Europe, excepting Spain, Ireland, and southern Italy. It is the precursor of the "Humanist Script" of the Italian Renaissance of the fifteenth century and of the modern printed Latin type.

The Carolingian manuscripts were richly adorned with miniature paintings and picturesque illuminations. The name "miniature" is derived from their prevailingly vermilion color (*minium, Mennig,* "cinnabar"), and the scribes were called "miniators." Special artistry was displayed in the beautifully designed initial letters and marginal adornments. They show Carolingian art at its best, revealing in their elaborate spiral and fretted designs Oriental-Byzantine, Oriental-Moslem, and Anglo-Celtic influence. There is a peculiar restraint in the rendering of natural objects and human characters, an absence of thematic variations, and a lack of verisimilitude that endows these miniatures with a solemn and sublime monumentality. From here a straight line may be drawn to the Rhenish schools of painting of the tenth and eleventh centuries. Most of the monasteries succeeded in developing their own style of miniature painting, so that when speaking of the art schools of Reichenau, Regensburg, Tours, etc., we are able to distinguish specific local characteristics.

Architecture. Byzantine influence is noticeable in Charles's famous palace church (*Palastkapelle, Münster*) at Aachen which shows a central octagonal ground plan of Oriental origin. The palace church was to represent a partial replica of the East Roman Emperor Justinian's *Hagia Sophia* in Constantinople, the symbol of the emperor's theocratic power and majesty. The Church of San Vitale in Ravenna had to serve the Carolingian architect as the nearest model. From Ravenna, too, Charles had transferred the bronze monument of Theoderic the Great, placing it in the court of his palace in Aachen.

The excavations at Ingelheim in the Rhineland give us an idea of the appearance and organization of a Carolingian palace (*Pfalz*). A vast building served as living quarters for the retinue of the imperial court. It comprised porticoes, chapels, and halls of varying size and shape. As an economically self-sufficient unit the palace included the surrounding dwellings of the laborers, artisans, brewers, bakers, weavers, spinners, carpenters, metalworkers, and so forth.

The ecclesiastical architecture of the Carolingian Age followed the model of the simple and longitudinal early Christian basilica rather than the more complex central or circular plan of the Byzantine and Iranian styles and of Charles's palace church. The form of the basilica itself had evolved from the late Roman court and market hall and the Roman *villa*. The early Christian basilica (*c.* 350–600) is a modest and ascetic-looking building, consisting of one high central nave and two (or four) lower aisles, a flat roof, and a semicircular apse which contained the altar and the throne of the bishop. In Carolingian times the primitive style of the basilica developed into the Romanesque style, so called because of the several motifs of Roman architecture embodied in it. The main innovation was the introduction of a transept that rendered the ground plan cruciform and provided additional space for the common recitation of the Office that had become the rule under Benedictine influence. In Germany churches of great age or large size were called *Münster* ("minster," from the Latin *monasterium*).

Despite his patronage of the arts and crafts, Charles was convinced that "the adornment which is derived from the moral goodness of a congregation is of greater value than a beautiful church." And in the *Libri Carolini,* which were written to reject the cult of images, we read: "In the realm that God has entrusted to Our care, the basilicas abound with gold and silver, with jewels and lovely ornaments, and even if we decline to burn candles and incense in front of images, we nevertheless adorn with the most precious of objects and materials the places which are dedicated to the divine service."

Music. In connection with the general liturgical reform Charles emphasized the importance of Church music. The primitive water organ, which had been invented in Alexandria in the second century B.C., was introduced in the Frankish kingdom through a gift of the Eastern Emperor Constantine V (757) to King Pepin. Charles had several instruments sent from the East to be copied by Frankish craftsmen and installed in the major churches of the Empire. To insure correct liturgical singing, he had Roman teachers instruct clergy and laity in different parts of the Frankish kingdom. Especially favored was the *Cantus Gregorianus* (*cantus plenus,* "plain song," "plain chant") which, originally derived from Greek and Jewish temple chants, had become an integral part of early Christian liturgy and had been revised and reorganized by Pope Gregory the Great (590–604).

Gregorian singing, which is unaccompanied and for one voice only, and characterized by its free rhythmical movement, flourished through the greater part of the Middle Ages but declined after the fourteenth century with the advent of polyphony. It experienced a modern revival at the end of the nineteenth century, when it recovered its ancient status as the official liturgical chant of the Roman Catholic Church. Its so-called "neumatic notation" (from Greek: *neuma* = "wink," "gesture," "sign"), of unknown origin, differs in tact, measurement, and appearance from modern notation, but we now know how to transpose the notes into their modern

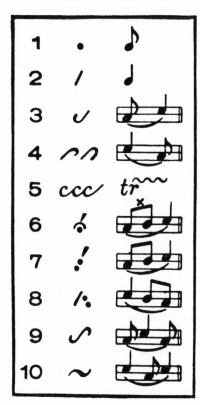

Neumes

1. Punctus, Punctum (short note)

2. Virga (higher tone)

3. Pes, Podatus (ascending interval)

4. Flexa or Clivis (descending interval)

5. Quilisma (tremolo)

6. Salicus (2 ascending tones with half-tone beat)

7. Scandicus (2 ascending tones)

8. Climacus (2 descending tones)

9. Torculus or Pes flexus (3 tones in the sequence: low, high, low)

10. Porrectus or Resupina (3 tones in the sequence: high, low, high)

equivalents. The most famous modern schools of Gregorian Chant are the Benedictine abbeys of Beuron and Maria-Laach in Germany and Solesmes in France.

Carolingian Culture After Charles the Great. The cultural revival that owed its splendid achievements to Charles the Great was more long lived than were his political and social creations and innovations. Carolingian culture grew into its full stature in the generation that followed Charles's death, finding home and shelter in the institutions of monastic learning. Under Charles the Bald the director of the Palace School was Johannes Scotus Erigena (810–877), a native of Ireland and the greatest scholar and philosopher of the ninth century, representing an important link between Neo-Platonism and the scholasticism of the twelfth and thirteenth centuries (cf. p. 141 sqq.).

Among the many pupils of Alcuin one of the outstanding men is Hrabanus Maurus (780–856), abbot and later on archbishop of Fulda, the author of an encyclopedia of knowledge and of poetical as well as catechetical works. At the head of the abbey of Reichenau at Lake Constance (*Bodensee*) we find his pupil Walafrid Strabo (809–849), a native Aleman, a scholar and poet

of vivid imagination and strong emotional appeal, who has left us a sample
of nature poetry in the descriptive poem "My Little Garden." In the
monastery of St. Gall taught Notker Balbulus (the "Stammerer," 840–912),
the greatest of the religious poets of the Carolingian epoch and the author
and compiler of the stories and legends concerning the life of Charles the
Great which are contained in the collection *Gesta Caroli Magni*. Likewise
at St. Gall we find Tutilo († 915), a man of universal tastes and interests,
equally versed in commercial and literary matters, architect, painter, goldsmith, poet, and composer.

The Carolingian Abbey. While war, famine, and death, the apocalyptic
triad, were driving the Carolingian empire to the brink of complete destruction, the Benedictine monasteries kept the flame of culture alive. The
Carolingian abbey, which provided the background for these many-sided
cultural activities, was at the same time a great social and economic center,
a great landowning corporation. In the eighth century the abbey of Fulda
owned 15,000 plowlands, while Lorsch possessed 911 large estates in the
Rhineland. But St. Gall in Switzerland perhaps more than any other
monastic community represented the ideal type of a Carolingian abbey.
A plan that dates from the beginning of the ninth century shows the abbey
as a miniature city, with churches, schools, workshops, granaries, hospitals,
baths, mills, breweries, farm buildings, gardens, and cemeteries. Material and
intellectual culture, agrarian economy, and the cultivation of the arts and
sciences went hand in hand.

It must have been relatively easy for an organization of such dimensions
and such resources to accomplish the difficult task of transforming waste
lands and swamps into flourishing settlements, clearing the forests, draining
the fens, and creating centers of agricultural and commercial life and
enterprise. The monasteries were among the first to establish markets and
to develop the institutions of banking and social insurance on a small scale.
Landowners could purchase pensions or become resident members of the
monastic community as "oblates." Freemen would surrender their liberty
in order to join the number of those serfs and tenants who were living within
the confines of the "patrimony of the Saint" in whose name an abbey or
church was dedicated. They were called *Homines Sanctorum* (the "Saint's
Men"; French: *Sainteurs*), and usually enjoyed the benefits of that mild and
humane rule that has given rise to the proverb: "There is good living under
the crozier" (*Unter'm Krummstab ist gut leben*).

Vernacular Literature in German Monasteries. It is to the credit of the
German monasteries that they bridged over the abyss that still separated
the Latin language of the educated from the *lingua theodisca,* the language
of the people. The "interlinear glosses," which provided the Latin texts with
an interspersed German vocabulary, and the "glossaries," a primitive type
of Latin-German dictionaries, represent the first attempts at making use
of the German language for the purposes of education. The oldest glossary
was compiled in Bavaria about the year 750. The still older "Wessobrunn

Prayer," discovered in the monastery of Wessobrunn in Bavaria, is written in Bavarian dialect and dates back to the missionary activity of Boniface. It consists of a description of the creation of the universe in alliterative verse, and concludes with a prayerful invocation in prose. As a cultural document it illustrates an early stage of the Germanic reception of Christian ideas.

The period of Charles the Great witnessed the translations of the Benedictine rule and the hymns of Ambrose (Reichenau), of the Psalms and several theological tracts (St. Gall), of the Gospel of Matthew, several sermons of Augustine, and a large number of liturgical and homiletic texts. A translation of Tatian's (second century) Gospel Harmony is dated in the ninth century, being a continuous narrative of the life of Christ based on the four Gospels. *The Lay of Hildebrand (Hildebrandslied)*, copied about the year 800 by two monks, who wrote the fragmentary alliterative poem on the outer leaves of a theological manuscript, was found in the abbey of Fulda. Representing the only surviving document of Old High German heroic poetry, the *Hildebrandslied* tells of the probably fatal encounter between Dietrich of Bern's (Theoderic of Verona, cf. p. 25 sq.) armor-bearer Hildebrand and his son Hadubrand.

A heroic poem, although of a different kind, is also the Old Saxon *Heliand (Heiland,* "Saviour"), written in alliterative verse by an unknown Saxon author during the earlier part of the ninth century. Here the life of Christ is assimilated to the everyday life and thought of the recently converted Saxon people. Christ is depicted as a great king and heroic leader, the Church is the king's palace, the disciples are the faithful thanes and vassals who have sworn lifelong fidelity in truly Germanic fashion. The landscape of Saxony with its fields, forests, and castles provides the scenic background. But we must not exaggerate the significance of certain deviations from the biblical account, recalling that early Christian art, literature, and liturgy quite generally cherish the conception of Christ as a victorious king rather than the humiliated sufferer on the cross. The Saxon *Heliand* combines Germanic form with Christian content in a true synthesis. While the advice to offer the attacker the other cheek would still have appeared incomprehensible to the Saxon temper, the poem nevertheless elaborates on the Sermon on the Mount, praising the hero whose heroism is tempered by gentleness, whose loyalty is adorned with the virtues of justice and charity.

In some respects the simple contours of the Old Saxon *Heliand* offer an even more eloquent testimony to the Christianization of the German mind than the velvety outline of its Frankish counterpart, Otfrid von Weissenburg's *Gospel-Harmony* of Christ (*Krist*), which was written by its scholarly author between 850 and 868. The rhyme at the end of the metrical line, familiar from Latin hymnology and vernacular charms and incantations, was adopted by the Alsatian monk, Otfrid, in place of alliteration. But both *Heliand* and *Krist* are German as well as Christian, each reflecting the tribal characteristics of their authors and the different ways in which Franks and Saxons responded to Christian ideas. The more immediate and naïve response is contained in the *Heliand*. Otfrid's narrative is more flexible and slightly sentimental, and at the same time more didactic, inspired by the monastic reform movement under Louis the Pious and its attempts to extirpate secular and pagan heroic poetry.

National Diversity and Cultural Unity. Such literary documents as *Heliand* and *Krist* are powerful manifestations of the new national life that for the first time began to assert itself at the end of the Carolingian period, coinciding with the dissolution of the Empire of Charles the Great. In view of this at first gradual and afterward phenomenal rise of the national states of Europe, it is a fact well worth remembering that Charles the Great, the creative master builder of the epoch that bears his name, is claimed as a national hero by Frenchmen and Germans alike, thus forcefully symbolizing the common cultural roots that underlie the two major branches of continental European civilization.

PART II. MEDIEVAL CIVILIZATION UNDER THE SAXON, SALIAN, AND HOHENSTAUFEN DY-NASTIES (919 - 1254)

1166   Frederick's third expedition into Italy: he captures Rome but is forced by an epidemic to withdraw to Germany

1176   Frederick's fourth expedition into Italy: he is decisively defeated by the Lombard army at Legnano

1177–1178   Peace between Frederick I and Pope Alexander III at Venice and truce between the emperor and the Lombard League

1183   Peace of Constance, confirming the preliminary peace treaties and granting a large degree of self-government to the Lombard cities

1184   The great *"Reichsfest"* of German Chivalry at Mayence, attended by over 70,000 knights

1189–1192   The Third Crusade under the leadership of Frederick Barbarossa

1190   Frederick Barbarossa is drowned in Asia Minor

1190–1197   Henry VI, son of Frederick Barbarossa

1190   Founding of the Order of Teutonic Knights

1191   Henry VI is crowned emperor in Rome

1194   Henry VI conquers his hereditary kingdom of Sicily, Hohenstaufen supremacy extends over all Italy, with the exception of the Papal States

1198–1208   Philip, duke of Swabia, younger son of Frederick Barbarossa, elected by the German nobles

1198–1215   The Welf, Otto IV of Brunswick, younger son of Henry the Lion, elected antiking by the Welf faction of German nobles, struggle for the throne between Welfs and Hohenstaufens

1208   Philip of Swabia is assassinated

1212–1250   Frederick II, son of Henry VI of Hohenstaufen

1220   Frederick II receives the imperial crown in Rome

1226   The Order of Teutonic Knights is called into Prussia for the purpose of Eastern colonization

1227   Frederick II is excommunicated by Pope Gregory IX (1227–1241) for his failure to fulfill his vow to undertake a Crusade

1228–1229   The Fifth Crusade under the leadership of Frederick II

1230   Peace between Frederick II and Gregory IX

1230–1283   Conquest of heathen Prussia by the Order of Teutonic Knights

1235   Legal enactment of the *Land Peace* at the Diet of Mayence, the first publication of an imperial law in Latin and in German

1236–1237   Victorious struggle of Frederick II against the cities of Lombardy

1237   Expansion of the territory of the Teutonic Knights to include Kurland, Livland, and Estland

1241   The Mongolians are repulsed at Liegnitz

1245   Following a resolution of the Council of Lyon, Frederick II is deposed and excommunicated by Pope Innocent IV (1243–1254)

1246–1247   Henry Raspe, landgrave of Thuringia, first antiking

1247–1256   William of Holland, second antiking

1250–1254   Conrad IV, son of Frederick II

1256–1273   *"Interregnum"* (*"die kaiserlose, die schreckliche Zeit"*): Germany without an emperor

1268   Conradin, the last member of the Hohenstaufen dynasty, executed at Naples; collapse of imperial government in Germany

Chapter 4

THE SAXON DYNASTY AND THE
REBIRTH OF THE EMPIRE

The Medieval Synthesis. The Carolingian ideal of a universal Christian empire under the leadership of emperor and pope survived the century of decline, and contact with the Carolingian tradition was restored by the ascendancy of the Saxon dynasty. The tenth and eleventh centuries completed the synthesis and cultural consolidation of Europe and at the same time allowed the individual nationalities to assert their character and express themselves freely within the general frame of a supranational civilization. Nationalism in the modern sense of the term, denoting the autonomous expansion and development of European nations and their cultures, did not become a historical reality until medieval society was being disrupted by the social, religious, and political upheavals of the fifteenth and sixteenth centuries. Until this happened Germany remained the leading member of the European commonwealth of Christian nations, owing her leadership primarily to the glamour and glory of the idea of the Empire which symbolically expressed the continuity of past, present, and anticipated future.

While presenting on the surface the spectacle of an organic unity, embedded within the structure of a universal State and a universal Church, Germany actually constituted a *coincidentia oppositorum*. She presented a unity of opposites, achieved and held together by virtue of the fundamental conviction that was shared by Greek and Christian civilization alike: that life could and should be molded according to ideal patterns, that religious and social ideas were to inform material reality and impress upon it the mark of the ideal and the spiritual. Within the Christian commonwealth of nations this ideal pattern had assumed the form of a natural-supernatural organism which, in a rationally arranged order, tied the particular to the universal, the individual to the group, the State to the Church, nature to supernature. It is this concept of the organic structure of society, derived from the biblical idea of the Church as the "Mystical Body of Christ" (1 Cor. 10:17; Eph. 4:22; Gal. 4:9), that made it possible to combine seeming opposites in a unified system of graduated orders and relations.

61

Every type of being receives its individual character and intrinsic value from its relation to its infinite source and cause, which permeates and sustains the entire cosmos of nature and mind. "Be what thou art" — realize all your potentialities in your God-given station in society — becomes the imperative of a Christian humanism which rests upon the foundation of Greek and Christian wisdom and is absorbed by the European mentality, so that it is as vigorously alive in Dante and the German mystics of the Middle Ages as in the thought of Leibniz, Goethe, and Hegel. Knowing himself as an instrumental cause in the hands of his Creator, man freely collaborates with the plans and designs of a metaphysically significant world and civilization. Cultural formation out of a philosophical and religious ideology becomes the ideal goal of the Christian and German Middle Ages.

It is only when looking at it in this way that the medieval "unity of opposites" becomes comprehensible. Life is full of contrasts, but they are ultimately reconciled in the synthesis of a God-centered civilization. Love of the world and flight from the world, the ideals of knighthood and the ideals of the cloister, cruelty and tenderness, sensuality and spiritual ecstasy, penetrating rational analysis and implicit and childlike faith, the claims of an authoritarian State and Church and respect for the dignity of the individual and the social group, exploitation of the peasant and tender consideration for the poor and downtrodden, for widows and orphans and the sick and suffering, for lepers and outcasts: the cleavage between the ideal demand and the imperfect reality is overcome by a generally accepted and approved standard of moral values whose violation is condemned as a sinful infringement upon a divinely sanctioned order. This medieval synthesis had constantly to be reconquered, with the supernational unity of medieval Europe as the scene of the struggle, harboring under its roof the three major forces of Greek, Christian, and Germanic cultures.

This European unity under Germanic leadership was one of faith and morals, of thought and action, manifesting itself in State and Church, in their antagonisms as much as in their common idealism and enterprise. Struggles were waged for the supremacy of State or Church, among and between classes and vocational groups, between emperors and popes: campaigns and crusades, peaceful colonization and violent conquests, irenic missionary activity and cruel inquisition, persecution, and extermination of heretics. And the Saxon emperors were destined to symbolize the vital cultural and social energies and ambitions of an ecclesiastically colored civilization, to resurrect the Roman Empire of the Frankish Nation in the more imposing structure of the "Roman Empire of the German Nation."

Saxon Leadership. The disintegration of the Carolingian dynasty had greatly encouraged the spirit of rebellion against a centralized authority among the hereditary sovereigns of the great tribal duchies of Germany. Saxony, Bavaria, Franconia, Swabia, and Lorraine formed the so-called "stem" duchies (*Stammesherzogtümer*), each of them representing a feudal state within the German realm. Any ruler who wanted to restore the dignity and authority of the imperial crown had first of all to restrain the ambitions and aspirations of the overbearing territorial lords. The situation was rendered even more complex by the fact that the dukes and other magnates constituted the electoral college and, in electing a new king, were naturally inclined to give their vote to a man whom they could hope to control to some extent and who would not endanger their relative independence. Considering this state of affairs, the historian marvels at the number of brilliant and powerful leaders who, with firm determination and farseeing vision, were to rule the destinies of the German nation through the centuries that followed the downfall of the Carolingian empire.

It was the tribal vigor and patriotism of the Saxons that was resplendent in the extraordinary qualities of some of the Saxon rulers. They succeeded in welding together into a new cultural unity the discordant and disjointed forces of the German lands. Under Henry I (919–936) and Otto I (the Great, 936–973) German cultural and political leadership in the Western World reached an unprecedented summit. The new Empire, it is true, rested on a narrower basis than the Carolingian Germanic-Romanic civilization. The western part of the Frankish kingdom had now become an independent national organism (France), and Italy as well as Burgundy were autonomous administrative units. However, this new Empire was more interested in serving the cultural advancement of the Western World than in establishing an imperialistic rule. The Germans of this period may therefore truly be called the great organizers among the European nations, taking upon their shoulders the world-historic responsibility of shaping the Christian Middle Ages. It was Otto the Great who saved the papacy from an abyss of depravity, who profoundly comprehended and realized the immense task of renewing German civilization in harmony with the spirit of the Christian and classical tradition.

As Saxons the rulers belonged to a racial group that had been scarcely touched by the culture of classical antiquity. As German kings and emperors, however, they soon transcended the narrow limits of tribal politics and restored a definite relationship with the social background and heritage of Western Christendom.

Of special significance for the future development of German civilization were the ties that soon began to link inextricably the German and Italian interests and policies. In 962 Otto the Great responded to several appeals of Pope John XII by entering Italy and restoring law and order, which for several decades had been at the mercy of rival secular and ecclesiastical factions. He married Adelaide (Adelheid), the heiress of the crown of Lombardy, and pronounced himself king of Italy. The Pope bestowed upon him the imperial crown, and this event marked the actual beginning of the "Holy Roman Empire of the German Nation" (*Sacrum Romanum Imperium Nationis Germanicae*), although the name itself was not applied until the fifteenth century.

The continuity of tradition with the ancient Roman as well as with the

Carolingian empire was virtually re-established. Northern Europe once more came in contact with Mediterranean and more especially with Byzantine civilization. Otto's and Adelaide's son, Otto II (973–983), married the Greek princess Theophano, the daughter of the Byzantine emperor, Romanos II. With her and even more with the son of Otto II and Theophano, Otto III (983–1002), Byzantine manners and customs were introduced into the life of the imperial court of the West, and were reflected in the arts and crafts as well as in social and religious practices and institutions. In Otto III the Christian empire had come to life again in its dual aspect of an Eastern and Western, a Byzantine Greek and Carolingian Roman ancestry. The emperor's scholarly friend and adviser, Gerbert of Aurillac (940–1003), the later Pope Sylvester II (999–1003), impressed upon Otto the superior claims and titles of the Western Roman tradition. It was he who made Otto see and appreciate the great heritage of Western civilization: "Ours, yea ours, is the Roman Empire. Its strength rests on fruitful Italy and populous Gaul and Germany. Our Augustus art Thou, O Caesar, the Emperor of the Romans. . . . " Gerbert and Otto visualized Dante's ideal Empire, the commonwealth of Christian nations, ruled by the dual authority of emperor and pope.

Under Otto III Rome became the capital of the Empire, the emperor exercising a practically unlimited control over the papacy, while at the same time his influence on German affairs was steadily waning. For more than one German emperor it proved an impossible task to rule both Germany and Italy, to do justice to German and Italian interests alike, and to wield both the secular and the spiritual sword. Otto III died at the early age of twenty-two, leaving to his successors the difficult task of once again restoring royal authority in Germany. With Henry II (the Saint, 1002–1024), a great-nephew of Otto I, the Saxon dynasty came to an end. Henry used the bishops, whom he had invested with their offices and endowed with land and administrative authority, to control and curb the unruly lay nobility.

The general physiognomy of the age is more and more characterized by the growing influence of Church civilization upon secular life, a development which began with the rule of Otto the Great and lasted unto the days of Henry IV (1056–1106) of the Salian-Frankish dynasty. The Saxon as well as the early Salian emperors were relying chiefly on the loyalty and support of the ecclesiastical princes. To insure this loyalty the king invested the bishops with the symbols of their ecclesiastical office. On the occasion of Henry II's coronation in Rome in 1014, Pope Benedict VIII handed the emperor a golden apple, richly adorned with jewels and a cross, the apple signifying the universal aspect of imperial power. But Henry had the apple sent to the monastery of Cluny, in order to indicate his devotion to the ideals of the ecclesiastical reform movement, which inspired the political and cultural activities of the Ottonian and the Salian periods and co-operated with the forces of secular and ecclesiastical administration.

The Beginnings of German Colonization. It has been pointed out that the German territory of the Saxon emperors compared unfavorably with that of the Carolingian empire. The Slavs in the east and the Hungarians in the southeast constituted an increasing danger to the stability of the Empire, so that the Saxon emperors considered it as one of their primary tasks to establish their supremacy in these outlying frontier districts. This was accomplished both by conquest and by peaceful penetration and colonization. Peasants and missionaries under the leadership of dukes and princes, abbots and bishops, acted as the emissaries and became the guarantors of German culture in these religions. But better protection of the frontiers was only one of the reasons for the Germanization of the eastern and southeastern districts. Another and even more compelling motive was the scarcity of land in view of a rapidly increasing population, subsequent to the restoration of order and security under Henry I and Otto the Great. Continuing the work of his father, Otto vanquished the Wends and established marches and bishoprics between the Elbe and Oder rivers. On the Lechfeld near Augsburg he dealt a decisive blow to the Hungarian invaders (955) and reconquered the eastern Bavarian march, thereby laying the foundations for a future Austria.

In his personal appearance Otto the Great exemplified the vigor and youthful optimism of the people over whom his rule extended and whose labors, struggles, and achievements he faithfully and joyfully shared. Physical and intellectual alertness made him equally fitted for warlike and peaceful pursuits. His erudition comprised a wide range of interests, and he spoke several languages, having acquired a mastery of Latin rather late in his life. The two Ottos that succeeded him were his equals in cultural and intellectual awareness but lacked his sense of proportion. This lack was the main cause of their inefficiency in handling the affairs of Germany.

The Electoral College. The German monarchy under the Saxon and Salian emperors was still hereditary, though not in name. Nominally, the ecclesiastical and secular electors (*Kurfürsten*) formed the electoral college, but in reality the more powerful ones among the German emperors exercised their authority to secure the succession of their eldest sons.

Up to the year 1257 the ecclesiastical electors were the archbishops of Mayence (Mainz), Cologne (Köln), and Treves (Trier); the secular electors were the Count Palatine, the duke of Saxony, and the margrave of Brandenburg. In that year, however, the number of secular electors was increased by one through the addition of the king of Bohemia. The number of seven electors in all was legally established by the "Golden Bull" (1356, cf. p. 165). In 1623 the electoral dignity was transferred from the Count Palatine to the ruler of Bavaria, while in 1648 the Palatinate was once more added as the eighth and in 1692 Hanover (Brunswick-Lüneburg) as the ninth electoral district. After 1803 additional electoral provinces were created in Baden, Hesse-Kassel (Kurhessen), Württemberg, and Salzburg. The title *Kurfürst* (elector), however, became meaningless after the dissolution of the "Holy Roman Empire of the German Nation" in 1806.

The Army. The old Germanic army, recruited from the people (*Volks-heer*), had been transformed into an army of vassals, of professional soldiers and warriors. The dukes, counts, bishops, and abbots who had been endowed with fiefs were to furnish the king a certain number of armed men, proportionate to the size of their holdings. These subordinate vassals usually dwelt in their castles (*Burgen*), and were summoned by their liege lord to render military service in time of war.

Castles and Cities. Up to the twelfth century the terms *burg* ("borough"; Greek: *polis*; Gothic: *baurg*) and *stat* (town, city) are used synonymously to designate a fortified place, surrounded by walls. This original meaning is still evident in the names of numerous German cities: Augsburg, Freiburg, Hamburg, and so forth. The inhabitants were called *Bürger* (burghers), their legal statutes, *Burgrechte* (burghership, civic rights).

The arts of fortification developed in the later Middle Ages from primitive beginnings to a high degree of perfection. From the early Middle Ages on methods and materials were frequently adopted from ancient Roman models. A fortified settlement enjoyed the special privilege of the "Peace of the King" (*Burgfriede; Königsfriede*), granting the inhabitants the king's protection in their peaceful pursuits and prohibiting feuds inside the city walls. It was this element of security that contributed greatly to the growth of the cities and to making their walled-in territories centers of trade and commerce. It was in the cities, too, that with a rising class of "burghers" a new conception of civic liberties and of personal freedom came into being that found its expression in the proverbial saying: *"Stadtluft macht frei"* (the air of the city makes a man free).

Even a small village might be fortified by a surrounding wall and moat, but it could not be called a city unless it had obtained the privilege of holding a weekly market. The inhabitants of the larger and more thickly populated settlements depended on the agricultural produce of the surrounding farming districts. The peasants, on the other hand, were in need of the commercial and industrial products of the cities. Thus the development of a fortified settlement into a marketing center was the outcome of a natural process of economic intercourse and expansion. The privilege of holding a market was granted by the king, who issued special charters, at first to the lord, later to the city magistrates. Frequently we find the medieval city simply designated as "market" or *koufstat* (trading place), its inhabitants are called *koufliute* (trading people); *marktrecht* (marketing right) is used synonymously with *statrecht* (city rights, civic rights).

The lord is the guarantor of the "King's Peace" and represents the judicial power within the territory of the city. He appoints a judge and puts him in charge of legal administration. While the lower judiciary powers were soon to be transferred to the city magistrates, the lord reserved for himself the higher judiciary and the power over life and death (*Blutbann*). As soon as the lords began to realize that the cities represented a new and substantial source of income, they proceeded to create a large number of new urban settlements upon their territories and secured for them the usual royal privileges. At least 350 new towns originated in this way in the course of the twelfth and thirteenth centuries in the northeast of Germany alone. Some of them never developed beyond the size of village communities. Among the most famous founders of German cities are the counts of Zähringen (Freiburg im Breisgau, Bern in Switzerland) and Henry the Lion (1129–1195; München, Braunschweig, etc.).

Social Organization. The social structure of the period of the Saxon emperors as well as that of the succeeding Salian-Frankish dynasty was characterized by the political and economic supremacy of the dukes and counts, the bishops and abbots as the representatives of the secular and ecclesiastical nobility. Their power rested upon the ownership of land. Several victories over the Hungarians and Slavs had added considerably to their territorial possessions. The royal domains, which had been temporarily increased by the conquests in the East, diminished rapidly in size under the later Saxon emperors, owing to the continued necessity of rewarding the services of the nobles by territorial grants.

To the steadily increasing power of the secular and ecclesiastical landowners corresponded the decreasing number and significance of the freemen. The free or partially free peasantry of former times was no more. The majority of the people were living in some form of bondage or serfdom. The status of actual slavery was restored to some extent following the wars of conquest in the eastern Slavic regions. Most of the Slavic prisoners of war were reduced to an extreme form of serfdom, and slave trading became once more a remunerative occupation. Legally the serf was still considered as a piece of merchandise: he could be sold, exchanged, or given away.

Agriculture, Trade, Commerce. Despite the seemingly low social esteem in which the tillers of the soil were held, this whole society of the early Middle Ages still rested upon a solid agricultural foundation. Agriculture and horticulture were closely allied, and men and women took an equal share in the cultivation of fields and gardens. The monasteries excelled in the cultivation of vineyards as well as of fruit, vegetable, and flower gardens.

Industrial activities were still in a rudimentary stage. Many of the articles of consumption were produced by the consumer, and the home industries flourished. The small homesteader built his own home and stables, manufactured his own plows, carts, and tools. Bread, butter, and beer were homemade. Spinning, weaving, sewing, embroidering were some of the favorite occupations of women and were practiced by women of every social rank.

The restoration of a reasonable amount of security under Otto the Great safeguarded and encouraged the development of trade and commerce. The new territories in the East furnished the raw materials and absorbed the finished products of the mother country. The trade routes to Italy and the Orient were opened anew, and the Saxon emperors held their protecting arm over the "emperor's merchants," as the German tradesmen were then called. Jews, Lombards, and Venetians held a kind of trade monopoly, particularly as far as the trade with foreign countries and money transactions was concerned. If the needy wanted to obtain small loans they usually turned to the monasteries, thus avoiding the payment of interest.

Those merchants who had their permanent abode in the city were artisans and craftsmen. Their commercial activities were confined to the city territory, while the traveling merchants exported domestic goods and imported the merchandise of foreign countries. Outstanding commercial centers in the eleventh and twelfth centuries were Zurich, Basel, Strasbourg, Konstanz, Augsburg, Regensburg in the south; Mainz and Köln in the west; Magdeburg in the east. The southern German cities were the intermediaries of the German-Italian-Byzantine trade; the western Rhenish cities were important outposts for the commercial intercourse with Flanders, France, and England, while Magdeburg occupied a key position in regard to the newly developed Slavic East.

Mining. City life with its increasing and much more complex demands, its luxuries, and the ensuing spirit of competition stimulated the development of free commercial enterprise. Not only were new industries created, such as the manufacture of glass, but old industries, such as mining, smithing, and the furrier's and currier's trade, experienced a vigorous revival. The ore deposits in the southeast of Germany, in the Tyrol, in Styria, Bohemia, the Hartz, the Ore Mountains (*Erzgebirge*), and the Giant Mountains (*Riesengebirge*) provided the raw materials for the manufacture of arms.

The eleventh and twelfth centuries witnessed the formation of the first trade unions: they were unions of miners, and it was the German miner who became the teacher of Europe in the art of mining.

Money. The significance of money and its circulation was greatly increased by the development of trade and commerce. The working of gold and silver mines resulted in new forms of wealth, and new methods in the acquisition and the administration of property were soon to be adopted. Money began to circulate more and more freely and accumulated in the urban centers of trade. Into a world that still lived and thought in accordance with the ideal patterns of the self-sufficing village community and the feudal hierarchy, the growth of city life and commercial economy introduced a new concept of the function and purpose of money. As soon as opportunities for investments offered themselves, money began to lose its stigma of sterility: money began to breed money. The seed of a capitalistic money economy was planted in medieval soil.

The Slavic and Italian regions abounded with precious metals, and the German rulers received tributes and various duties and taxes in silver or gold coin from these countries. The right of coinage, originally a royal privilege, was gradually extended to the dukes and counts, the bishops and abbots, and finally to the cities, where the "master of the mint" occupied an important and respected position. As the local coins frequently differed in value according to their place of origin, the traveling merchant found himself compelled to go through the troublesome and costly process of a repeated currency exchange. To forge coin was considered a capital crime and avenged by capital punishment. In this as in other respects economic theory and practice is characterized by its strong ethical implications, an ethical bias which is prompted by theological and philosophical considerations and which remains practically unchanged until the advent of modern times.

Chapter 5

THE SALIC-FRANKISH DYNASTY AND
THE REFORM MOVEMENT OF CLUNY

Imperial Power Under the Early Salic Franks. After the death of the last Saxon emperor, Henry II, in 1024, the crown passed to Conrad II (1024–1039), duke of Franconia, who became the founder of the Salic-Frankish dynasty. He followed the example of Henry II in further strengthening the royal power and creating respect for lawful authority. Under his rule the kingdom of Burgundy (not to be confused with the duchy of Burgundy which belonged to France) became through inheritance part of the German Empire (1032). It occupied the region of the Rhone Valley, territories which today belong partly to France, partly to Switzerland.

Both Henry II and Conrad II had prepared the way for the further extension of imperial power that took place under Conrad's son, Henry III (1039–1056), with whom the Salic-Frankish rule reached its greatest dignity and strength. Once more the German emperor was able to assert his authority in ecclesiastical as well as in secular matters. Once more it was the Empire which came to the rescue of a degraded papacy, the emperor deposing three rival popes and appointing to the papal see Clement II, formerly bishop of Bamberg. A number of German popes, following each other steadily by imperial appointment, were to become the exponents and leaders in the ecclesiastical reform movement that had its origin in the tenth century in the French-Burgundian monastery of Cluny. Its strongest and most efficient supporter and protector was Emperor Henry III. It was due to his relentless activism and enlightened idealism that for a brief interval Empire and Papacy harmoniously co-operated in a combined effort to purify and renovate Church and society.

Growing Antagonism Between Empire and Papacy. But Henry III's successful attempt to strengthen the spiritual power and influence of the Church, and to free the clergy from secular bonds and attachments, was to result in new and unprecedented complications and conflicts, which came to a dramatic climax shortly after the emperor's death, stirring the Christian commonwealth of nations to its very depths.

When Henry III died in 1056, his son Henry IV (1056–1106), who was to succeed him on the throne, was only six years old. The king's widow, Agnes, who acted as regent until 1062, was unable to uphold the imperial authority in view of the unreliability and unbridled selfishness of the secular nobles. As chaos and anarchy threatened anew, it became all the more essential for the imperial government to preserve its prerogatives in appointing bishops and abbots. The ecclesiastical vassals, endowed with nonhereditary fiefs, were the emperor's most valuable advisers in time of peace and his most loyal supporters in time of war. It was therefore understandable from a political point of view that the emperors made every effort to oppose the attempts of the Church to free herself and her episcopate from secular control and influence.

As an outgrowth of the austere spirit of Cluny, the monastic rule of celibacy was made binding on all priests. It was imposed on the clergy in their entirety, in the face of stubborn resistance and widespread opposition among the German priests. Shortly after the death of Henry III a decree enforcing earlier enactments was passed by the Lateran Council, which vested the right of electing a pope in the College of Cardinals and the clergy of the City of Rome, thereby eliminating the influence of the Roman aristocracy and the German emperors.

Pope Gregory VII. The most outspoken advocate of the ecclesiastical demands was the Cluniac monk Hildebrand, who, in 1073, succeeded to the papal throne as Gregory VII (1073–1085). At the time when Henry IV had reached maturity, then, he found himself confronted with a powerful papacy, led by a representative of the ascetic rule of Cluny, where Benedictine monasticism had been restored to its original purity. The pope counted among his friends and allies not only the counts of Tuscany, but the Lombards in northern Italy and the Norman conquerors of southern Italy as well. After their first landing at Salerno in 1016 the Normans had returned at regular intervals, building up their own small but powerful states in the southern part of the Italian peninsula and especially in Sicily. In return for aid and protection that he had received from the Normans, Pope Nicholas II (1058–1061) had invested the Norman leader, Robert Guiscard, with power over Apulia, Calabria, and Sicily. In this way the papacy had prepared itself for the coming contest with the Empire.

Simony and Lay Investiture. Under the leadership of Pope Gregory VII the Church launched its major attack upon the practice of *simony* and upon *lay investiture. Simony* denotes the sale of ecclesiastical offices, which had become a widespread abuse as a consequence of the holding of temporal powers and possessions by the clergy. Lay investiture refers to the right of the king, or the feudal lord of a bishop or abbot, to invest these clerical dignitaries with ring and crozier, the symbols of ecclesiastical power. It was the contention of the popes of the Cluniac reform and especially of Gregory VII that the insignia of a Church office carried a spiritual significance, and that no layman should have the right to bestow them. The spirit of Cluny demanded the complete liberation of the Church from imperial and secular influences. But Gregory VII demanded more than that: with his iron will and all the tenacity that he had inherited from his peasant ancestors, he fought for the absolute supremacy of the ecclesiastical authority over both spiritual and temporal affairs, thus actually trying to reduce the imperial dignity to a position of vassalage. As the soul is superior to the body, he argued, so spiritual authority is superior to temporal authority. It is the duty of the successors of Peter, the Prince of Apostles, to admonish and, if need be, depose wicked rulers, because the vicar of Christ is responsible for the souls of all men.

Thus the prohibition of lay investiture was only one item in Gregory's far-reaching and revolutionary program. For the emperor, however, it was an issue of capital importance, not only his prestige but the very structure of imperial power and authority being involved. And so the attack upon the practice of lay investiture was bound to develop into a life-and-death struggle between Empire and Papacy, a struggle which could only end with the virtual obliteration of one of the two powers.

The German bishops, as we know, were at the same time members of the nobility, holders of royal fiefs and therefore vassals of the king-emperor. To give up the right of investiture meant in the emperor's opinion that he had to divest himself of the support of his ecclesiastical vassals and to put himself at the mercy of the lay nobility. On the other hand, to grant the emperor continued control of ecclesiastical appointments and elections meant that the pope had to abandon his plans of gaining complete independence from secular interference in Church affairs.

Henry IV at Canossa. The struggle for supremacy that raged between these two powers unleashed not only torrential floods of human passion, but also strong currents of idealism and enthusiasm. It cut into the very marrow of State and Church, entailing division and disruption of empire and papacy, the banishment of kings, and the deposition of kings and popes, undermined religious convictions and social institutions, and broke the heart and spirit of both Gregory and Henry, the two principal characters of the tragedy.

Gregory VII, in the year 1076, demanded universal renunciation of the practice of lay investiture. Henry IV's answer was the convocation of a synod of German bishops, who declared Gregory deposed and proceeded to elect an antipope. Gregory, in turn, excommunicated the emperor, absolving his subjects from their oath of allegiance. The German lay nobles promptly seized the opportunity to start a rebellion against the emperor. As Henry's situation grew more and more desperate, he made up his mind to offer his unconditional submission to the papal demands and to ask for absolution. In 1077 Henry and Gregory met at Canossa, in the castle of Countess Mathilda of Tuscany, where the pope, interrupting his intended journey across the Alps and into Germany, had sought shelter and protection in view of the approaching imperial forces. After having spent three days barefoot in the snow in front of the gates, Henry, wearing the garb of a penitent sinner, was admitted and freed from the ban of excommunication. Considering the spirit of the age, this scene in itself — an emperor humbly confessing his sins and begging for the priestly absolution — is by no means unusual, but Henry, in recognizing the authority of a pope whom he himself had deposed and declared unworthy of wearing the triple crown, had silently acknowledged political defeat.

Nevertheless, the immediate result of Canossa was a temporary restoration of imperial prestige that enabled the emperor to regain the support of a majority of the German nobles and bishops. Was Henry's submission prompted by a temporary change of heart or was it merely a shrewd political move on his part? The emperor was a spoiled, ego-centered young ruler, passionate, impulsive, and lacking in self-control. Yet his character shows traces of a genuine nobility of heart and mind, coupled with a sincerity of endeavor that seems to preclude mere deceptive scheming and cheap hypocritical dissimulation.

The reconciliation, at any rate, was of short duration. When Henry resumed the practice of lay investiture, he was once more deposed by Gregory, and Rudolf, duke of Swabia, the choice of the rebellious nobles, was given papal recognition. But the situation had changed: with the moral and active support of the greater contingent of the German nobility and clergy, Henry deposed Gregory a second time and had Clement III elected as antipope. With his victorious army the emperor entered Rome in 1084 and was crowned by Clement, while Gregory, seemingly defeated, died in exile in southern Italy where he had sought refuge in Norman territory.

The Concordat of Worms. Henry's triumph, to be sure, was short lived. While in the Church the schism continued, the emperor's own son Henry V (1106–1125) concluded an alliance with the papacy and rose in arms against his father, imprisoning the emperor and forcing him to renounce the throne. Henry IV, however, escaped and was about to begin a punitive campaign against his treacherous son when death put an end to his colorful and tragic career. The struggle continued between Church and State. Henry V carried on his father's fight for the imperial control of ecclesiastical elections. A pope was imprisoned and another rebellion occurred in Germany before the struggle was brought to a temporary conclusion by a .compromise that was actually a victory for the papal claims.

In the Concordat of Worms (1122) it was decided that bishops and abbots were to be invested with their fiefs (as a symbol of their secular office) by the emperor, but that they were to receive ring and staff (the insignia of their spiritual authority) from the pope. In Germany the act of consecration was to follow the act of investiture, whereas in Burgundy and Italy consecration was to take precedence. Being represented at the elections, the emperor retained a limited control over ecclesiastical appointments and over the German clergy. But just the same, the struggle over investiture left the imperial authority considerably impaired and greatly contributed to that turbulent and unsettled state in which the German nation found itself upon the death of Henry V in 1125. Since the emperor died without a direct heir, the Salic-Frankish dynasty came to an end, and once again the princes were offered the opportunity of exercising their legal rights in electing a new monarch.

Kingship and Priesthood. It is an ingredient of the Germanic tradition that the political organization of the State expresses a community of interests that rests on the two pillars of royal authority and individual freedom. The Germanic chieftains, princes, and kings were never absolute rulers in the Oriental and Byzantine fashion. They were the leaders of their people and as such they were held personally responsible for the common welfare of all and could be deposed if they failed to fulfill the terms of the unwritten contract from which they derived their title of leadership. Furthermore, royal power, according to the Germanic concept of government, is never above the law but always subject to its rules. "The royal power, like the whole people," we read in the *Forum Iudicum,* an early Visigothic law code, "is bound to observe the laws."

The attitudes taken by both Henry IV and Gregory VII signified a departure from these ancient principles of Western political theory. Henry IV, and after him Frederick Barbarossa (cf. p. 89 sq.), appealed to certain principles in Roman Law to substantiate their absolutistic claims, principles that were opposed to those upon which medieval civilization had risen under Germanic leadership. Likewise, the divinely ordained sovereignty of Dante's (1265-1321) concept of a universal monarchy introduces an idea which is foreign to the Germanic tradition. In his *Monarchia* the principle of liberty is sacrificed to a legalistic concept of order that is arbitrarily divorced from the demands of reason and the natural law. Gregory VII's attempted establishment of a theocracy (a Church-State) as well as Henry IV's and Barbarossa's inclination toward "caesaro-papism" (imperial absolutism, totalitarianism) tended to undermine the constitutional structure of the Germanic Middle Ages. However, it should be noted that even during their most heated controversies the representatives of Empire and Papacy never surrendered the idea that State and Church mutually depended on each other and that their destinies were therefore closely intertwined. It was not in order to destroy the papacy that Henry IV launched his attack against Gregory VII, but in order to depose a pope who in his opinion endangered the unity and harmony of the ecclesiastical and secular powers: "For our Lord Jesus Christ has called Us to the Kingship but not Thee to the Priesthood" (*Mon. Germ.* LL. II, p. 47).

It was the same ideology that motivated the actions of Henry's papal opponent. The fight against simony and lay investiture and the enforcement of celibacy among the secular clergy were means to the same wished-for end, the harmony of *regnum* and *sacerdotium,* this time, to be sure, emphasizing the supremacy of the papacy.

Canossa, therefore, is a symbol as well as a turning point. It marks the end of Charlemagne's and Otto the Great's protectorship and actual domination of the ecclesiastical realm. Henceforth the German emperor and the Empire as such relinquish their claims to the spiritual sword. The monasteries, in accordance with the demands of the Cluniac reform movement, are placed under the direct supervision and authority of Rome, so that the struggle over lay investiture constitutes the first major phase in the creation of a strictly ecclesiastical medieval civilization.

The Church in Germany. An external symptom of a religious revival and a direct outgrowth of the reform movement was the foundation of several new religious orders, all animated by the desire to restore the rigorous discipline of the earlier stages of western monasticism. Bruno, a canon from Cologne, retired with several companions into a solitary wilderness, the Chartreuse mountains near Grenoble, and became the founder of the Carthusian Order (1084); Robert, abbot of Molesme and founder of the Cistercian Order (1098), introduced into his monastic communities the revised and invigorated Benedictine rule; St. Norbert of Xanten on the Rhine founded the Premonstratensian Order at Prémontré (1121).

The Carthusians were to become famous as writers and copyists of manuscripts, while Cistercians and Premonstratensians indulged in hard, bodily labor, contributing to the economic development of their age and taking a prominent part in the work of colonization in the eastern frontier districts of Germany. As missionaries they penetrated into the region between the Elbe and Oder rivers, clearing the forests, draining the swamps, and teaching the German settlers who had followed them from different parts of Germany how to cultivate the soil and protect alluvial lands against floods and other elemental forces of nature. Thus numerous German villages grew up in the immediate neighborhood of these eastern monasteries.

But the spirit of Cluny also made itself felt in the ranks of the secular clergy, where the vices of venality and bribery had exerted a corrupting influence, ecclesiastical offices being sold or given away by the secular lords who were the owners of churches and church lands. The decrees of Gregory VII which imposed celibacy upon all the members of the clergy caused, as we have heard, a storm of indignation in Germany; priests, bishops, and even synods expressed their violent opposition. But Gregory did not yield and even went so far as to forbid the people to receive the sacraments from married priests or to attend their services. It is an interesting fact that in Italy as well as in Germany the pope found his strongest support among the laity. In Italy popular feeling ran high against the worldly possessions and the luxury of the higher clergy, while in Germany the people at large approved of the ascetic ideals of Cluny and showed themselves deeply concerned with the reformation and purification of the Church.

The ecclesiastical penal codes are contained in the Penitential Rituals (*Bussbücher*). Under the influence of the reform movement disciplinary measures became more and more severe. To understand the significance of this ecclesiastical administration of justice it is necessary to point out that the medieval church in many respects performed judiciary functions that were later entrusted to the State. Lacking an organized police force and a centralized judicial power, the State was frequently not in a position to exercise or even command a judicial authority.

Faith and Superstition. The Penitential Rituals and the Communion Books give evidence of the amount of ancient pagan beliefs which still survived in a Christian garb. Throughout the medieval centuries pagan superstitions and Christian faith were closely allied, particularly among the peasant population with their stubborn adherence to ancient customs and traditions. The Cluniac reform destroyed many of these pagan remnants of the Germanic past, while the preceding and again the following period frequently made use of pagan beliefs and practices in order to give the Christian message a wider popular appeal. The unlettered people, living in close contact with nature, its phenomena and forces, were unfamiliar with the finer distinctions of theological and philosophical speculation, and attributed magical powers to their favorite saints and even to the sacraments of the Church. The relics of saints, sacred numbers, altars, altar cloths, the vestments of priests were supposed to be endowed with miraculous powers.

The blessings with which the Church consecrated and elevated nature and its implements, salt, oil, bread, wine, wax, herbs, fields, and pastures, were frequently mistaken for magical rites and in this way encouraged superstitious beliefs. The most sinister and consequential residue of ancient paganism was the belief in witchcraft and sorcery, an offshoot of the demonology of the Chaldeans, the Jews, the Greeks, the Romans, and other ancient peoples. Germanic mythology and religion knows of evil spirits who dwell in the forests and are the enemies of man, threatening to destroy or corrupt him. In the Christian era these superstitions sometimes blended with the Christian doctrine of the fallen angels (devils), repeatedly gripping the imagination of an entire epoch of Western civilization with the force of a mental disease and associating themselves with the most inhuman perversions and aberrations. The historically and culturally significant "Penitential Ritual" of Bishop Burchard of Worms (*c.* 1020) opposes many of the superstitious beliefs of his age and prescribes severe punishments for uncritical credulity in such matters.

Symbolism and Emotionalism. According to the medieval view of the world, all natural and human life is symbolical and analogical: it points beyond itself to its eternal source and cause. Life thus assumes the appearance of a monumental morality play in which everything receives significance in view of the momentous decisions that precede and determine the end. This symbolical character of reality adds weight and meaning to the seemingly most indifferent things, words, thoughts, and deeds. Life itself thus becomes a kind of continuous liturgical ritual. This explains the important part that gestures and attitudes, formal social etiquette, religious ceremonial, meaningful verbal patterns, play in the plastic and literary arts of these centuries.

Men and women of every station in life were given to violent outbursts of emotionalism. In an age of contrasts the free and easy flow of tears alternated with childlike expressions of gaiety, laughter, and merrymaking. Self-abasement in public was quite commonly practiced, and at times assumed the curious forms of a standardized ritual: it was customary that a bishop-elect at first refused to accept the dignity conferred upon him, fleeing into the wilderness to hide his unworthiness. The emperor was expected to weep profusely at his coronation. A penitent sinner had to lie prostrate on the ground, manifesting his repentance by moaning and weeping. Embraces and kisses were freely exchanged on every conceivable occasion. Expressions of love and hatred, joy and sorrow, gentleness and cruelty were found side by side, symbols and symptoms of a life that was manifold in its outlets and manifestations, but unified and single-tracked in purpose and end.

"Treuga Dei" (The Truce of God). Under Feudal Law (*Fehderecht*) private feuds and wars were practically unrestricted in number and extent. It is one of the greatest merits of the ecclesiastical reform movement, and one of the symptoms of the growing influence of Church legislation, that the French bishops succeeded at the end of the tenth century in imposing the so-called Peace of God (Latin: *Pax Dei*) upon the lawless nobility, compelling the nobles under penalty of excommunication to respect the person and property of peasants, merchants, churchmen, and other noncombatants. As a direct outgrowth of the spirit of Cluny must be considered the institution of the "Truce of God" (Latin: *Treuga Dei*), promulgated by a French synod and prohibiting any kind of private warfare from every Wednesday evening until the next Monday morning, the days that were hallowed by the suffering, death, and resurrection of Christ, and during the season of Lent.

Later on the "Truce of God" was extended to include certain other seasons and feasts of the ecclesiastical year. The Salic emperors worked unceasingly for the general promotion and the universal acceptance of the Truce of God. Henry IV regulated its observance by legal decree (1085). And when Pope Urban II in 1095 called upon the knights of Europe to come to the rescue of the Holy Sepulcher in Jerusalem, he referred to the "Peace of God" in these words: "Those who formerly have misused their feudal right in fighting against the faithful, shall now start out upon a battle that is worthy of their efforts and that will end in victory. Those who formerly have taken the field against their brethren and blood-relations shall now wage a just war against the barbarians."

Family Life and the Position of Woman. It was due to the generally strengthened position of the Church that it gained an increasing influence upon family life. The priest, taking the place of the guardian (*Muntwalt*), now joined man and woman in holy wedlock, and the marriage ceremony was held in the church and followed by a nuptial Mass. But married life was anything but pure happiness and bliss. Sexual appetites were only partly checked by moral and religious restrictions and inhibitions, and adultery was widespread among both sexes. Abortions were frequent, and malformed or crippled children were often exposed or killed.

Aside from general religious instruction only a small percentage of the young men and women received a liberal education or some kind of intellectual training. Those who were given the opportunity of attending the cathedral or convent schools were usually either members of the nobility or candidates for the priesthood and ecclesiastical offices.

The civilization of the Middle Ages shows a strongly masculine character. Men are the dominating agents in Church, State, and society. Despite the chivalresque glorification of love and womanhood, women occupied an inferior social position throughout the Middle Ages. The social prejudices of ancient biology and sociology were too firmly entrenched to be overcome by a Christian dogmatics which theoretically recognized in woman man's equal, destined to reach the same degree of perfection in this life and in the life to come. But in practice even the leading philosophers of thirteenth-century scholasticism considered woman as a biologically underprivileged male and withheld from her the equality of social status. "She exists for the sake of man, and yet she is not a slave; she is free, and yet she is not a full-fledged citizen; there is no strict legal relationship between man and woman as there is between free man and free man, and yet she is man's partner and his companion of equal rank" (Thomas Aquinas, *Summa Theologica,* 2-2, q. 10, a. 8).

It is nevertheless true that we meet with a large number of highly educated women, some of them of noble birth, some outstanding in literary accomplishments or adepts of mystical theory and practice, yet all of them confined to a circle that is marked by the cultural domination of the Church. Secular education and therefore also the education of women in secular pursuits is the exception rather than the rule.

The legislative power of the Church (Canon Law) made itself most strongly felt in the enactment and enforcement of marriage laws. While in other respects Roman Law served as a suitable basis for ecclesiastical legislation, the marriage laws were an immediate expression of Church doctrine. According to Roman and Germanic Law the marriage bond could be solved either by mutual agreement of the two parties to the marriage contract or by the wish of one of the partners. The Church, on the other hand, maintained that only death solved and terminated the marriage bond. As one of the seven sacraments, marriage was endowed with religious sanctions and consecrated by the Church. The Church, therefore, claimed exclusive legislative and judicial power in all matters pertaining to the state of matrimony. The tenth and eleventh centuries witness the gradual disappearance of state legislation in matrimonial affairs.

Nature, Animals, and Plants. Medieval man, still largely depending on the soil for his livelihood, was firmly rooted in maternal Nature. He was deeply attached to reality in all its aspects, the visible and the invisible, the sensuous and the spiritual. His confidence in the world of phenomena was sustained and guaranteed by that supreme reality of which everything else was a symbol and feeble image. Field and forest, wind and cloud,

Wehmeyer, Hildesheim

St. Michael's Church, Hildesheim

Interior of St. Godehard's Church, Hildesheim

plants and animals evoked brotherly thoughts and affections. The plant and animal ornaments with which the copyists adorned their manuscripts and the masons their handiwork in sculpture and architecture give evidence of their faithful and accurate observation. The philosophers never doubted that mind and reality were proportioned to each other, so that the theory of knowledge plays a rather negligible part in medieval speculation.

The artists and poets loved to personify the forces of nature, endowing sun and moon, wind and cloud with human features as they share emotionally the moods of sadness and joy, of crucifixion and resurrection. Animals were honored and commemorated in legend and satire, they were man's inseparable companions at home and in public. Knights and noble ladies surrounded themselves with falcons, magpies, daws, starlings, ravens, cranes, and parrots. Hunting with hounds or hawks was a favorite pastime of both sexes. The presents that kings and princes received from foreign potentates regularly included some lions, leopards, or monkeys. Legal procedure dealt with animals as with intelligent and responsible beings that were indicted, judged, sentenced, punished, and sometimes executed.

Arts and Crafts. At the beginning of the eleventh century the arts of the Western World found themselves in a new situation. The persecutions of Christianity and the struggles for recognition were a matter of the past, and the Romanesque style (*c.* 950-1150), having come into its own, proudly displayed its riches in the different countries of Europe. Christian doctrine, reinforced by the reform movement of Cluny, provided the inspiration for the artistic accomplishments in architecture, sculpture, painting, and the minor arts and crafts. The supernational unity of this inspirational source did not result, however, in uniformity of artistic creation, but left room for the individual national temperaments to speak in their own voices.

German architecture of the Romanesque period is characterized by an intense struggle between the horizontal and vertical forces and directions, verticality being emphasized by the tallness of an increasing number of church towers and spires. The Romanesque church rests upon the earth in its walls, its round arches, its vaults, its pillars, and its porches, but it rises toward heaven in its towers, its choirs, and its gables. It combines the massive and plastic self-sufficiency of classical antiquity with the soaring flight of Christian spirituality. Romanesque church architecture in Germany grows out of the German landscape: it embodies the hopes, fears, beliefs, and superstitions of the period of which it is a monumental symbol. The Romanesque style expresses that graduated and hierarchical order of values that characterizes the civilization of the Middle Ages, a hierarchy that, reaching down from God to the atom, allots to each type of being its proper place in the universal organism of Church, State, and society. Life, nature, and art acquire a symbolical value by sharing in that cosmos of Nature and Grace which, by means of the sacramental system of the Church, consecrated the objects of nature and daily life: vegetative life, animal life, and life on the human level.

It is in two major points that the Romanesque style in church architecture departs from the earlier type of the Christian basilica: (1) pillars replace the columns, supporting the arches of the nave areade; (2) the nave is divided into a series of sections or "bays," retarding the continuous horizontal movement of the basilican interior and introducing in its place a diversity of clearly proportioned and self-sufficient architectural parts.

In view of future developments special emphasis must be placed on the resumption of the ribbed groined vault (already known to the Romans), which in the eleventh century replaced the early wooden ceiling as well as the intermediate form of the barrel vault. The ribbed groined vault was supported by a series of six arches, resulting normally in a vault of domical shape.

Bishops, abbots, and princes tried to outdo each other in their building activities and in their encouragement and sponsorship of the arts. St. Gall, Regensburg, and Hildesheim continued to stand out as illustrious centers of artistic activities and accomplishments. Bishop Bernward (993–1022) of Hildesheim, the tutor of Emperor Otto III, was one of the most influential protectors of the arts and is especially remembered as the builder of St. Michael's Church in Hildesheim (1001–1022), the most outstanding contribution of Saxony to the early Romanesque style. The cathedral of Magdeburg owes its existence to Emperor Otto I, that of Bamberg to Henry II. The great Rhenish cathedrals of Spires (Speyer), Mayence (Mainz), Worms, the abbey church of Maria-Laach, and the several Romanesque churches of Cologne (Maria im Kapitol, Apostelkirche, St. Gereon) were erected during the rule of the Saxon and Hohenstaufen emperors. Many of these monuments were completely destroyed during World War II.

Secular architecture played a rather insignificant part in a prevailingly ecclesiastical age. Of the representative secular architecture of the Saxon and Salic epochs only a few samples have survived. The most beautiful and the one best preserved is the Imperial Palace (*Kaiserpfalz*) at Goslar in the northern part of the Hartz Mountains that was begun by Henry II and completed by Henry III (*c.* 1050). Within its walls Henry IV was born. The building was restored during the years 1867–1878. Secular building activity was greatly aided and stimulated by the rise of a knightly aristocracy, the spread of the ideals of chivalry, and the growth of the cities.

Romanesque architecture ruled over the other arts of the period. Sculpture as well as painting were subordinated to architecture, which provided their *raison d'être*. Romanesque sculpture is filled with a sense of lasting existence, abiding in childlike confidence in the manifold forms of reality that are presented as sensible symbols and images of the purely intelligible.

The arts and the crafts are still undivided, united by the general characteristics and criteria of skill, usefulness, beautiful shape, and social significance. The anonymous masters, those artist-monks, who created altar tables, choir screens, baptismal fonts, crucifixes, ornate columns and capitals, and the solemn cathedral sculptures: they were both artists and craftsmen. The art of goldsmithing reached a high degree of perfection in the creation of altar vessels and cultic furniture, of tabernacles, monstrances, reliquaries, book covers, and chandeliers. The cathedral of Aachen contains a pulpit wholly wrought of gold, dating back to the days of Emperor Henry II.

The pelican, who nourishes his young with his own blood; the phoenix, who rises to a new life out of his own ashes: they are symbols of Christ. The poisonous glance of the basilisk signifies the spirit of evil; the virginal bee tells of Mary, the immaculate maiden. Minerals, plants, animals, men, and angels, the book of nature and the book of life repeat a thousandfold the story of creation, fall, and redemption. The arts are integral parts of the lives of the people, and life itself in its plenitude is enshrined in artistic creation.

Romanesque painting, like sculpture, served the adornment and enhancement of the architectural frame and background. The huge wall spaces of the cathedrals were frequently decorated with representations of biblical themes of the Old and New Testaments. The figural composition in its rigid and angular design seems to be influenced by the style of miniatures and mosaics. The illumination and illustration of manuscripts, missals, gospel books (*Evangeliare*), psalters, legends, calendars, and Latin classics reached new heights of perfection with the gradual emancipation from Irish and Byzantine patterns. In the art school of Reichenau originated the "Evangeliary" of Otto III, containing a famous miniature painting of the nations doing homage to the emperor. The art of painting on glass, being still in the earliest stage of its development, was practiced in Romanesque times at St. Emeram (Regensburg) and at Tegernsee near Munich. Some of the stained-glass windows in the cathedral of Augsburg date from the middle of the eleventh century and are among the oldest specimens of this sublime art which achieved its full splendor in the later Gothic period.

Music. Together with architecture and its allied arts, music also served religious, social, and educational ends. To be sure, there were the popular tunes of the wandering students and minstrels, who accompanied their songs on the harp or the fiddle, the former being one of the most ancient musical instruments, while the latter was introduced from Asia by way of Byzantium in the tenth century. But music as a fine art occurs in the early Middle Ages chiefly in the form of the ecclesiastical and monastic choral chant, which in the Romanesque period at times introduces even polyphonic motifs. The music of the Antiphonaries (choral songbooks) of St. Gall in Switzerland of the ninth and tenth centuries represents the authentic version of the liturgical Gregorian Chant (cf. p. 54 sq.).

The Latin system of *neumatic* notation was developed in Rome before the eighth century, and remained in use to the end of the fourteenth century. The neumatic signs were derived from the signs and accents of the grammarians. The necessity of fixing the intonation of the notes led to the invention of several tentative systems of notation after the ninth century and to the introduction of the "staff," consisting at first of one, then of two, and finally of four lines (five lines in modern notation). The transformation of the neumatic signs into square notes was practically completed at the end of the thirteenth century. Of greater importance were the several modal systems, because they expressed the psychological and sociological implications of different musical styles. The three major phases of modality are represented by the Greek, the medieval (Church modes), and the modern polyphonic modes which date from the beginning of Renaissance polyphony in the fifteenth century.

The first theoretical treatises on the medieval Church modes were written at the beginning of the ninth century. Hermann Contractus of Reichenau († 1054) gives a complete description of eight modes which he calls *tropi,* while the Italian Benedictine monk Guido d'Arezzo († 1050) first introduced the term *modus* instead of *tonus* or *tropus.* Adam of Fulda, an outstanding German musicologist of the fifteenth century, quotes a little poem by Guido d'Arezzo that illustrates the changing emotional contents that are expressed by the different Church Modes:

"For every mood the first will be good; the second so tender to grief;
If anger the third one provoke, then the fourth will bring the relief;
The fifth be the mood for the joyous; the sixth one the pious will prize;
The seventh is pleasing to youth, but the last is the mood of the wise."

On the whole it may be said that medieval German and European music followed the peculiarities of the Latin language with its characteristic measuring or counting of syllables, the same principle that has left its indelible impress upon the metric forms of all the Romance languages and literatures. It took Germany several more centuries to emancipate herself in her musical and literary arts from this foreign rhythmical and metrical technique and to rediscover the qualitative principle of accentuation. Of all the Indo-European nations the Germanic peoples alone emphasize the quality rather than the quantity of word syllables, putting the stress on the root syllable, the one that imparts substantial meaning to the verbal pattern. Medieval liturgical chant, on the other hand, depended entirely on the quantity of syllables, the neumes being sung as a succession of long and short tones, following the example of oratory and the declamation of poetry. The German manuscripts of St. Gall, Einsiedeln, and Metz of the ninth and tenth centuries mark the long and short tones by means of signs and letters. The growing influence of the spoken vernacular languages after the close of the tenth century tended to corrupt the classical tradition of Latin elocution and likewise the ancient style of musical performance.

Literature. Latin was the language of the Church; it was the language of the clergy, who represented learning and culture in most of its aspects. The vernacular Old High German language with its full sounding vowels and sonorous endings appeared as inferior to the velvety smoothness and the elegant flow of the Latin rhymes and rhythms. Whoever wanted to be recognized as a poet had to write Latin verse, carefully heeding the metrical rules of the ancient classical authors.

The poetry of monks and nuns dealt with the most diversified subject matter: biblical themes and the lives of Christian saints, historical events and legends, proverbs and satires. While all the German monasteries encouraged the practice of poetry and song, the didactic and epical elements prevailed, and only a few of the writers excelled in the field of the drama and the creation of church hymns. The Benedictine abbeys of Gandersheim, Tegernsee, and St. Gall stood out as centers of literary activities.

Hrotsvitha (Roswitha, c. 932–1001), a learned canoness of a secular convent for ladies of the Saxon nobility, affiliated with the monastery of Gandersheim, commemorated about the year 980 the accomplishments of Otto the Great in her epic *Gesta Odonis*. In her poems she celebrated the foundation of Gandersheim, the resurrection of Christ, the life of Mary, and, basing her story on a Greek model, she approached the *Faust* theme in *The Conversion of Theophilus*. The latter is a poetic description of Theophilus' pact with the devil and his final salvation through the intercession of the Virgin Mary. In her dramas, which were written in rhythmical prose and were to serve as substitutes for the widely read but objectionable pagan comedies of the late Roman playwright Terence (c. 190–159 B.C.), she described the conversion of harlots, glorified Christian virgins and martyrs, and gave evidence of great skill and a naïve and sprightly sense of humor. The period of the Saxon emperors could offer no equivalent to the stage of the age of Terence, so that Hrotsvitha's dramatic works were not written with a view to stage production. While Hrotsvitha composed these clever and amusing dialogues, medieval drama, properly so called, originated at about the same time from the liturgy of the Church.

Religious poetry flourished above all in the monastery of St. Gall in Switzerland. It was the home of Germany's leading poets, writers, and teachers in the tenth century. Out of the spirit of music was born the literary form of the "sequence," in which words and music blended and whose influence is noticeable in the works of the *"Minnesänger"* of the age of chivalry (cf. p. 155 sq.).

Latin in their form, but German in their content are the epic poems of *Walter with the Strong Hand* (*Waltharius Manu Fortis*) and *Ruodlieb*. The *Song of Walter* (*Waltharilied*) was written about 930 in Latin hexameters by Ekkehard I and metrically revised by Ekkehard IV († 1060). The poem tells of Walter and his betrothed Hildegund, who flee from the court of Attila, king of the Huns, their encounter with the greedy King Gunther of Burgundy, and the final triumph of their love and loyalty. It is typically Germanic in its mixture of heroism and tenderness, and Walter appears as the first German representative of Christian knighthood, the undaunted yet humble protector of noble womenhood.

In *Ruodlieb* (c. 1030) the colorful world of the eleventh century has come to life. The anonymous author, belonging to the Bavarian monastic community of Tegernsee, has been called the first master of realism in German literature. The description of the knightly hero's travel experiences and adventures manifests not only an accurate factual observation, but reveals wisdom, human understanding, love of nature, and a keen sense of humor.

During the eleventh and twelfth centuries a growing missionary zeal finds its literary equivalent in an increasing output of didactic poetry and prose. The attempts at popularization issued in the gradual adoption of the German vernacular, in sermons as well as in religious poetry. Closely related to the ascetic spirit of Cluny is the *Ezzoleich* (*Lay of Ezzo, c.* 1060), a lyric poem, written in German, but following the formal model of the Latin sequences. Linguistically it marks the transition from Old High German to early Middle High German. As to its content, it represents the first lyrical attempt to tell the story of creation and redemption in the German tongue. Ezzo, its author, deserves high credit for the harmonious combination of didactic and poetic values.

The institution of the Feast of the Immaculate Conception in Lyon (*c.* 1140) led to the creation of hymns, sequences, and epic poems in praise of the Virgin Mary, the mediatrix between Christ and suffering mankind. At the beginning of the twelfth century many members of the clergy began to turn to worldly themes. *The Lay of Anno* (*Annolied*), composed between 1080 and 1110 by a monk of the monastery of Siegburg near Bonn on the Rhine, is a kind of world chronicle, centering in the figure of St. Anno, archbishop of Cologne (1056–1075) and tutor of the young Emperor Henry IV. The *Lay of Alexander* (*Alexanderlied*) was written between 1120 and 1130 by the cleric Lamprecht (*Pfaffe Lamprecht*), who used as his model a French epic of the same name. The life of the great conqueror Alexander is described as futile and misspent because of his entanglement in worldly concerns.

At about the same time (*c.* 1130) Conrad, a priest from Ratisbon (Regensburg) in Bavaria, adapted his *Lay of Roland* (*Rolandslied*) from the French *Chanson de Roland,* telling of the heroic deeds of the most famous of Charlemagne's paladins (cf. p. 43). Roland is depicted as the typical knight of the age of the Crusades, the servant of God whose life has been consecrated by his exalted calling. Despite this religious tinge the description of camp life in the army of Charlemagne emphasizes the worldly aspects and elements of the period. *The Emperors' Chronicle* (*Kaiserchronik*), the work of a Bavarian priest (*c.* 1150), goes so far as to praise the power of worldly love (*minne*) over all creatures, as an indispensable requisite for knightly and courtly education. The work belongs in the category of popular rhymed chronicles, presenting a medley of historical and legendary elements.

Secular literature of an inferior order is represented in the poetry of the gleemen (*Spielmannsdichtung*), of wandering students and scholars who included among their number all kinds of entertainers, jugglers, and jesters. These in their own way perpetuated the ancient heroic legends and sagas, but primarily fulfilled the role of a living news chronicle, singing of contemporary events in Church and State, telling fairy stories and fables, performing on the village green or in the castle, catering in every way to the taste of the popular fancy of the unlettered and worldly minded. It was only later in the twelfth century that the wandering minstrel recovered a finer sense of literary values and prepared himself for the great task that the age of chivalry had in store for him.

Scholarship and Education. The primary goal of learning and education in the Ottonian and Salic periods was the formation of a religious and moral personality. The pre-Christian classical curriculum of the seven liberal arts was to provide the foundation upon which the structure of Christian dogma should rest. As in Charlemagne's time, the higher learning was patronized and greatly encouraged by the German emperors. But the members of the clergy were the representatives and carriers of intellectual life. Many of the bishoprics became now important seats of learning.

Each monastery had two separate schools, one of which served the education of the future clergy, while the second one was attended by the sons of nobles who aspired to leading positions in secular life. The strictest discipline ruled in both schools, corporal punishment being frequent and severe. Next in importance and influence ranked the cathedral schools which were attached to each bishopric. The director of the cathedral school was called "Master" (*Magister Scholarum, Scholasticus*), and to him was entrusted the supervision of the several parish schools of his bishop's diocese.

The curriculum in both monastery and cathedral schools consisted of a preparatory course, followed by instruction in rhetoric, dialectic, music, astronomy, arithmetic, and geometry. The preparatory training included the reading, recitation, and memorization of Latin psalms, writing upon wax tablets and parchment, and the acquisition of a vocabulary comprehensive enough to enable the student to begin with the reading of the more popular Latin authors of antiquity. The study of grammar made the student familiar with the classical Roman grammarians, writers, and poets, reading and translation being equally stressed. The class in rhetoric had to learn the art of letter writing, the drawing up of legal documents and diplomas, the making of wills, and all the agenda of the medieval chancery. Style and composition were further improved by the study of Cicero, Quintilian, St. Augustine, or some compendium of the art of rhetorics. The study of dialectic served the sharpening of the intellect to make it a suitable instrument for logical thought and disputation. Some of Aristotle's works were read in Latin translations alongside with Boëthius (cf. p. 26), Cassiodorus (cf. p. 52), and other pagan and Christian philosophers. Greek was not taught in these early medieval schools, and consequently very few had any knowledge of it.

The *Trivium* of sciences was, as we know (cf. p. 26), followed by the *Quadrivium*. The class in music studied the Church modes and the interrelation of tonal values, following in the main the theories laid down in Boëthius' tract *On Music* (*De Musica*). Astronomy was chiefly concerned with calendaric calculations in connection with the fixing of ecclesiastical feast days and seasons, and the hours of monastic devotions. Arithmetic, following in the footsteps of Pythagoras († 497 B.C.) and the Church Fathers, was closely tied up with speculations on the symbolism of numbers. More realistic but less popular was the study of geometry, including geography and the rudimentary beginnings of natural science. Maps and globes were known and frequently used. The maps of the world showed Asia with an indication of the location of the biblical Paradise in the upper half, Europe in the lower left, Africa in the lower right part of the map. The continents, surrounded on all sides by water, were arranged in the form of a "T" (T-maps).

The convent schools for women, attached to their respective monasteries, were attended by girls who were preparing themselves for a religious vocation as well as by daughters of noble families who would leave the convent after their educational curriculum was completed. Versatility in the reading, writing, reciting, and singing of Latin was emphasized, while the curriculum of the seven liberal arts was otherwise reduced to a minimum of fundamental principles of general education.

Outside of the monastic and metropolitan schools education was at a low ebb. Even in the ranks of the nobility the eleventh century witnesses a growing contempt of the higher learning. We find, for example, honorable mention of the fact that Emperor Henry IV was able to read the letters that he received. And even the splendor of the following period of courtly culture is not without the blemish of widespread illiteracy among the laity.

Chapter 6

THE HOHENSTAUFEN DYNASTY AND THE AGE OF CHIVALRY

Lothar and Conrad III: Welf and Waiblingen. With the death of Henry V in 1125 the Salic-Frankish dynasty had come to an end, and the German nobles, in choosing Lothar of Supplinburg (1125–1137) as their new king, reasserted once more the validity of the time-honored elective principle of Germanic kingship. Henry V had died without direct heirs, and the electors had disregarded the hereditary claims of the two nephews of the late emperor, Frederick of Hohenstaufen and his younger brother Conrad. Thus originated the feud between the two powerful feudal families of the *Welfs* (Guelfs) and the *Waiblingens* (Ghibellines; their name possibly derived from one of the family possessions of the *Hohenstaufens*), which later on spread to Italy and continued for several centuries.

Lothar's election caused the Hohenstaufens to rise in armed rebellion and to wage private warfare against Henry the Proud (1126–1139). Henry was head of the Welfs; son-in-law and heir of Lothar; duke of Bavaria, Saxony, and Swabia; count of Tuscany; and, by the end of Lothar's reign, the most powerful territorial lord of Germany. True to their traditional policy of checking any considerable growth of the imperial power, the electors chose the Hohenstaufen, Conrad III (1138–1152) to succeed Lothar. Now it was the Welfs' turn to feel themselves slighted and offended, and this Welf-Waiblingen family feud added to the general turmoil and confusion that characterized this period of feudal license. Conrad's participation in the unsuccessful Second Crusade (cf. p. 107), undertaken in alliance with the king of France, tended to undermine further the prestige of the German emperor.

Frederick I (1152–1190) and the Consolidation of the Empire. Conrad III wisely passed over his own young son in favor of his nephew, Frederick, who was destined to rescue the Empire from anarchy and disintegration. Being the nephew of Henry the Proud through his mother, he was half Welf and half Waiblingen, thus acceptable to both parties and able to reconcile temporarily their conflicting ambitions.

Frederick I, named *Barbarossa* (red beard, *Rotbart*), is the most brilliant and attractive figure among the Hohenstaufen emperors, the symbol of all chivalrous virtues, and the favorite of the Romantic writers of the early nineteenth century. It was the ambition of his life to resurrect the ancient glory and power of the Roman Empire under German leadership, and he succeeded to a remarkable extent in realizing his aims. True representative of the social standards and prejudices of knighthood that he was, he underestimated the significance of the rising commercial and industrial forces embodied in city life and their new ideals of citizenship. An idealist in his vision of a greater empire and in his exalted view of the mission of chivalry, he was a realist in the execution of his far-reaching plans and in the practical application of his sound and noble principles.

His first major objective, the restoration of order and stability in the German lands, was at least partly achieved by the promulgation of a general land peace (*Landfriede*), forbidding private wars and feuds, and guaranteeing a stricter enforcement and a more universal application of the existing local enactments. Next he re-established imperial supremacy over Poland, Bohemia, Hungary, and Burgundy.

The emperor's nephew and the current head of the Welfs was Henry the Lion (1156–1180), the son of Henry the Proud. To gain the friendship and military support of this ambitious prince, Frederick made him duke of Saxony and Bavaria and thereby the most powerful lord in the Empire. Henry accompanied Frederick on the first two of his six expeditions into Italy, and aided German expansion and colonization in the East (cf. p. 110 sq.). He is also remembered as the founder of the bishoprics of Lübeck, Ratzeburg, Schwerin, and of the city of Munich (München). Banned by the emperor in 1179 for his refusal to come to Frederick's aid in the Italian campaign of 1174, he went into exile in England, retaining only Brunswick (Braunschweig) and Lüneburg as his family possessions. The duchies of Saxony and Bavaria were divided up into smaller units, and the greater part of Bavaria was given to Otto Wittelsbach, whose descendants occupied the Bavarian throne until the German revolution of 1918.

Frederick experienced a most severe setback in his attempt to recover imperial control of Italy. His relations with the Roman Curia appeared to be of a friendly nature when he started upon his first Italian expedition in 1154. Pope Adrian IV (1154–1159), the first and only Englishman to sit on the papal throne, had sought Frederick's aid against the citizens and the Senate of Rome, who under the leadership of Arnold of Brescia attempted to regain the ancient freedom of the city from papal supremacy. Frederick had Arnold of Brescia executed and, in 1155, received the imperial crown from Adrian. However, when Frederick refused to act as the pope's squire by holding his bridle and stirrup, and thus seemed to deny implicitly the papal claim that the imperial crown was a feudal benefice conferred by the pope — affirming rather the origin of imperial power from God through the election of the princes — the relations between the two potentates became very strained. These incidents, as a matter of fact, marked the beginning of the last great struggle between Empire and Papacy that finally led to the decline and almost complete disintegration of both powers in the four-teenth century. Both emperor and pope tried to substantiate their claims by legal argumentation, having recourse to Roman and Canon Law respec-tively. Both legal branches had received a new impetus from the revival of learning in the twelfth century, and Canon Law, mainly based on the Scriptures and the decrees of popes and Church councils, received its classical form in the *Decretum* of Gratian (*c.* 1140), famous jurist of the University of Bologna.

The natural allies of the papacy were the cities of Lombardy, which felt themselves hampered in their commercial and industrial growth and thwarted in their desire for civic rights and self-government by imperial administration and supervision. Most of these North Italian communities were involved in factional and internecine strife, and Milan in particular exercised an oppressive rule over her smaller neighbors. Frederick took it upon himself to have the royal privileges formulated by a council of jurists from Bologna, and to appoint royal officers to safeguard these imperial prerogatives. On his second expedition to Italy in 1158 Frederick captured Milan and publicly promulgated his imperial rights before the Imperial Diet at Roncaglia. These rights included the appointment of imperial admin-istrative officers and the collection of taxes from tolls, markets, mints, and law courts. But the Lombard cities offered at first passive and later active resistance, and turned to the pope for protection.

In the meantime, Adrian's death had caused a papal schism, a majority of the cardinals voting for Alexander III (1159–1181), a minority for Victor IV. The emperor's support of Victor and several other antipopes was of no avail, as practically all the rulers of Europe stood solidly behind Alexander. Thus Frederick found himself facing the combined opposition of a united Italy, and in Alexander III he was confronted by a masterful politician who was fully his equal in circumspection, determination, and practical realism. Despite all the odds against him, the emperor at first seemed successful in the execution of his plans. He destroyed Milan in 1162, crushed the Lombard cities on his third expedition to Italy in 1166, and even besieged and captured Rome, while Alexander had to seek refuge in Sicily. But this victory was almost immediately followed by disaster: a pestilence destroyed the imperial army, and Frederick had to withdraw to Germany.

His withdrawal was the signal for the Lombard cities to unite in renewed efforts to offer an organized and impregnable resistance. Under the leader-ship of a newly risen Milan they formed the Lombard League, building at the same time a strongly fortified city which they named Alexandria in honor of their papal ally. When the emperor returned to Italy in 1174, this city withstood all his attempts to conquer it, and in 1176 Frederick was decisively defeated at Legnano. The Lombard cities emerged triumphant from the struggle for their civic liberties, and Frederick had to come to terms with the Lombard League as well as with his papal adversary. He ended the papal schism by making his peace with Alexander, and in 1183 he confirmed the self-government of the Lombard cities in the Peace of Constance. The royal prerogatives had to be surrendered, but the cities in return recognized the imperial sovereignty.

Although Frederick seemed to have failed in his struggle against the papacy, neither emperor nor pope had abandoned their respective claims to supremacy, so that at best a new compromise was effected which bore in itself the symptoms of latent discontent and a future crisis. Stubbornly persisting in the traditional aims of imperial policy, Frederick brought about the marriage of his eldest son Henry with Constance, heiress of the kingdom of Sicily, thus paving the way for a future alliance between southern Italy and the Empire that would be a formidable asset in a renewed conflict with the papacy, while at the same time it established a new basis for the commercial relations with the Orient.

Frederick paid his final tribute to the spirit of the age when he took the cross in 1189 and led twenty thousand of his knights on the noble adventure of the Third Crusade. He was seventy years of age when he started upon this crowning event of his colorful career, only equaled in splendor and enthusiasm by the great festival of Chivalry of the year 1184 at Mayence (Mainz), where more than seventy thousand nobles had gathered to witness the knighting of the emperor's sons, Frederick and Henry. Frederick Barbarossa never reached the Holy Land, meeting his death in 1190 in the icy waters of the river Saleph in Asia Minor. The chaotic times of the *Interregnum* (cf. p. 96) gave birth to the Kyffhäuser legend, which attached itself first to Barbarossa's grandson, Frederick II, then to be transferred in the sixteenth century to his great ancestor. Popular imagination, coupled with certain prophecies of the Italian Benedictine historian Joachim of Fiore (*c.* 1140-1205) relating to the coming of the Third Empire, pictured the emperor asleep in the depths of the Kyffhäuser Mountain in Thuringia, waiting for the day of his return to lead his people to unity and renewed glory.

Frederick II and the Disintegration of the Empire. The Hohenstaufen period is marked from its beginning by an intense nationalization of both the imperial and the papal claims and ambitions. While the German historian Otto von Freising (*c.* 1111-1158) still visualized the ultimate realization of Augustine's universal kingdom of peace and justice under imperial leadership, the Church as well as the Empire nourished the idea of national independence. The Hohenstaufen emperors saw in the Empire the source of all law, investing the imperial dignity with totalitarian titles and predicates.

a) The Imperial Policy of Henry VI. Potentially Frederick Barbarossa's son Henry VI (1190-1197) represented the gravest threat to the power of the papacy, and his final victory was only prevented by his premature death. He succeeded in isolating the pope in central Italy by enforcing his authority in the kingdom of Sicily, to which he had a claim through his wife

Constance, and at the same time he secured the loyalty of northern Italy by granting the largest measure of independence to the Lombard cities. He appointed his own vassals in the Papal States, thus limiting the suzerainty of the pope to the duchy of Rome. His cruel and relentless will to power envisaged a hereditary Empire of the Hohenstaufens, with Italy as its center, extending over the territories of both the Western and the Byzantine Empires. Feeling himself the true heir of the Roman Caesars, he revived and invigorated the political ideology of Otto III (cf. p. 64). During the seven years of his reign he built up a system of personal power and imperial influence that is almost unparalleled in medieval history.

b) *Frederick II and Innocent III*. Once more the tense drama that had reached its climax at Canossa (cf. p. 72 sq.) was re-enacted on the European stage, but this time the two major characters were more evenly matched than Henry IV and Gregory VII.

When Henry VI died he left as his heir his four-year-old son Frederick, and immediately rival candidates began to struggle for the imperial crown. Philip of Swabia, Henry's brother, was the choice of the Waiblingen faction, while the candidate of the Welfs was Otto of Brunswick, son of Henry the Lion. After ten years of factional strife Philip was murdered in 1208, Otto was proclaimed German king and received the imperial crown in 1209. When he tried to assert his imperial claims in Italy and threatened the Papal States, he met with the opposition of Pope Innocent III (1160–1216), the most powerful of the medieval popes, who carried the theocratic ideas of Gregory VII to their logical conclusion. As a result of the excommunication of Otto of Brunswick a Hohenstaufen rebellion in Germany returned Frederick, king of Sicily, the son and heir of Henry VI, to the throne of his ancestors. Civil war continued in Germany to the year 1214, when Otto of Brunswick was defeated by Philip Augustus, king of France (1180–1233), who was one of the supporters of Frederick's claims to the imperial crown. After having received the desired assurances and guarantees, including Frederick's promise to give up the kingdom of Sicily to his infant son Henry, Pope Innocent confirmed the election of the new emperor, who now ascended the throne as Frederick II (1212–1250).

In Barbarossa's grandson one of the most fascinating personalities of Western civilization enters upon the historical stage. Frederick II has been called the first modern man, a precursor of the great figures of the Renaissance, a humanist, and a skeptic. To his friends he appeared as the Messiah, the herald of universal peace, the god-emperor of a new age, while his enemies saw in him a ruthless tyrant and the incarnation of the antichrist whose coming spelled ruin and the end of the world. The modern historian recognizes in Frederick the antagonistic elements of a historic constellation in which two epochs meet and clash: the ecclesiastical civilization of the Middle Ages and the secularized modern world.

When Frederick at the age of eighteen proceeded triumphantly from Sicily to his northern German kingdom to receive the royal crown at

Aachen (1215), he completed the encirclement of the Papal States and precipitated the beginning of the final phase of the life-and-death struggle between Empire and Papacy.

From his father, Henry VI, Frederick had inherited the cunning that was needed to master the adverse forces of political intrigue, and an implicit consciousness of his exalted mission. The cosmopolitan environment of Sicily with its mixture of racial, religious, and social forces had equipped his mind with keenness of observation and a mild, sometimes cynical, skepticism. And Pope Innocent, to whose guardianship the years of his early intellectual formation had been entrusted, had not only influenced the future emperor's ideas of rulership and statecraft but had also put at his disposal the broad educational facilities of the new age of learning, thus laying the foundations for those extraordinary mental qualities which made Frederick one of the most advanced and independent thinkers of his epoch.

Pope Innocent III had been trained in the law schools of Bologna and Paris, and he based his universal claims on the tradition embodied in Canon Law. "God," he proclaimed, "has instituted two high dignities: the Papacy, which reigns over the souls of men; and Monarchy, which reigns over their bodies. But the first is above the second." Innocent III lived entirely in the world of medieval ideas, and he attempted to formulate and realize his political plans according to the principles and methods of scholastic philosophy and theology (cf. p. 141 sqq.). In contrast to the inspirational asceticism of Gregory VII, the papal adversary of Frederick II represents a legalistic and casuistic mentality which is guided by considerations of formal logic. Accordingly, the gigantic struggle between the two potentates had now become a competitive contest of legal principles rather than a conflict between historical powers.

c) Frederick's Struggle With the Papacy. The final act of the Hohenstaufen tragedy began with Frederick's return to Italy in 1220. Pope Innocent III had died in 1216. After having wrested from Innocent's successor, Honorius III (1216–1227), the concession to remain in possession of his Sicilian kingdom, Frederick reorganized the whole governmental system of Sicily, issued a new legal code based on the principles of Roman Law, and lent his encouragement to industry, commerce, and agriculture. He founded the University of Naples and made southern Italy a center of intellectual and cultural activities. Although the emperor was primarily interested in Italy and cared but little about Germany, he did not lose sight of the idea of a universal and united empire. Less than eight of the thirty-eight years of his rule were spent in Germany, where imperial government was almost exclusively carried on through the princes. In order to gain the support of the German secular and ecclesiastical lords he gave them almost absolute sovereignty within their domains. The "Constitution in Favor of the Princes" (*Constitutio in Favorem Principum*), promulgated by the emperor in 1231, created a fateful community of interests and privileges among the nobility as against the rising citizenry of the towns, and established a legal basis for the future particularistic dismemberment of the Empire.

While in this way the Church in Germany gained a much desired independence of imperial control, in Italy Frederick's territorial ambitions came into sharp conflict with the sovereign rule of the popes in the Papal States and their feudal supremacy over Sicily. Honorius' successor, Gregory IX (1227-1241), took advantage of Frederick's unfulfilled promise to undertake a Crusade and excommunicated the emperor. When Frederick finally started upon his Crusade in 1228, he did so in defiance of the pope, and succeeded in winning Jerusalem by diplomatic negotiations with the sultan. A peace treaty, concluded in 1230, established a temporary truce between Empire and Papacy.

When Frederick returned to Italy from Germany where, in 1235, he had subdued a rebellion instigated by his son Henry, he found himself confronted with an alliance between the Lombard League and the papacy, the same combination of forces that had brought disaster to his grandfather, Frederick Barbarossa. Pope Gregory's fight for the theocratic claims of the Church was carried on by his successor, Innocent IV (1243-1254), and the struggle was still undecided when Frederick's death in 1250 released the forces of anarchy in the German lands.

d) Frederick, the "Antichrist"? In judging Frederick's character and in trying to evaluate the struggle between waning and rising cultural forces that are symbolically expressed in his conflict with the papacy, one does well to take into consideration the emperor's own estimate of his world-historic mission. After his peaceful conquest of Jerusalem he issued a manifesto in which he interpreted his victory as a token of the Lord Almighty, who is powerful and terrible in His glory, who changes the times to make them suit His will and welds the hearts of the nations to unity. The emperor speaks here as the Chosen One of the Lord, who has been raised miraculously above the princes of the earth. Making use of the terminology of the Old Testament, Frederick assumes the full autocratic power of the reborn Roman Imperator, and he rationalizes his political philosophy by means of the newly discovered Aristotelian metaphysics (cf. p. 143). The ancient Roman idea of the universal rule of peace and justice within the framework of a totalitarian State, thoroughly organized by the power of the sword, takes the place of the Augustinian ideal of the Peace of the City of God.

Gregory IX, on the other hand, the last of the papal representatives of the medieval philosophy of life and civilization, recognized the fundamental change that was involved in the imperial proclamations and policies and publicly declared the emperor to be the self-avowed emissary of the Prince of this World and the personification of the antichrist: "Out of the depths of the sea rises the beast, filled with the names of blasphemy, raging with the paw of the lion and opening the lion's mouth to blaspheme the Divine name. . . . Openly it displays its machinations . . . to destroy the Tables of the Covenant of the Saviour! Behold the head, the middle, and the end of this beast, Frederick, the so-called Emperor."

The emperor, in turn, calls the pope the Pharisee occupying the chair of perverted dogma, planning the reversal of the divinely established order of the Realm, an apocalyptic monster, the red horse risen from the sea, the great dragon, the antichrist, the false vice-regent of Christ. The Roman Curia is characterized as the Council of the High Priest, scheming against the "Anointed One of the Lord." The Romans must be awakened from their sleep of inertia to rise once more to their ancient greatness. The Messianic age has arrived when everyone must be converted to worship the new and true Messiah. From the emperor's birthplace, as from a new Bethlehem, will come forth the new leader, the *Dux,* the Prince of the Roman Empire. The emperor is the supreme lawgiver whose will must be done, whose name must be adored, to whom earth and sea pay homage.

When the emperor was on his triumphal march upon the city of Rome, it was Gregory, then one hundred years of age, who rallied the wavering Romans to his support, pointing to the relics of Peter and Paul, and who, crowning them with the papal tiara (triple crown), explaimed: "This, Romans, is your antiquity." Frederick passed by the city of Rome, and afterward all his remaining plans were doomed to failure.

In viewing the profound significance of these events the modern historian is forced to the conclusion that both Empire and Papacy failed to recognize the mutual interdependence of *Imperium* and *Sacerdotium,* that both powers overstressed their claims to absolute supremacy, and that both thereby not only undermined the foundations of their own political power but contributed to the dissolution of the supernational unity of Western civilization.

The End of the Hohenstaufen Dynasty. As if to seal outwardly the ultimate failure of the imperial policy of the Hohenstaufens, the last member of their family, Frederick II's grandson Conradin, was captured by Charles, duke of Anjou, and executed together with his friend, Frederick of Baden (1268).

The German nobles had used Frederick II's Italian entanglements to establish fully their own independence. During the last ten years of Frederick's reign the antikings, Henry Raspe and William of Holland, were elected by the papal party. After Frederick's death his son Conrad IV (1250–1254) carried on the campaign in Italy, and his short reign was followed by the *"kaiserlose, schreckliche Zeit"* (the terrible period of Germany's being without an emperor, 1256–1273) of the so-called *Interregnum,* leaving the Empire deprived of a central power and at the mercy of rival factions.

Disregarding for the moment the frustration of the Hohenstaufen policies, with the resultant political disintegration of the Empire, we recognize the age of Hohenstaufen rule as the most brilliant period of medieval civilization, its climax as well as its beginning decay. It is the age of the great accomplishments in philosophy and the arts, in the realm of mind and letters, and it marks the consummation of the formative forces of a religiously guided and inspired civilization and the incubation period of the modern world.

The Age of Chivalry. The Hohenstaufen emperors embody in their personalities and their interests the type of culture that is generally associated with the Age of Chivalry and the ideals of knighthood. For the first time in the history of Western civilization we meet here with a genuine class culture that is characterized by secular or semisecular features. Ecclesiasticism and monasticism have moved from the center to the periphery, and their place has been occupied by the knightly castle and the princely court.

The fully developed knightly culture of the twelfth and thirteenth centuries was the result of a gradual transformation of the social organism. One of the factors that contributed to the formation of the international society of knights (French, *chevalier;* German, *Ritter* — "horseman") was the development of a mounted army, replacing the foot soldiery of the early Middle Ages. This change dates back to the time of Charles Martel and his fight against the Saracens in the eighth century (cf. p. 30) and the Mongolian invasions of the ninth century. The feudal environment with its social and cultural implications provided the setting for the evolution of knightly etiquette and class consciousness. The fourteenth century saw the decline of knighthood, heralding at the same time the phenomenal rise of the new burgher class with their corresponding social ideology. During the twelfth and thirteenth centuries, when the spirit of chivalry was at its height, knighthood had become a legally established institution, to the extent that only descendants of three generations of freeborn nobles were admitted to the Order of Knighthood, while in the period of decline the class restrictions were virtually obliterated, and an intermixture with the newly developed city aristocracy took place.

Knightly culture (*höfische Kultur*) was characterized by definite rules of social behavior, stressing the knightly virtues of moderation (*diu mâze*), discipline, self-control, courage, perseverance, and loyalty. The law of the strong hand or the principle that might creates right (*Faustrecht,* "club-law") gave way gradually to the rules of the "Peace of God" (cf. p. 77), which protected the poor, women, and traveling merchants from the former lawlessness of feudal aristocracy. Promulgated as an ecclesiastical commandment by Pope Urban II (1088–1099), the *Treuga Dei* was embodied in Canon Law in the twelfth century. It expressed the endeavor of the Church to infuse religious motivations into the institutional etiquette and the practices of knighthood. The ideals of Cluny (cf. p. 70 sq.) are reflected to some extent in the concepts of knightly honor and knightly virtue. It is this aspect of chivalry that is strikingly presented in the romances of the twelfth century, of which the French *Chansons de Geste* are beautiful examples and notably, among them, the *"Chanson de Roland."*

The knightly cult of noble womanhood likewise shows a peculiar mixture of purely secular and religious or even mystical elements. It was chiefly due to the influence of the French *Troubadours* that the German *Minne-*

sänger (cf. p. 155 sq.) developed a highly conventionalized etiquette in the service of the noble Lady who was, at least in theory but frequently also in reality, placed upon a pedestal of exalted dignity. However, the artificiality of this rationalized sexuality of chivalry, the external gloss of courtliness (*hoevescheit*) or courtesy (*courtoisie*) only thinly veils the inherent frivolity of a knightly ethics which does not hesitate to make God the confidant of lovers and the helper and guardian of adulterers. Furthermore, it is the married woman and frequently the one of higher social rank who is made the object of knightly yearning and wooing; an ideal object that is all the more worthy of devotion and veneration because its attainment would of necessity meet with innumerable obstacles and difficulties. On the other hand, the more religious and ascetic components of the spirit of chivalry were further developed by the knightly orders and especially by the Order of Teutonic Knights (cf. p. 113 sq.), whose members solemnly forswore the knightly love code and submitted to a semimonastic discipline.

The cradle of knighthood as a social order is to be looked for in southern France, in the homeland of the *Provençal Troubadours,* and it is there that the secular elements are most conspicuous. Fashion and poetry, etiquette and external behavior of the French knights of the *Provence* developed in close contact with and under the influence of the highly civilized Arabs, the conquerors of Spain, who had established cultural centers at the courts of the caliphs, especially the court of Cordova. The Crusades (cf. p. 106 sqq.) further strengthened the influence of Islam and its culture upon those knights and their retinue who visited the Moslem countries and observed at firsthand the social and cultural customs and conditions of the Arabs. At the same time the Crusades contributed to the greater refinement and cultural education of the German knight by subjecting him to the polishing influence of French elegance of manners and a highly cultivated sense of literary and artistic form. Thus the creation of a supernational knightly aristocracy is largely to be attributed to the supernational enterprise of the Crusades. But whatever significance may be attached to these foreign importations and adaptations, they acted merely as external stimuli to which the German mind responded in a thoroughly original way. They left their marks on the cultural surface without changing the essential indigenous forces of German civilization. Thus German *Minnesang,* the German court epic, German mysticism, German Gothic reflect to a large extent the Romanic pattern, but they nevertheless represent typically German adaptations and variations of a general European theme.

German Knighthood. As far as Germany is concerned, the new culture of chivalry is associated with the Swabian, Bavarian-Austrian, and Frankish regions. Southern Germany was in closer touch with the international movements of the age and therefore more susceptible to influences from East and West. The Saxons of the German Northwest were more conservative by nature and at the same time geographically farther removed from the new focus of cultural exchange. The splendor of the rule of the Swabian dynasty of the Hohenstaufens made their native stem duchy the actual center of the courtly display of German knighthood.

In an age of feudal aristocracy with vertical rather than horizontal divisions of social strata, it is not surprising to find the structure of the knightly pyramid hierarchically ordered and graduated. The king was the knight supreme. Then followed in a descending scale the dukes, margraves, counts, and nobles. Lowest in the social scale of knighthood ranked the "ministerials," the descendants of those unfree tenants who in the Frankish empire of the Carolingians had become the personal attendants of the lord and thus the nucleus of a new caste of the lower nobility. During the twelfth century they had obtained the right to acquire independent fiefs, and the thirteenth century witnessed their ascendancy to the class of free knights.

Strict dividing lines separated the various ranks of knights from other social groups and estates, from which they were distinguished by social etiquette, dress, standards and manners of living and habitation, and the code of feudal law.

Knightly Education. The training for the profession of knighthood started at an early age. The small boy who was destined to become a future knight was usually sent to the castle of his father's liege lord or some other nobleman to serve as a page (*Knappe*) and to be educated in the social etiquette of chivalry. Not infrequently he was sent to the court of some French noble or was given a French tutor. Military education began at the age of fourteen. As one of his lord's squires he received a thorough training in the knightly sports and games, such as racing, jumping, swimming, wrestling, riding, fencing, hunting, the art of archery, and the intricate ceremonials and finesses of the knightly tournament. He had to learn the full etiquette of social behavior, the rules of dressing, walking, conversation, salutation, and the strict requirements of social intercourse. At the age of twenty-one the young squire was considered sufficiently prepared to be solemnly received into the order of knighthood.

The ceremony of knighting (*Schwertleite*) provided an occasion for an elaborate display of knightly splendor and was an exorbitantly expensive affair for the youth's family. The Church took an important part in the proceedings. The night preceding the great event was spent by the knight-to-be in vigil before the altar of the family chapel. After having attended Mass in the morning and having received the sacraments of Penance and Communion, the youth had his sword blessed by the priest and he was once more entreated to be loyal to the virtues of his new calling: to be magnanimous, helpful, courteous, truthful, loyal, and brave; to aid the Church; to protect and defend widows, orphans, pilgrims, and the poor and oppressed; to obey the Roman emperor in all temporal matters; and to keep himself untainted in thoughts, words, and deeds. The ceremony reached its climax with the handing over of shield, sword, and golden spurs, followed by the "accolade" (*Ritterschlag*), three blows on neck or shoulder, administered by the king, the prince, the liege lord, the bishop, or some distinguished knight or noble lady. The festivities were usually concluded by a tournament, the favorite and most picturesque of knightly sports and entertainments. The actual tournament (German: *Turnier;* from Latin, *torneamentum;* French verb, *tourner:* "to turn") was distinguished from the lighter and less hazardous sportly encounters of two knights in single combat: the *Buhurt* (from late Latin, *hurtus:* "thrust"; French, *heurter*) and the *Tjost* (Latin, *justa;* French, *jouste:* "joust"), by its almost warlike character: two groups of knights meeting in armed contest, with prisoners being taken and ransomed, frequent fatalities being the rule rather than an exception.

An important and indispensable element of these knightly spectacles was the presence of noble ladies, whose favor and admiration was coveted by the display of knightly courage, skill, and cunning. Many a knight took part in the tournament in honor of the lady of his choice, wearing upon his shoulder or helmet her veil or colors as a symbol of his devotion. A flower wreath, a belt, a falcon, a sword bestowed upon him by his beloved seemed ample reward for his bravery.

Knightly Armor and Knightly Warfare. The armored knight is still a favorite subject of popular imagination, and it is indeed hard to conceive of knightly life without evoking at the same time the colorful picture of knightly armor, which was considered a habit of honor and a symbol of social distinction. The armor consisted of a cone-shaped steel helmet, a shield, and a loose cloak of linked mail which covered the body from the helmet to the knees. Closed visors to protect the face, and full-plate armor as well as the more fanciful types of headgear and silk coats, made their appearance toward the end of the thirteenth century. The knight's offensive weapons were sword, dagger, and spear. The dagger, sometimes called the *misericorde,* was used as a "dagger of mercy" to administer the coup de grace to a mortally wounded enemy. The knight's horse was protected by a heavy blanket, consisting of metal rings, which was covered by a more elaborate *covertiure,* a second cover of costly material and adorned with the coat of arms. The foot soldiers among the knight's attendants wore a partial-plate armor and were equipped with swords, spears, and halberts (from *helmbarte,* "battleax"), clubs, bows and arrows (*Armbrust,* popular adaptation from Middle Latin, *arcubalista,* "crossbow"). This foot soldiery was made up of mercenaries and servants, frequently recruited from urban communities. Although snubbed by the knights as their social inferiors, they represent the nucleus of all modern armies and were soon to outgrow the knights in military efficiency and strategic significance.

The knightly armies were of relatively small size, rarely exceeding two thousand in number, not including the attendants and the baggage train. The crusading army of Frederick Barbarossa is estimated to have numbered one hundred thousand, an exceptionally formidable contingent of soldiers. Army discipline was strictly regulated by the decrees of martial law. Barbaric cruelty frequently characterized the treatment of wounded or captured

Evangeliary of Otto III

Rheinstein Castle

enemies; and the conquered territories, cities, and castles were ruthlessly pillaged and destroyed; the men killed, the women violated, the children murdered.

The Castles and Their Inhabitants. The castle is as inseparably linked with knightly life and culture as is military training, feudal warfare, and knightly armor. It was home and fortress in one, the knight's abode in time of peace as in time of war. To get a true insight, therefore, into the spirit of chivalry it will be necessary to observe the nobleman's life inside the castle walls.

The German equivalent for castle is the word *Burg,* derived from the verb *bergen,* denoting a protecting and protected dwelling. The beginnings of the medieval type of *Burgen* date back to the ninth and tenth centuries. The plans of fortification followed in the main the rules laid down by the Roman writers and architects Vitruvius (88–26 B.C.) and Vegetius (*c.* A.D. 400). Important innovations and improvements were due to the influence of Oriental military science during the period of the Crusades.

The invention and perfection of firearms toward the end of the Middle Ages greatly diminished the military significance of the castles, many of which were destroyed during the peasant wars of 1524–1525 and again during the Thirty Years' War (1618–1648), and a large number decayed and fell to ruins when their owners abandoned them and moved into the cities. It was the Romantic movement of the early nineteenth century that rediscovered the rugged beauty of these witnesses and symbols of knightly civilization, glorifying them in poetry, songs, and pictures, and reviving a general public interest in their preservation and restoration. The total number of *Burgen* on German soil at the end of the Middle Ages was in the neighborhood of 10,000, about 400 of which are still extant and habitable.

The site of the *Burg* was chosen for its defensibility rather than for the beauty of the surrounding scenery or easy accessibility. Preferred locations, therefore, were hilltops, islands, or marshy regions. The castle could be approached from one side only, and a series of obstacles had to be overcome by an attacking enemy. The moat (*Graben*) which wholly or partly surrounded the castle was usually filled with water and spanned by a drawbridge. Above the moat rose the mighty wall (*Mauer*), built of solid blocks of stone and crowned with battlements (*Zinnen*). To render the defense more efficient towers of various shape were intermittently inserted in the wall, the center of which was occupied by the great gate, wrought of heavy oakwood and reinforced with iron bands.

In case the attackers succeeded in breaking through this outer wall, they found themselves in the outer courtyard and had to face a second line of defense. In this outer courtyard were located the stables and barns, the bakery and the washhouse, a small fruit and vegetable garden, the lady's rosary, and frequently a small square where, in the shade of linden trees, knightly sports and games would be practiced by the lord's sons and their companions. In the inner court rose in lonely majesty the main tower with its thick and heavy walls (*Bergfried;* Old French, *beffroi;* English, *"belfry"*), overlooking the countryside, thus permitting to spy an approaching enemy from afar, and serving as the last refuge of the castle's inhabitants in time of war. In its lower stories the great tower contained the storerooms and the subterranean dungeon. Next to this fortresslike and awe-inspiring structure was located the lord's palace (Latin, *palatium;* German, *Pfalz*), with kitchen, bath, storerooms, and the servants' living quarters on its main floor, and the big festival hall, the sleeping rooms, and the lady's apartments (*Kemenate,* from Middle Latin, *caminata;* Old High German, *cheminata:* a room equipped with a "chimney") in the upper stories. In the larger castles the women's living quarters frequently occupied a separate building. The palace-chapel was architecturally connected with the palace.

The knightly castle as a whole was a very imposing structure from a military point of view, but crude and primitive as far as comfort, convenience, and hygienic conditions were concerned. As glass windows were unknown well into the thirteenth century, the openings that were set in the masonry were narrow open slits through which wind and rain could pass practically unobstructed, or they might be covered with horn sheets, parchment, oiled paper, or linen. Despite the fire that burned in the open chimneys of the larger rooms, cold, dampness, and drafts must have caused great inconvenience.

Social life in the castle centered in the big vaulted hall, benches running alongside the walls, chandeliers and candles shedding their light, Oriental rugs being spread out on the floors or being affixed to the walls, and cushions of precious materials being used for added comfort as well as for decorative purposes. Indoor games of various kinds, such as chess, checkers, backgammon, and dice games, were enjoyed by the inhabitants of the castle in the wintertime. Otherwise, the winter must have been a most dreary and depressing season, so that spring was universally hailed as the great harbinger of joy, the bringer of all the good things in nature as well as in human life. But despite the narrowness and primitivity of his home life the knight felt such a strong sentimental attachment to his castle that he even made it an integral part of his family name (*Herr Georg von Frundsberg; Herr Heinrich von Mindelberg,* etc.).

Knightly Dress, Manners, and Customs. The Crusades were in part responsible for the more extravagant tastes and habits of living, for the increased craving for luxuries as manifested especially in the manner of dressing, eating, and drinking. Precious silks and furs added to the splendor and dignity of the personal appearance of lord and lady. Lively and even glaring colors were quite fashionable, red and yellow being highly favored, before the later Middle Ages made yellow the distinguishing color of harlots and Jews. Make-up, which had been popular with the peoples of antiquity, was now lavishly used by noble ladies, and the women of Austria were so entranced by the new custom that even the peasant women began to imitate it. The trains of men's and women's costumes became so long that they had to be carried by pages. Some of the preachers refer to them as the "devil's coaches." The shoes became narrow and pointed. The upper garment had detachable sleeves which were widened and lengthened to such an extent that they would drag on the ground. Men and women adopted the fashion of having the dress cut low about the neck and tightly fitting about the body, with slits in various places allowing for freer movement and at the same time adding a new decorative element.

The manners and pleasures of the table were largely influenced by the French. A growing variety of food and drink from different parts of the world was gradually made available. The extensive use of spices called for heavy drinking, wine being the most popular beverage. Knives were used but forks were still unknown in the fourteenth century. One plate, one knife, and one drinking cup usually served two persons, a lord and his lady. The knight was fond of a generous and lavish display of food, drink, and social entertainment in the presence of guests, but left alone with the members of his family he practiced the virtue of economy and was satisfied with a most frugal bill of fare.

The knights were skillful and enthusiastic hunters, both for sportly and utilitarian reasons. The kitchen had to be provided with meat, and the forests had to be cleared of wild animals, such as lynx, bear, wolf, boar, bison, and so forth. The knight reserved for himself the right to the chase of big game, while small-game shooting (rabbits, squirrels, partridges, etc.) was left to the peasant. The taming of falcons for hunting purposes was originally an Oriental custom but became one of the most distinguished forms of the knightly chase. Frederick II and Albert the Great (cf. p. 144 sq.) are among the famous authors of special treatises on the art of falconry and falcon breeding. The tamed falcon was taught how to hunt and kill herons and other game in an air fight. For centuries the falcon hunt remained one of the favorite entertainments of the knightly aristocracy.

The ceremonious and rhythmical dances were accompanied by singing and the playing of the lute or the fiddle, the latter being the forerunner of the violin that was introduced from the Orient via Byzantium in the tenth century. Customarily the noble lords and ladies were skillful makers of verse and tunes which they sang and accompanied on their own instruments. The nobleman's and noblewoman's musical teacher was the wandering minstrel (*Spielmann,* pl., *Spielleute*). He was messenger, news reporter, singer, and poet in one, and he was hailed and feted in the knight's castle, at the bishop's court, and on the village green.

The small, heatable bathroom of the castle contained a wooden bathtub in which the knight would spend many hours, enjoying the aromatic fragrance of his perfumed bath, being waited on by maidservants, taking his meals or carrying on lengthy conversations.

The feudal marriage was one of convenience and was entered into on the basis of economic considerations, usually involving a transfer of land

or the union of two families of nobility. The formal consent of the bride
had become a prerequisite for the validity of the marriage contract, although
the husband was as a rule chosen by the parents or other relatives of the
bride-to-be or even by the feudal overlord of the knightly family. The
nuptial festivities would last for days or even weeks, the attending knightly
guests adding to the splendor of the occasion by arranging tournaments,
dances, and other social entertainments.

The general political disintegration of the waning Middle Ages, together
with the gradual dissolution of the agrarian basis of medieval society and
its replacement by the rising money economy, resulted in the material
and cultural decay of the knightly class. It was only in the newly colonized
territories of the Germanic East that the spirit of chivalry experienced a brief
and glorious belated flowering in the stern and ascetic heroism of the
Teutonic Knights (cf. p. 113 sq.).

The Crusades. The phenomenal rise and spread of the religion and
culture of Islam after the death of Mohammed (570–632) had led to
the foundation of great Mohammedan states in the Near East, in North
Africa, Spain, and Sicily. Islamic culture in the early medieval centuries
was far superior to the still semibarbarous civilization of western Europe.
It was not until the beginning of the eleventh century that the stupendous
dynamic force of Mohammedanism began to slacken, while Christian
Europe, on the other hand, was well on its way to political and intellectual
superiority. The two cultural forces which, due to their mutually exclusive
ideological convictions and their strong missionary zeal, had developed a
growing antagonism, were nearing the crucial moment of a decisive clash
and contest.

During the eleventh century the Saracens were driven out of Sicily, and
the firmly entrenched Moslem outposts in Spain became the object of the
awakening crusading spirit of the West. The earlier phases of the disputes
and struggles between Empire and Papacy had sufficiently enhanced the
authority of papal power to allow its representative in Rome to speak as
the leader and exponent of a united Christendom. The ascetic spirit of
Cluny (cf. p. 70 sq.) and the monastic reform movement had in turn aided
in creating a religious enthusiasm that was eager to spend its pent-up
energies.

Thus the way was well prepared when Pope Urban II (1088–1099) summoned the peoples of Europe to take up arms to recover the Holy Land and
the City of Jerusalem from the hands of the infidels. The Byzantine emperor,
Alexius I, had appealed to the pope to aid him in his defensive struggle
against the Seljuk Turks who, after having taken over the remnants of
the once flourishing empire of the caliphs of Bagdad, were advancing westward and threatening Constantinople.

Pope Urban's appeal found ready and universal response, and his message
was carried to the corners of the Christian commonwealth of nations by

Peter the Hermit and other preachers whose oratory aroused the enthusiasm of feudal Europe.

There were seven Crusades in all, not including the grotesque adventure of the "Children's Crusade" of the year 1212, which brought death or slavery to many of the thousands of boys and girls from France and Germany who did not get farther than to the ports of Genoa and Marseilles. Although Germany was profoundly stirred and vitally affected by each one of these expeditions to the Holy Land, only three of them were conducted with the official support and participation of German knighthood and under the full or partial leadership of the German emperor.

The first Crusade (1096–1099) was also the most successful one, leading to the conquest of Edessa, Antioch, and Jerusalem, and to the establishment of several Christian feudal states in the East, among them the kingdom of Jerusalem. The crusaders' army consisted chiefly of Flemish, French, and Norman knights. The high command was given to the papal legate, Adhemar of Puy. Among the knightly leaders were Count Raymond of Toulouse and Duke Godfrey of Bouillon.

The second Crusade (1147–1149), which was given its start and its élan by the powerful preaching of St. Bernard of Clairvaux (1090–1153), and in which King Louis VII of France and the Hohenstaufen Emperor Conrad III were the leading figures, turned out to be a complete failure. As a consequence the situation of the Christian population in the Holy Land became increasingly precarious, especially as rivalries and jealousies had caused multiple divisions among the Christian settlers, while on the enemy's side the great Sultan Saladin succeeded in uniting most of the Moslem world under his rule.

Saladin's conquest of Palestine and the City of Jerusalem in 1187 was the danger signal that was needed to prepare the European mind for the effort of the third Crusade (1189–1197). This time the German emperor, Frederick Barbarossa, was the first one to start upon the new expedition, followed by the kings of France and England, Philip Augustus and Richard the Lion-hearted. But Frederick Barbarossa was drowned while crossing the river Saleph in Asia Minor. The command was taken over by his son, Frederick of Swabia, who died during the siege of the city of Acre on the coast of Palestine. After futile battles with the Moslem armies and quarrels between the kings of France and England and their followers, Philip Augustus returned home, while Richard the Lionhearted concluded a truce with Sultan Saladin in 1192. The Christians were given a strip of the Palestine Coast from Acre to Ascalon and obtained the permission of free entry to the City of Jerusalem.

The fourth Crusade (1202–1204), inaugurated by Pope Innocent III, got under way while civil war raged between the rival emperors in Germany (cf. p. 93). The campaign became a series of shameful dealings between the French crusaders and the Venetians, whose greedy doge, Enrico Dandalo, was largely responsible for diverting the Crusade from its original purpose and turning it into a looting expedition that ended with the capture of Constantinople and the establishment of the Latin Empire of Constantinople (1204–1261).

The fifth Crusade (1228–1229) was undertaken by the excommunicated Hohenstaufen Emperor Frederick II (cf. p. 95), who succeeded in gaining Jerusalem by peaceful negotiations with the sultan, thus resurrecting once more the kingdom of Jerusalem in his own name.

France's saintly king, Louis IX (1226–1270), was the leader of the remaining two expeditions. The sixth Crusade (1248–1254) was aimed against Egypt, whose sultan had conquered the kingdom of Jerusalem (1244). The French king was captured with his army and had to be ransomed. He died in Tunis in the course of the seventh Crusade (1270), while the crusaders under the leadership of Prince Edward of England went on to Syria without accomplishing anything. After the loss of Tripolis (1289) and Acre (1291) the Christians had to give up their claims to the Holy Land.

Significance and Motivations of the Crusades. It can easily be seen that the Crusades were a strange combination of various motives and impulses, ranging from the loftiest to the basest. Medieval man is fully human in that he exhibits all potentialities from the greatest exaltation and sublimity to the most pitiful depravity. It is not surprising, therefore, to find among the crusaders those inspired by religious idealism and true devotion side by side with those who had left their native soil because adventure, lust, and rich booty beckoned in the mysterious East. And religious enthusiasm, the spirit of adventure, and the love of fighting not infrequently resided in the same breast. It is true: the fight against the infidels was all too often taken as a pretext for plunder or as a subterfuge to satisfy the land hunger of a feudal society that was beginning to feel the effects of the growing shortage of land. But there was also to be found that splendid conception of the loyalty of the Christian knight to his divine Liege Lord who had called him to arms through His representative, the pope. And there were the large numbers of knights who were desirous of expiating their human failings by a life of heroic sacrifice, by joining the army of pilgrims on their way to the sepulcher of Christ.

Results of the Crusades. The political failure of the Crusades is obvious enough. Lack of adequate leadership, and those frequent dissensions in the ranks of the crusading armies that reflected the factional discord of medieval Europe, contributed to the ultimate paralyzation of even the most heroic and unselfish efforts. The consequence was a growing disillusionment and a steadily diminishing enthusiasm, while at the same time the interests of the European peoples were diverted into new channels. With military feudalism involved in a slow but inevitable process of decline, the national monarchies and the new commercial middle class were manifestly establishing themselves as the dominating forces of the future. Although the Church had taken a leading part in inaugurating and encouraging the Crusades, the fact that neither the political nor the religious aspirations of the papacy in the East were realized, engendered, in the end, a loss of ecclesiastical prestige. The new cultural and religious contacts that were established with the Mohammedan and Byzantine civilizations resulted not only in a broadening of interests and the acquisition of new departments of knowledge but likewise in the growth of criticism and even skepticism.

As far as Germany was concerned, there had been some cultural and economic intercourse with the Arabic-Islamitic world long before the beginning of the Crusades. But these commercial and cultural bonds were now strengthened and broadened. Eastern science, philosophy, artistry, nautical knowledge, military science, manners and customs of living began to exert a direct influence upon the German lands. Among the newly imported products of the soil were maize, rice, sugar, pepper, cinnamon, lemons, and oranges (Arab., *nârandsch*); among the new fabrics were damask, baldachin silk (*Baldach* = "Bagdad"), colorful Oriental rugs and embroideries, and leather articles. The Germans began to grow fond of the use of Oriental dyes, cosmetics, salves, and perfumes; they decorated their homes and castles with Oriental mattresses, cushions, and divans; they learned from the Arabs a more courtly and genteel social behavior, so that much of the courtly etiquette of knighthood may be traced to Arabic or Byzantine sources; they adopted from the Arabs new methods of fortifying their German cities and castles and learned to prepare a kind of gunpowder from sulphur, charcoal, and saltpeter; they enlarged their knowledge of stellar constellations and enriched the sailors' language by Arabic terms, such as zenith (*Zenit*), *Bussole* (compass), admiral, and so forth; the merchants' language by such words as bazaar (*Basar*), magazine (*Magazin*), tare (*Tara*), tariff (*Tarif*), and so forth. In architecture the horseshoe arch and the highly ornamental "arabesques" are of Arabic origin. The art of goldsmithing received new inspiration from the Oriental smiths and carvers in whose Eastern workshops some of the German goldsmiths had been apprentices in the age of the Crusades. Arabic legends and sagas provided new motifs for the German epic and lyric poetry of the Age of Chivalry.

But it was chiefly Arabic science and philosophic speculation that left its profound impress on all Western civilization. The Arabs became the teachers of Europe in astronomy, geography, arithmetic, physics, and alchemy, and the influx of the new scientific ideas was due to the newly established contacts with the Arabic outposts in Spain as well as in the Near East. Their medical science was highly developed, not only theoretically but in practical application, as is documented by the model organization of their hospitals and the variety of their medicaments. In theology and philosophy Arabic thinkers such as Alfarabi (philosopher, † 950), Avicenna (physician and philosopher, 980–1037), Ghasali (Algazel; philosopher and theologian, 1059–1111), and Averroes (philosopher, 1126–1198) proved themselves masters of original and ingenious speculation and presented the West with their translations of and commentaries on the works of Aristotle, thus facilitating the Christian-scholastic synthesis of the Platonic and Aristotelian traditions (cf. p. 143).

The results and consequences of the Crusades in the intellectual and cultural spheres were manifold, and while some of these results would have been achieved by way of Spain and Sicily, that is, without the direct contacts established by the Crusaders, the whole process of the intellectual and cultural expansion of Europe was intensified and speeded up by the crusading spirit with its emotional stimuli and by the actual acquaintance with life and thought in the Near East.

It is, however, symptomatic of the growing astuteness of German culture that neither the Romanic nor the Oriental influences that acted upon the German mind in the Age of Chivalry, and especially during the two centuries of the Crusades, were able to silence the voice of a genuine Germany that speaks so unmistakably in German art and poetry, in the games of war and the diversions of peace, in bold political action and in the silence of mystical contemplation.

Colonization and Expansion in the East. The territories to the north and east of Germany were the scene of a number of crusading enterprises in the broader sense of the term, campaigns that had for their goal as much the conquest of new arable land and the security of the outlying frontier districts of the German empire as the conversion of heathen populations. These expeditions were rewarded by lasting success not only because of a more competent leadership but because they found an invaluable ally in the healthy energy and inexhaustible working capacity of the German peasantry.

Byzantine missionaries had begun the conversion of the Bohemian Slavs in the ninth century. These Bohemians soon turned their allegiance from the Greek Orthodox to the Roman Catholic Church. Otto the Great incorporated Bohemia in the Empire but granted its rulers a fair degree of autonomy. In the second half of the tenth century Roman missionaries succeeded in converting the Slavic population of Poland. St. Stephen, king of Hungary (997–1038), converted the partly Slavic but predominantly Magyar population of Hungary, Poland's southern neighbor, at the beginning of the eleventh century. He organized the nomadic peoples of his country in a unified state that followed closely the Frankish pattern. During the thirteenth century Poland and Hungary together acted as buffer states of the Empire to ward off the repeated attacks of Mongolian hordes.

But most important and consequential for Germany was the expansion of the Germans in the northern and eastern frontier districts and the subsequent colonization of the newly acquired territories. The beginning of the colonization of the regions east of the Elbe dates back to the days of Henry I (cf. p. 65) and Otto I (cf. p. 65), but the preoccupation of imperial policy with the problems of southern Europe and especially with Italy had nullified many of the initial results. It was not until the twelfth century that colonization in the North and East was consistently and energetically resumed by some of the powerful princes of northern Germany, among them Henry the Lion, duke of Saxony and head of the Welf party, Albrecht the Bear, Adolf II of Schauenburg, and the archbishops of Bremen and Magdeburg.

In a proclamation of the year 1108 the secular and ecclesiastical princes of northeastern Germany issued the following appeal to the various tribes of Germany: "Oppressed by many and unending calamities and acts of violence that we have endured at the hands of the heathen, we implore your mercy, that you may come to our aid in halting the ruin of your mother, the Church. The most cruel of heathen peoples have risen against us and have become all-powerful: men without mercy, glorying in their inhuman malignity. Arise, then, spouse of Christ, and come! Thy voice shall sound into the ears of the faithful, so that all will speedily join the army of Christ. Those peoples are the most wicked of all, but their land is the best of all, abounding in meat, fowl, honey, and corn. It need only be cultivated in the right manner to overflow with all the fruits of the soil. . . . Well, then, you Saxons, you people of Lorraine, you Flemings, you renowned conquerors of the earth: here is an opportunity not only to save your souls but, if you wish, also to acquire the finest land as your dwelling place. . . . "

This is a manifesto that is as strange as it is illuminating. Even if it should be verified that it was penned not by the nobles of eastern Saxony but by a Flemish author who dwelt in the Slavic border regions, this proclamation would still reveal in a very striking way the several motives that prompted the Germans of the later Middle Ages to start upon their eastward drive into the wide open spaces beyond the river Elbe.

The motivations are threefold, and they are stated with naïve and almost disarming frankness. In the first place, the princes and nobles of northeastern Germany felt it necessary to protect the open and almost defenseless boundary line, beyond which dwelt semibarbarous and politically unstable populations. Widukind of Corvey, famous Saxon historian of the tenth century, tells of the stubborn resistance of the Slavs who "preferred war to peace, ignoring the greatest of misery when it was a question of defending their precious freedom." But, as time went on, Slavic resistance weakened, and the Germans began their advance beyond the boundary lines of the old marches.

The second impulse to eastern colonization was a direct outgrowth of the crusading spirit of the twelfth century, as exemplified by the campaign against the heathen Wends in the year 1147, the harsh alternative as formulated by Bernard of Clairvaux allowing only for conversion or destruction. In this second impulse, missionary zeal and a very worldly will to power were mingled in constant interaction. The military subjugation of the heathens was immediately followed by missionary efforts, the religious activities being frequently contaminated by all those inconsistencies and ambiguities that forever attach to the use of physical force and coercion in the realm of the spirit. Charlemagne's conversion of the Saxons and the deeds and misdeeds of the Spanish Conquistadores in South and Central America belong in the same category with the methods employed in the colonization of the Slavic lands in the Germanic East. The chronicles of the twelfth century tell of the greed and cruelty of some of the Saxon dukes and margraves and make them responsible for the refusal of the Slavs to submit voluntarily to Christian-Germanic rule.

The third impulse was the desire to find an outlet for a growing population and to relieve the economic pressure caused by an increasing scarcity of arable soil.

National ambitions and national consciousness were still in a very rudimentary stage, and they are not even mentioned in our manifesto. It is only the retrospective view of the modern historian that ascribes a momentous national significance to the colonization of the Germanic East. The feeling of racial superiority was likewise conspicuously absent, and marriages between Germans and Christian Slavs were frequent and were considered unobjectionable.

Despite the fact that the German emperors and imperial policy had no direct share in the Eastern colonization, it is nevertheless obvious that the authority of the *Imperium Christianum* provided the indispensable foundation for German policy in the East. Ever since the days of Charlemagne the emperors considered themselves as the protectors, defenders, and pioneers of Christendom and were always prepared to extend their claims to heathen territories and populations. It was Charlemagne himself who had started the drive to the East in his powerful thrust against the Avars that opened up the regions of the lower Danube and the vital road into Austria. It was Otto the Great who had succeeded in incorporating in the Christian-Germanic realm the vast territories of the Northeast. But it was only in the period of Hohenstaufen rule and afterward under the leadership of the Teutonic Knights that the policy of colonization received its solemn sanction as a partial realization of the universal mission of the Christian Empire of the German nation.

Knights, clerics, peasants, and burghers shared in the colonization and settlement of the Germanic East. These settlements went economically through the same stages as the motherland, the establishment of marketing centers being followed by the founding of cities. The thirteenth and fourteenth centuries witnessed the growth of important urban communities in Brandenburg, Pomerania, Saxony, Silesia, Prussia, and Livonia (Livland). Most of the settlers came from the Low German lands, i.e., from Holland, Flanders, Friesland, and from the Rhenish districts. The farmers in particular were attracted by promises of a higher standard of life, better working conditions, and increased personal liberties.

The villages that originated east of the Elbe were distinguished from those of the motherland by their regularity, the houses with their apportioned lots of land being located alongside the main road (*Reihendorf, Marschen-*

dorf). In tenacity and working capacity the German peasant was superior to the Slav and therefore considered as a desirable settler even by Slavic princes who would call German peasants to their territories and permit them to live and work there "under German law."

The Order of Teutonic Knights ("Deutscher Ritterorden"). Beyond the Vistula, in the territory between Poland and the Baltic, lived the heathen Prussians, a savage and warlike tribe of Letto-Lithuanian stock. Early in the thirteenth century the Poles appealed to the Order of Teutonic Knights for aid in their struggle with their Prussian neighbors. After they had been promised the exclusive possession of all the territory they would be able to conquer, and after this promise had been confirmed by the special privilege of Emperor Frederick II of the year 1226, the Knights started upon their crusade in 1230 and, by the year 1283, had made themselves the uncontested masters of Prussia. They established a strong German state on the eastern Baltic and thereby created a political organism which combined in a perfectly unique way certain fundamental character traits of medieval and modern times.

In its origins the Order dates back to the year 1190, when it was founded during the siege of Acre by the armies that took part in the Third Crusade. The Knights pledged themselves to the care of the poor, the sick, and the wounded, and to the fight against the infidels. The members comprised German knights, priests, and lay Brothers. A white mantle with a black cross was the distinguishing feature of their habit. White and black subsequently became the national colors of Prussia. The fifteenth century marked the beginning of the Order's decline. Its remaining possessions in the German Reich were secularized in 1805, while its Austrian branch still existed early in the twentieth century.

The state that was founded by the Teutonic Knights at the end of the thirteenth century was the embodiment of contrasting ideas: a belated fruit of the waning Middle Ages, based upon a spiritualistic conception of chivalry, including the ascetic features of monasticism and the religious fervor of the Crusades, but at the same time vigorously documenting the absolutistic and centralistic tendencies of modern statecraft. This ideal of a monastically colored knighthood was merely one more manifestation of that spiritualistic absolutism that animated the political aspirations of the papacy in the final phase of its struggle with the secular totalitarian ambitions of the Empire. And when, at the beginning of the sixteenth century, the realm of the Teutonic Knights was nearing its doom, it was Martin Luther who, in 1523, commented on the situation in a letter addressed to the Order of Teutonic Knights: "Your Order," he wrote, "is truly a strange order, and especially because it was founded to fight against the infidels. For this reason it must make use of the worldly sword and must act in a worldly manner, and yet it should be spiritual at the same time, should vow chastity, poverty, and obedience, and should keep those vows like the members of other monastic orders. How well these two things harmonize we know from daily experience and from the use of our reason."

Sociologically the Teutonic Order was organized according to the Germanic principle of leadership and loyalty, the members blindly obeying their freely chosen "leader" who could be deposed by the community only in case of serious infractions of fundamental rules and laws of the Order. Out of this centralized administration grew an absolutely reliable officialdom that facilitated the exact and efficient handling of state finances and guaranteed a maximum of political and economic self-sufficiency. But this very same sociological structure produced a certain inflexibility in the theory and practice of government, and prevented the Order from adapting itself to the changing conditions of time and environment. As a social organism the Order was and remained a foreign element in the conquered Prussian lands, and it failed to educate the indigenous population in the rights and duties of citizenship and thus to employ them usefully and constructively in social and political life. It was therefore not unnatural that the native burghers and nobles in their growing opposition resorted successively to treasonable conspiracies with the Polish enemy, to revolution, and finally to outright desertion in the decisive battle of Tannenberg (1410).

The Order of Teutonic Knights owes its fame to its accomplishments in the field of rural and urban colonization and economico-political administration. Its cultural achievements are limited to the creation of a certain type of architecture that is a true mirror of the ideas that inspired its life and work. The East Prussian castles of the Order, above all the magnificent Marienburg, the seat of the Grand Master (*Hochmeister*), are a remarkable combination of monastery, castle, and palatial residence. This architecture is stern, solemn, and matter of fact. Although the characteristic features of the Gothic style (cf. p. 148 sqq.) are unmistakable, it lacks all the more intimate charm of an artistically refined taste.

The Order of Teutonic Knights enacts the final chapter in the story of Eastern colonization. The result of this ruthless and heroic conquest of land as well as of the earlier stages of the eastward drive was the approximate doubling of the area of habitable and arable German territory. The frontiers that were reached and secured at the end of the Middle Ages are the racial frontiers of Germany to the end of Word War II. It is the settlement of the Eastern marches (*Ostmarken*) that has laid the foundations for the growth of the modern state organisms of Brandenburg-Prussia and Austria-Bavaria.

Social Divisions in the Middle Ages. Individualism in the modern sense was unknown in medieval society. The individual received his sanctions from the group with which he shared his concepts of right, honor, and responsibility. The social order was conceived as an essentially static one, in which each class or estate had to fulfill definite God-given functions. All the members of the social organism were expected to collaborate for the good of the whole. This was the ideal. It permeated to some extent the

Marienburg Castle

The Town Hall in Braunschweig

whole edifice of feudal society: the property concepts of the nobles, the labor concepts of peasants and craftsmen, the concepts of honor and bravery of the warriors. "The health of the whole commonwealth will be assured and vigorous, if the higher members consider the lower and the lower answer in like manner the higher, so that each is in its turn a member of every other" (John of Salisbury, bishop of Chartres, 1115–1180). It was a faultless theory whose attempted realization met with all the imponderabilities of human nature, human frailty, greed, and passion.

But medieval man was more than a mere member of his social class (*Stand*): as a social being (*animal sociale*) he was at the same time a moral personality, endowed with reason and the faculty of moral self-determination. This personal quality remained theoretically unaffected by his social position, so that master and servant were both considered as equals before God but as legally distinguished according to their social function. These social distinctions were largely dependent on the definitions of Roman Law which as such was rooted in the traditions of antiquity.

This system of social order is ideally fashioned in analogy to the graduated order and continuity of the universe and its divine rulership, so that Thomas Aquinas (cf. p. 145 sq.) could designate the principle of order as "the most excellent thing in the universe" (*Ordo est Optimum Universi*). Man, by virtue of his intellect, shares in the government of the universe and is called upon to realize the principle of order in the cosmos of human relations. Every title of human authority, from the head of a nation to the head of a family, is derived from this divinely instituted universal order. The "law of nature," reflecting divine law, is recognized as the all-pervading universal law that serves as a guiding principle and an absolute norm for the ordering of human relations and the fulfillment of the demands of social justice. Human reason establishes the identity of the natural and the moral law and by doing so becomes capable of collaborating with the aims and ends of the universe.

The Peasants. The agricultural basis of medieval society made for an economic system that reduced the peasant quite generally to the position of a serf. In the graduated scale of estates the peasant, therefore, ranged at the bottom. He had to perform compulsory labor, he was expected to pay all kinds of special fees and taxes, and he was legally tied to the lord's manor. If he wanted to leave the manor, he had first to obtain the lord's permission and pay a special fee. He was subject to the private court of justice of his lord, he had to grind his grain at the lord's mill and bake his bread in the lord's oven. In case of death the serf's personal belongings, his cattle and household goods, could be seized wholly or in part at the lord's pleasure, and the heir would have to buy a special license to acquire the movable property that was bequeathed to him.

It is an undeniable fact that the medieval mind was firmly convinced that the institution of some sort of servitude was contained in the natural law and could never be entirely done away with. And yet the position of the peasant was better than that of a slave. The corporative spirit of the Middle Ages created the march and village associations, where the peasants united for the protection of their interests, and by means of which they secured for themselves a certain minimum of human dignity and economic independence. The peasant could generally be assured of food, clothing, and shelter for himself and his family. He was required to work on the lord's demesne land from two to four days a week and was frequently called upon to perform various extra services (*Frondienste*), but he was usually able to devote several days of the week to the cultivation of his own land.

The Church insisted that the serfs were not tools but men, although Canon Law seems to have recognized and enforced serfdom, and Pope Innocent III (1198–1216) merely described an actual situation when he wrote: "The serf serves; he is terrified with threats, wearied with forced labor, afflicted with blows, despoiled of his possessions; for, if he possess nought, he is compelled to earn; and if he possess anything, he is compelled to have it not; the lord's fault is the serf's punishment; the serf's fault is the lord's excuse for preying on him. . . . " (*De Contemptu Mundi:* "On the Contempt of the World.") And yet the disappearance of serfdom was chiefly due to the general shift of economic forces and not to interference on the part of the Church. The peasant revolts in England (1381), Flanders (1382), and Germany (1524–1525) reveal a deep-seated resentment on the part of the peasant class that finally resulted in desperate acts of violence.

There were groups of peasants in Saxony, Flanders, Friesland, and in the valleys of the Alps who were practically freemen, dwelling on their own land and only subject to the emperor. They had to pay military taxes and were entitled to take part in the judicial administration of their county. The majority of the German peasants, however, were half-free or unfree tenants.

At the end of the thirteenth century the peasant's lot had considerably improved, owing primarily to the general change in economic conditions and the opening up of new markets and new colonial territory. The value of arable land had increased many times over, and the cultivation of fruits and of the vine would yield a rich surplus that could be traded at the lord's market or in the nearest city. Many peasants, of course, joined the huge army of emigrants to the Eastern marches to establish themselves as free tenants.

The Medieval German City. Despite the fact that the city dwellers did not rank as a real class or estate in the social pyramid of the Middle Ages, it was nevertheless the burgher who proved the most dynamic and disruptive element of medieval society, who in the end successfully opposed his own independent concept of culture to the medieval idea of a universal cultural organism. In his own personal self he discovered the power of his own thought and will, the bases of his new concept of freedom. Thus the medieval city became the cradle of a new middle class, a new corporative legal code, a new economic system, and a new philosophy of life.

The new money economy was developed first in the Italian cities, whose leading merchants and bankers created a number of free and legally independent republican communes. Their fight against the feudal privileges of the ecclesiastical and secular princes is paralleled by a similar struggle of the German and French cities for a complete autonomy of city trade and city administration. Some of the German cities developed likewise into free city republics, while others joined the newly formed city leagues.

In Germany alone about two thousand cities and towns of varying size were founded during the medieval centuries, the most important of which were Cologne (Köln) in the Rhineland, the largest of medieval German cities, with a population of about fifty thousand; Nuremberg (Nürnberg) in Franconia; Munich (München), later the capital of Bavaria and the cultural center of southern Germany; Augsburg, likewise in Bavaria, one of the foremost commercial centers, an important link in the trade route from Italy to northern Europe and home of some of the wealthiest burgher families of the later Middle Ages; Strasbourg in Alsace; Mayence (Mainz), the "golden city," one of the foremost centers of the secular and ecclesiastic culture of the Empire; the great seaports of Hamburg (at the mouth of the Elbe), Bremen (at the mouth of the Weser), and Lübeck (on the Baltic); Danzig, the port for German-Polish trade; and Vienna, southeastern outpost of the Empire, the leading city of the Eastern march and later on the capital of the Austro-Hungarian monarchy. Most of the principal cities of Germany had an average population of from ten to twenty thousand. The important commercial centers were connected by trade routes, one such commercial artery leading from Venice across the Alps via the Brenner Pass, through Germany, and up the Rhine valley to the prosperous cities of Flanders.

City Leagues. The Hanseatic League. The Lombard League, which had fought for the freedom of the cities of northern Italy against the ambitions of the Hohenstaufen emperors (cf. pp. 91, 95), furnished the pattern for the formation of several German city leagues, among which the Rhenish League (founded 1254-1255), the Swabian League (founded 1331), and the *Hanseatic League* were the most powerful. The word *Hansa* (Gothic and Old High German: "union," "group," "association") was applied in the thirteenth century to the guild of Rhenish-Westphalian merchants in their London settlement, the Steel-Yard (*Stahlhof*), and was later used to designate the character of the German city leagues as co-operative associations for the protection of mutual commercial interests. By the end of the thirteenth century the Hanseatic League controlled the mouths of the Elbe, Weser, Oder, and Vistula (Weichsel), and had secured trading privileges and foreign markets in London, Bruges (Netherlands), Bergen (Norway), and Novgorod (Russia). The League comprised the most important cities of northern Germany, among them the new cities of the Germanic East, in the territory that had been recently acquired from the Slavs. With the emperor busying himself in Italian affairs, these cities, for the sake of self-protection, had to rely on close co-operation. Only in this way were they able to maintain a fleet that was large and strong enough to guarantee safe trading. Hamburg and Lübeck had started the movement about the middle of the thirteenth century, and the largest known membership in the League at any one time was close to one hundred. Leading cities were Danzig, Lübeck, Brunswick, and Cologne. The League held a monopoly in the Baltic trade and controlled especially the important herring and cod industries. But the Hanseatic merchants also shipped furs, amber, lumber, grain, and flax from Russia, Sweden, Poland, and Prussia, and traded these articles in Bruges and London for raw wool, cloth, and minerals. The settlements in these foreign lands were equipped with extensive warehouses and living quarters and protected by surrounding walls.

The Hanseatic League reached its greatest prosperity in the second half of the fourteenth century. In the course of the fifteenth century the power and prestige of the League were steadily weakened by the rise of a capitalistic economy, the growth of the commercial power of the Netherlands, that caused the shifting of trade routes to the West, and by the disintegration of the Baltic and Russian trade as a consequence of the Polish conquest of the Teutonic Knights and the political unification of Scandinavia (Union of Kalmar, 1397). Nominally the Hansa existed for two more centuries, and the cities of Lübeck, Bremen, and Hamburg were still known as the three "Hansa-Cities" at the end of the nineteenth century.

Trade Fairs. Any merchant, whether an inhabitant of the city or not, who paid his toll and the rent for his booth could trade freely at the international city fairs which were held once or twice a year under the protectorate of either the municipal government or, more frequently, the king, bishop, abbot, or lord. The German city fair is known as *Messe* (Mass), because it usually began on solemn religious feast days, immediately following the celebration of the Mass. It lasted for several days or several weeks, and after it was all over the foreign merchants would pack up their remaining goods and would continue their troublesome and dangerous voyage to the next city where a fair was to be held. The most celebrated city fairs in the middle of the twelfth century were those in the prosperous district of Champagne in France. But they were soon equaled in fame by the fairs of Bruges.

The External Appearance of the City. The medieval city was small in extent, the streets were narrow, and the houses crowded together. But the general appearance was highly picturesque and never monotonous. Regular city planning can only be observed in the colonial cities in the conquered Slavic regions, while ordinarily the city presented a highly irregular maze of streets, squares, nooks, and corners.

The city was surrounded by a high, massive wall and a deep moat. Numerous inserted towers surmounted the wall, and admission was gained through several city gates which in turn were strongly protected by bridges, towers, and palisades. Many medieval city gates are beautiful examples of the exquisite craftsmanship of the medieval stonemason.

The contour of the city was dominated by the cathedral with its towers and spires, symbolically expressing the subordination of all secular life to religious incentives. One or more main streets, from fifteen to twenty feet wide, led from the gates to the centrally located market square, and from there on to the opposite gate. The remaining streets were crooked, narrow, usually unpaved, and without a drainage system. As the city grew it frequently became necessary to enlarge the encircling wall or to construct a second and even a third one with a larger diameter.

Surrounding the market square were the main municipal buildings: the church, the town hall (*Rathaus*), and the merchants' hall (*Kaufhaus*). The large size of the market place corresponded to its significance as the focus of municipal life, its civic center for trading, public assemblage, and city administration and jurisdiction.

The houses were usually four or five stories high, the upper stories jutting out beyond the lower ones so as to utilize every bit of available space. As a result of these building methods the already congested living conditions in the cities often became quite intolerable. Frequent epidemics were a natural outgrowth of these unsanitary surroundings.

Public Buildings. Special care was taken to make the public buildings true symbols of the dignity and self-assurance of the burghers. Many surviving city halls are marvels of architectural art, testifying to the excellent taste and the great wealth of the cities. Among the most renowned of German city halls are those of Braunschweig, Goslar, Hildesheim, Hanover, and Lübeck in the north, and Regensburg, Ochsenfurt, and Überlingen in the south. Most of the famous southern town halls are of later date and therefore largely influenced by models of the Italian Renaissance (Konstanz, Augsburg, Nürnberg, etc.).

The interior of the city hall contained the subterranean city prison or dungeon, called the "dogs' hole" (*Hundeloch*) or "black bag" (*Schwarzer Sack*). Likewise in the basement was located the *Ratskeller* (council cellar), where the municipal supply of wine and beer was stored, on which the city usually held a monopoly. The City Council, one of whose duties was the arrangement of public festivals, employed a "city cook" and provided rooms for banqueting and dancing in the city hall. The main floor contained a certain number of booths that were used as shops and rented to trades people. The larger part of the second floor was occupied by the imposing and richly decorated *Ratssaal* (council hall), which served as the assembly hall of the City Council, as municipal courtroom, and as official reception room.

The *Kaufhaus* vied with the *Rathaus* in the artistic taste and solemn dignity of its external appearance. The oldest *Kaufhäuser* date from the thirteenth century, but most of them were built during the following two hundred years. From the merchants' halls we must distinguish the "guild halls" constructed and owned by the members of the different merchant and craft guilds (cf. p. 125 sq.), to serve as places of consultation and social recreation. Of simpler taste and appearance were the remaining municipal buildings, such as the granary (*Kornhaus*), the weighhouse (*Waage*), the mint (*Münze*), the armory (*Zeughaus*), the apothecary's shop (*Apotheke*), and the bathhouse (*Badestube*).

Private Residences. Even less ostentatious was the dwelling place of the ordinary citizen. The protruding upper stories of the houses were adorned with bays (*Erker*) and bay windows (*Erkerfenster*). Most of the houses were built of wood and covered with thatched roofs. Quite popular but in the main confined to Germany was the technique of supporting stone walls with timber framing (*Fachwerk*). Up to the thirteenth century only the bishop's residence and the houses of wealthy patricians were built of stone. This explains the large number of devastating conflagrations. Leather buckets and a big water tub were the only known implements for extinguishing a fire. The first fire engine was invented in Nuremberg in the fifteenth century.

Almost every house bore the owner's special mark on its front; it was either related to his calling or derived from the name of his patron saint. The owner's mark imparted a kind of personal life and dignity to his dwelling place. Windows were few in number; they were small, and could be closed with wooden shutters, oiled paper, parchment, or wickerwork. The beginning of the thirteenth century brought Germany the benefits of imported Venetian glass windows. They consisted of several small sections of glass panels with leaden frames (bull's-eye glass, *Butzenscheiben*).

If a benignant moon was not shedding some rays of light, the city was enveloped in darkness during the night, the interiors of the houses being scantily lit by means of tallow candles, small oil lamps, lanterns, and chandeliers. For heating purposes the stove was given preference over the open hearth that was quite universally used in the Romanic countries. Originally made of bricks, after the beginning of the thirteenth century the German type of stove was built of green or yellow glazed tiles which were covered with relieflike ornaments and figurative compositions of biblical themes, mostly of high artistic quality.

The household furniture included several heavy oak benches, running alongside the walls and provided with solid backs and arms; some chairs and stools; a heavy rectangular table; a large, iron-plated chest; a tall, massive, and artistically decorated cupboard. The beds were large and wide, and so high that a footboard was needed to climb in. They were crowned by a rooflike canopy (baldachin) that was covered with paintings or carvings, with curtains hanging down on either side.

City Administration. Personal freedom was the one precious possession that all the inhabitants of the city had in common. If a serf escaped from some manor and lived in a city for a year and a day, he was free and could no longer be claimed by his former lord. On the basis of this consciousness of personal liberty there developed the specific laws and regulations of the social and economic life in the city as manifested in democratic forms of self-government. Some cities in Germany acquired an almost complete independence (*Freie Reichsstädte,* "free imperial cities"), while others voluntarily accepted the overlordship of the king or some powerful noble. They paid their taxes to the legitimate political authority and were otherwise left free to manage their own affairs. Many of the cities had to fight for their freedom and their civic rights, while others obtained charters from the king or the lord by peaceful negotiations. A city could consider itself fully emancipated when it was granted representation in the Imperial Diet.

The city administration was in the hands of the City Council (*Stadtrat*), whose members were chosen either jointly by the burghers and the over-lord of the city or, in free cities, by the burghers alone. The City Councils could usually rely on the co-operation and sympathy of the emperors, who were their natural allies in their struggle against the ambitions of the territorial princes. The weakening of imperial power toward the end of the Middle Ages was therefore the cause for the subjection of many a German city to princely rule.

Membership in the City Council was at first limited to the indigenous city aristocracy, the nobles and ministerials (cf. p. 99) who had achieved the liberation of the city from the domination of the overlord. Gradually the big landowners and the merchants were admitted to the governing class, whose members constituted a distinct patrician aristocracy. The cities grew strong and prosperous under their rule. But it was not long before the demands of the lower classes for a proportionate share in city administration led to severe struggles for political power and supremacy, which in turn were followed by a progressive weakening of the political influence of the cities. In many cases these social conflicts ended in compromise. In the Hansa cities the patricians maintained their supremacy, in other places (Augsburg, Nürnberg, Ulm) the patricians as well as the merchant and craft guilds were represented in the City Council, while in the city of Mainz the guilds became the uncontested masters of their city in 1444.

One or several Bürgermeister (mayors) presided over the City Council. The councilors (*Ratsherren*) employed a number of paid officials, the most important of whom was the city clerk (*Stadtschreiber*) who was in charge of records, protocols, and city archives, and who was originally a member of the clergy. He had to be an experienced jurist and was aided by several legal advisers.

Imperial cities obtained the status of independent republics and combined the functions of city and state government. They had to concern themselves with foreign politics, they waged wars, and they made treaties and concluded alliances with other cities or with territorial princes.

The City Council also administered the judicial branch of government. The city had its own code of civil and criminal law that was binding upon all citizens with the exception of the clergy, whose members were subject to Canon Law. Another important function of city government was the organization of military defense. In the beginning every citizen was bound by duty to take up arms, the poorer classes providing the foot soldiery, the patricians the cavalry. Most of the city armies were excellent, outstanding in attack and defense. When the growing economic development of the cities made it desirable to release the burghers from military service, the City Councils began to employ mercenary soldiers, sometimes even hiring impoverished knights and princes.

The privilege of coining money was a right of the city government that had only been won after a long struggle. Their administration of the mint contributed to the stabilization and unification of the currency. A unified system of currency had not yet been attained by medieval economy, and the granting of the right of coinage to great and small lords had created an increasing monetary confusion.

At the end of the Middle Ages the *Pfennig* could be considered as a kind of monetary unit. Half a *Pfennig* was a *Heller,* so named after the city of Halle in Swabia, the place of its coinage. Twelve pfennigs made up one *Schilling;* 240 pfennigs were one *Pfund* (pound). Various silver coins, such as the *Groschen* (from Latin, *grossus,* "thick pfennig") or the *Weisspfennig* (*Albus*), were used locally. In the latter part of the thirteenth century the standard basis of currency became the Rhenish *Goldgulden* ("gold guilder," "florin," first coined in Florence in 1252). The currency agreement of the Rhenish Prince-Electors of 1386 fixed the value of one *Goldgulden* at 20 *Weisspfennigs* which was the equivalent of 240 *Heller*. The Saxon *Gulden-groschen* (a silver coin) and *Joachimstaler Silbergulden* were used side by side with the Rhenish *Goldgulden* from the beginning of the sixteenth century. The standard currency in the German north and northeast was the *Mark,* the equivalent of half a *Taler*. Several currency unions (*Münzvereine*) worked for a unification of the different currencies. The fraudulent devaluation of coins was a frequent occurrence and led to the enactment of stringent city laws against counterfeiting. According to a register from Niederaltaich in Bavaria of the year 1243 a large horse cost three pounds, a pig 25–50 pfennigs, a sheep 10 pfennigs, a package of special Christmas cheese 1 pfennig, a bushel of oats 14 pfennigs. Skilled masons received a weekly pay of 38 pfennings, unskilled laborers 19 pfennings. Money had, of course, quite generally a much greater purchasing power than it has today.

The life of the citizens was regulated and controlled by a number of city ordinances that laid down rules for the construction and maintenance of houses and streets, for the preservation of public health and the prevention of the spread of epidemics, for the prevention of fires, against immodesty and indecency in dress and entertainment, for the protection of the consumers of food and drink, together with a host of similar regulations that might pertain to almost any department of human and social activity.

Care of the Poor and the Sick. The care of the poor and the sick was in the hands of several monastic and semimonastic orders which were founded toward the end of the Middle Ages. Very numerous were the members of the sisterhood of Beguines who spread from the Netherlands over the greater part of Germany. Their congregations could be found in almost every German city of medium size. They answered a real social need in a period when Crusades, wars, and epidemics had led to a definite surplus of women, a considerable proportion of whom could never expect to get married. The Beguines took the vows of chastity and obedience for the period of their stay in the beguinage (*Klause, Samnung*), earning their livelihood with spinning, sewing, nursing, and teaching. Frequently there developed in their circles enthusiastic and exaggerated forms of piety which brought upon them accusations of heresy and persecutions by the ecclesiastical and secular authorities.

Outside the city walls were located the hospitals for the sufferers from leprosy (*Siechenhäuser*). They were built during the twelfth and thirteenth centuries when this disease began to claim more and more victims, partly because of the crowded and unsanitary conditions in the cities. A specially assigned priest ministered to the lepers in their own hospital chapel, and they were buried in their own church yard. They were excluded from human society by solemn ecclesiastical rites. They were then given a gray or black habit, gloves, a cane, a drinking cup, and a bread bag, and were escorted to the lepers' home where they would have to spend the rest of their earthly days. They were forbidden to drink from public wells, and they had to warn the approaching stranger by the sound of a rattle or a horn. The order of St. Lazarus that was founded in Palestine in the twelfth century was especially devoted to the care of lepers. St. Elizabeth of Thuringia (1207–1231), the wife of landgrave Ludwig, and St. Hedwig, duchess of Silesia (1174–1243), founded *Siechenhäuser* and personally nursed the unfortunate ones who were afflicted with leprosy.

Merchant and Craft Guilds ("Gilden" and "Zünfte"). While the city as a corporate economic unit of marked independence· presented a united front to those who were not members of its community of interests, the social divisions within the city were in turn corporatively organized and strictly delimited. The organizations of the merchants and artisans who represented the most numerous classes of the population were known as guilds. The German word *Zunft* is derived from the Old High German verb *zeman* (to become, befit, beseem) and refers to the regulative and restrictive character of the guilds. The guilds were the channels through which the city government exercised its control of business. The "masters" worked out the rules, the magistrates confirmed them, and henceforth they were considered as binding on all the members of the guild.

The origin of the guilds is rather obscure. They may derive from the old Germanic religious brotherhoods, or they may simply be an outgrowth of the desire of the merchant and artisan classes for mutual protection and social security. The first records of organized guilds date from the twelfth century.

The guild was closely linked with the religious life of its members, and religious and social incentives were intertwined in all their activities. Each guild had its patron saint, whose image was represented on its banners and shields and whose feast day was solemnly commemorated. In fraternal intercourse they cultivated the social virtues. They revolutionized the conventions of the feudal age and revived the social heritage of the German past for the benefit of a new epoch of German civilization.

Sociologically the guild is a corporation of individuals that become a unity by means of the voluntary association of its members. This association imparts to the individual a new consciousness of his personal value, freeing him from his attachment to the soil and placing him in an organic relationship to city, state, and corporation. While the individual thus frees himself in one respect, he imposes upon himself new ties and obligations.

To safeguard the efficient control of social economy, to uphold the "honor of the trade," and to serve the interest of the common good, membership in the guild was made compulsory, so that ordinarily nonmembers could neither buy nor sell at retail within the city. The guilds regulated prices, set definite standards for wages and hours of labor, and controlled the quality of goods. But more important than these restrictions on unlimited profits and unfair competition was the positive promotion of trade and commerce, and the encouragement that the individual merchant and craftsman received from a reasonable equality of opportunity.

The merchant guilds achieved their greatest power and influence in the twelfth century. While their main purpose remained an economic one, they began to take an active part in the administration of the city. With the growing specialization of industry the influence of the merchant guilds declined, and their place was taken by the craft guilds, whose members were artisans. They sold the products of their hands directly to the consumer without needing the services of a middleman.

The craft guilds were highly specialized, and each branch of industry was represented by its own guild. Membership was limited to the skilled trades, and the guild statutes and regulations were even more strict and exclusive than those of the merchant guilds. The methods of manufacture, the quality of materials, prices, and wages were closely supervised, and the total number of local masters, journeymen, and apprentices was limited by special rules.

A long period of training was required to advance from apprenticeship to mastership. The master had to obtain the permission of the guild if he wanted to take on an apprentice. The permission was granted if the apprentice was of free and legitimate birth and of German nationality, and if the particular trade was not crowded. The apprentice (*Lehrling*) was usually ten or twelve years of age when he entered the service of his master. He lived in the master's house, but his training was supervised by the guild. The master gave him food and clothing and a small fee. The master exercised the authority of a father and was responsible for the boy's physical and moral well-being. The apprenticeship would last from two to ten years, depending in part on the skill that was required in a particular trade. At the end of this period the apprentice was promoted with solemn rites to the rank of a journeyman (*Geselle*). He was given a certificate (*Lehrbrief*) and was now free to set out upon several years of travel (*Wanderjahre*) in order to acquire more experience and greater skill. He was paid by the day or by the week and tried to save enough money to be able to stand on his own feet at the earliest possible time. His working day lasted from five or six o'clock in the morning until darkness and often late at night. But holidays were frequent, and Monday was the journeyman's special day off, so that he would be able to attend to his personal affairs, visit the bathhouse, and cultivate his social and political interests ("good Monday," "blue Monday").

When the end of his years of travel had come, the journeyman would apply for full membership in the guild. He was required to submit a sample of his work (*Meisterstück*) and had to pass an examination before being received into the guild as a master (*Meister*). He would then establish a workshop in his own house, where he would manufacture his goods with his own hands and hire his own journeymen and apprentices. As an employer he considered himself as socially on the same level as his employees, who would some day be masters themselves. The self-imposed rules of the guild prevented him from making excessive profits at the expense of his competitors, while at the same time they guaranteed him a decent standard of living.

The rise of capitalistic tendencies at the end of the Middle Ages tended to undermine the bases of the guild system. The guild principle of "production for use" gave way to the methods of "production for profit," and the masters began to misuse their monopolies to the detriment of their competitors.

Medieval Economic Theory. The new economic system that was no longer based on the personal tenure of land, but on the impersonal power of money, found its strongest supporters in the cities. It was there that the new kind of wealth was created and the methods for its acquisition developed. Payments in the feudal age were mostly made in the form of services or produce, and trade was carried on primarily by barter. Money, if it existed, was usually hoarded. With the revival of trade that followed the Crusades, and with the rise of the new urban centers of commerce, the opportunities for investment increased, and the new money economy began to revolutionize the structure of medieval society. Economic forces no longer have their meaning circumscribed by the needs of the consumer, but they become the instruments of the producer, who artificially creates ever new needs that in turn require ever new satisfactions.

The economic theories of the Middle Ages, as embodied in the works of the scholastic philosophers and theologians of the thirteenth and fourteenth centuries (cf. p. 141 sqq.), were prompted by and immediately concerned with those economic and social transformations that were gradually brought about by the growth of trade and the rise of the cities. Their economic speculations dealt in the main with private property, money, prices, and the taking of interest (usury).

a) *Private Property.* They maintained that the right to own property was a natural and moral one, springing from the nature of man and finding its expression in the institution of private property. On the other hand, it was considered as equally obvious that the actual distribution of private property was in no way sacred or absolute but a matter of social convenience and human relations. "Man has a twofold relation to external things, of which one is the power of producing and consuming. For this it is lawful that man should possess property. . . . The other relation to external things is their use, and as far as this goes no man ought to have anything proper to himself but all in common, so that thus each may communicate easily to another in his necessities" (Thomas Aquinas, *Summa Theologica,* I, 2, 66, 2). The reasons listed in defense of the institution of private property were derived from Aristotle and were repeated over and over again in medieval treatises on social science.

The principle of contract that permeated all human relationships in the feudal age and that was binding on king and serf alike, knew only of the conditional exercise of the right of ownership. The owner was a steward, and while the means of production were thus actually in private holding, they remained theoretically in the hands of the community.

b) *Money.* The medieval attitude in regard to money, its nature, acquisition, and use, was based on the fundamental conviction that economic goods were mere means and as such subordinated to the moral ends of life, and that any economic activity was subject to the moral law. In his *Commentary on the Politics of Aristotle* (Parma edition, Vol. IV, p. 390), Thomas Aquinas wrote: "Political economy, which is concerned with the using of money for a definite purpose, does not seek unlimited wealth, but wealth such as shall help towards its purpose, and this purpose is the good estate of the home." If the prime object of the trader was to make money, he was engaged in a condemnable economic activity. If he was motivated by the desire to provide a decent living for himself and his family, his profession was lawful and laudable, provided that his business practices were beyond reproach. "He who has enough to satisfy his wants," wrote Heinrich von Langenstein (1325-1397), "and nevertheless ceaselessly labors to acquire riches, either in order to obtain a higher social position, or that subsequently he may have enough to live without labor, or that his sons may become men of wealth and importance — all such are incited by a damnable avarice, sensuality, or pride" (*Tractatus Bipartitus de Contractibus Emptionis et Venditionis,* 1, 12). About two hundred and fifty years later Martin Luther used even stronger language to condemn the same economic practices.

c) *The Just Price (Justum Pretium).* It was the conviction of the medieval thinkers that a "just price" for articles that were bought and sold could be determined and fixed by law. It was admitted, however, that the price level would have to be adjusted to local conditions and circumstances. "Sometimes the just price cannot be determined absolutely, but consists rather in a common estimation, in such a way that a slight addition or diminution of price cannot be thought to destroy justice" (Thomas Aquinas, *Summa Theologica,* II, 2, 77, 1, ad m). The ideal standard by which the justice of economic practices could be measured was provided by the natural law: "Every law framed by man bears the character of a law exactly to that extent to which it is derived from the law of nature. But if at any point it is in conflict with the law of nature, it at once ceases to be a law; it is a mere perversion of law" (Thomas Aquinas, *Summa Theologica,* I, 2, 95, a. 2). The just price would guarantee a man a sufficient profit to live his life according to the standards that public opinion associated with his social status.

d) The Taking of Interest. The prohibition of the taking of interest was defended in the Middle Ages by reference to the Scriptures, to the Church Fathers, to Aristotle, and to the law of nature. It had thus become an integral part and a major issue of medieval economics. It was a prohibition well suited to a system of agricultural economy but out of tune with the new money economy that depended more and more on the credit system. Paradoxically enough, the very Church which had promulgated and for centuries enforced the laws and decrees prohibiting the taking of interest, joined the State in becoming in many instances a protagonist of money economy and of the spirit of early capitalism.

The ethical theory of the Middle Ages in regard to the taking of interest held that money was barren and sterile and therefore could not breed money. It was considered contrary to the natural law that a man should live and earn without labor. It was considered immoral to charge money for a loan on which no such payment should have been asked. The profits raised by a monopolist, the beating down of prices, the rack-renting of land, the subletting of land by a tenant at a higher rent than he paid himself, the cutting of wages, the refusal of discount to a tardy debtor, the excessive profits of a middleman — all these practices were condemned by medieval ethics, which grouped them all under the title of "usury."

There were, however, certain loans on which interest might be lawfully demanded. Thus it was considered lawful to charge interest if the lender, in loaning the money, suffered a loss which he would not have incurred otherwise; or if the lender by loaning the money deprived himself of a profit which he would otherwise have made; or if the borrower of the money used it in a manner that involved the risk of losing it, and if he had mentioned the nature of that risk to the lender. There were other exceptions to the general rule, but they were few, and most of them could be grouped among the above cases.

The Church councils which were strongest in their condemnation of usury in any form were the Lateran Councils of 1139 and 1179, and the Councils of Lyon (1274) and Vienne (1311). Any kind of financial speculation was branded as illegal and immoral. The moneylender was considered virtually an outlaw. Under pain of excommunication or interdict individuals and communities were required to expel usurers from their midst, and they were to be refused the sacraments and Christian burial until they had made restitution. The Council of Vienne decreed that moneylenders be compelled to submit their accounts to examination, and those who defend usurious practices are to be punished as heretics.

e) *The Jews and Lombards as Moneylenders.* One of the results of this ecclesiastical legislation on interest was the concentration of credit transactions in the hands of the Jews who were not bound by the prohibition laws of the Church. An imperial edict of the fourteenth century decreed a rate of 43 per cent as the upper limit of charges on loans! However, the Jews not only demanded excessive rates of interest but dead pledges (*Faustpfänder*) and promissory notes as well, so that they became the possessors of increasing wealth in the form of money, land, and real estate. By the payment of large sums they secured the protection of emperors, princes, and cities. The people at large, however, began to hate and despise them as usurers and oppressors. They were excluded from citizenship, restricted in their movements, relegated to certain streets and quarters of the city (*Judengassen, Judenviertel*). They were not admitted to the public baths and places of social entertainment and had to wear special dress and other distinguishing marks. Despite the enactment of protective laws, violent outbreaks against the Jews were frequent. They were reproached with ritual murders, sacrilege, and blasphemy, with the poisoning of public wells and a host of other crimes. In 1285 the Synagogue in Munich was burned by an angry populace, with one hundred Jews who had sought refuge in the building, and the long series of cruel persecutions reached their climax about the middle of the fourteenth century, when there raged wholesale murder of Jews in Switzerland, along the Rhine, in Swabia, Bavaria, and Austria. They were banished from Augsburg in 1438, from Munich in 1440, from Würzburg in 1488.

The repression of the Jews was good news for the financially no less efficient and equally ruthless Lombards, who took the place of the Jews as moneylenders and, by cunning and casuistry, successfully endeavored to circumvent the ecclesiastical laws. The Italians in general felt no scruples in asking interest, not even from the pope when he needed money to finance his undertakings. To protect the poor from the exploitation of Jews and Lombards the cities established special organizations in the form of fraternities, guilds, and hospitals, where money could be borrowed cheaply. Such loan banks were called *Montes Pietatis* (Mounts of Piety); they were founded in most European countries in the course of the fifteenth century.

But the most dangerous competitors of Jews and Lombards were the big merchants who began to monopolize the money trade toward the end of the Middle Ages. The bulk of their income was derived from the working of rich mines of silver, gold, iron, copper, zinc, quicksilver, and lead. The mining industries of Bohemia, Bavaria, Saxony, Silesia, Styria, Carinthia, and the Tyrol provided all Europe with the much coveted metals, ores, and minerals. The fifteenth century witnessed a regular "gold rush" in Germany. According to tradition the mines were still owned by the territorial lords. But the big merchants took them over as security for loans and began to exploit them for themselves, so that the masters of the mines soon became the owners of the precious metals as well. When they found out that money trade was the most lucrative of all, most of them went into the banking business.

The papal Curia became involved in the practices of the new money economy after the beginning of the thirteenth century, when the papacy had reached its peak as a political power and when scholastic philosophy had just completed its anticapitalistic system of economic ethics. The Curia needed money to keep up its world-wide political organization, but money could only be obtained by taxing the clergy and the laity and by paying interest to lenders. Many representatives of the Church, becoming more and more entangled in worldly affairs, were in the end more interested in the raising of funds than in the salvation of souls. Some popes became the most important customers of the new Italian and German bankers. These latter had their agents and advisers at the papal court, and they were in charge of the administration of the receipts from indulgences, and other sources of papal income. Like the emperors, some of the popes began to take part in the competitive economic struggles and established capitalistic monopolies for certain industries. Thus Church and State both paid their tribute to the changing spirit of the age, and the Church in particular became in many instances the ally of forces that undermined the foundations of medieval civilization.

Religion and the Church. In Germany as elsewhere the Middle Ages were formed, dominated, and permeated by religious forces. Even the seemingly most insignificant event or activity was endowed with a strong religious accent, so that practically nothing was relegated to a sphere of neutrality or indifference. A definite scale of values was accepted as inherent in the universal order of things, establishing a "hierarchy of being" (minerals, plants, animals, human beings, angelic beings, God) that might be resented, criticized, or challenged, but which was entrenched strongly enough in the medieval mind to constitute a general rule of life and a standard of public opinion.

The sacramental system of the Roman Catholic Church was accepted as the normal framework within which Christian life and culture displayed themselves, and for centuries the Church and religion were almost synonymous. This implicit confidence in the legitimacy of ecclesiastical authority was challenged for the first time by the contact of the Christian West with non-Christian forms of civilization that followed the Crusades (cf. p. 108 sq.). It was further undermined by the growing secularization of Church institutions and practices and a general lowering of moral standards among the members of the ecclesiastical hierarchy. It was finally destroyed by revolutionary movements in theology, philosophy, economics, politics, art, and literature. At the end of the Middle Ages regional nationalism in Church and State began to replace the universal ecclesiastical rule.

The administrative center of the medieval Church was the papal Curia with its head, the pope, the College of Cardinals, and its large number of clerical officials. The right of the cardinals to elect the pope had been established by the decree of Pope Nicholas II in 1059. The chief administrative officers in the many national provinces of the Church were the archbishops and bishops who presided over their dioceses. Most of the members of the higher clergy were of noble birth, and many of them lived the lives of feudal lords and were oblivious of the spiritual significance of their position. They surrounded themselves with vassals and servants, court singers and entertainers. They loved the excitement of the hunt and the adventures of war, and they were so thoroughly entangled in worldly affairs that a popular saying in Germany maintained: the hardest thing to take on faith was the salvation of a German bishop.

The cathedral, which was located in the principal city of each diocese, was the church of the bishop. The "cathedral chapter" consisted of a certain number of canons (priests) who were in charge of the services, took part in the administration of the diocese, and elected the new bishop. The acquisition of land made the cathedral chapters more and more independent of the bishop. As many of the canons likewise belonged to the nobility, they frequently neglected their priestly duties, appointed a poorly paid curate (vicar), and lived like the worldly lords and knights. The "prebend" (office) of a canon was coveted by many a young nobleman because it guaranteed a considerable revenue from some piece of land. Many such officeholders were attracted by nothing but these material advantages and were therefore utterly lacking in the spirit of religion and morality.

In contrast to the richly endowed prebends of the canons, the income that the average parish priest drew from his share in the land of the village, town, or manor was very small. The payment of the tithe (*der Zehnte*), representing a compulsory tax on one tenth of the agricultural and industrial produce and originally promulgated by the Carolingians as a compensation for the confiscation of Church property, was exacted only in a few places. Besides, part of the parish priest's income went to the bishop in the form of taxes and another part to the "patron" of the church who had bestowed the parish upon the priest as a feudal "benefice."

Most of the parish priests were recruited from the peasant class. They were poorly equipped for their office, and frequently they lacked even the most elementary forms of secular and religious education. Many of them tried to increase their incomes by engaging in secular businesses, such as agriculture, trading, medical or legal practice, or more despicable activities. In the later Middle Ages the law of celibacy was frequently not observed, and the wives and concubines of priests became the objects of popular resentment and of the eloquent denunciations of the preaching friars.

The rise of the cities and the newly founded universities (cf. p. 137 sqq.) contributed greatly to the gradual improvement of clerical training. But at the same time the improved and increased educational facilities created a kind of academic proletariat, as many of the students, after having completed their university course, were unable to find positions. These "goliards" (from Goliath, their patron) roamed about as wandering minstrels and vagabonds, as composers and singers of *Vaganten-Lieder,* praising wine, women, and song. One of their number, "Walther, the arch-poet," is known as the author of the Latin student song *"Mihi est propositum in taberna mori"* (it is my destiny to die in a tavern). Its author belonged to the retinue of Reinald of Dassel, archbishop of Cologne (1120–1167).

Ecclesiastical jurisdiction was exercised in the episcopal courts according to the rules of Canon Law. Episcopal jurisdiction extended to all the members of the clergy, including students and deacons, likewise to widows and orphans and to those who took part in a Crusade; also to all who were engaged in dealings of a moral and religious nature, such as marriages, certain business transactions that were sanctioned by an oath, and offenses against religion (heresy, sacrilege, blasphemy, etc.). The sentences imposed by the ecclesiastical courts were usually lighter than those of the civil courts, and never involved the death penalty. According to Canon Law the Church should never shed blood, and formally the ecclesiastical authorities complied with this principle by reserving the imposition of capital punishment to "the secular arm" of the civil government, to which an unrepentant sinner was ordinarily handed over. In doing so, however, the Church knew exactly what the judgment would be, with what methods it would be executed, and how the admissions of guilt were obtained.

The Religion of the People. Religious life in the Middle Ages was essentially informed by the theological concepts of the Church, but it was enriched and colored by the imagination of the common people.

The people were anxious to have visible and tangible objects for their devotion and adoration. During the period of the Crusades the veneration of the relics of the saints increased greatly in fervor and frequency. Jacobus de Voragine's "Golden Legend" (Latin, *Legenda Aurea*) describes the mourning and the great devotion of the people when they learned of the death of their benefactress, St. Elizabeth of Thuringia (1207–1231). They cut off some curls of her hair and pieces of her garment to keep them as relics of the dead saint. The people rejoiced when Frederick Barbarossa in 1164 had the bones of the Three Wise Men of the East (*die heiligen drei Könige*) transferred from Milan to Cologne. In their honor the artisans of Cologne created in the thirteenth century one of the most imposing cathedrals and one of the most magnificent reliquaries of Germany. The "shrine of relics" soon became quite generally the most precious implement of the churches and the object of innumerable pilgrimages.

Pilgrimages became more numerous and gained greatly in popularity during the age of the Crusades. The new shrines in Canterbury (England), Mont-Saint-Michel (France), St. Patrick's Cave (Ireland), and Maria-Einsiedeln (Switzerland) began to attract as many pilgrims as the ancient ones in Rome, Jerusalem, and Santiago de Compostela (Spain). But very much like the Crusaders, some of the pilgrims were prompted by worldly incentives, by love of adventure, curiosity, or greed. Brother Berthold of Regensburg († 1272), one of the most popular and influential German preaching friars of the Franciscan Order, expressed the opinion that it was better to journey to find devout people who are alive than to see dead saints: "I pity you, because every now and then you journey to St. James. And what do you find at Compostela when you arrive? St. James's head! That is all right; but, after all, it is only a dead skull whose better part is in the heavens beyond. But you run to St. James and neglect your business at home, so that your children and good wives grow poorer and poorer, and you yourself become more and more indebted and oppressed."

The Mendicant Orders: Franciscans and Dominicans. Some of the ancient Benedictine monasteries had been responsible for the reform movement of Cluny (cf. p. 70 sq.). The Cistercian and Carthusian Orders represented reform movements which led to a revival of strict monastic discipline within the Benedictine Order itself (cf. p. 36 sq.). In the meantime however, the Benedictine monasteries had again fallen into decline, chiefly owing to their excessive wealth. The Church in general had greatly relaxed its moral discipline and turned from the purity and simplicity of the early Christian centuries, when Francis of Assisi (1182–1226) and Dominic, a native of Caleruega in Castile (1175–1221), appeared and became the founders of the Franciscan and Dominican Orders respectively. Both the Italian and the Spaniard were sons of wealthy parents, but both renounced the possessions and honors that awaited them and chose poverty as their lot. No member of the two new orders was allowed to possess more than the bare necessities of life, and their communities lived entirely on the charity of their fellow men. They were therefore called the mendicant or begging orders and were also known as *friars* (from Latin, *frater:* "brother").

While St. Francis stressed the preaching of the Gospel and the imitation of Christ in aiding the poor, the sick, and the sinners (*Ordo Fratrum Minorum;* abbr.: O.F.M.; "minor brothers," "little brothers"), St. Dominic and his followers were more exclusively concerned with the task of preserving and restoring the purity of religious doctrine by scholarly sermon and disputation (*Ordo Praedicatorum;* abbr.: O.P.; "preaching friars"). St. Francis was a man of great simplicity, animated by a childlike devotion to Christ and the Church; Dominic was a penetrating thinker, a born leader and organizer, whose mind was endowed with a rare sense of proportion and moderation. Both men wanted the members of their congregations to come in close contact with the people, and the Dominicans more than the Franciscans were destined to play an active part in social and political affairs.

Whereas the Benedictine settlements were mostly located in the country-side, the Franciscans and Dominicans established themselves in towns and cities. Even while Francis of Assisi was still alive Franciscan settlements were founded in such German cities as Augsburg, Regensburg, Mainz, and Worms. And the Dominican Order likewise gained a foothold in Austria before the death of its founder. The German Dominican, Jordanus of Saxony († 1237), was chosen to succeed Dominic as general of the order in 1222.

The greatest of medieval theologians, philosophers, and scientists in all European countries were either Franciscans or Dominicans. They met at the new centers of learning, the universities, and added greatly to their growth and reputation. But soon rivalries and heated controversies disturbed the good relationship between the two orders, and they began to oppose each other on doctrinal grounds.

The Franciscan friars were closer to the hearts of the people than the learned Dominican preachers. David of Augsburg (1200–1272) and his pupil, Berthold of Regensburg, were both Franciscans, and the common people enjoyed listening to them because in their sermons they recognized their own language, their own thoughts and emotions, their own joys and woes.

Albigenses and Waldenses. The same dissatisfaction with the actual con-ditions in Church, State, and society that led to the foundation of the mendicant orders was at the root of a number of heretical movements which threatened the Church from within, and whose adherents were persecuted and finally suppressed by force. The several heretical sects that originated in the twelfth century were all opposed to the sacramental system of the Church and to the clergy as a privileged and socially distinguished class or caste. Like the Franciscans, they demanded the return to the apostolic ideals of primitive Christianity, proclaiming the general priesthood of all Christians.

The Albigenses (from the city of Albi) and Waldenses (the followers of the merchant Peter Waldo from Lyon; also called *Cathari:* "the pure ones") lived and preached in the south of France, but their teachings soon spread to Germany. They denounced avarice and selfishness but went so far in their extreme asceticism as to identify everything material and physical with the forces of evil. They thus revived the ancient Manichaean doctrine of the radical corruption of nature and matter, to which St. Augustine had given allegiance before his conversion to Christianity. They rejected all external symbols, such as sacraments, liturgical ceremonies, sacred vessels, vestments, and images. They denounced marriage, private property, the eating of meat, the use of force, and the shedding of blood. They threatened the unity of Church and State with anarchy and nihilism by preaching a double morality for two essentially different classes of men: the chosen ones who belonged to the inner circle of the religious elite and were no longer in need of religious and civil authority; and the uninitiated masses who still walked in utter darkness. Peter Waldo and his followers were more moderate in their views, and several groups of Waldenses escaped persecution and were allowed to survive in various European countries.

Heresy and the Inquisition. Ever since the days of Emperor Constantine heresy had been considered as a major crime that implied an attack against God and a divinely instituted authority, and that was to be punished in accordance with both ecclesiastical and secular legislation. Thomas Aquinas makes a distinction between those who, like pagans and Jews, have never known and professed the Christian faith, and actual apostates. The former should be left free to follow their consciences, while the latter are to be considered as traitors and are to be dealt with by force. Generally speaking, he thinks, no one should be compelled to accept the teaching of Christianity, and even children should not be baptized against the wish of their parents to whom God had given authority and responsibility in their regard. But anyone who had once voluntarily accepted Christianity should be compelled to live up to his promises. To the medieval mind such a promise constituted a simple contract whose legal obligations were enforceable by law. And the law of heresy followed the pattern of the law of treason: no one could be compelled to belong to one State rather than another, but once he had sworn allegiance to a certain State, he could then be compelled to fulfill his obligations toward that State.

Many a ruler encouraged the destruction of heretics as a welcome means to enlarge his possessions at their expense or to rid himself of dangerous enemies and rivals. In 1232 Emperor Frederick II decreed for the whole Empire that heretics should either be burned or have their tongues cut out. At about the same time Eike von Repkow's *Sachsenspiegel,* the oldest law-book written in German, whose legal concepts are based on national tradition and custom as well as on imperial legislation, demands that heretics be burned at the stake.

Finally, the extermination of heresy was methodically organized by Pope Gregory IX (1227-1241), who authorized certain religious orders, and especially the Dominicans, to try cases of heresy, thereby establishing the Papal Inquisition or Holy Office. The trials were held in secret, a counsel of defense was often denied, the names of the accusers remained unknown to the accused, and the confessions were extorted by the application of torture. The cruelty of these trials, in which accuser and judge were united in the person of the inquisitor, contributed to the growth of anticlerical feeling. Conrad of Marburg, inquisitor of Germany and confessor of St. Elizabeth of Thuringia, was assassinated in 1233, and his fate could hardly claim any sympathy on the part of the German hierarchy. Bishop Conrad I of Würzburg was killed on his way to the cathedral in 1202. It is not surprising, therefore, that Pope Boniface VIII (1294-1303), the last of the great medieval pontiffs, speaks of the hatred of the laity for the clergy as if it were a matter of course. Both the sectarian heretical movements and

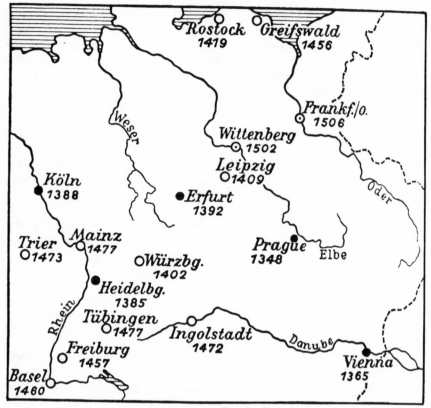

From *Der Grosse Herder*, Herder, Freiburg i. Br.

The Oldest German Universities (to 1500).

the growing opposition of the orthodox laity indicate the dangers with which the ecclesiastical structure was being threatened from without and from within. The clerical element is gradually outnumbered and outweighed by a laity whose members adopt the self-contained culture of the new urban civilization.

The Universities: Organization and Curriculum. The expansion of trade and commerce and the concentration of prosperity and culture in the cities made not only for a richer life but for a more complex concept of living. New problems had to be faced whose solution demanded a depth and acuteness of mental training that could no longer be provided by the old monastery and cathedral schools (cf. p. 87 sq.). And so there arose between the twelfth and the sixteenth centuries — mostly under the sponsorship of the Church — those institutions of higher learning which became known as universities and which were henceforth the main carriers of theoretical and practical knowledge.

By the beginning of the thirteenth century six such Centers for General Studies had been established, among them Salerno and Bologna in Italy, Paris in France, and Oxford in England. Eight more developed during the following hundred years in Italy, Spain, Portugal, France, and England. Twenty-two more universities were founded during the fourteenth century, five in Germany, and by the year 1500 their number had increased to eighty.

While the intellectual life of Germany suffered from the aftereffects of the struggles between Empire and Papacy, France more than any other nation experienced a cultural and intellectual rebirth. As early as the eleventh century Paris had become the center of learning and the "city of philosophers." Its university served as a model for all the *Studia Generalia* in the northern countries, including Germany and England. The neighboring outposts of Arabic and Jewish learning that had been established in Spain proved a mighty stimulus in the educational renascence of France. The University of Paris, where the liberal arts as well as theology and philosophy were especially cultivated, had developed out of the cathedral school of Notre Dame. Among its famous professors in the eleventh and twelfth centuries we find Peter Abelard (1069–1142), the "master of opposites," who first developed the scholastic method of argumentation (cf. p. 145 sq.); Hugh of St. Victor (1069–1141), of German origin, who was called the "second Augustine"; and Peter Lombard († 1164), the author of the famous *Four Books of Sentences* that became the standard text for all the theological schools up to the sixteenth century.

The first university on the soil of the German empire was established in Prague, the capital of Bohemia, in 1348, by Emperor Charles IV, to be followed by the foundation of the Universities of Vienna (1365), Heidelberg (1385), Köln (1388), Erfurt (1392), Würzburg (1402), Leipzig (1409), Rostock (1419), Greifswald (1456), Freiburg (1457), Basel (1460), Ingolstadt (1472), Trier (1473), Mainz (1477), Tübingen (1477), Wittenberg (1502), and Frankfurt on the Oder (1506).

The organization of the medieval university followed the general sociological pattern of the craft guilds (cf. p. 125 sqq.). Students and professors were related to each other like the members of a guild who had united for the purpose of study. The students were the apprentices, the bachelors the journeymen, the professors the masters (*Magister Artium*: Master of Arts, M.A.). The master's degree was granted after the student had passed a thorough examination in which he had proven his ability in defining, discussing, and defending certain propositions. The doctor's degree was granted to those who wished to specialize in one of the professions, and an examination in public was one of the requirements. The term *Artium Baccalaureus* (A.B.) merely indicated that a student had started to do advanced work.

As an essentially ecclesiastical institution the university was exempt from civil jurisdiction and subject to the disciplinary powers vested in the faculty, whose members were only responsible to the pope. The charter for the founding of a university might be granted by the emperor, the king, or the pope.

The students flocked to the universities from different countries, attracted by the reputation of certain schools in their respective fields. They were not hampered by language barriers, Latin being the universal language of higher learning. The university usually consisted of four "faculties": liberal arts, theology, law, and medicine. Each faculty was headed by a dean who was subordinate to the rector and possibly a chancellor, who was the representative of the bishop. Masters and students were divided into several "nations" (*Landsmannschaften*) according to the countries of their origin, and the rector was chosen by these national societies. In the thirteenth century four "nations" were represented at the University of Paris: the French, the Picards, the Normans, and the English. The latter group included the Germans, Scandinavians, Poles, Hungarians, and Bohemians. All the "nations" together were called *universitas nationum*.

The material equipment of the medieval university was of the most primitive kind: there were no campus grounds, no lecture halls, no laboratories, no libraries. Teachers and students were practically the only assets that the university possessed. The professor would lecture in his own home or in a hired hall, surrounded by a group of students who might be seated on the floor. The lectures were based on standard texts, and the professor would dictate the text itself, together with his commentaries (glosses). To the beginning of the fifteenth century the students used wax tablets on which they inscribed their notes.

The course in the liberal arts included the work of the beginners, part of which was taught in the monastery and cathedral schools. The *trivium* and *quadrivium* (cf. p. 87 sq.) still provided the general framework of the curriculum, but more emphasis was now placed upon the strictly philosophical disciplines, while grammar and rhetoric were merely considered as valuable tools for the better mastery of the more important subjects of logic and metaphysics.

The study of nature was still in its infancy. The "book of nature" presented a panoramic display of divine works, "written by God Himself, so that in it man might be able to read eternal truths" (Hildegard of Bingen). In flower and tree, mountain and river, rock and animal, medieval man saw symbolic hieroglyphics of a supernatural design. The originally Oriental collection of allegorical descriptions of the world of animals and minerals, known as the *Physiologus,* presents a true picture of the medieval outlook on nature, traces of which are also found in art, literature, and culture. According to Freidank, a German poet of the thirteenth century, nothing on earth is without symbolical or allegorical meaning (*bezeichenheit*).

On the other hand, the thirteenth century shows considerable progress in the accuracy of scientific observation and in the empirical collection and classification of scientific facts and data. It was the conviction of Albert the Great (1193–1280, cf. p. 144 sq.) that "a logical conclusion that contradicts sense perception is not acceptable. A fundamental principle which does not agree with the experimental data of sense knowledge is in reality no fundamental principle at all but a fundamental error." Albert recognized that the milky way consisted of a multitude of stars, he knew about the existence of our antipodes, discussed the influence of the axial direction of mountain ranges on climatic conditions, and he gave accurate descriptions of plant and animal organisms. His English colleague, the Franciscan friar, Roger Bacon (1214-1294), the "admirable doctor" (*Doctor Mirabilis*), was the most progressive scientist of his age. He was actively engaged in mathematical, astronomical, optical, chemical, and medical research. He recognized the laws of the refraction of light and described the phenomenon of the rainbow and the burning glass. He constructed optical instruments and designed plans for automobiles, microscopes, telescopes, steamboats, and airplanes. In order to determine the nature of the original human language he developed the idea of a science of comparative linguistics. Being thus far advanced beyond the scientific knowledge of his time and very outspoken in his criticism of contemporary conditions and institutions, he was suspected of heresy, until he found a protector and defender in the person of Pope Clement IV (1265-1268).

Medieval chemistry was almost invariably linked with the pseudo science of alchemy, just as astronomy seemed inseparable from astrology. The alchemists were still in search of the philosopher's stone (*Stein der Weisen*), the fundamental substratum of all metals, and they tried with indefatigable zeal to change iron into gold or copper into silver.

In the absence of anatomical studies the students often had to be satisfied with the book knowledge gathered from the works of the ancient Greek and Roman physicians Hippocrates (the "father of medicine," 490 to *c.* 370 B.C.) and Galenus (second century A.D.) and their Arabic translators and commentators. It was Emperor Frederick II who prescribed practical studies in anatomy and on the dissecting table for all the medical schools of the Empire. The people at large had little confidence in new medicinal methods and medicaments and clung steadfastly to their old beliefs in the healing power of magical charms and miracle-working salves, roots, and plants.

Contacts with the Orient stimulated and enriched geographical and ethnological studies. The earth was still considered the center of the universe and the stage for a divinely directed drama. It was believed to be of globular shape, immovably fixed in space, while around it revolved the celestial spheres, consisting of fire, water, air, and the different constellations and circles of stars. Beyond these starry circles were the dwellings of the blessed in heaven, while the place of the condemned was thought to be located in the interior of the globe. The surface of the earth came to be better known in consequence of Crusades and commercial and missionary expeditions, the latter leading some members of the mendicant orders into the interior of Asia even before the fourteenth century. Nevertheless, the people were only too willing to believe the most wondrous tales of distant countries and continents.

The study of law was chiefly concerned with Roman civil law as embodied in the Code of Justinian (482–565) and Canon Law, based largely on Gratian's *Decretum*. The Universities of Bologna, Padua, and Orléans were among the most renowned centers of legal studies, while Salerno, Toulouse, and Paris were famous for their medical schools.

The Revival of Learning: Theology and Philosophy. The curriculum of the medieval university received its formal justification from the place that was allotted to theology and philosophy, the supreme sciences, from which all knowledge and learning had to take its directions. It is because of the major changes and innovations that occurred in the course of the twelfth and thirteenth centuries in these sciences and their mutual relations, and because of the cultural significance of these transformations, that theology and philosophy occupy a unique position in the general revival of learning and therefore require special treatment.

a) Scholasticism. Up to the twelfth century the leading clerical scholars of the West had been primarily interested in theological speculation from a theological point of view, leaving little or no room for rational argumentation, but referring their discussions and arguments to divine authority as supreme arbiter. There is, therefore, hardly any systematic and independent philosophical thought from the decline of the Neo-Platonic Greek schools of the second and third centuries to the medieval schools of the thirteenth century, if philosophy be understood as a natural interpretation of the universe and a general evaluation of being from the point of view of pure reason. The centuries that lie in between were taken up by the development of theological doctrine and dogma as embodied in the works of the Church Fathers of early Christian times (patristic epoch) and the writers of the early medieval centuries (Origines, Clement of Alexandria, Gregory of Nyssa, Augustine, etc. — Scotus Erigena, Gerbert of Aurillac, Anselm of Canterbury, etc.).

In the period from the sixth to the ninth century a new civilization was gradually built up on the ruins of the Roman empire and with the aid of the northern barbarians. Roman Law was adopted and codified, and the Carolingian Renaissance (cf. p. 51 sqq.) emerged from the "dark ages" of the migrations like a symbolical synthesis of the pagan and the Christian, the southern Mediterranean and the northern Germanic-Frankish forces of civilization. And this first great cultural awakening, retarded as it seemed by political anarchy, was nevertheless soon followed by decisive developments in the sphere of human thought. The period from 900 to 1200 prepared the way for the formation of a so-called "scholastic" theology and philosophy, whereby the limitations and respective claims of both disciplines were redefined, the problem of universals (universal ideas) received its classical formulation, and a definite method of rational disputation was worked out.

The redefinition of theology and philosophy amounted in reality to a declaration of independence on the part of human reason within its own proper sphere. Was human reason then henceforth considered as capable of grasping all the truth that there is? The philosopher-theologian would reply with Thomas Aquinas that there were certain truths which by their very nature transcended the capacity of human reason and would therefore have to be accepted on divine authority. Reason and revelation both proceeding from the same divine source, it seemed inconceivable to the scholastic philosopher that they could ever contradict each other, as long as man made the proper use of his God-given faculties.

In the fourteenth century the followers of the Franciscan friar William of Occam (c. 1300–1349) introduced the doctrine of the so-called "twofold truth," maintaining that what was philosophically true might be false theologically, and vice versa. This Occamist teaching, which exercised such a strong influence on Martin Luther's theological concepts ("I am of Occam's school"), grew out of a disregard for human reason for the sake of an overemphasis upon a supernaturally infused faith. Scholasticism, on the other hand, as developed by the Thomistic schools (the schools influenced by Thomas Aquinas) insisted that the theologian must refer in his arguments to God as the first cause of all things, whereas the philosopher's argumentation must be strictly rational, in that he considers things as they are constituted individually in themselves and, by making use of his sensory and intellectual experience, step by step works his way upward to the First Cause. The theologian argues deductively from cause to effect; the philosopher argues inductively from effect to cause. Under the influence of this revolutionary departure in the field of philosophical speculation Thomas Aquinas created a new theory of knowledge and completely reshaped the proofs of the existence of God as well as the traditional philosophical groundwork of moral philosophy.

The solution of the problem of universal ideas at which Thomistic scholasticism arrived is known as moderate or Aristotelian realism. It has been erroneously stated that scholasticism was nothing but an endless theorizing about the nature of universal ideas. The problem, however, is one that every philosophy in every part of the world has had to face. It concerns the reality of human concepts or ideas. To the so-called extreme realist (e.g., Plato) universal ideas, such as humanity, goodness, whiteness, have a real existence independent of the objects in which they are embodied. For the "nominalist" (e.g., Epicurus, William of Occam, our contemporary pragmatists and behaviorists, etc.), on the other hand, ideas have no reality whatsoever but are merely conventional symbols and names (nomen, nomina) that serve to signify and classify human perceptions.

Moderate realism or the realism of the Thomistic schools strikes a middle path between these extreme positions, admitting both the ideal and real validity of the universal concept. Perceptions inscribe the experiences of particular, individual objects of thought upon the mind as upon an "empty slate" (tabula rasa), but the spontaneity of the "active intellect" (intellectus agens) is capable of abstracting the universal qualities that are inherent in the individual objects of thought, thus forming an idea or universal concept. According to this theory, then, the individual is the real substance, and the universal idea owes its clear formulation to the abstractive and conceptual faculty of the human mind.

Thus the Thomistic philosopher affirmed with strong arguments the significance of individual objects and their lawful activities, and thereby established a solid basis for the investigations of natural science. Once created, each individuality rests in itself, standing on its own ground, but is sustained in its substantiality by that divine power to which it owes its existence. All created things together in their manifoldness and their individualization resemble their Creator and reveal His perfection in varying degrees. Individually and united they partake of the highest good, thus constituting an ordered universe. Man, finding himself placed in the center of such a universe, at the crossing point of matter and spirit, the highest animal and the lowest spirit, evidently a "mixed being," endowed with the irrational nature of the brute as well as with the faculties of intellect and free will, became more convinced of his personal value as philosophy encouraged him to be conscious of his own self, telling him that only a free contractual agreement could bind him to any individual or any authority.

b) *Aristotle Rediscovered.* The great intellectual revival of the thirteenth century would have been impossible without the abundance of philosophical stimulation that was received from the acquaintance with the great Arabic, Saracen, and Jewish thinkers whose works were introduced in Latin translations in the schools of France, England, Germany, and Italy. The Spanish city of Toledo provided an ideal meeting ground for Moslem and Christian civilization. The Arabic thinkers had not only preserved the Neo-Platonic tradition which was partly embodied in the Augustinian and Franciscan schools of Europe, but in Syria and Persia they had also become familiar with Aristotle (384–321 B.C.), the greatest speculative and scientific mind of antiquity and the tutor of Alexander the Great. It was through Arabic translations and interpretations that European speculation became re-acquainted with the writings of the great sage from Stageira, whose major works for centuries were believed to have been lost, following the suppression of philosophical studies in Athens by Emperor Justinian in 529. To the end of the twelfth century the knowledge of Aristotle had been confined to his *Logic* as expounded by the Neo-Platonist Porphyry and in the translation of Boëthius (470–525).

But the Aristotle who was now transmitted to the West was so strongly colored by the philosophical and theological convictions of the Mohammedan world that he had to be retranslated and reinterpreted to make his philosophy a suitable instrument for the expression of Western thought. Two Dominican scholars, Albert the Great ("the German") and his pupil, Thomas Aquinas, accomplished the great synthesis of Platonic, Aristotelian, and Christian philosophy.

Such an undertaking required courage as well as genius, at a time when Aristotelian philosophy was opposed in many quarters as being at odds with Christian doctrine, and when some Aristotelian writings had been condemned by the Church Synods of 1210 and 1215. Notwithstanding these obstacles, Albert and Thomas went about to demonstrate that Christian doctrine could find a natural support and solid foundation in the Aristotelian physics, metaphysics, and ethics.

c) *St. Albert the Great* (Albertus Magnus, *1193–1280*) *and St. Thomas Aquinas* (*1226–1274*). Being the greatest German scholar of the Middle Ages, Albert the Great was surnamed "the universal Doctor" (*Doctor Universalis*). He was a descendant of the counts of Bollstädt and a native of the town of Lauingen in Swabia. He was won for the Dominican Order by its general, Jordanus of Saxony. He taught in Hildesheim, Freiburg, Regensburg, Strasbourg, Cologne, and Paris; acted as provincial for the German Dominicans from 1254–1257; became bishop of Regensburg in 1260; and resumed teaching in Cologne in 1269. He built up his encyclopedic structure of knowledge on the foundations of Aristotelian thought, following the example of Aristotle in using both the inductive and deductive methods and in showing great interest in the natural sciences. In his long life he learned how to combine action with contemplation, never losing sight of the human, social, and practical implications and obligations of knowledge and wisdom. From the study of books he turned to his laboratory to work on the construction of mechanical instruments, to carry on chemical research, or to experiment with animals. And from the laboratory he might turn to the monastery gardens to give the gardener some advice as to the care of vineyards and vegetables or to tell some peasant about the best methods of cattle breeding. He trained falcons, wrote a book on falconry, and displayed great skill as an artisan.

In medieval legends Albert the Great lives on as a miracle worker and a magician. Nature and life were to him open books of whose perusal he never tired. He studied the literatures and philosophies of the Jews, the Arabs, and the Greeks; he devoted twenty years of his life to the commentation and interpretation of the works of Aristotle. His zeal led him far beyond the confines of his monastery, his pulpit, and his confessional. It became one of his major concerns to work for peace and co-operation among men, classes, and nations, so that he was many times called upon to settle religious, social, and political disputes by arbitration.

Albert's thoroughly human nature comes out frequently in his dealings with philosophical opponents. When accused of teaching indiscriminately the system of Aristotle, he answered that his commentaries represented an explanation of Aristotle rather than his own doctrine, and went on to say: "I mention this point because some of my opponents have grown so petrified in their indolence that they read and search the books of more talented writers for the sole purpose of exhibiting their own destructive criticism. It was this type of men who murdered Socrates; they drove Plato from Athens; they intrigued and plotted against Aristotle. They are in the councils of scholars what the liver is in the human body. For when the bile which issues from the liver flows into the body, it makes it bitter. Similarly, there are some scholars who are very bitter and bilious. And they pour their biliousness over all the others because they cannot tolerate the thought that others want to strive harmoniously for the attainment of the truth."

The sane and practical nature of Albert's thought and of his art of living is well summed up in these excerpts from his sermons: "That you weep one tear of love: that is more pleasing to God than that you weep tears of sorrow, even if they would flow as abundantly as the waters of the Danube. . . . Go out and find God yourself. That is more profitable to you than that you send all the saints and all the angels. . . . Judge and condemn nobody. That is more pleasing to God than that you shed your blood. . . . Accept with patience the dispensations of God's providence. That is more pleasing to Him than that you be carried away in rapture and ecstasy."

It was in Paris, the "city of philosophers," that the first meeting took place between Albert the German and his great pupil, Thomas Aquinas, the "angelic doctor" (*Doctor Angelicus*), who was destined to complete the imposing synthesis of ancient and medieval wisdom. Thomas was born at Rocca Secca in Italy, in the hereditary castle of the counts of Aquino. After having received his earliest education at the ancient Benedictine abbey of Monte Cassino, he took up the study of the liberal arts at Naples. In 1244 he joined the Dominican Order despite the protests of his family, and suffered a year's imprisonment at the hands of his brothers. After having regained his freedom he went to Paris (1245), and followed Albert to Cologne when the latter took charge of the new house of studies in that city. He returned to Paris in 1252 and passed the regular examinations to obtain the higher degrees. He taught at the University of Paris from 1256–1259, at the Pontifical Curia in Rome from 1259–1268, and returned to Paris once more to take a hand in the struggles between the Aristotelians and the followers of ·the Arabic philosopher Averroes as well as the conservative Augustinian-Franciscan theologians. In 1272, Thomas began to teach at the University of Naples, the foundation of Emperor Frederick II. He died in 1274, forty-eight years of age, on his journey to the General Church Council that was to be held in the French city of Lyon.

Seventy major works are listed in the official index of Thomas' writings, the most important ones being his commentaries on the Aristotelian physics, ethics, and metaphysics, the *Summa Contra Gentiles* (against the errors of the non-Christians), and the *Summa Theologica* (in three major parts, unfinished). The latter work contains a comprehensive exposition of the system of nature and grace in their hierarchical interrelation, intended as an irrefutable basis of Christian civilization. The method used in the *Summa Theologica* is the dialectical one, first developed in a rudimentary form by Peter Abelard (1069–1142) in his *Sic et Non* (Yes and No) principle, presenting successively argument and counterargument. The method was perfected by the English Franciscan philosopher, Alexander of Hales (1170–1245), and Thomas Aquinas. In its classical form it involves a triadic process, consisting of a prefatory statement of the arguments and counter-arguments of a given proposition, then follows the solution of the problem (the "body" of the article: *corpus articuli*); and, finally, the initial objections are answered point by point on the basis of the solution contained in the main part of the article.

When Thomas Aquinas first entered the University of Paris, his heavy build and his taciturnity caused his fellow students to nickname him the "dumb ox." After his death the faculty of arts referred to him as "the shining morning star, that sublime light that is destined to enlighten the whole world."

d) Mysticism. Scholasticism as such includes both theological and philosophical speculation. As a philosophical discipline it considers in its Thomistic form the intellect as the highest of human faculties, convinced that human reason is capable of penetrating deeply into the mysteries and causal relations of the universe, and of acquiring an analogical knowledge even of the supernatural. Mysticism, on the other hand, is a branch of theology and as such is concerned with a knowledge that transcends the realm of physical nature, in its mode as well as in its object. Christian mysticism aspires to the ultimate reunion of the spiritual soul with its divine origin, brought about by a contemplating love that is informed and infused by divine grace. The "mystical union" (*unio mystica*), of which all the mystics speak as the culminating point of their experience, signifies the blending of cognition and love, of intellect and will, and their unification with the divine will. Visions, ecstasies, and other extraordinary phenomena are entirely lacking on the highest levels of mystical experience. On the other hand, the mystic is transformed into what the Flemish mystical writer Ruysbroek (1294–1381) calls "the true social being," and what Thomas Aquinas has in mind when he discusses the interrelation of the active and contemplative forms of life. To the mystic all earthly things are interwoven with eternity. Elevated to the life of contemplation, he returns to his daily life and occupation to do the works of charity with a higher degree of intensity and efficiency. The pinnacle of Christian mysticism, therefore, is nothing but the highest possible earthly development of Christian life.

e) Mysticism and the German Language. It becomes quite intelligible, then, why Christian mysticism is not opposed to scholastic philosophy, even if some of the mystics use their own terminology to express experiences which have a tendency to escape hard-and-fast verbal patterns. Many of the great leaders of medieval philosophy were both philosophers and mystics, simply because they were both philosophers and theologians. This is especially true of the German mystics of the thirteenth and fourteenth centuries, men and women alike, even if they clothed their religious experiences at times in Neo-Platonic phraseology. Whenever they avail themselves of the German tongue they become linguistically creative, coining new words and imparting new meaning to old and conventional ones. If, like Meister Eckart, they are given charge of convents or beguinages (cf. p. 125), they find themselves compelled to adapt their sermons to the mental capacity of their listeners, thereby simultaneously softening and vitalizing the formalistic rigidity of the scholastic syllogisms. Thus they must be credited with having created a German philosophical language and terminology.

Meister Eckart (1260-1327) is the first German philosopher to use the German language in discussing problems of psychology, metaphysics, ethics, and speculative and practical theology. Not until the eighteenth century did the German language become the accepted medium of philosophical speculation, when Christian Thomasius (1655-1728, cf. p. 360 sq.) departed once more from the traditional use of Latin. Many of the German abstract nouns ending in the suffixes *"-heit," "-keit,"* and *"-ung"* owe their origin to the German mystics (e.g., *Wesenheit, Heiligkeit, Tröstung*).

f) Mysticism and German Literature. One of the centers of mystical devotion in the second half of the thirteenth century was the Cistercian convent of Helfta in the present province of Saxony, the home of Gertrud the Great, Mechthild of Hackeborn, and Mechthild of Magdeburg. While Gertrud and Mechthild of Hackeborn wrote in Latin, Mechthild of Magdeburg's *Fliessendes Licht der Gottheit* (the effluence of the divine light) is the first great mystical work in the German language; it is saturated with the sentiments of mystical lyricism and makes use of the motifs and verbal patterns of knightly and courtly culture. It was in the latter part of the thirteenth century that the Dominicans were given charge of a large number of convents in Germany. Out of sermons, lectures, and letters developed a special category of mystical literature, consisting of tracts, legends, verse, epistles, prayers, sentences, and biographies. A favorite literary form was the dialogue. Centers of German mysticism and mystical literature were Cologne, Basel, Strasbourg, and numerous Dominican monasteries and convents in Switzerland, Swabia, and Franconia.

Francis of Assisi's *Hymn to the Sun* sounded the *leitmotif* of mystical nature feeling and the love of nature. The world is resplendent with a beauty that the mystic does not esteem for its own sake but as the raiment of its Maker. Henry Suso (1295-1366) sees everywhere in nature the radiation of the uncreated Light: "If you take a close look, there is no creature so small that it could not serve as a stepping stone to carry you nearer to God."

g) Eckart, Suso, Tauler. Meister Eckart of Hochheim (1260-1327), a native of Thuringia, is the most ingenious of the German mystics, a metaphysician, preacher, and speculative theologian whose Latin works grow out of the Thomistic tradition of the Dominican Order. He has influenced later Catholic and Protestant mysticism as well as the nature philosophy and speculation of the German Romanticists and idealists of the nineteenth century. The "little spark of the soul" (*das Fünklein*) is the innermost part of the human being, the apex of the human mind, where the birth of the divine Logos and the mystical union with the Godhead takes place. Meister Eckart's style is dialectical, antithetical, and full of paradoxes, his terminology colored by Neo-Platonism; his statements are hyperbolical, unconventional, and daring to such a degree that he was not spared the accusation of heresy and the censorship of the Inquisition. Despite the sublimity of his speculative intuition he never lost sight of the near and the concrete, as is evidenced by this often quoted and characteristic utterance: "If a man were carried away in ecstasy like St. Paul, and he knew of a sick person who was in need of a plate of soup: I should consider it far better that you leave your rapture for charity's sake, so that you might serve with greater love that needy person."

Henry Suso (1295–1366), likewise a Dominican friar of noble descent and a native of Swabia, is the *Minnesänger* among the German mystics, a pupil of Meister Eckart's but less intellectualistic and more given over to lyrical sentiment. His *Booklet of Eternal Wisdom* is one of the most precious gems of mystical literature and the most widely read manual of devotion of the German Middle Ages.

John Tauler (*c.* 1300–1361) of Strasbourg, a Dominican preacher like Eckart and Suso, is more ethically and practically inclined than either of them. His style is popular and direct, but not lacking in depth and formal beauty. His personality and his writings are in conformity with the religious outlook of the new middle class, the inhabitants of the cities and the builders of the Gothic cathedrals. He was greatly admired by Martin Luther and exercised a profound influence on Luther's theology in its earlier phase.

Gothic Architecture. It has been said that the Gothic cathedral is a theological *Summa* in stone, the architectural manifestation of those spiritual forces that are alive in scholasticism and mysticism. But Gothic architecture is more than that: it embodies the culture and splendor of knighthood, the enthusiasm of the Crusader, the individualism of the burgher. It is, in short, the most striking expression of the changing and changed spirit of the age, the symbol of a new rhythm and meaning of life. It expresses the longing of a heart whose attachment is divided between heaven and earth, and whose restlessness heralds a radical break in the continuity of European civilization.

Gothic architecture is a European phenomenon, and Germany received it from northern France, where it had developed in the course of the twelfth and thirteenth centuries, only to adapt it to her own needs and shape it according to her own national spirit. A transitional style with mixed Romanesque and Gothic characteristics is occasionally found in the first half of the thirteenth century, while strict Gothic becomes the general method of building in Germany after the middle of the thirteenth century.

The term "Gothic art" was first used by Giorgio Vasari and other Italian artists and art critics of the sixteenth century who, enthralled by the art works of antiquity, considered Gothic architecture as a creation of the northern barbarians, the "Goths." The German Romanticists of the beginning nineteenth century in their enthusiasm for medieval art and culture made the epithet "Gothic" a title of honor.

The transformation from Romanesque to Gothic was then a gradual one. As an artistic style Gothic held sway over most of Europe to the middle of the fifteenth century. According to certain stylistic changes it is divided chronologically into early, high, and late Gothic.

The later examples of the Romanesque style (cf. p. 81 sqq.) suggest an increasing vertical tendency, owing especially to the tallness and the growing number of towers and spires. But the Romanesque architect was unable to achieve that strict verticality and extreme height of the building that seemed to be desired by the northern temperament, as long as he continued to use round arches for the construction of the nave vaults. The Gothic master builder broke with this tradition by dividing the nave into a series of oblong bays in place of square ones, and he vaulted these spaces with pointed arches instead of semicircular ones. As a result, the whole building began to take on a different shape, suggesting a dynamic vertical movement and rising to much greater height. However, the full utilization of the new structural tendencies depended on the even more important invention of the buttressing system. The flying buttresses and the nave piers, while introducing fascinating new aesthetic motifs in the external appearance of the building, fulfilled at the same time the practical function of carrying the lateral thrust of the roof and the vaults to the outside of the cathedral, so that the walls become actually disembodied. Being no longer required to carry the heavy load of masonry, they serve as a framework for the increasingly large stained-glass windows which in their turn add a new element to the artistic effects of the interior.

Ground plan and general appearance of the Gothic cathedral are characterized by a complication of detail and a simultaneous simplification of the structural whole. The choir frequently becomes double aisled, providing for an ambulatory with many small private chapels that radiate from it, indicating a growing desire for private devotions and a more personal relationship to the Deity. The façade becomes the dominating part of the building and symbolizes the Gothic striving for extraordinary effects.

The Gothic cathedral stands in the world no longer as a stranger as did the early Christian basilica, but as a princely ruler, conscious of the tasks and functions of the *Sacrum Imperium* of medieval civilization at its height. The interpenetration of spiritual and secular rulership and the increasing secularization of life appear in the many plant and animal motifs that characterize Gothic tracery and ornamentation. The artisan carves naturalistically and in motley array the foliage of maple, ivy, thistle, hops, strawberry, geranium, clover, violets, and others. The slender spires are crowned with the cruciform finial flower, the symbol of faith, hope, and charity, the theological virtues.

While Romanesque architecture was a monastic type of art, executed under monastic leadership, Gothic architecture is largely the result of the communal religious spirit of the laity in the cities. The guilds of stone-masons have their own local workshops (*Bauhütten*), their patron saints, their special trade-marks, carefully guarding the secrets and symbolisms of their profession. For the first time in the history of Western architecture the will of the masses becomes a decisive element in the stylistic development. They are the creators of those immense spaces of naves and aisles, the centers of the worshiping thousands (the Dome of Milan has a capacity of forty thousand) who listen to the oratory of preaching friars, watch the display of the colorful liturgical drama, and take part in religious spectacles and processions. "Here body and soul are immersed in a deep sea. . . . Human intellect loses itself in divine intellect. It is drowned as in a bottom-less sea" (John Tauler). Here the "pure inwardness" (*reine Innerlichkeit*) of Martin Luther and early Protestantism, the idea of a general priesthood, and the pantheistic nature-philosophy of the Renaissance are foreshadowed. The interior of the cathedral of the "late Gothic" style (*Spätgotik*) acquires, especially in Germany, more and more the character of a huge hall (*Hallenkirche*), the nave and side aisles reaching equal height and the pillars growing slender and tall like ever so many trees that spread their branches across the vaulting, where they form a netlike pattern of inter-twining lines (*Netzgewölbe*).

Gothic Arts and Crafts. Gothic sculpture has no independent existence but is subordinated to the laws and requirements of architecture. The body seems to move under a transcendental law. Its well-known *S* line appears as a fragment of an infinite movement that aims beyond itself and beyond the natural sphere. The female figure is depicted in frail and soft outlines, of slender build, with narrow shoulders and long, sensitive hands.

Worldly motifs and grotesque forms again indicate an increasing secular tendency. The glass windows of the northern aisle of the cathedral of Strasbourg depict the idealized portraits of the twenty-eight German kings who had ruled up to the year 1275. A wild and grotesque sense of humor is rampant in the gargoyles (*Wasserspeier*) and masks, in the stone-cut demons, goblins, dragons, and other phantastic imagery that were attached to buttresses, choir stools, moldings, vaulting shafts, and so forth.

The statuary of the cathedral in its inexhaustible wealth of invention confronted the individual with the totality of life, its possibilities and realities, embracing nature and supernature, birth, growth, and decay, health and sickness, alertness, weariness, and soft melancholy. The cathedral sculpture relates the epic of the Christian economy of salvation, beginning with the Old Testament (creation, patriarchs, prophets, kings, and queens), then proceeding to the dramatic events of the New Testament (birth and life of Christ, Apostles, confessors, virgins, martyrs), and finally culminating in the scenes of the Last Judgment and the themes of the Apocalypse (resurrection of the dead; the angels with the trumpets of doom; St. Michael with the scales; Christ in His glory, surrounded by the nine choirs of angels, etc.). Side by side are portrayed the Synagogue (Old Testament) with veil and broken lance and the *Ecclesia Triumphans* (New Testament). The starry sky with the signs of the zodiac, the motherly earth with the seasonal symbols of growth and decline, the months with their respective activities and benefits, the seven liberal arts as friendly helpers in the intellectual and moral formation of the Christian personality: they all share in illustrating and paraphrasing the meaning and the end of human life; they all want to impress upon man the necessity of that momentous decision that involves his sanctification and eternal happiness.

The special contribution of the Gothic style to the art of painting was the creation of the stained-glass window with its peculiar and intricate technique that has never again been equaled. Considering that some of these windows consist of several thousand pieces of glass, it is obvious that great skill and patience were required for their creation. The glass had to be cracked with the aid of glowing iron or coal, and in each and every piece the color had to be fixed by firing. Then the pieces had to be fitted together and held in place by strips of lead. The black lines of the leading served at the same time to separate color from color and keep the different colors from fusing in the eye of the spectator.

In the later phases of the development of Gothic architecture the stained-glass windows began to occupy more and more space, so that in the end the artists created veritable walls of glass, color, and light. But the life of the colored windows depends on the co-operation of the sunlight. They change their appearance according to the changing hours of the day and the changing seasons of the year. Living an unreal and transfigured life, they are the last thin walls to separate the church interior from the world outside, the last frail barrier erected between nature and spirit.

A special significance attaches to the "rose window," one of the favorite decorative motifs of the Gothic style. It is a large circular wheellike window that was inserted in the façade or other prominent parts of the building and consists of a multitude of glass panels separated by spokes of masonry. The "rose window" is a kind of mystical mathematics, symbolizing the convergence of supreme lawfulness and impenetrable mystery in the concept of the divine. From the inside of the cathedral it looks like a wheel of fire or a whirling sun of the skies.

The excellence of Gothic craftsmanship is manifested in the many works of the minor arts and crafts. Great care was taken in preparing dignified monuments for the dead. On top of the sarcophagus the defunct person was usually represented in either lying or kneeling position, clothed with the insignia of his office and dignity. Goldsmiths used the ornamental patterns of Gothic architecture in their shrines, reliquaries, monstrances, chandeliers, and crucifixes. The art of manuscript and book illumination flourished to the end of the medieval period. The Gothic miniatures frequently turn to secular subject matter, such as the description of tournaments, festivals, and hunting scenes. The *Hortus Deliciarum* (Garden of Delight) of the Abbess Herrad of Landsperg is a kind of encyclopedia, illustrated with 636 drawings.

The most outstanding German monument of miniature painting and book illumination is the Heidelberg Manesse Codex (*Heidelberger Liederhandschrift*) which originated in Zürich in Switzerland about 1330 and on its 854 pages contains about 7000 stanzas of 140 German *Minnesänger* and 131 illustrations. This manuscript belonged originally to the Swiss Councilor Manesse von Maneck, was temporarily in the possession of the Vatican Library, and, in 1888, was given to the University of Heidelberg by the crown prince of Germany. The artist-monks and secular painters began to take an equal share in the creation of this and similar works.

While the Gothic period was not favorable to the development of an independent art of painting, the stained-glass windows occupying most of the available clear wall space, the easel picture made its appearance at the end of the medieval period, calling for new techniques, new subject matter, and new objectives.

Court Epic; Folk Epic; Didactic and Lyric Poetry.

a) Court Epic. The age of the Hohenstaufen emperors, the struggles between emperors and popes, the adventures of knights and crusaders, the period of scholasticism, mysticism, and Gothic art gave Germany her first great literary awakening. The French versions of Greek, Byzantine, Carolingian, and Celtic themes, the French *chansons de geste,* the romances dealing with Charlemagne, Roland, Alexander, King Arthur, Parzival, Tristan provided the German authors with their subject matter. They sang and told about the heroic and idyllic past and present in a language that is known as Middle High German (*c.* 1100–1450) and Middle Low German (*c.* 1200–1600) and that was distinguished from Old High German by a flattening of the full sounding middle and end syllables (from *o* and *u* to *e:* OHG *salbôtum* to MHG *salbeten,* etc.) and by the partial diphthongization of *î, û, iu* to *ei, au, eu* (*hûs* to *haus,* etc.) and the monophthongization of *ie, uo, üe* to *î, û, û̂* (*stuol* to *stûl,* etc.).

The German court epic is truly national in tone and feeling, in its passionate longing, its joyous exaltation, its sweet melancholy, its somber brooding and doubting. It is international and cosmopolitan in its themes, its social and conventional setting, and in the characters of its heroes. The higher and lower nobility are the standard-bearers and protectors of poetry. Princely courts, such as the Babenbergers in Vienna or the counts of Thuringia on the Wartburg, become centers of literary movements. The place of the old Germanic hero is taken by the courtly cavalier. This new society was partly educated by its poets and singers, who were its servants as well as its rulers. It was the function of poetry as a social art to serve the entertainment and cultural education of the knightly class.

Henry of Veldeke (twelfth century), the first of the great German *Minnesänger,* is also the founder of the courtly epic, the singer of the love of Dido and Aeneas (*Aeneid*). The Swabian ministerial, Hartmann von Aue (*c.* 1160–1210), the perfecter of a classical Middle High German style, adopts some of the themes of the Old French poet, Chrestien de Troyes (*c.* 1140–

1191) in the Arthurian romances of *Erec* and *Ivein* and creates his own version of *Oedipus Rex* in the legend of Gregorius, the "virtuous sinner" who atones for having unwittingly married his own mother by lifelong penance on a barren rock in the open sea. In his *Poor Henry* (*Der arme Heinrich*) he strikes a theme that was later on treated by both Longfellow (*The Golden Legend*) and Gerhart Hauptmann: the Swabian knight who is cured of leprosy by the unselfish devotion and sacrifice of a peasant girl from the Black Forest.

Wolfram von Eschenbach (1165–1220) was an unlettered ministerial of the lower nobility. He never achieved in his works Hartmann's formal perfection and harmony of style, but his personality was richer and deeper, his language dark and heavy, expressing a dynamic vitality of thought, emotion, and imagination that would never submit to the clarity and symmetry of the literary conventions of the age.

A comparison of Wolfram's greatest work, *Parzival,* with its French source, *Li Conte de Graal* by Chrestien de Troyes, shows the originality and thoroughly Germanic quality of Wolfram's epic. The theme of the inborn nobility of man who through doubt, error, and complexity unwaveringly proceeds on his way to the castle of the Holy Grail and to that simplicity and wholeness of thinking and doing that constitutes the ideal of spiritual knighthood, is really an early version of the *Faust* problem and a true mirror of German mentality in the Hohenstaufen age.

The saga cycle centering in the Holy Grail is closely connected with the legends of King Arthur (*Artus*) and the knights of his Round Table. Arthur is the leader of the British Celts in their campaigns against Scots, Angles, and Saxons. Gavein, Ivein, Erec, Tristan, Parzival are among the most distinguished knights of the Round Table. The Holy Grail (German, *Gral;* from Romanic, *gréal;* Middle Latin, *gradalis:* "vessel") is that precious vessel that was used by Christ at the Last Supper and by Joseph of Arimathea to receive the blood of the Crucified. To be a guardian of the Grail is the privilege and reward of that highest order of spiritual knighthood whose members are called Knights Templar. According to the legend, Titurel, the son of a French king, erected the castle of the Holy Grail, Montsalvage (MHG: *munsalvâtsche,* "wild mountain") on Spanish soil, in the midst of a wild, impenetrable forest.

Parzival's life receives its meaning and sanction from the German knightly culture of which he is a part, and his vocation to the kingship of the Holy Grail reads like a commentary on the political and spiritual implications of the Hohenstaufen claims to the *Sacrum Imperium*. Parzival's doubts are alleviated and resolved not by the administration of the sacrament of penance and the priestly absolution, as was the case in Chrestien's version, but by his trust in the consoling word of Trevrizent, his uncle, and by divine grace, whose all-pervading presence he has divined in the awakening of nature on Good Friday morning: "First of all he thought of his Creator who had made this whole world."

The author of the first German literary work that glorifies the passion
of earthly love was probably a cleric. Master Gotfrid von Strasbourg's
(† *c.* 1215) epic fragment, *Tristan and Isolt,* surpasses even Hartmann von
Aue's epic art in its clarity and purity of form. Gotfrid's poem follows the
model of the story told by the Anglo-Norman poet, Thomas, but the subject
matter is treated with originality and ingenuity. All the forms and forces
of the age of chivalry, with light and shade evenly distributed, refined and
with a considerable amount of sophistication, are psychologically interwoven
with the overmastering passion that draws the hearts of Tristan and Isolt
inevitably into an abyss of sinful bliss and moral anarchy.

b) Folk Epic (Heroic Epic). Unknown poets are the authors of those
great literary monuments of the twelfth and thirteenth centuries that are
known as folk epics or heroic epics (*Heldenepos*). They differ in form and
content from the knightly and courtly literature of the same period and
seem to follow different ethical standards and social ideals. The author of
the *Lay of the Nibelungs (Nibelungenlied, c.* 1170) draws his themes from
the Germanic past, especially from the centuries of the migrations, and he
uses a style that is less refined and more rugged than that of the court epics.
In place of the knightly virtues of steadiness (*staete*), discipline (*zucht*),
moderation (*mâze*), we find the irrepressible and imponderable forces of
unrestrained passion, in love and hatred, in doing and suffering, in victory
and defeat, in life and death, loyalty (*triuwe*) being the only Germanic
character trait that is glorified in folk and court epics alike. The knightly
and Christian concepts are merely an external gloss, barely covering the
brutal and unbridled rule of the instincts of a seemingly different race of
men and women. A sense of tragic frustration permeates the *Lay of the
Nibelungs,* which in its unmitigated pessimism deprives this monumental
work of a final metaphysical significance. The Middle Ages added a sequel
to the poem, entitled *The Lament (Die Klage),* in which the attempt was
made to explain the inexorable immensity of the Nibelungen tragedy and
to introduce into it an element of conciliation.

Siegfried's death through the treachery of Hagen, and Kriemhild's
revenge that leads to the destruction of the Nibelungs, are the major themes
of the poem. Interest is focused upon the personal destiny of its heroes and
heroines, and no attention is paid to the world-historic setting or the social
background of its events. From the point of view of the Middle Ages the
geographical setting of the *Lay of the Nibelungs* must have appeared as
an unreal one, reaching back into the remoteness of the fifth and sixth
centuries of the Christian era. Even more unreal in its setting and almost
wholly lacking in distinct historical contour appears the second of the
great heroic epics of the German Middle Ages, the *Lay of Kudrun (Gudrun-
lied)* that was composed about 1230. The scene is laid in the North Germanic
regions of the North Sea. If the *Nibelungenlied* conjures up the period of
the migrations, the *Lay of Kudrun* re-creates the atmosphere of the Viking
Age, thereby again transcending and evading the conventional requisites

of the age of chivalry and the courtly epic. The poem tells of the abduction of Kudrun by an unsuccessful suitor, her years of trials and sufferings, and her final rescue by her lover, Herwig. This main theme is preceded by a parallel set of motifs in the Viking story of the abduction of Hilde, the daughter of Hagen. While artistically the Kudrun epic equals the poem of the Nibelungs, it does not reach the latter's scope as a symbol of Germanic mythology and psychology. It combines the features of family chronicle and idyl, relating its episodes of Viking raid, rape, revenge, reunion, and happy end in orderly sequence, but lacking the dramatic intensity and suspense of the Nibelungen tragedy.

c) Didactic Poetry. In a category by itself but not without a didactic implication is the poem *Meier Helmbrecht,* which was composed about the middle of the thirteenth century by Wernher "the gardener." Written in the vein of the later village novel, it presents a vivid and realistic picture of the age of decaying chivalry, relating the story of a young farmer who, dissatisfied with his lowly social position, becomes a highwayman and is finally hanged by angry peasants.

Didactic rules of life as well as acrimonious attacks upon immoral practices in Church and State are contained in Freidank's poem *Bescheidenheit* (a book of useful advice, *c.* 1230). Manuals of knightly discipline and behavior were composed by the author who is known by the name of "Winsbeke" (*Herr von Windsbach*) and by Thomasin von Zirclaria (*c.* 1216). With a didactic purpose the Franconian poet named "Stricker" wrote the story of a clerical impostor (*Der Pfaffe Amis, c.* 1230), and moralizing tendencies are embodied in Hugo von Trimberg's realistic poem *Der Renner* (1300) and in the Dominican friar Ulrich Boner's *Edelstein* (*Jewel,* 1330), a collection of fables and parables.

d) Lyric Poetry ("*Minnesang*"). The period of court epic and heroic epic was also the great age of a unique type of lyric poetry known as *Minnesang* (love song). It is a form of social love poetry and as such is distinguished from the later *Liebeslied* as well as from the simple *Volkslied.* It is the expression of the knight's homage to some noble lady and is therefore determined in form and content by the code of knightly etiquette.

The literary pattern of *Minnesang* was originally developed in the Arabic court circles of Andalusia and later on adapted to the social environment of the knightly aristocracy of the Provence, where the Hellenistic and Latin sense of poetic form had never been lost. The art of the Provençal *troubadour* (inventor) was intimately associated with music. His song was accompanied on the lute or the fiddle.

From the Provence, where it had developed at the beginning of the twelfth century, the art of the *troubadour* migrated to the north of France and from there to the German Rhineland. The forms of the *Minnesang,* however, soon became stereotyped and artificial, and only poets of more than average talent were capable of breaking through the wall of conventions to give vent to natural and personal feeling.

Among those who were thus able to rise above the limitations of a poetic honor code, Walther von der Vogelweide (*c.* 1170–1230) stands out as the greatest lyrical genius prior to Goethe. What imparts to his poetry its distinctive character is the perfect blend of form and content, the universality of his outlook, the integral realism and absolute sincerity of his poetic experience.

Walther was in all probability a native of the southern Tyrol. As a member of the lower nobility and a man without means he wandered as a gleeman from court to court, from country to country, from the Adriatic to the Baltic, from Styria into France, thereby gaining that broad knowledge of human nature and worldly affairs that is reflected in his works. He was drawn into the feud of the Welfs and Waiblingens (cf. p. 89), and in the end the young Hohenstaufen, Frederick II (cf. p. 92 sq.), rewarded Walther's allegiance with a small fief that brought with it long-desired economic security.

Walther's poems are based on personal experience, and they deal with every phase of life that entered into the circumference of his personal vision. He affirmed wholeheartedly the universalistic tendencies of his age, which confronted him practically in the rival claims of Empire and Papacy. He sided with the Hohenstaufens in their rejection of papal theocracy. The education, outlook, and social form of knightly culture are Walther's own, but he animates them with the breath of his genius.

In accordance with the broad scope of his interests and his knowledge Walther's poetry extends from the praise of "uncourtly" love (*niedere Minne*) to the mystical veneration of the Madonna; from trifling yet intimate observations to the passionate call to arms in the interest of some great political, social, or religious cause. The treasury of Walther's lyrical themes is thus well-nigh inexhaustible. He sees the universal significance in individual things and events, and he derives personal applications from general rules and universal principles. His nature poetry combines realism with idealism; it is as naïve and direct as it is artful and thoughtful. His ardent love for his German land, for German breeding, German women, German scenery, for everything German made him wish for the rebirth of an enlightened German-Christian Imperium under Hohenstaufen leadership.

Thus in Walther von der Vogelweide the disparate forces of medieval German culture were once more united, integrated, and poetically transfigured, while in State and Church the cleavage of minds had already begun to disrupt the ideological bases of medieval society. In one of his last poems Walther looks back upon his life and upon the waning splendor of knightly culture, and he realizes that the world that is his world begins to grow old, and that winter and death are approaching. Thus his singing, that had begun with the joyous jubilation of the awakening spring, ends with a note of resignation, intimidation, and sadness.

The Medieval Theory of Art. It is rather amazing that in an age that abounded with works of sublime beauty there should not be developed a definite philosophy of art. As a matter of fact, medieval views on art and beauty have to be gleaned from the works of philosophers who, aside from occasional remarks, gave no special attention to the aesthetic problem as such. Art in the Middle Ages, it seems, was a social phenomenon to such an extent that its manifestation in human works was taken for granted, constituting an integral element in the everyday experience of every man, woman, and child.

If we try to disengage the few references to artistic creation in the works of the schoolmen from their metaphysical frame, it appears that a work of art was considered as proceeding from the exercise of right reason in the sphere of creative activity. It was the business of the artist to make things that needed making and to make them as well as possible, so that they would fit their purpose. In this way art signified a triumph of mind over matter, impressing some ideal form upon some proportionate material.

Prudence was required for *doing* things in the right way. Artistic skill was required for *making* things in the right way. Prudence was primarily concerned with the effect of an action upon the doer; art was primarily concerned with the effect of the creative act upon the work that was to be created. Both activities proceeded from the exercise of right reason.

Any human work that was governed by the rule of right reason was therefore a work of art, whether it was a question of making shoes or illuminating manuscripts or building cathedrals. God, as the world's Creator, was the supreme Artist; man was "His workmanship," "His husbandry," but also the continuator of God's creation and so His collaborator and a creator in the second degree. Thus there was no distinction between artist and artisan: every artisan was an artist and every artist an artisan.

All the arts were considered both useful and beautiful; all were socially and religiously significant. Some arts are more closely related to matter, while some are of greater appeal to the mind, and so the medieval philosopher made a distinction between "servile" and "liberal" arts. In the contemplation and appreciation of beauty, mind, will, and sense rejoice because they are immersed in the superabundance of being. In other words, the beautiful is a free gift that is superadded to works that are properly planned, fashioned, and executed.

It was the opinion of Thomas Aquinas that art followed the ways of nature, and that nature followed the ways of God (*Summa Theologica,* I, 145, 8). That does not mean that it is the task of the artist to imitate or duplicate the works of nature, but rather to follow nature in its ways of operation. Thus the medieval artists did not copy nature, but interpreted, deciphered, transfigured it. Nature was a sealed book, full of miracles and mysteries. It was the privilege of the artist to open its seals and to disclose the meaning of its pages, pictures, and signs. The artist was an interpreter of life, having experienced life in the fullness of its meaning and having touched the splendor of that form that determines the essence of all things.

PART III. DECLINE, REVOLT, REFORM, RESTORATION

1261   Rudolf wages war against King Ottokar II of Bohemia
1273–1291   Rudolf of Hapsburg, king and emperor of Germany
1278   Rudolf's victory over Ottokar on the Marchfield establishes the dynastic power of the house of Hapsburg
1291   Foundation of the Swiss Confederation of Schwyz, Uri, and Unterwalden
1292–1298   Emperor Adolf of Nassau, a Rhenish count, Rudolf's successor, is defeated and slain in 1298 by Rudolf's son, Duke Albrecht of Austria
1298–1308   Emperor Albrecht I of Austria; assassinated by a member of his own family (John Parricida, duke of Swabia)
1308–1313   Emperor Henry VII, count of Luxemburg
1309–1376   The "Babylonian Captivity" of the popes at Avignon
1310–1313   Henry VII's expedition to Italy and his coronation in Rome. He wins Bohemia for his son, John
1313–1330   Frederick "the Fair" of Hapsburg and Louis, duke of Bavaria, struggle for the imperial crown
1314–1347   Emperor Louis IV, the Bavarian, opposed by Pope John XXII (1316–1334)
1327–1330   Louis's expedition to Italy and his coronation by the people of Rome
1338   The "Electors' Union" (*Kurverein*) of Rense establishes the validity of imperial elections without papal approval
1347–1378   Charles IV, of the House of Luxemburg, German emperor and king of Bohemia, son of King John of Bohemia
1349–1350   The "Black Death," the flagellants, and the persecution of the Jews
1356   The "Golden Bull," defining the methods of imperial elections, making the electoral princes virtually independent sovereigns
1378–1400   Emperor Wenceslaus (Wenzel), the elder of Charles's two sons, deposed by the Rhenish Electors in 1400
1378   Beginning of the "Great Schism" in the Western Church
1386   Victory of the Swiss Confederation over Duke Leopold of Austria near Sempach
1400–1410   Emperor Rupert (Ruprecht), count palatine of the Rhine
1410–1437   Emperor Sigismund, king of Hungary (since 1387), younger brother of Wenceslaus
1410   Battle of Tannenberg: the Poles vanquish the Teutonic Knights
1414–1418   Church Council of Constance; end of the "Great Schism"
1415   John Huss is burned at the stake
1419–1436   The Hussite Wars
1438–1439   Emperor Albrecht II, son-in-law of Sigismund; the imperial crown returns to the house of Hapsburg
1440–1493   Emperor Frederick III, cousin of Albrecht II
1440–1450   Civil war in Switzerland. The last Hapsburg possessions in Switzerland are lost.
1448   Concordat of Vienna between Frederick III and the Holy See

c. 1450   Invention of the art of printing by John Gutenberg (*c.* 1400–1468) of Mainz

1452   Frederick III receives the imperial crown in Rome, the last coronation of a German emperor in Rome

1457   The "Marienburg," stronghold of the Teutonic Knights, taken by the Poles

1460   Personal Union of Schleswig-Holstein with Denmark

1466   The territory of the Order of Teutonic Knights (West Prussia plus Ermland) is ceded to Poland; East Prussia becomes a feudatory of Poland

1477   Frederick's son Maximilian, by his marriage to Mary, the daughter and heiress of Charles the Bold of Burgundy, secures the Netherlands and the Free County of Burgundy for the Hapsburg family possessions

1483–1546   Martin Luther, reformer

1491–1556   Ignatius of Loyola, founder of the Society of Jesus

1491   Frederick III negotiates a treaty with Ladislas IV, the Polish ruler of a united Bohemia and Hungary, to secure for the Hapsburgs the hereditary succession in Hungary

1493–1519   Emperor Maximilian I, son of Frederick III

1495   The Diet of Worms; constitutional reform and promulgation of a perpetual Land Peace (*ewiger Landfriede*)

1504   Francis of Taxis establishes the first postal route between Brussels and Vienna

1508   Maximilian I accepts the title "Chosen Roman Emperor"

1512   The Diet of Cologne; the Empire is divided into ten major judicial districts (*Landfriedenskreise*)

1517   Martin Luther nails ninety-five theses on the portal of the castle church in Wittenberg

1519   Ulrich Zwingli's reformation in Zurich (Switzerland)

1519–1556   Emperor Charles V, son of Philip the Fair and Joanna the Insane

1520   Publication of Luther's three revolutionary pamphlets: (1) *To the Christian Nobility of the German Nation;* (2) *On the Babylonian Captivity of the Church;* (3) *On the Freedom of a Christian Man* — Condemnation of forty-one sentences in Luther's writings by the Papal Bull *"Exsurge Domine"* (June 15) — Luther is threatened with the ban of the Church; he burns the papal Bull and a copy of the book of Canon Law (Wittenberg, December 10)

1521   Luther is banned by the Church (Bull, *"Decet Romanum"* of January 3) — Diet of Worms — Luther refuses to recant and is declared under the ban of the Empire by the "Edict of Worms" — Charles V's brother Ferdinand receives the Austrian possessions of the Hapsburgs

1521–1526   Charles V's first war against Francis I, king of France

1522   First edition of Luther's translation of the *New Testament;* 1534: first edition of his translation of the entire *Bible*

1522–1523   Diet of Nuremberg — revolt of the knights of the Empire

1524–1525   The Peasants' War

1525   Luther's marriage to Katherine of Bora (June 13); he publishes his pamphlet *Against the Murderous and Rapacious Hordes of Peasants*

1526   Peace of Madrid between Charles V and Francis I — the First Diet of Speyer — Ferdinand (I) inherits Bohemia and Hungary

1526–1529   Charles V's second war against Francis I

1529   Peace of Cambrai between Charles V and Francis I — The Second Diet of Speyer: the "evangelical" estates of the Empire protest against the decrees prohibiting the spread of the Lutheran doctrines ("Protestants") — Vienna is threatened by the Turks — Disputation of Marburg between Luther and Zwingli, concerning the doctrine of the Eucharist (the Lord's Supper)

1530   Coronation of Charles V in the cathedral of Bologna by Pope Clement VII, the last coronation of an emperor by a pope — Diet of Augsburg: Presentation of the Protestant "Augsburg Confession" (*Confessio Augustana*), composed by Melanchthon — Formation of the Protestant League of Schmalkalden — Promulgation of the *"Carolina"* (imperial code of criminal law)

1531   Ferdinand (I) becomes Roman-German king — Death of Zwingli in the battle of Kappel against the Catholic cantons of Switzerland.

1532   The religious peace of Nuremberg

1533   Peace between King Ferdinand and Sultan Soliman

1534–1535   Rule of the Anabaptists in Münster

1536–1538   Charles V's third war against Francis I

1540   Foundation of the Society of Jesus (Jesuit Order) by Ignatius of Loyola

1541   John Calvin's reformation in Geneva

1542–1544   Charles V's fourth war against Francis I

1544   Charles V invades France; Peace of Crespy — Diet of Speyer: Charles V and the Protestants unite for the purpose of defending the Empire against France and the Turks

1545–1563   Council of Trent: the Catholic Restoration

1546–1547   War of Schmalkalden between Protestants and Catholics

1548   The Diet of Augsburg accepts the "Interim," a provisional settlement of the religious dispute

1552   Duke Maurice of Saxony betrays the cause of the emperor; Occupation of the bishoprics of Metz, Toul, and Verdun by King Henry II of France — Treaty of Passau, favoring the Protestant cause — Unsuccessful campaign of Charles V against Henry II

1555   The religious peace of Augsburg

1556   Emperor Charles V abdicates and retires to a Spanish monastery; he dies in 1558

1556–1564   Emperor Ferdinand I, brother of Charles V

1564–1576   Emperor Maximilian II, son of Ferdinand I

1576–1612   Emperor Rudolf II, son of Maximilian II

1583–1634   Albrecht von Wallenstein, duke of Friedland and Sagan

1585–1642   Cardinal Richelieu

1602–1661   Cardinal Mazarin

1608   Foundation of the Protestant Union, headed by Frederick IV, elector palatine

1609	Foundation of the Catholic League, headed by Duke Maximilian of Bavaria
1612–1619	Emperor Matthias, brother of Rudolf II
1618–1623	*The Bohemian Revolt.*
1619–1637	Emperor Ferdinand II, grandson of Emperor Ferdinand I, cousin of Emperor Matthias
1619	Election of Frederick V, Elector Palatine, son-in-law of King James I of England, as king of Bohemia
1620	The combined armies of the emperor and the Catholic League under General Tilly defeat the Bohemians on the White Hill near Prague
1623	Duke Maximilian I of Bavaria (1598–1651) receives the Upper Palatinate and Frederick V's Electorate
1624–1629	*The Saxon-Danish War*
1626	Wallenstein defeats Count Mansfeld at Dessau — Tilly defeats King Christian IV of Denmark at Lutter am Barenberg (Brunswick)
1628	Wallenstein besieges unsuccessfully the city of Stralsund
1629	The Edict of Restitution, restoring to the emperor all ecclesiastical estates, secularized after the Treaty of Passau (1552)
1630	Dismissal of Wallenstein
1630–1635	*The Swedish War*
1630	Gustavus Adolphus, king of Sweden (1611–1632), lands on German soil (Pomerania)
1631	Tilly storms the city of Magdeburg and is defeated by Gustavus Adolphus at Breitenfeld
1632	Wallenstein is called back and given the supreme command of the imperial armies — Death of Tilly — Death of Gustavus Adolphus in the Battle of Lützen
1634	Wallenstein is assassinated in Eger (Bohemia)
1635	Peace of Prague
1635–1648	*The Swedish-French War*
1637–1657	Emperor Ferdinand III, son of Emperor Ferdinand II
1640–1688	Frederick William, the Great Elector (of Brandenburg)
(1643–1715)	Louis XIV, king of France
1644–1648	Peace assemblies at Münster and Osnabrück (Westphalia)
1648	*Peace of Westphalia*
1683–1699	The Great Turkish War
1683	Siege of Vienna
1684	Formation of the "Holy League" between Austria, the republic of Venice, and the papacy
1687	Victory of the "Holy League" at Mohács (Hungary)
1697	Victory of Prince Eugene of Savoy at Zenta (Hungary)
1699	Peace of Karlowitz
1715–1718	The Second Turkish War
1716–1717	Victories of Prince Eugene at Peterwardein and Belgrade
1718	Peace of Passarowitz

Chapter 7

THE END OF THE MIDDLE AGES: DISINTEGRATION OF THE EMPIRE AND THE RISE OF THE TERRITORIAL STATES

The End of the Interregnum. Rudolf of Hapsburg. The period of the *Interregnum* with its unchecked lawlessness was brought to an end in 1273, when the leading German princes elected Rudolf of Hapsburg as German king, thus at least nominally restoring the "Holy Roman Empire of the German Nation." The fourteenth and fifteenth centuries saw the continuance of the imperial dignity under different houses, finally reverting to the Hapsburgs, who were to retain the imperial title until the dissolution of the Empire in 1806. But while France and England developed during the following two centuries into powerful centralized nations with a unified civilization, the German Empire developed a progressive weakness in its political organization that found only partial and temporary compensation in the flourishing culture of its individual territorial states, under the rule of secular and ecclesiastical princes. The emperors no less than the territorial lords were primarily interested in the aggrandizement of their family possessions or their social prestige, and thus they mostly lost sight of the greater national and international issues at stake. Protective leagues of cities and districts within the Empire were organized for the defense of national and communal interests, a defense which the emperor could not and would not provide.

Rudolf of Hapsburg (1273-1291) owed his election to the fact that the German princes had been on the lookout for a ruler who would be strong enough to put an end to the anarchical conditions in the Empire, yet whose prestige and personality would constitute no danger to their own particularistic and dynastic ambitions. The new emperor was a prince of moderate wealth and influence, whose family possessions were located in the German south, extending from the Alpine passes into the Alsatian regions. His upright and noble character won him the confidence of the people, and he succeeded in checking lawlessness and securing peace in the Empire.

He wisely abstained from reviving the Italian policies of the Hohenstaufens, but concentrated his energies on the acquisition of land and power for his family, thus laying the foundation for the future greatness of the Hapsburg dynasty.

Ottokar II of Bohemia, who had refused to recognize the validity of Rudolf's election, was defeated and fatally wounded on the Marchfield near Dornkrut (Lower Austria) in 1278, and Rudolf took from him Austria and its dependent territories. The emperor gave some of these conquered lands to his son Albrecht and thereby aroused the fear and suspicion of the electoral princes to such an extent that upon Rudolf's death in 1291 they passed over Duke Albrecht of Austria and gave their vote to Adolf of Nassau (1292–1298), an obscure Rhenish count, adventurer, and ruthless politician, who was defeated and slain by a dissenting group of German princes under the leadership of Duke Albrecht.

The Hapsburg, Wittelsbach, and Luxemburg Emperors (1298–1438). Emperor Albrecht I (1298–1308) is described in contemporary chronicles as a stern and energetic ruler, "hard as diamond." In his attempt to stand up for his imperial rights he had to cross swords with the electoral princes and was assassinated by his own nephew, John "the Parricide," duke of Swabia. The Electors had gotten a rather bitter taste of the menacing power of the house of Hapsburg and decided to offer the crown to Count Henry of Luxemburg, who succeeded Albrecht as Emperor Henry VII (1308–1313). His exalted conception of the imperial dignity prompted him to embark on an expedition to Italy to pacify the warring members of the Welf and Waiblingen factions and to receive the imperial crown in Rome in the traditional fashion. He was hailed by the exiled Florentine poet Dante (1265–1321) as the bringer of peace and justice and was crowned Roman emperor in 1312. But he proved himself a partisan of the Waiblingen cause and died only one year later, without having succeeded in settling the family feud. Before leaving for Italy Henry had secured an Eastern outpost for the territorial power of the house of Luxemburg by obtaining the election of his son, John, as king of Bohemia.

In Germany Henry's death was followed by another disputed election, and this time the Hapsburgs in the person of Frederick "the Fair," son of the late Emperor Albrecht I, met with the opposition of Louis of Bavaria, pretender of the house of Wittelsbach. A civil war that broke out after Frederick and Louis had both been crowned by their respective adherents ended with Louis' victory and Frederick's imprisonment. Louis subsequently used Frederick as a pawn in his dealings with Pope John XXII (1316–1334), the last great character on the papal throne in the drawn-out struggle between Empire and Papacy in the Middle Ages. Frederick was released after a captivity of two years and a half and was later on accepted by Louis as coregent.

When Pope John XXII interfered in the struggle between Louis and Frederick, claiming that Louis should have appealed to Rome for arbitration, and demanding Louis' resignation under penalty of excommunication, it seemed as if the times of Henry IV, Frederick Barbarossa, and Frederick II had once more returned, with accusations and counteraccusations being hurled back and forth. But the political constellations had changed, and the events that had preceded the papal threat aided in rendering it ineffective. Louis had started upon an expedition to Rome and had been crowned on the Capitoline Hill by the Roman people and anointed by two excommunicated Italian bishops. The pope's residence was no longer in Rome but in Avignon, where the papacy in its "Babylonian Captivity" (1309–1376, cf. p. 172 sq.) was more and more becoming a servile instrument of the French monarchy. Louis heaped a flood of invectives upon John XXII, declared him deposed, and secured the election of an antipope. But only ten weeks later both emperor and antipope had to flee from Rome for fear of being stoned by the populace. Louis tried to make his peace with Benedict XII, the successor of John XXII, but was appalled by Benedict's demands, including unconditional surrender of all his imperial rights and dignities until his claims and titles should have been vindicated by the Church. The result was a joint proclamation of the "Electors' Union" (*Kurverein*), issued at Rense (1338), in which the Electors came to the defense of Louis and the imperial prerogatives. The proclamation stated that "since the Empire depends on God alone, he who is elected by a majority of votes can take the title of king and exercise all sovereign rights without need of consent or confirmation of the Pope."

Louis failed to take advantage of the strength of his position and antagonized the German princes by the inconsistency and selfishness of his political moves. The opposition party rallied around the house of Luxemburg, demanded the deposition of Louis, and secured the election of Charles of Luxemburg, one year before Louis' death (1347). The new emperor, Charles IV (1346–1378), had inherited the kingdom of Bohemia from his father, King John, the son of Emperor Henry VII. He had been educated in France, Bohemia, and Italy, and had received an intellectual training and diplomatic schooling that proved a great aid in the troublesome times into which he was born and in which he tried to steer a middle course between social, political, and religious extremes. It was his supreme ambition to restore the glory of the German empire, with his native and hereditary state of Bohemia as the center of gravity, and with the acceptance of a hereditary succession of the house of Luxemburg. In his autobiography he appears as a man of strong religious convictions with definite leanings toward mysticism.

Charles's interest was so much centered in his Bohemian lands that Emperor Maximilian I (cf. p. 167 sq.) was to refer to him later on as "the arch-father of Bohemia and the arch-stepfather of the Empire." Bohemia developed under his rule into one of the best organized states of the Empire, and its flourishing culture found an external expression in the foundation of the University of Prague (1348), the first university in German-speaking lands and the personal creation of Charles IV. By means of diplomatic schemes, financial transactions, and marriage unions he incorporated in the Bohemian kingdom the territories of Brandenburg, Lower Lusatia, and part of the Upper Palatinate. Brandenburg, which he took from the house of Wittelsbach, fell to his son, Sigismund, upon the emperor's death in 1378, who bestowed it on Frederick of Hohenzollern in 1415. Alliances with Poland and Hungary assured the security of the eastern boundaries of the Empire.

As far as the Empire at large was concerned, Charles nourished no illusions as to the solidity of its political and social structure. He was conscious of the inherent weakness of the Imperial Diet and of the partyism among princes and nobles which was to blame for the internal disintegration and for a weak and vacillating foreign policy. He felt that the best he could do was to take a number of measures to prevent further decline and to enforce at least a semblance of order. At the Diet of Nuremberg in the year 1356 Charles IV promulgated the famous "Golden Bull," whose significance has been compared by some authors with that of the British *Magna Charta Libertatum* of 1215. It defined the powers of the electoral princes, dealt with the proceedings at elections and the order of succession to an Electorate, and most of its provisions remained valid to the very end of the Holy Roman Empire in 1806. One of its major effects was a remarkable increase in the prestige and independence of the members of the electoral college. They were to have full sovereign power within their territories, and from the judgments of their courts no one could henceforth appeal to the emperor. The electorates were to be hereditary, and the territories of the secular electors were to be inherited according to the rule of primogeniture (succession of the first-born son). There were to be seven electors, four of them secular princes (the king of Bohemia, the duke of Saxony, the margrave of Brandenburg, the count palatine of the Rhine), and three ecclesiastical princes (the archbishops of Mainz, Köln, and Trier).

In laying down the provisions of the rudimentary form of a written national constitution Charles had tried to make the best of an extremely precarious situation. Without curtailing the privileges of the territorial princes he had managed to secure the possession of two of the most important electoral votes, those of Bohemia and Brandenburg, for the German emperor and the house of Luxemburg. The elections in the future were to be held at Frankfurt, and the ceremonious display of the imperial insignia, the crowns of Aachen and Milan, the orb, the staff, the scepter, and the sword were to enhance the splendor of such an occasion.

While Charles had thus undeniably consolidated the power of his house and outwardly added to the territorial possessions and the prestige of the Empire, it is none the less apparent that the prestige of the imperial office itself had suffered greatly from the surrender of so much power to the territorial princes. The rule of Charles's sons marked a further step in the gradual decline of imperial power. Wenceslaus (Wenzel, 1378–1400), the elder of the two, was an habitual drunkard, and in 1400 he was deposed by the electors and replaced by Rupert, count palatine of the Rhine (1400–1410). After his death the crown was offered to Wenzel's younger brother, Sigismund (1410–1437), who had been king of Hungary since 1387 through his marriage with the heiress of that country. While his diplomatic skill in directing the proceedings of the Council of Constance (1414–1418) achieved a major triumph by putting an end to the "Great Schism" of the Church (cf. p. 173 sq.), he became involved in the ferocious Hussite Wars that followed the burning of John Huss (cf. p. 176 sqq.) in 1415. It was in the same year that Sigismund gave the March of Brandenburg to Frederick of Hohenzollern (the name derived from the ancestral castle atop Mt. Zollern in Swabia), Count (*Burggraf*) of Nuremberg, whose descendants became the creators of the kingdom of Prussia and the later German empire of the Hohenzollern dynasty.

Under Wenzel's and Sigismund's rule disorder in the German lands increased, the Burgundian state in the West and the Polish nation in the East reaping the profits of the virtual breakdown of imperial power. The Teutonic Knights were decisively defeated by the Poles at Tannenberg (1410, cf. p. 114), and the Swiss peasant communes in the South emancipated themselves from the domination of the house of Hapsburg (1386).

The Rise of the Hapsburg Dynasty. When Sigismund died without a male heir in 1437, the crown reverted once more to the Hapsburgs. The short reign of Albrecht II (1438–1439) was followed by the election of his cousin, Frederick III (1440–1493), who devoted most of his energy to the consolidation of his family possessions, so that the power of the Hapsburgs soon overshadowed completely the other principalities of the Empire, and the imperial dignity was never again wrested from the Hapsburg dynasty to the very end of the Austro-Hungarian monarchy in 1918.

During the fifty-three years of Frederick's rule German affairs of state were drifting from bad to worse, while the emperor looked on, unable to make up his mind one way or the other. Verifying the traditional saying *"Bella gerant alii; tu felix Austria nube"* ("Let the others wage wars; you, happy Austria, may rely on marriage alliances"), he secured the Burgundian succession for his house by joining his son, Maximilian, in matrimony to Mary, the heiress of Charles the Bold of Burgundy. In addition, he negotiated a treaty in the East, whereby the Hapsburgs were to become the heirs of Ladislaus, king of a united Poland and Bohemia, upon the expiration of the male line of succession. The son of Mary of Burgundy and Maximilian, Philip "the Handsome" (*Philipp der Schöne*), was to inherit not only the Burgundian estates, including the Free County (*Freigrafschaft*) of Burgundy, but also Luxemburg and the wealthy provinces of the Netherlands. Philip was married to Joanna (1496), the daughter of Ferdinand and Isabella of Spain and the heiress of Castile and Aragon. When Philip died and Joanna was pronounced insane (1509), their young son Charles inherited not only the immense territorial possessions of his parents but, upon the death of his maternal grandfather Ferdinand in 1516, became the sovereign of the kingdoms of Spain, Sardinia, Sicily, Naples, and the Spanish-Castilian possessions in the New World. When Emperor Maximilian I died in 1519, the domains of his grandson, Charles, were further increased by the vast hereditary Hapsburg territories in Germany, so that Emperor Charles V stated the truth when he said: "In my realm the sun never sets."

When Charles was nineteen years of age, his Empire extended over Germany, Burgundy, Italy, and Spain with her possessions overseas, an aggregation of power that was unparalleled since the days of Charlemagne. However, it was too artificial a structure, composed of too many heterogeneous elements, to last for any considerable length of time.

Maximilian I (1493–1519), "the last of the knights" (*der letzte Ritter*), was a ruler of charming personality; a poet and a scholar; a patron of art, culture, and education. His interests were broad and cosmopolitan, his ideas lofty and often spectacular, but he lacked the realistic sense of proportion that makes the great statesman. He attempted to remedy the clumsy and inefficient administrative and political organization of the Empire by decreeing several constitutional reforms at the Diet of Worms (1495), including the establishment of a standing national court of justice (*Reichskammergericht*) and the promulgation of a perpetual Land Peace (*ewiger Landfriede*).

The realization of some of his major projects was seriously hampered by rising war clouds and political complications in the East and West of the Empire. In the East the Turks were sweeping across the plains of Hungary, threatening Austria with invasion, while, in the West and Southwest, France and Spain were embarking on a definitely imperialistic policy of expansion, with the conquest of Italy as one of their major objectives. Owing partly to his constant lack of funds, partly to the unreliability and indifference of the German princes, Maximilian was unable to prevent the French from becoming the masters of northern Italy and the Spaniards from conquering Naples and Sicily. If Maximilian had not reverted to the traditional Austrian policy of letting peaceful matrimonial alliances make up for military losses, the Empire would undoubtedly have had to bow before the rising stars of Spain and France.

"The last of the knights" was at the same time one of the foremost among the moderns, and actually dealt the knightly form of warfare a deadly blow by adopting the new methods and inventions of military science, replacing the old-fashioned cavalry with their heavy armor and their elaborate showing by artillerymen and foot soldiers whose organization followed the model of the Swiss mercenaries (*Landsknechte*). The emperor himself invented new types of cannon and transport wagons, taking a lively interest in all matters pertaining to military science.

All the external splendor of which Maximilian himself was an exponent cannot obscure the fact that the German empire at the end of the Middle Ages lacked the essential elements of order, solidarity, and unity. The processes of decentralization went on practically unchecked, and the larger territorial principalities of the Electors were surrounded by a growing number of the smaller domains of sovereign barons and free knights, and of the ecclesiastical estates of archbishops, bishops, and abbots. To these must be added some fifty to sixty free imperial cities, subject only to the nominal authority of the emperor. The fourteenth and fifteenth centuries witnessed innumerable private feuds, border skirmishes, wars of succession, and endless struggles and clashes between princes, cities, and nobles, between clergy and laity, patricians and guilds. But despite the absence of a central, controlling, directing, and law-enforcing power the general cultural level was high, trade and commerce flourished, and the prosperity of the burgher class favored the development of higher education and creative endeavor in the arts and crafts.

The Rise of Austria. It seems necessary, at this juncture, to trace the growth of that German state which, with the rise of the Hapsburg dynasty, assumed the cultural leadership of Germany for centuries to come. That state is Austria.

After Otto the Great (cf. p. 65) had successfully checked the westward migration of the Magyars (Hungarians) by his victory on the Lechfeld (955) and driven the Slavs eastward from the river Elbe, he re-established the eastern march (Ostmark), which had been created originally by Charlemagne after his victory over the Avars (790–803). The name Austria (*Ostarrichi*) was first used in the tenth century to designate the German settlements of the eastern marches, which owned nominal allegiance to the duke of Bavaria but which, since 976, actually had been governed quite independently by the margraves of Babenberg. Frederick Barbarossa made Austria an independent duchy in 1156. In the course of the twelfth and thirteenth centuries Styria (*Steiermark*), parts of Carniola (*Krain*), and Upper Austria were added to the Austrian domains.

The last member of the house of Babenberg died in the battle against Bela IV of Hungary (1246), and the duchy of Austria as well as the province of Carinthia (Kärnten) were occupied by King Ottokar II of Bohemia (1251). Rudolf of Hapsburg seized the German fiefs of Ottokar II and gave Austria, Styria, and Carniola to his sons, Albrecht and Rudolf, thereby firmly establishing the stronghold of Hapsburg supremacy in southeastern Germany.

The Austrian regions had become predominantly Germanic in the centuries of the migrations, their ethnological and national structure being decisively influenced by the immigration of the Bavarians in the beginning of the sixth century. The Bavarians were the descendants of the ancient Marcomans, who had originally occupied the territory of Bohemia and for that reason had been named "Boivarii." They were an agricultural Germanic tribe of great vitality and tenacity and endowed with other qualities that predestined them for cultural leadership. They rapidly acquired the habits of a frontier people, dwelling in partial autonomy in the outlying eastern border regions of the Frankish empire. They were severely hampered in the peaceful cultivation of their lands and even found their territorial possessions endangered by the onslaughts of the fierce Avars and several auxiliary Slavic peoples with independent cultures of their own. Partly subjected by the Avars, who drove the rest of them westward, they advanced into the Alpine valleys and had reached Styria and Lower Austria by the end of the sixth century. Charlemagne's victory over the Avars led to the definitive incorporation of the eastern marches in the Frankish empire and to the creation of an ecclesiastical province with its center in Salzburg. Politically and ecclesiastically these eastern Alpine regions, extending far into the plains of Hungary, formed part of Bavaria. The subsequent subjection and absorption of the several Slavic enclaves, according to the opinion of some scholars, led to the verbal and semantic equation of *servi, sclavi, Slavi* (slaves, Slavs).

The day of the battle on the Lechfeld (955), with its decisive victory over the Magyars, was the actual birthday of Hapsburg Austria. It reestablished the eastern march and created for Bohemia and Hungary the foundation for their later unification with Austria. At the same time it provided a suitable background for the cultural achievements of these regions in the Middle Ages. It was in the Eastern March that the *Lay of the Nibelungs* (cf. p. 154) and the Gothic and Bavarian saga cycles were given their final touch. These were the regions where *Minnesang* achieved its most vital expression in Walther von der Vogelweide (cf. p. 156), where Austrian historiography developed in intimate connection with a specific monastic culture, where during the seventeenth and eighteenth centuries flourished the courtly as well as the popular arts, crafts, and literatures of the Austrian Baroque and Rococo (cf. p. 337 sqq.).

It was in the tenth century, then, that the genius of Austria came to life, that very definite and homogeneous type of national culture that perpetuated itself through the centuries, displaying its humane and artistic riches in song and dance, fashions and manners, arts and crafts, political and social formations, religious and philosophical ideas.

Rudolf of Hapsburg was responsible for the shift of the center of gravity of German dynastic rule to the eastern part of the Empire. It was this shift that made the combination Hapsburg-Austria a constellation of world-historic significance. Even the Mark Brandenburg, the nucleus of the later kingdom of Prussia, and the German empire under Prussian leadership, were an outgrowth of this development. When Napoleon I destroyed the last remnants of the Holy Roman Empire of the German Nation, political leadership passed to the combined East German powers of Austria and Prussia, an alliance which successfully defended the German heritage and freed Germany from French domination and oppression. It is for this reason that the history of Austria can only be understood with a view to the larger context of the history of central Europe.

The House of Hapsburg and the Swiss Confederation. The independence of Switzerland was achieved in a prolonged struggle of the free Swiss peasant and city communes against the absolutistic claims of the rising territorial state of Austria. The Swiss Confederation originated in the league of the three Alpine cantons of Schwyz, Uri, and Unterwalden. The inhabitants of these rural districts had formed a defensive alliance against their Hapsburg overlords and more specifically against Rudolf of Hapsburg. After the latter's death the league developed into a formal confederation, whose peasant armies won their first decisive victory over the Hapsburg knights at Morgarten (1315). They were afterward joined by neighboring cities and cantons and defeated the Hapsburgs again at Sempach (1386) and Näfels (1388), thereby consolidating their political autonomy. The last Hapsburg attempt at restoration of the *status quo ante* was successfully frustrated in the so-called "Zurich-War" (*Zürich-Krieg*) of 1436–1450. By 1516 the number of cantons had increased to 13, including Zug, Glarus, Lucerne, Zurich, Berne, Basel, the southern French-speaking Valais with the valley of the upper Rhone, and the Italian-speaking Ticino (*Tessin*), south of the Saint Gotthard Pass.

The new Swiss peasant democracy of Europe rested ethnologically upon a combination of Alemanic and Romanic tribal and racial characteristics; it rested politically and culturally on the semiautonomy of individual cities and cantons. During the following centuries various subdivisions brought the number of cantons to 22, and this cantonal system of administration was acknowledged and preserved by the powers at the Congress of Vienna (1814–1815, cf. p. 454 sqq.). Nominally the Swiss Confederation remained a part of the Holy Roman Empire to the end of the Thirty Years' War (1648).

Decline of Feudal Law, and the Holy Veme. The victories of the Swiss peasant armies over the heavily armored Austrian knights was one of the many symptoms of the approaching doom of the age of knighthood. The knights would indeed have become the forgotten men of the new age, if a goodly number of them had not disgraced their name and calling by exhibiting a complete disregard for law, order, and decency. As highwaymen and robber-knights they became the parasites and playboys of the age. The rising money economy had reduced their means of livelihood, while the new methods of warfare steadily reduced their military superiority. When they were not passing their days in enforced idleness in their castles, they would ravage and ransack the countryside, taking their revenge on the prospering though despised "pepper-bags" (merchants) from the cities, who had undermined the bases of their subsistence. Feudal law, whose provisions for self-defense were deeply rooted in ancient Germanic legal concepts, now degenerated into "club law" (*Faustrecht*) and was used as a pretense for attacks upon monasteries, villages, and traveling merchants. Imperial power had grown too weak to act as a law-enforcing agency. The people, therefore, unwilling to tolerate the outrages of the knightly robber bands, began to organize for the suppression of crime and lawlessness.

The "Holy Veme" was originally a Westphalian peasant court, deriving its methods of legal procedure from the old free courts of Carolingian times, judgment being passed by bailiffs (*Schöffen*), who were presided over by a *Freigraf* (count). The Veme developed into a secret society of vigilantes, who counted among their members many noblemen and even Sigismund, the German emperor, who welcomed the organization as an efficient means to check the legal anarchy that had risen in the Empire. The trials were surrounded with great secrecy, and a solemn oath bound all members "to hold and conceal the Holy Veme from wife and child, from father and mother, from sister and brother, from fire and wind, from everything upon which the sun shines or the rain falls, from everything between earth and heaven." The proceedings were conducted with elaborate rites and ceremonial symbolisms. The death penalty was inflicted by hanging. In case the accused person refused to appear before the court, he was solemnly pronounced as outlawed (*vogelfrei*), and every member was in duty bound to carry out the dread sentence of the law. The later development of the Veme in the fifteenth century led to an increasing abuse of its power and to its final suppression by law. The authority of these secret tribunals had never been established by due legal process but was based chiefly on the moral force of public opinion.

Emancipation of the State and Beginning Decline of the Church. The three major events that left their indelible mark on European civilization in the fourteenth and fifteenth centuries were the struggle between Emperor Louis the Bavarian and Pope John XXII; the "Babylonian Captivity" of the papacy at Avignon; and the Conciliar Movement.

a) Boniface VIII and the Bull "Unam Sanctam." When Pope Boniface VIII (1294–1303) tried to restate and reassert the political claims of the papacy, he met with the strong resistance of the rising territorial monarchies of France and England. Although Boniface was as firmly convinced as Gregory VII (cf. p. 71 sqq.) that there was only one real head of the Christian commonwealth and that the papacy had been endowed by Christ with temporal as well as spiritual power, the feudal might of the Church was thoroughly broken, and the days of the feudal state were likewise numbered. Boniface, whom Dante's *Divine Comedy* relegates to the "Inferno," was a character of the early Renaissance: haughty, vainglorious, avaricious, and also extremely practical minded, a canonist who was fond of any outward display of power but oblivious of all strictly spiritual motivations. In his Bull *"Unam Sanctam"** of 1302 he solemnly declared that "for salvation it is absolutely necessary for every creature to be subject to the Roman pontiff." A few years earlier (1296) the Bull *"Clericis Laicos"* had forbidden the clergy of any country to pay subsidies to secular rulers without the pope's consent. Both documents had been drafted in connection with Boniface's quarrels with King Philip IV (the Fair) of France. The immediate result of these controversies was an open rebellion of the French

---

* Papal bulls and encyclical letters are usually named after the first two words of their text.

king and the French National Assembly and their appeal to a general Church council. Boniface was taken prisoner by the French chancellor but released shortly afterward. He died in 1303, leaving the authority of the Papal See at the mercy of the French crown.

b) Louis the Bavarian and Pope John XXII. The king of France succeeded in persuading the College of Cardinals to elect Clement V (1305–1314), a Frenchman, to the papal throne. Clement then established the papal capital in the city of Avignon (1308), which was a fief of the Holy Roman Empire and, though located on the border of France and thus within the sphere of French influence, was not actually a French city. Clement V appointed twenty-eight cardinals, twenty-five of whom were Frenchmen, in this way ensuring an unbroken line of French popes, seven in all. The period of predominating French influence in papal elections and papal policies is known in the history of the Church as the "Babylonian Captivity" (1309–1376).

Clement V was followed by John XXII (1316–1334), who revived the claims of Boniface VIII and went so far as to demand the right to appoint the German king. The result was his clash with Louis the Bavarian, one of the two claimants to the imperial crown.

c) The "Defensor Pacis." In his counterattack Louis made use of the services of his court physician, Marsilius of Padua (c. 1290–1342), who with his famous political tract *Defensor Pacis* (Defender of the Peace) popularized the traditional medieval theory of the State which in its essential features was based on the political philosophy of Aristotle and Thomas Aquinas and only deviated from tradition when it subordinated papal authority to the State and denied the primacy of the bishop of Rome (the pope). It had been one of the main tenets of medieval political theory in the West from the ninth to the thirteenth century to extol the supremacy of the law of the State over all its members, even over kings and princes. This theory maintained that positive State law, in order to be valid, must be based on the natural law and that as such it expressed the traditions, customs, and wishes of the whole community.

It is this point of view that distinguishes the political philosophy of Thomas Aquinas or John of Salisbury (c. 1115–1180, scholastic philosopher of the School of Chartres) from the concepts of an Oriental State absolutism, based on the presumption of a "divine right of kings." The community being the ultimate source of all State authority, its members may legitimately take action against unjust rulers and unjust laws. The idea of the sovereignty of the people is thus deeply embedded in medieval political theory, but inseparably linked with the sanctions that are embodied in the divine law, the natural law, and the law of reason. According to John Quidort of Paris, a Dominican friar of the end of the thirteenth century († 1306), royal power is derived from God but with the consent and elective power of the people (*a populo consentiente et eligente*). The innovation in Quidort's position is his rejection of the temporal power of the papacy and the strict separation of ecclesiastical and secular jurisdiction. The Church is confined to the sacramental order, while the State is conceived of as an autonomous and completely secularized organism. As Christ rules only over a spiritual kingdom and not over earthly goods, so the pope can claim no domination but only ministration.

These arguments are repeated with even greater emphasis in regard to the autonomy of the secular State by Marsilius of Padua and John of Jandun († 1328), his collaborator. Quidort's political liberalism issues in undisguised naturalism, anticipating Machiavelli's complete emancipation of politics from moral sanctions (cf. p. 247 sqq.).

The *Defensor Pacis* calls the claims of the Bull *"Unam Sanctam"* — papal jurisdiction over the affairs of the Empire and the right of controlling elections — a "laughable arrogation." No bishop is head of the Church by any other title than by a spiritual life and by human delegation. But the Roman bishop has usurped secular power and thereby perverted ecclesiastical legislation. He intends to destroy the authority of the princely electors by denying that the king or emperor-elect is invested with full legal power. By opposing such papal claims to temporal authority, the emperor acts as "defender of the peace." As the adviser of Louis the Bavarian, Marsilius of Padua staged a practical demonstration of his political theories when, in 1328, he had Louis proclaimed emperor by the people of Rome and, shortly afterward, had an antipope (Nicholas V) chosen in the same way.

d) The Great Schism and the Conciliar Movement. Marsilius had de-manded that in all matters of dogma and doctrine the final decision should not rest with the pope but with a general council of the whole Church. Not being derived from the Scriptures, papal authority, according to Marsilius, could only be delegated by a general council or by State legislation.

The popular movement that favored the authority of a standing com-mittee of the Church or a general Church council to replace the centralized power of the Roman pontiff received a new impetus from the events which led to the "Great Schism." The "Babylonian Captivity" ended with the return of Pope Gregory IX (1371–1378) to Rome. He died shortly afterward, and the following conclave (the electoral assembly of cardinals) conferred the papal dignity on the Neapolitan Urban VI (1378–1389). Because of the latter's refusal to return to Avignon, the French cardinals, maintaining that the election had been influenced by the pressure of the Roman mob, elected Clement VII (1378–1394) as antipope and thereby started that disastrous division of the Church known as the "Great Schism" (1378–1418). The rival pope set up his residence at Avignon.

The Council of Pisa (1409) summoned both popes, and upon their re-fusal to appear and to recognize the authority of the council, it declared them deposed and proceeded to elect Alexander V, formerly archbishop of Milan; after Alexander's early death (1410) they gave their votes to the wily and energetic John XXIII, whose shady past (he had been a freebooter) could but further discredit the dignity of his office. Since neither the aged Gregory XII (1406–1415), the third of the successors of Urban VI in Rome, nor Benedict XIII (1394–1424), Clement VII's successor in Avignon, would recognize the decisions of the Council of Pisa, the year 1410 witnessed three rival claimants to the papal throne, while in the same year three rival candidates — Wenceslaus, Sigismund, and Jodocus of Moravia — contended for the secular rulership of the Christian commonwealth.

At the Council of Constance (1414–1418) all three popes were forced to abdicate, the schism was ended with the election of Martin V, a Roman cardinal of the Colonna family (1417–1431), and the papacy returned to Rome. While the Council of Constance could do little to do away with the abuses which had led to the schism, it issued a decree which asserted the superiority of a general council over the pope, and aided the Conciliar Movement by providing for future convocations and deliberations of general councils of the Church.

A new attempt to accomplish what the Council of Constance had failed to bring about was made at the Council of Basel (1431–1449). Its main objectives were: reform of the Church "in head and members," and reunion with the schismatic Greek Orthodox Church, which had been separated from Rome since the eleventh century. Both moves failed to materialize in the end, and factional disputes as well as a general lack of clear thought and concerted action were soon to paralyze the efforts made in behalf of the conciliar theory.

Pope Martin V had been succeeded by Eugenius IV (1431–1447), who was uncompromisingly opposed to the theory that the pope should be merely the first official of a constitutional assembly. He tried to gain control of the general council by transferring it from Basel to Ferrara and later to Florence. Thereupon the members of the rump council who stayed in Basel, ignoring a papal decree of dissolution, declared the pope deposed and elected Felix V as antipope. Eugenius, however, succeeded in rallying most of the European powers to his support, thus forcing his papal rival into submission and resignation. By declaring itself dissolved in 1449, the Council of Basel silently acknowledged the defeat of the Conciliar Movement.

The principle that the decisions of general Church councils should take precedence over papal decrees, which had been agreed upon at Constance and Basel, was voided by Aeneas Sylvius Piccolomini, who had been Frederick III's secretary and poet laureate at his court, and who ascended the papal throne as Pius II (1458–1464). He was one of the leading Humanists (cf. p. 244 sqq.) and without any doubt the greatest representative of the papacy in the fifteenth century. After having at first supported the antipope, Felix, he afterward sided with Eugenius IV and was instrumental in bringing about the Concordat of Vienna (1448). In concluding this solemn treaty with the Holy See, Germany followed the example of France which had secured her national and political autonomy by the "Pragmatic Sanction" of Bourges (1438), which clearly defined the limits of papal interference in ecclesiastical elections as well as in matters of papal taxation and jurisdiction. The Concordat of Vienna contributed to the temporary appeasement of the relations of State and Church, redefining the mutual spheres of influence, and conferring certain benefits and material advantages on both partners. In his Bull *"Execrabilis"* (1460) Pius II denounced any future appeal to a general council as an "execrable abuse," thereby giving the lie to his own former convictions and wiping out the last vestiges of the conciliar theory.

Black Death, Flagellants, Persecution of the Jews. In the years 1349–1350 Europe was visited by the most devastating epidemic in all its history, the Black Death or bubonic plague. It was an event of such enormous dimensions that it left a lasting impress on the physiognomy of the age, and some historians have even attributed epochal significance to the plague and its consequences. It added to the many sinister forebodings of the waning Middle Ages an aspect of gloom and despair, so that henceforth the dreaded figure of Death and the "Dance of Death" becomes a familiar theme in preaching and teaching, thinking and living, in theology as well as in literature and the arts.

It is estimated that twenty-five million of the population of Europe died as victims of the plague, which in all probability had been introduced from the Far East, spreading from Asia Minor and North Africa to the ports of southern Europe and from there across the whole continent, including England. In Germany there was hardly a village that was spared the horrible visitation.

The populace and their ecclesiastical and secular leaders felt inclined to look upon the plague as a judgment of God, passed upon a faithless generation whose members in Church and State had rent the seamless garment of Christ by revolt, discord, and anarchy. The bloody struggles between the Welfs and Waiblingens (cf. p. 89 sqq.), the Mongolian invasions, earthquakes, floods, and upheavals of every kind were the common experience of everyone and, together with the prophecies of the Benedictine theologian Joachim of Fiore († 1202) and others, had given rise to the general expectation of the approaching end of the world.

As early as the thirteenth century groups of penitents had organized mass processions and pilgrimages in the Romanic countries, but the movement reached its climax in the years of the Black Death. Intimidated and frightened people from every walk of life joined the processions of the "Flagellants," religious fanatics who went from town to town, carrying crosses, singing hymns, burning candles and incense, and lashing themselves with iron-spiked scourges. Wherever they went, they were met by large numbers of enthusiastic and credulous people, often by the entire population of a town or village, so that they themselves became the most dangerous carriers of the plague. They preached repentance and mortification, attacking not only the widespread and flagrant abuses in State and Church but all civil and ecclesiastical authority. It is hardly surprising, then, that in the end they were branded as heretics and proscribed as enemies of society.

The cruel and fanatical persecution of the Jews that took place about the middle of the fourteenth century was partly instigated and generally encouraged by the Flagellants. The Jews were suspected of having poisoned the wells and thereby caused the Black Death. Social, religious, and racial hatreds combined brought about the massacres of the years 1348–1351. A contemporary Strasbourg chronicle describes the burning of Jews on a funeral pyre that was erected in the cemetery. Similar scenes were enacted in scores of towns. In many cases the Jews put fire to their own houses and perished in the flames. The imperial government made no attempt to punish the excesses. The property of the victims was confiscated and fell to the crown or the municipalities.

John Huss and the Hussite Wars. The trial and burning of John Huss (1369–1415) and the bloody civil war that followed it offers an interesting illustration of the growing nationalistic feeling in Europe. John Huss was the hero, leader, and exponent of a movement that represented a compound of religious, national, and social motivations. Theologically Huss was influenced by the doctrines of the Oxford scholar, John Wyclif (c. 1324–1384), who demanded that the Church be expropriated and reduced to the simplicity and poverty of the early Christian centuries. Wyclif defended the superiority of the State over the Church in temporal matters, defined the Church as the community of those who are predestined for salvation, appealed to the authority of the Bible as against that of dogma and canon law, and denied the dogma of "transubstantiation" (the real transformation of the substance of bread and wine into the substance of Christ's body and blood in the consecration of the Mass).* He insisted that only a worthy priest could validly administer the sacraments and thereby renewed the Donatist heresy against which St. Augustine in the fifth century had asserted the objective character of sacramental grace. He urged a thorough reform of ecclesiastical organization and discipline, and attacked the veneration of saints, the granting of absolution from sins in the sacrament of penance, and the practice of indulgences (the remission of temporal punishment, as distinct from eternal punishment, through the application of the accumulated merits of Christ and the saints). Wyclif was expelled from Oxford but enjoyed the backing of the British crown and parliament. After the peasant revolt in England of the year 1381 his followers, the "Lollards" ("lullers," poor, singing priests), were persecuted as heretics.

Wyclif's ideas had spread to Bohemia, where they provided John Huss, who held a professorship at the University of Prague, with his arguments against the corrupt Bohemian clergy. But Huss went beyond an attack on religious doctrines and practices. He was a Czech nationalist and a fierce and eloquent preacher of social reform, and as such he advocated the use

---

* The dogma of "transubstantiation" maintains that while the "substance" is thus transformed, the "accidents" or properties (color, shape, extension, etc.) remain unchanged.

of the vernacular in the liturgy and launched a campaign against the wealth of the clergy as well as against the dominating influence of German ecclesiastics in the Bohemian Church. His demand for the use of the vernacular in the liturgy became the battle cry and symbol for a national revival movement of the Czechs. After the "Golden Bull" (1356, cf. p. 165) had confirmed the independence of the kingdom of Bohemia and had urged the teaching of the native Czech language, Slavic nationalism rose in full force, extending to secular and religious matters alike. A national Czech literature was in the making, and the Bible was translated into the national language. Thus the political implications of the Hussite movement were soon to overshadow its religious significance.

John Huss, who enjoyed the backing of King Wenceslaus and a large part of the population of Prague, was urged by Emperor Sigismund to appear before the Council of Constance to answer to the charge of heresy. As early as 1412 Huss had been indicted and excommunicated by the archbishop of Prague, but now he received from the emperor a guarantee of safe-conduct and hoped that once he were given a chance to answer his enemies in public, he would easily sway them with the power and fire of his oratory.

However, Huss reached Constance before Sigismund, and the emperor upon his arrival learned with dismay that the safe-conduct had been violated and that after a brief hearing Huss had been thrown into a dungeon. Huss's enemies argued that, first, a heretic was beyond the pale of even the protection of the emperor and that, second, it was not necessary to keep faith with one who himself had broken faith with God. On the other hand, it seems that only now did the emperor learn the seriousness of the charges that were advanced against Huss, and that he was shocked and horrified by the radical views of the would-be reformer. Huss was given no opportunity to explain and defend his doctrines, but at four council hearings was urged to recant. After the second hearing the emperor left John Huss to his fate with these words: "If you persist in your errors, it is for the council to take its measures. I have said that I will not defend a heretic; nay, if anyone remained obstinate in heresy, I would burn him with my own hands." Huss was found guilty of heresy, handed over to the secular arm, and burned at the stake.

The Hussite party of Bohemia almost immediately rallied to avenge the martyrdom of their national hero. The clergy, nobles, and cities sent a strongly worded protest to Constance, while a group of Huss's followers seized half a score of the city councilors of Prague and hurled them through the windows of the city hall to the street below, where the frenzied mob tore them to pieces. This event marked the beginning of the Bohemian revolt and the Hussite wars (1415–1436).

The uprising, aside from being anti-German, soon became distinctly socialistic in character, giving exaggerated emphasis to certain democratic and liberalistic aspects in Wyclif's and Huss's teachings. The war was waged on the part of the Hussites with all the ferocity and fanaticism of a national crusade. Imperial armies were repeatedly sent against the Bohemians, but they crumbled before the invincible courage of the rebels. Not until the year 1436 could actual peace be restored, and then only by a compromise on the part of the Empire and the Church. The so-called "Compactates of Prague" secured for the Bohemians some of their religious objectives: communion in both kinds (the host and the chalice as well, which in the Roman Catholic rite is allowed to the celebrating priest only), the free preaching of the Gospel, and the right to try members of the clergy before secular courts. The more radical wing of the Hussite party formed the nucleus of the sect of the "Moravian Brethren" whose members were to play an important part in the pietistic revival movement of the seventeenth and eighteenth centuries (cf. p. 364 sqq.). King Wenceslaus had died as one of the first victims of the war. Emperor Sigismund, his brother, could enter Prague in 1436 as king of Bohemia, but he died in the following year.

William of Occam, Nicholas of Cusa, and the Political Reform. It was significant that at the meetings of the Council of Constance the participating nations and their ecclesiastical representatives were holding separate sessions, formulating their policies by majority vote, before they met the other nations in plenary session. In doing so they acted as national parliaments, and it was undoubtedly the parliamentary type of government in England, as established in a rudimentary form by the Magna Charta of 1215, which provided the pattern for the proceedings at general councils of the Church, the cardinals constituting a standing committee of the Church, and the pope presiding as the chosen executive.

a) William of Occam and Nominalism. Two essential innovations are implied in the theories that underlie the political structure of the Council of Constance. The one points to the nationalization of the Church, the other to the transfer of the idea of the sovereignty of the people from the State to the Church. The credit for having provided the intellectual bases of these fundamental changes belongs to William of Occam († 1349 in Munich), a Franciscan theologian and philosopher, who was born in England, taught at the University of Paris, was excommunicated in 1328, and found refuge and protection at the court of Emperor Louis the Bavarian. A great scholar and a prolific writer, he must be considered as the most important forerunner of Martin Luther, some of whose central theological convictions he anticipated.

As a representative of the nominalistic branch of scholastic philosophy (cf. p. 142), Occam deprives religion of its rational foundations, substituting the irrationality of a dark, miraculous, and paradoxical unintelligibility. Tertullian's (*c.* 160–220) famous saying: *"Credo quia absurdum"* (I believe, because the object of my faith is an incomprehensible paradox) expresses the quintessence of Occam's theology. His God is an arbitrary and absolutistic ruler, who is bound neither by the laws of nature nor by the laws of reason. In his denial of the law of causality Occam anticipates

Hume's and Kant's criticism, while in his denial of substances and universals he is in essential agreement with the pragmatism and behaviorism of today. His denial of an objective universal order of nature leaves no room for a rational ethics which could be based on such an order. If realities, such as good, evil, order, law, truth, falsehood, and every kind of universal concept and predication is a mere nominal label and an expedient convention, there remains nothing but the testimony of the individual conscience, whose authority and judgment must be final, because it constitutes the only certainty which exists. In this emphasis upon the subjective certitude of individual consciousness Occam points forward to Descartes's (1596–1650) *"Cogito, ergo sum"* (I think, therefore I am), who made this kind of certitude the starting point of his philosophy. Furthermore, the denial of causality implies the denial of finality, and with the rejection of a teleological universe (one of graduated causes, means, and ends) the road is cleared for the rise of the *"nuova scienza"* (new science) of mechanical physics.

In his social ideals as well as in his struggle against the papacy William of Occam is to some extent determined by his Franciscan heritage. He belonged to that radical group of "Spiritual" Franciscans who had been condemned by Pope John XXII for their uncompromising adherence to the ideal of absolute poverty and a voluntary communism on a religious basis. In opposing the theories on property and private ownership advanced by John XXII, Occam wrote a monumental work on social philosophy (*Opus Nonaginta Dierum,* "The Work of Ninety Days"), outlining in 126 chapters a comprehensive system of Christian communism, designed for the reorganization of the Church. The secular order, on the other hand, is pessimistically conceived as being perverted and corrupted by sin and therefore subject to the rule of force and violence. William of Occam no longer believes in the possibility of a just and reasonable social order in the secular sphere, and therefore relinquishes the norm of the natural law, on which Thomas Aquinas had built the system of his social and political philosophy. Occam quite logically, then, proclaims an almost complete autonomy of the political and economic spheres. In his teaching, Church and laity, God and world, supernature and nature are separated by an unbridgeable chasm.

Occam's masterpiece is the *Dialogus* (Dialogue), in which he attacks the papal claims to temporal authority and sets definite limits to the spiritual power of the papacy by appealing to the authority of the Bible. It is in this work that he applies the principle of the sovereignty of the people to the ecclesiastical realm. All rulers, including the pope, have received their power indirectly from God but directly and immediately from the people and the commonwealth. The sovereignty of the people may be exercised in the form of a referendum, each parish or community delegating their representatives to a bishop's council or royal parliament, whose members in turn elect delegates for a general council, in which laymen as well as women may be represented. The pope like any other ruler is limited in his authority by the will and the general welfare of his constituents.

In examining the leading ideas of the political and religious reformation in the following centuries it is impossible to avoid the realization of the fact that William of Occam's thought has proven a most vital influence in the making of the secularized modern world.

b) Nicholas of Cusa's Attempted Reform. The period from the middle of the fourteenth to the middle of the fifteenth century marks the beginning of the modern world. The major events and movements — the "Great Schism," the Councils of Constance and Basel, the rise of the great city republics of Italy and Flanders, the German city leagues, the European peasant revolts — they all signalize the dissolution of medieval civilization and the approaching political, social, and religious revolution and reformation.

While in England and France the nationalistic tendencies in the Church were firmly anchored in the national State, in Germany the mystical movement prevented such a consolidation. German mysticism (cf. p. 146 sqq.), the *"philosophia Teutonica,"* prepared the way for a nonecclesiastical form of piety, a religion without a priestly hierarchy, a devotion with an anticlerical bias. Especially in the Netherlands this new form of piety (*devotio moderna*) gained considerable influence on the thought and culture of the new age. It was here, in the circles of the "Brethren of the Common Life," that the *Imitation of Christ* originated, a manual of Christian devotion, which, notwithstanding its strict orthodoxy, owes its modernity and universal appeal to the same practical and communal bent of mind that made the schools of the Brethren in Deventer and Windesheim model institutions of humanistic education. In Deventer (Holland) the great Erasmus of Rotterdam (cf. p. 249 sq.) received his early training.

A similar religious atmosphere and environment furnished the background for the life and thought of Nicholas (Krebs) of Cusa (1401–1464), a native of the Moselle district, who grew up in the still orthodox but broad and many-colored world of ideas as advanced by men like Gerard Groote (1340–1384), Florentius Radewyn (1350–1400), and Thomas à Kempis (1379–1471). These influences left their marks on the mind of the future bishop and cardinal, while at the same time the numerous heretical, anticlerical, and antiauthoritarian societies in the Rhineland and in Holland, the "Brethren of the Free Spirit," the "Friends of God," and the "Lollards," impressed upon him the need for ecclesiastical reform. In 1432 we find Nicholas of Cusa at the council tables of Basel and afterward of Florence and Ferrara. We see him turn against the conciliar theory which he had at first defended and become an eloquent advocate of papal rights at the Diets of Mainz, Nuremberg, and Frankfurt. As a papal legate he traverses Germany, Austria, and the Netherlands, carries on negotiations with the Hussites and the Greeks, trying to arbitrate and to reconcile opposing points of view in political and religious matters.

Nicholas of Cusa is one of the great philosophers of Germany and the first one of her speculative geniuses in modern times. In a unique way he combines tradition and progress, being as much at home in antiquity as in the medieval and modern worlds. He combines a Greek sense of form, proportion, and moderation with Gothic spirituality and modern individualism. His keen critical sense recognized the shortcomings of the feudal system and the danger of a narrow and selfish particularism and partyism for Church and State. If he could have had his way, Germany might have been spared many of the upheavals that followed the Lutheran reformation. "Nicholas of Cusa appeared in Germany as an angel of light and peace in the midst of darkness and confusion. . . . He was a man of faith and love, an apostle of piety and learning," wrote John Trithemius, abbot of Sponheim (1462–1516).

The scholastic pattern of his philosophy was enriched and invigorated by a strong overtone of Neo-Platonic mysticism. His God is the "unity of opposites" (coincidentia oppositorum); He is beyond all that is knowable and finite and yet the innermost essence of everything that there is; the greatest and the smallest ("Deus est omnia, quae esse possunt, maximum et minimum"), comprising in Himself every type of being and becoming, while the universe, conversely, in its entirety and in every part is a mirror and representation of the Godhead. All human knowledge is a "learned ignorance" (Docta Ignorantia), and only the Socratic philosopher who realizes his own ignorance may hope to approach the mysteries of reality and to explore the depths of the unknown. All creatures are related to God, glorifying Him as the supreme Artist, the Creator, and Father of all.

Some of the ideas of the great Cardinal of Cusa live on in the philosophical system of Leibniz (1646–1716); his mathematical speculations in Leibniz' discussions of the infinitesimal calculus; his theory of individual monads — vital centers of energy, forming the ultimate constituent parts of the universe — in Giordano Bruno's (1548–1600) and Leibniz' Monadology. And, like Leibniz, Nicholas of Cusa drew up a program for the reunion of the separated churches and the unification of religious creeds, inspired by a visualization of a unified Christendom under the rule of Christ the King.

The New City Culture. The inhabitants of the newly developed city communes were the creators of new forms of life and civilization, which they cultivated in conscious opposition to the medieval culture of chivalry. The feudal idea of a social pyramid and the system of mutual services and obligations which it entailed was replaced by the self-sufficiency and the pride of the burgher class. Human value was no longer inherent in social functions and in privileges of birth but was found in human nature as such, in personal vision, individual initiative, and in critical search and research.

Rudolf of Hapsburg (cf. p. 162 sq.) was the first German ruler whose personality bore the imprint of the new age and who was therefore an emperor with a great popular appeal. When he was still governor (Landvogt) in his ancestral province of Alsace, he sided with the citizens of Strasbourg in their struggle with their bishop, and he held his protecting hand over the merchants who traveled across the peaks of the Alps. He preferred the company of simple city folk, of artisans and craftsmen, to that of minnesingers and courtiers.

a) Fashion in the Fifteenth Century. The increasing wealth of the burgher class as well as their contact with foreign manners and customs led to a growing extravagance in the world of fashion. Many city ordinances and imperial as well as local statutes attempted to put a check on the immoderate indulgence in luxuries. In 1445, the city of Regensburg enacted a law that set eighteen dresses and eighteen coats as an upper limit for a woman's wardrobe.

The modes of apparel for men grew more and more effeminate. The lords and knights began to wear their hair long and curly and tried to imitate women in dress and gait. They bared their necks and shoulders and wore necklaces and bracelets. Men and women alike were fond of many-colored costumes, fashioned of costly imported materials, such as damasks interwoven with gold and silver threads, velvet, brocade, fur, and Flemish lace. The shoe points became so long that they rendered walking difficult and had to be tied to the knees by means of a chainlet. (A Regensburg city ordinance of 1485 restricts the maximal length of shoe points to two inches.) The detachable sleeves of the upper garments were either so tight that they hindered the freedom of movement or so wide that they would drag on the ground. The tight-fitting costumes, as they prevailed especially in the Burgundian fashion, were slit open at different places, showing the silk lining and the finely plaited silken French shirt underneath. Bells of different size and shape were often attached to hems, belts, and shoes.

b) Family Life. Craftsmen, artisans, merchants, and professional men who kept careful records of their families in the form of chronicles give evidence of a strong clannish feeling. The overplus of women still forced a large number of the female members of the family to join religious communities, either regular convents or semimonastic beguinages (cf. p. 125).

Sex life in the fourteenth and fifteenth centuries had become very irregular. Adultery and concubinage were no longer as strongly resented by law and public opinion as in the earlier medieval centuries or in Germanic antiquity. Illegitimate children were often brought up together with the legitimate ones, and they even inherited part of the family possessions.

The dowry of a burgher's daughter usually represented a considerable amount of money, and each house father took pride in providing in the best possible way for the security and comfort of his offspring. Marriages were contracted at an early age, and frequently, especially in the wealthier classes, the married couple continued to live in the parental household. Early marriages among the poorer burghers and peasants, on the other hand, caused a good deal of social misery and destitution.

Prolific families were the rule rather than an exception, and infant mortality was correspondingly high. Ecclesiastical and secular legislation protected mother and child and provided severe penalties for abortion.

The number of servants was much larger than in later centuries. They were considered as part of the family, sharing in the weal and woe of their employers. Wages were very low, legal protection was entirely insufficient, and there were no provisions for old age and sickness. The relationship between employer and employee was accordingly a patriarchal one, based on considerations of charity rather than of social justice.

All classes indulged in eating and drinking without any sense of moderation, especially on festive occasions. The culinary arts developed under foreign influence. Spices were used in increasing quantities, and every kind of food and drink was strongly seasoned. Meat was preferred to any other food, and strongly salted gravies were served with meat, fish, and vegetables. Many varieties of pastries, puddings, cakes, and tarts are indications of the growing refinement of the German cuisine. The first cookbooks were written by hand and date back to the fourteenth century. The most comprehensive of the earliest printed cookbooks is the one by Marx Rumpolt (Frankfurt, 1576). When Bishop John II of Speyer solemnly took office in 1461, the bill of fare on this festive occasion consisted of the following courses: (1) Mutton and chicken in almond milk; fried baby pigs, geese, carp, and pike, with baked dumplings; (2) venison in black pepper sauce; rice with sugar and baked trout, gingered all over; sugar cakes; (3) fried geese, filled with eggs; carp and pike in gravy and berry jam; (4) baked pastry with white and red wine.

Wine and beer were the most popular drinks. Mead was consumed chiefly by peasants. Brandy was at first (fourteenth century) used exclusively as a medicine. "Whoever drinks half a spoonful of brandy every morning, he will never be sick," says a pamphlet of the year 1483. Beer was consumed in large quantities, and its quality had considerably improved. Home-brew was less frequently manufactured, while the community breweries became more and more numerous. Beer trade increased greatly in volume, especially in the North, where the Hansa-cities acquired almost a monopoly. The North also produced the best-quality beers, the brews of Erfurt, Naumburg, Einbeck (*Bock*), Goslar, and Magdeburg taking the lead. The famous Brunswick brew (*Braunschweiger Mumme*) was the favorite beer of Martin Luther.

In the South, Nuremberg and Schwabach were outstanding brewing centers. But the South quite generally gave preference to the excellent products of the growing wine industry, the wines of the Rhine, Moselle, and Neckar regions, and those of Franconia ranking highest in quality. From Austria came the Tyrolese and Danubian wines, from Hungary the "Eastern wine" (*Osterwein*), from foreign countries the various Greek and Italian wines. The Swabian city of Ulm was the center of the German wine trade. The Scandinavian countries were Germany's chief customers.

Drunkenness, which the Roman Tacitus had mentioned as one of the weaknesses of the Germanic tribes, again became the national German vice in the fifteenth and sixteenth centuries. We read in Aventinus' (1477-1534)

Chronicle of Bavaria: "All the other nations speak evil of us, scolding us as a people who are no good except in carousing and revelling, drinking and slumming, and they call us the coarse, senselessly drinking Germans, always intoxicated, never sober."

Drinking bouts were held in the private drinking rooms of the guilds and in the homes of patricians as well as in hostels, taverns, and public houses. The day laborer, the servant, the wandering student, the peasant, the journeyman would frequent the public houses and taverns, where manners were coarse and service poor. The tavern (*Weinhaus*) could be recognized by its house mark, from which its name was usually derived. This symbolic emblem might have the shape of a green wreath, a barrel hoop, or a jug; or it might represent the coat of arms of some distinguished traveler who had stopped over and hung up his escutcheon.

Tablecloths and table utensils were now quite generally used, the plates being made of tin or wood. Knives and spoons were fashionable but forks were still missing, and the fingers were still considered the most suitable instruments in eating.

c) *Feasts and Holidays.* Most of the feasts of the ecclesiastical year were family festivals as well. At the end of the Middle Ages they were celebrated with greater splendor than ever before. Early in Advent, on December 6, St. Nicholas (Santa Claus), accompanied by his servant Rupert (*Knecht Ruprecht*), the mythical wanderer, in whom Odin (Wodan), the supreme god of the Germanic pantheon, lived on, went from house to house offering apples, walnuts, sweets, and pictures to well-behaved children. The children placed little paper boats in front of doors and windows so that St. Nicholas, the patron of skippers, might fill them with his gifts.

The sacred twelve nights between Christmas (*Weihnacht*) and Epiphany were the period of the turning of the year, and were filled with mysterious forebodings. Green branches adorned with colored ribbons and tinsel served as decoration, later replaced by the Christmas tree (first mentioned in Alsace about the middle of the sixteenth century). The crib with the Christ Child originally derives from the Christmas celebration of St. Francis of Assisi (1223), but in its present form it is a German creation of the later Middle Ages. The realistic rendition of the events of the holy night was developed to artistic perfection in the sixteenth century, in connection with the popular Christmas plays. From that time on the art of crib making can be traced through the centuries, experiencing unprecedented heights in Sicily and Naples at the beginning of the eighteenth century and later on in Bavaria, Austria, Silesia, the Rhineland, and Westphalia. In the later Middle Ages the children, masquerading as angels, shepherds, and kings, would wander from house to house, singing Christmas carols. Street singing likewise introduced the New Year (*Neujahr*); and Epiphany, the feast of the Three Wise Men from the East (*Dreikönigsfest*), again offered an opportunity to do homage to the child in the manger. At nightfall three boys in royal attire would carry a star on top of a tall pole, singing their "star-songs" (*Sternlieder*).

Preceding the season of Lent the old pagan instincts would come to life again in the celebration of "shrovetide" (*Fastnacht*). Reverting to the tradition of the Roman *"Saturnalia,"* men, women, and children, clergy and laity alike, disguised their identity and plunged into unchecked merriment and sensual pleasure. Among the floats of the shrovetide pageant (*Fastnachtszug*) was the *carrus navalis,* a ship filled with masqueraders, from which the word "carnival" is derived. The ship symbolized originally the resumption of the shipping trade and traffic after the gloomy winter season.* The climax of the pageant was usually the performance of a shrovetide play in the market square.

The hilarity of the shrovetide was followed by the sorrow and lament of Ash Wednesday. Equipped with torches and lanterns people would go out and search for the defunct *Fastnacht;* they would conduct a mock funeral for her, while in the church choir the huge Lenten veil (*Fastentuch*) would be affixed to the wall, on which various scenes of Christ's Passion were depicted.

On Palm Sunday the children brought to the church bundles of palm leaves, which were blessed by the priest. They were then carried in solemn procession, children and members of the clergy impersonating young Hebrews and disciples, drawing or carrying a wooden statue of Christ, seated on a donkey. During Holy Week, Passion plays were performed in many German cities.

Easter, commemorating the resurrection of Christ, was the central feast of the Christian world. Its events, as they are embodied and dramatized in the liturgy of the Church, formed the nucleus for the development of a European drama. Many of the popular Easter customs point back to pre-Christian times. The jubilant sound of the Christian Easter bells mingled with the old Germanic joyful welcome extended to the awakening spring. In the countryside the Maypole was surrounded by dancing lads and maidens, a May Queen (*Maienkönigin*) or a May Count (*Maigraf*) was chosen and paraded about village and town. The "Easter fires" (*Osterfeuer*) were believed to protect the crops and to aid the fertility of the soil. The blessing of the elements at the entrance of the church on the morning of Holy Saturday includes the solemn kindling and blessing of fire. The most popular custom, however, was the giving away of the motley-colored Easter eggs (*Ostereier*), known and practiced all over Europe and apparently dating back to very ancient times. The Easter rabbit (*Osterhase*), who is supposed to lay the Easter eggs, probably owes this title of honor to his being widely known as a symbol of fertility, while the Easter lamb (*Oster-*

---

* Sebastian Brant appropriated this symbol when he wrote his *Ship of Fools* (*Das Narrenschiff*).

lamm) symbolizes the Paschal Lamb of the Old Testament, which fore-
shadows Christ's sacrificial death.

The most magnificent ecclesiastical pageant was the Corpus Christi
procession, which was held on the Thursday after Trinity Sunday and
was instituted in 1246. It was a feast of thanksgiving to the eucharistic Christ
and was celebrated with the participation of all classes of the population,
clergy and laity alike. The day of *Corpus Christi* (*Fronleichnam:* the body
of the Lord) stimulated the creation and production of "sacramental plays"
(*Sakramentsspiele*), of which the great Spanish playwright Calderón de la
Barca (1600–1681) became the unsurpassed master (*Autós Sacramentales*).

The festival enjoyment of the summer season was climaxed by the celebration of St. John's day (*Johannistag*), the birthday of John the Baptist,
fraught with memories and superstitions of Germanic-pagan antiquity.
As in olden times it was celebrated as the feast of the summer solstice, with
fires kindled on the mountain peaks and the young folk jumping across the
flames. Fiery wheels were rolled down the slopes and hillsides, while the
ashes of the fires of St. John were poured over the fields.

Many German cities celebrated their own local feasts of a semisecular or
secular and popular character, some of which have survived to the present
day. Festivities were also customarily connected with the visits of high
dignitaries of State and Church and with secular and ecclesiastic gatherings
(diets and councils).

The knightly tournament (cf. p. 100) had become in the fourteenth and
fifteenth centuries a favorite sport and entertainment not only of patricians
but of members of the merchant class and even of peasants. Each city had
its special playgrounds and rose gardens, which served for recreation and
diverse kinds of sports and amusements, such as bowling, handball, dancing,
and fencing. The love of dancing became a craze, so that not only guild
halls, dance halls, and taverns would be invaded by dancing crowds, but
churchyards, monasteries, and church porches were at times used indiscriminately as public ballrooms. Quite different from the light, loose, and lively
popular dances of the younger generation were the solemn and heavy dance
rhythms that had survived from the age of courtly culture. Obscenity and
licentiousness characterized not only the peasant dances but sometimes those
of the educated classes as well. The popular dance tunes of former times
were partially replaced in the fourteenth and fifteenth centuries by instrumental accompaniment, the favorite instruments of the wandering minstrels
and gleemen being the fife, the pipe and the bagpipe, the trumpet, the
trombone, the harp, the lute, and the drum. Music was introduced in the
urban home as a new form of social entertainment.

The riflemen of the cities were organized in guilds, the so-called brotherhoods of St. Sebastian, whom they had chosen as their patron saint.
In the course of the fourteenth century the crossbow began to replace the
heavy wooden bow, which with the invention of gunpowder gave way to
the firearm. The great festivals of the rifle guilds (*Schützenfeste*), originating

in the fourteenth century, were usually held in the season of Pentecost. The outstanding marksmen were given awards that varied in value and kind, such as geese, oxen, horses, cloths, banners, beakers, rings, belts, coins, and so forth. The winner of the first prize was pronounced "king of the marksmen" (*Schützenkönig*).

Card and dice games became a favorite pastime in the fourteenth and fifteenth centuries and were practiced openly or clandestinely in gambling houses. Playing cards, which had originated in the Orient, came to be manufactured in large quantities, especially as the invention of the printing press (cf. p. 189 sq.) facilitated mass production. Some of the foremost engravers tried their artistic skill in the making of playing cards. The oldest extant German deck, consisting of forty-eight cards, dates from the year 1475 and was printed in Ulm.

d) *Public Baths, Immorality, and Prostitution.* Of cultural interest are the customs and abuses connected with public and private bathing. It was generally believed that frequent bathing was an effective weapon against diseases and epidemic plagues. Private bathing facilities were provided in monasteries, castles, and the homes of the well-to-do burghers. The public bathhouses of the cities were leased to bath keepers (barber; German, *Bader*). These bathing establishments became more and more houses of public amusement and finally of moral depravity and prostitution. The bathers would spend many hours in the bathhouse, being waited on by maid-servants, eating, drinking, gambling, singing, gossiping, and talking politics. Instead of being an aid to public health and hygiene, the bathing houses thus became centers of contagion, favoring the spread of epidemic diseases, such as cholera, syphilis, and the plague.

Besides these private and public baths there were the spas or natural mineral-water baths (*Wildbäder, Heilbäder, Naturbäder*), for the benefit chiefly of the upper strata of society. We have a description of Baden in the canton Aargau in Switzerland by Francesco Poggio Bracciolini, a citizen of Florence, who visited this spa when he attended the Council of Constance in 1417. He found gathered together there a motley crowd of statesmen, army officers, members of the secular clergy, monks, and nuns. The bathing establishments were frequented by men and women alike, and the baths were equipped with floating tables, upon which food and drink was served. The evenings were spent in dancing and other social diversions.

Public morals were quite generally at a low ebb in the fourteenth and fifteenth centuries, and no social class was exempt from the decline and confusion of ethical standards. Brothels (*Frauenhäuser*) were condoned by public opinion and legalized by the administration. On the occasion of princely receptions these houses were festively adorned with flowers and garlands, and the distinguished visitors of the town were greeted and presented with bouquets by the inmates (*Hübscherinnen*). The life of a prostitute was regulated by city ordinances. She was required to wear distinctive dress or a special mark, such as a yellow or red veil, a green or yellow cloak and red headdress. In old age they were abandoned to misery, destitution, crime, and disease, unless they had mended their ways and found refuge in one of the many "homes of St. Magdalen" (*Magdalenenheime*).

e) Commerce, Banking, Mining. Despite political factionalism and growing social unrest the country was still prosperous and filled with the spirit of venture and enterprise. At the turn of the fifteenth century the expansion of German commerce was evidenced by the thriving Hansa cities in the North, the fishing industries of the North Sea, the wealthy communities of the Rhine valley; the rich iron, copper, and silver mines of Austria, Bohemia, and central Germany. Frankfurt, Nuremberg, and Augsburg had their equals only in the leading Italian trade centers, such as Venice, Florence, or Genoa. The Medicis of Florence and the Fuggers of Augsburg were the most influential banking-houses of the fifteenth century.

These bankers were the pioneers of international finance in the modern sense. When Hans Fugger, a weaver from the district of Augsburg, died in 1409, he left his sons a considerable fortune. The younger son, Jacob († 1469), became the actual founder of the trading company of Fugger, while in turn his three sons, Ulrich, Georg, and Jacob, Jr., carried on their father's business, intermarried with noble families and, in 1473, received a patent of nobility from Emperor Frederick III. In 1519 the three brothers established in their native city of Augsburg a model settlement for the poor, consisting of fifty-three duplex houses (*Fuggerei*), constituting a section of the city that was well preserved at the beginning of World War II and was one of the major attractions shown to tourists. Emperor Maximilian I borrowed from the Fuggers the equivalent of two and one half million dollars, and Charles V as well as several of the popes obtained similar loans. Like the Medicis of Florence the Fuggers were generous patrons of the arts and of learning.

Much of the Fugger fortune was acquired by the exploitation of the German silver mines and by securing a monopoly of mining rights for certain districts. Banking and mining mutually depended on each other, banking capital facilitating the introduction of improved technical methods and wielding sufficient political and economic power to make the operation of the mines a worth-while and productive undertaking. With the general growth of the volume of trade and commerce the opportunities for profitable investment became more numerous and money circulation increased, especially with the importation of gold and silver from the mines of Mexico and Peru in the sixteenth century.

f) Means of Transportation and Communication. The use of the compass had been known to the Arabs, and important discoveries in the fields of cosmography and meteorology during the fourteenth and fifteenth centuries led to a notable advancement of overseas traffic. The ships of the Hansa advanced to the entrance of the Mediterranean. Nautical geography was greatly aided by the calculations of the German cosmographer, Martin Behaim (1459–1507), who undertook an expedition to the west coast of

Africa (1484–1486) and constructed the first globe. Transportation on land, on the other hand, was carried on in traditional primitive forms. The ordinary traveler usually rode across the country on horseback, while elderly and sickly people were either carried in a sedan chair or traveled in a closed carriage or coach.

Regular postal service was established at the end of the fifteenth century. Up to that time the exchange of written communications was complicated and difficult. In the Middle Ages princes, cities, monasteries, and universities had transmitted their messages by a special messenger and courier service. The Teutonic Knights had developed a very efficient system of relay posts. The cities in the interior of Germany followed their example in developing their own system of postal messengers. The imperial chancellery of the Hapsburg rulers employed special couriers and developed a fairly regular postal communication system during the reign of Frederick III.

From 1489 on we find members of the family of Taxis (later Thurn and Taxis) as imperial postmasters. In 1520 they were given charge of postal administration in all imperial territories. They controlled two main postal highways, the one running from the Netherlands through France and Spain, the other through southern Germany and Austria down to Venice, Milan, Rome, and Naples. In 1595 Emperor Rudolf II appointed Leonard of Taxis as "postmaster general." Later on, the territorial princes and the great urban trade centers established their own postal services, thereby becoming competitors of the imperial post and cutting in on its big revenues. The dissolution of the Holy Roman Empire (1806) invalidated most of the postal privileges of the Taxis family. The German-Austrian Postal Union of 1850 created a unified postal territory for the German and Austrian states. After the unification of the German states and the foundation of the new German Empire of 1871 the Imperial Postal Administration (*Reichspostverwaltung*) absorbed all the remaining local administrative units, with the exception of Bavaria and Wurtemberg (*Swabia*), which retained some degree of autonomy until 1919.

The Invention of Printing. The expansion of trade, commerce, and industry in the fifteenth century was accompanied by a growing desire for more efficient means and methods of education, which would give the average citizen access to the intellectual and scientific achievements of the past and present. The new craving for reading and for a broad general education was satisfied and received an even greater impetus through the invention of book printing with movable type.

Up to the middle of the fifteenth century books had to be written by hand. The manuscripts (*manu scribere;* "to write by hand") were the work of monks, and they were almost exclusively used in monastic libraries. The "Brethren of the Common Life" (cf. p. 180) were among the first professional copyists of religious books who tried to make their products available to the people at large. The fifteenth century witnessed the growth of a class of professional scribes in the cities.

It is only partly correct to speak of the "invention of printing" in the fifteenth century and to credit John Gensfleisch Gutenberg (*c.* 1400–1468) of Mainz with this discovery. The art of printing had been known to the Chinese, the Babylonians, the Romans, and other peoples of the ancient world. The Chinese had produced printed books before the beginning of the eleventh century A.D. Pictures, playing cards, pamphlets, and even books had been printed in Europe since the twelfth century by means of carved metal or wooden blocks (woodcuts, block prints). The invention of the manufacture of paper from rags considerably reduced the cost of the manuscripts and led to the gradual development of a regular book trade, which was in the hands of the so-called *stationarii* (stationers).

Gutenberg's important contribution to the art of printing was the invention of the movable metal types, which were cast separately with the aid of a "matrix" or model and could be assembled in any desired combination for any number of books. It was the great advantage of this innovation that books could now be printed in large quantities and at very moderate cost. Before the close of the fifteenth century more than one thousand printing presses had been established in Europe and more than thirty thousand editions had been published. In the sixteenth century Germany alone contributed nearly one million volumes to the general output. The most famous of the early printing firms were the Aldine Press at Venice, the Froben Press at Basel, and the Plantin Press at Antwerp. Five presses had been established at Mainz, six at Ulm, sixteen at Basel, twenty at Augsburg, and twenty-one at Cologne. More than one hundred German presses were operated in Italy. The first geographical maps were printed by Konrad Schweinsheim in 1471, and Erhard Oeglin invented the art of printing musical notes in movable type.

The earliest books printed with movable type are called *incunabulae* (*Inkunabeln, Wiegendrucke*). In type, format, and material they follow closely the old paper and parchment manuscripts. The Latin (*Antiqua*) type of letters, which resembled the old minuscules (cf. p. 53), was introduced into Germany from Italy, partly replacing the Gothic characters.

The invention of movable type aided greatly in providing the broadest possible forum for the teachings of the Humanists and the Reformers, and in arousing a widespread popular interest in political, social, and religious affairs. In the age of the Reformation the art of printing served as one of the most efficient weapons in the religious struggle. Germany as a nation prided herself on having given to the world a new method of education and public enlightenment. Everyone probably agreed with Jacob Wimpheling, one of the leaders of early German Humanism, when he wrote in 1507: "As in former times the apostles of Christianity, so now the disciples of the new sacred art of printing go out from Germany into all the lands, and their printed books become the heralds of the Gospel, the preachers of truth and knowledge."

Arts and Crafts.   The German craftsman and artisan of the fourteenth

Section of the Virgin's Altar in Creglingen, by Tilman Riemenschneider

and fifteenth centuries was justly proud of his exquisite workmanship. The products of his hands were highly praised and esteemed at home and abroad. The "Tomb of St. Sebald" in St. Sebald's Church in Nuremberg, containing the relics of the city's patron saint, and the famous tabernacle in St. Lawrence Church (*St. Lorenz*), in the same city, are adorned with the self-portrayals of their makers, Peter Vischer (*c.* 1460–1529) and Adam Krafft (*c.* 1455–1508), the former depicted with his leather apron and hammer, the latter shown in the company of two of his journeymen. The fame of the goldsmiths and metalworkers of Augsburg, Nuremberg, Cologne, Vienna, Ratisbon, Prague, and Ulm extended all over Europe, their crafts being greatly aided and encouraged by the brief revival of the spirit of knighthood under Emperor Maximilian I. The Tyrolese masters excelled in cabinetwork, such as the making of chests, cupboards, decorative portals, chancels, and choir stools.

In the age of prospering cities and expanding trade the wealthy merchants became the patrons of the arts. The artists themselves were little concerned about the originality of their work or their personal fame, so that it is often difficult to distinguish between the creations of the masters and those of their apprentices and journeymen. The public buildings, secular and ecclesiastic, were the result of the communal effort of the city, each social group contributing its proper share. Thus an intimate contact was established between the people, the artists, and the art works. The interrelation of art and life in the fourteenth century is reflected in the more realistic observation of the near and the concrete, the occurrences of everyday life, the small, the genrelike, and the idyllic.

German architecture of the fifteenth century lacks the depth and vitality of many monuments of the preceding age, but it excels in magnificent and imposing creations of ecclesiastical and secular art, cathedrals, town halls, and castles. The great works of late Gothic sculpture forego the solemnity and sublimity of the high Gothic and, in accordance with the taste of the burgher class, turn to the descriptive, the intimate, and the psychological. The statues partake of the fast and vigorous rhythm of city life. They are close to nature and indulge in phantastic decorative design, the abstract lineament of folds, exaggerated gesticulation, and a complex scale of emotions. In Nuremberg we find the artists Veit Stoss, Adam Krafft, and Peter Vischer; in Würzburg Tilman Riemenschneider (*c.* 1460–1531), the master of late Gothic wood sculpture in Franconia, whose works combine the religious inwardness of medieval sculpture with the psychological realism of the early Renaissance. In the peasant wars of 1524–1525 (cf. p. 240 sq.) this master joined the peasant armies who fought against the bishop of Würzburg, was captured and subjected to severe torture.

The growing realism and individualism in the arts was most strikingly manifested in the Netherlands, whose culture was strongly and proudly Germanic and where the full national emancipation of occidental painting was brought about in the fifteenth century by such ingenious innovators as the brothers Hubert (*c.* 1370–1426) and Jan van Eyck (*c.* 1385–1440), the creators of the famous Altar of Ghent, who had been educated in the tradition of book illumination. Together they painted the Ghent altarpiece, the central panel depicting the "Adoration of the Lamb," symbolizing Christ and his sacrificial death, an illustration of the words of the Apocalypse: "I looked, and Lo, a Lamb stood on Mount Sion." In the background is the likewise symbolic Fountain of Life, in the foreground a realistically rendered landscape, while the groups of worshipers represent the different strata of Christian society. The altarpiece consists of twenty separate panels, reaching a new height of individualistic portrayal and a richness of color which bears witness to the greatly improved technique of oil painting. This newly perfected technique of the artists of the Netherlands and those of Burgundy became the model for the great painters of Italy, Spain, England, and especially Germany. Under the leadership of the Van Eycks oil painting on canvas or wood replaced the older method of painting on a specially prepared panel with colored pigment that had been mixed with egg (*tempera*-technique).

The classical land of book painting (illumination, miniature painting) was Burgundy, but the Netherlands and Germany benefited from the achievements of the Burgundian schools, appropriating and imitating their advanced technique of perspective and verisimilitude. The school of miniature painting in Prague enjoyed the friendly interest and support of Emperor Charles IV and King Wenceslaus.

The school of Cologne took the lead in the development of oil painting in Germany. The works of the Rhenish masters combine the spiritual depth of the mystics of the Rhineland with the gracefulness and fragrant beauty of the painters of Burgundy. Stephan Lochner († 1451), the most prominent member of the Rhenish school, is the author of many religious paintings, among which his Madonnas and especially the solemn and sublime "Adoration of the Child" in the Cathedral of Cologne (*Dreikönigsbild*) rank highest.

After the middle of the fifteenth century the leadership in oil painting passed to the south of the Empire, with the Swabians, Lukas Moser and Konrad Witz, and the Tyrolese, Michael Pacher (painter and carver), forcefully striking a new and more virile note. In the Alsatian regions Martin Schongauer's (*c.* 1450–1491) workshop attracted the outstanding talents among the younger generation, and from him they adopted a new sense of form and proportion. His influence is especially noticeable in the works of the masters of Ulm, Augsburg, and Nuremberg.

Dürer, Holbein, and Grünewald. It is against this general artistic background that the three greatest geniuses of German painting — Albrecht Dürer, Hans Holbein the Younger, and Matthias Grünewald — must be seen to be fully appreciated. In Dürer and Holbein the inner life of the late Gothic style in the North blends with the formal beauty of the Italian Renaissance, while in Grünewald the spirituality of the Germanic North reaches out even beyond the stylistic boundaries of the sixteenth century

Knight, Death, and the Devil, by Albrecht Dürer

Madonna With Child, by Matthias Grünewald

and anticipates the religious fervor of the period of Baroque (cf. pp. 330–354) and Catholic Restoration (cf. pp. 253–259).

a) *Albrecht Dürer* (*1471–1528*). The sober realism and solid craftsmanship that characterize the Frankish school of painting, and that were practiced in the workshop of Michael Wohlgemut (1434–1519) in Nuremberg, were to reach unprecedented heights in the timeless art of Wohlgemut's greatest pupil, Albrecht Dürer. A native of Nuremberg, a city which in the fifteenth century embodied everything that was great and admirable in German culture, Albrecht Dürer learned the art of drawing in the workshop of his father, who was a well-known goldsmith. From 1486–1490 he worked as one of Wohlgemut's apprentices. As a journeyman he traveled along the valley of the upper Rhine, to Colmar, Basel, and Strasbourg. Twice he visited Italy, and in his later years he journeyed to the Netherlands.

During his travels he eagerly absorbed new experiences and technical innovations but never lost his identity and strongly marked personality. Foreign lands and their people, personal contacts and social intercourse rather proved an invaluable aid in developing his individual style, and the acquaintance with foreign mentalities helped him to understand more profoundly himself, his own art, his country, and his people. Some of the leading Humanists he called his friends, and during his stay in the Low Countries he met Emperor Charles V and Erasmus of Rotterdam (cf. p. 249 sq.). Clever and ingenious artist and craftsman that he was, Albrecht Dürer never lost sight of the material and mechanical bases of his work and happily combined sound theory with faultless execution. In the graphic arts he stands out as a bold innovator who perfected the techniques of woodcut and engraving, both arts having originated in Germany during the first half of the fifteenth century, while the technique of etching was invented by Daniel Hopfer of Augsburg about the year 1500.

The sentiments of the age as well as Dürer's own outlook on life are symbolically illustrated in two of his most celebrated engravings: "Knight, Death, and Devil" (1513) and "Melancholia" (1514). The former shows a knight on horseback, in heavy armor, proceeding on his way through vale and forest, in grim determination and with courage undaunted, while the weird specters of Death and Devil try in vain to waylay him and shake his trust in life. The engraving that bears the title "Melancholia" depicts an enigmatic woman, seated on the ground and surrounded by all the paraphernalia of sciences old and new, but with the despairing glance of utter skepticism and frustration in her eyes. Clearly, Albrecht Dürer is suggesting the growing complexity of life as it weighed heavily on the individuals of a new epoch that was about to emerge from the shelter of a common heritage of faith and order, embarking upon adventures of body and soul, which were as alluring as they were intimidating.

b) *Hans Holbein the Younger* (*1497–1543*). The second of the great German masters in the sixteenth century deserves the predicate "classical" in a fuller sense than even Dürer did. He emancipated himself completely from the Gothic tradition which was as yet unbroken in the warm color harmonies of his own father, Hans Holbein the Elder (*c.* 1470–1524), a prominent member of the Swabian school of painting. The son owes his fame to the purity of his artistic form and the clarity of pattern which helped him to achieve a detachment and tranquillity that make him a faithful recorder of reality and one of the greatest portrait painters of all time. In him the northern Renaissance reaches its culminating point.

At the age of seventeen Holbein moved from his native city of Augsburg to Basel in Switzerland, where he had intercourse with Erasmus of Rotterdam and other scholars and publishers of the humanistic circles. The iconoclast movement of some groups of the reformed churches in Switzerland forced him to abandon religious painting and finally prompted him to leave his native land to become the official painter to the court of King Henry VIII of England.

Even the religious paintings of Holbein's early period are religious in name and theme only, but classical, cool, and worldly in their matter-of-factness and in the calculated stateliness of their poses. His "Madonna of the Burgomaster Meyer" is a German family picture, the document of a ripe city culture and of bourgeois taste. An element of irony and mild skepticism permeates many of Holbein's works, introducing a satirical note even into his treatment of the "Dance of Death," a series of woodcuts that present a running commentary on one of the favorite themes of the later Middle Ages: the gruesome figure of Death approaching the representatives of different social groups and impressing upon them the universal democracy of the great Reaper's merciless rule: "Here God judges justly, the masters lying with the servants: now mark well and, if you can, tell the master from the servant!" (from the so-called *Little Dance of Death* of Basel). In these woodcuts Holbein becomes the spokesman of his age as well as of his class, the defender of the democratic claims of the cities against the aristocracy of imperial and princely rule.

c) Matthias Grünewald (c. 1470–1528). The most unconventional and extraordinary of the three German master painters, entirely untouched by the Italian Renaissance and deeply rooted in the intellectual clime and maternal soil of the Germanic North, is Mathis Gothard Neithard, better known as Matthias Grünewald. Beyond the fact that he was born in Würzburg, died in Halle on the Saale, and worked in Mainz, Frankfort on the Main, and Aschaffenburg, little is known about his life. In his masterpiece, the "Isenheim Altar" in Colmar (Alsace), he appears as the great mystic visionary among the German painters, the interpreter of the inner life, in whose works a sense of inexorable tragedy is mitigated only by the spiritual powers of mercy and love. His colors are symphonically arranged, with loud dominants striking the key notes.

The "Isenheim Altar" was originally painted for a hospital church in southern Alsace and depicts, on some of its panels, scenes of the Annunciation, the Birth of Christ, the Crucifixion, and the Resurrection. Grünewald's treatment of the theme of the Crucifixion illustrates best the artist's indifference to conventional concepts of beauty, harmony, and symmetry, whenever it was a question of expressing inner experiences that transcend the normal scope of human joy or human suffering. The body of Christ is rendered in proportions much larger than life, yet with a naturalistic over-description of somber detail, in livid, greenish colors as if in the process of decomposition. It is suspended from the cross against the backdrop of a dark night sky, the emaciated arms outstretched, with hands nailed to the cross-beams and fingers convulsively upturned. Beneath the cross the pointing finger of John the Baptist gives pictorial emphasis to his spoken words: "He must grow, and I must diminish," offering an effective counterbalance to the group of mourners on the opposite side: Christ's mother in the protecting embrace of John the Evangelist, and the kneeling figure of Mary Magdalen, with hands raised in fervent supplication.

Gloom and suffering of the Crucifixion are contrasted with the jubilant tones and colors of the Incarnation and the "Angels' Concert": one panel, but divided into two parts, with a dual background of late Gothic decoration and a bright, sunlit landscape. The minute and naïve observation of human life adds to the poetic and idyllic beauty of the composition.

As the ripest bloom of the Gothic-medieval world the "Isenheim Altar" with its masterly orchestration restates and summarizes the spirituality of the past, anticipating at the same time the synthesis of nature and super-nature which was to become the central problem and the supreme ambition of Baroque art (cf. p. 337 sq.). The antithesis of life and death, the dualism and tension that penetrates reality to its innermost depth, but is reconciled in the ecstatic exuberance of feeling, point forward to the mystical and pietistic forms of devotion that characterize the religious temper of the age of the Catholic Restoration (cf. p. 253 sqq.).

Language and Literature. During the thirteenth, fourteenth, and fifteenth centuries the German language was used in an increasing number of legal documents, deeds, and contracts of sale, donation, and arbitration. The law code of the Saxons (*Sachsenspiegel*), originally written in Latin, had been translated into German by Eike von Repkow about the middle of the thirteenth century. The Swabian law code (*Schwabenspiegel*) was written in German about 1275. Various imperial edicts, such as Rudolf of Hapsburg's Land Peace of 1287, were likewise promulgated in German. The German language became more and more a true mirror of the social changes that were taking place and, owing to the influence of the German mystics (cf. p. 146 sqq.) and the rising city culture, acquired a closer affinity to the everyday life of the people. Poetry descended from its aristocratic heights and put on the simpler and popular features of a workaday world of burghers and peasants.

a) Folk Songs. The singers, too, descended from the castles to the valleys and plains, mingled with the people, singing with them the songs of their loves and yearnings, their woes and worries, their deeds and aspirations: working songs, hunting songs, nature songs, religious songs, pastoral songs, drinking songs, student songs, soldiers' songs, and so forth. Some of the oldest German folk songs have the form of the ballad, and they frequently manifest, in their moods, themes, and rhythms, dramatic and tragic elements.

The folk songs of the Germans, like every type of folk song, are an expression of the communal experiences of an entire people. They mirror the folk spirit that is shared by the many individuals that constitute the natural units of the several social groups, classes, and estates. Melody and text become inseparably linked, after having undergone a process of gradual mutual adaptation and solidification. As to the question of authorship, it seems impossible to establish a general rule: many of the German folk songs are anonymous, while others were composed by well-known poets but were appropriated by the people and underwent considerable transformations.

Stylistically the German folk songs are simple and direct in text and tune without ever becoming monotonous. The dialogue and the refrain are favorite devices, adding rhythmical stress and color accents.

The oldest German folk songs date from the middle of the thirteenth century. The first collection is contained in the *Locheimer Liederbuch* of 1460. Herder (cf. p. 396 sq.) in the eighteenth and the Romanticists of the beginning nineteenth century (cf. p. 470 sqq.) extolled the folk poetry of all nations as genuine manifestations of the folk spirit (*Volksgeist*). The very term *Volkslied* was coined by Herder. He published an anthology of the folk songs of forty-eight different nations (*Stimmen der Völker,* "Voices of the Nations," 1778). The most popular collection of German folk poetry was edited by the two Romantic writers, Achim von Arnim and Clemens Brentano (*Des Knaben Wunderhorn,* "The Boy's Magic Horn," 3 vols., 1806–1808). The interest in German folk song was revived in recent decades by the several groups of the German Youth Movement (cf. p. 709 sq.).

Next to the folk songs the folk books (*Volksbücher*) stand out as monuments of German life and German culture. Like the folk songs they were handed down from generation to generation, wandering from village to village and from one German tribe to the other. They, too, were probably written down originally by some individual author but soon became the property of the people as a whole. Historical personages (Faust, Eulenspiegel, Kaiser Octavianus, etc.) were frequently surrounded with a wreath of poetic fancy, embodying the thoughts and feelings of the people. Again the Romantic writers of the early nineteenth century must be credited with the rediscovery and just appraisal of these literary documents of the German past.

b) The Beginnings of German Drama. Medieval drama originated in the liturgy of the Church and therefore was essentially an accessory of the religious service. It was closely associated with the sacrifice of the Mass, its stage being the church choir and its purpose the dramatization of the mysteries of the Redemption. Its spiritual center was the Gospel narrative of the Incarnation and Resurrection of Christ. The absence of all the elements of metaphysical or individual tragedy sets this liturgical drama apart from Greek and modern drama alike. The gloom of Golgotha was always followed by the gladness of Easter, so that in the end tragedy issued in "Divine Comedy."

In Italy, France, and England the origins of these morality and miracle plays can be traced back to the eleventh and twelfth centuries, while in Germany they were not universally known and produced until the beginning of the fourteenth century. The oldest plays were all performed in Latin, the texts strictly following the biblical and liturgical books; later on, German and Latin passages were used alternatingly. A purely German drama finally emerged in the fourteenth century.

The actors were originally priests, who dramatized the antiphonies of the Easter chants, especially the scene that depicts the two Marys and the angel at the tomb of the risen Christ. This so-called "Easter-Tropus" (verses which introduce and surround the liturgical texts) was composed around the biblical question: "Whom do ye seek?"; the answer of the two Marys: "Jesus of Nazareth, the Crucified," and the angel's response: "He is risen, He is not here; go ye and make it known." To this nucleus new and more realistic motifs were gradually added, until the preponderance of satirical and comical elements made it necessary to transfer the performance from the interior of the church to less cultic surroundings, monastic chapter halls or public buildings and squares. Additional religious themes were provided by the inclusion of other parts of the liturgy, so that in the end medieval drama embraced almost every major event of the ecclesiastical year, including the prefigurative symbols and prophecies of the Old Testament.

The development of the Passion play marks a certain humanization and secularization of the purely religious and cultic character of the early miracle plays. The dramatization of Christ's Passion required not only a more elaborate display of technical and artistic devices, made possible by the share that the inhabitants of the prosperous cities of the fifteenth century took in these spectacles, but it also put the emphasis on the human and emotional elements in the performance of the actors: torture and agony, human suffering, and motherly care. The Passion and morality play of the fifteenth century becomes a cyclical and panoramic spectacle, the production of which might occupy a period of several days, enacted no longer by priests and clerics but by students and choirboys, burghers and lay brotherhoods. Of the several Passion plays which have survived the disintegration of religious drama, the one of Oberammergau in Bavaria is the best known. It owes its origin to a revised edition and compilation of two Augsburg moralities of the fifteenth and sixteenth centuries. The oldest authentic text dates from the year 1662. Its periodical performance (normally every tenth year) was instituted by a solemn vow of the population of Oberammergau in 1633, when the town was visited by the plague.

A purely secular type of play developed apart from religious drama, but was of less decisive influence on German dramatic art. It dates back to the farces and burlesques of the Carolingian period and, in the form of the "shrovetide play," reached its maturest form in the *Fastnachtsspiele* of Hans Sachs (1494–1576), Hans Rosenplüt (*c.* 1450), and Hans Folz (*c.* 1450–1515), all connected with the circles of the *Meistersinger* Schools of Nuremberg, but none of them ascending to the level of a pure dramatic style.

c) *The Schools of the "Meistersinger."* With the decay of the culture of chivalry the "Minnesänger" (cf. p. 155 sq.) had become silent, and the castle could no longer serve as the abode of the Muses. The art of poetry had to adapt itself to the simple and sober tastes of the burgher class, and it found a new home in the workshops and festival halls of the guilds and glee clubs. These so-called schools of the "mastersingers" emerge at the beginning of the fifteenth century, and their members apply the strict rules and statutes of the guild system to the free spirit of poetry, thus cutting the wings of poetic imagination and stifling creative genius.

The apprentice of the art of poetry had to undergo a rigid training until he would be allowed to graduate from "scribe" (*Schreiber*) and "friend of the schools" (*Schulfreund*) to the rank of "poet" (*Dichter*) and "master" (*Meister*). The rules were set forth in the "tablature" (*Tabulatur*) and had to be pedantically observed, if the candidate wished to avoid failure. Meter and subject matter were likewise meticulously prescribed, and specially appointed judges (*Merker*) presided over the public competitions to add up the errors and the infractions of the rules and to award the winner a silver chain with a medallion. The whole procedure was, of course, profoundly oblivious of the true spirit of poetry. Even Hans Sachs, the Nuremberg shoemaker-poet and the greatest talent among the members of the schools, hardly ever succeeded in transcending the unnatural limitations imposed on his art by the social prejudices and artistic misconceptions of his age. Among his 6200 poetic creations there are 4275 master songs. However, some of his *Fastnachtsspiele* and farces (*Schwänke*) stand out as models of wit, healthy realism, and common sense. Hans Sachs joined the forces of the Reformation, praising Luther as the "nightingale of Wittenberg."

Education and the Schools. The changing standard of living, the difference in vocational training and interest, and the increasing number of people who actively participated in the social, economic, and cultural life of the cities required new means and methods of education. Many of the secondary schools of the fourteenth and fifteenth centuries were founded, administered, and supervised by the city councils. The cathedral and monastery schools continued in existence, but had grown too small to take care of the rapidly growing number of pupils. The schoolmaster (*Schulmeister*), appointed by the city council, was in most cases a layman who had acquired his education at some university. He was assisted by one or several teachers (*Unterlehrer, Provisoren, Locati*). The larger part of the headmaster's and the assistants' salaries was paid from tuition fees. In addition, the pupils were required to present their teachers with various contributions paid in kind, such as Christmas hens, shrovetide cakes,

Easter eggs, flour, wood, and so forth. The teacher might earn some extra money by making woodcuts or drawing up legal documents.

The well-to-do children had their private tutors or preceptors, who supervised their homework and accompanied them on their way to and from school. The poorer children obtained the money needed to pay their board and tuition by begging or singing, if they were not fortunate enough to secure one of the few available stipends (endowments for choirboys, etc.).

The curriculum usually included writing, reading, reckoning, religion, liturgical singing, and Latin. The three standard textbooks were the *tabula* (primer), Donatus' time-honored grammar, and the *Doctrinale puerorum,* composed by the Franciscan grammarian, Alexander de Villa Dei, in 1199. According to the texts used on different class levels the students were known as Tabulists, Donatists, and Alexandrists. Discipline was severe and corporal punishment frequent.

Private German schools, as distinguished from the public and municipal Latin institutions, make their appearance after the middle of the fourteenth century. Coeducation was not infrequently practiced in private German schools as early as the fifteenth century. Separate public schools for girls (*Maidlin-Schulen*), with women as teachers, are traceable in the fourteenth century. They were mostly attended by the children of the poor, while the daughters of wealthy burghers and nobles received their training in convent schools. The standard of general education was relatively high in the fifteenth century. It seems evident that the majority of the population had acquired the essentials of reading, writing, and arithmetic.

Students attending the university lived together in a students' hall or dormitory (*Burse*), under the supervision of a *Magister* (master). Here, too, an almost monastic discipline was rigidly enforced. Dress, the hours of study and recreation, and rules of conduct were prescribed in every detail. The student's day began at four o'clock in the morning and ended at nine o'clock at night. Meals were taken in the common refectory. The strictness of the rules was perhaps responsible for the many infractions of academic discipline, as evidenced by unending complaints and reprimands. Various excesses were traditionally committed during the initiation ceremonies for freshmen. In the presence of the *Magister* the newcomer would be subjected to almost any imaginable kind of mischief and vexation; with his face disfigured by mud or salves, teeth broken or pulled out, his beard shorn, and powerful purgatives administered by force, the neophyte must have cut a sorry figure, especially when he considered that he had to pay for the ensuing drinking bout. Nevertheless, he had the satisfaction that henceforth he was entitled to call himself "scholar" or *Bursche*.

The Changing Spirit of the Age. The fourteenth and fifteenth centuries witnessed the growth of modern humanity as it stands revealed in the movements of Renaissance, Humanism, Reformation, and Catholic Restoration, which stir and occupy the following two hundred years. The symptoms of the impending transformation are manifold, and they affect life and civilization in all their aspects. The change is primarily one of religious ideology and social philosophy, and it is therefore most clearly manifested in the religious attitudes of individuals and groups and in their relationship to life and death.

The religion of the later Middle Ages bears the marks of paradoxical contrasts: superficiality and carefree hedonism on the one hand, and a terrifying metaphysical anxiety, loneliness, and a frenzied and almost hysterical preoccupation with the mysteries of the supernatural and preternatural on the other. Church festivals are celebrated with an ever increasing splendor and the outward display of lavish popular entertainment. The interior of the church building becomes a favorite social meeting place: the people attending the services in the company of their dogs or other pets; the traveling merchants offering their wares for sale; and announcements of public auctions being read from the pulpit. But this desecration of the spiritual and this intemperate joy of living was accompanied by morbid fear, resignation, and wayless despair — a mood that is well expressed in a touching little poem, composed by a certain Master Martinus of Biberach in the year 1498:

> Ich leb', weiss nit wie lang
> Ich sterb und weiss nit wann;
> Ich geh', weiss nit wohin:
> Mich wundert dass ich fröhlich bin.*

The hour of death is filled with all the horror of the awful unknown. The soul is overwhelmed by dryness, lack of faith, distrust and doubt, and by its attachment to things transitory. The dying person, however, clings desperately to the sacraments and the other aids and consolations that the Church has to offer, such as extreme unction, holy water, blessed candles. The funerals become most elaborate and even extravagant affairs. The mourners wear black garments and carry crosses, candles, torches, and banners. The burial is followed by a funeral repast or burial feast.

This dualism, which sounds so shrill and discordant in the death throes of the Middle Ages and the birth throes of the modern world, finds a remarkable illustration in a literary document of the early fifteenth century. Johan von Saaz, author of *Der Ackermann aus Böhmen (The Ploughman of Bohemia,* 1400), after having lost his beloved wife, has a plowman and Death discuss in dialogue form the position of man in the universe, in view of death, retribution, and eternal salvation. The plowman defends the intrinsic value of earthly beauty, vigor, and joyfulness, of human life in its plenitude, as against the medieval subordination of creature to Creator, of nature to supernature. This glorification of life and nature as ends in themselves — however problematic and restrained its expression — sounds the major theme of Renaissance and Humanism.

---

* I live, don't know the end;
I die, and don't know when;
I go, and don't know where;
I wonder I am free from care.

Chapter 8

REFORMATION, PEASANT WARS, AND CATHOLIC RESTORATION

Charles V and the Empire. After the death of Emperor Maximilian I, in 1519, the choice of the Electors was his grandson Charles, the son of Philip the Fair, duke of Burgundy, and Joanna the Insane, the eldest daughter of Ferdinand and Isabella of Spain. At the age of sixteen Charles had become king of Spain, and he was nineteen years old when he assumed the burden of governing one of the vastest empires of all time. The dominion of the new ruler of the Hapsburg dynasty extended over the hereditary Hapsburg possessions in Germany: the Burgundian states of Franche-Comté, Luxemburg, and the Netherlands; the newly conquered Spanish possessions in South America; the Spanish kingdoms of Castile and Aragon; as well as Naples, Sicily, and Sardinia, Spain's possessions on Italian soil.

In contrast to France, which had achieved unity and strength as a centralized monarchy, Charles's possessions were scattered through many lands, and communications were difficult. The royal power was further weakened by the lack of a hereditary imperial succession, the absence of a definite political center of gravity, and the constant rivalry of the several princely houses.

The election of 1519 had been preceded by an electoral campaign, in which King Francis I of France (1515–1547), King Henry VIII of England (1509–1547), Charles's own younger brother Ferdinand, and Frederick, the prince-elector of Saxony, were at various times candidates for the imperial office. Leo X (1513–1521), the Renaissance pope of the Medici family, only reluctantly withdrew his initial objection to Charles's election and his support of the candidacies of Francis I and Frederick "the Wise" of Saxony. When the German Electors finally voted unanimously for Charles, their decision was chiefly influenced by the fact that, with the withdrawal of Frederick of Saxony as a candidate and with Charles's refusal to withdraw his own claims in favor of his brother Ferdinand, the choice left to them was between a member of the Hapsburg family and a potentate of wholly foreign blood and nationality. They also hoped that personal interest in the fate of his hereditary Austrian lands would impel Charles to take up the fight against the Turkish menace in the eastern provinces of the Empire, and that the strongly Catholic tradition of the Austrian and Spanish Hapsburgs would make the new emperor a stanch defender of the Roman Catholic position against the rising tide of the Reformation. Nevertheless, before giving Charles their votes, the Electors had made him sign a "capitulation" (electoral compromise) that was to guarantee their own prerogatives as well as safeguard Germany from the infiltration of Spanish soldiers and officials and from a cultural prevalence of Spanish influence.

The solution of the problems with which the young emperor found himself confronted would have required a large measure of statesmanlike vision, determination, and actual power, a combination of qualities which Charles could in nowise call his own. He grew but slowly into the stature required by his exalted calling, and was at all times both too sensitive and too inflexible to direct or control the rapidly shifting events on the European scene. Being no match for the shrewd and frivolous king of France, and the scheming territorial princes of Germany, and handicapped besides by the fact of his never ceasing to be a foreigner on German soil — a Spaniard in his manner, his tastes, and his mentality — Charles experienced a long series of partial achievements and total disappointments. Finally, reaching a point where, in his utter loneliness, dynastic power had no more allurements for him, he laid down the burden of ruling the mightiest empire on earth and retired to a Spanish monastery (1556).

Charles V and Francis I: The Conflict Between Hapsburg and Valois. The main factors that decided the future destiny of the Empire were the conflict between the houses of Hapsburg and Valois and the Lutheran revolt in Germany. Most of the wars that Charles waged against Francis I were fought on foreign soil, which necessitated the absence of the emperor from Germany and provided the German princes with the opportunity of strengthening their territorial independence and of preventing the centralization of the imperial government. Charles's foreign entanglements required his exclusive attention and used up most of the material resources of the Empire, so that little consideration could be given to the settlement of the religious disputes and to the readjustment of the social order.

Between the two opposing monarchies of Hapsburg and Valois stood the less powerful but equally determined and ever watchful representative of the house of Tudor, Henry VIII of England. He and his minister of state, Cardinal Wolsey, encouraged, chiefly with vague promises, either side at different times, thus upholding what is euphemistically known as the "European balance of power."

The ruler of France, finding his country surrounded by the Hapsburg lands in the south (Spain) and in the east (the Empire), had set his mind on the destruction of what he considered the Hapsburg menace. In Italy, the possessions of the two houses were spread out over the peninsula, Francis holding the duchy of Milan and Charles ruling over the kingdom of Naples, with both monarchies challenging the legality of each other's claims.

The cause of Charles was hampered not only by the traditional shortage of money and supplies of the German emperors, but likewise by the political, social, and religious unrest in different parts of the unwieldy Empire. Hostilities started in 1521, after Charles had presided over the Diet of Worms, and had entrusted his brother Ferdinand with the administration of the German and Austrian crown lands of the house of Hapsburg. While Charles was engaged in his struggles with the house of Valois, the task of protecting the eastern frontiers of the Empire from the attacks of the Turks was left to Ferdinand. He became king of Bohemia and Hungary by marriage, after his wife's brother, Louis II, the last king of Hungary, was killed by the Turks at Mohács in 1526.

Charles's first war against Francis was fought in Italy and ended with what looked like a decisive victory for the emperor — the capture of the French king. In the Treaty of Madrid (1526) Francis solemnly renounced the duchy of Burgundy as well as the French claims to the disputed territories in the Netherlands, Navarre, and Italy. In this first campaign Henry VIII and Pope Leo X had been the allies of the German emperor.

Francis, however, never intended to keep the solemn pledges of the Peace of Madrid. Once safely back on French soil he succeeded in organizing the "League of Cognac," which included the Italian states as well as the successor of Leo X, Pope Clement VII (1523-1534), another Medici on the papal throne, during whose reign the separation of the Anglican Church from Rome was consummated. In Germany, meanwhile, the affairs of State were carried on by a "governing council" which had been created by the Diet of Worms and which was composed of delegates chosen by the Electors and the emperor. It was during this second campaign against Francis I that the ill-famed and brutal "sack of Rome" (1527) occurred. The constable of Bourbon, after having deserted the cause of the French king and after having obtained the command of the imperial army in northern Italy, led his mutinous troops to the Eternal City so that they might collect their overdue pay from the spoils of pillage and plunder. Spanish troops and German mercenaries vied in acts of wanton savagery and sacrilege.

Clement VII, after an imprisonment of seven months in the castle of San Angelo, conferred the imperial crown on Charles V in the cathedral of Bologna in 1530, this being the last coronation of a German emperor by a pope. In the Peace of Cambrai (1529) Francis I again renounced his claims to the contested territories in Italy, but was allowed to retain the duchy of Burgundy. Several times Charles's impending defeat had been turned into victory, and by 1529 Hapsburg domination of Italy was definitely established.

The *"Sacco di Roma"* had taken place without Charles's knowledge, but though he disapproved of the acts of violence, the conquest of Rome and the siege of Clement VII in San Angelo served his ends and strengthened his strategic position. The terms of the Treaty of Cambrai gave him sufficient prestige and a free hand to deal with the dual dangers of Turkish aggression and religious revolt.

The Turks had captured Constantinople in 1453 and had constantly advanced westward during the following decades. At the time of Charles's election they were in possession of the territory of the ancient Byzantine empire and of the Balkan States, carrying their advance under Sultan Suliman "the Magnificent" (1520–1566) up the river Danube and threatening Vienna in 1529. After a temporary setback they resumed their march on Austria in 1532, when Charles V joined forces with his brother Ferdinand, repulsing the aggressors and liberating part of Hungary. In 1533 a peace was concluded between Ferdinand, who in 1531 had been elected Roman-German king, and Sultan Suliman. The final result of twelve years of warfare with the Turks was the partition of Hungary in 1541, which left the greater part of the country in the possession of the enemy. The Turkish domination of Hungary lasted for some 150 years and brought the country to the brink of ruin. Not until the end of the seventeenth century did the house of Hapsburg succeed in restoring the integrity of Hungary.

The Peace of Cambrai was hardly more than a truce, and hostilities between Charles and Francis started again in 1536, with a French attack on Milan and Piedmont, ending in another truce (Nice) and another treaty (Toledo, 1538). The French king repeatedly sided with the Protestant princes of Germany and with the Turks against Charles V. The year 1542 witnessed the grand alliance of the French, the Turks, the Swedes, and the forces of the duke of Cleves, and in 1544 Charles invaded France and advanced on Paris. In the Peace of Crespy (1544) Francis surrendered all his former gains, renouncing all his claims to Hapsburg territory but retaining Burgundy and the towns of the Somme districts. The feud was once more resumed under the successor of Francis, King Henry II (1547–1559), when through the treachery of Duke Maurice of Saxony and other rebel princes of Germany the German bishoprics of Metz, Toul, and Verdun were lost to France (Treaty of Chambord, 1552). The self-styled "vindicator of the liberties of Germany" (Henry II) was to hold the three bishoprics as "Vicar of the Holy Empire."

Charles V and the Reformation: The Wars With the German Princes. It becomes necessary at this point to recount the major events of the reform movement that had been initiated by Martin Luther, as far as they affected the course of German political history in the sixteenth century. The religious, cultural, and literary aspects of the Reformation will be treated separately.

When German mercenaries, most of them Lutherans, stormed Rome on Easter, 1527, they actually made Charles V the undisputed master of Italy, a fact that was later on confirmed by the Treaty of Cambrai, 1529. The march on Rome was almost symbolical, inasmuch as it gave vent to a general and popular German resentment against the papacy. Oddly enough, the emperor's victory over Clement VII and the following reconciliation of the two rulers made it possible for Charles to turn now with full vigor against the Lutheran reform movement. When Charles returned to Germany in 1530, it was with the firm resolve to settle the religious issue once and for all.

Charles was a native of the Spanish Netherlands, a Spaniard at heart, and a foreigner in Germany and Italy alike. His religious and political convictions were predetermined by his strictly Catholic education and by the ideas of the Catholic Reform in Spain that had been inaugurated by Francisco Ximenez de Cisneros (1436–1517), cardinal and primate of the Church in Spain and later on regent of that kingdom. Charles furthermore was intellectually and emotionally attached to the tradition of the Holy Roman Empire and its universal mission, as the embodiment of the Christian commonwealth of nations. He was therefore by nature as well as by inherited characteristics opposed to political and religious particularism and regionalism. These were the factors that influenced his attitude in dealing with the Lutheran Reformation.

On October 31, 1517, Martin Luther had posted his ninety-five theses on the portal of the castle church in Wittenberg, attacking the practice of the sale of indulgences and other abuses as well as dogmatic teachings of the Catholic Church. Luther's refusal to recant at the Diet of Augsburg (1518), the ensuing controversy with the famous theologian Dr. John Eck of the University of Ingolstadt (1519), and the burning of the papal bull of excommunication (1520) had made the German Augustinian monk a figure of international significance and the logical protagonist of ecclesiastical reform.

The disputation with Eck at Leipzig almost coincided with the election of Charles V as German emperor. In the following year (1521) Charles solemnly opened his first imperial diet in the city of Worms. According to ancient imperial law the ban of the Church called for an immediate proclamation of the ban of the Empire. The diet, because Luther's position had already grown so strong, decided to grant him another hearing with an added guarantee of safe-conduct. The "Edict of Worms," declaring Luther under the ban of the Empire, was pronounced and signed by Charles and a number of the German princes, after Luther had again refused to retract any of his statements, unless he should be convinced "by witness of Scripture or by plain reason." Charles decreed that the safe-conduct should be respected but that henceforth Luther should be prosecuted as a convicted heretic. To avoid any possible resistance on the part of pro-Lutheran forces, the edict, which had been drawn up on May 8, was not published until May 26, when most of the representatives of the Estates of the Empire had left the city.

Instead of quelling the incipient reform, the Edict of Worms had the opposite effect of strengthening the adherents of Luther and of further weakening the authority of the emperor. Charles's renewed absence from Germany made it possible for the Lutherans to complete their organization and to overthrow the established ecclesiastical regime in all the territories they controlled. At the First Diet of Speyer (1526) the States of the Empire passed a "recess," in which they agreed that each of them should be permitted to manage its own religious affairs according to the dictates of conscience, until the time when a general council would decree a permanent settlement of the religious issues. This declaration, which practically made ecclesiastical policy a matter of the independent sovereignty of individual states, was supported by the Lutheran and Catholic princes alike. It was repealed, however, by the Second Diet of Speyer in 1529, where it was decreed that the existing dividing lines between the religious factions should be recognized and respected, but that further interference with the religious practices of the Catholic tradition should not be tolerated. The six princes and fourteen cities whose signatures were obtained for a formal protest against these decrees were henceforth known as the "Protestant" party.

In the following year (1530) Charles returned to Germany and presided over the Diet of Augsburg. The "Confession of Augsburg," drawn up on the emperor's request by Luther's friend and collaborator, Melanchthon, and designed to prepare the way for a mutual understanding and a possible reunion between Catholics and Lutherans, was read in public. Its conciliatory tone was met by a firm Catholic "confutation," adopted and confirmed by Charles in its entirety. The emperor then gave the Protestant party six months to reconsider their position, after which their heresy should be suppressed by force. Luther, still under the ban of the Empire and the Church and therefore prevented from being personally present at the Diet of Augsburg, was kept well informed of every phase of the proceedings and threw the weight of his influence and advice on the side of those who were convinced that reconciliation was impossible and that civil war had become virtually unavoidable.

In 1531 a number of Protestant princes and delegates of free cities joined together in a defensive alliance, known as the League of Schmalkalden (the name of a town in Hesse). The leadership was alternately in the hands of the Elector John of Saxony and Duke Philip of Hesse. The League became the spearhead of all opposition against the imperial regime, and was at various times supported by the kings of France and England and even by the Catholic Dukes of Bavaria. When the Turkish menace became more acute, the members of the League refused to defend Germany against foreign invasion unless they were granted freedom of religious propaganda in all the territories of the Empire. The so-called First Religious Peace of Nuremberg (1532) established another truce between the opposing forces and provided the basis for joint action against the Turkish aggressors. The following fourteen years, during which Charles V was preoccupied with embroilments and military campaigns in the Mediterranean, in France, and in the Netherlands, gave the members of the League ample time to consolidate their position. Their cause was further strengthened by the death of Duke George of Saxony, a stanch Catholic, who was succeeded by his Protestant brother, Henry (1539), and by the inclusion of Brandenburg among its member states. The German North had now become a solid bulwark of the Lutheran faction, which by the year 1546 could boast of a following that included more than half of Germany and four of the seven Electors of the Empire.

If Charles V nevertheless could open his campaign of 1546 with a fair chance of success, it was due not only to the inadequate leadership of the armies of the League but also to the discords, rivalries, and selfish policies of the Protestant princes. The Spanish foot soldiers of Charles's army, though inferior in numbers, represented the crack troops of the military forces of Europe and were commanded by the duke of Alva, one of the greatest and at the same time most ruthless military leaders of his century.

Another contributing factor to the eventual defeat of the Protestant League was the unexpected alliance of Landgrave Philip of Hesse with the emperor, the outgrowth of an unsavory family affair of this prince. With Luther's and Melanchthon's consent the landgrave had contracted a second marriage, while his first wife was still alive, and though Luther had urged that the whole affair be kept secret, the truth had come out, alienating many of the members of Philip's own party. The additional fear of having to face indictment and punishment for bigamy caused the landgrave to become a traitor to the cause of his allies and to join secretly the imperial forces. Although according to Canon Law the validity of Philip's second marriage was not recognized, he was satisfied as long as he was allowed to stay with Margarete von Sale, his second wife.

Charles very shrewdly used the discord among the Protestant princes to his own advantage, and succeeded in winning over two Hohenzollern princes as well as Maurice, duke of Saxony, the successor of Duke Henry. Pope Paul III (1534-1549), successor to Clement VII, concluded an alliance with Charles and supported the emperor with troops and money. The defeat of John Frederick, Elector of Saxony,* in the battle of Mühlberg (1547) broke the resistance of the League of Schmalkalden, leaving the Protestant princes at the mercy of the victorious emperor. Martin Luther had died in the previous year, and the Catholic Reform Council of Trent (cf. p. 257 sqq.) had held its first session in 1545. King Francis I of France and King Henry VIII of England died in 1547. Charles V could feel himself for once the undisputed master of the Empire, and as such he is represented on Titian's famous painting: in full armor, seated on horseback, with "dark red, golden-fringed saddle-cloth; a broad red, gold-edged sash over his burnished breastplate; on his head a German helmet, in his hand a short spear."

The Diet of Augsburg (1548) brought a provisional settlement of the religious dispute, known as the "Interim," which, it was hoped, would soon be superseded by the definitive and lasting decrees of the general Church

---

* The electorate of Saxony had been divided in 1485 between the Dukes Ernst and Albrecht (Ernestine and Albertine line) of the Wettin dynasty, Ernst receiving the electoral title, the duchy of Saxony, northern Thuringia, and part of Franconia, while Albrecht was given the Mark Meissen and southern Thuringia. John Frederick belonged to the Ernestine, Maurice to the Albertine line of succession.

council. But the terms of the "Interim" were never really accepted in good faith, nor were they observed by the Protestant princes and their subjects, who felt that the concessions of the Catholic party were by no means far reaching enough. Any hopes that Charles might have nourished as to the durability of the religious truce were bitterly disappointed by the rebellion of the Protestant princes of 1552. This time Duke Maurice of Saxony made common cause with King Henry II of France (1547–1559), and Charles narrowly escaped being captured by Maurice's troops at Ingolstadt.

The emperor not only had failed to take advantage of a situation which in every respect favored his cause, but had wasted the fruits of his victory by a series of tactical and psychological mistakes. He had alienated many of his sympathizers by the continued presence of Spanish troops on German soil and, above all, by his attempt to secure the imperial succession for his son, Philip of Spain. At a meeting of the German princes at Passau, Charles's brother Ferdinand presided as the representative of the emperor, securing the latter's consent to a treaty which was to grant equal protection to Catholics and Protestants. Ferdinand, in his capacity as Roman-German king, was again commissioned by Charles to preside over the Diet of Augsburg in 1555, negotiating the Religious Peace of Augsburg, which finally settled by decree some of the most controversial issues, and whose enactments served to maintain an armed peace for the rest of the sixteenth century. The compromise arrived at in the deliberations of the Diet was by no means to the liking of Charles, who remained unwaveringly opposed to the concessions as contained in the major provisions of the Treaty of Augsburg. He had staked his life and his honor on the destruction of Protestantism, and he withdrew from the political arena when he realized his failure and partial defeat.

The Diet of Augsburg laid down the following four principles as a *modus vivendi* for the Catholic and Lutheran factions: (1) The Lutheran principalities and free cities should be free to choose between the Catholic and Lutheran creeds, but the rulers were entitled to impose the religion of their choice upon their subjects. Those people who professed a religion different from that of their rulers were permitted to move with their belongings to other territories. This principle is expressed in the phrase: *cuius regio eius religio* (the religion of the ruler determines the religion of those ruled). (2) An "ecclesiastical reservation" (*reservatum ecclesiasticum*) decreed that ecclesiastical princes who wished to join the Lutheran faith were to surrender their territories, which would then remain under the control of the Catholic Church. Lutherans living in such ecclesiastical holdings should be permitted to practice their religion. (3) Protestant states should retain all Church property that they had confiscated prior to 1552. (4) The principle expressed in the phrase *cuius regio eius religio* should apply only to Catholics and Lutherans, but not to Calvinists.

The terms of the Religious Peace of Ausburg as contained in these declarations marked one further step in the dissolution of the traditional order of Europe. By endowing the secular princes with the prerogatives of ecclesiastical (episcopal) dignity and jurisdiction it prepared the way for the absolutistic and totalitarian forms of secular government in the following centuries. Additional power and prestige was added to princely rule and accelerated the disintegration of the Empire.

Armed Peace and Formation of Rival Leagues. Charles V, realizing that the Electors could not be persuaded to accept the Spanish Philip as his successor, had finally decided to divide his inheritance between his son Philip and his brother Ferdinand, the former receiving Spain and Burgundy, the latter the German Hapsburg possessions as well as the imperial crown. The new German emperor, however, was a weak monarch. Repeatedly he had to call upon the aid of his Hapsburg cousins in Spain to defend his lands against foes within and without.

The German princes, Protestant and Catholic alike, had acquired too much secular and ecclesiastical power to accept the dictates of imperial rule. They embarked upon separatistic policies and adventures and frequently crossed and counteracted the political designs of the emperor. All the same, the Religious Peace of Augsburg might have provided a workable basis for a stabilized national policy if the selfishness of the princes had not been greatly encouraged by the constant interference of foreign powers. The situation was further complicated by the gradual shift in the religious balance of power that had been brought about by the Catholic reform movement following upon the successful conclusion of the Council of Trent (cf. p. 257 sqq.).

The Religious Peace of Augsburg coincided with the first vigorous attempts on the part of the Catholic Church to recover its former power and prestige, and to regain Germany for the Catholic faith. The Roman Curia, aided by the militant Order of Jesuits (cf. p. 254 sqq.), had become exceedingly active in all parts of the world, but especially in the territories of the Empire. The larger part of southern Germany and the ecclesiastical principalities of the Rhineland were thus recovered for the Catholic faith, and the principles of the Peace of Augsburg were rigorously enforced. Lutheranism, on the other hand, had fallen into a state of political apathy, thereby manifesting some of that passive quietism in regard to political authority that had characterized Luther's own theological attitude in his earlier years. On the Protestant side the law of political action, backed by strong moral conviction, was now dictated entirely by the forces of Calvinism (cf. p. 236), which had established its German strongholds in some parts of the upper Rhineland in the West and in Bohemia in the East. It had gained the adherence of the elector palatine and the elector of Brandenburg and was prepared to challenge the Catholic Restoration. Any co-operation between Calvinists and Lutherans was precluded by the sharp cleavage of minds that separated the two denominations from each other as much as from the Catholic Church. Thus the Lutheran princes remained passive onlookers in the initial stages of the Calvinist-Catholic struggle, trying to follow a policy of detached neutrality.

To appreciate the rapid and dynamic growth of Calvinism, we do well to remember that in the Religious Peace of Augsburg its adherents had not even been given a legal status. Now, only seven years later (1572), the Calvinists felt strong enough to incite the Rebellion of the Netherlands under the leadership of Prince William of Orange, which led to the secession of the seven northern provinces from Spain and from the Empire (1581), followed by the destruction of the Spanish Armada by the English in 1588.

The struggle for the possession of Cologne was fought in the years 1582–1584. Westphalia and the lower Rhenish districts were saved for Catholicism with the aid of Spanish troops and owing to the indifference of the Lutheran princes as well as the fervor of the Catholic population. The incident which at last aroused the Lutherans from their lethargy and from a false feeling of security was the forced conversion of the Bavarian city of Donauwörth by Duke Maximilian of Bavaria (1598–1651), the militant leader of the Catholic princes. At Donauwörth Protestant interference with a Catholic procession had led to the military occupation of the town and the ensuing religious decrees.

These events occurred in 1608, and in the same year a number of Protestant princes under the leadership of the Calvinist elector palatine, Frederick IV, united to form a defensive alliance, known as the "Protestant Union." The Catholic answer was given in the following year (1609), when Maximilian of Bavaria assumed leadership in the newly organized "Catholic League." Civil war was not far off, and an immediate outbreak of hostilities was perhaps only halted by the realization that the impending conflict would soon assume the dimensions of a general European war and that it would have to be fought on German soil.

The mere fact that the German emperor was not a member of the Catholic League speaks eloquently of the rather pitiable role that the imperial government played in national affairs. The Hapsburg emperors, Ferdinand I (1556–1564), the brother of Charles V; his son, Maximilian II (1564–1576); and the latter's son, Rudolph II (1576–1612), all Catholics, were chiefly concerned with preserving and expanding their hereditary lands, including the kingdoms of Bohemia and Hungary. The Catholic princes of the Empire, on the other hand, were ever watchful lest the central authority might be strengthened by a decisive imperial victory over Protestantism. And, as it was perfectly obvious that any war would involve both the Austrian and Spanish branches of the Hapsburg family, none of the Catholic princes was anxious to precipitate such a concentration of imperial power as would inevitably result from an armed conflict.

But the events that issued in the final catastrophe happened in such rapid succession that considerations of diplomacy and expediency had to be disregarded. Emperor Rudolph II, a lover of astrology and black magic and the admiring protector of John Kepler and Tycho de Brahe, was politically unstable and incompetent and in his later years suffered from persecution mania. Under pressure, and while his brother Matthias in union with the Hungarian and Austrian nobles was working for his deposition, he attempted to appease the Protestant Estates of Bohemia and to win their support by issuing the Bohemian "Royal Charter" of 1609, granting free exercise of religion to all his Bohemian subjects. The head of the Catholic opposition against these concessions was Duke Ferdinand of Styria, the emperor's cousin, a docile pupil of the Jesuits and, together with Maximilian of Bavaria, champion of the Catholic Restoration in the Empire. Matthias finally achieved the overthrow of his brother's regime in Bohemia and, upon Rudolph's death in 1612, succeeded him as German emperor (1612–1619). After some attempts at conciliation Matthias aroused the violent opposition of the Bohemian Protestants when he designated as his heir and the future king of Bohemia his cousin Ferdinand, who was known and feared for his intolerance and for the ruthless suppression of Protestantism in his own lands. An open rebellion of the Czech nobles in 1618 gave the signal for the beginning of the Thirty Years' War (cf. pp. 284–293). Emperor Matthias died in the following year, after having been deprived by Ferdinand of his Bohemian, Austrian, and Hungarian possessions. Exactly one hundred years after the election of Charles V as emperor of the Holy Roman Empire the electors met again in Frankfurt on the Main to cast their votes for a successor to Emperor Matthias, this time under the shadow of the great religious war which had become a grim reality.

Martin Luther: His Personality and His Work. There are few characters in the history of civilization who have caused such profoundly revolutionary changes in the general outlook of their age and who have determined the destiny of their own nation to such an extent as Martin Luther. Although his thought and work were in many respects a continuation and fruition of certain tendencies of the preceding centuries, supplemented by influences of education and environment, the amount of spontaneous and creative innovation that remains Luther's personal contribution to his age testifies to a unique and ingenious personality. Although the picture of Luther has been colored by partisan likes and dislikes, by prejudice and wishful thinking, his dynamic vitality as well as his passionate sincerity have seldom been denied, and it thus becomes the privilege of the historian to view and evaluate the significance of the reformer and his work with the dispassionate detachment of a retrospective analysis.

a) Childhood and Early Manhood. Martin Luther was born on November 10, 1483, at Eisleben, in the province of Saxony. His father, Hans Luther, a small peasant and mine digger, had moved with his family to the Saxon town from Möhra in Thuringia shortly before Martin's birth. One year later (1484) the father was again on the move, this time settling at Mansfeld, the center of the growing mining industry of Saxony. "My great-grandfather, my grandfather, and my father were real peasants," says Martin Luther in his *Table Talk*. His proud assertion: "I am the son of a peasant," receives added emphasis in the further statement: "Kings and emperors have been of peasant stock."

Martin's childhood was by no means a very happy one. The sternest discipline ruled in the house of his parents as well as in the Mansfeld school where he received his elementary education. The son complained later on that father and mother were incapable of understanding the inner life of their children and that their strictness had driven him into a state of pusillanimity (*usque ad pusillanimitatem*). At the age of fourteen Martin was sent to the school of the "Brethren of the Common Life" (cf. p. 180) in Magdeburg to continue his studies. The schools of the Brethren counted among their more famous pupils such men as Thomas à Kempis, the mystic; Gabriel Biel, one of the German followers of William of Occam (cf. p. 142); Nicholas Copernicus, the great astronomer; and Cardinal Nicholas of Cusa (cf. p. 180 sq.), the ingenious philosopher. Their doctrines were on strictly orthodox ground, but in their devotional life they stressed the social aspects and impulses of the *devotio moderna*.

Luther spent only one year with the Brethren in Magdeburg. In 1498 he entered the Latin school in Eisenach in Thuringia, following his father's wish, who wanted him to get acquainted with some family relations in that city. In Magdeburg as well as in Eisenach Martin had to earn his livelihood by begging and singing in the streets. We are told by Luther's pupil, Mathesius, that even the sons of well-to-do parents were sent on these begging and singing tours to acquire the virtue of humility and to develop a feeling of compassion with the poor and unfortunates. Martin soon found a home and with it the warmth and benignity of family life in the house of Kuntz Cotta and his wife, Ursula, who began to take a motherly interest in the development of the boy.

Hans Luther wanted his son to become a jurist, and Martin again followed his father's advice when he left Eisenach after a stay of three years and entered the Saxon University of Erfurt (1501). The city had become known as the "new Prague," after the mass emigration from the capital of Bohemia that followed the Hussite struggles (cf. p. 176 sq.). Before taking up his professional studies Luther had to complete his course in the faculty of arts, including the study of the classics (Ovid, Vergil, Horace, Terence, etc.), and an extensive training in the essentials of philosophy. The leading philosophical authority was still Aristotle, but Erfurt more than most of the other European institutions of higher learning was committed to the nominalistic (cf. p. 142) interpretation of the Greek master, following the example of William of Occam and other members of the Franciscan schools. It was the period of decadent scholasticism, and the classical philosophical synthesis of Thomas Aquinas (cf. p. 145 sq.) was no longer sufficiently known and appreciated. The Bible was familiar to Luther at that time only in the form of homilies (*Postillen*), pericopes (passages of the Gospels and Epistles, used in the liturgy), and of the "Biblical Histories" (*Historienbibeln*), all of which were known in German translations to clergy and laity. Luther tells us that he was twenty years old when he first saw the complete Bible in the university library at Erfurt.

Luther received the degree of Bachelor of Arts in 1502, that of Master of Arts in 1505. Soon afterward he began his studies for the legal profession. His later criticism of the contents and methods of jurisprudence indicates that his rich emotional life found itself thwarted by the unimaginative dryness of his subject matter. He may have found an emotional outlet in his association with some of the members of the Humanist movement (cf. p. 251 sq.), known as the "Erfurt poets." Luther was especially attracted by the brilliance of their literary style and admired their proficiency in the Latin tongue. His enthusiasm for the Latin classics bore fruit in the fluency and formal perfection of his own literary style, both in Latin and German. The pagan aspects of the Humanist movement left no impression on Luther's mind. His growing interest in the Bible made him virtually immune to any such influence.

b) Luther, the Augustinian Monk. It seems that the cheerless atmosphere of his parental home predisposed Luther to take a gloomy and pessimistic view of life and human nature. A letter of the year 1528 speaks of an innate inclination to religious melancholy and even despair. It must have been such a state of mind that prompted his sudden decision to quit his legal career and enter the local monastery of the Augustinian Eremites. On his way back to Erfurt, from Mansfeld, where he had paid a visit to his parents, he was thrown to the ground by a stroke of lightning and, convinced of having received a sign and call from heaven, he immediately vowed to become a monk. Luther was twenty-two years old when the portals of the monastery closed behind him. In 1506 he was made a subdeacon and deacon, and in 1507 he was ordained to the priesthood. While celebrating his first Mass he was so overcome with the tremendous majesty of the Almighty that the assisting priest had to restrain him from running away.

In 1508 Luther was sent by his superiors to the new University of Wittenberg, recently founded by Frederick the Wise, elector of Saxony. He stayed at the Augustinian monastery in that city and was immediately commissioned to teach a course on Aristotle's Nicomachean Ethics. Upon the recommendation of the vicar of his order, John Staupitz, Luther was made a Bachelor of Sacred Scripture in 1509.

His inner life during these years was darkened by the unbearable thought of an eternal predestination of man for either heaven or hell: "My heart trembled when I thought of God's grace. The name of Jesus frightened me, and when I looked at Him crucified, He appeared to me as a flash of lightning." Luther had such a strong sensation of the terrors of God's judgment that he felt his hair stand on end. Some of his lecture notes reveal his beginning rejection of Aristotle, whom he calls a "rancid philosopher" and a comedian whom he intends to unmask. At the same time we read of his growing admiration of the writings of St. Augustine, whose teachings were traditionally given preference in the Augustinian and Franciscan Orders.

In the late autumn of 1510 we find Luther on a journey to Rome, where he went as a delegate of his order to settle some disputed matters of ecclesiastical administration. He had expected to find a holy city and was shocked and grieved when he discovered that the Rome of the Renaissance was a center of art, taste, sophistication, and luxury, but that the religious spirit was drowned in worldliness and moral corruption. Luther stayed in Rome for about four weeks and then returned to the Augustinian monastery in Wittenberg, where he resumed his teaching at the university and, in 1512, received the degree of Doctor of Theology.

The lectures of the new professor dealt with scriptural exegesis and showed a strongly mystical inclination. He was particularly fond of the sermons of John Tauler (cf. p. 148) and an anonymous mystical treatise, known as *Theologia Germanica*. He was fascinated by his discovery that these mystical doctrines emphasized the weakness of the human will and the all-pervading efficiency of divine grace. For Luther these teachings seemed to imply a complete passivity of human nature in the process of salvation, a quietude born of the conviction — which resulted from his own tormenting experiences — that all human endeavor was incapable of overcoming the fatal consequences of original sin. Shortly after having prepared a new edition of the *Theologia Germanica* he declares in a sermon of the year 1516: "The man of God goes wherever God may lead him. He never knows whither he goes. He does not act himself, but God acts through him. He is on his way, whatever this way may be. . . . Such are the men who are guided by the divine spirit."

In 1515, Luther had been chosen as his order's vicar of the districts of Meissen and Thuringia and entrusted with the supervision of eleven monasteries. His many administrative duties left him little time for the observation of monastic rules: "I could use two clerks or chancellors. My chief occupation is writing letters. Besides, I have to preach in the monasteries, in the refectories, in the parish church. I am director of studies and vicar, i.e., I do the work of eleven priors. . . . I lecture on St. Paul and collect the explanations of the Psalter. . . . Rarely do I have time to recite the canonical office and to celebrate Mass, to say nothing of the temptations of the flesh, the world, and the devil."

Luther's interpretation of certain mystical doctrines led him to more and more violent attacks against the Catholic teaching on the merits of "good works" (*Werkheiligkeit*), such as the veneration of saints, sacraments, pilgrimages, indulgences, fasting, and almsgiving. While he was still a devout member of his monastic congregation, the seeds of his new gospel had already been firmly embedded in his soul. Why should there be confession of sin and penance, if good works were unsuitable instruments to procure a lasting peace with God? When Luther was told by his friend and superior, Staupitz, that peace and consolation were hidden in the love of Christ, these words were balsam for Luther's aching and longing heart. He was ready to challenge a religious and social system that had grown too complacent to see that its own faults were writing its doom.

c) Luther's New Gospel. The dramatic events that made Luther's name and personality a blazing signal of opposing creeds were a direct outgrowth of his religious scruples concerning the problem of predestination and the share of divine grace and human works in the economy of salvation. While lecturing on Paul's Epistle to the Romans, Luther was struck by the Apostle's insistence that neither the natural law nor the Mosaic law could justify a man before God, but that justification was exclusively due to God's grace as revealed in the New Testament. This statement was interpreted by Luther as implying the negation of the natural human faculties, so that man would be "justified by faith *alone,* through the merits of Christ being attributed to the sinner." If that was true, then "good works" were not only unnecessary, but they were actually impossible, due to that weakness and corruption of human nature that was the consequence of the "Fall of Man" (original sin). Human self-abnegation was thus effectively contrasted with God's all-pervading power and majesty. There was no doubt in Luther's mind that those who were predestined for salvation would be given the gift of faith and, with faith, the confidence and conviction of being children of God, saved by His redeeming love. The stain of corruption remains, but the sinner uses the merits of Christ as a shield to cover up his weakness and sinfulness.

The position of the Roman Catholic Church in this matter makes clear the extent of the innovation: according to the pre-Reformation as well as post-Reformation Catholic teaching, man's essential natural faculties and the freedom of his will were not radically corrupted but only deeply wounded by original sin. As it is God's will that all be saved, everyone is called upon to co-operate freely with divine grace. The amount of grace given is sufficient to enable the sinner to remain a child of God by his own free choice, after having been adopted by Christ through the sacrament of baptism. The disposition for sin is constantly diminished, and the potency for moral action strengthened by the aid of the other sacraments.

Luther calls William of Occam (cf. p. 142) his spiritual ancestor, and it is interesting to note how much of the substance of Luther's teaching can be attributed to that dynamic court theologian of Louis the Bavarian. Occam had denied that the existence of God, the freedom of will, and the spirituality of the soul could be rationally demonstrated. He had espoused the doctrine of the "double truth" (what is true philosophically may be false theologically, and vice versa), and he had exalted the Deity beyond the distinctions of good and evil, thus making the divine will entirely arbitrary and irrational.

Luther follows Occam in his contempt of reason and in his ideas on the nature and all-pervading power of God, whose testimony in the "inner word" enlightens the faithful as to the true meaning of the Scriptures, independent of ecclesiastical authority. The contention that God's exalted majesty had been minimized by Catholic theologians and philosophers in favor of the human faculties of reason and free will is Luther's main argument against the scholastic *Sautheologen*. On the other hand, he characterized William of Occam, Gabriel Biel (1430–1495), and other nominalists as empty dialecticians, who had neglected the study and testimony of the divine "word" as revealed in the Bible. Positively as well as negatively, therefore, the influence of Occamistic teaching, together with the main body of traditional Franciscan theology that it contains, represents an important force in the formation of Luther's religious convictions.

d) Luther's Ninety-Five Theses; Fight Against Indulgences; Disputation of Leipzig. The event that brought the latent crisis into the open was the public sale of indulgences by the Dominican friar, John Tetzel, in the year 1517. Pope Leo X (1513–1521), the friend and protector of Raphael and Michelangelo, the splendor-loving Renaissance pope of the Medici family, had proclaimed a papal indulgence in order to obtain the funds needed for the reconstruction of St. Peter's Cathedral in Rome in accordance with the designs of Michelangelo. Leo had commissioned Albrecht of Brandenburg, archbishop of Mainz, with the task of collecting the money in Germany. Tetzel, in his turn, acted on the orders of his superior when he went from town to town, offering varying spiritual benefits upon the payment of certain amounts of money.

"Indulgences" were customarily granted by the Church on different occasions, not to effect remission of sins but in return for penances consisting in the performance of good works. Not until the fourteenth century do we find the partial substitution of money gifts for works of mercy and charity. In Luther's time the theory and practice of indulgences was rather indefinite, lending itself to all kinds of misinterpretation and abuse. Yet as late as 1516 Luther himself had been of the opinion that whatever abuses might be connected with the practice of granting indulgences, "it is a great benefit that indulgences are offered and obtained." It was therefore not the institution or practice as such that aroused his anger and prompted his attack when, on the eve of the Feast of All Saints, 1517, he expressed his disapproval in the form of ninety-five theses, which he nailed on the door of the castle church in Wittenberg.

Although Luther's theses were written in Latin, they immediately caused a sensation. They voiced a resentment that was quite universally felt, aggravated by the overbearing manner in which such contributions had been solicited in Germany and by their matter-of-fact acceptance by the Roman Curia.

Luther had declared his willingness to discuss and defend his theses in public, but the immediate result was the publication of a number of counter-theses by Tetzel and a summons to Luther to appear before a chapter meeting of his order at Heidelberg. Luther knew that at Heidelberg he would be asked to recant and that his refusal to do so might bring upon him the severest penalties. He therefore appealed to the Elector Frederick of Saxony, whose interference in his behalf was to make it possible for him to return safely to Wittenberg.

Contrary to his own expectations, the disputation at Heidelberg in 1518 resulted in a victory for his cause, and on his way back to Wittenberg he enjoyed the further satisfaction of being allowed to preach in Dresden before Duke George of Saxony and his court. Greatly encouraged by his success, he now edited a revised edition of his theses in the form of "resolutions," in which he further elucidated his new dogmatic views and which he dedicated to Pope Leo X. Although firm in his insistence that he could not recant, he asked Leo for advice and guidance and concluded with the following fervent supplication: "Most holy father! I prostrate myself at the feet of thy Holiness with all that I am and all that I have. Do what thou wilt, give life or death, call or revoke, approve or disapprove! In thy voice I will recognize the voice of Christ, who dwelleth and speaketh in thee. If I have deserved death, I do not refuse to die."

When Luther was asked to appear in Rome within sixty days to answer the charges preferred against him, Frederick the Wise of Saxony again interceded, with the result that the inquiry was entrusted to the famous Dominican theologian, Cardinal Cajetanus de Vio, and Luther was allowed to stay in Germany. He met Cajetanus at Augsburg in 1518, where the Imperial Diet was in session, and again he refused to recant, claiming that he had not contradicted any papal definition. He appealed to the pope against his accusers and asked that his case be submitted to a general Church council. In this appellation he promised to speak or do nothing against the Roman Church and the pope, as long as the latter was "well advised" (*bene consultus*). Frederick the Wise also took the stand that Luther's teachings had not been proven heretical.

To secure the co-operation of the Saxon elector in the Lutheran controversy, the pope ordered the papal notary and chamberlain, Charles von Miltitz, a Saxon nobleman, to present Frederick with the "golden rose," which had been blessed by the pope and which was customarily awarded each year to some prince as a symbol of special favor. Miltitz approached Luther and succeeded in effecting a further truce by persuading the reformer to dispatch a conciliatory letter to Rome.

In the meantime, the quarrel over the granting of indulgences had begun to develop into a more fundamental controversy concerning the primacy of the Roman See. It was this ancient claim of papal supremacy and authority over the universal Church, redefined by a papal decree of the year 1518, that was next attacked by Luther and that became the major issue in the Disputation of Leipzig in 1519.

The disputation was held between Martin Luther and his friend, Andrew Bodenstein, called Carlstadt, on the one side, and John Eck (Mayr), professor of theology at the University of Ingolstadt, on the other. The verbal duel took place in the largest hall of the Pleissenburg, in the presence of the duke and his court and a large number of local and visiting scholars. Eck succeeded in evoking from Luther the reluctant admission that he even questioned the authority of general Church councils, and that he considered some of the condemned teachings of John Huss (cf. p. 176 sq.) as Christian and evangelical.

e) Revolutionary Writings and Excommunication. In 1520, John Eck was called to Rome to report on the Lutheran struggle, and he took with him copies of Luther's publications. Immediate action on the part of the Curia had been delayed by the imperial election of 1519 (cf. p. 205). In order to gain the support of Frederick the Wise, Charles V had promised that Luther should not be condemned without having been given an opportunity to present his case before the Imperial Diet. This delay was used by Luther to formulate his convictions in several writings, some of which are equally important as theological and literary documents.

In June, 1520, he published his book *On the Papacy in Rome.* It was written in German and demonstrated for the first time his ability to adapt his style to the taste and understanding of the broad audiences to which many of his writings were henceforth addressed. He proclaimed that, being a spiritual, invisible realm, the Church needed no visible head and that its mark of identification was the community of the faithful, united and distinguished by baptism, communion (the Lord's Supper), and the preaching of the divine word. The "power of the keys" (power to forgive sins) was not confined to the priesthood or an ecclesiastical elite, but was possessed by all Christians who were capable of awakening in the consciences of their brethren the certitude of divine mercy.

News had reached Luther that Rome was about to bring his trial to conclusion by pronouncing the Great Ban against him. Far from being intimidated by this prospect, he was roused to passionate and almost feverish literary activity. His *Address to the Christian Nobility of the German Nation on the Improvement of the Christian Estate* and the following pamphlet *On the Babylonian Captivity of the Church* have become famous as the two major polemical manifestoes of the Lutheran Reformation. The former was written in German and contained an ardent appeal to the Estates of the Empire to revolt against the tyranny and corruption of the papacy. The Roman Curia is accused of having exploited the good-natured Germans for the sake of material gain and political power. The distinction between priesthood and laity is termed a hellish invention, and the doctrine of a general priesthood of all the faithful is proclaimed for the first time. The national states are called upon to establish their secular jurisdiction over the ecclesiastical hierarchy. The papacy is designated as the embodiment of the antichrist, and among the ecclesiastical institutions that are attacked, monasticism and the law of celibacy rank foremost. The violent language of this pamphlet won Luther the enthusiastic support of the revolutionary knights Ulrich von Hutten (cf. p. 251 sq.) and Franz von Sickingen (cf. p. 251 sq.), and of some of the younger set of Humanist writers.

In the same year in which Luther published his *Address to the Nobility* and was working on the Latin pamphlet *On the Babylonian Captivity of the Church,* he addressed a letter and a "protestation" to Charles V, in which he calls himself an obedient son of the Holy Catholic Church, who only reluctantly, against his will and for the sake of truth, had left the solitude of his cell to take part in the theological controversies: "In vain do I ask forgiveness, in vain do I offer silence . . . in vain do I ask for better information." He concludes by asking the emperor for a just trial, addressing Charles as the "king of all kings," before whom he (Luther) appears "humbly as a little flea." When the letter was handed over to Charles V at the Diet of Worms, he tore it to pieces with his own hands.

The pamphlet *On the Babylonian Captivity of the Church* identifies the papacy with the kingdom of Babylon, which has subjugated and corrupted the Church of Christ. Only three sacraments as against the seven* of the Catholic tradition are recognized as valid: baptism, penance, and the Lord's Supper. The doctrine of "transubstantiation" (cf. p. 231) is denied, and the reception of the sacraments is described as a voluntary act of the individual, not demanded by Christ. The celebration of the Mass has no sacrificial significance and is not even a meritorious act. "Neither Pope nor bishop nor anybody else has the right to impose even one syllable on a Christian without his consent."

Shortly after Luther had learned that the bull of excommunication had arrived in Germany, he published the famous tract *On the Liberty of a Christian Man,* in a German and Latin edition. Following the advice of Miltitz, he sent the Latin version to Leo X, together with a letter in which he once more emphasized his peaceful intentions, but at the same time asserted that the institution of the papacy was dead: Leo was like a sheep among the wolves and like Daniel in the lions' den. The Roman Church was a den of thieves and rogues.

In his treatment of the concept of Christian liberty Luther reiterates his definition of faith, which is an act of simple confidence in God's mercy. The result of such an act is the true liberty of a Christian: "That is Christian liberty: we no longer need any works to attain true devotion. . . . By virtue of his faith a Christian man is raised so highly above all things that he becomes their master in a spiritual way: nothing can impair his road to beatitude" (*Seligkeit*). However, the Christian as a social being must exercise self-control and be charitable to others. Such charity grows out of his faith and his pure love of God. The works of mercy are without merit in themselves and cannot lead to beatitude. Therefore, it is quite useless to look upon the good works and count their number: "Good works never make a good, devout man, but a good, devout man does good and devout works." He does them, knowing that Christ has already fulfilled for him all the commandments, and that therefore a just man needs neither the law nor good works. Luther's argumentation was intended to refute the

---

* (1) Baptism; (2) confirmation; (3) Sacrament of the Altar [Eucharist, the Lord's Supper]; (4) penance [confession and absolution of sins]; (5) extreme unction [of the dying]; (6) holy orders [ordination of priests]; (7) marriage.

Catholic teaching that hope of eternal reward and fear of eternal punishment were legitimate motives of Christian faith and works.

Meanwhile, Luther's case had been judged by the Roman Curia, and the Bull *Exurge Domine et iudica causam tuam* ("Rise, O Lord, and judge Thy cause") of 1520 had condemned forty-one of Luther's propositions and had threatened him with excommunication unless he retracted within sixty days. Among the condemned teachings were those that referred to man's inability to perform good acts, those that dealt with justification by faith alone; with the efficacy of the sacraments; his teachings concerning purgatory, penance, and indulgences; and those that denied the authority of the pope and of general councils.

Luther took this condemnation of his major tenets as a declaration of war and answered immediately with another pamphlet, entitled *Against the Execrable Bull of the Anti-Christ (Adversus execrabilem Antichristi bullam)*. In his own German edition of this pamphlet he asked the question: "Who would be surprised if princes, nobles, and laymen should beat the Pope, the bishops, priests, and monks over the head and drive them out of the country?" On December 10, 1520, a gathering of students and professors of the University of Wittenberg, who had assembled in front of the Elster-Gate, witnessed the solemn burning of a collection of the papal decretals and the canon law. Luther himself stepped forward and, committing a printed copy of the papal bull (*Exurge Domine*) to the flames, exclaimed: "As thou hast destroyed the truth of God, so the Lord today destroyeth thee, by means of this fire. Amen." This symbolic act was the signal for the actual beginning of religious revolution in Germany.

After the time limit set for Luther's submission had expired, a new bull (*Decet Romanum Pontificem*), dated January 3, 1521, declared the excommunication in force. Copies of Luther's writings and a wooden statue of the reformer were ceremoniously burned in Rome. Leo X addressed a letter to Charles V, asking for the full co-operation of the Empire in making the ban of the Church effective.

A meeting of the Imperial Diet had been called in the city of Worms, for January, 1521, and Luther, upon the suggestion of Frederick the Wise, declared his willingness to appear before the assembled Estates to have his cause tried and judged. Over the objections of the papal legate the Estates petitioned the emperor to summon Luther to Worms, in order to prevail once more upon him to retract, before pronouncing over him the ban of the Empire.

The summons reached Luther in Wittenberg on March 26, together with an imperial safe-conduct. The reformer's journey from Wittenberg to Worms was one triumphal procession, confirming his conviction that he could rely upon the sympathy of the majority of the German people, an experience which strengthened in him the resolution not to recant, come what might. Defiance and self-assurance are the characteristic traits in Luther as portrayed by Lucas Cranach in the year of the Diet of Worms.

The first hearing before the assembled electors, princes, prelates, nobles, and other delegates took place in the palace of the local bishop. Luther seemed intimidated by the august assemblage and, when asked by the speaker whether he was ready to recant, answered with a subdued voice, demanding that he be given more time for deliberation. He was granted a delay of twenty-four hours. The emperor, unimpressed by Luther's appearance, remarked: "That man will never make a heretic of me."

At the decisive second hearing that was held on the following day, Luther had regained his courage and composure and delivered the famous speech, in which he defended his convictions, with a firm and steady voice. After he had finished, the speaker asked him for an unequivocal answer: was he willing to recant or not? Whereupon Luther declared: "Unless I shall be convinced by witness of Scripture or by valid argument, I shall stay convinced by those sacred Scriptures which I have adduced, and my conscience is imprisoned in the word of God. I neither can nor will recant anything, for it is neither safe nor right to act against one's conscience. So help me God. Amen."

Luther left Worms a few days after the hearing. Meanwhile, Frederick the Wise had worked out a plan that would protect Luther against the dangerous consequences of the impending ban of the Empire. Five of the elector's horsemen, feigning an attack on Luther's traveling coach, kidnaped him on the road that leads from Möhra to Gotha, and brought him safely to the Wartburg near Eisenach in Thuringia, the property of the elector of Saxony. The hiding place had been selected by the councilors of Frederick who, claiming complete ignorance as to Luther's whereabouts, thus saved himself unnecessary embarrassment.

The "Edict of Worms," dated May 8, declared Luther under the ban of the Empire. He was condemned as a heretic, ten times worse than John Huss; as the author of writings which served to incite revolt, schism, and bloody civil war; as a subverter of all law, and a devil in human form. No one might shelter him or offer him food and drink. When apprehended, he must at once be handed over to the emperor. Whoever should protect him would share in his crime and incur identical penalties.

f) Luther in the Wartburg.   Clothed in knightly attire and partly disguised by a beard, Luther stayed in the Wartburg as "Squire George" (*Ritter Görg*) for almost a full year. He occupied a small room and used his enforced solitude to continue his writing. He tells of temptations of the flesh and of frequent vexations by the devil, who appeared to him in various shapes and disguises. He calls the Wartburg his "Patmos,"* because of the large number of visions and hallucinations that he experienced there. There is no evidence, however, that Luther threw his inkstand at the devil, thereby causing the famous stain on the wall of his cell that is even to this day shown to visiting tourists.

---

* The name refers to the city of Patmos on the Dodecanese Islands where St. John the Evangelist is said to have written the inspired text of the Apocalypse.

Luther's *Interpretation of the Magnificat,** written in the Wartburg and dedicated to the son of the Saxon elector, rejects the Catholic belief in the intercession of Mary in behalf of the faithful, but retains the doctrines of the virgin birth and of the Immaculate Conception (Mary's being born without the stain of original sin, in view of her being destined to become the mother of the Redeemer).

The greatest and most far-reaching accomplishment of the year in the Wartburg, however, was Luther's translation of the *New Testament* from Greek into German, a work whose literary significance was almost immediately recognized by friend and foe alike. It is hard to understand how Luther could have completed this monumental work, in addition to all his other plans and labors, within the short span of one year. The translation of the *Old Testament* followed later, and Luther's complete German Bible was published in 1534. The fifth printing of the year 1545 is regarded as the standard edition.

Luther's desire to fortify his theological system and especially to anchor his doctrine of "justification by faith alone" (fiducial faith) in scriptural authority induced him to consider the different sacred books as of unequal value and to eliminate several of them, among others the Epistle of James, which he called an "epistle of straw." By using for his translation the written language of the Saxon chancelleries and by blending this Middle German with elements of High German dialects, while at the same time he imparted to his work the flavor, vigor, and vitality of his own personality, he became the creator of a unified High German language, whose structure, syntax, and vocabulary have remained essentially unchanged to the present day. His acquaintance with mysticism on the one hand, and with the life, thought, and speech of the people on the other, made him capable of enriching his native tongue by means of individual and communal experience, which called for and issued in new and striking word formations.

As it was Luther's intention to substitute the authority of the Bible for almost the entire body of discarded Church tradition, he employed every device to make his work as readable and easily accessible as possible. Woodcuts served to emphasize the anti-Catholic tendency of his translation. Thus, the scarlet woman of the Apocalypse is crowned with the papal tiara, and Catholic dignitaries as well as the German emperor pay homage to this symbol of blasphemy and iniquity.

g) Luther's Return to Wittenberg and His Marriage. While Luther was working in his cell on the Wartburg, some of his followers in Wittenberg and elsewhere had carried his teachings to such extreme conclusions that he felt his presence was needed to call a halt to such excesses as the burning of sacred images, and the demolition of the statues of saints. Even more dangerous was the movement of the "Prophets of Zwickau,"

---

* *"Magnificat anima mea Dominum"* (my soul doth magnify the Lord): Mary's hymn of praise, in which, during her visit with her cousin Elizabeth, she gives thanks for being chosen to become the mother of Christ. The "Magnificat" forms part of the canonical office.

who adopted the teachings of the Anabaptists and their leader, Thomas Münzer (cf. p. 242), and who turned against Luther's doctrine on infant baptism, arguing that if Luther's contention was true and faith was the only requisite for the efficacy of the sacrament of baptism, then children must not be baptized until they had reached the maturity that was required for an act of faith.

Luther was fully conscious of his religious mission when he defied all the dangers that threatened him and returned to Wittenberg in 1522. He soon disappointed many of his friends and followers by turning out to be much more conservative in his views than they had anticipated. It had become clear to him that religious and social anarchy could only be avoided if he succeeded in organizing a church in which freedom was curbed by unity through authority. Although many vital changes in cult, liturgy, and dogmatic theology were introduced, much of the traditional Catholic doctrine and practice was retained. The authority of the Scriptures was declared supreme, but the practical exercise of the new creed was placed under the absolute control of the civil government. Superintendents, replacing the Roman Catholic bishops, were the appointees and officers of the state.

If the religious and social radicals felt repelled by Luther's conservatism, many of his Humanist sympathizers were estranged by the schismatic character that the Lutheran reform movement had assumed. Thus their hopes were frustrated that the reform could be carried out within the old Church by a gradual process of enlightened education. They were also unable to accept Luther's metaphysical and ethical rigorism and pessimism, his denial of free will, and his denunciation of human nature.

Luther's ideas were realized step by step in the organized structure of the new church: of the sacraments there now remained only baptism and the Lord's Supper; pilgrimages, fasts and abstinence, the veneration of the saints and their relics were done away with; the monastic orders were dissolved, and all the members of the clergy were allowed to marry. Thus the barriers that had separated ecclesiastics and laymen were broken down. Luther resumed his lectures in the University of Wittenberg and at the same time reorganized the religious cult and ecclesiastic discipline of his church. The liturgy of the Mass was largely retained, the Latin texts being gradually replaced by German translations (*German Mass and Order of the Service,* 1526). The sacrificial character of the Mass, however, was definitely denied.

As time went on, more and more significance was attached to congregational singing. Recognizing in the religious hymn a powerful force in spreading the new faith, Luther delved into the treasury of the past and drew on his own religious experience, utilizing his poetic gifts to provide the Lutheran Reformation with its great, warlike, lyric manifestoes. Ancient Latin hymns were translated into German, secular songs were revised and turned into church hymns. Luther himself created thirty-six hymns, for which his friend, John Walter, the musician, composed the melodies. Twenty-four of these songs were first published in 1524 (*Geistliches Gesangbüchlein*). The powerful and defiant *Trutzlied: "Ein' feste Burg ist unser Gott"*) ("A Mighty Fortress Is Our God"), whose melody is based on motifs of medieval "plain song" (Gregorian chant, cf. p. 83 sq.), originated in 1527, reflecting a period of critical strife and strain in the progress of the Lutheran Reformation. Frequently the melodies of ancient Latin church hymns or of pre-Reformation German religious and folk poetry served as textual and musical patterns.

In 1524 Luther threw off the habit of the Augustinian Order, and in the following year married the former Cistercian nun, Katherine of Bora. His friends were jubilant, his opponents scandalized. The newly married couple made their home in the former Augustinian monastery in Wittenberg, and Luther's "Käthe" rented the former monastic cells to university students, who henceforth shared the family life of Luther's household.

h) Luther and the Peasants. The same year 1525 marked the climax of the great German Peasants' War (cf. p. 240 sq.), with whose origin, conduct, and infamous end Luther was at first indirectly and later on directly concerned. The views that he had expressed in his book *On the Freedom of a Christian Man* had been interpreted by the peasants as a vindication of their revolt against social injustice and oppression. Luther's *Exhortation to Peace* (April, 1525) referred to the "Twelve Articles" of the peasants, their demand of the "Gospel without human addition," and was an attempt on his part to reconcile the opposing parties by mediation. He addressed both lords and peasants, telling them that they were both wrong and at odds with Christian teaching: "Both tyrants and mobs are enemies of God." His admonition having failed to persuade either party, Luther then turned passionately against the peasants in his pamphlet "Against the Murderous and Rapacious Hordes of the Peasants," in which he not only claimed that the peasants have no just cause of complaint, but ended by calling them "mad dogs and specters of hell," urging the princes and lords to "strike them down, throttle and stab them in secret and in public": "A prince can now deserve mercy better by shedding blood, than others can by prayer." Even years after the revolt had been savagely put down, Luther, himself a peasant's son, was to write: "I am very angry at the peasants, who cannot see how well off they are, sitting in peace through the help and protection of the princes. You impudent, coarse asses, can you not understand this? May thunder strike you dead!"

Such violent outbursts of anger can only be understood if we remember that Luther had originally attacked ecclesiastical and secular authorities, not because he found them too rigorous and too exacting but because of their laxity and corruption. With most of the medieval writers he shared the conviction that society rested on serfdom. In addition, the sharp dividing line that he had drawn between the external realm of secular power and the inner kingdom of the spirit had issued in a political theory that favored an extreme absolutism of the secular powers, whose function it was to act as law-enforcing agents in a world that was hopelessly entangled in sin and corruption. Thus, when the peasants wrote: "Christ has delivered and redeemed us all, the lowly as well as the great, without exception, by the shedding of His precious blood," Luther felt all the horrors of approaching anarchy and answered promptly: "This article would make all men equal and so change the spiritual kingdom of Christ into an external, worldly one. Impossible! An earthly kingdom cannot exist without inequality of persons. Some must be free, others serfs, some rulers, others subjects." The problems of social ethics and social reconstruction were to be left to the discretion of the state. They were foreign to Luther's conception of the functions of the Church: "Christians are rare people on earth. Therefore, stern, hard, civil rule is necessary in the world, lest the world become wild, peace vanish, and commerce and common interests be destroyed. . . . No one need think that the world can be ruled without blood. The civil sword shall and must be red and bloody."

i) Predestination and Free Will. In 1523 Erasmus of Rotterdam (cf. p. 249 sq.) had published his work on the freedom of the human will (*De Libero Arbitrio Diatribe*), in which he attacked Luther's determinism. Luther's answer was given in 1525, in a work that he himself considered his masterpiece and the capstone of his theology, and to which he gave the title *De Servo Arbitrio* (On the Enslaved Will). Employing a large number of biblical quotations, Luther tries to establish once and for all that God works everything in everyone and that man, by his own nature, is entirely unable to recognize and choose the good: "Everything that is created by God, is moved by His omnipotence. . . . " Human will, like a saddle horse, stands between God and the devil: "If God mounts into the saddle, man goes as God wills it. . . . If the devil mounts into the saddle, man goes as the devil wills it. It is not in man's power to run to one of the two horsemen and offer himself to him, but the horsemen fight against one another to gain hold of the horse. . . . If we believe that Satan is the Prince of this World, who constantly besets the Kingdom of Christ and does not release his grip on the enslaved human beings unless he is forced to do so by the power of God, then it is evident that there can be no free will." In this way Luther tries to explain the predestination of the condemned souls, who will suffer the torments of eternal hell-fire. But if man lacks the freedom of choice, who then is responsible for the sins he commits? Luther answers: "God is God, and for His will there is neither reason nor cause. . . . He is the rule of all things." We are reminded once more that Martin Luther was "of Occam's school."

j) The Two Catechisms and the Book on Marriage. The more Luther's reformation lost the character of a sectarian movement and acquired the sociological characteristics of a church organism, which received and embraced saints and sinners, the more was he compelled to stress the authoritarian elements as against the individualism and liberalism of religious enthusiasts and pseudomystics. In the end he was to deny explicitly the mystical inclinations of an earlier period of his own life and to construe instead an antagonism between a "faith," which was based on the objective authority of the Scriptures, and a "mystical" subjectivism, which claimed personal illumination by an "inner light."

The development in the direction of authoritarianism included the justification of force, compulsion, and persecution of heretics as means to crush divergent views and movements within and without the Lutheran Church. The demand of freedom of conscience and religious conviction was completely abandoned. In serious cases of heresy, such as adherence to the teachings of the Anabaptists (cf. p. 241 sq.), capital punishment was recommended, while in milder forms of disbelief or in the case of moral offenses the disciplinary action consisted in the exclusion of the sinner from the sacrament of communion. The Lord's Supper in the Lutheran congregations was now (after 1526) generally administered in both kinds, the bread and the wine.

In 1529 Luther published two manuals of religious instruction, known as the *Little* and the *Great Catechisms*. The *Little Catechism,* designed "for children and people of a simple mind," was a model of clear and straightforward exposition of doctrine, omitting all polemic agitation against the Catholic Church. The *Great Catechism* was primarily intended for the use of Lutheran pastors. No reference was made to the right of individual interpretation of the Bible, nor to Luther's previous emphasis on the fatal consequences of original sin and the dogma of predestination for eternal damnation. After Luther's death the two catechisms were incorporated in the "Form of Concord" (*Konkordienbuch*) as *"symbola"* (articles of faith) of the Lutheran Church.

In his book *On Matrimony* (*Von Ehesachen*) of 1530 Luther emphasizes that marriage is not a sacrament but "an external, worldly thing, like clothes and food, home and hearth, subject to secular authority." Nevertheless he praises the state of married life as a worthy and even sublime and divine institution. Divorce he considers permissible in the case of adultery and desertion.

k) *Luther and Zwingli.* At about the time when Luther had taken his monastic vows at Erfurt, Huldreich (Ulrich) Zwingli (1484-1531) was ordained a priest. His relations to the radical wing of the Humanist movement awakened his interest in the ideas of the Lutheran reform. Shortly after having accepted the ministry of the Great Minster (*Grossmünster*) in Zurich, he succeeded in winning the city council over to his views, and in introducing the "reformed" creed in that city. Celebration of the Mass was prohibited, all images were either destroyed or removed from the churches, and all citizens were in duty bound to listen to Zwingli's sermons. Even singing and organ music were originally excluded from church services.

In a Socratic manner Zwingli declared that virtue was the result of knowledge. Yet, quite inconsistently, he denied the freedom of the will and taught absolute predestination. His radicalism and rationalism, however, resulted in several clashes with Luther, especially concerning the words of institution in the commemoration of the Lord's Supper. It was Zwingli's conviction that Christ's sacramental words "This is My body, this is My blood" must be understood symbolically, not literally, meaning "this signifies My body, this signifies My blood," while Luther insisted on a strictly literal interpretation, maintaining that Christ was really present on the altar, but only for those who believed in His presence and only as long as the ceremony lasted (doctrine of *impanation*).

In 1529 Luther and Zwingli met in the city of Marburg for a disputation (*Religionsgespräch*) on the controversial issue. Despite Zwingli's conciliatory attitude Luther refused to yield to the rational arguments of the Swiss reformer, with the repeated assertion: "Your spirit is different from ours." In the same year the rural cantons of Switzerland, which had preserved their Catholic heritage, concluded an alliance with Catholic Austria, and the following armed conflict ended with the defeat of the reformed forces in the battle of Cappel (1531). Zwingli died on the field of battle.

l) Luther and Melanchthon. With the "Protestation" of the Lutheran princes and cities of the year 1529 (cf. p. 210) a "Protestant party" had come into actual existence. At the Diet of Augsburg in 1530 the Lutherans presented the so-called "Augsburg Confession" (*Confessio Augustana*) that had been drawn up by Philip Melanchthon (1497–1560), Luther's close friend and collaborator. It was a carefully and shrewdly worded document that left the door ajar for a compromise with the Catholic party. Some of Luther's main tenets, such as the doctrine of the general priesthood of all the faithful, the denial of the primacy of the Roman See, the denial of free will, and the doctrine of absolute predestination, were not even mentioned.

The author of this document was a classical philologist and a teacher of great erudition, whose impressionable mind had been fascinated by Luther's genial and dynamic personality. He was a man of letters rather than a man of action, and it was in his capacity as a scholar that he effectively supplemented the Lutheran teachings, by providing the reformed theology with a philosophic basis, thus systematically preparing the way for the development of a Protestant scholasticism that was indebted to Cicero and Aristotle. A native of Bretten in Baden, he showed his predilection for the Humanist trend of the age by adopting the name "Melanchthon," a Greek translation of his family name, Schwarzerd. Retiring, introspective, and peace-loving by nature, of frail physical constitution, he was drawn into theological controversies and political quarrels against his will, so much so that he remarked in the hour of his death that he felt happy to be freed at last from the wrath of the theologians (*a rabie theologorum*). The great services that Melanchthon rendered to his country by reorganizing the system of higher learning, especially his reforms in the field of Protestant secondary education, earned for him the title of honor, *"Praeceptor Germaniae"* (the Teacher of Germany).

Although Luther had somewhat reluctantly approved of Melanchthon's formulation of the *Confessio Augustana,* he subsequently declared himself opposed to all further attempts at mediation and compromise. He admitted that he was not able "to tread as gently and softly" as Melanchthon. On April 15, 1530, he had arrived at the castle of Coburg on the southern slope of the Thuringian mountains; to watch the proceedings at Augsburg. From here he sent an *Admonition to the Ecclesiastics Assembled at the Diet of Augsburg,* designed to impress upon the members of the Diet the momentous importance of their decision. "If I live," he exclaims in this pamphlet, "I shall be as a pestilence to you; if I die, I shall be your death; for God has called me to run you down. . . . I shall not leave you in peace until you either mend your ways or perish."

m) Completion of the German Bible. Twelve years after the edition of his translation of the New Testament, the entire Bible in German, richly illustrated with woodcuts, was published by Hans Luft in Wittenberg. Luther had taken as a basis for his translation the original Greek text of the Scriptures in place of the Latin Vulgate. In this he followed the humanistic tendencies of his age. Erasmus of Rotterdam (cf. p. 249 sq.) had pointed the way with his Greek edition of the New Testament. But it was Luther's great merit that the Bible soon became the most widely read book in German lands.

Many of the illustrations are violently polemical. The scarlet women of Babylon and the apocalyptic dragon appear again, crowned with the papal tiara, and the title page of the Wittenberg edition of 1541 portrays the devil with a cardinal's hat, driving a man into the jaws of hell.

Luther's translation of the Bible was a work of eminent literary merit, but it was by no means the first German translation. The author of the first complete German Bible, printed by Mentel in Strasbourg in 1466, is unknown. One hundred and fifty-six different Latin editions of the complete Bible were printed between the years 1450 and 1520. Thereto must be added a large number of earlier manuscripts as well as the numerous editions of specific parts of the Scriptures in Latin and German, especially the Psalter and the Gospels and Epistles of the ecclesiastical year, taken from the Old and New Testaments. They were collected in the so-called "plenaries" or "homilies" (*Postillen*), which had gained great popularity among people of every walk of life.

n) Luther's "Table Talk." The students who lived as boarders in Luther's household, friends of the family, and invited guests gathered almost daily around the family table to listen to Luther's informal talks or to carry on spirited discussions. Luther's utterances were usually written down in shorthand by some zealous student or friend, and it is to these gatherings in the family circle that we owe the famous collection of "Table Talks" (*Tischreden*), dealing with various theological and philosophical problems,

MARTINVS   LVTHERVS

Luther at the Age of 37, by Lucas Cranach

Erasmus, by Hans Holbein

personal experiences and reminiscences, and multiple related subjects. The *Tischreden* are an invaluable aid in any attempt to establish a historically reliable picture of Martin Luther, his personality and his work. The directness and spontaneity of the speech, the blend of natural simplicity, genial humor, and biting satire make this collection a source of genuine delight, notwithstanding an obvious lack of consistency, moderation, and premeditation. The almost unbelievable coarseness of many passages and expressions must be largely attributed to the growing degeneration of taste and style in the sixteenth century. The records begin with the year 1531 and extend to the end of Luther's life. "Frau Käthe" was not only an attentive listener but frequently took part in the discussions.

Luther's family life was a happy one. The children were brought up in a deeply religious atmosphere, and Katherine Luther proved herself a strong and brave comrade in the many struggles that weighed dark and heavy on the last decades of Luther's life.

o) Luther's Last Years and Death. Dissensions in the ranks of his own church, controversies with the leaders of separatistic sects, the realization of the gradual regeneration of the Catholic Church, and, in addition, Luther's failing health were factors that produced in his mind frequent moods of doubt, weariness, skepticism, and even despair: "Let everything fall to pieces, let it stand, let it perish, let it go as it will . . . , " he exclaims in 1542. And again: "Germany is no more; never again will she be the same that she was in the past."

The "invisible" church that Luther had hoped to establish in the hearts of all the faithful had grown into a very visible human institution, which had to rely on the support of the secular state for its existence and perpetuation. In order to preserve the unity of his creation, Luther found himself compelled to maintain it by force and to turn against his own principles of individual freedom and toleration.

From the beginning of the fourth decade of the sixteenth century the thought of his approaching death recurred again and again. When he celebrated his sixty-first birthday in the company of friends (1545), he thought that he would not live through the Easter season of that year. He spoke gloomily of a threatening defection of the brethren in the faith, by which they would do more harm to the Gospel than the mostly ignorant and epicurean papists.

Once more, however, his hatred of the papacy prompted Luther to take up his pen to denounce the Church of Rome as the creation of Satan (*Against the Papacy in Rome, an Invention of the Devil,* 1545). Lucas Cranach's drawings and woodcuts, inspired and commentated by Luther and designated by himself as his "testament to the German nation," served the same purpose. In other writings of this last period he dealt with the practices of usury and the part played by the Jews in the money trade. While in an earlier period of his life he had hoped to convert the Jews to his new gospel, he now attacked their race and religion in most violent terms. In his views on usury Luther adhered strictly to the medieval tradition, in an age in which the gradual adoption of the credit system in trade and commerce had rendered meaningless the prohibition of the taking of interest. He felt that the devil himself is in the complicated mechanism of financial organization: "The greatest misfortune of the German nation is the traffic in interest. . . . The devil invented it, and the Pope, by giving his sanction to it, has done untold evil throughout the world." Usurers should be refused the Lord's Supper and Christian burial. The luxury trade with the East, the machinations of international finance, speculation, and monopolies are denounced: "Foreign merchandise which brings from Calicut and India and the like places wares such as precious silver and jewels and spices . . . and drain the land and people of their money, should not be permitted."

In 1541 John Calvin (1509–1564) had established his theocratic rule in Geneva. Born in Picardy (France) and educated in Paris and in the law schools of Orléans and Bourges, he had been influenced by the reading of Luther's works, when he began to work out his own version of the reformed creed and gave it a doctrinal foundation in the *Institutes of the Christian Religion* (1534). His legally trained mind made him averse to all halfhearted measures, and though he recognized his indebtedness to Luther, he became the most relentless advocate of the doctrine of absolute predestination and an integral determinism that went far beyond Luther's position. Luther's separation of the worldly and ecclesiastical spheres he likewise rejected and, by conceiving of God as an all-powerful, all-penetrating, stern, and unbending Judge, he established the moral code of Calvinism on the basis of an Old Testament concept of divine law.

Calvin's theocratic state embraced the most minute details of public and private life and tried to realize a commonwealth of saints by the application of the most rigid discipline and a system of constant control and supervision. By denying the real presence of Christ in the Eucharist Calvin approached the position of Zwingli. His teachings, accordingly, were sufficiently at variance with Luther's fundamental convictions to make an open conflict between the two men highly probable. Luther's death, however, forestalled this. In the following decades Calvinism spread from Switzerland to other countries, notably France, the Netherlands, Bohemia, and Scotland, making also considerable inroads into southern Germany, where in some districts it replaced Lutheranism.

Martin Luther died on February 18, 1546, of a prolonged heart ailment, at Eisleben, the city of his birth. He had gone there to mediate a quarrel between the counts of Mansfeld. Two of the friends who surrounded his deathbed asked him whether he wished to remain faithful to his teachings. His affirmative answer was his last utterance. His wife and children had remained in Wittenberg and could not be with him in the hour of his death. He lies buried in the castle church in Wittenberg.

p) Germany and the Reformation. It depends upon the historian's point of view whether he looks upon the Lutheran Reformation as a blessing or a curse. To designate it as a typically German phenomenon, and to oppose it as such to a Romanic or un-Germanic type of religious devotion, may be correct in so far as Luther's movement shows a definite preference for a religion of "pure inwardness" (*reine Innerlichkeit*) and personal experience as against a form of worship which stresses the importance of external form and dogma, liturgical ritual, and cultic imagery. However, we shall do well not to put too much emphasis on such distinctions, in view of the fact that Luther's ideals of spiritual freedom, individual judgment, and pure inwardness were never actually embodied in the completed structure of his church; most of the ideas that had brought about his break with Rome had to seek refuge in the shelter of those separatistic sects that were persecuted with fire and sword by the three reformed churches.

On the other hand, while Luther's own mentality was undoubtedly more medieval than modern, he nevertheless inaugurated that secularization of life and culture which came to its fruition partly without his doing and partly even against his will. As far as Germany is concerned, the fatal consequence of his movement was the division of the German nation, its best minds and its cultural energies, into antagonistic camps, intellectually, socially, politically. But even here it is hard to determine whether the searching thoroughness of the German mind, its· deep and vital concern with the ultimate problems of human existence, with truth, goodness, and beauty, was not intensified rather than crippled by the spiritual challenge that was Luther's gift to the German people.

Revolution and Civil War. The Lutheran Reformation represents only one aspect of the deep-seated unrest and dissatisfaction that produced the violent social reactions of the early sixteenth century. Socially and politically, the age was characterized less by attempts at reform than by the spirit of revolt, issuing in class warfare and social disintegration. The end of the Middle Ages and the beginning of modern times is marked by the revolt of the have-nots, the socially disinherited, those who for some reason or other were not able to keep pace with the changing economic and political constellations of the time. But, as is always the case, these economic and political transformations were only surface phenomena which pointed to a more fundamental change in the intellectual and moral attitudes and convictions. The have-nots in the beginning of the sixteenth century were the peasants, the proletarians in the cities, and the impoverished knights.

a) *Peasantry and Early Capitalism.* The peasant, who had been relatively well off in the agrarian society of the early Middle Ages, had become virtually a slave in the course of the fourteenth and fifteenth centuries, concomitant with the advent of the new money economy, city trade, and capitalistic enterprise. The rights to the piece of land that he held either on a long or short lease (*Erbpacht* and *Zeitpacht*), had been constantly diminished, while at the same time his duties had become correspondingly heavier and, finally, almost unbearable. With the waning of imperial power questions of right and social justice had become more and more questions of might, to the exclusion of any moral motives and obligations.

Roman law, after the eleventh century, had been gradually adopted by most European countries and had supplanted the traditional tribal laws in Germany during the fourteenth and fifteenth centuries. It was used with legalistic ingenuity and seemingly inexorable logic to the advantage of princely and capitalistic interests. It superseded and invalidated the principles that had been embodied in the ancient law codes of the peasants (*Weistümer*). "According to the damnable teaching of the new jurists, the prince is to be everything in the country, but the people nothing, the people having nothing to do but obey, serve, and pay taxes," wrote Jacob Wimpheling (1450–1528), a priest and one of the leaders of early Humanism. Furthermore, the steady increase in population led to a growing scarcity of available land and to the parceling out of farmland in smaller and smaller units.

The peasantry at the end of the Middle Ages was becoming more and more dependent on city capital. This increasing indebtedness led to hatred and resentment against the professional money lenders, the Jews, usurers, merchants, and quite generally· against all the representatives of the new money economy, who dominated and cornered the markets, controlled the prices, and destroyed the bases of agrarian activity and economy. The great merchants and merchant-princes of the fifteenth century, such as the Medicis in Italy and the Fuggers, Welsers, and Hochstetters in Germany, represented the growing power of international finance and were the powers behind the European thrones and the directors of the destinies of European states. They fixed the prices of commodities and necessities at their will and controlled the domestic and foreign markets. Mining and banking were the two main sources of the income of these early capitalists. The Fuggers in Augsburg, for instance, acquired the greater part of their wealth through the operation of German silver mines. With an organized credit system still in its infancy, the possession of coined money in gold and silver was an absolute prerequisite for business transactions on a large scale. The restrictions imposed on unrestrained competition by the guilds (cf. p. 126) were felt as so many shackles and were thrown off to give way to the freedom of capitalistic venture and initiative. Merchant companies and, later on, joint-stock companies were to provide added opportunities for profit for their individual members and facilitated the formation of monopolies. The joint-stock company, which appears fully developed in Germany at the end of the sixteenth century, implies joint liability for the indebtedness of the whole company, while in the ordinary merchant company each member carried on his transactions on his own capital and risk.

The anticapitalist spirit called forth plans for social reconstruction as well as many get-rich-quick schemes, supposed short cuts to Utopia. Some writers suggested that all merchant companies should be done away with. Ulrich von Hutten (cf. p. 251 sq.) fought against merchants, knights, lawyers, and clergymen, while Geiler von Kaisersberg (1445–1510), the famous preacher and moralist, found the monopolists more detestable even than the Jews and asked that they be exterminated like wolves.

A resolution passed by the Austrian Diet of 1518 reads as follows: "The great companies have brought under their control . . . all goods which are indispensable to man, and they are so powerful by the strength of their money that they cut off trade from the common merchant who is worth from one to ten thousand florins; they set the prices at their pleasure and increase them at their will, by which they visibly grow fewer in number; but a few of them grow into a princely fortune to the great detriment of the country." Some of the inflated big business houses broke down after a short-lived boom, involving in their downfall the savings of small investors. The failure of the Hochstetters in 1529 amounted to 800,000 florins, about $6,500,000 in our present value of money. With the disintegration of the craft and merchant guilds the hitherto friendly relations between masters and journeymen gave way to growing antagonism. Labor was on the way to become a commodity that could be bought and sold, and the working-man, selling his labor to the highest bidder, was gradually forced into a proletarian existence.

The revolts of the peasants were essentially a last attempt of an agrarian society to hold its own against the superior forces of the new capitalistic system of economy. The peasants appeared as the reactionary and retro-gressive forces in an age that had introduced the profit motive as the chief factor in economic endeavor and that adhered to the formerly condemned and despised theory that money can breed money. With increasing opportunities in commercial enterprise the investment of capital in ever so many ways became the order of the day and was universally practiced by states, cities, and individuals. The newly discovered trade routes to Africa, India, and the Americas added even greater stimulus and allurement to an expanding international trade, based on large-scale invest-ment and commercial credit. But this whole process of transforming an agrarian into a financial society was accompanied by almost constant con-flicts, convulsions, and explosions.

It is not surprising that despite his conservatism the peasant, too, wanted his share of the goods of this world; that he, too, had been seized by the desire to advance his social position and to raise his standard of living. In addition, Luther's message concerning the "Freedom of a Christian Man" had provided him with a moral incentive and justification in his demand for social justice and for due consideration of his human rights. The spirit of revolt was fanned by the news of the successful struggle of the Swiss peasants against the oppressive rule of the Hapsburgs (cf. p. 170) and by the sympathizers among the city proletariat, groaning under the burden of excessive taxation. From the beginning, therefore, we find the lower classes in the cities involved in the uprisings of the peasants.

b) Beginnings of the Peasants' Revolt. The first revolutionary wave started in the southwestern corner of the Empire, those districts that were closest to the free peasant republic of Switzerland. Within a short time the movement spread to Swabia, Franconia, and Thuringia. The symbol of the rebellious peasants was the *"Bundschuh,"* the common laced boot worn by the peasants, which was depicted on their banners — a sign of protest against the costly buckskin footwear of the nobles.

The first major uprising occurred in the Alsatian regions in 1493. It was prematurely discovered and bloodily crushed. The same fate befell the second major revolt of the year 1502. But Joss Fritz, the leader of the peasants, escaped and, after another unsuccessful attempt and another escape, he reappeared in 1525, when the Great Peasant War had already gotten well under way. Minor uprisings in Württemberg and in the eastern part of the Empire had likewise ended in failure.

c) The Great Peasant War (1524–1525). "Nothing but God's Justice" had been the battle cry of the peasants at the beginning of the revolt, but now they demanded the liquidation of all the intermediate powers that stood between the emperor and the people: (princes, lords, bishops, abbots, etc.). They formulated their demands in the famous "Twelve Articles" of 1525, to which the peasants in all parts of Germany subscribed. The authors of the articles accepted Luther's new gospel as their spiritual creed and designated all opponents as enemies of Christ. In the name of the gospel they demanded freedom of choice in the election of their pastors; the abolition of serfdom and the tithe; the free use of water, woods, and pastures; and the abolition of the death tax (*Todfall*) which deprived widows and their children of a large part of their inheritance. Reference to scriptural authority was again made in the concluding words: "If one or several of these articles be contrary to the word of God, we will not defend such propositions."

The more considerate among the ruling powers recognized that there was just cause for complaint on the side of the peasants, and if their counsel had been heeded, the following excesses could have been averted. A number of city magistrates and several territorial and imperial Diets passed resolutions against usurious practices and trade monopolies. Berthold of Henneberg, the imperial chancellor, elector, and archbishop of Mainz, had spoken for the cause of the peasants when he advocated a thorough reform of imperial administration at the Diet of Worms in 1495. However, the shortsightedness and selfishness of the imperial and local governments prevented the adoption of any socially progressive legislation.

After the rather moderate demands of the Twelve Articles had been rejected, the peasant movement developed into a social revolution. Direct communications between the peasants and the dissatisfied elements in the cities were soon established. The armies of the peasants received further moral and material support from the ranks of the rebellious imperial knights who, in 1522–1523 under the leadership of Ulrich von Hutten (cf. p. 251 sq.) and Franz von Sickingen, had risen in revolt against ecclesiastical and secular princes to establish an empire that was to be free from Rome and from princely domination. Some of the knights and nobles came to the aid of the peasants for idealistic reasons, among them Götz von Berlichingen and Florian Geyer, who even assumed temporary leadership of the peasant troops. Fanatics, adventurers, mercenary soldiers, and others were prompted by ambition, lust of adventure, or greed to join the ranks of the peasants. In Würzburg we find on their side Tilman Riemenschneider, the sculptor.

The Great Peasants' War which had started in May, 1524, in the region of Lake Constance (*Bodensee*) near the Swiss border, had soon spread to most parts of southern and central Germany. An assembly held at Memmingen in Bavaria voted death to all nobles and asked for the destruction of all monasteries. During the following period of violence cities were captured, castles destroyed, monasteries and churches desecrated and burned, and the instincts of the peasant mobs satisfied their desire of revenge in many acts of savage cruelty. In the course of seven major encounters the peasants were finally subjugated by the well-trained armies and the superior strategy of their opponents. The peasant armies were well equipped but lacked adequate, unified, and unselfish leadership. The lords followed Luther's advice and drowned the revolt literally in blood. Over one hundred thousand peasants were slain, many other thousands were wounded, tortured, and crippled for life. Terrible vengeance was meted out to the survivors: their arms were confiscated, their liberties revoked, their burdens increased. An official estimate puts the number of those executed at ten thousand. The lords devised the most inhuman tortures for their victims.

The lot of the peasants after the end of the war was much worse than it had ever been before. The winners were the princes and territorial lords. They made the Lutheran Reformation, that had been so enthusiastically welcomed by the peasants, serve their own selfish and dynastic ends, feeding their lust for power on both social revolt and religious reform. In 1555 serfdom was legally recognized throughout the Empire. The lower classes fell into a state of apathy and degradation, while the educated classes cherished a pedantic Latin culture, built on legalistic concepts and rationalized theological formulas.

d) *The Anabaptists.* In the cities the revolutionary movement had its center in the sect of the Anabaptists. In their literal interpretation of the Scriptures they went to such extremes as to run about without clothes or to play with toys in order to appear "as little children." They gathered together, waiting for the food that their heavenly father would send them, if only they "took no heed as to what they should eat." They refused military service, would not bind themselves by oaths, denied the doctrine of eternal damnation, the existence of the Trinity, the divinity of Christ, and derived the sanctions for their actions from visions and inspirations. They were opposed to private property and the authority of State and Church and, above all else, they denied the validity of the baptism of infants.

From Switzerland, where the movement originated, the Anabaptist teachings spread to the North and gained an enthusiastic following in the Saxon towns of Zwickau and Wittenberg, at the time when Luther was a voluntary prisoner in the Wartburg (cf. p. 225). Their leader, Thomas Münzer (1498–1525), a native of Thuringia, adopting a hammer as the symbol and emblem of his party, led his followers in their fight for a new communistic society, built on the inspired guidance of those in whom the divine word burned as a living flame that devoured all "godless," that is, all who were opposed to the new order. The Anabaptists succeeded in converting Luther's friend, Carlstadt, but Luther's unexpected return from the Wartburg shattered their hopes of making Wittenberg the center of their movement.

After the outbreak of the Great Peasants' War Thomas Münzer dreamed of making Mühlhausen in Thuringia the nucleus of his kingdom of God on earth. He secured for himself a position in the city government, established a "Christian regime," raised (contrary to the antimilitarist creed of his sect) an army, and called for the extermination of all his opponents, especially of all monks, priests, and nobles. Scores of churches, monasteries, and castles were sacked and burned by his fanatical followers. Countless works of art and literature were destroyed.

Thomas Münzer reappeared on the day of the decisive battle of Frankenhausen (May 15, 1525), leading his peasant hordes to their destruction. He was captured, subjected to torture, and executed, after having confessed and received Communion according to the Catholic rites.

After Münzer's death the Anabaptist movement was revived in 1531 in the city of Münster in Westphalia. The cruel persecutions of the preceding years had strengthened rather than weakened the vitality of the sect. Under the leadership of Bernard Rothmann, Bernard Cnipperdolling, and John of Leyden the Anabaptists overthrew the magistrates of the city, took the government into their own hands and banished all the "godless" from the city. A communistic regime was established and polygamy was officially decreed, the women being distributed among the men. What was to happen again in the days of the French revolution of 1789 was proclaimed in the "Kingdom of Zion" of 1534: all church towers were to be cut down, so that "everything that is exalted might be humbled." John of Leyden assumed the title of king, calling himself "John the Just, on the throne of David," proclaiming his dominion over all the world and sending out twenty-eight apostles to preach the new dispensation.

After a year's duration the "Kingdom of Zion" succumbed to the imperial armies that had been sent against the city of Münster. The Anabaptists and their leaders offered heroic resistance, and those who had to pay with their lives died with the fortitude of religious conviction. The doctrines of the Anabaptists were once more revived in a milder and saner form by Menno Simmons (1492–1559), the founder of the Mennonite sect.

The Age of Discoveries. The Spaniards and the Portuguese were the great seafaring peoples and the discoverers of new continents at the beginning of modern times (fourteenth and fifteenth centuries). The Germans, who had practically no share in the expeditions themselves, were nevertheless deeply affected by the cultural changes that followed the discovery of new countries, peoples, and entire civilizations. Their outlook was broadened, their geographical and astronomical concepts revolutionized, their thinking and living was directed into new channels.

The first great family of explorers were the Polos of Venice, Nicolo, Matteo, and Nicolo's son, Marco, who undertook two expeditions to Asia, in the closing decades of the thirteenth century. They reached the Chinese city of Pekin, and young Marco Polo spent seventeen years in the service of the Tartar emperor, Kublai Khan. Up to this time trade between Italy and the Far East had been controlled by Moslem middlemen, who had reaped immense profits. It was for this reason that the Western merchants were eager to discover a direct sea route which would make it possible for them to avoid the difficult and costly journey through central Asia and to establish direct communication with India and China. Their spirit of enterprise and adventure was soon encouraged and backed by the centralized states and the money interests of Europe.

After Henry the Navigator (1394-1460), a Portuguese prince, had devoted his untiring efforts to the exploration of the west coast of Africa, his country-man, Bartolomeu Diaz, reached the Cape of Good Hope, the southern-most point of Africa, in 1486. About one decade later (1497-1498) another Portuguese, Vasco da Gama, discovered the sea route to the East Indies and landed in the harbor of Calicut. In the meantime, Cristoforo (Juan) Colombo (latinized form: Columbus; germanized form: Cristoffel Dauber, 1451-1506), a native of Genoa (Italy) in the service of the Spanish crown, had set out to explore the eastern coasts of Asia and had discovered the islands of Guanahani (San Salvador), Cuba, and Haiti. He undertook four expeditions in all and died in the conviction that all he had accomplished was to find a new sea route to East India, when in reality he had re-discovered the American continent, once known to the seafaring Norman Vikings and long since forgotten.

The final conquest of the American continent was due to the initiative of Spanish military leaders and adventurers, such as Fernando Cortez and Francisco Pizarro, who in the opening decades of the sixteenth century conquered Mexico and Peru. Streams of gold and silver began to flow from the New to the Old World, greatly strengthening the capitalistic trends in European society and at the same time making Spain its foremost and most powerful exponent.

The newly discovered continent received its name (America) from the Florentine cartographer, Amerigo Vespucci († 1512), who had made several journeys to the New World. The name "America" was first proposed by Martin Waltzenmüller, a native of Freiburg, in his *Cosmographiae Introductio* ("Introduction to Cosmography," 1507). Fernando Magellan, a Portuguese nobleman in Spanish services, was the first explorer who succeeded in sailing completely around the world (1519–1522).

The Germans, like all other Europeans, were fascinated and entranced by the fabulous treasures and luxuries that the age of discoveries had made available for Western civilization. They stood amidst a changing world with mixed feelings of jubilation, awe, admiration, and a pride which throve on visions of unlimited power and manifested itself in greed, unrest, and dissatisfaction. When Albrecht Dürer was shown in Brussels a display of all the wondrous and precious things imported from Mexico, he wrote: "Never in all my life have I seen anything that has elated me as much as these goods; for among them I noticed wonderfully artistic things, so that I marvel at the subtle ingenuity of these peoples in foreign lands."

The Renaissance. The beginning of modern times is generally associated with the *Rinascita* or "Renaissance," as the movement was called by Voltaire and the French Encyclopaedists. The term signifies an attempted revival of the arts, literatures, and ideas of classical Graeco-Roman antiquity, a culture that was characterized as much as the medieval philosophy of life by a definite concept of man, who now enthusiastically experienced his newly acquired power in the conquest and technical mastery of the realms of nature and mind. The objects of nature are subjected to closest scrutiny and to the test of the scientific experiment, while at the same time they are divested of the partly symbolical and partly mystical veil which had enveloped and harbored them in the cosmic universe of a spiritually and ecclesiastically determined world view. Nature and supernature are broken asunder, and the natural provinces of life, the realms of philosophy, morality, art, politics, economics, and so forth, are proclaimed autonomous, subject only to their own intrinsic laws.

Properly speaking, the Renaissance is a phenomenon of the European South and more specifically of Italy, where the spirit of antiquity had never died. It was still alive to some extent in the structures of ancient temples and palaces, in Roman Law, and in the documents of classical Greek and Roman literature. But the philosophic, artistic, and literary Renaissance forced these ancient contents into new molds, and its great representatives proudly felt themselves to be the legitimate sons and heirs of the classical past of their nation.

Dante Alighieri (1265–1321), the great Florentine poet, had summarized for a last time the medieval system and mode of life in the tripartite setting of his *Divine Comedy,* man's journey through hell, purgatory, and paradise. But the personal style, national consciousness, and strongly individualistic outlook of this master foreshadowed the spirit of a new age. The vernacular Tuscan dialect had served him as the medium of his literary language and, together with Petrarch (1304–1374) and Boccaccio (1313–1375), he created the modern Italian idiom. Petrarch, like Dante, embodied contradictory motives in his life and work: the lover of solitude and introspection praises friendship and social intercourse; the ascetic despiser of things transitory hungers for the acclaim and applause of the masses; the lover of freedom humbly submits to ecclesiastical rule and discipline; the defender of an enlightened and supernational humanism passionately proclaims the political and cultural supremacy of Rome. While Petrarch in the sonnets that he addressed to Laura created a distinct pattern for the poets of the Italian Renaissance, the witty, sensuous, and superbly balanced prose style of Giovanni Boccaccio's *Decamerone* became the model for the later Italian novelists. Translations of Boccaccio's works were among the first books printed in Germany.

The Renaissance movement and the largely secularized Church of the fifteenth and early sixteenth centuries were on excellent terms, the representatives of the Roman Church giving their sanction and blessing to the cult of Christian as well as pagan antiquity. Clerical writers adopted the style of the Attic comedy, and the Vatican became one of the great centers of Renaissance culture. Girolamo Savonarola (1452–1498), the ascetic Dominican prior of San Marco in Florence, who had raised his lonely voice in passionate protest against the extravagance and moral depravity of the papal court of Alexander VI (1492–1503), was burned at the stake as a heretic, while Pope Leo X of the house of Medici (1513–1521) surrounded himself with the most famous artists, writers, and orators of his age. The popes of the Renaissance were no hideous monsters but splendor-loving secular princes, who shared in the virtues and vices of their contemporaries. Some were even very able administrators, but most of them had little realization of the spiritual responsibilities of their office.

The most distinguished protagonists of the political and artistic Renaissance were the Florentine Medicis. Cosimo de Medici (1389–1464), the son of a merchant, founded the Platonic Academy in Florence and made himself the undisputed political leader of his native city. His grandson, Lorenzo "the Magnificent," himself a poet and art collector, told his son Giovanni, the future Pope Leo X, that the fine art objects and beautiful books of antiquity were of much greater value than gold and other material possessions. He held his protecting hand over the arts and sciences and employed the famous painters Ghirlandajo (1449–1494) and Botticelli (1444–1510) at his court. He founded the academy for sculptors in which Michelangelo received his training.

One of Giovanni's closest friends was the philosopher Pico della Mirandola (1463–1494), in whose works the Jewish, Greek, and Christian traditions blend. In his *Discourse on the Dignity of Man,* Pico gave expression to the religious creed of a Christian Platonist, when he had God address Adam in these words: "Thou hast the seeds of eternal life within thyself. I have set thee in the center of the universe, so that thou mayest see everything that existeth therein. I have created thee neither a heavenly nor an earthly being, neither mortal nor immortal, so that thou mayest be thine own sculptor and conqueror, so that thou mayest model thine own countenance. Thou canst degenerate into an animal, but by virtue of thy free will thou canst also regenerate thyself and become a godlike being." Pico della Mirandola and his contemporary, Marsilio Ficino (1433–1499) signify the turn from Aristotle to Plato that characterizes the philosophical outlook of the foremost thinkers of the Italian Renaissance.

The first of the Renaissance popes was Nicholas V (1447–1455), who told the College of Cardinals shortly before his death: "I have adorned the Holy Roman Church with magnificent buildings, with the most beautiful forms of an art that abounds with pearls and jewels, with books and tapestries, with vessels of gold and silver, with precious vestments. I have practiced every kind of magnanimous liberality, in building activities, in the purchase of rare books and manuscripts, in the copying of Latin and Greek masterpieces, in the employment of great scholars." One of his collectors of manuscripts, whom he had sent to Germany, discovered the long-lost *Germania* of Tacitus (cf. p. 5) in the monastery of Hersfeld. Lorenzo Valla (1405–1457), one of the pope's advisers, a master in the new science of literary and historical criticism, offered conclusive proof that the so-called "Donation of Constantine" (cf. p. 41 sq.), on which the medieval papacy had based their claims to Italian territory, was a bold forgery of the ninth or tenth century.* The fraudulent nature of the document of the "Donation" was independently substantiated by Cardinal Nicholas of Cusa and by the English Bishop Reginald Pecock. Pope Nicholas' lasting creation was the foundation of the Vatican Library, which grew to approximately five thousand volumes during the period of his pontificate.

Pope Pius II (1458–1464), the former Aeneas Sylvius Piccolomini, who succeeded Nicholas after the short reign of Calixtus III, acquired fame as a scholar, poet, and orator. For years he had been the secretary of the Imperial Chancellery and was therefore excellently acquainted with conditions in Germany, on which he comments at length in his "History of Europe." Under the pontificates of Sixtus IV (1471–1484), Innocent VIII (1484–1492), and Alexander VI (1492–1503) the institution of the papacy became almost completely secularized and corrupted, chiefly by the practice of "nepotism."**

Under Julius II (1503–1513) the reconstruction of St. Peter's Cathedral was begun, which was completed under his successor, Leo X (1513–1521), the last of the Renaissance popes. It was Julius who called Michelangelo (1475–1564), the great architect, sculptor, painter, and poet, to his court and entrusted to him the task of adorning the Sistine Chapel with monumental paintings and of designing the pope's own tomb.

Raphael (Santi), 1483–1520, a native of Urbino, worked as court painter and architect under Julius II and Leo X. In his "Disputa" Raphael depicted the most brilliant figures of world history, gathered around the exposed Eucharist, and in his monumental "School of Athens" he conjured

---

* This, of course, does not invalidate the legitimacy of the donations of Pepin and Charlemagne (cf. p. 41 sq.).

** Nepotism (from Latin, *nepos* = "nephew"): favoritism, practiced among the members of the papal families in order to increase their dynastic power, including appointments to important offices and the creation of entire new principalities.

up the entire culture of antiquity in the figures of its leading representatives. A large number of mural paintings record the high points of ecclesiastical history and the victories of the papacy.

Under Leo X Rome became the capital city of the Renaissance, the magnificent center and meeting place of a motley array of artists, writers, and scholars, but also of vainglorious courtiers and venial parasites. Under Leo's two successors, the Dutch Hadrian (1522–1523), the last of the popes of non-Italian nationality, and Clement VII (1523–1534) of the house of Medici, the structure of the Church was badly shaken by the storms of the Lutheran Reformation. In 1527 Rome was pillaged by Spanish and German mercenary soldiers, and the death knell had been sounded for the splendor of the Roman Renaissance. Among the defenders of Rome we find Benvenuto Cellini (1500–1571), the illustrious goldsmith, sculptor, musician, and engineer, whose autobiography was to be translated by Johann Wolfgang von Goethe.

All the smaller Italian courts of the Renaissance vied with Rome in the attempt to become centers of art, learning, and brilliant social culture. The great Florentine painter Leonardo da Vinci (1452–1519), a master of all the arts and an engineer and scientist besides, worked at the court of the Sforza in Milan. In the literary atmosphere of the court of Urbino, Baldassare Castiglione (1478–1529) wrote his *Cortegiano* ("The Courtier"), glorifying the social ideals of the Italian Renaissance. Venice, the great commercial metropolis, abounded with art collections and libraries, palaces and churches. Here Giovanni Bellini (*c.* 1430–1516) and Titian (1477–1576) created their immortal works, and here also Aldus Pius Manutius (*c.* 1449–1515) had established his famous printing press, the cradle of many highly artistic and rare specimens of printing, known as the Aldine books.

The ecclesiastical as well as the secular Renaissance paid homage to the ideal of an individualism that realizes all the potentialities of human nature, striving for a harmonious development of the physical and intellectual faculties of the *uomo universale* (the "total man"). In the political perspective the "total man" is Nicolo Machiavelli's ideal "Prince," who became the model of all the political absolutisms of the following centuries. This "Prince," as depicted in Machiavelli's famous book of the same title, bore the features of Cesare Borgia (1475–1507), the most ruthless and unscrupulous of the Renaissance rulers, who paid his own peculiar tribute to his age by developing even murder into a fine art. Divorcing political action from all principles of morality, Machiavelli makes the political leader a law unto himself, whose might creates his right, and who feels justified in using any conceivable means that serves the end of political power. "Whoever makes the attempt," we read in the fifteenth chapter of *The Prince,* "to act morally in all things, must of necessity perish among a crowd who pay no heed to morality. Therefore, a prince who wishes to assert himself must know how to act immorally whenever the opportunity arises, always conforming his actions to political necessity."

To be sure, the prince must use frequently such terms as "justice" and "religion," but only to cater to the fools. Moral values are determined by power, not by religion. Christianity in particular is to blame for having emasculated the political will and, by educating man for a world to come, made him an easy prey for scheming scoundrels.

German Humanism. When the Renaissance crossed the Alps about a century after the death of Petrarch and Boccaccio, it underwent a thorough transformation. Despite the many points of contact and interrelation between Germany and Italy, the spirit of the *Rinascita* never became an adopted philosophy of life in the north. The Italian Renaissance was too much and too essentially a culture of external form and a philosophy of sensuous beauty to suit the serious and introspective mood of the northern mind. The Germans in particular were traditionally much more concerned with the substances than with the appearances of things. The Lutheran Reformation had strengthened rather than weakened this innate tendency. But there was one aspect of the southern movement that struck sensitive organs in the north: the intellectual leaders of the German nation were deeply in sympathy with those scholarly efforts that dealt with the timeless values and interests of humanity.

When the Turks conquered Constantinople in 1453 many of the Byzantine scholars had sought refuge in Italy, making their living by copying and translating Greek manuscripts. The Italian scholars who subsequently devoted themselves to the study of the classical writings in Greek and Latin, the *litterae humaniores,* and who brought about a splendid revival of ancient literature, called themselves "Humanists." German students attending Italian universities, and those Italians who represented their nation at the Church councils in the north, carried the movement across the Alps. But whereas Italian Humanism had been essentially an intellectual and philological movement, in Germany it became a strong moral and educational force. The Italians were interested primarily in the pagan documents of Greece and Rome, while the Germans rediscovered many of the treasures of Christian antiquity, the writings of the Church Fathers, and the original texts of the Scriptures.

Just as in Italy, German princes took pride in becoming the patrons and protectors of the new movement and its representatives. Emperor Charles IV (cf. p. 164 sq.), the founder of the University of Prague, has been called the "father of German Humanism." His son Sigismund surrounded himself with poets and scholars, and Emperor Maximilian, the "last of the knights" and the contemporary of Pope Leo X, cultivated more than any of the other rulers the humanistic spirit in his many-sided interests and activities. The courts of Wurtemberg, Saxony, Brandenburg, and the Palatinate became centers of humanistic culture and education. By the end of the fifteenth century the movement was firmly entrenched in the Universities of Heidelberg, Vienna, Prague, and Erfurt. Among the ecclesiastical princes, Cardinal Albrecht, elector and archbishop of Mainz, stood out as a patron of humanistic culture, and Bishop Johann von Dalberg of Worms was on friendly terms with some of the foremost Humanist writers. Humanists were employed in the imperial, princely, and municipal chancelleries, and the cities of Augsburg and Nuremberg were renowned Humanist havens. Ulrich von Hutten (cf. p. 251 sq.) voiced the general conviction of his contemporaries when he exclaimed: "The arts and sciences are gaining more strength and vitality, the spirits wake up; banished is barbarism; Germany has opened her eyes."

a) *John Reuchlin and the "Letters of Obscure Men."* "The two eyes of Germany" was the epithet applied to John Reuchlin (1455–1522) and Desiderius Erasmus (*c.* 1466–1526), the two leading Humanists in the north. Reuchlin had revived the study of Hebrew and published the first Hebrew grammar in Germany. A jurist by profession, he mastered Greek and Latin with equal ease, and his scholarly endeavors encouraged the critical and comparative study of the scriptural texts. Although he was on orthodox ground in his theological convictions, he became involved in a partly theological, partly linguistic controversy which brought him into close alliance with some of the antiecclesiastical Humanists.

His intense interest in the mystical doctrines of the postbiblical Jewish *Cabbala* made him oppose a scheme for the destruction of all nonbiblical Hebrew books, as advocated by John Pfefferkorn, a baptized Jew. Asked for his opinion by Emperor Maximilian, Reuchlin condemned Pfefferkorn's proposal as an unjust and barbarous undertaking. The following personal quarrel with Pfefferkorn soon became a public issue, the Humanists siding with Reuchlin, and a number of obscurantist theologians supporting Pfefferkorn. In the course of this struggle the Humanists dealt a blow to their opponents which made these the laughingstock of Europe. Some of Reuchlin's friends and sympathizers, among them Ulrich von Hutten, published anonymously the famous 118 *Letters of Obscure Men* (*Epistolae Obscurorum Virorum,* 1515 and 1519), addressed to Ortuin Gratius, a theologian of Cologne and one of Reuchlin's chief opponents. The letters were supposedly written by a number of anti-Humanist theologians, and in their barbarous mixture of Latin and German were a most convincing exhibition of vanity, ignorance, stupidity, and obscenity. So skillfully were they composed that the deception went at first unnoticed. When the truth finally leaked out, the discovery proved decisive for the victory of Humanism in Germany.

b) *Desiderius Erasmus of Rotterdam.* The "Prince of the Humanists" was "the shadow of a man" — of frail physique, sensitive and mildly skeptical, but endowed with a penetrating mind that embraced with its keen observation the widest possible range of interests. Witty, a good entertainer, yet not free from vanity, Erasmus knew how to gain the favor of the mighty by flattery and adulation. Opposed to extremes and excesses, he loved moderation, harmony, peace, and in all things the golden mean, avoiding a clear "Yes" and "No" whenever possible. Cosmopolitan of mind, he felt himself to be the intellectual ruler of the most illustrious minds of a European family of nations, and he considered it his major duty to live the life of a true Humanist, to develop in himself a perfect harmony of human faculties and performances. His life was spent in the great cultural centers of France, England, Italy, Germany, and Switzerland.

Erasmus was born in Rotterdam, the son of a cleric; he was educated in the school of the Brethren of the Common Life (cf. p. 180) in Deventer and entered one of the monasteries of the Windesheim Congregation of the Brethren. He was ordained a priest in 1492 but soon afterward left the cloister with the permission of his superiors to start on his wanderings and to pursue the studies which made him the most brilliant scholar of his age. Not unlike Dürer and Holbein the painters, Erasmus combined Germanic inwardness with a Romanic sense of form and proportion. As a man and a thinker he lived in the ancient past rather than in the present, feeling perfectly at home in the Greek and Latin tongues and developing a classical diction entirely his own. As a philosopher and theologian he advanced the studies of textual and biblical criticism by his new editions of the classical writers, the Church Fathers, and the Greek New Testament (1516), preparing the way for the rationalistic sociology and theology of the age of Enlightenment.

On his first visit to England in 1499 he met the leading Christian Humanist in that country, Sir Thomas More. More was the internationally known author of the *Utopia,* a work that visualized an ideal pagan Humanist state established on the bases of natural reason, and as such a trenchant reproach against the so-called "Christian" states of Europe. Thomas More eventually suffered martyrdom for his opposition to King Henry VIII. Erasmus was bound to him by a lifelong friendship. Adhering to Christianity as the guiding philosophy of his life, Erasmus was nevertheless very outspoken and full of scorn and sarcasm in his criticism of ecclesiastical personalities and institutions, of scholastic philosophy and monastic theory and practice. His most widely read book, the *Praise of Folly (Encomion Moriae,* 1509), presents Dame Folly, bragging about her large following among all nations and estates, while her most faithful sons and servants are the theologians, especially the monks. Despite such attacks on the Catholic tradition Erasmus disappointed the expectations of those who had hoped that he would join the forces of the Lutheran Reformation. His initial admiration of Martin Luther turned gradually into aversion and definite opposition. Commotion, excitement, and revolt had never been to his liking. To the same men who had hailed him as the shining star of Germany, he appeared after his defection from Luther's cause as a snake in the grass, a cowardly renegade, a sophistic juggler.

In his *Querela Pacis* (Lament of Peace) of the year 1517 Erasmus appears as an ardent advocate of enduring peace among the members of the Christian family of nations. He shows himself influenced by the political ideas of Cicero, Seneca, St. Augustine, and even the scholastics, Thomas Aquinas and Cardinal Cajetanus de Vio, agreeing with the latter in their rejection of an unqualified pacifism. In his capacity as privy councilor of the young King Charles of Spain (the future Emperor Charles V) he composed, in 1515, an instruction for the guidance of a Christian ruler (*Institutio Principis Christiani*), an interesting and noteworthy refutation of Machiavellian principles in political theory. When Paul III (1534-1549) succeeded Clement VII on the papal throne, and the idea of a Catholic Reform Council was nearing its realization, Erasmus declared his willingness to co-operate in the restoration of peace and order in the Church. There was even some talk of making him a member of the College of Cardinals. But Erasmus for once recognized his limitations: he knew he was a king in the realm of letters and learning, but a stranger in the arena of political action.

c) Ulrich von Hutten, Franz von Sickingen, and the "Younger Humanists." The most colorful, spectacular, and erratic figure among the German Humanists was Ulrich von Hutten (1488-1523). He and his companions, who called themselves "the poets," belonged to a group of so-called "Younger Humanists," most of them highly talented but ruthless and undisciplined, and in their boundless vanity thinking of themselves as the reborn Homers, Ovids, and Ciceros. Beyond the fact that they adopted Greek and Latin names in place of their inherited German ones, there was little that they had in common with the world of antiquity.

Ulrich von Hutten was a descendant of Franconian nobility, whose family shared in the general decay of the knightly estate to such an extent that in Hutten's generation they had sunk to the level of robber-knights. However, Ulrich had been destined by his father for the monastic life, and his first act of rebellion was to flee from the monastery of Fulda and join the ranks of the Humanists. He was above all a fiery German nationalist who was untiring in his efforts to arouse Germany to wage a life-and-death struggle against the power of the Roman Catholic Church and all "ultramontane" influence in the north. He used the brilliance of his mind and the dynamic force of his pen to castigate and excoriate the objects of his wrath. Through his great talents as a writer, poet, and orator he gained the favor of Emperor Maximilian who, in 1517, personally crowned him with a laurel wreath. But, living recklessly, Hutten wasted his gifts, ruined his health, and died prematurely of the dread "French disease" (syphilis).*

For a short time Hutten's name was associated with that of Martin Luther, but Hutten's radicalism led to an early estrangement. With words of unrestrained hatred and wild passion the warring knight called upon his countrymen to rise in bloody revolt against Rome: "They have sucked our blood, they have gnawed our flesh, they are coming to our marrow; they will break and crush our every bone! Will the Germans never take to arms, will they never rush in with fire and sword?" To render his appeal

---

* This disease, first recorded toward the end of the fifteenth century, is said to have been brought to Western Europe by the Spanish conquerors of South America.

more effective Hutten relinquished the Latin tongue and began to write in German. He made common cause with Franz von Sickingen (1481–1523), one of the robber-knights, whose deeds and misdeeds were often inspired by noble motives and by his compassion with the oppressed and down-trodden. Sickingen played a leading part in the revolt of the Imperial Knights of 1522–1523 and, in the end, having failed in his attempt to better the economic and legal position of the knightly estate by means of constitutional amendments, was mortally wounded during the siege of his castle of Landshut in the Palatinate. From the Ebernburg near the city of Worms, where Sickingen had been born and where in the days of the Diet of Worms he offered shelter to a number of friends and sympathizers of the Lutheran Reformation, Hutten sent out a veritable flood of pamphlets, attacking and vilifying the assembled delegates: "The measure is full," he wrote. "Away from the pure springs, ye filthy swine. Out from the sanctuary, ye cursed money-lenders. . . . Can ye not see that the breezes of freedom are blowing; that men are wearied of the present state of things and want to bring about a change?"

Hutten's end was tragic: after the Diet of Worms and Sickingen's defeat he lost all his bearings, so that his actions began to resemble those of a common highway robber. Without means of subsistence and tormented by his disease, broken in body and spirit, haunted by his enemies, he fled to Basel, where he hoped Erasmus of Rotterdam, with whom he had once been on friendly terms, would give him shelter, so that he might die in peace. But Erasmus sent word that he was very much afraid Hutten might not be able to live in his unheated rooms, for he, Erasmus, could never endure the heat of a stove! Hutten gave vent to his disappointment in one last pasquil, in which he referred to Erasmus' vanity, thereby inviting an answer which for once was stripped of all subtle irony and showed the dignified Humanist in a genuine, red-blooded rage. Banished from Basel, Hutten spent his last days on the tiny islet of Ufenau on Lake Zurich, which had been offered him by Huldreich Zwingli, from whose report we learn that Hutten "left behind him positively nothing of value: no books, no household effects — nothing but a pen."

The German Humanists expressed their ideals in poetry and prose, in speeches and epistles, in word and in deed. Here and there they followed the example of the Italian academies and formed literary societies. Heidelberg and Vienna became outstanding centers of the movement. It was not easy for the new spirit to gain a foothold in the universities of the Empire, but gradually the faculties of art and letters had to adapt their curriculums to the demands of the Humanists, who had their largest following among the younger generation. Basel, Erfurt, and Heidelberg became the foremost seats of Humanist education. The Latin secondary schools in the cities benefited greatly from the Humanist influences. The increased enrollment and improved methods of instruction prompted Luther to write in 1521: "A boy of twenty knows more today than twenty doctors did formerly."

Nevertheless, despite the wider range of studies and a definite enlargement of the historical and scientific horizon in the upper strata of society, the people at large were hardly affected by the Humanist movement. It remained essentially confined to scholarly circles, who drew a sharp line of demarcation between themselves and the uneducated rabble. Many a German Humanist, on the other hand, pursuing historical studies and witnessing the pride the Italian people took in the glories of their national heritage, came across some of the important documents of the Germanic past. This slowly awakening nationalism was greatly stimulated by the strong antipathy to everything that was associated with the Roman Curia. This explains the temporary alliance between the younger German Humanists and the leaders of the Lutheran Reformation. They had in common the objects of their hatred but were divided by what they loved and esteemed. It did not take the younger Humanists long to discover that Luther was not greatly interested in dialectics, aesthetics, and linguistics, but rather in theology, faith, and the Bible. And when the Lutheran Reformation had really gotten under way, its reverberations proved vital enough to overshadow completely the scholarly endeavors of the Humanists.

The Catholic Restoration (Counter Reformation). Of those European countries which remained practically untouched by the waves of the Protestant Reformation (Italy, Spain, Portugal, Poland, Ireland), Spain ranked foremost as a political power. Emerging successfully from her armed contests with France, she had been able to assert her will in the north and south of Italy as well as in the Netherlands and in the Free County of Burgundy. The family relations between the courts of Madrid and Vienna made the house of Hapsburg the European center of gravity. Owing to this political constellation it had been possible for Spain to approach and solve the question of ecclesiastical reform at a time when the Roman Curia had not even been awakened to a full realization of the threatening dangers, and several decades before the beginning of the Lutheran Reformation in Germany.

The leader of the reform movement in Spain was the archbishop of Toledo (1495-1517), Cardinal (1507) Ximenes de Cisneros (1436-1517), the confessor of Queen Isabella of Castile and a member of the Franciscan Order. Supported in his efforts by the rulers of Castile and Aragon, Ximenes restored the integrity of the Catholic Church throughout Spain, revived and vitalized the theological and philosophical studies, and founded the University of Alcalá (1500). Like the Protestant and Humanist leaders he was convinced of the necessity of a thorough reform, but he also felt certain that this could and should be accomplished within the framework of the established Church. It was the spirit of this Spanish Restoration that dominated and permeated the Catholic reform movement in other European countries.

While official Italy in Church and State was still imbued with the semi-paganism of the Renaissance, increasing numbers of devout individuals began to organize in religious brotherhoods, aiming at a revival of the religious spirit among the masses. Under the pontificate of Leo X the "Oratory of Divine Love" was founded, and in 1524 Bishop Gian Pietro Carafa of Naples established the new Theatine Order (Theate or Chieti was the name of his episcopal see), while the Capuchin Order, founded in 1526, restored the original rigor of the Franciscan monastic discipline.

Within a relatively short period (c. 1535–1648) the Catholic reform movement had not only restored faith and order in the Roman Church but had impressed its ideas on the culture of those countries in which it was victorious. The Catholic Restoration, in the countries of its origin as well as in the territories that were reconquered and reconverted from Protestantism, succeeded in rallying once more the intellectual, social, religious, artistic, and literary forces around an ideological center, manifesting itself in the élan of the Baroque style (cf. p. 337 sq.) which superseded the Renaissance. It was a form of expression that was less naïve and more fraught with inner contradictions than the preceding Christian styles, but it was forceful and aggressive, a blend, as it were, of pagan and Christian elements, of Gothic spirituality and the sensuous beauty of the Renaissance. Its chord of emotions with a corresponding scale of formal values reached from the ecstatic heights of the mystical revival in Spain (St. Teresa of Ávila, St. John of the Cross) to the gay and colorful exuberance of ecclesiastical and secular architecture, sculpture, and painting in Spain, Italy, southern Germany, and Austria; from the austere serenity of Calderón de la Barca's (1600–1681) dramas and sacramental plays to the dazzling phantasmagoria of the new Jesuit stagecraft (cf. p. 346 sq.); from stern religious asceticism to festive courtly splendor, uniting Church and State in powerful and soul-stirring displays of undisguised propaganda.

a) Ignatius of Loyola and the Jesuit Order. In spite of the fact that with the accession of Paul III (1534–1549) the Catholic reform movement began to make itself felt in the leadership and guidance of the Church, its sweeping successes and victories would have been impossible without the two events which marked a turning point in the history of the Catholic Church: the foundation of the Jesuit Order and the Council of Trent.

Ignatius (Íñigo) of Loyola (1491–1556), the founder of the Jesuit Order, a native of the province of Guipúzcoa, was of Basque origin and the heir of the knightly traditions of his family. Born in the ancient castle of his ancestors, near the town of Azpeitia, and having received a knightly and military education, he was thirty years of age when his normal career as an officer in the Spanish army was abruptly cut short by a serious wound which he received while defending the fortress of Pamplona against the French. During a long period of convalescence, partly spent in the ancestral castle, being aware of the fact that his physical injury would never permit him to re-enter the military service, and influenced by some spiritual readings, he conceived of the idea of devoting his future life to the service of

Christ, his divine Liege Lord. His health restored sufficiently, he made a pilgrimage to the Benedictine abbey on the Montserrat. After a knightly vigil before the image of the Madonna, he deposited his armor and his sword on the altar, continuing on his way in the garb of a penitent, equipped only with a pilgrim's staff. The harbor of Barcelona being closed on account of an epidemic, Ignatius had to relinquish temporarily his plan of boarding a ship for Jerusalem. He stayed in Manresa for almost a year, during which time he familiarized himself with some of the important documents of medieval mysticism and with the spirit of the *"devotio moderna"* (cf. p. 180). He was especially impressed with the "Spiritual Exercises" (*Ejercitatorio de la Vida Espiritual*) as devised by Garcia de Cisneros, the abbot of Montserrat, which manual in turn was based on the teachings of some of the leading French, German, and Dutch mystics of the Middle Ages.

Garcia's spiritual meditations suggested to Ignatius the principal structure of his own *Spiritual Exercises* (*Exercitia Spiritualia*), which were to become the theological, ascetic, and psychological basis of Jesuit training, education, character formation, and institutional organization. Ignatius' original contribution and addition to the older methods of meditation lie in his profound psychological insight, his knowledge of the human soul and its faculties. He used these means to the end of training the human mind and bending the human will so as to become obedient instruments of any purposeful direction and command: instruments hard as steel, ready to submit to any kind of sacrifice or privation, willing to serve at any place, any time, and in any circumstances. All the senses and all the powers of the imagination are called upon to contribute their full share to the formation of mental and moral habits and decisions. The *Imitation of Christ* is made a tangible reality by contemplating vividly and in drastic nearness the Lord's suffering and humiliation in order to arouse the Christian's generous love and devotion, in view of an ultimate union with the source of all beauty, goodness, and truth.

The most conspicuous element of the *Spiritual Exercises* is the spirit of military regulation and discipline, transferred to a set of spiritual ends. Man is to be so transformed that he no longer "prefers health to sickness, wealth to poverty, honor to disgrace, a long life to a short one — and so on in everything else, so that we learn to desire and choose only those things which are helpful in reaching the end for which we have been created." Christ is depicted as the supreme War Lord, whose honor and glory are the final goal of the individual's every thought and deed. All disorderly inclinations are to be ordered, adjusted, and subordinated to the divine will. Education for Christian action is considered as all important, and it is this principle of activity, *"Ad Maiorem Dei Gloriam"* (for the greater glory of God), which further distinguishes Ignatius' *Exercises* from purely contemplative forms of devotion, and which greatly appealed to an age of political conquest, geographical expansion, and scientific invention.

After having finally satisfied his yearning for a pilgrimage to the Holy Land (1523), Ignatius returned to Barcelona by way of Venice and Genoa and subsequently completed his liberal and theological education at the Universities of Alcalá, Salamanca, and Paris. He received the degree of Magister of Arts from the College of Ste. Barbe in 1534. In the same year he and six of his companions and disciples on the Montmartre solemnly vowed to devote their lives to missionary activity in the Holy Land, or, if this plan should prove impracticable, to offer their services to the pope for whatever kind of work he would assign to them.

Several times Ignatius and his companions suffered persecution and in-carceration at the hands of the Inquisition and had to clear themselves of the suspicion of being sympathizers of Martin Luther. Their apostolic zeal among the poor and unlearned and the plain gray habit which they had chosen as their dress seemed to make them conspicuous as innovators and agitators. In 1535 we find Ignatius back in his home town, to recover from a chronic infection of the gall bladder, taking up his residence in the asylum for the homeless, preaching and teaching in the immediate neighbor-hood of the castle of the Loyolas. A reunion with his Paris companions in Venice was followed by a recurrence of his illness. After his recovery he decided to make Italy his abode and the center of his future activities.

On their way to Venice the companions of Ignatius visited the tomb of Erasmus of Rotterdam in Basel. After their arrival in Venice Ignatius ordered them to proceed to Rome to obtain the papal permission for their pilgrimage to Jerusalem. The permission was granted by Paul III, but the threatening war between Venice and the Turks prevented them from making the journey. Shortly afterward Ignatius and his companions were ordained to the priesthood.

Meanwhile, in Rome, the friends of the ecclesiastical reform had greatly strengthened their influence. The scholarly statesman and diplomat, Gasparo Contarini, had been made a member of the College of Cardinals and of the committee in charge of the preparations for the forthcoming Church council. He and a group of like-minded friends became the nucleus of a new generation of cardinals who carried the reform to its final victory.

After Ignatius and his companions had offered unconditionally their services to the pope, the "Society of Jesus" (*Compañia de Jesús*) was formally instituted in June, 1539. A special vow of absolute obedience to the pope was added to the customary three monastic vows of poverty, chastity, and obedience. The members were to be freed from the observance of the choral recitation of the liturgical office, so that more time might be avail-able for the service to their fellow men. They were not required to wear monastic habit, so that they might not be mistaken for just another variety of the then ill-famed and partly degenerate older religious orders. The original decree of the foundation was confirmed by a special bull of Julius III on July 21, 1550, and Ignatius was elected general or *praepositus* of the Society. Despite his feeble health he guided the destinies of his order with circumspection and indefatigable energy for fifteen years. The absolute authority with which the constitution of the Society invested the office of its general reflected the spirit of the age of rising absolute monarchies and national armies. The democratic-parliamentary constitutions of the mendicant orders (cf. p. 134 sq.) had given way to the spirit of autocracy, with the principles of leadership and subordination as its bases.

When Ignatius died, his foundation comprised fifty-eight colleges, in addition to numerous seminaries and novitiates. The first companions of Ignatius had received a humanistic education during their years of study in Paris, and they retained their high respect for the principles of liberal education and handed it down to their associates and successors. During the lifetime of the founder, houses of study were established in most of the larger cities of Europe and in all the centers of academic learning. The spirit of Ignatius was the lifeblood of all these institutions of higher learning, the spirit of a personality whose genius for organization was akin to that of John Calvin, and whose depth and breadth of religious experience was comparable to the spiritual fire that burned in the soul of Martin Luther.

b) The Council of Trent (1545–1563). It was not long after the foundation of the Jesuit Order that the papacy itself took the lead in the Catholic reform movement. In vain had Cardinal Contarini made the attempt to bring about a reconciliation of Protestants and Catholics at the Diet of Regensburg in 1541. He had only drawn upon himself the suspicion of heresy and had died in the following year without having been able to clear his reputation. The same year, 1542, witnessed the resurrection of the Inquisition (cf. p. 136) for the suppression of heresy, wherever it might raise its head. At the same time a strict censorship of the printing press was set up to stamp out all heterodox opinions, preparing the way for the publication of the *Index of Forbidden Books* and the creation of a permanent *Congregation of the Index* (1571), the former promulgated during the Council of Trent, the latter under the pontificate of Pius V (1566–1572).

The preliminary efforts to restore the doctrine and discipline of the Church were finally crowned by the convocation of the Council of Trent (Trient), so named after the southernmost city of the Empire, where the assembly was solemnly opened in 1545. Four popes (Paul III, Julius III, Marcellus II, Paul IV) died during the eighteen years that the council was in session. The deliberations were several times interrupted and the meeting place temporarily removed to Bologna and back again to Trent. The militant leader of the reform was for some time Pope Paul IV (1555–1559), the former Gian Pietro Carafa, the compiler of the first *"Index,"* who attempted to recover for the papacy the power and prestige that it had possessed in the Middle Ages. His failure to understand the vastly different spirit of his own age, his ineptitude in dealing with political realities, and his anti-Spanish bias involved him in a number of futile controversies and in a useless and unsuccessful war with King Philip II of Spain (1555–1598), the son of Emperor Charles V. He reproached Ferdinand I (cf. p. 214) for being too lax in dealing with German Protestantism, and refused to recognize him as German emperor. He made the Inquisition the supreme tribunal in all matters of faith and morals, and by his uncompromising attitude he provoked a rebellion of the Roman people, who gave vent to their anger by setting fire to the building of the Inquisition.

It was Paul IV's successor, Pius IV (1559–1565), who brought the Council of Trent to a successful conclusion. A sober and sane student of jurisprudence, he preferred mediation and persuasion to force. The twenty-fifth and last session of the council was held in December, 1563. Among the 255 assembled ecclesiastics there were 4 cardinal legates, 2 cardinals, 3 patriarchs, 25 archbishops, 168 bishops, 7 abbots, 39 procurators (representing absent members), and 7 generals of religious orders.

While the council failed in healing the breach between Catholics and Protestants, still its chief objective was fully secured, namely that of firmly laying the foundations for a thorough restoration of the Roman Catholic Church. The hierarchical constitution had been preserved, abuses had been recognized and rectified with utter rigorism, and the ancient ideological structure of the Church had been reaffirmed and redefined.

Some of the more important decrees dealt with the contested nature of the process of justification. Luther's doctrine of "justification by faith alone" was rejected; the human will was declared to be not entirely unfree; human nature, human emotions and passions were considered as not radically corrupted but as capable of being educated, ordered, and used for moral ends. Special decrees dealt with the intellectual and moral training of the clergy, the importance of the integrity of the Christian family, and the indissolubility and sacramental character of the marriage bond. As against the Protestants' appeal to the exclusive authority of the Bible, the council decided that Scriptures and Tradition (all the dogmas and definitions preserved and handed down by the teaching office of the Church) were equally valid sources of divine authority and revelation; that Church Tradition existed prior to the Scriptures, and that therefore the Bible was merely an inspired written documentation and reflection of oral tradition.

c) *Peter Canisius and the Catholic Restoration in Germany.* The pontificate of Pius V (1566–1572) marks the climax of the Catholic reform movement. "Fra Scarpone" (Brother Sabot or "Wooden Shoe"), as the new pope was called on account of his monkish habits, was neither a warrior nor a politician but exclusively interested in the salvation of souls. Frugality, strictest economy, and moral austerity began to rule at the papal court. It was under Pius V's successor, Gregory XIII (1572–1585), whose name remains associated with his reform of the calendar (cf. p. 274 sq.), that the Catholic Restoration made itself felt as a formative cultural force beyond the confines of the Italian nation.

The Jesuits had exerted considerable influence on the proceedings of the Council of Trent, and they had been active in near-by and distant countries (China, India, etc.) in ever so many fields of religious and educational endeavor. But their order derived the greatest amount of encouragement from the favor of Pope Gregory XIII. The fifth general, Claudius Aquaviva (1581–1615), the author of the famous *Ratio Studiorum* ("Order of Studies"), obtained from the pope a new confirmation of the original constitution and invaluable support in the organization of theological seminaries and institutions of higher learning.

Some of the most significant educational work of the Jesuits was done in Germany, where Catholic education was revived under the leadership of Peter Canisius (1521–1597), to whom the German Catholics refer as a "Second Apostle of Germany" (the first being St. Boniface, cf. p. 39). A native of Nymwegen in Holland, he had been influenced by the *devotio moderna* as cultivated by the Brethren of the Common Life (cf. p. 180) and by the reading of manuals of mystical contemplation of the later Middle Ages. He had attended the first sessions of the Council of Trent as the "procurator" of Cardinal Otto Truchsess von Waldburg and soon afterward had been called to Rome by Ignatius of Loyola himself. The special field of his activity was to be a number of southern German districts, where he succeeded in winning over the Catholic princes for his plans and where he worked as a teacher and preacher.

Canisius considered it one of his major tasks to raise educational standards among the Catholic youth, so as to match the unquestionably superior training and discipline of the Protestant schools, which had attained such great efficiency under the influence of Philip Melanchthon's (cf. p. 231 sq.) school reforms. Canisius was engaged in educational work in Vienna, Ingolstadt, Augsburg, and Fribourg (Switzerland), and was commissioned by Emperor Ferdinand I to compose the new Catholic catechism, first in Latin (1555) and later on in German (1560). The Antwerp edition of 1589 was illustrated with 102 engravings. The *Imperial Catechism* was translated into twenty-five languages and was still used in many Catholic schools as late as the nineteenth century.

Peter Canisius was the first German member of the Society of Jesus. Shortly after his death the *Ratio Studiorum* was officially introduced in the German schools of the Jesuit Order. The curriculum included the humanities as well as mathematics and the natural sciences. The scholastic standards were high enough to make the Jesuit secondary schools model institutions of their kind. Gradually the Jesuits extended their influence to the leading Catholic universities of the Empire, and the great successes of the Society as the vanguard of the Counter Reformation were mainly achieved by means of their firm grip on the educated classes, especially on the future political and dynastic leaders. Under the direct or indirect guidance of the Jesuits the Catholic Restoration was carried forward by force in several German lands. Protestantism was utterly destroyed in Bavaria. When the archbishop of Cologne joined the Protestant reformers, he was driven from his see by Bavarian and Spanish troops, and a Bavarian prince was placed at the head of his diocese. At the end of the sixteenth century all the bishoprics in the German West were held firmly by the Catholic Church. The eastern dioceses had been secularized by the Protestant princes. In the Austrian Alpine regions Duke Ferdinand of Styria carried the Counter Reformation to a complete victory. Catholic and Protestant princes alike adopted and enforced the principle *"cuius regio eius religio"* (cf. p. 212).

Social and Cultural Conditions: (*a*) *Peasants, Burghers, Nobles, and Princes.* Of the four estates (*Stände*) of the Empire, as they existed after the Great Peasants' War of 1524-1525 (clergy, nobility, burghers, and peasants), the *peasants* ranked so low in the social scale that Wimpheling, one of the spokesmen of German Humanism, does not even consider them a *Stand* in the juridical sense of the term. Their condition was worst in the German East, where they were completely at the mercy of the powerful feudal landowners, and where in some districts (Mecklenburg, Pommern) they were reduced to the status of actual slavery. But everywhere the peasant was an object of social oppression and exploitation, especially after serfdom had been legally established by the Imperial Diet of 1555.

The *burghers* enjoyed prosperity and social prestige in the earlier part of the sixteenth century, but their estate began to show symptoms of decline and diminishing influence after 1550. The trading privileges of the Hansa (cf. p. 119 sq.) were revoked by Queen Elizabeth of England in 1579, and the Steel Court (*Stahlhof*) in London was closed in 1598. Hamburg was the only one of the member cities of the Hanseatic League which succeeded in maintaining and improving its trade relations with England and in establishing commercial contacts with Amsterdam, the new Dutch trading center, thereby developing into the "most flourishing emporium of all Germany."

The commercial districts of upper (southern) Germany were able to maintain their prosperity to the end of the sixteenth century, when they gradually had to give way to the competitive pressure of the British and Italian money interests. The Dutch revolt against Spain and the sack of Antwerp by Spanish mercenaries (1576) eliminated one of the chief markets of the merchants of upper Germany, but at the same time it established the commercial supremacy of Amsterdam and the Dutch trading interests. Frankfurt on the Main, on the other hand, benefited by the fall of Antwerp, as is indicated by the growing significance of the *Frankfurter Messe* (Trade Fair).

The numerous bank failures and crashes of the second half of the sixteenth century were partly caused by the growing indebtedness and final bankruptcy of Spain and France, partly by reckless financial speculation and the excessive luxury that characterized the wealthy burgher class. The static nature of the guild system (cf. p. 125 sq.) made it too rigid to provide the frame for the rapidly shifting forces of the money trade. Capital rose as a monstrous and wholly impersonal power that could only with difficulty be controlled by the undeveloped financial techniques of the age of early capitalism. The wholesale middleman, a figure that had been unknown to the Middle Ages, began to dominate the markets and to secure trade monopolies. The separation of the producer from the consumer transformed and finally destroyed the fundamental character of the guild system. The guilds were becoming more and more exclusive, the masters establishing themselves as an oligarchic group, subjecting to their financial power not only the journeymen but also those fellow masters who lacked the means to invest the capital required for wholesale production, or who were determined to preserve their independence. A sharp social division began to line up merchant employers against a class of wage earners whose members had little chance of ever rising from the rank of journeyman to that of employer. In the sixteenth century the journeymen began to form their own guilds to defend their rights against the vested interests of capitalist masters who, in their turn, established employers' guilds to impose their will on the wage earners and to facilitate mass production.

The burgher who, in the fifteenth and the early sixteenth century, had been proud of his social status and had developed cultural, artistic, and literary tastes, forms, and standards, began to cast envious glances at the members of the nobility, trying to imitate their style and manner of living. The outward appearance of the burgher's residence assumed more and more the palatial pomp and elegance of the Italian Renaissance, and many a wealthy citizen moved into the abandoned castle of some impoverished nobleman. Increasing numbers of burghers' sons attended the universities of the Empire and of neighboring lands to prepare themselves for a career in the imperial or princely chancelleries or, as privy councilors, professors, and members of the higher clergy, to exert an influence on political and cultural affairs.

The social and cultural crisis of the *nobility* had preceded the decline of the burgher class by more than a century. It has been pointed out how the nobles were deprived of their livelihood and the *raison d'être* of their social existence by the transformations that had taken place in the technique of warfare and in military science. The manufacture of gunpowder and the introduction of firearms had largely done away with the mounted armies of knights, replacing them with mercenary foot soldiers.* As a disinherited class, the nobles hated and despised the burghers. Nevertheless, marriages between the two estates were frequent, the burgher coveting a distinguished name and an exalted rank in the social ladder, the nobleman frequently trying to salvage his shattered finances by choosing a bride from among the city plutocracy. In the German East more than in any other part of Germany the nobility shared in agricultural and commercial activities, trading and speculating in wool, wine, wood, and grain. Only in a very few instances were the nobles interested in the intellectual and cultural

---

* The Chinese were familiar with gunpowder and the use of hand grenades in the twelfth century, and in the thirteenth century the Arabs had brought this knowledge to the Western World, where both Albert the Great and Roger Bacon, the most advanced scientific observers of their time, had described it in detail (*c.* 1250). About 1380 the German, Berthold Schwarz, is said to have considerably improved the efficiency of gunpowder as an instrument of warfare.

pursuits of their nation, and the majority of them are reprimanded and denounced in contemporary chronicles for their extravagance and their riotous living. The honor code and etiquette of the old-time knight and noble became an object of ridicule and satire in Bojardo's (1434–1494) *Orlando Innamorato* ("The Enamored Roland"), in Ariosto's (1474–1533) *Orlando Furioso* ("The Raging Roland"), and especially in Cervantes' (1547–1616) immortal *Don Quixote*.

A new avenue for members of the nobility was opened up by the development of a centralized system of administration at the princely courts. The creation of a large number of professional court officials (*Berufsbeamtentum*) made it possible for a new generation of nobles to obtain positions as councilors, ambassadors, chamberlains, pages, and so forth.

The *princes* themselves, with their prestige greatly enhanced after their decisive victories over the peasants and other social rebels, their coffers swelled with the expropriated Church possessions, moved swiftly in the direction of absolutism. In the case of Protestant princes, their newly acquired position as titular heads of national and regional churches had brought the administration and supervision of ecclesiastical affairs, public morals, education, public health under their jurisdiction. Economically, they became the protectors and promoters of capitalistic interests, realizing that the welfare of their states depended on a prosperous business life and on a maximal amount of taxable income. By creating a unified territorial economy they were able to finance the maintenance of the official bureaucracy of their chancelleries and to meet the growing expenditures of their mercenary armies. In many cases they monopolized the mining privileges, leased the rights of coinage, pawned the princely domains, and sold the secularized Church properties. Thus their policy of aggrandizement and enrichment was strictly guided by Machiavellian principles. Considerations of honor, square dealing, or patriotism were in most instances subordinated to economic and financial calculations. Although the fully developed system of "mercantilism" (cf. p. 328 sq.) and State paternalism is a creation of the seventeenth and eighteenth centuries, its beginnings are clearly distinguishable in the sixteenth century.

The wasteful extravagance of the princely household, with its constant need of money and the ensuing search for new sources of income, explains the profound interest of the rulers in the art of "gold making" and the pseudo science of alchemy. "Gold makers" are found in the service of practically all the princely courts, and many of the princes spent days and weeks of hard labor in their court "laboratories," in the vain hope of producing gold synthetically. Emperor Rudolph II (1576–1612) kept two hundred alchemists busy at his court, and the princes of Saxony, Brandenburg, and others followed his example.

The social and intellectual culture of the courts of the Italian Renaissance is conspicuously lacking at the German courts. In its place there is found an external and superficial display of gorgeous pageantry and perpetual festive entertainment. The great passion of the average prince was the hunt, with all the sportly thrills that it involved and all the infringements on the property rights of the peasantry that it entailed. Tremendous sums of money were spent on artificial fireworks, mythological *tableaux vivants,* romantic and exotic pageants and masquerades.

Some of the German princes were collectors of all kinds of rarities, curiosities, and antiquities, and in this way the arts and crafts derived some benefit from the princely tastes and interests. It was the chief task of the court painters to flatter the vanity of their employers by idealized portraiture of the different members of the princely families. "Art chambers" (*Kunstkammern*) were established at most courts to house the many oddities that the traveling collectors of the prince had brought together from many lands and regions. Genuine artistic taste was shown by the Hapsburg Emperor Rudolph II, the "German Medici," who had assembled 413 valuable paintings in his art gallery in Prague, by Archduke Ferdinand of Austria, the founder of the splendid collection of the castle of Ambras, and by some of the Bavarian princes. Augustus I of Saxony (1533-1586), who was chiefly interested in astronomical and mechanical instruments, started the court collection in Dresden which was to become famous under his successors. Of the higher arts, music was greatly appreciated at the Bavarian court, where Albrecht V (1528-1579) appointed Orlando di Lasso (1532-1594), the great composer, as conductor of the princely orchestra (1563).

The gradual weakening of the indigenous national elements in German culture in the course of the sixteenth century was responsible for an increasing admiration of foreign modes of living and the imitation of un-German artistic and literary styles. The German princes and nobles visited the famous Italian universities and learned to live and breathe in the atmosphere of Italian Humanism. The graphic and decorative arts copied Italian models and motifs, and princes as well as wealthy patricians had their residences either built by Italian architects or by German workmen who had learned their trade in Italy.

The family relations between the German Imperial and the Spanish courts account for the influence of Spanish style and etiquette in fashion, behavior, and literary expression. The Spanish writers Antonio Guevara (c. 1480-1545) and Luis de Gongora y Argote (1561-1627) had developed an *"estilo culto,"* a pompous, flowery, and ornate but empty and shallow style, which became known as "Gongorism." It had its equivalents in Italy and in England, in the works of Giambattista Marini (1569-1625) and John Lilly (1554-1606), known as "Marinism" and "Euphuism" (from Lilly's novel *Euphues, Anatomy of Wit*), respectively. Likewise from Spain came the phantastic and bombastic novel of *Amadis,* the son of King Perion of Wales and the British Princess Elisena, who, after numerous adventures, marries the daughter of King Lisuarte of England. The novel conquered all Europe and had reached the monstrous size of twenty-four volumes when the German translation of 1569 was published by Sigmund Feyerabend in Frankfurt. For a long time the *Amadis* was considered as the manual of correct and exemplary social behavior. It represents a last flickering of the courtly chivalresque tradition and was duly satirized in Cervantes' *Don Quixote* (1605, 1615). The Spanish "picaresque" novel (*Schelmenroman*) inspired Grimmelshausen's masterpiece, *Simplicissimus* (cf. p. 300). Popular taste in Germany reacted negatively to these foreign fads and fashions, but the people at large had no say in the matter, and by the end of the sixteenth century the Spanish style in dress and social behavior had become widely accepted.

Much of the Spanish influence reached Germany by way of France. Under Louis XI (1461–1483) and Louis XII (1498–1515) the French court had become the center of the national and cultural life of the country and, as in the days of chivalry, the German princely aristocracy considered France as the model country of the refined arts of living and learning. While the ruling dynasty of France was involved in its struggles with the Hapsburg emperor (cf. p. 206 sq.), the French court made capital out of the selfishness and greed of the German princes, many of whom received "pensions" from the French king, their reward for political services or even for treasonable activities. Many of the German nobles joined the French armies and fought the battles of the French monarchy. French tutors were called to Germany to educate the sons of nobles and princes, and German students traveled to France to attend the Universities of Paris, Orléans, and Montpellier, to learn the French language, acquire the polish of French manners, and get acquainted with the much heralded French culture.

The general fondness of everything foreign reached its culminating point during and following the Thirty Years' War (cf. p. 284 sqq.). But even at the end of the sixteenth century the national substance of Germany had become so diluted that Pastor Johannes Sommer, in the preface to his *Ethnographia Mundi* (a description of the modern world), published in 1609, was quite serious in asserting that people who had died twenty years ago would not recognize their own children: if they were to step back into life, they might think that there were no Germans left but "only Frenchmen, Spaniards, Englishmen, and other peoples." Those foreign countries and cultures, to whose influence and dictates the Germans too willingly submitted, seemed to share this opinion: they looked down upon Germany with scorn and contempt, calling her inhabitants semibarbarians, brutal, uncultured, and intellectually inferior. "No nation is more despised than the Germans," exclaims Martin Luther. "The Italians call us beasts, and France, Italy, and all the other countries heap ridicule upon us."

Social and Cultural Conditions: (*b*) *Clergy and Scholars. Religion and Superstition.* Reformation and Counter Reformation alike had stimulated the interest in theological problems and religious discussions among all classes of the population, but after the middle of the sixteenth century this preoccupation assumed the nature of a real obsession, with all the earmarks of religious fanaticism. Not only the Bible but theological pamphlets and dogmatic compendia were read and discussed by men and women, by princes, scholars, burghers, artisans, and peasants. Political and social life, the arts and the sciences bore the imprint of theological tutelage, and the court theologians became more and more the intellectual leaders of the age. Religion was the topic of conversation in universities and on street corners, in chancelleries and taverns, in cities and villages. The rapidly multiplying sects, all convinced of their exclusive possession of religious truth and all basing their claims on the concept of "evangelical freedom," engendered a spirit of hatred, suspicion, abuse, and persecution. The pulpits and lecture halls, hymns and morality plays, paintings, engravings, and woodcuts served to indict and calumniate the religious opponents. Protestant artists pictured the pope and the cardinals suffering the tortures of hell-fire, while the Catholic artists meted out the same punishment to Luther and his followers. Parties and individuals accused each other of being possessed by the devil, of being the devil's allies, of being devils in disguise.

In Geneva, John Calvin (cf. p. 236) had established his tyrannical regimentation of faith, and there, in 1553, the physician Michael Servet was burned because of his anti-Trinitarian views. In Basel, the Dutch Anabaptist David Joris, the founder of the Jorist sect, was exhumed three years after his death (1556), to be solemnly burned, together with his portrait and his writings. Similar tyranny and bigotry were prevalent in Catholic Austria: in 1527 Leonard Käser, a priest who had embraced Lutheranism, was seized at the deathbed of his father and burned. Many who had accepted the reformed doctrines had done so because of the promised liberties, completely forgetting about the sacrifices and obligations that were implied. Thus Melanchthon complains as early as 1528 that "no one hates the Gospel more bitterly than those who claim it as their own." When he looks at the conditions of the age he feels fear that transcends all imagination, and twenty years later (1548) he speaks of the hatred of the majority of the German people for the Gospel and its preachers. As a matter of fact, in the later decades of the same century the dogmatism and fanaticism of the theologians meets with a growing indifference, laxity, and ignorance on the part of the masses.

In 1549 Johann Oldecop, a German chronicler of Hildesheim, had the following inscription affixed to his house: "The Church is shaken; the clergy is corrupt; the devil rules." While popular religious devotion and the people's participation in ecclesiastical life were on the decline, it was the element of fear that now as formerly in the fourteenth and fifteenth centuries held sway over men and women.

The decline of religious life was due in part to the corruption of the clergy. Both the Catholic and Protestant clergy had become the objects of popular hatred. Many of the priests and pastors lived in dire poverty, like beggars, and many others lacked the most elementary training for their office. Those few who held the flame of the Gospel alive were usually disliked and defamed by their colleagues or even denounced as heretics. Thus,

Johann Arndt (1555–1621), the author of the *Four Books of True Christianity*, was attacked as an enthusiast, a Calvinist, a papist. "The devil will give him his reward for his heretical doctrines," wrote John Corvinus, a Lutheran pastor.

The devil quite generally was uppermost in the imagination, the speeches, and the writings of all and sundry. Superstitious beliefs, partly inherited from the previous centuries, partly rediscovered in the documents of antiquity and in the panpsychism of Platonic and Neo-Platonic nature philosophy, generated a pathological craving for the miraculous, the mysterious, and the occult. Some of these superstitions showed a host of morbid, sinister, and pernicious aspects and components. The unexpected, extraordinary, unheard-of might occur at any time and in any place. In 1522 a cow was said to have given birth to a monster, and Luther promptly published an *Explanation of the Monkish Calf of Freiberg in Saxony,* wherein he described the monster as a symbol and counterfeit of the horrible institution of monasticism, a miracle wrought by God Himself. Melanchthon followed with a publication on *The Popish Ass in Rome,* referring to the offspring of a donkey that had been found in the Tiber, pointing to an early end of the papacy. Tales were rampant of animals that had given birth to human children, of women who had begotten young devils, of dragons who had caused conflagrations, of dead persons who had risen from their graves, of angels who had descended from heaven, of all kinds of evil forebodings: events that are recorded in letters, chronicles, house books, dream books, nativity books, books of magic and sorcery. Prophetic visionaries claimed to be able to read the future in the stars (astrology), in the storm, in the fire, in metal mirrors, in human features, or in the lines of the palm.

An atmosphere of black magic and sorcery surrounds the mysterious figure of Doctor Georg Faust (*c.* 1507–1540), a native of Knittlingen in Swabia, the archsorcerer, physician, and alchemist, the "philosopher of all philosophers," who claimed with his black magic to have effected the victory of the imperial army at Pavia and the conquest of Rome (1527). He captivated the imagination of his contemporaries and inspired the poetic fancy of centuries to come (Marlowe, Lessing, Goethe, Lenau, Grabbe, etc.). The first *Faust-Book, the Story of Doctor Johann* Faust, the Widely Renowned Sorcerer and Magician,* was first published by Johann Spiess in Frankfurt.

The hero of the Faust-Legend, the *Faust-Book,* and the popular puppet play of the archsorcerer is in a way a true mirror of the sixteenth century. Faust's pact and companionship with the Evil One illustrates the importance that was attributed to the influence of the demonic powers and the vile, cruel, and sinister tyranny of the devil. In Luther's life and works references to the devil are frequent. While in the Wartburg, he claims to have seen him twice in the disguise of a dog. In Wittenberg he saw him

---

* In legend, fiction, and drama Georg Faust lived on as "Johann" Faust.

in the form of a black cat, and in Eisleben he beheld him from his window, seated on a near-by fountain, his mouth opened in a wide grin. "The devil is about us everywhere; he puts on a mask, as I have seen with my own eyes, appearing in the guise of a sow, a bundle of straw, and the like," we read in Luther's *Hauspostille*. Everything that stands in the way of the spread of the Gospel is the work of the devil. Even the best man must fall if the devil rides him. Theologians of all denominations agreed with Luther, suspecting His Satanic Majesty as the cause of every human passion, weakness, and vice. The "trouser-devil" was responsible for the bizarre fashions of mercenaries and burghers; the "drink-devil" caused drunkenness and debauchery; the "dance-devil" lurked behind the immorality of dance-crazed couples; and the "hunting-devil" inspired the passion of the chase. This preoccupation with the devil produced a special type of literature (*Teufelsliteratur*), works that were often profusely illustrated, the devil frequently being clothed in the habit of a monk.

Persons afflicted with mental diseases, also sleepwalkers and epileptics, were suspected of being possessed by the devil. "Far and near, on all sides the number of possessed persons is getting so large that it is a pity and a wonder," wrote Andreas Celichius, superintendent of Mecklenburg (1595). Exorcisms designed to drive out devils were practiced by Catholics and Protestants. Celichius published a treatise on "Possessions," in which he pointed out that most of the afflicted persons were women. This he finds not surprising, in view of the fact that sin and death were brought into the world by a woman and that women were full of pride, curiosity, and sensuality, and therefore more attracted by devilish sorcery than men.

The darkest chapter in this story of aberrations of the human mind was written by the instigators and perpetrators of the trials for witchcraft. It was the crowning superstition of all and it swept over Europe with the irresistible force of an epidemic, affecting the young and the old, the wise and the unlettered, men and women of every station in society. The *Witches' Hammer* (*Malleus Maleficarum*), edited by the two Dominican inquisitors, Heinrich Krämer (Institoris) and Jacob Sprenger (1487), makes it possible for us to gain some insight into the follies and manias that poisoned the imagination of the waning Middle Ages and that came to life again after the middle of the sixteenth century.

In 1484 the two authors of the *Witches' Hammer* succeeded in inducing Pope Innocent III to issue the Bull *"Summis Desiderantes,"* which defined witchcraft as a form of heresy and thereby placed the prosecution of alleged witches under the jurisdiction of the Inquisition. In the first decades of the sixteenth century the numerous accusations still met with a healthy skepticism, and Hans Sachs very soberly speaks of "vain imaginings." But the majority of scholars and educators, both Catholic and Protestant, were of a different opinion. After initial doubts even Luther became firmly convinced of the actual existence of witches, whom he denounced from his pulpit as milk thieves and weathermakers who traveled on magic carpets and induced people to fornication and prostitution. "I would burn them myself, according to the custom of the Law, as the priests of old stoned the evildoers," he wrote. John Calvin, too, demanded the merciless destruction of witches, and the prisons in Geneva were overcrowded with the unfortunate victims of superstition. Although himself a mortal enemy of the Dominicans, the German poet and satirist Johann Fischart (*c.* 1546–1590) prepared a new edition of the *Witches' Hammer* in 1588 and translated the *Daemonomania* of the French jurist, Jean Bodin (1530–1596), a work which served as a great encouragement to one of the worst persecutions.

As a matter of fact, many people actually engaged in fortunetelling, stargazing, gold making, and manifold other magical practices, and it was by no means exceptional that overscrupulous or hysterical persons voluntarily accused themselves of having had sexual intercourse with the devil and other evil spirits and of having committed other horrible crimes. The number of trials increased greatly after the middle of the sixteenth century, when the cruelty and semibarbarism of the age, the sadism of judges, spectators, and executioners, and the application of the most inhuman devices of torture added new notes of terror to the proceedings. The "witches" were forced to confess that they had traveled through the air on broomsticks, on goats, calves, and pigs, that they had attended the "Witches' Sabbath" on a desolate mountain peak in the Hartz, known as the "Brocken" or "Blocksberg," there to celebrate "Walpurgis-Night" (the eve of May 1) in wild orgies with Satan. They were forced into the admission that they had paid homage to demons, sacrificed children, and practiced cannibalism.

In the later sixteenth century and throughout the seventeenth century the witchcraft trials extended all over Germany. It is estimated that during that period approximately one hundred thousand victims were executed. Among them were men, women, and children, princesses and other ladies of noble birth, councilors and princes, priests, monks, and pastors, and even some of the judges and accusers were themselves accused and convicted.

Rules for the legal procedure in trials on witchcraft had been laid down by the *Carolina,* the law code of Emperor Charles V (1532), which served as the standard for German criminal law for a period of about 250 years. Its statutes were relatively moderate and sane, but they were frequently invalidated and disregarded by the territorial law courts. In Germany, the tribunals of the Inquisition played an insignificant part in the trials, the "secular arm" becoming more and more the sole administrator of justice. Absolute lawlessness characterized the final phase in the evolution of this collective insanity. No one was safe and beyond suspicion and, once accused, he was considered an outlaw, caught in a legal net from which there was no escape.

The belief in witchcraft and the persecution of witches was not a German but a European disease and affliction, and in some countries the mania persisted even after it had died down in Germany. In Scotland, where the trials were especially cruel, the legal statute dealing with witchcraft was not repealed until 1735. In North America we read of sporadic persecutions during the seventeenth century in Massachusetts, Connecticut, Virginia, culminating in the outbreak of a regular epidemic in Salem, Massachusetts, in the year 1692. The last burning of a "witch" in Germany took place in Würzburg in 1749. In Glarus (Switzerland) a servant girl was accused of witchcraft and executed by the sword in 1782.

The first German author who courageously expressed his condemnation of the trials for witchcraft was the Calvinist physician Johann Weyer, whose Latin work on sorcery and demonology was translated into German in 1565 and was almost immediately placed on the *Index* of forbidden books. Gradually the voices of reason grew stronger, and Protestant as well as Catholic theologians and scholars attempted to put an end to the trials and executions. In the seventeenth century the Jesuits, Adam Tanner (1572–1632) and Friedrich Spee (1591–1635), stood in the forefront of those who were opposed to the witchcraft trials. In 1631 Spee published anonymously his *Cautio Criminalis,* a book of 400 pages whose contents were the fruit of the personal experiences of the author who, in his capacity as a priest and confessor, had accompanied many of the victims on their way to the stake and had convinced himself of their innocence. The brunt of his attack was aimed at the injustice of the procedure, especially as regards the application of torture: "Is torture to be abolished?" he asks. "I answer: either torture must be wholly done away with or it must be so changed that it no longer endangers innocent persons. This is a matter that concerns the consciences of the princes, a matter for which they as well as their councillors and confessors will have to render account before their eternal judge. . . . My blood boils when I hear mentioned the names of those unjust inquisitors who even declared our devout Father Tanner as deserving of torture, for the sole reason that he has written very reasonably concerning these witchcraft trials. This is one of their arguments for indicting persons and committing them to torture. Why don't you make me an inquisitor! I should immediately proceed against all German magistrates, prelates, canons, and religious. If they want to defend themselves, I will not listen to them, but I will torture them, good and solidly, and they will yield, and: behold! I shall exclaim, where the witches hide themselves . . . I declare: we are all witches as soon as we are subjected to torture."

The venom of theological strife and the cancerous growth of superstition had by no means deadened the voices of true and simple faith and devotion. Mystical piety had withdrawn from the official churches but was alive in private conventicles and in the hearts of religiously inspired individuals. Caspar Schwenckfeld (1489–1561) of Ossig (Luther called him "Stänkfeld" or Stenchfield) was a Silesian nobleman whom the intolerance of the Protestant orthodoxy had forced to roam about without rest or haven. Sebastian Franck of Donauwörth (1499–1542) was first a Catholic priest, then a Protestant preacher, then a soap boiler and a printer, but always a

"Schwarmgeist" (enthusiast), a mystic visionary, and the author of the first comprehensive history of Germany (*Chronicle,* 1531). Valentin Weigel (1533–1588), a native of Saxony, lived the quiet life of a saintly Protestant parson, stressing the value of mystical inwardness and placing the kingdom of God in the individual soul: "Paradise, Christ, or the Kingdom of God is then not outside but within. Therefore we must not seek heaven here or there. If we do not find it within ourselves, if we do not feel and taste it there, we shall seek it in vain and shall never find it."

Quaint and fanciful was the life, personality, and work of Jacob Böhme (1575–1624), the unlettered shoemaker-philosopher of Görlitz in Lower Silesia, whose mystico-theosophical speculations on God, man, and the world were drawn from his rich inner life, and whose originality of style and thought have exercised a decisive influence on the German thinkers of the early nineteenth century, especially on Fichte, Schelling, Hegel, Novalis, and Franz von Baader. For Böhme a strong dualism is inherent in the "abyss" of the Deity. Purity, goodness, and beauty are from eternity opposed by darkness and evil, and out of this aboriginal antinomy God constantly generates His own essence into the world, which consequently includes good and evil as the necessary requisites of the process of cosmic evolution. In contemporary philosophy Max Scheler's anthropology with its dualism of "urge" and "spirit" is indebted to Böhme's theosophy. But his influence extends even to British and North American speculation. The English theosophists, Bromlay and John Pordage, and the visionary, Jane Leade, adopted Böhme's fundamental ideas, and the "Behmenists" play a significant part in English Church history in the seventeenth century. In modern times the vitality of Böhme's thought is reflected in some of the concepts of Ralph Waldo Emerson and the New England Transcendentalists.

With the exception of Jacob Böhme, these mystical representatives of unorthodox Protestantism continued the medieval tradition of Eckart, Suso, Tauler, and the *Theologia Germanica* (cf. p. 218), with an added pantheistic note which made them maintain with Sebastian Franck that "God is all in all: nature, happiness, the essence of all beings and natures, the virtue of all virtues, He in whom all things are contained." Not sharing in the vilification of opponents and the intolerance of the orthodoxy, they also agreed with Franck when he wrote: "To me a Papist, a Lutheran, a Zwinglian, a Baptist, yes, even a Turk is a dear brother."

Both the old and the new churches in some of their best representatives gave testimony of their conviction that any true faith must be tested and proven in acts of mercy and charity. Faith and charity in their interplay are described by Luther in his book *On the Freedom of a Christian Man* as follows: "A Christian man does not live in himself but in Christ and in his fellow men; in Christ through his faith, in his fellow men through his love. By virtue of his faith he rises above himself to God; from God he descends again by virtue of his charity, and yet he always remains in God and in the divine love."

Social and Cultural Conditions: (c) *Education and the Schools.* Scholastic-dogmatic interests on the one side and humanistic tendencies on the other determined the educational ideas of the sixteenth century. The humanistically trained scholar was the standard-bearer and model type of intellectual culture. Those who had hoped that the German written language would preserve and further develop the fluency and brilliance with which Luther's tongue had endowed it were bitterly disappointed. The New High German language had to face the dangerous competition of the New Latin idiom of the scholars with its pedantic and unimaginative conventionality, whose influence was felt in the official German style of the chancelleries. Many of the scholars and educators went so far as to discourage the instruction and use of the German language altogether and, by means of the strictest supervision of the students, to enforce the exclusive use of Latin. The cultivation of a neo-classical style became the primary aim of the philologically minded Humanist teachers.

Martin Luther, on the other hand, was chiefly interested in religious education, and he seized upon every means that seemed to further that end. To combat certain destructive forces in education, such as a popular hostility toward the higher learning, a widespread distrust of scholars and clergymen, and a growing neglect of learning in favor of money-making, Luther wrote his address *To the Councillors of All German Cities: that they may uphold and reconstruct the Christian Schools* (1524). Melanchthon, the author of the constitution of the schools of the province of Saxony (1528), praised the sciences as the most splendid ornament of religion and emphasized their importance for the well-being of the national state. His grammars were adopted in a large number of secondary Latin schools, and in his capacity as a professor in the University of Wittenberg he influenced and educated a generation of prospective teachers. The spirit cultivated in these circles was that of Christian Humanism. Special emphasis was placed on religious instruction, prayer, church attendance, and the development of moral habits. Greek and Latin were the major subjects in the liberal curriculum, and dramatic productions in Latin were to facilitate self-expression in the languages of the classical masters.

To be sure, Melanchthon's beneficent influence did not extend much beyond his lifetime. Toward the end of the sixteenth century complaints about the Protestant secondary schools became very outspoken. We learn that the teachers were poorly paid, that they had to petition annually for their reappointment, that they had to earn extra money as musicians, innkeepers, and fortunetellers. Even more numerous are the complaints about the studying youth: their lack of discipline and due respect for authority; their indecent dress; their drinking, fighting, and swearing.

The Catholic schools which went through the same critical stage were greatly improved by the endeavors of the Jesuit teachers. The curriculum followed the directions laid down in Ignatius of Loyola's *Ratio atque Institutio Studiorum Societatis Jesu* (cf. p. 254 sqq.), but in their Christian-

Humanist aim they were very similar to those institutions which had adopted Melanchthon's educational ideals.

The universities began to flourish again after an initial decline that had followed the religious upheavals of the beginning Reformation. New foundations of the sixteenth and early seventeenth centuries were the Catholic universities of Dillingen (1549), Olmütz (1574), Würzburg (1582), Graz (1586), Paderborn (1615), and Salzburg (1623); and the Protestant universities of Marburg (1527), Königsberg (1544), Jena (1558), Helmstedt (1574), Giessen (1607), Rintelen (1621), and Altdorf (1623). Most of the newly founded Catholic institutions served primarily the education of the future clergy and had only a philosophical and theological faculty.

All of the new universities were founded by territorial princes; they were no longer self-governing but State institutions; the professors had become the servants and employees of the princes and had lost many of their former privileges. The denominational character of the university was strongly marked, and the freedom of teaching was much more restricted than in the Middle Ages. Whenever the prince found it expedient to change his religious affiliations the teaching staff of the university had to follow suit. Objectors were summarily dismissed or imprisoned. The professors were poorly paid and had frequently to rely on extra earnings as tradesmen, innkeepers, court jesters, and so forth. Their venality, servility, and indolence became the subject of many complaints. The Catholic universities came more and more under the exclusive influence of the Jesuit Order.

With the dissolution of monastic and clerical institutions the medieval students' unions (*Bursen*) had gradually disappeared. They lived on only in the seminaries of the Catholic universities. Numerous sources tell of the breakdown of academic discipline, of dueling, carousing, strikes, and revolts among the students, and of their clashes and quarrels with the townspeople.

Although there were no essential changes in the program of studies, and most of the universities had retained the four medieval faculties, scholarship as such became less and less creative and constructive but was either controversial or purely factual, historical, and philological in a narrowly restricted sense of the term.

The Sciences. Renaissance, Humanism, and the era of discoveries had greatly stimulated the general interest in man and the physical world that was his abode. But nature was still a great mystery, and science and occultism were close allies. Chemistry and alchemy, astronomy and astrology were still inseparably linked together. Sebastian Münster's *Cosmographia* (1543), pretending to be a compendium of geography, history, physics, and linguistics, gives evidence of a queer mixture of careful observation, child-like credulity, and uncontrolled imagination. The sixteenth century finds Germany taking the lead in cartography and in the manufacture of globes. Gerhard Krämer's map of the world of 1569 served as a model for the cartographers of other European countries. Mineralogy and geology were considerably advanced by the investigations and studies of Georg Bauer

(Agricola, † 1555), a physician who spent many years of his life in the mining district of Joachimsthal and published the results of his research in numerous writings (*Bermannus, Sive de Re Metallica; De Re Metallica Libri XII,* etc.). Though a scientific mind in the modern sense, he nevertheless believed firmly in the existence of gnomes and mountain goblins.

The science of botany had made but little progress since the days of Albert the Great (cf. p. 144 sq.). It was due to the influence of the Humanists that the botanical works of antiquity and of the Middle Ages were studied anew, leading to a growing preoccupation with living plant organisms. Conrad Gesner († 1565), professor of natural science and a physician in the city of Zurich, composed two comprehensive works on botany and zoology and grew rare alpine and exotic plants in his private botanical garden. The "herb-books" (*Kräuterbücher*) by Hieronymus Bock and Leonard Fuchs (the fuchsia is named after him) acquired great popularity.

The sciences of anthropology and anatomy benefited from the physicians' new interest in the mysterious functioning of the human body. Andreas Vesalius († 1564), physician at the imperial court, saw in the authority of the ancient Roman physician Galenus (second century A.D.) the most formidable handicap for a fruitful development of medical science. Vesalius' *De Humani Corporis Fabrica Libri VII* (Basel, 1542), richly illustrated with excellent woodcuts, was the result of his anatomical studies and marks the beginning of modern medical science.

A pioneer in the fields of medical science and nature philosophy and likewise opposed to the chiefly theoretical knowledge of ancient medicine was Theophrastus Bombastus Paracelsus von Hohenheim (1493–1541), a Swiss physician, scientist, and theosophist, and one of the most fascinating personalities of the sixteenth century. A revolutionist in his thoughts and methods, he favored practical observation and experimentation and burned in public the works of Galenus and Avicenna (Arabic physician and philosopher, 980–1037). Nature he considered the greatest of all teachers and healers, and man was the mediator and interpreter of its laws. He placed chemistry in the service of medicine, praising the human mind, imagination, and will as the most important sanative powers. He criticized the use of Latin and Greek in writing and teaching and was the first professor to deliver his lectures in German (Basel, 1526–1528). His philosophical teachings may be characterized as a kind of panpsychism, claiming a magical affinity between plant organisms and certain organs of the human body and stressing the influence of the planets on human life. His eccentricity and doctrinal rigorism won him many enemies and few friends. Wandering restlessly from place to place, he died in poverty and misery at the age of forty-seven and lies buried in the Church of St. Sebastian at Salzburg. His writings have been re-edited and reinterpreted in recent years.

With surgery still in its infancy and medical science in general on a low level, ignorance and superstition were widespread among the members of the medical profession, and most people had to entrust their well-being to the crude methods and medicaments of the barbers. The majority of physicians were firm believers in the "science" of astrology, but their preoccupation with the planets and their movements prepared the way for the rise of astronomy.

Nicholas Copernicus (1473-1543), the son of a merchant of German ancestry, a native of the then Polish city of Thorn (East Prussia), and a canon of the Cathedral of Frauenburg, the father of modern astronomy, roused a storm of opposition with his epochal work *De Revolutionibus Orbium Coelestium* ("On the Revolutions of Heavenly Bodies"; completed in 1535 and published shortly before his death), wherein he described the sun as a fixed body in the center of the universe, around which revolve the earth and the other planets. He furthermore contended that the earth rotated on its own axis once every twenty-four hours (heliocentric view). The Middle Ages, on the other hand, had considered the earth the immovable center of the universe, around which the other heavenly bodies revolved once in every twenty-four hours (geocentric or Ptolemaeic theory, advanced by Ptolemaeus of Alexandria, second century A.D.). The theologians found fault with the discovery of Copernicus because it seemed to be at variance with the Scriptures. Nevertheless he dedicated his work to Pope Paul III. It was temporarily placed on the *Index of Prohibited Books* (1616-1757), in connection with the controversies concerning the teachings of Galileo.

Following in the footsteps of Copernicus, the great Swabian astronomer, John Kepler (1571-1630), expressed the planful motion of the universe in three fundamental laws: (1) the orbit of the planets has the form of an ellipse, the sun being fixed in one of the foci; (2) the radius vector of a planet traverses equal areas in equal times, its speed increasing and diminishing in proportion to its nearness to or remoteness from the sun; (3) the time interval required by a planet to complete its way around the sun depends on its average distance from the sun: the square of a planet's periodic time is proportional to the cube of its mean distance from the sun.

But even Kepler, great scientist that he was, devoted himself to the making of calendars, prognostics, and horoscopes. "I serve," he said, "the foolish little daughter Astrologia, so that her highly rational mother, Astronomia, may not have to starve." Theological bigotry was up in arms against Kepler's scientific discoveries, and his Protestant coreligionists attacked him severely for having recommended the acceptance of the "new calendar," promulgated by Pope Gregory XIII in 1582. In Protestant Germany and the Netherlands this "Gregorian Calendar" was not adopted until 1700. In Denmark it was introduced in 1710 and in England and the American colonies in 1752.

The hitherto accepted "Julian Calendar," introduced by Julius Caesar in 46 B.C. and improved by Emperor Augustus in A.D. 4, had been based on an assumed solar year of 365¼ days, whereas actually the solar year is eleven minutes and a few seconds shorter. This accumulated annual error prompted Gregory XIII to publish his Bull *Inter Gravissimas* of 1582, annulling ten days and restoring the original date of the equinox to the twenty-first of March. A leap year was proposed for every fourth year, but three of the leap years occurring within a period of 400 years were to be considered as common years (leap years at the close of the centuries, ending in 00 and not divisible by 400). The improvement that was achieved by the new calendar is indicated by the fact that on its basis an error of only one day would accumulate after a period of approximately 4000 years. Before the final steps for the adoption of the calendar were taken, the Fifth Lateran Council (1512–1517) and the Council of Trent (1545–1563) had devoted some of their deliberations to this much disputed question, and in 1514 the papal commission had asked for and received the advice of Corpernicus. The Gregorian Calendar in its final form was largely the work of the Bamberg Jesuit, Christopher Clavius (1538–1612), who furnished an explanation of the reformed calendar in his *Apologia* (1588) and *Explicatio* (1603).

Foremost among the great minds of the age of the rising natural sciences ranks the genius of Galileo Galilei (1564–1642) of Pisa, the inventor of the telescope, the discoverer of the mountains of the moon, the rings of Saturn, the moons of Jupiter, the phases of Venus and Mercury, and the sun spots. His defense of the Copernican system led to his being compelled by the Inquisition to forswear his belief in the movement of the earth. Summoned to Rome in 1615, he promised neither to teach nor defend henceforth the heliocentric theory. Nevertheless, he wrote a defense of the Copernican system in form of a dialogue (1632).

A worse fate befell Giordano Bruno (1548–1600), the brilliant Italian nature philosopher who, influenced by Stoic and Neo-Platonic trends of thought, taught a system of aesthetic pantheism, in which he proclaimed the infinity of the world and the identity of man, God, and the universe. Returning to Italy after a stay of five years in Germany, he was arrested by the Inquisition, accused of heresy, and after a lengthy trial handed over to the secular authorities to be burned at the stake.

Philosophy and Historiography. The revival of Aristotelianism and Thomistic Scholasticism (cf. p. 141 sqq.) in the seventeenth century was preceded by a period of philosophical stagnation, eclecticism, and decadence. The reformers, with the exception of Melanchthon, had no use for philosophy as a rational discipline, and it was therefore neglected in the curriculums of the Protestant schools. In the Catholic system of education, on the other hand, Aristotle retained his time-honored position, but Germany and Europe in general lacked philosophical ingenuity and preferred the dusky labyrinths of occultism and mystagogy to the light of reason.

Historiography flourished in the sixteenth century in both the ecclesiastical and secular fields. Among the new and improved editions of historical documents of the past were the works of the Church Fathers and the acts of the Church councils. Matthias Flacius (1520–1575), one of the leaders of the Lutheran orthodoxy, wrote with several collaborators the first Protestant church history (1559 sq., 13 vols.), the so-called *Magdeburg Centuries* (*Magdeburger Zenturien*), which found its Catholic counterpart in the *Annales Ecclesiastici* (1588–1593, 12 vols.) of the Italian historian, Cardinal Caesar Baronius (1538–1607).

The classical historiographical works of Switzerland and Bavaria respectively are Gilg Tschudi's (1505–1572) *Swiss Chronicle, 1000–1470* (first printing, 1735), and John (Aventinus) Turmair's (1477–1534) *Annales Boiorum* (Bavarian Annals), first written in Latin (1554) and later on in German (1566). Of equal merit from the point of view of political and cultural history are the historical works of the Swabian Lutheran preacher and mystic, Sebastian Franck (1499–1542), whose sincerity and objectivity have netted him the title of a "modern thinker of the sixteenth century" (*German Chronicle, Cosmography,* etc.). Both his historical and mystical writings are inspired by his belief in the manifestation of a divine principle in the changing forms and aspects of historic evolution, as reflected in the destiny of peoples. The "Eternal Word" is "spirit and life, not just a letter, not written with ink or pencil on paper, parchment, or stone, but impressed as a seal into the hearts of all men by the finger of God."

Language and Literature. Martin Luther's significance in connection with the history of the German language has been mentioned (cf. p. 226). Luther's language and style as well as the depth of his religious experience exercised a decisive influence on the form and content of German prose and poetry in the sixteenth century, an influence which is even noticeable in the writings of his most bitter foes. The people as a whole, every group and each individual, had been taught to read, sing, and pray in Luther's tongue, thus gradually imparting color and life to the adopted idiom of the Saxon chancellery. The philologico-grammatical exercises and the Ciceronian mannerisms of the younger German Humanists could not prevent the final and permanent victory of popular feeling and expression in language and literature. The printed and written German script (Gothic letter type) owes its modern form to John Neudörffer (1497–1563), who taught students from all parts of Germany in his Nuremberg writing school.

As far as German literature is concerned the century of the Reformation is a period of decline. Most of the literary products of theological zeal, whether written in German or Latin, were didactic, academic, and eclectic. The greatest literary talent in the ranks of Luther's Catholic opponents was the eloquent Franciscan friar, Thomas Murner (1469–1537). A native of Alsace, he became the leader of the Upper Rhenish branch of German Humanism and earned international fame by his passionate German satire *On the Great Lutheran Fool* (*Von dem grossen lutherischen Narren*). A masterful German satirist like Murner, influenced by François Rabelais' (*c.* 1494–1553) great French satire of *Gargantua and Pantagruel* (1532), was John Fischart (*c.* 1546–1590), who used polemical wit and a baroque ornamental and gaudy style in his violent attacks on Catholic institutions and traditions. Ulrich von Hutten (cf. p. 251 sq.), likewise writing with a strong anti-Catholic bias, is next to Luther the first German author whose German style achieves true greatness of lyrical expression and whose revolutionary pathos is born of the depth of social and personal experience.

Following in the footsteps of Martin Luther, the singers of Protestant hymns impart in their songs religious significance to the entire breadth of life and culture. Defiance, fear, trust, and jubilant rejoicing are the principal motifs of their lyrics, varying according to temperament, mood, and religious climate. Many of the Protestant church songs were taken over into Catholic hymnals before the close of the sixteenth century. The realization of the fact that the production of hymns had proven an invaluable aid in spreading the Protestant convictions led to the publication of several Catholic songbooks (Michael Vehe, 1537; John Leisentritt, 1567).

Next to religious poetry the historical folk song came into its own during and immediately following the Reformation. It was inspired by the great events of the early sixteenth century: Luther's and Hutten's fight against Rome and the national resistance to the advancing Turks. Many of these folk songs originated around the campfires of mercenary soldiers, and their texts and tunes expressed the soldier's longing for home, love, happiness, and peace. The creative forces of poetry were still alive among the common people, nourished by the reminiscences of inherited motifs of the *Volkslieder* and *Minnelieder* of the fourteenth and fifteenth centuries.

The endeavors of the Humanists and of Hans Sachs in the dramatic field were chiefly documents of pedagogical tendencies, issuing in the post-Reformation period in a new type of "school drama" that combined ancient classical with contemporary elements, didacticism with psychological introspection. The German drama of the sixteenth century consciously cultivates a "bourgeois" atmosphere and a set of emotions and ideals that were characteristic of the new middle class of the cities: inwardness (*Innerlichkeit*), righteousness, honesty, simplicity of heart and mind, humility, morality, and all the virtues of a healthy and homely family life. The treatment of the biblical parable of the Prodigal Son by Burkard Waldis (*c.* 1490–1556) and others gives evidence of the same emphasis upon the redeeming and forgiving love of the father for his lost child that appears so strongly accentuated in Luther's translation of the Bible and in his doctrine of "salvation by faith alone."

German narrative prose in the sixteenth century exists in the two major forms of the folk tale or folk novel (*Volksroman*) and the art novel (*Kunstroman*). The folk novel has its roots in traditional popular anecdotes and is always close to the events that move the hearts and minds of the common people. The art novel, on the other hand, is more intimately linked to the social pattern of the new middle class (*Bürgertum*). The mostly anonymous folk novel reaches its peak in the *Faust-Book* of 1587 (cf. p. 266), the most characteristic example of the didactic middle class literature of the period following the Reformation. The typical art novel of the age was created by George Wickram (1520–1561), the founder of the "Meistersinger School" of Colmar in Alsace. The art novel does not grow out of the anecdotal tradition but follows the pattern of courtly and knightly fiction, with a new emphasis on social distinctions and a growing self-assertion of middle class consciousness. Wickram's *Goldfaden* ("Golden Thread") presents the civic virtuousness of the German middle class in effective contrast with knightly decadence. The entire set of knightly virtues and courtly emotions and passions is viewed with growing suspicion and disgust. But already the following generation adopts an attitude of scorn, disdain, and critical satire toward the self-centered complacency of middle class morality, and the era of princely despotism leads to a devaluation of conservative civic ideals.

Arts and Crafts. The Reformation had shown its hostility toward the plastic arts in the iconoclast movements which were inspired by the theological spiritualism of the reformers and which were especially violent in those countries and regions where the teachings of Calvin and Zwingli had been adopted. Religious paintings and sculptures, altars, organs, monstrances, crucifixes, chalices, and chandeliers were in many places removed from the churches and destroyed. We have observed how Luther successfully tried to halt the misguided enthusiasm and fanaticism of the despoilers of religious art. Though opposed to the veneration of saints and their relics and to those cultic practices (the sacramental system, the Mass, etc.) around which the arts had crystallized in the past, he was not hostile to religious art as such and found words of highest praise for ecclesiastical music, "that magnificent gift of God, which is so close to sacred theology."

The secularization of ecclesiastical institutions and possessions was another factor that worked to the detriment of religious art, depriving especially the Protestant churches of the necessary means to carry on their protectorate over the arts and crafts. The new employers of the artists were the princes, nobles, and patricians.

As in former times they had worked for the greater glory of God and the Church, so now the artists and artisans served the glorification of the secular State and its princely rulers. The architects, mostly of Italian and Dutch nationality, were entrusted with the task of constructing a host of magnificent princely palaces and castles, with flights of halls and chambers, with huge courts and extended parks and gardens. The castles of Heidelberg and Stuttgart and the Belvedere in Prague are some of the outstanding monuments of princely pride and splendor in sixteenth-century Germany. Compared with these palatial residences even such stately and ornate structures as the city hall in Bremen or the Peller-House in Nuremberg appear rather small and insignificant.

The courts of the castles and palaces and the public squares in front of them, the parks, portals, and stairways were adorned with a rich display of statuary and plastic ornamental design. The castle church or chapel was lavishly decorated and equipped with imposing altars and pulpits. An

Heidelberg Castle

artistically designed tombstone, sarcophagus, or mausoleum was to perpetuate the name of the ruler. German cities, gardens, residences, public fountains, even churchyards and churches, abounded with mythological sculptures of a pagan pantheon of gods and goddesses, of nymphs and dolphins, of Greek heroes and courtesans.

German *painting* of the sixteenth century likewise reflects the tastes and whims of the princely or patrician employers. Mythological scenes and figures animate the atmosphere of landscape painting, and "nothing was dearer to the heart of the most august princes and lords and their most serene spouses and relations than the glorious portraits of their own countenances." It goes without saying, therefore, that the art of portrait painting achieved new and unprecedented heights under the influence of an exaggerated cult of personality. Most of the princes gave steady employment to specially appointed court painters.

The *graphic arts,* including engraving, etching, and woodcut, had greatly aided the propagandistic activities of the adherents as well as the opponents of the Reformation. These relatively new techniques had facilitated the inexpensive mass production of polemic subject matter without excluding or diminishing artistic values. Many of the leading painters of the age (Dürer, Holbein, Altdorfer, Aldegrever, the brothers Barthel and Hans Sebald Beham, etc.) created outstanding graphic works in the form of book illustrations or designs for goldsmiths and other craftsmen, some of them owing the greater part of their fame to their masterful command of the new techniques (the Neat Masters or *Kleinmeister*).

The applied and mechanical arts and crafts flourished in the workshops of the goldsmiths, carvers, and cabinetmakers. The products of southern Germany, profiting by close contact with the accomplishments of the Italian Renaissance, were superior in number and quality to the output of the German North. In the year 1588 we find in Augsburg alone 170 masters in the art of goldsmithing. The preferred materials in which the German artisans exercised their craftsmanship were ivory, alabaster, mother-of-pearl, amber, gold and other precious metals, ebony and cedarwood. Many of the finished products served to enrich the "art chambers" of princes and patricians.

The art of *music* had been introduced into secular society by the Italian Renaissance, whose favorite form of musical expression was the madrigal, based on lyrical texts and sung by from four to six different voices, with or without instrumental accompaniment. The form of the madrigal marks the disappearance of the Ecclesiastical Modes (cf. p. 83 sq.), the upper voice taking the lead and dissonances becoming the common device of musical composition. Among the German practitioners of this new musical form Hans Leo von Hasler (1564–1612) of Nuremberg stands out. He had held a Fugger scholarship in Venice and had been taught by the great Venetian master, Andrea Gabrieli (*c.* 1510–1586). For the Lutheran Church Hasler created a famous book of chorals.

The first of the great German composers is Heinrich Finck (*c.* 1445–1527), whose works reveal the influence of the great Dutch masters, William Dufay (*c.* 1400–1474) and Josquin des Près (*c.* 1450–1521). German music like German painting received decisive inspiration in the sixteenth century from Italy as well as from the Netherlands. The Dutch composer Josquin des Près spent the last years of his life in the service of the German imperial court. The courts of Vienna, Munich, Heidelberg, and Dresden opened their portals to music and song and took pride in employing some of the outstanding composers of the age.

Dutch and German polyphony reached its classical height in the works of Orlando di Lasso (1520–1594). He had received his musical training in Italy and had traveled in England, France, and the Netherlands. From 1557 until his death he lived in Munich at the court of Duke Albrecht V. Emperor Maximilian II raised him to the status of nobility and the pope conferred upon him the title of a "Knight of the Golden Spur." He is to the North what the great Palestrina (1526–1594) is to Italy, and his *Seven Penitential Psalms* rank with Palestrina's *Missa Papae Marcelli* (a Mass dedicated to the memory of the Reform pope, Marcellus II) as crowning achievements of modern polyphony.

Luther's description of the polyphonic technique of vocal composition gives evidence of his appreciation and understanding of this musical form: "Is it not remarkable and admirable," he says, "how one sings a plain melody or tenor voice against which these four or five voices take part, gamboling and playing round this single tune, decking it with wondrous art and sound; seeming to take the lead in a heavenly dance, meeting, greeting, and embracing one another, so that all who have an understanding for such art agree that there is nothing in the world more remarkable than such a song decked round with many voices." Luther himself had some of the Protestant chorals polyphonically arranged, in the manner of the Dutch Motets. The collection of *New German Sacred Hymns* (*Neue deutsche Geistliche Gesänge*) of 1544 contains polyphonic arrangements of the works of the early composers of the Lutheran Reformation, among them the Swiss master, Ludwig Senfl, and Arnoldus de Bruck, conductor at the court of Vienna. The singing of polyphonic chorals required specially trained church choirs, under the direction of a precentor (*Kantor*). The schools took an important part in the rendition of these works, and Luther strongly insisted that instruction in musical theory and practice be made compulsory.

Gradually, in the course of the sixteenth century, the strict boundary lines between ecclesiastical and secular music disappeared, and instrumental music acquired an increasing significance. Among the favorite musical instruments were the horn, bassoon, flute, cornet, trumpet, trombone, violin, and the newly improved organ which, with the varieties of its tonal expression, represented an orchestra by itself.

At the beginning of the sixteenth century the medieval fiddle (rebec) with only three strings gave way to the modern violin, in the dual form of the *viola da braccio* and the *viola da gamba* (violincello). Violinmaking has been practiced as a craft and an important home industry in Füssen and later on in Mittenwald in Bavaria ever since the beginning of modern times.

Chapter 9

THIRTY YEARS' WAR AND
TURKISH WARS

The Bohemian Revolt and the "Winter-King" (1618–1623). The war which started with the violent uprising of the Bohemian nobles, in answer to the enforced acceptance by the Bohemian Diet of the Catholic Duke Ferdinand of Styria as future king of Bohemia, was to last for thirty years and, as time went on, it involved almost every state in Europe. Its first phase is marked by the fierce opposition of Bohemian Calvinism to the religious and dynastic ambitions of the Hapsburgs. By designating his cousin Ferdinand as his heir and successor on the Bohemian throne, Emperor Matthias had violated the ancient elective principle embodied in the Bohemian monarchy. The opportunity beckoned for the Czech nationalists to free their country once and for all from the hated Hapsburg domination.

On May 23, 1618, a group of nobles entered the council chamber of the royal palace at Prague and hurled the emissaries of the emperor into a ditch below the window, where they landed unharmed. With this somewhat symbolical act the Bohemians had given the signal for the outbreak of open rebellion. Their representatives met at a specially convened Diet and pronounced Ferdinand dethroned. When Emperor Matthias died early in 1619, the duke of Styria succeeded him as Emperor Ferdinand II, and this newly added prestige gained for him the support of Spain, the Catholic League (cf. p. 214), and the papacy. The Bohemians, on the other hand, turned for aid to Frederick, the young Calvinist prince-elector of the Palatinate, the head of the Protestant Union (cf. p. 214) and the son-in-law of King James I of England, offering him the Bohemian crown. They hoped that in so doing they would be able to enlist the active support of England as well as of the Protestant princes of Germany. Both parties involved in this struggle thus must bear the responsibility for having turned a local rebellion into a European religious war.

The hopes of the Bohemian Calvinists were not fulfilled: King James of England, who was engaged at that time in negotiations for a marriage alliance with Spain, was unwilling to aid Frederick's campaign, and the Lutheran princes of Germany felt utterly reluctant to risk possible defeat at the hands of the powerful Catholic League by throwing in their lot with the Calvinists. The combined armies of the emperor and the Catholic League under the command of General Tilly defeated the Bohemians in the battle of the White Hill near Prague (1620), and Frederick had to flee the country, leaving Ferdinand in undisputed possession of Bohemia and Austria. Thus the bold adventure of Frederick's campaign had come to an inglorious end, and the Jesuits had been proven right in their prediction that the reign of the "winter-king" would not last a full year.

The Catholic reaction was ruthless, the persecution of Calvinism violent in the extreme. All the religious privileges that had been granted to the Bohemians were revoked, the estates of the rebel nobles were confiscated, and large parts of the population were faced with the alternative of either conversion or emigration. Duke Maximilian of Bavaria, whose armies had had a major share in securing the victory for the emperor, was awarded the electoral title and the domains of Frederick (1623). The scene of action had been shifted to the Palatinate, where Spanish troops had been quartered and where the outlawed Frederick, aided by the soldiers of General Mansfeld and the margrave of Baden-Durlach, had made a last stand. The Palatinate was subjugated by Tilly, and the Protestant troops retired in a northerly direction, leaving the combined forces of Austria, Bavaria, and Spain as the victors in this first major phase of the war.

Albrecht von Wallenstein and the Saxon-Danish War (1624–1629). The collapse of German Protestantism on the field of battle had given a vastly superior strength to the forces of the Catholic League and to the house of Hapsburg, thus seriously upsetting the religious balance of power. Fear of a complete re-Catholization of Germany aided in enlisting foreign support for the cause of the German Protestants and at the same time led to a fateful extension of the bases of warlike operations. The neighboring Protestant nations, Holland, England, and Denmark, were aroused by the impending danger of a Catholic supremacy in Europe, while the French monarchy, though Catholic, disliked the increasing power and prestige of the rival Hapsburg dynasty and was ready to offer subsidies and diplomatic aid to the German Protestants. James I's marriage negotiations with Spain had come to naught, and the British ruler had decided to improve the relations between England and France by marrying Henrietta Maria, the sister of King Louis XIII of France. He was busy with cementing a coalition of states to force the restoration of Frederick of the Palatinate to his hereditary possessions. Holland was anxious to join any alliance directed against Spain, and King Christian IV of Denmark was willing to lend material aid to his German-Lutheran coreligionists in their fight against the German emperor and the Catholic League.

It was at this juncture that the brilliant and enigmatic figure of Albrecht von Wallenstein stepped into the limelight of European affairs to dominate the theater of war during the following decade. A native of Bohemia of Protestant parentage, but nominally a Catholic, he twice rose to power to become the generalissimo of the imperial armies and to save the emperor from imminent disaster, and twice he fell from the heights of success, to be dismissed in disgrace and deposed. Wallenstein belongs among those mysterious and fascinating political or military genuises who, like Alexander, Caesar, Napoleon, or Hitler, consider themselves as the chosen instruments of fate or providence and who, exclusively possessed by the dynamic force of an idea and impelled by demonic ambition, follow a meteorlike course to their inescapable downfall. Compared with the far-flung planning and scheming of Wallenstein, Tilly's military bravery appears as the efficiency of a devout and honest but utterly unimaginative subaltern officer.

Having acquired a considerable fortune and social prestige by the purchase of lands that had been confiscated after the Bohemian revolt, Wallenstein raised an army for the emperor at his own expense, demanding in return the right to support his soldiers by levying contributions in conquered territories, and to be invested with almost unprecedented political power. His army included the most heterogeneous elements, Catholics as well as Protestants, men picked from various nationalities, all blindly devoted to their leader, unified and co-ordinated in aim and action by Wallenstein's personal magnetism.

With over fifty thousand men the generalissimo marched northward to join the army of the Catholic League. His troops broke the resistance of Count Mansfeld of Savoy, leader of an army of mercenaries and an ally of the Bohemians. Mansfeld was defeated at Dessau on the Elbe and withdrew into Bohemia, hotly pursued by Wallenstein, while Tilly at the same time (1626) defeated the Danes at Lutter am Barenberg and forced them to withdraw from German soil. With the Catholic-Imperial forces gaining a firm foothold in northern Germany, Wallenstein envisioned the establishment of a sovereign state of his own in the conquered territories along the Baltic coast. Emperor Ferdinand appointed him as general of the imperial navy and of the Baltic and North Sea and made him "Duke of Friedland."

It was Wallenstein's favorite idea to make the German emperor as absolute and independent a sovereign as the kings of France and England and, to achieve this end, to make the imperial office hereditary. A powerful imperial fleet in the Baltic was to forge an important link between the Hanseatic cities and the Spanish sea power. The great general's interest in the religious issues of the war was completely overshadowed by his political plans and ambitions, which in turn could only be realized if the German emperor were willing to sacrifice the issues of the Catholic Restoration to the ideal of a superdenominational German monarchy. This, however, Ferdinand was not prepared to do. Even if he could have been persuaded to follow Wallenstein in his visionary political ideology, he would have met with the stubborn opposition of the princes of the Catholic League and the ecclesiastical electors. The members of the League were apprehensive lest a strong and centralized imperial authority might endanger their sovereign prerogatives, while the ecclesiastical princes were most anxious to gain back for the Church the confiscated, secularized, and protestantized ecclesiastical domains.

Wallenstein suffered his first setback in 1628, when the city of Stralsund withstood successfully the siege of his army. In the following year Emperor Ferdinand issued the "Edict of Restitution," calling for the restoration to the Catholic Church of all ecclesiastical lands which had been handed over to the Protestants since the Treaty of Passau (1552, cf. p. 212). Wallenstein, well aware that the enforcement of the "Edict" would lead to a severe aggravation of the religious conflict and necessitate the continuation of the war, declared himself opposed to it. Faced with the choice of losing the support either of the Catholic League or of his commander in chief, Ferdinand decided on the latter course. In carrying out the resolution of the Diet of Regensburg (1630), Ferdinand notified Wallenstein of his unqualified dismissal and appointed Tilly as supreme commander.

Gustavus Adolphus, Wallenstein, and the Swedish War (1630-1635). In the very year of Wallenstein's dismissal Gustavus Adolphus, king of Sweden (1611-1632), the "Lion of the North," had landed on the coast of Pomerania. A descendant of the house of Vasa, he was enthroned at the age of seventeen and in scarcely two decades had made Sweden one of the most formidable and best organized military powers of Europe. He had driven the Russians back from the Baltic and had concluded a treaty with Poland, which gave him access to a number of Prussian ports and strengthened his resolution to make the Baltic a "Swedish Lake."

The two pillars of Swedish supremacy in the North were the spiritual force of Lutheran Protestantism and the political domination of the Baltic. Both appeared to be threatened by the sudden expansion of the Catholic-Hapsburg empire along the Baltic coast. It is doubtful, nevertheless, whether Gustavus Adolphus would have acted without the encouragement and the assurances he received from France's Cardinal Richelieu, the powerful prime minister of King Louis XIII (1610-1643). It was the political combination of the power politics of Sweden and France which proved decisive for the final stages of the Thirty Years' War and which forced the religious ideologies to yield to the objectives of Spanish-Austrian, Swedish, and French imperialism.

In 1629 Richelieu persuaded his king that it was necessary to intervene in the European conflict in order to guarantee France's greatness and security for centuries to come. In bringing about an alliance between Catholic France and Protestant Sweden Richelieu placed political expediency above religious loyalty and sacrificed the Catholic to the nationalistic idea.

It was Swedish aid which had encouraged the inhabitants of Stralsund to resist successfully Wallenstein's attack in 1628. Now, with the promise of financial support from France, Gustavus Adolphus decided to start armed intervention on a large scale. Strange to say, he was not favorably received by those forces whom he came to rescue. Not only were the Lutheran princes intimidated by the strength of the imperial forces, but they also seemed to be apprehensive of the political implications of further foreign intervention. Thus, the elector of Brandenburg could only be won over to the Swedish cause by force, after his territory had been invaded. The tactical mistake on the part of Tilly, of attempting to scare John George of Saxony to his side by threats of force, caused the Saxon elector to join hands with the Swedes. Thus reinforced by an alliance with the two leading Protestant powers of northern Germany, Gustavus Adolphus attacked and defeated the imperial army at Breitenfeld near the city of Leipzig (1631). From then on the Swedish king proceeded on a triumphal march, westward through the bishoprics on the Main and Rhine rivers and finally southward into Alsace and southeastward into Bavaria. He entered Munich in the company of the outlawed "winter-king," Frederick of the Palatinate. Tilly had been defeated again at the crossing of the Lech river and had died shortly afterward of the wounds received on the field of battle (1632).

Emperor Ferdinand was quick to realize that there was only one man who could save the imperial armies from annihilation — Wallenstein! Living in involuntary retirement on his estates, smarting from the blow to his dignity and his pride, and still resenting what he considered ignoble ingratitude on the part of the emperor, Wallenstein had to be begged to raise an army and to accept the supreme command. When he finally agreed it was with the understanding that he be given dictatorial powers and princely prerogatives.

Gustavus Adolphus and Wallenstein, the two greatest military geniuses of the age, met in the bloody battle of Lützen near Leipzig (1632). The Swedes were victorious, but the victory cost them their king and leader, who died in action. The Swedish military command was taken over by Duke Bernard of Weimar, while the political destinies of Sweden were entrusted to chancellor Oxenstierna, acting as regent for Queen Christina who was not yet of age. Despite partial successes the Swedish cause waned with the death of Gustavus Adolphus, while the stars of the Duke of Friedland and his emperor ascended.

Wallenstein, too, was nearing the end of his dramatic career. Encamped in Bohemia and Silesia with his army of sixty thousand, he relapsed into political dreaming and scheming, being determined that his own political ambitions should receive their full share in the remaking of the political map of Europe. He visualized himself as the future elector of Brandenburg and as the sovereign ruler of a state that was to extend from Friedland in Bohemia to the Baltic and North Sea. Convinced that his destiny was written in the constellations of the stars, he let his judgment be influenced by astrological speculation and began to lose more and more of his freedom of choice and determination. His inactivity as well as his personal ambitions aroused the suspicion of the imperial court in Vienna. Suspected of carrying on secret and treasonable negotiations with the Swedish enemy with a view to dictating a political peace to the Empire based on the equality of religious creeds, Wallenstein was deserted by most of his officers and men and assassinated in the Bohemian town of Eger by the Irish Colonel Butler and some fellow conspirators (1634).* His fortune and extended possessions were confiscated by the emperor and distributed among the officers and troops of the dead general.

In the year of Wallenstein's assassination the Swedes under Bernard of Weimar were defeated by an imperial army at Nördlingen in Bavaria and had to give up most of the territories that they had previously conquered. In the following year (1635) the emperor negotiated the Peace of Prague with the electors of Brandenburg and Saxony. Under the terms of this treaty the two electors were to relinquish their alliance with Sweden, and all disputed German Church lands were to be restored to those who had held them in 1627. The "Edict of Restitution" of 1629 was thereby virtually annulled.

Richelieu, Mazarin, and the Swedish-French War (1635–1648). With the signing of the Treaty of Prague peace could have been restored if the aims of French imperialism had not prevented it. Richelieu had not yet achieved the ardently desired destruction of Hapsburg power in Europe. He found a willing tool to carry out his political plans in the Capuchin monk, Père Joseph of Paris, the former François du Tremblay, Baron de Maffiers. In lending his aid to Richelieu's Machiavellian policies Père Joseph was attempting to revive the mystical dream and prophecy that dated back to the times when King Louis VII of France started on the Second Crusade. In this prophecy the French king was described as the future supreme sovereign of a universal Christian empire that was to embrace Orient and Occident. The house of Hapsburg appeared as the major obstacle in the realization of this ambitious scheme.

In 1635 France declared war on Spain and concluded an alliance with Holland and Savoy. Bernard of Weimar, the Swedish commander, was placed on the French payroll. Thus France was not only responsible for the continuation of the war for another thirteen years, but she also became the leading power as far as military strategy and efficiency were concerned. Most of the battles were fought on German soil, and the final peace negotiations were conducted under French pressure and concluded at the expense of Germany.

In 1642 Richelieu was succeeded by Cardinal Mazarin, an ambitious politician of Italian descent, who assumed truly dictatorial powers and continued with even greater energy and ruthlessness the struggle for the aims of French imperialism. It was chiefly due to his influence that France now became a thoroughly militarized nation. The French armies under the command of General Turenne and the prince of Condé fought with varying success on the Neckar and Rhine and in the Spanish Netherlands, where the Spaniards suffered a crushing defeat at Rocroi in 1643. In 1646

---

* Cf. Friedrich Schiller's Wallenstein trilogy (*Wallenstein's Camp; The Piccolomini; Wallenstein's Death*) and the same author's *History of the Thirty Years' War*.

the Swedish army under General Wrangel and a French army under Turenne joined their forces on Bavarian soil, and in 1648 the Swedes stormed Prague, while the prince of Condé annihilated a Spanish-Austrian army near Lens (France). Peace negotiations had been under way for the past four years, carried on by two parallel assemblies, the Catholic and Protestant powers meeting separately in the Westphalian cities of Münster and Osnabrück. On October 24, 1648, the peace treaty of Westphalia was signed.

The Peace of Westphalia (1648). The peace treaty of Münster and Osnabrück marked the end of the Holy Roman Empire of the German Nation as a political power. From 1648 on, it existed only nominally and on the map. The profits of the war were reaped by those foreign powers whose intervention had prolonged the conflict and whose armies had devastated the German lands. In the Westphalian Peace Conference Sweden and France sat in judgment on the destiny and the future boundaries of Germany, with the German princes and the German emperor too powerless to withstand their dictation. Each of the almost three hundred petty principalities of Germany was represented at the conference table, and each of them was given sovereign rights, including the privileges of coining money, raising their own armies, and concluding alliances with foreign powers *("ius foederis")*. And in addition to their votes, those of France and Sweden were required in any important decision that was to be taken by the Imperial Diet.

France and Sweden were doing a thorough job in paralyzing the arm of the central government and in destroying German unity of purpose and political action. The war which had begun as a religious struggle ended with a peace that bore all the earmarks of modern imperialism, leading to the economic and national strangulation of the weaker by the stronger. The injustices embodied in the terms of the settlement bore in themselves the seeds of future armed conflicts, of a series of wars that were to be fought for dynastic supremacy, territorial gains and readjustments, and for economic domination.

In the Treaty of Westphalia the Thirty Years' War was described as a "struggle of liberation," waged by the German Estates and Principalities against the autocracy of the emperor, and France and Sweden came forward as the guarantors of "German Liberty." Freed from its diplomatic verbiage and elaborate trimmings, this meant simply that Germany had become a French protectorate.

France accordingly received the largest share of the booty: the Hapsburg possessions in Alsace, in addition to the bishoprics of Metz, Toul, and Verdun, which she had held since 1552 (cf. p. 208). Richelieu in his memorandum of 1629 had already designated the acquisition of Lorraine and the city of Strasbourg as objectives of France's foreign policy, *"pour acquérir une entrée en Allemagne"* (in order to gain a gateway into Germany). With the possession of these territories France would obtain a strategic position in the German Southwest; from here she would be able to control the activities of the princes of southern Germany and check the movements and designs of Austrian politics. Although the free city of Strasbourg was not included in the French grab at the end of the war, the new boundary was marked by the Rhine river, from the Rhenish Palatinate (*Rheinpfalz*) up to the Swiss border.

Sweden, the second great European power to entrench itself on German soil, received the bishoprics of Bremen and Verden and the western part of Pomerania. She thereby gained a strong foothold on the southern coast of the Baltic and control of the Oder river and the mouth of the Elbe.

Brandenburg, in return for the surrender of western Pomerania to Sweden, received several secularized bishoprics and a guarantee of her territorial rights in eastern Pomerania. The Palatinate was divided between Duke Maximilian of Bavaria and Charles Louis, the son of the "winter-king" (Frederick V), each of them receiving the electoral title. Holland and Switzerland, which nominally had still belonged to the Empire, were formally recognized as independent European powers. The great German seaports on the North Sea and the Baltic, Hamburg, Bremen, and Lübeck, lost their freedom and were made subject to the political and economic influence of Denmark and Sweden.

As to the religious settlement, the status of the year 1624 was to be recognized as a binding norm, and secularized Church lands were to remain in the hands of those who held them at that time. In this way a large number of north German bishoprics as well as the lands of Wurtemberg and the Palatinate were retained by the Protestants. On the initiative of the elector of Brandenburg the Calvinists were now included in the privileges of the Religious Peace of Augsburg (cf. p. 212). Calvinist princes thus were given the right to determine the religion of their subjects. Although theoretically the three major rival denominations, Catholic, Lutheran, and Calvinist, were granted equal rights, religious toleration was no more in evidence at the end of the great war than it was at its beginning.

Cultural Collapse. The Thirty Years' War engraved itself on the consciousness of contemporaries as the greatest scourge of mankind since the days of Attila and his Huns. Its horrors are vividly described in memoirs and letters, in sermons and pamphlets, in chronicles and narratives. These documents speak of an *"excidium Germaniae"* (the destruction of Germany), of a *"Germania expirans"* (a dying Germany). They tell a sordid tale of the lust of bloodshed; of slain and tortured men, women, and children; of destroyed cattle and farm land; of devastated and pillaged cities, towns, and villages. We read of the rapidly shifting alliances and allegiances and of how, as time went on, everybody became everyone's foe: Swedes, Croats, Spaniards, Frenchmen, and mercenaries from all countries ravaging and ransacking the German lands. We learn of a whole generation growing up and knowing the blessings of peace only from hearsay. We are told about the deserted schools and universities, the decline of morality and religion, about empty workshops, burned churches and desecrated church-yards. It is hardly surprising then that Gustav Freytag (1816–1895), in his *Pictures from the German Past* (*Bilder aus der deutschen Vergangenheit;* first printing in 5 vols., 1859–1867), wonders how "after such losses and such corruption of the survivors, a German people has remained in existence, a people which was able after the conclusion of the peace to till the soil, to pay taxes and, after miserably dragging along for a hundred years, to bring forth new energy and enthusiasm, and a new life in the arts and sciences."

And yet, truthful as some of the contemporary reports on the social and cultural collapse of Germany may be, many others will have to be accepted with reservation. For one thing, the seventeenth century in general leans toward exaggeration, no less in its historiographical accounts than in its art, its literature, its fashion, its social behavior. Again, we have learned today from experiences that are close to our own memories that times of extraordinary stress and duress generate various modes of wishful reportage and outright propaganda, born of the urge to indict the political, social, or religious opponent and to blacken his record by atrocity tales which usually are a composite of truth and imagination. To judge the frightful events of the war adequately it becomes necessary to submit the above-mentioned horror tales to the tranquil searchlight of historical criticism and thus reduce them to their true proportions.

It is obvious that the Thirty Years' War, judged by its original motivating causes and aims, was one of the most futile and unnecessary wars ever fought. During its last phases the war dragged on by its own momentum. In viewing its dire course from the beginnings of the conflagration down to its last flickerings, it becomes almost impossible and evidently quite meaning-less to even raise the question of war guilt: the war had been born of the convulsions of a disintegrating civilization, and its changing constellations were merely symptoms and symbols of one of the major crises in the history of the European peoples.

Some figures may illustrate the extent to which the vitality of the German people was taxed and depleted by the successive waves of destruction. The city of Augsburg lost 62,000 of its 80,000 inhabitants. The population of the duchy of Wurtemberg was reduced from 400,000 to 48,000. It is reliably estimated that the density of the population of Germany as a whole decreased by nearly two thirds. The national health was weakened for generations to come by hunger and epidemic disease. The purity and strength of the native stock suffered from miscegenation as well as from inbreeding. The economic decline which in its beginnings reached back to the preceding century was fatally accelerated and consummated by the war. The work of reconstruction was hampered by the lack of raw materials, building mate-rials, and skilled labor. Peasants, craftsmen, artists, and merchants were equally hit by the instability of the times and by the reduction of national income. The chaotic conditions of trade and commerce led to an increasing confusion of the money market and a devaluation of the currency, while on the other hand money became a mere commodity and the object of reckless speculation. The disproportion between the increasing prices and the decreasing purchasing power grew appalling.

Bleeding from innumerable wounds, Germany in a supreme effort had to draw upon the moral and spiritual reserves of her people if she wanted not only to survive but also to revive. That strength of conviction, a strong will to action, and a realistic appraisal of the difficult tasks ahead were not wholly lacking, is evidenced by the text of a pamphlet of the year 1647, in which the anonymous author appeals to the national spirit of the German people in words like the following: "The Frenchmen and Swedes boast loudly of having subdued Germany. Our banners are displayed in Paris and Stockholm. . . . Kings, formerly obeying the call of the German Emperor . . . have become our masters by our own discord. . . . These so-called liberators approach us as with the kisses of Judas. . . . From the Rhine, from the North Sea, and the Baltic they look out from their watch towers, spying for every opportunity and conflict that might arise . . . and not unlike the ancient Romans in Greece, they begin as friendly advisers, then become arbiters, and finally masters. Awake, O Germany! Consider what thou really art! Arise from this deadly fight! The Empire can only be revived by the Empire; Germany can only be reborn by Germany. . . . As members of one body, of one state, as brethren we all must embrace each other in love, and with all our faculties and virtues strive heroically toward the great goal. . . . "

Austria Amidst Warring Ideologies. The Thirty Years' War in its later phases had developed into a life-and-death struggle between the French Bourbons and the Austrian-Spanish Hapsburgs. With the steadily diminishing prestige of the Spanish crown the burden of defending the dynastic aims and possessions of the Hapsburgs against French aggression fell more and more on the Austrian branch of the Hapsburg family. In the seventeenth century we find Austria engaged in a world-historic struggle on two fronts, *France* launching her attack from the West and the *Ottoman Turks* advancing from the East.

The battle that had to be fought against the encroachment of the dynastic interests of France, the ally of the Turks, was rendered all the more difficult because it required both repulsion of foreign attack and defense of the central authority of the Empire against the autonomous German princes, some of whom had concluded alliances with the French crown.

Three rival interests and ideologies clashed in the Thirty Years' War, Emperor Ferdinand II representing the unity of imperial power and Catholic tradition, Gustavus Adolphus advancing the idea of a Nordic Protestant empire, and Wallenstein fighting for a centralized monarchy, based on religious toleration and headed by the house of Hapsburg. It was Wallenstein's dream to create a monumental German superstate extending from the Baltic in the North to the Adriatic Sea in the South. Such a German imperium if realized would have established German hegemony in the Western World and would have provided an impregnable basis for unified operations against the Turks.

But it was the idea of religious toleration and a political unification without unity of faith which was unacceptable to Emperor Ferdinand and which caused Wallenstein's defection and downfall. The emperor felt in duty bound to follow the example of his much admired Spanish cousin, King Philip II, in restoring the Christian-Catholic unification of the Western World. The idea of political unity without unity of faith was inconceivable to him. Thus Wallenstein was dismissed, and France and the autonomous German princes became the beneficiaries of his defeat. The emperor, in turn, had to compromise his religious ideology by concluding a separate peace with the Protestant Saxons, and the religious war became a regional struggle for a European balance of power. The house of Hapsburg was forced to concentrate its efforts on the creation of a strong Danubian state within the confines of its hereditary domains. Mazarin's war aims culminated in the separation of the Spanish and Austrian branches of the Hapsburg dynasty; the separation of Austria from the rest of the Empire; and the establishment of the French-German boundary on the Rhine. In 1658 the first Rhenish League, headed by the archchancellor of the Empire, lined up the German princes against the central imperial power; while the Peace of the Pyrenees of 1659, terminating the struggle between France and Spain, marked the decline of Spanish power and the rise of France to European supremacy. The Peace of the Pyrenees was sealed by the marriage of the young French king, Louis XIV (1643–1715), to Maria Theresa, the daughter of King Philip IV of Spain. The political ambitions of Richelieu had finally reached their goal.

In the East, on Austria's second frontier, the Ottoman Turks, who had invaded the Balkan Peninsula about the middle of the fourteenth century, had held the European continent in suspense over a period of three hundred years. As the Franks under Charles Martel had saved the Christian civilization of the West from the advancing Arabs in the eighth century, so the house of Hapsburg preserved the essential integrity of Europe by the repulsion of Turkish-Islamitic expansion.

In 1453 the Turks had conquered Constantinople and subsequently driven the Venetian Republic from its outposts in the Aegean Sea and in Greece. They threatened the entrance to the Adriatic and conquered Egypt in 1516, thus erecting a wall between the economic spheres of the Mediterranean and Indian Oceans. Under Soliman II (1520–1566), their greatest sultan, they crossed the Danube and advanced into Hungary, took the city of Belgrade and annihilated the Hungarian army in the swamps of Mohács in 1526. Once again the claims of emperor and pope to supremacy over the Christian West was met by the Ottoman Sultan's idea of a theocracy of the East, including in its orbit the Western World.

By 1529 the Turks had advanced to the gates of Vienna, to put an end to the rule of "those miserable lords of Vienna." A small contingent of scarcely 20,000 defenders, drawn from the hereditary Hapsburg domains and from other parts of the Empire, was faced with the almost impossible task of holding the city against a besieging army of 150,000 men. The Turks were masters in the art of mine-warfare but unequal to the superior strategic resourcefulness of western military science. Their indecision and several blunders saved Vienna, but the westward advance of the Turks resulted nevertheless in the tripartition of Hungary, leaving the invaders in possession of the largest slice of that country. Austria had to agree to pay an annual tribute to the Turkish "Sublime Porte" and went through a period of constant anxiety, insecurity, and incessant border warfare which ended only in 1606, when the sultan was compelled to recognize the political equality of the Hapsburg emperor.

The remainder of the Turkish drama was enacted in the latter part of the seventeenth century. The second siege of Vienna of 1683 opened the period of the Great Turkish War, in the course of which the house of Austria, united with the pope, the king of Poland, and the republic of Venice in the "Holy League," and entrusting its armies to the brilliant leadership of Duke Charles of Lorraine and Prince Eugene of Savoy, gained victory after victory over the Turks. With the decisive battle near Zenta on the Theiss river, the resistance and military prestige of the enemy were shattered, and the kingdom of Hungary with its dependencies was regained for the Austrian crown. The great victories of Prince Eugene of 1716 and 1717, at Peterwardein and Belgrade, were won in alliance with Venice in the course of the third major Turkish war. The heroic deeds of the great Savoyan leader live on in the stanzas of the dramatic folk ballad *"Prinz Eugenius, der edle Ritter . . . "* (Prince Eugene, the Noble Knight . . .). The house of Hapsburg extended its influence far into the Balkans and began even to nourish dreams of a revived Byzantine Empire under Hapsburg leadership. Prince Eugene is commemorated as the statesman and general who, though of Italian birth and French breeding, fought his battles for the liberation of Europe from French and Ottoman imperialism, co-ordinating the dynastic interests of the Hapsburgs with the vital necessities of German and European civilization as a whole.

Soldiers and Military Science. The period of the Thirty Years' War had further developed and perfected the system of mercenary armies and the methods of recruiting these hired troops from many lands. The princes entrusted the business of recruiting to their generals, who were frequently held responsible for the maintenance of the armies and who reimbursed themselves by marauding, pillage, and by the imposition of heavy contributions on conquered territories and populations. The soldier was attracted to the colors not by love of country or other ethical motives but primarily by greed and love of adventure. Some of the great military leaders, such as Wallenstein, Tilly, and Gustavus Adolphus, made repeated attempts to enforce discipline and the observance of some degree of lawfulness among their troops. Thus Wallenstein's *Military Law* of 1617 enjoins the soldiers to refrain from "ungodly, frivolous, and evil living; from blasphemy, oppression of the poor, and debauchery. Therefore, all lords, squires, and their servants shall listen to the word of God every Sunday and whenever the sound of the bugle calls them to service or sermon. Likewise, though money or payment may not always be ready in due time for distribution, everyone shall observe the rules of equity and fair play and shall make out receipts and keep accounts." However, there was a wide gap between theory and practice, and after the death of the great generals the last remnant of discipline and humane consideration was thrown to the winds, and cruelty and inhumanity became the order of the day.

Military science was directed into new channels by that eminent military strategist, Gustavus Adolphus. He reorganized the Swedish army and made it the most powerful military machine of Europe. He was the first to introduce compulsory military service (conscription) among some of his Swedish contingents. He armed his foot soldiers with muskets instead of pikes, emphasized the tactical and strategical significance of the cavalry, and heightened the flexibility of his armies by introducing new and lighter uniforms and more adequate equipment. The square formation of the troops was replaced by formations of threefold echelons, resulting in a considerable lengthening of the fighting line. Light artillery units were created by a general diminution of the cylinder bore (caliber) of the cannon, by the shortening of the gun barrel, and by the introduction of "leather cannon" whose barrels were made of thin copper sheathing, covered with leather.

It was the soldier as a social type who became the symbol and the ruler of the age. Booted and spurred, a martial-looking and colorful figure and an insufferable braggart, this new *"miles gloriosus"* is portrayed in the Silesian dramatist Andreas Gryphius' (1616–1664) satire *Horribilicribrifax*. Informed of the conclusion of a peace treaty between the emperor and the king of Sweden, he thunders indignantly: "Can he make peace without even asking me? . . . Does he not owe all his victories to me? Have I not shot down the Swedish king? . . . Have I not conquered Saxony? Have I not earned my reputation in Denmark? How would the battle on the White Hill have ended without me? What glory have I not earned in the battle with the Grand Turk? Fie upon you! Get out of my sight; for I get mortally vexed when I fly into a real rage: overpowered by hot and boiling wrath and savage ire I am capable of seizing the spire of St. Stephen's Cathedral in Vienna and bending it down so hard that the whole world will turn upside down like a skittle-ball."

The horrors of the great war had made the soldier an object of popular fear, hatred, and contempt. It was the general conviction that the calling of a soldier was outside the pale of decent and humane occupations. The soldier had made himself an outlaw and an outcast.

Fashion "à la Mode." The superiority which France had achieved as a result of the Thirty Years' War strengthened greatly the French prestige and influence in matters of artistic taste and social behavior. Even during the initial stages of the war the French *monsieur à la mode,* the fashionable beau, made his appearance in German cities and at the German courts. The stiff and tight Spanish fashion for which the standard had been set by Emperor Charles V and his court, with its "millstone collars" and the enormous wire constructions which had become a requisite of women's dresses (the "farthingale" or *"cache-bâtard"*), familiar from Velasquez' paintings, gave way to looser, wider, and softer garments of precious materials and imposing splendor.

About the middle of the seventeenth century the change from the Spanish to the French fashion was completed: the men wore wide, soft, sacklike pleated breeches, adorned with laced ribbons. The upper part of the body was covered with a sleeveless vest and a comfortable long-tailed coat. The stiff frill was replaced by a soft, broad linen or lace collar. The hair was worn either braided on one side or in long, flowing curls, covered usually with ribbons and jewels. A soft felt hat with broad rim, adorned with colorful feathers, took the place of the tall and stiff Spanish headdress. A pointed "Vandyke" beard or goatee, long gauntlets, a rapier dangling from a sword belt, and spurred boots completed the martial appearance of the gentleman: a queer mixture of Frenchman and Swede, of dandy and ruffian.

The ladies relinquished the wire contraptions of their crinolines or hoop petticoats, and the contours of the female figure reappeared under the easy and natural flow of the folds. The skirts were very long and ended in a train. The upper garments were cut low around the neck and were framed by a lace collar. The sleeves were wide, pleated, and likewise adorned with costly lace and multicolored ribbons. The loud colors gradually gave way to subdued halftones and nuances of blue, green, pink, brown, and yellow. The "tower coiffure" or *"Turmfrisur,"* with the hair combed over tall frames of wire, was abandoned in favor of freely flowing curls, parted in the middle, braided, and dressed in the form of a chignon on the back of the head. Powder was used to give the hair the desired color to match the dress. Men and women covered their faces with tiny black plasters, the "beauty patches" or "mouches." "I noticed many women," remarks Hans Michael Moscherosch (1601–1669), one of the leading satirists of the age, "whose faces looked as if they had had themselves cupped, pricked, or hacked. For in all those places to which they wanted to draw attention, they were pasted with small black plasters and with round and pointed little flies, fleas, and other quaint man-traps."

Literary Trends. German literature in the period of the Thirty Years' War presents a medley of eclectic imitations of foreign models, living mainly on borrowed form and subject matter. The reaction against such an artificial and colorless internationalism found its expression in the linguistic societies whose endeavors to purify and invigorate the national German idiom reach back to 1617, the year of the foundation of the "Fruitbringing Society." Other groups with similar aims were organized during the following decades, but on the whole the literary products of their members were no less pedantic, artificial, and lacking in social significance than the works which they criticized and upon which they wanted to improve. It was their conviction that poetry could be taught and learned like any trade or craft, and one of their number, the Nuremberg councilman George Philip Harsdörffer, composed the famous *Poetischer Trichter* ("Poetic Funnel"), to "pour in the German art of verse and poetry within six hours."

Like the members of the "Meistersinger Schools" these writers preferred biblical subjects, but introduced pastoral and idyllic motifs to emphasize their desire for the primitive and indigenous. Others cultivated a ceremonious courtly formalism with which they paid their tribute to the fashions and tastes of princely despotism. Conspicuously lacking were the truly poetic elements of creative imagination, melodious rhythm, and the warmth and sensuous richness of life and nature. They did not write and sing out of the fullness of their hearts, but as the representatives of a certain class, group, or convention. Nevertheless, their works were indicative of a significant social transformation which was characterized by the disintegration of the middle class and the birth of the aristocratic culture of the gentleman *à la mode,* with its petrified code of a conventional and unreal philosophy of life.

At the same time these writers mark the transition from a poetry that was limited by religious precepts and patterns to a secular style and worldly themes. The world is seen as a play of the forces of good and evil, but sensuous and natural beauty are positively valued and affirmed. In the religious speculation of Jacob Böhme (cf. p. 270) the forces of evil figure as vital and formative necessities. It is this thought that Böhme names as the fundamental cause of his spiritual unrest which was born when he "contemplated the great depth of this world, the sun and the stars and the clouds, rain and snow and the whole of creation, and man, that little spark, and what he may be worth in the judgment of God as compared with this great work of heaven and earth. But because I discovered that good and evil dwelled in all things, in the elements of nature as well as in creatures, and that in this world the ungodly fare as well as the devout . . . I was seized by a deep melancholy."

The strong note of doubt and insecurity which is felt in Jacob Böhme's utterances is almost wholly absent in the poetic works of those writers who continue the tradition of the Protestant and Catholic church hymn. Here trust in the rational administration of world affairs, confidence in the dispensations of divine providence, are the prevailing motifs, while the praise of nature as a revelation of the wisdom and supreme beauty of the Godhead is added as an element of mystical piety. While Luther's hymns (cf. p. 227 sq.) had been expressions of the religious experiences, longings, and victories of his social-ecclesiastical group, the lyrics of Paul Gerhardt (1606–1676) and

Paul Fleming (1609–1640) sing of the yearning of the individual soul, rising at the same time above the artificial conventions of their contemporaries. Friedrich Spee (1591–1635), the Jesuit writer and poet, and the convert Johann Scheffler, surnamed "Angelus Silesius" (the Silesian Angel, 1624–1677), the two outstanding Catholic hymn writers of the seventeenth century, show themselves influenced by the mystical speculation of past centuries as well as by the pastoral poetry of their own time. The works of both authors reveal originality of form and depth of ideas despite the shackles imposed upon them by mechanical rules and patterns. On Andreas Gryphius (1616–1664), on the other hand, the horrors of the times weighed too heavily, inhibiting and stunting a creative genius who under more favorable conditions might have become one of the leading dramatists and lyricists of Germany. His sensitivity was struck by the disheartening breakdown of all those values that he cherished, and his sonnets paint a gloomy picture of the transitoriness of all earthly things.

What the seventeenth century relished and desired was not a great poet but a clever theorist who could offer a clear-cut and comprehensible program. Martin Opitz (1597–1639), a member of the "Fruitbringing Society," was so widely acclaimed because he offered just such a program in his *Prosodia Germanica (Book on German Poetry,* 1624). It proved a most influential work whose rules and prescriptions were gratefully obeyed by several generations of German writers, and whose author was enthusiastically proclaimed as the "father of modern German poetry." It was Opitz' ambition to teach his German contemporaries how to achieve a literary greatness that equaled that of ancient Greece and Rome. He succeeded to some extent in freeing the secular forces of German culture from the dogmatic bonds of Protestant Reformation and Catholic Restoration alike and in utilizing literary talent for social purposes. Both he and Friedrich Spee independently established a new principle for German poetics and metrics by their demand that the mechanical counting of syllables in German verse should be replaced by the alternating use of stressed and unstressed syllables, in accordance with the normal and natural rhythm and meaning of the word. By following the model of Dutch literary patterns he transformed the Romanic metrical devices so as to adapt them to the Germanic laws of prosody.

The German imitation of foreign fashions and the corruption of courtly culture find a severe critic in the Silesian epigrammatist, Friedrich von Logau (1604–1655), and in the prose satires of Hans Michael Moscherosch (1601–1669). Logau speaks of Germany as the slave of France, a "lumber-room where other nations store their crimes and vices," and Moscherosch asks questions like the following: "Are you a German? And you wear your hair like a Frenchman? . . . Why do you wear that silly French kind of a beard? Your ancestors considered an honest full-grown beard their greatest pride, and you . . . treat and trim and curl it every month, every week, every day! . . . Is nothing good enough for you that is made in your own country, you despisers and traitors of your fatherland?"

The greatest cultural and literary document of the period of the Thirty Years' War is, however, the masterly novel that bears the title *The Adventurous Simplicissimus* (1669) and whose author was Jacob Christoffel von Grimmelshausen (1625-1676). After his conversion to Catholicism he became an advocate of the reunion of all Christian denominations and emphasized the practical values of religious conviction. His *Simplicissimus* has often been compared with Wolfram von Eschenbach's epic *Parzival* (cf. p. 153), and the parallelism of theme and character development is very close indeed. Though largely autobiographical and highly personal and direct in style and atmosphere, Grimmelshausen's work achieves the objective plasticity of the great epic. The novel tells us of the physical and spiritual growth of its hero from early childhood to a manhood tempered and balanced by that practical wisdom which is the result of experience, great suffering, and frequent trial and error. The ways of both Parzival and Simplicissimus lead from original harmony and childish innocence through complexity and sinful entanglements to a second and richer unity and simplicity in the vision and possession of God. But Parzival's social "milieu" was that of courtly culture at its best, while the cultural barrenness in the environment of Simplicissimus offers a sharp contrast and an almost insurmountable obstacle to the spiritual aspirations of the hero. While the cultural and social frame of Wolfram's epic is essentially static, that of *Simplicissimus* is dynamic, depicted in a continuous process of change and evolution and beset with conflicts and tensions which symbolically reflect a world composed of good and evil, beauty and sordidness, orderliness and chaos. Simplicissimus is a fool like Gerhart Hauptmann's *Emanuel Quint,* Dostoievski's *Idiot,* and Wolfram's *Parzival,* a fool before God in the end, after having been nature's and the world's fool in the earlier parts of the novel. The author seems to visualize the end of an historic epoch, the end of his time, and with the apocalyptic laments over the impending dissolution are mingled the voices of faith in humankind, hope for regeneration, and love of this strange world of incomprehensible mystery.

PART IV. RATIONALISM – ENLIGHTEN. MENT – GERMAN IDEALISM – ROMANTICISM

1658–1705	Emperor Leopold I, son of Emperor Ferdinand III
1658	Formation of the first "Rhenish League" (*Rheinbund*) for the preservation of the terms of the Peace of Westphalia
1663–1806	The "Permanent Diet" at Regensburg
1670	Louis XIV drives Duke Charles IV out of Lorraine
1674	The Empire declares war on France
1675	Frederick William, the "Great Elector" (of Brandenburg) defeats the Swedes at Fehrbellin
1678	Peace of Nymwegen; Freiburg im Breisgau is ceded to France; continued French occupation of Lorraine
1679	The Peace of St. Germain compels the Great Elector to return all his Pomeranian conquests to Sweden
1680	Louis XIV institutes his "Chambers of Reunion" to determine the historical territorial rights of France and to justify Louis' annexations in Alsace, Lorraine, and Franche-Comté (Free County of Burgundy)
1681	The French occupy the city of Strasbourg
1684	Truce of Regensburg with Louis XIV
1687	The Diet of Pressburg confers the male line of succession in Hungary on Austria
1688–1697	Louis XIV's invasion of the Palatinate
1688	Alliance of the emperor, Spain, Sweden, the foremost imperial princes, England, Holland, and Savoy against France
1689	Devastation of the Palatinate by the French armies under General Mélac
1697	Peace of Ryswyk: France retains the occupied regions of Alsace but returns Freiburg and the territories on the right bank of the Rhine — The duke of Lorraine is reinstated in his rights
1699	Peace of Carlowitz: Hungary, Transylvania (*Siebenbürgen*), part of Slavonia, and Croatia are united with Austria; the Austro-Hungarian monarchy becomes one of the Great Powers of Europe
1701	Frederick III, elector of Brandenburg, son of the "Great Elector," assumes the title of "King *in* Prussia" (Frederick I)
1701–1714	The Spanish War of Succession
1705–1711	Emperor Joseph I, son of Emperor Leopold I
1711–1740	Emperor Charles VI, younger brother of Emperor Joseph I, the last in the male line of Hapsburg succession
1713	Promulgation of the "Pragmatic Sanction" by Charles VI, proclaiming the indivisibility of the Hapsburg possessions and providing for the succession of the emperor's daughter, Maria Theresa
1713–1740	Frederick William I, king of Prussia, son of the elector of Brandenburg, Frederick III (Frederick I, after his adoption of the royal title)
1740–1786	Frederick II (the Great), king of Prussia, son of King Frederick William I

1740–1780	Maria Theresa, empress of Austria (queen of Hungary), married to Francis Stephen, duke of Lorraine
1740–1742	The First Silesian War
1741–1748	The Austrian War of Succession
1742–1745	Emperor Charles VII (of Bavaria), the only non-Hapsburg emperor between 1438 and 1806
1744–1745	The Second Silesian War
1745–1765	Emperor Francis I of the Lorraine-Hapsburg line, husband of Maria Theresa (cf. above), elected as German emperor after the death of Charles VII
1756–1763	The Seven Years' War (Third Silesian War)
1765–1790	Emperor Joseph II of the Lorraine-Hapsburg line, son of Maria Theresa
1772	The first partition of Poland (between Prussia, Austria and Russia)
1778–1789	The Bavarian War of Succession
1781	Emperor Joseph II issues the Edict of Toleration
1785	Foundation of the League of Princes (Fürstenbund) by Frederick the Great
1786–1797	Frederick William II, king of Prussia, nephew and successor of Frederick the Great
1789	Outbreak of the French Revolution
1790–1792	Emperor Leopold II, brother of Emperor Joseph II
1790	Convention of Reichenbach between Prussia and Austria
1792–1797	First Coalition War between Prussia-Austria and France
1792–1806	Emperor Francis II (Francis I as emperor of Austria, 1804–1835) of the Lorraine-Hapsburg line, son of Emperor Leopold II
1793	The second partition of Poland (between Prussia, Austria and Russia)
1795	Separate peace between Prussia and France at Basel — The third partition of Poland (between Prussia, Austria and Russia)
1797–1840	Frederick William III, king of Prussia, son of Frederick William II
1797–1799	Congress of Rastatt
1799–1802	Second Coalition War between Austria and France
1803	Principal Decree of the Imperial Deputation (Reichsdeputations-hauptschluss) of Regensburg concerning the secularization and expropriation of all ecclesiastical principalities and imperial cities — The French occupy the electorate of Hanover
1804–1814	Napoleon I, emperor of the French
1805	Third Coalition War between Austria and France
1806	Creation of the Rhine Confederation (Rheinbund) — Abdication of Francis II as German emperor — The End of the Holy Roman Empire
1807	Peace of Tilsit between France and Prussia
1809	Peace of Schönbrunn between France and Austria

Chapter 10

RISE AND DECLINE OF ABSOLUTISM AND ENLIGHTENED DESPOTISM AND THE END OF THE HOLY ROMAN EMPIRE

Princely Despotism and the Theory of the Absolute Monarchy. The Thirty Years' War had carried France to a leading position in European affairs, but it had greatly weakened Austria, Spain, and the German principalities. The Holy Roman Empire dragged on merely by its historical momentum, and the feudal system was discredited and damaged beyond repair. The Treaty of Westphalia had given full sovereignty to the German princes and, lending every encouragement to their selfish ambitions, had taught them how to reap personal benefits from the conclusion of foreign alliances and from their disloyalty to the emperor. Imitating the pattern of the French court, they established an autocratic type of regime, disregarding the traditional prerogatives of the Estates and provincial Diets. Their principalities became autonomous (self-governing) territorial units, ruled by absolute monarchs who exercised the functions of government by "Divine Right" and who were thus the originators and infallible interpreters of divine, natural, and human law. The code of princely absolutism had been written by Machiavelli (cf. p. 247 sq.), and Louis XIV followed its precepts to the letter. Though he may never actually have spoken the words *"L'Etat c'est moi"* ("I am the State"), they summarize admirably his political philosophy.

In his *Instructions for the Dauphin* Louis XIV wrote: "My first step was to make my will supreme; everything that is comprised in our states, all the money in public treasuries as well as all the money in circulation, belongs to us. You, the Dauphin, must be convinced that the kings, as good patriarchs, have the absolute disposal of all property, whether it belongs to clergymen or laymen. The life of the subjects belongs to their princes, and the princes must preserve it as their property. . . . We are the representatives of God. Nobody has a right to criticize our actions. Whoever is born as a subject must obey without asking."

Similar ideas were expressed in England by the philosopher Thomas

Hobbes (1588–1679), to whom the State appeared as a "mortal God" and who saw in despotism the only efficient protection against anarchy. The change that political theory had undergone between the fifteenth and seventeenth centuries becomes evident when we compare the above statements with certain pronouncements of Cardinal Nicholas of Cusa (cf. p. 180 sq.), who expressed the sentiments of his age when he wrote: "It is much better that the commonwealth should be ruled by laws than even by the best man or king" (*De Concordantia Catholica,* Book III). This principle of the supremacy of the law had been upheld by political theorists throughout the Middle Ages. The German *Sachsenspiegel* of the thirteenth century (cf. p. 199), speaking of the right of free election, states that this principle is not derived from the authority of one man but from the natural and divine law. All "majesty" comes from God, but also from man, so that any monarchical rule is limited and conditioned by law and the common good of the citizens.

In the earlier part of the sixteenth century this principle of the relative and limited authority of the ruler was still upheld by some of the most important writers on political theory, and even Machiavelli insisted upon the subordination of rulers to the law, citing France as a kingdom that lived in security because its rulers were bound by many laws. Martin Luther's position is somewhat ambiguous, and while in his earlier writings he defended the absolute authority of the ruler as the representative of God, whose will must not be resisted even if he be a tyrant, we find that after 1530 Luther took account of the constitutional law of the Empire, admitting that the electors might agree to depose of an unjust ruler.

The Jesuit writers of the sixteenth and seventeenth centuries (Vitoria, Mariana, Suarez, Bellarmine, etc.) are unanimous and very definite in their rejection of the theory of an absolute "Divine Right" and in their insistence that the community is the ultimate natural source of political authority and therefore of all law. They declare that it is the characteristic vice of the tyrant to invalidate existing laws and to show no consideration for legal traditions. These authors are joined in their condemnation of the claims of the absolute prince by most of the political thinkers and the theologians of the Established Church in England (Richard Hooker, George Buchanan, William of Orange, etc.), by the leaders of the Whig party (John Selden, Edmund Burke, etc.), and by the Huguenot writers in France. Some of them go even so far as to defend tyrannicide.

The theory of the Absolute Monarchy, or the doctrine that the king was above the law, was systematically defended for the first time by Jean Bodin (1530–1596), the French jurist, in his work *On the Republic.* Absolute monarchy appeared to him as the best form of government, and even the rule of a tyrant he deemed better than the rule of the people. William Barclay, a Scotch jurist, in a work on royal power published in 1600, maintains that it is the king who decides what is to be law, that the ruler's authority is truly divine, and that to revolt against the king is to revolt against God. Theory and practice blended in the personality of King James I of England (1603–1625) who, as James VI of Scotland, before he succeeded to the English throne, had written a work on *The True Law of Free Monarchies* (1598, 1603), in which he combined the secular theory of the absolute monarch with the theological doctrine of absolute authority by divine right.

Like Luther and the early Church Fathers, James referred to the scriptural testimony of the appointment of the Old Testament kings, Saul and David, directly by God, thus making God the remote cause of all constituted authority. The major components of this theory are the ideas of government as embodied in Roman Law, the Oriental conception of royal power, and the Judaistic idea of the king as the appointee of God. In holding such views James I reverted to the political convictions of the early Christian centuries, when the injustices of the political and social order were regarded as a consequence of the fall of man from his original innocence and therefore had to be passively accepted and endured. The Jesuits, St. Robert Bellarmine (1542–1621) and Francisco Suarez (1568–1617), on the other hand, resumed and continued the medieval tradition, and the latter urged the people to retain supreme power in themselves and to delegate the task of legislation to a senate or some appointed leader who was to act in conjunction with some legislative body. The same doctrine had been stated in the thirteenth century by the famous jurist and cleric Bracton in these words: "The king is subject to God and to the Law."

When Charles I of England (1625–1649) tried to carry further his father's absolutistic claims he provoked the rebellion that sent him to the block of the executioner. Nevertheless, the same claims were revived by Charles II (1660–1685), and by the year 1660 royal absolutism was firmly established in every part of Europe, with the exception of Holland and Switzerland. In England the absolute supremacy of the crown was finally done away with by the "Glorious Revolution" of 1688 which made the ruler responsible to a parliament.

The Calvinists, in the course of their struggles with Catholic governments, took exception to the doctrine of the Divine Right of Kings, asserting the right of resistance to "ungodly rulers." The representative system as embodied in the Reformed Presbyterial Church-Order offers one of the first examples of representative government in the modern sense, based on a "social contract" that was fashioned in accordance with the model of the covenants of Israel, from which the Jews derived their kings and laws. The Calvinist idea of the State, however, was strictly governed by religious principles, and truly democratic institutions were anticipated only in the administration of the New England states, where the European class system was nonexistent and where political institutions were derived directly from church institutions. And yet there was a vast difference between these patriarchally ruled state organisms with their stern ethico-religious discipline, anchored in the divine and natural law, and Rousseau's (cf. p. 376) naturalistic Contract State, the product of the arbitrary will of fluctuating majorities.

Despite the changes from limited to unrestricted absolutism that took place in most European countries in the course of the seventeenth century, the real and radical break with the medieval idea of civilization occurred first in Oliver Cromwell's (1599–1658) "Commonwealth," in which the separation of State and Church was proclaimed and different denominations were (in theory) to be tolerated side by side.

Louis XIV and the German Empire. The Peace of Westphalia had given France the much coveted opportunity to influence and control to a large extent the future destinies of Germany. Louis XIV was firmly resolved to continue his anti-Hapsburg policies and to bring about the permanent enfeeblement of Austria. To achieve this end and at the same time to keep the Empire in a state of confusion and disruption, he made use of the princes' opposition to the emperor, assuming the role of a protector of their prerogatives. When Emperor Ferdinand died in 1657 Louis tried in vain to secure the succession of the elector of Bavaria. Much against his wishes, the Hapsburg Leopold I (1658–1705), archduke of Austria and king of Bohemia and Hungary, received the votes of the electoral princes. But the new emperor found himself immediately confronted by the "Rhenish League" (*Rheinbund*), a powerful combination of German princes, headed by the elector of Mainz and in alliance with France. The avowed purpose of the League was the protection of the liberties of the princes against possible imperial encroachments, and the preservation of the terms of the Westphalian Peace.

A few years later the Imperial Diet, as constituted by the same peace treaty, composed of the three colleges of the princes, the nobility, and the cities, established itself on a permanent basis in the city of Regensburg, the several states and principalities being represented by delegates and ambassadors. This "Permanent Diet" continued its shadowy existence for the next 143 years (1663–1806) and died a belated death in the year of the dissolution of the Holy Roman Empire. It was merely a debating society, in which France's voice carried more weight than all the others combined, and it accomplished little in the realm of practical politics. The imperial court (*Reichskammergericht*), established in Frankfurt on the Main in 1495, was moved to Speyer in 1527 and to Wetzlar in 1693, where it likewise lingered on to the end of the Empire in 1806, when it was found that 6000 law suits were still pending and that some of the unfinished business dated back one hundred years. The German empire as such included over 1700 independent or semi-independent princes and nobles, vassals of the emperor in name only, three hundred of whom were secular or ecclesiastical sovereigns of German principalities.

Louis XIV, conscious of the strength of his position and well aware of the inherent weakness of the Empire, carried out a comprehensive program of national aggrandizement at German expense. His designs aimed at the realization of what he called France's "natural frontiers," meaning the acquisition of all of Alsace and most of the other territories on the left bank of the Rhine, including Franche-Comté, the Rhenish Palatinate, the Spanish Netherlands, and part of the Dutch Republic. If these plans were crowned with success, Louis would not only be strong enough to prevent a reunion of the Spanish and Austrian Hapsburgs, but he would be able to establish an undisputed hegemony of France in Europe. Feeling himself to be the heir of Charlemagne, he dreamed of disinheriting the Hapsburgs and of resurrecting the Frankish Empire under French leadership. In this grandiose political scheme the river Rhine was to become the natural and national boundary of France. In advancing his claims Louis could count not only on the sympathy and support of most of the German princes, but also on the aid of Sweden, which owed her position as a great power to her collaboration with the policies of Richelieu and Mazarin (cf. p. 287 sq.). The anti-imperial sentiment in Poland and the Franco-Turkish alliance (cf. p. 293 sq.) forged the remaining links in the combination of powers which encircled the German Empire on all sides.

All the odds seemed to be against the Empire. If Louis had confined himself to his anti-imperial policies he might have succeeded in his far-reaching plans. However, the aspirations of French imperialism transcended Louis' continental European ambitions. In his attempt to extend French political and economic supremacy to the colonial possessions overseas, he challenged the rival claims of Spain, England, and the Netherlands alike. Louis overreached himself and, though partly successful in his aggressive policies against the Empire, suffered ultimate defeat at the hands of the Great Powers of Europe.

In 1667 Louis attacked the Spanish Netherlands and in the following year invaded Franche-Comté. Sweden decided to join a Dutch-English alliance against the French king, and in the Peace Treaty of Aix-la-Chapelle (Aachen, 1668) Louis returned Franche-Comté but retained eleven cities in Flanders. In 1670 he drove Duke Charles of Lorraine out of his hereditary domains and annexed this province of the Empire. In 1672 he launched an unprovoked attack against the Dutch who, commanded by Prince William of Orange (1650–1702), the subsequent King William III of England, broke the force of the invasion by opening the dikes and flooding the countryside. In its defensive war Holland was aided not only by Emperor Leopold and the elector of Brandenburg but eventually also by Denmark, Spain, and England. An ironclad alliance between the Empire and Spain was answered by Louis with the annexation of the ten imperial towns of Alsace and the first devastation of the Palatinate by the troops of General Turenne. In the Peace of Nymwegen (1678) France obtained Franche-Comté from Spain and retained a number of border towns in the Spanish Netherlands and the imperial city of Freiburg im Breisgau.

In the years after the conclusion of the Peace of Nymwegen Louis tried to achieve one of his major aims, the annexation of Alsace. He instituted the

"Chambers of Reunion" (*Chambres de Réunion*), specially appointed French law courts, whose task it was to establish by means of casuistry and sophistry the historical French titles of sovereignty to the contested territories. Military occupation followed promptly every legal decision of these courts, and the seizure of the imperial city of Strasbourg in 1681 completed the annexation of Alsace.

While a number of German princes gradually awoke to a realization of the ignominious position of the Empire, concerted opposition to France was hampered by the pro-French sympathies of some of the most influential principalities, among them Brandenburg, whose elector was completely drawn into the orbit of French imperialism. Nevertheless, many of the princes joined with the emperor and the kings of Spain and Sweden in the defensive League of Augsburg (1686). When Louis violated the terms of the Truce of Regensburg of 1684 (which had left him in possession of all the recently annexed territories) by a renewed attack on the Rhenish Palatinate (1687), he found himself confronted not only by a suddenly aroused and united Germany but simultaneously by a European coalition of powers, headed by England.

In the meantime the Turks, France's allies, had been halted in their westward advance, and this Franco-Turkish friendship as well as Louis' persecution of the French Protestants (Huguenots) had alienated many of France's sympathizers among the Protestant princes of Germany. About 200,000 Huguenots, deprived of the freedom of worship and education, left France and found refuge in Holland, England, and Prussia, the same powers that were now solidly lined up against further French aggression.

The winter of 1688–1689 witnessed a second and even more cruel and senseless devastation of the Palatinate by order of General Mélac, and the destruction of the cities of Worms, Speyer, Mannheim, and Heidelberg with their historic monuments and art treasures. The Heidelberg castle, beautiful even in ruins, stands to this present day as an eloquent witness of wanton destruction.

The Peace of Ryswik (1697) marked the end of the war against the Palatinate and brought humiliating terms for Louis: he was forced to return all the territories which had been adjudged to France by the Chambers of Reunion, with the exception of the city of Strasbourg and the occupied regions of Alsace, and the duke of Lorraine was to be reinstated in his sovereign rights and lands. That Louis was able to retain part of his booty on the left bank of the Rhine was due to the fact that the attention of the Empire was absorbed a second time by the Turkish threat of invasion in the East. The emperor decided to sacrifice Alsace in the West in order to be able to put up an impregnable wall of defense in the East. The Peace of Carlowitz (1699) made Hungary part of Austria and raised the Austro-Hungarian monarchy to the rank of a Great Power.

With the following War of the Spanish Succession the Empire was only indirectly concerned. That it was eventually drawn into the conflict was due to the fact that Charles, the Hapsburg pretender to the Spanish crown, was the son of the German emperor (Charles VI, 1711–1740). The other claimant to the Spanish throne was Philip of Anjou, the grandson of Louis XIV, whom the testament of King Charles II of Spain had named as his successor. When Louis XIV tried to press the claims of his grandson by threat of arms, he met with the determined opposition of the *"Grande Alliance,"* consisting of a coalition of Austria, England, Holland, Savoy, and Brandenburg. The French suffered defeat at the hands of John Churchill, the Duke of Marlborough, who deployed his brilliant strategy in the North, and of Prince Eugene of Savoy in the South. The fact that after ten years of struggle Charles, the candidate of the *"Grande Alliance,"* was called to succeed his brother Joseph on the imperial throne, reviving the threat of a reunited Spanish-Austrian Hapsburg empire, created uneasiness and dismay in the war councils of the allies and more particularly among the English and the Dutch, who were as much opposed to a European hegemony of the Anjous and Bourbons as they were to that of the Hapsburgs, considering either one to be contrary to the cherished principle of the European "balance of power." The peace treaties of Utrecht (1713) and Rastatt (1714) reflected the conflicting ideas among the member states of the *"Grande Alliance"* and their endeavor to keep France powerful enough to check Hapsburg ambitions.

The Bourbon Philip V was allowed to succeed to the Spanish throne, with the stipulation that the crowns of Spain and France were never to be reunited. The emperor received the Spanish Netherlands, Milan, and Naples, while the elector of Brandenburg, Frederick III (cf. p. 312), obtained the privilege of assuming the title of "King *in* Prussia." France retained Alsace but had failed in her designs to dominate Germany by making the Rhine her national boundary. The states of Louis XIV were financially exhausted by a series of long and costly wars, whose net gain was out of proportion to the material waste and physical exertion involved. Germany's position as a nation was not much stronger than it had been after the catastrophe of the Thirty Years' War: she was still a pawn in the hands of scheming European politicians; foreign potentates were still represented among the German Estates; and German princes were still entangled in foreign political interests and alignments. The Swedish king ruled part of Pomerania and was represented in the Diet at Regensburg, while the elector of Saxony became king of Poland in 1697, and a member of the Welf dynasty of Hanover ascended the English throne as George I (1714–1727), thus linking Hanover to England by a bond of personal union. The imperial house itself had large possessions in Hungary, the Netherlands, and Italy, finding it more and more difficult to harmonize its European with its specifically German interests and obligations.

The Rise of Brandenburg-Prussia. The constellation of the European powers experienced a decisive change toward the end of the seventeenth and at the beginning of the eighteenth century. Two newcomers, Prussia and Russia, had been added to the three Great Powers of Europe: France, Austria, and England. While the gigantic struggle for economic and colonial supremacy between France and England eventually overshadowed every other event, the attempted realization of a balance of power met with ever increasing difficulties, and the two youngest arrivals among the European nations advanced their national and territorial claims with great vigor and determination.

The great Nordic War (1700–1721), fought by King Frederick IV of Denmark, Augustus the Strong of Saxony-Poland, and Tsar Peter the Great of Russia against the young ruler of Sweden, Charles XII, had ended with Sweden's defeat in the battle of Poltawa (1709). The allies were joined in 1714 by Prussia and Hanover, and the Peace of Stockholm (1720) restored to Prussia the larger part of Pomerania (annexed by Sweden during the Thirty Years' War), including the mouths of the Oder and Vistula rivers. Sweden yielded her position as a Great Power to Russia, which had been able to conquer Estonia and Livonia and thus dominated the Baltic. In their pursuit of the Swedes the Russian armies had advanced into the territories of Pomerania, Mecklenburg, and Holstein, and during one phase of the war Peter the Great had visualized the acquisition of these lands for Russia. French-Russian rivalry finally prevented the full realization of the Russian ambitions, but Russian influence nevertheless extended henceforth into the German empire, adding another element of foreign pressure and thereby increasing the internal instability.

a) The Great Elector (1640–1688) and the Construction of the Prussian State. The meteoric rise of Brandenburg-Prussia from a petty North German state to a leading European power was due to the political and military leadership of three members of the Hohenzollern family: Frederick William (the "Great Elector"), King Frederick William I (grandson of the Great Elector, 1713–1740), and King Frederick II ("the Great," great-grandson of the "Great Elector," 1740–1786). Frederick III of Brandenburg (1688–1713), the son of the Great Elector, was inefficient and wasteful in his administration but a patron of the arts and sciences and, as a reward for his support of the emperor in the Spanish War of Succession, was given the privilege of calling himself "King Frederick I *in* Prussia" (West Prussia still being part of Poland).

The Hohenzollerns of both the Swabian and the Frankish-Brandenburg-Prussian Line derived their name from their ancestral castle on top of Mount Zollern in Swabia. As counts of Nuremberg the members of the family increased their possessions by inheritance as well as by their repeated support of imperial policies and military campaigns. Frederick VI was given the Stadtholdership and later on the hereditary possession of the Mark Brandenburg (1415). The Great Elector, margrave of Brandenburg, after having freed East Prussia from Polish overlordship in the course of the Thirty Years' War, acquired eastern Pomerania and some other territories in the Treaty of Westphalia. By inheritance the three small duchies of Cleves, Mark, and Ravensberg on the lower Rhine had become part of Brandenburg-Prussia in 1614. All these territories were widely scattered, disorganized, and without natural cohesion. It was the Great Elector's historic accomplishment to have turned this conglomeration of lands into a unified state that was animated by the definite political and cultural will to assume leadership among the principalities of northern Germany and to make Brandenburg-Prussia the foremost Protestant power of the Empire.*

The Great Elector achieved his goal by circumspection, thrift, and political shrewdness. Despite the tenacity with which he clung to his constructive ideas for Prussia, he did not lose sight of the larger issues of imperial policy, and when Louis XIV in 1658 attempted to bribe him into supporting the French king's aspirations to the imperial throne, Frederick William gave his decisive vote to the Austrian candidate (Leopold I). In 1672 he came to the defense of the Dutch Republic against Louis' unprovoked attack, and when the Swedish allies of France invaded the Mark Brandenburg in 1675 and the armies of the Great Elector found themselves outnumbered two to one, he achieved a major victory over the enemy in the battle of Fehrbellin. In 1686 his army joined the imperial troops in the war that was waged against Turkey for the reconquest of Hungary, and in 1688 he concluded a secret treaty with Prince William of Orange, according to which 6000 Brandenburg soldiers were to assist the prince in his struggle for the British throne.

If the Great Elector's foreign policy was naturally confined to efforts that aimed at territorial unification and national consolidation, his internal reforms offered remarkable evidence of prudent and constructive government. A small standing army represented a powerful weapon of defense and provided that amount of security that was necessary to carry out the intended social reforms. The Great Elector, realizing that the well-being of his state rested on a well-balanced system of production and consumption, on a healthy integration of agrarian and industrial interests, improved the system of land tenure and the methods of soil conservation and at the same time encouraged trade and industry.

Colonists from Holland and Huguenot exiles from France were settled on Prussian soil, and their efficiency and skill contributed greatly to the rising prosperity of the country. The desertlike regions around Berlin developed into flourishing provinces, and the capital itself doubled its population during Frederick William's reign. A regular postal service connected outlying districts of the state, breaking down the monopoly of the Empire-supported Thurn and Taxis posts (cf. p. 189). The Frederick William Canal was constructed, connecting the Spree with the Oder and, by joining up with the Havel and Elbe rivers, provided an uninterrupted waterway to the North Sea. The colonial foundations overseas, however, the East India Company, and the settlements on the West Coast of Africa, while

---

* Lutheranism was first overtly adopted by the Elector Joachim II of Brandenburg in 1539.

proving the Great Elector's spirit of enterprise, did not warrant the expenditure involved and were short lived. When Frederick William died the Prussian State was strong enough to command the attention and respect of the leading European statesmen.

b) King Frederick William I (1713–1740) and the Growth of Prussian Militarism. The Great Elector's son, Frederick III (Frederick I as "King *in* Prussia," 1688–1713), proved unworthy of the heritage bequeathed to him, and his love of splendor and ostentation as well as the corruption and extravagance of the royal household brought the state to the verge of bankruptcy. An iron will was needed to restore the continuity of the policies pursued by the Great Elector. Frederick's son and successor, Frederick William I, the soldier-king, was a ruler who possessed those qualities that were to make Prussia not only respected but feared as well. He possessed a brutal and tyrannical will, free from the inhibitions of sentiment and untouched by the refinements of taste and culture, an indefatigable working capacity coupled with frugality and economy, and a sense of duty that was rooted in religious convictions. These were the qualities that made Frederick William I at once admired and feared, a tyrant in the family circle and an autocrat in his country. What adds a human touch to the harsh features of this character is his unswerving devotion to the service of his country, an almost humble modesty in his personal needs and wants, his high sense of responsibility, and a self-effacement that was ever willing to sacrifice personal happiness for the sake of the commonweal. If he demanded much of others, he demanded even more of himself, and his own life was a perfect paradigm of the sternest of discipline.

During the rule of Frederick William I, Sweden ceased to exist as a great military power, and the Treaty of Stockholm (1720), concluded at the end of a series of wars with Poland, Russia, Denmark, and Prussia, adjudged the greater part of western Pomerania to the Prussian king. When Frederick William I died he left to his heir a state that was recognized as the most thoroughly militarized power of Europe and one of the most self-sufficient and prosperous of contemporary absolutistic monarchies. The king of Prussia had created an army that in numerical strength was surpassed by few in Europe and in military efficiency was second to none. The "long fellows" (*die langen Kerle*) of the regiment of the royal guards, recruited from many lands by notoriously dubious methods, were the king's greatest pride, and he took a childish delight in everything that pertained to military drill and soldierly display. He went even so far as to force marriages between especially tall men and women, in the hope of breeding a generation of giants.

Following the mercantilistic trend of his age, Frederick William I furthered the development of domestic agriculture, encouraged the home industries by protective tariffs, and strove in every way to make his country economically self-supporting. In his *Instructions for the General Directory of Finance, War, and Domains* he pledged his adherence to the creed of all absolute monarchs: "We are lord and king, and can do what we will." He strove to do away with inefficiency in government, with "red tape" and legal quibbling. If the members of the General Directory keep their minds on the service of the king, they "will all have their hands full and will not need to campaign with law suits against each other. But the lawyers, these poor devils, will be as futile as the fifth wheel on a cart."

The king had achieved his aim and established Prussian sovereignty on a "rock of bronze." He had built an impregnable political organism which the superior statesmanship of his son was to endow with the social and cultural substance of a civilized state.

c) King Frederick II ("the Great," 1740–1786) and Prusso-Austrian Dualism. Emperor Charles VI had died in 1740 without a male heir. Before his death he had secured the Hapsburg territories for his daughter Maria Theresa by invoking the "Pragmatic Sanction" of 1713. Frederick II had succeeded his father as king of Prussia in the same year (1740) in which Maria Theresa, the archduchess of Austria, became queen of Hungary and Bohemia and advanced her claims to the imperial succession. Frederick, who at the age of thirty had become the ruler of the powerful Prussian State, made his recognition of Maria Theresa's succession dependent on the cession of the province of Silesia to Prussia. Under the pretext that Austria was no longer strong enough to protect the liberties of the Silesians, Frederick occupied that province in a surprise coup, at the same time offering Maria Theresa an alliance in return for a full recognition of his claims to the Silesian crownlands. Maria Theresa's refusal led to the first Silesian war (1740–1742), running concurrently in part with the Austrian War of Succession (1741–1748), which was fought for the possession of the imperial crown. Both the Elector Charles of Bavaria and Frederick Augustus of Saxony had married daughters of the late Emperor Joseph I and laid claims to the imperial succession.* Following the example of Prussia, and with the approval and support of France, the German electors gave their votes not to Francis Stephen of Lorraine, Maria Theresa's husband, but to the Elector Charles of Bavaria (1742–1745) who, as Charles VII, thus became the only non-Hapsburg emperor between 1438 and 1806. Austria's claims

---

*

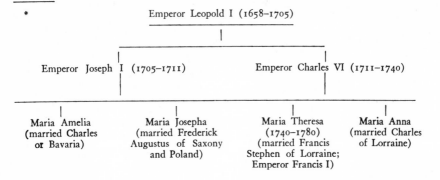

Emperor Leopold I (1658–1705)

Emperor Joseph I (1705–1711)   Emperor Charles VI (1711–1740)

Maria Amelia (married Charles of Bavaria)   Maria Josepha (married Frederick Augustus of Saxony and Poland)   Maria Theresa (1740–1780) (married Francis Stephen of Lorraine; Emperor Francis I)   Maria Anna (married Charles of Lorraine)

were supported by Russia, Holland, and England, while France, Spain, Bavaria, and Saxony fought on Frederick's side. In the Treaty of Breslau (1742) Prussia gained Upper and Lower Silesia.

In the second Silesian war (1744–1745), Prussia, France, and Bavaria were opposed by Austria, England, and Sardinia, and the Treaty of Dresden (1745) confirmed Frederick in the possession of Silesia. The death of Emperor Charles VII and the election of Francis Stephen (Francis I, 1745–1765) as emperor strengthened Maria Theresa's cause by adding considerably to the prestige of the house of Hapsburg. The general European war ended with the Treaty of Aix-la-Chapelle (Aachen) in 1748, whereby Frederick's annexation of Silesia was once more confirmed.

As far as the adversaries, Austria and Prussia, were concerned, the results of the two Silesian wars were undecisive, inasmuch as the fundamental issue, the rivalry between the houses of Hapsburg and Brandenburg-Prussia, remained unsettled. The struggle of France and England for supremacy in their colonial empires in the New World (the "French and Indian War") coincided with the Seven Years' War (1756–1763) on the European continent, which was fought by Frederick almost singlehanded against a triple alliance of Austria, Russia, and France. Political allegiances and coalitions shifted so rapidly that it is sometimes difficult to give a rational account of the changes on the European chessboard which made partners in arms one day, implacable foes the next. While in the War of the Austrian Succession (1741–1748) England and Austria stood together against France and Prussia, in the Seven Years' War France and Austria were aligned against England and Prussia. Hapsburg and Bourbon, archenemies for the past two hundred years, made common cause against the king of Prussia, whose aggressive policies seemed to constitute the latest threat against the European balance of power.

Frederick invaded Saxony and Bohemia and for five years fought with varying success, aided only by insignificant military forces from some of the minor German princes and by subsidies from England. Nevertheless, he held at bay a coalition of three empires whose population outnumbered that of Prussia twelve to one. The labors of Frederick's ancestors now bore fruit, and the long-established discipline of the Prussian armies, the solid structure and admirable organization of the Prussian State, combined with Frederick's strategic genius, were rewarded by the successive victories over the French at Rossbach (Province of Saxony, 1757), over the Austrians at Leuthen (Silesia, 1757), and over the Russians at Zorndorf (Brandenburg, 1758). Serious reverses failed to shake the Prussian king's confidence in his ultimate triumph. In the sixth year of the war the Empress Elizabeth of Russia died (1762) and Tsar Peter III followed her on the throne; he was an admirer of Frederick and proposed an immediate peace and a Russo-Prussian alliance. France, exhausted by her colonial war with England, likewise deserted the Austrian cause by concluding the separate Peace of Fontainebleau (1763). Maria Theresa, in the Peace of Hubertusburg of the same year, had to reconcile herself to the definitive surrender of Silesia to Prussia.

Despite the fact that as far as the geographical map of Europe was concerned the Seven Years' War had resulted in but few territorial changes, it had created an entirely new situation with respect to the prestige and relative significance of Prussia and Austria. Prussia had proven and established herself as the second great power within the German Empire. The Prusso-Austrian dualism of interests and ambitions had come into the open and provided a keynote in the following struggle for national unity and the cultural integration of modern Germany. The cession of Silesia to Prussia made Austria more than ever before a southeastern border state of the Empire. Austria's foreign policy in the second half of the eighteenth century was determined by her desire to revenge the rape of her former province. This explains the otherwise incomprehensible alliance with the French monarchy, an alliance which involved the severance of those ties that had bound Austria to England ever since the days of Prince William of Orange. It was this new alignment of powers that provided the bases for England's victorious colonial wars against France, so that William Pitt was correct in saying that England conquered America in Germany. The distribution of the colonial empires of the future was in part at least decided on German soil, with Germany having neither a say nor a share in the matter.

The Prusso-Austrian dualism was not only due, however, to rival political claims, but just as much to the dynamism of spiritual forces that were embodied in the two powers. Austria was the traditional bulwark of German Catholicism, while Prussia had made herself the spearhead of an active and aggressive Protestantism. The two countries developed their respective cultures in accordance with different intellectual and moral patterns. The almost constant political tension provided not only for frequent conflicts and clashes, but likewise in the end for a growing enrichment and variety of German civilization as a whole. The integration and utilization of these polar forces within the political structure of a "Greater Germany" loomed as a faint possibility even in the eighteenth century, but the factors that worked against its realization — the particularism of the German principalities, the shortsightedness or selfishness of political leaders, and the complexity that characterized the general European struggle for spheres of interest and economic power — were obstacles that proved too formidable. Thus the following two centuries offer the sad spectacle of a relentless Prusso-Austrian contest for supremacy rather than that of a constructive effort for co-ordination and unity.

A most unfortunate result of the Prusso-Austrian rivalry in the eighteenth century was the ever growing influence of foreign powers in German politics. Austria, to gain the support of France and Russia, sacrificed the formerly Spanish Netherlands (the territory of Belgium) to France, and East Prussia to Russia (Russian occupation, 1758–1762). Almost in the same measure in which the French danger in the West subsided, the Russian pressure in the East increased. The rival interests of Prussia and Austria offered an opportunity for Russia to assume the role of an arbiter in German affairs. Both Austria and Prussia tried to further their political interests by courting the favor of Russia. When Catherine II of Russia (1762–1796), who succeeded her husband, Tsar Peter III, after the latter's assassination, showed her determination to make Poland part of the Russian empire, it was Frederick the Great who suggested the first partition of Poland (1772) between Prussia, Russia, and Austria. Although Prussia's share in that shady deal was smaller than that of either Austria or Russia, Frederick acquired West Prussia, which for the past three hundred years had been under Polish sovereignty, and thus united East Prussia with the province of Brandenburg. The city of Danzig* remained Polish for the time being owing to the pressure of England, which had a big stake in the Polish trade and did not want to see that important Baltic seaport change hands.

The empress of Russia felt that it was to her country's advantage to perpetuate the Prusso-Austrian dualism. She showed her hand again in negotiating the Peace of Teschen (Silesia), ending the Bavarian War of Succession (1778–1789), the last in the series of wars that Frederick the Great waged against Austria, in which he frustrated the attempt of Maria Theresa's son, Emperor Joseph II (1765–1790, cf. p. 302) to annex part of Bavaria. The peace treaty gave Austria only a tiny fraction of the desired territory, while Prussia emerged from this conflict without any territorial gain. The foundation of the "League of Princes" (*Fürstenbund*) in 1785 represented Frederick's final and crowning attempt to check Hapsburg expansion in the empire.

d) Frederick the Great: An "Enlightened Despot." The forty-six years of Frederick's rule were almost evenly divided between the exploits of war and the works of peace. The twenty-three years that followed the bloody Seven Years' War were only interrupted by the brief campaign of the Bavarian War of Succession. It was in his peaceful and constructive endeavors that Frederick proved himself the model representative of "enlightened despotism."

The king considered himself "the first servant of the state" and ruled his country in a benevolent and patriarchal, but nevertheless thoroughly autocratic and absolutistic, fashion. The evaluation of his accomplishments as a German prince and statesman differs in accordance with the political theories and attachments of his biographers. Those who favor the idea of a "Greater Germany," either with the inclusion of both Austria and Prussia

---

* Danzig, first mentioned in 997, was added in 1308 to the territories of the Teutonic Knights and, after the decline of the Order, was linked with Poland by Personal Union (after 1454). It reached the peak of its prosperity about 1600 and lost much of its former significance in the following period of Polish decline. In 1793 Danzig was given to Prussia, was made a "Free City" by Napoleon (1807), returned to Prussia in 1814, and became the capital of West Prussia in 1878. It was separated from Germany by the Treaty of Versailles (1919) and declared a "free city" under the protectorate of the League of Nations. The Treaty of Potsdam (1945) gave Danzig to Poland.

and the co-ordination of their forces and spheres of interest or under Hapsburg leadership, see in him the destroyer of the integrity and prestige of the Holy Roman Empire. Those who read and interpret German history from the Prussian point of view praise him as the great pioneer of the unification of Germany under Prussian leadership, the ruler who laid the foundations for the powerful national state of Bismarck and William II (cf. p. 546 sqq.). Whatever judgment the individual historian may feel inclined to make his own, it is certain that Frederick, like most of the other German princes, was guided in his political plans not by the interests of Germany as a whole but by the interests and needs of his own Prussian State and its aggrandizement.

It makes one of the most startling chapters in the study of human psychology to follow the development of this enigmatic character from a rather effeminate and indolent poetical dreamer to one of the most imposing and uncompromising political figures of modern history. The hard school of experience through which Frederick went under the one-sided military education of his early youth, in humiliating subjection and violent opposition to the tyrannical regime of his father, explains in part the bitter cynicism and utter disillusionment of his later years. His thwarted emotional life and the forced marriage to Princess Elizabeth Christine of Brunswick undoubtedly contributed to making Frederick the avowed misogynist he was, whose anti-Austrian policies were stimulated and intensified by the fact that the Hapsburg lands were ruled by a woman, and who in the course of the Seven Years' War complained that he was persecuted by the "Three Furies" (Maria Theresa of Austria; Elizabeth of Russia; and Madame de Pompadour, the all-powerful mistress of King Louis XV of France). His attempted and frustrated desertion and flight and the following execution of his youthful friend and accomplice, Lieutenant Hans Hermann Katte, marked the decisive break in the life of the crown prince of Prussia, after which he resigned himself to the destiny that his position imposed upon him.

After his accession to the throne Frederick's primary concern was the development of the army to an even greater efficiency. He considered the heritage of military organization that his father had bequeathed to him as the most precious asset in the consolidation of the Prussian State. By the end of the seventeenth century standing armies had become a common institution in all German principalities. At the end of the Seven Years' War Frederick had raised the strength of his armed forces from eighty thousand to two hundred thousand men. Prussia had become one of the foremost military powers of Europe, and as most of the contingents of the Prussian army were recruited among the native population, the Prussian soldier developed a sense of duty and a patriotic sentiment which were invaluable in both war and peace. Prussia became the first and foremost of modern nations to cultivate a Spartan ideal of military discipline, combined with a consciousness of national solidarity.

The internal policies of Frederick the Great were inspired by certain principles that he had adopted from some of his favorite writers and philosophers: among the ancients, the Stoics; and among the moderns, Leibniz (1646–1716), Christian Wolff (1679–1754), and Voltaire (1694–1778). "Philosophers should be the teachers of the world and the guides of princes," he wrote. In his youth he had written a book entitled *Anti-Machiavell* (1739), in which he set forth his own ideas on the obligations of the ruler toward his subjects, and in general opposed the amoralistic political doctrines of Machiavelli (cf. p. 247 sq.). But in practice and especially after the bitter experiences of the Seven Years' War Frederick developed more and more into one of Machiavelli's most docile disciples. By that time "the first servant of the state" had become an exceedingly lonely individual, cut off from all family ties and associated with hardly any man or woman whom he could call his friend. He had correctly foreseen that his marriage would turn out to be a failure and that there would be "one more unhappy princess in the world." Even in the colloquial atmosphere of the "tobacco college" at Potsdam and Sans-Souci, where the king used to spend merry evenings in the circle of scholars and artists whom he had drawn to his court, where he would play the flute or read from his own manuscripts — even here real human warmth was strangely lacking and Frederick's lonely majesty seemed to erect invisible but unscalable barriers. The king's real friends were his dogs and horses, with whom he would converse in German, while on most other occasions he gave preference to French.

Frederick's admiration for French *esprit,* the French language, French literature and culture was almost boundless, while he was unaware of the great classical revival of German literary and intellectual life that was gradually taking shape under his very eyes. He had nothing but praise for the tragedies of Corneille and Racine and despised the works of the young Goethe (cf. p. 407 sqq.) as a "detestable imitation of the abominable plays of Shakespeare." Among the famous Frenchmen who contributed to making his court a great center of enlightened thought was Maupertuis (1698–1759), the French physician and mathematician, who conducted an arctic expedition to Lapland to prove the flattening of the poles of the earth. In 1741 Frederick made him president of the Academy.

With Voltaire, whom Frederick had likewise invited to his court and whom he considered the greatest genius of the age, his relations were more complex. It was a kind of love-hate that bound him to the great French "philosophe," historian, playwright, and satirist. Frederick was fascinated by Voltaire's keen and critical mind, by his wit and *esprit,* and by his courageous fight for a humanitarian morality, freed from dogma and sectarianism. The initial familiarity between Frederick and Voltaire ended abruptly when the king ordered the confiscation of one of Voltaire's satires, aimed at Maupertuis. Voltaire's intercepted flight from Prussia and his following arrest were the remote cause for the satirist's publication of *The Private Life of the King of Prussia,* the bitter fruit of a pent-up resentment.

In accordance with his moral and political convictions Frederick proceeded in his work of social reform in the highhanded manner of paternalistic government. He imposed his ideas and his will on men and institutions alike. The royal decrees extended to the procedures of criminal and civil law; to military, financial, and social administration; to agriculture, industry, and commerce; to the modes and manners of thinking and living.

One of his first measures provided for the abolition of torture in Prussia. In matters of religion he favored a spirit of toleration that was to make it possible for "everyone to get to heaven in his own fashion" (*Jeder kann nach seiner Façon selig werden*). Accepting the ideas of eighteenth-century "Deism" (cf. p. 356 sq.), he had no use for theological dogma and established churches, although he would not interfere with their cults. He considered it politically expedient to grant complete freedom of worship and even invited the Jesuits to teach in the Prussian schools after their order had been expelled from most European countries and temporarily suspended (1773–1814) by papal decree.

The hardest work of social reconstruction had to be done after the sufferings and devastations of the Seven Years' War. Within a few years Frederick had accomplished the task of healing most of the wounds inflicted on Prussia by the invading armies and the prolonged state of siege. By means of a state-controlled inflation of the currency he managed to emerge from the war with a balanced budget. By a systematic policy of colonization and settlement he added several thousand people to the population of Prussia, increased the area of the arable land, and, by encouraging agriculture and the home industries, made his states practically independent of foreign markets. The manufacture of silk was introduced by a royal decree which commanded the planting of mulberry trees and the cultivation of the imported silkworm. Settlers from foreign countries were granted exemptions from taxes and customs duties, and with their aid 225,000 acres of waste land and marsh were reclaimed along the shores of the Oder, the Warthe, the Vistula, and the Netze. High protective tariffs practically eliminated foreign competition, and an administrative board, composed entirely of French officials, was entrusted with the enforcement of these highly unpopular measures. As coffee could not be grown in Prussia, Frederick had his "coffee smellers" enter and search private homes at will, to prevent wholesale smuggling.

The same Spartan discipline that ruled in the Prussian army was made the basis of the life and occupations of the entire aristocracy. They were under the constant supervision of the crown and had to pay dearly for belonging to a caste whose special privileges were outweighed by the heavy burdens they had to carry in the service of their government. Frederick's attempted abolition of serfdom among the peasantry met with the determined opposition of the landed nobility of Pomerania and proved unsuccessful for that reason.

In all his endeavors Frederick II was guided by a fundamental conviction that is best expressed in the preamble of the *"Codex Fridericianus,"* the code of Prussian common law that was published after the king's death: "The welfare of the state and its inhabitants is the object of society and the limit of legislation; laws must limit the liberty and the rights of the citizens only in the interest of general welfare."

The king's mind was as fertile in the speculative as in the practical realm: his collected works, including historical writings, poetry, and musical compositions, fill thirty-one volumes in the edition of the Berlin Academy (1846–1887), to which the over forty-odd volumes of his political correspondence (1879–1931) must be added.

Austria and Prussia After Frederick the Great. Maria Theresa's eldest son, Emperor Joseph II (1765–1790), was another representative of the ideas of "enlightened despotism." His noble intentions, however, lacked so much in practical sense and moderation that Frederick the Great could justly say of him that "he always wishes to take the second step before he has taken the first." In the brief span which followed his mother's death and during which he ruled independently (1780–1790), his far-flung undertakings met with such wholesale failure that in his self-composed epitaph he spoke of himself as a man "who, with the best of intentions, was unsuccessful in everything that he undertook."

In his foreign policy he made the mistake of attacking the Turks (1788) in alliance with Catherine of Russia, thereby strengthening Russia's hand in the region of the Black Sea at the expense of Austria's Eastern sphere of interests. His attempts to follow the example of Prussia in creating a strong military state by winning the Bavarian lands for Austria, in exchange for the Austrian Netherlands, were frustrated by Frederick's watchfulness and superior diplomacy. With the aid of his recently created "League of Princes" the Prussian king succeeded in checking Joseph's every move. His endeavors to make German the official and "universal" language in all the territories of Austrian administration, and to Germanize racially and ethnically non-Germanic populations, resulted in dangerous uprisings in Flanders, Hungary, and the Tyrol. When he tried to enforce by decree the principles of enlightened despotism, abolishing torture, advocating religious toleration ("Edict of Toleration," 1781), curtailing the autonomy of ecclesiastical administration and the privileges of the nobles, and in general aiming at a more equitable social order, he met with a negative response, with passive resistance, censure, or open rebellion in each individual case.

Whatever may be said in just criticism of many of Joseph's hasty and sometimes ill-considered reforms, there is little doubt that both he and his brother Leopold II (1790–1792), who succeeded him on the throne, were undeviating in their loyalty to the idea of the German empire as the embodiment of a unified Central Europe. They kept this idea alive amidst all the vicissitudes of the Prusso-Austrian struggle for power and supremacy. It was their profound conviction that the Empire was doomed if a way could not be found to unite and rally Austria and Prussia in a common effort for a common cause.

To the detriment of the Empire neither King Frederick William II of Prussia (1786-1797), the nephew and successor of Frederick the Great (his marriage remained childless), nor Emperor Francis II (1792-1806), the son of Emperor Leopold II, who succeeded his father and, in 1804, assumed the title of Emperor of Austria (1804-1835) — neither of these two rulers was big and farseeing enough to place the interests of the Empire above small regional politics. Frederick William II was a frivolous despot who possessed none of the moral qualifications of his predecessor, whose anti-Austrian policy he abandoned without offering any constructive political idea as a substitute. He showed himself opposed to the plan that had been advocated by Duke Charles Augustus of Weimar, calling for the transformation of the "League of Princes" into a North German League under the leadership of Prussia. But the attempted co-operation with Austria, symbolically sealed by the Convention of Reichenbach (1790), was rendered

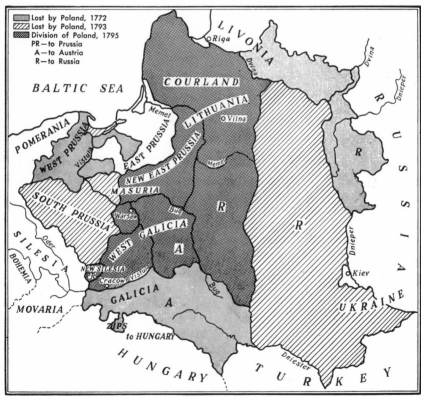

From *Der Grosse Herder*, Herder, Freiburg i. Br.

Partitions of Poland.

ineffective by continued rivalry and mutual distrust. Francis II likewise was motivated in his policies by Austrian rather than common German interests. He dealt a deathblow to the idea of the Empire when, contrary to imperial law, he made himself emperor of Austria.

It was during the reign of Francis II and Frederick William II that the *second and third partitions of Poland* took place. The first dismemberment of the Polish State (cf. p. 316) had been followed by a political and social reform movement in the territory that was left of the once proud Polish kingdom. But to prevent Poland's recovery and to create a new pretext for foreign intervention, Catherine of Russia fostered a rebellion against the new Polish constitution, and in 1793 Russia and Prussia agreed to renew the criminal procedure of 1772. Russia took by far the largest slice, while Prussia received Danzig, Thorn, and the districts of Posen and Gnesen.

In the third partition, which followed in 1795, Austria was once more allowed to share in the robbery: Prussia was given Masuria and the districts around Warsaw; Austria received West Galicia; Russia took the rest. Poland had ceased to exist as a State and was resurrected only when Russia, Germany, and Austria-Hungary were defeated in World War I (1914–1918).

The three partitions of Poland and especially the last one had given Prussia a considerable increase in territory, but at the same time a foreign population which became more and more unmanageable and whose assimilation proved impossible. Russia, on the other hand, had not only gained territorially but also ethnically and politically by bolstering her power with the annexation of a Slavic country.

French Revolution. Coalition Wars. Napoleon. The End of the Empire. While both Prussia and Austria became forgetful of the obligations imposed upon them by their common German destiny and nationality, most of the other European countries went through revolutionary developments which in the end proved fateful to Germany as a whole. England, which had become the foremost maritime and colonial power of the world, lost her North American colonies in the American War of Independence (1773–1783). The North American Republic was founded and based on a constitution which embodied those principles of the sovereignty of the people and the supremacy of the natural law that in part had been handed down from the political theorists of the Middle Ages and their interpreters in the sixteenth and seventeenth centuries (cf. p. 304 sq.) and in part were derived from the political doctrines of the contemporary philosophers.

Sentiment against all absolutistic state governments was running high, and wherever tyranny exercised its oppressive rule popular reaction appealed to the "inalienable rights" of the individual. The extent to which even enlightened despotism in Germany had become susceptible to the social trend of the times is shown by the fact that Frederick the Great had been the first monarch to acknowledge the young American republic, and that Prussia was the first sovereign state to conclude a treaty with the new nation overseas.

a) The French Revolution. France, burdened with debts and faced by national insolvency, was drifting along under the benevolent but weak and shiftless regime of Louis XVI (1774-1792). The *"ancien régime"* was overthrown in 1789, and the king died under the guillotine in 1793.

But the French revolutionary movement did not stop at the boundaries of France: in its aggressive dynamism it spread to the Spanish Peninsula and the Netherlands and could only be halted by the force of arms. The German reaction to the revolution was chiefly emotional for the time being. Before the reign of terror dispelled the beautiful dreams of an earthly paradise under the banners of "liberty, equality, and fraternity," the German intelligentsia had welcomed the French uprising in speeches and poems. The alienation between the two countries that resulted from disappointed hopes was all the more radical, and it was only two generations later that the political reverberations of the ideology of 1789 were definitely felt in Germany.

King Frederick William III of Prussia (1797-1840) was in no way a match for the statesmen and generals of the French Revolution. His attempt to preserve Prussia's neutrality in the Coalition Wars against France proved suicidal, and when Prussia finally, singlehanded, took up arms against Napoleon Bonaparte, it was too late.

The adversaries that France had to respect and fear were England and Austria. The British Isles, owing to their geographical position and the constitutional and moderately parliamentary form of the British government, were comparatively safe from being infected by the germ of the Revolution. England was only too willing to lend a hand in halting the revolutionary wave and in this way to preserve the proverbial European "balance of power" and keep France from challenging Britain's naval superiority. The German Empire, on the other hand, lay directly in the pathway of the advancing French armies, and only the fullest amount of co-operation between the leading German states could have stemmed the tide. Both England and Austria felt themselves as the defenders of human freedom against revolutionary terror and nihilism, but without the active participation of Prussia the victory of France over the Empire was a foregone conclusion.

b) The Aims of French Aggression. It is interesting to note that the leaders of the French Revolution resumed Louis XIV's policy of national expansion, that they tried to carry to a successful conclusion what the greatest of the French monarchs had been unable to accomplish, and that they reproached Louis' decadent successors for having forgotten and betrayed France's traditional national interests. Napoleon Bonaparte knew what he was talking about when he told one of the Prussian envoys: "I shall play the role that Richelieu has assigned to France."

We recall that it had been Louis XIV's great ambition to overthrow the dominion of the Hapsburg emperors, to gain possession of the left bank of the Rhine, and to subject the German states to French supremacy. It would have been the crowning achievement of his life if all these designs had finally converged in the resurrection of the Empire of Charlemagne, with Louis in the possession of the imperial crown. Louis had succeeded in realizing only a fractional part of these far-reaching aims, but the leaders of the Revolution were as good imperialists as their one-time monarch. In 1793 Danton, who at that time had assumed dictatorial powers, declared: "In vain, I say, they try to scare us with the idea that this Republic might grow too large. Its boundaries are marked out by nature. We shall definitely reach them — on the Rhine! It is there that the marches of our Republic must end, and no power on earth shall prevent us from attaining them."

c) *The Coalition Wars.* This, then, was the prize at stake in the several wars between France and Germany that were fought between 1792 and 1805 and that ended with the destruction of the Holy Roman Empire and the temporary extinction of Prussia and Austria as sovereign states.

The Convention of Reichenbach (1790) had made it possible for Austria and Prussia to enter upon the first Coalition War side by side. The legend that this war was forced upon France by the enemies of the Revolution deserves little credence. It is true that Emperor Francis II was impressed by the plea of the French refugees and the plight of Louis XVI. But it is also a well-established fact that the war was declared by the revolutionists when Francis II turned down a French demand for disarmament. There is no doubt that the French leaders needed success in the foreign field in order to be able to master an increasingly complex situation at home.

In 1792 small detachments of the Austrian and Prussian armies marched into the French Champagne but withdrew after the battle of Valmy (cf. Goethe's description in his *Campaign in France*). The French Republican Army of the Rhine followed the retreating allies beyond the Rhine and carried its march of conquest into Flanders. In the following year the First Coalition was formed, comprising England, Holland, Spain, Sardinia, Naples, and Portugal. Two years of warfare proved indecisive, and the Coalition broke up when Prussia concluded with France the separate Peace of Basel (1795). In the following year Archduke Charles of Austria, brother of Emperor Francis II and generalissimo of the Austrian armies, forced the French out of Franconia and Bavaria and back across the Rhine. Prussia, preoccupied with the consolidation of her Polish spoils (cf. p. 322), declared herself completely disinterested in the affairs of the Empire and even gave up her resistance against the annexation of the left bank of the Rhine by the French. Austria and England continued the fight, but in the Treaty of Campo Formio (1797) Austria had to agree to the cession of the left bank of the Rhine.

In the meantime the star of Napoleon Bonaparte (1769–1821) had started on its dazzling course. At the age of twenty-seven the heir, executor, and conqueror of the French Revolution had become commander in chief of the French armies. When the second Coalition War (1799–1802) began, he had made himself "First Consul" of the French Republic. This time Russia, England, Austria, Turkey, Naples, Portugal, the Italian and the Papal

States were united against France, while Prussia stood passively aside. The Austrians, successful in southern Germany and in Switzerland under the command of Archduke Charles, were defeated in the battles of Marengo and Hohenlinden (1800). Several Russian defeats in Switzerland and Holland were followed by Tsar Paul I's withdrawal from the Coalition. In the Peace of Lunéville (1801) the cession of Flanders (Belgium) and the left bank of the Rhine to France was confirmed and Lombardy was added to the French conquests. An imperial deputation was to compensate those German princes who had sustained losses by the French annexation of their territories on the left bank of the Rhine. The result of the *Principal Decree of the Imperial Deputation* of Regensburg (1803) was a complete remaking of the map of Germany. The secularization of all ecclesiastical territories provided the indemnification demanded by the princes of Prussia, Wurtemberg, Bavaria, Baden, Hesse, and Nassau. This arbitrary redistribution of lands and possessions signified the destruction of the ancient imperial constitution and absolutely ignored and denied the rights and prerogatives of the emperor. The German empire was transformed into a loose federation of medium-sized states.

The new order, inspired and supervised by Napoleon, marked the final triumph of all the aims of French imperialism. It was only logical when, in 1804, Napoleon crowned himself emperor of the French. Europe's answer was the formation of the third Coalition, including England, Russia, Austria, Sweden, and Naples, Prussia again maintaining her neutrality. In the Peace of Pressburg (1805) that followed the Austro-Russian defeat in the "Three-Emperors' Battle" (Francis II, Tsar Alexander I, Napoleon) at Austerlitz, Nemesis descended upon Prussia. While Napoleon rewarded his servile vassals and allies, Bavaria, Wurtemberg, and Baden with German land and promoted the dukes of Bavaria and Wurtemberg to the kingship, Prussia was compelled to enter into a humiliating alliance with France (1806). The principalities of southern Germany formally announced their resignation as member states of the Empire and formed the "Confederation of the Rhine" (*Rheinbund*) under the protectorship of France. On August 6, 1806, Emperor Francis II abdicated, and the Holy Roman Empire had come to an inglorious end.

Prussia had actually gained territorially by the secularizations, and her policy of neutrality had saved her from the afflictions of the war. But she had lost in power and prestige, and under the rule of a weak and irresolute king, isolated politically, she had to suffer further humiliations from the Corsican conqueror. And Napoleon was firmly determined to complete his work by the destruction of the last independent state on the European continent.

By breaking solemnly sworn treaties and by a series of other provocations Napoleon finally forced the wavering Frederick William III into the dreaded armed conflict. The Prussian armies and with them the Prussian State were defeated and crushed in the battles of Jena and Auerstedt

(1806), and in the following year the emperor of the French staged his triumphant entry into Berlin. Frederick William III fled to East Prussia, and in the Peace of Tilsit Prussia was forced to cede half of her territory, including all the formerly Polish provinces. All that remained in her possession was the lands east of the Elbe.

French occupation, heavy war indemnities, compulsory disarmament: Prussia was spared none of the humiliations of a nation that had been deprived of her independence and her honor by a merciless victor. Napoleon's brother, Jerome, was made king of Westphalia, and the elector of Saxony was presented with the newly created duchy of Warsaw. France ruled over Holland and the greater part of Germany. The Empire and Crown of Charlemagne had been restored and usurped by Napoleon. Austria survived in a greatly weakened state, and her population was composed of many non-Germanic (Slavic, Magyar, Italian) and heterogeneous elements. In 1809 she made one more attempt to challenge Napoleon's domination of Europe. This time Napoleon marched upon Vienna, and the Peace of Schönbrunn deprived Austria not only of her position as a great power but of some of her most valuable provinces as well. It left the state on the verge of complete financial collapse. Once more the future of Germany looked very dark indeed.

Chapter 11

CIVILIZATION IN THE AGE OF ABSOLUTISM AND ENLIGHTENED DESPOTISM

The Growth of the Absolutistic State. The world which emerged from the turmoil of the Thirty Years' War, and which bears all the earmarks of the civilization that extends into our own time, was characterized by the central position occupied by the secular State and its representative, the prince. In the following centuries the concept of the State becomes more and more abstract, divorced from the personality of the ruler: the absolutism of the prince is followed by the absolute sovereignty of "the State." But during the period which begins with the Renaissance and ends with the French Revolution of 1789 all political power is concentrated in the person of the sovereign who is responsible to no one but himself, in accordance with the political principles of Machiavelli (cf. p. 247 sq.) and the juridical maxims of Jean Bodin (cf. p. 304). "The royal throne is not the throne of a man but the throne of God Himself. . . . The King's majesty is an adequate expression of God's majesty," wrote Jacques Benigne Bossuet (1627-1704), bishop of Meaux, the most celebrated theologian in the age of Louis XIV.

This absolutistic concept of the State and its leader was the exact reverse of the social and political ideas of the Middle Ages, when the State was linked up with universal and other-worldly ends, and when a vocational division of powers and functions had given the individual his share in social and political administration. In the medieval cities this graduated order of rights and duties had received its fullest realization. But it was there, too, that some of the essential features of the modern State could be recognized: the unified economic territory of the city was strictly regulated and disciplined by local administration, and this administration itself resembled closely the political rule of the later absolutistic monarchies. Whereas the chancellors of the medieval emperors had been bishops and feudatories, the city clerk was a professional jurist, a layman, and thus the precursor of the chancellors of the absolutistic monarchs.

A further important characteristic of the absolutistic State is its predominantly or even exclusively secular nature, which in itself is indicative of the complete secularization of politics and morals that was the fruit of Renaissance and Reformation. The absolutistic State, in proclaiming its autonomy, refused to share its power with any other agency or to recognize any law and sanction beyond or above itself, and therefore was as much opposed to a universal empire as to a universal Church. The territorial State was the ideal absolutistic State and the "reason of State" (*ratio status, Staatsraison*) was its supreme law, whose exigencies fully justified alliances with "heretics" and pagans.

The absolutistic idea of State omnipotence, waging relentless warfare against every rival power and corporative organization, led logically to the destruction of the last remnants of feudalism and to the paralyzation of parliamentary government, wherever it existed. While it is true that social divisions and class distinctions in the age of absolutism were as conspicuous as ever, they were practically nullified by the fundamental and all-important distinction between the "sovereign ruler" and the "subject." The members of all social ranks were equally without rights and powers as against royal omnipotence. In thus eliminating the intermediate steps of a grad-uated social order the absolutistic State unknowingly prepared the way for the revolutionary ideas of social equality.

State and society were no longer conceived as organisms, as had been the case in the sociological speculation of Aristotle and Thomas Aquinas. The absolutistic State became a gigantic mechanism, a wonderfully con-structed machine, thus reflecting the all-pervading influence of the new mechanical and mathematical sciences. Frederick the Great compared a well-conducted government with the faultless consistency of a well-constructed philosophical system. He was convinced that social and political structures can be scientifically calculated and mechanically preconditioned, in accord-ance with the laws of induction, observation, comparison, and generalization. Reason and nature join in the construction of the well-ordered police State, in which nothing is left to chance but everything controlled and directed by the will of that abstraction called "the absolute State."

Economy in the Absolutistic State. The economic system which served to provide the abundance of material means for the satisfaction of the selfishness of absolutistic government is associated with the name of Jean Baptiste Colbert (1619–1683), Louis XIV's minister of finance, the creator of "Colbertism" or "mercantilism" in national economy. Mercantilism is merely another name for economic absolutism. The absolutistic State was truly totalitarian in the modern sense, in that it deprived all its subjects of their personal rights and liberties in order to enlist all their physical and mental faculties in the supreme effort of assuring internal prosperity and external security.

Colbert and his imitators in other countries considered a State-controlled economy an essential prerequisite for national aggrandizement. He tried to achieve his aim by devising a new system of taxation and internal revenue, in which the major burden fell on the economically and socially privileged classes; by encouraging domestic trade and commerce and the home industries, in order to make the State self-sufficient and independent of foreign imports; and by creating a favorable balance of trade by means of steadily increasing exports of finished goods and prohibitions on the export of raw materials. Such a favorable balance of trade was to fill the coffers of the mercantilist State with precious metals, while colonies were to provide both raw materials and markets. The absolutistic State used its military and political power to gain economic advantages, and it utilized in turn its increasing economic prestige to feed its political and national ambitions. In this process the absolutistic State and the rising middle classes were natural allies. They were both opposed to the medieval system of land tenure and agricultural economy, and the "Third Estate" (the middle class) was willing to sacrifice liberty and self-respect for the sake of material gain and the economic security and protection that was guaranteed by the new State paternalism. When finally, in 1789, the *Tiers état* (Third Estate) had acquired economic strength and self-sufficiency, its members felt that the moment had come to reclaim their civic and human rights and to revolt against the centralized State.

The secularization that characterizes the tenets of absolutistic political theory is no less in evidence in the economic sphere. Political economy shows itself no longer inspired by religious or moral motivations but by the scientific calculations of mathematics and physics. Economy in the absolutistic State anticipates the essential principles of the "economic liberalism" of Adam Smith (1723-1790) and the French "Physiocrats" in that it makes economic self-interest the source of all values in State and society. Self-interest, being inherent in the operation of a providential plan, must not be stifled but rather developed, enlightened, and rationalized. The striving for material abundance must be made the basis of social ethics. A pre-established harmony is said to permeate the cosmic as well as the social universe, so that the individual who seeks his own advantage works at the same time for the well-being of all: the progress of society as a whole is nothing but the sum total of the progress of all the individuals of whom it is composed.

With François Quesnay (1694-1774), the court physician of King Louis XV of France, the French Physiocrats and their German disciples demanded that all governments conform to the "natural order of things." They were convinced that economic laws were as fixed and inexorable as the laws of nature. The main function of the State is the removal of impediments that prevent nature from following its lawful course. The best government, therefore, is that which governs least. Stressing the importance of agriculture for the well-being of society, they denounced the mercantilistic theory as unsound and maintained that the real wealth of a State did not consist in the accumulation of gold but in the natural resources of the soil, the *"produit net"* — the surplus of natural products. They advocated a single tax, the ground tax, and defined the peasant as "the prime motor of the social machine."

Art and Culture of the Age of Baroque and Rococo. The period that follows the great upheavals of the age of the Reformation and that ends with the triumph of "Enlightenment" (cf. p. 368 sqq.) in the eighteenth century is known as the Age of Baroque and Rococo. The latter term designates the end phase of Baroque, coming to a rather abrupt termination in the years of the French Revolution at the end of the century. The Baroque* runs parallel in part with such intellectual movements as the Catholic Restoration, the theory of the absolutistic State, Rationalism, and Pietism. As a matter of fact it embraces unreconciled such opposites as rationalism and irrationalism, sensuality and spirituality, cynical sophistication and mystical ecstasy, stilted artificiality and the craving for the simplicity and harmony of nature. It is a period and a style filled with paradoxical antitheses and deriving its dynamic vitality from the unceasing and ever failing endeavor to overcome these dualisms in the synthesis of a newly conquered unity of thought and culture.

a) Origins of Baroque Culture. As an artistic style and a specific medium of cultural forms and forces Baroque represents the last great universal manifestation of the unity of Western civilization. It is Catholic in its essence, both in the denominational and the more general sense of the term, and its beginnings are inseparably linked with the militant and aggressive spirit of the Catholic Restoration (cf. p. 253 sqq.). It recognizes nevertheless its indebtedness to the cultural and artistic achievements of the Renaissance, whose individualism and cult of sensuous and natural beauty it adopted, rejecting however its paganism and subjecting man and nature to the dictates of a spiritually informed and divinely ruled universe. It may not be amiss, therefore, to characterize the Baroque age as a combination of certain characteristics of the Gothic and Renaissance cultures.

Baroque culture originated in Rome, the seat of the papacy. The popes were the chief patrons and propagators of the new style of thinking, building, and living, employing those artists (e.g., Michelangelo, Bernini) who created the resplendent symbols of the spirit of incipient and mature Baroque: the new circular structure of St. Peter's Cathedral and its adjacent colonnades and buildings.

b) Political Aspects of Baroque Culture. The political exponents of Baroque culture were the absolutistic princes and those ecclesiastical rulers who, like Richelieu, made the Church subservient to princely ambitions and the imperialistic designs of nationalistic policies. The result of this fusion of nationalism and religion was a steady weakening of ecclesiastical authority, until in the eighteenth century the popes became mere puppets in the game of Franco-Spanish power politics, finding their influence almost completely restricted to the small territories of the Papal States. The idealism that had inspired the reforms of the Council of Trent (cf. p. 257 sq.) had in many instances degenerated to a mere formalism whose emptiness had to be

---

* The name is derived from the Portuguese word *barocco:* "an odd-shaped pearl." The name "Rococo" is derived from the French word *rocaille,* denoting "shell ornament."

artificially filled with the pathos of heroic gestures and exaggerated emotions. The political reality was endowed with an accent of pessimism and melancholy resignation.

As early as 1637 the Spanish Jesuit, Baltazar Gracian, one of the greatest stylists of Spanish literature, wrote in his *Manual of the Art of Worldly Wisdom* (*Oráculo manual y arte de prudencia*): "Unhappy is he who like myself has been living among men, for every one is like a wolf unto the other, if not worse." And: "Believe me: neither wolf nor lion, nor tiger, nor basilisk are as cruel as man." And again: "Whoever does not know thee, oh life, he may well esteem thee; but he whose eyes have been opened, would prefer to proceed from the cradle straightway to the coffin." It is not surprising that Arthur Schopenhauer (1788–1860), the philosopher of an all-pervasive pessimism, became the best German translator of Gracian's *Manual*.

It is evident that this Spaniard's political pessimism represents the reaction of a sensitive intellectual to the general adoption of Machiavellian principles in national and international life. The traditional idea of the State as an organism based on the natural and moral law and informed by reason, custom, and freely determined human action, had been abandoned in favor of the new doctrine of the "Reason of State," serving as the sole criterion for every deed and misdeed.

c) Social Significance of Baroque Culture. With its special liking of the spectacular, theatrical, and representational, Baroque culture expressed most adequately the world of courtly form and etiquette as it was embodied in the two foci of the age — State and Church: the former more and more encroaching upon the ancient prerogatives of the latter.

If Rome was the birthplace of Baroque culture, the typical Baroque State was first realized in Spain and subsequently in France, where its political implications were most fully and effectively developed. Its artistic form language was most distinctly in evidence, however, in southern Germany and Austria and, with some racial and national modifications, in the southern part of the Netherlands, in Spain, Portugal, and their colonial possessions overseas. In France the king and his court were the center of the social culture of the Baroque age, representative of a style of life in which the solemn measures of classical antiquity and the worldly splendor of the Renaissance blended with Spanish *"gravidad"* and French grace and frivolity. German and Austrian Baroque, on the other hand, was not confined to a courtly social elite but penetrated all social groups and met with an enthusiastic response among the common people and peasants. This is especially true of the religious and artistic components of Baroque culture as manifested in a newly flourishing monastic life, a revival of the liturgical arts, colorful processions and pilgrimages, and a wave of mystical devotion.

In France the death of Louis XIV in 1715, the brief regency of Duke Philip of Orléans, and the following rule of Louis XV (1715–1774) brought about a relaxation of the shackles of courtly conventions and marked the triumph of the more lighthearted and careless social climate of the Rococo. This final phase of Baroque culture is characterized by many symptoms of social decay; by a lack of vitality, an atmosphere and attitude which is artistically expressed in the preference for subdued and broken colors and shaded autumnal nuances, by the virtual obliteration of all formal barriers between architecture, sculpture, and painting, with a marked emphasis on rhythmical musicality and pictorial decorative design.

d) Fashion in the Age of Baroque.   As in every other department of civilization so in the realm of fashion France and her all-powerful king set the absolute standards. By the manner of his dress the *galant homme,* style Louis XIV, tried to convey the impression of majestic and imposing splendor. His head was crowned with a leonine periwig with long, flowing curls that covered neck and shoulders. He wore short and tight knee breeches, silken stockings, buckled shoes, a richly embroidered vest, and a long laced coat with narrow waist. A lace necktie, lace cuffs, and a rapier added to the picturesque appearance of the typical *gentilhomme.* The beard was sacrificed for the greater glory of the periwig.

The age of Louis XV favored a fashion of softer and more graceful design, and King Frederick William I of Prussia, in protest against the artificiality of the periwig, introduced the famous pigtail or queue (*Zopf*) and made its adoption compulsory in the Prussian army. It was soon adopted by the military and other classes in every country. Later on, the *Zopf* came to be considered as a somewhat grotesque symbol of every philistinism, bureaucracy, and pedantry in past and present. In art the *Zopfstil* designates a mode of the decorative design of the dying Rococo, comparable to the French *"Louis Seize"* (style under Louis XVI), that reigned about 1770 and was characterized by sober plainness, a peculiar lack of imagination, and regularity in ornament.

The noble lady in the age of Louis XIV wore a narrow-waisted upper garment with laced sleeves of moderate length. As in the preceding period the richly pleated skirt ended in a long train, and the entire dress was lavishly decorated with lace embroidery and multicolored ribbons. After the second decade of the eighteenth century (*c.* 1720–1760) the hoop petticoat (farthingale, crinoline) returned and became known in Germany as the *Hühnerkorb* (chicken coop). Its framework was made of hoops of iron, wood, or whalebone, and it was covered by a petticoat, skirt, and robe of the finest silk, in choicest colors, and adorned with ribbons, laces, embroideries, and artificial flowers. The upper part of the body and the almost disappearing waist were enclosed and compressed by a tight corset. The towering laced hood (*Fontange*) that served as headdress in the age of Louis XIV disappeared after the king's death and gave way to a simple laced bonnet, worn on top of the combed-out hair. In the seventies of the eighteenth century the towering coiffures of the "fashion *à la mode"* staged once more a victorious comeback.

From Spain the artistically decorated fan, wrought of costly lace and covered with dainty paintings, had been imported. It was as indispensable to the fashionable lady as was the rapier to the well-dressed beau. Ladies of social standing were rarely seen without their snuffboxes, which were made of silver, ivory, steel, horn, or wood and adorned with delicate relief work or miniature paintings upon enamel. When out-of-doors, the lady carried a cane to which colored ribbons and flowers were attached, or a parasol to protect her face from the glaring sunlight.

The age of Baroque and Rococo paid less attention to even the minimum requirements of personal and public hygiene than any other period in European history. Beyond a water can and bowl the costly equipment of castle, palace, and private residence did not normally include any facilities for bathing and washing. One may even say without exaggeration that bathing and washing were most unpopular. Public bathhouses were ill reputed, and bathing in rivers and brooks was considered as indecent or in bad taste. This neglect of the most primitive demands of physical hygiene explains the universal use of enormous quantities of cosmetics, smelling salts, perfumes, and so forth, of "fragrant essences and ingredients."

e) Eating and Drinking. Table manners and the arts of the cuisine took their directives from France. Courtly etiquette exerted a restraining influence on the habitual German overindulgence in food and drink. The nonalcoholic beverages, such as coffee, tea, and chocolate, became very popular after they had conquered the society of the French court at the end of the seventeenth century. The first German coffeehouse was opened in Hamburg in 1680, and these establishments together with the "coffee gardens" gained the favor of the middle class and became centers of social intercourse, divertisement, and relaxation.* The politically interested *galant homme* would spend many hours in the coffeehouse, reading the latest newssheets, playing billiard or card games. The great popularity of coffee and tea resulted in the sharply decreasing consumption of wine and beer. In the year 1721 no less than 4,100,000 pounds of tea were imported into Europe by English, French, and Dutch trading companies.** These nonalcoholic drinks, as well as the newly acquired habits of smoking and snuffing, captured the imagination of all classes by their novelty and exotic charm and soon became the objects of poetic panegyrics. Foreign tobaccos were imported and taxed by the governments, and in the period of mercantilism (cf. p. 328 sq.) the princes encouraged the planting of tobacco in their own territories. At the end of the seventeenth century tobacco was grown in Alsace, the Palatinate, Hesse, Saxony, Thuringia, Brandenburg, and Mecklenburg.

---

* Coffee was brought from Africa to Arabia (Mecca = Mocha) in the seventh century A.D.; it reached Constantinople (via Asia) in 1554 and was imported into Europe in the seventeenth century.

** Tea has been known and used as a beverage by the Chinese since the fourth century A.D. and by the Japanese since the eighth century A.D. Dutch traders made it known in Europe about the middle of the sixteenth century. About a hundred years later it became popular with the European aristocracy.

f) Eros. Sexual relations, moral concepts, and the resulting love codes and conventions of the Age of Baroque and Rococo were partly conditioned by the position and evaluation of women during this period. The total abandonment of moral standards that became the conspicuous characteristic of the French court under the rule of Louis XV and among his German imitators is scarcely found in the age of Louis XIV. But even during the lifetime of the *"roi soleil"* that new and refined eroticism was developed that permeated and saturated the culture of the Rococo. Although in some respects the cult of the noble lady looked like a revival of the chivalresque *"Minne"* (cf. p. 155), this latest fad of European society was too much imbued with sophistication, frivolity, and morbidity to be mistaken for anything but the hectic proliferation of a waning civilization.

From the beginnings of European history to the end of the seventeenth century European society had shown distinctly masculine features, despite the fact that occasionally women would rise to positions of leadership in the spheres of religious and secular culture. But in the main women had been confined to the home and had recognized man as the natural political and social leader, finding their own happiness and contentment in the care of household and children and in rather narrowly limited social activities. During the seventeenth century, however, the European lady gradually advanced to a central position in society. Women began to play their part in the scholarly culture of the age.

Princesses and noblewomen of great erudition and culture became renowned for their genuine interest in intellectual pursuits and broke down the social prejudices that had hitherto barred them from the precincts of the arts and sciences. The "scholarly woman" (*das gelehrte Frauenzimmer*) becomes a familiar type in seventeenth-century culture.

Sophie Charlotte, the wife of the first king of Prussia, studied the philosophical systems of Descartes, Spinoza, and Leibniz and is known as one of Leibniz's closest friends. Anna Maria Schurmann, a deeply religious personality of pietistic leanings, a native of Cologne, wrote verses and letters in Latin, Greek, Hebrew, and French, and is said to have mastered fourteen languages. She was proficient in music, painting, etching, and wood carving and deeply interested in mathematics, history, philosophy, and theology. Elizabeth Charlotte of Orléans (*"Liselotte von der Pfalz,"* 1652–1722), the wife of Louis XIV's brother Philip, a German princess of the Palatinate, was a woman of remarkable originality and independence of judgment, retaining the integrity and naturalness of her character in the midst of the frivolous environment of the French court and showing wit and a keen sense of observation in her letters, in which she offers a running commentary on her startling experiences.

In the period of the Rococo, fashion, manners, and customs point to the growing effeminacy of the general taste and to the predominating influence of the feminine element in society. The decadent and effeminate *cavalier* became the obedient and abjectly admiring slave of a lady and mistress of superior taste, culture, and education. The marriage ties were loosened to such a degree that adultery on the part of both sexes was considered a conventional rule rather than a deplorable exception. Social honors were showered on famous and infamous courtesans and mistresses, the debauchee was celebrated as a hero, and a general reversal of moral values raised the unnatural to the status of the normal and natural.

g) Festivities and Social Amusements. Following the example of the ancient Roman emperors, the absolutistic princes tried to keep themselves and their subjects in good humor by never ending cycles of brilliant festivities and spectacular social entertainments. Marriages, baptisms, coronations, receptions, military victories offered a variety of occasions for colorful parades, processions, fireworks, ballets, masquerades, and multiform other theatrical and musical divertisements. The favorite dance was the gracefully stilted Minuet, an adaptation of a peasant dance of Poitou in France, introduced at the court of Louis XIV in 1663. It became an integral part of the preclassical and classical sonata and symphony of the seventeenth and eighteenth centuries and was transformed into the "Scherzo" movement by Ludwig van Beethoven. At the court balls and masquerades (*Redoute:* from the Italian *Ridotto*) nobles and burghers were carefully separated by a rope or railing.

Everyone paid his tribute to the gambling and card-playing craze, and gambling tables were never missing at social entertainments. In the accounts and balance sheets of wealthy burghers the gambling allowance for their wives figured as an important item, and in princely families definite figures for gambling money were included in the marriage contract. The most popular card game was the "royal" *L'hombre,* of Spanish origin, introduced into France and other European countries in the period of Louis XIV.

A favorite pastime during the winter season was the elaborate sleighing parties, combined with carnival festivities, with phantastically decorated sleighs, jinglets, masked noblemen and their ladies, and a long train of horsemen, lackeys, pages, and trumpeters. In summertime the princes arranged encampments (*Lustlager*) in the open air, with military display, concerts, ballets, *tableaux vivants,* and the varied pleasures of the chase.

The complexity and artificiality of the culture of Baroque and Rococo stood as barriers between nature and society. Even if at times in sentimental yearning men and women dreamed of nature as a haven of repose and an escape from the tyranny of rules and conventions, they were too much the children of their age not to value these laws and rules above everything else. The frail beauty of their culture shines forth from the pleasure castles (*Lustschlösser*) which they erected in the countryside and whose very names suggest a secret longing for solitude, peace, and rest (*Solitude, Sans-Souci, Eremitage,* etc.); yet even in the pastoral costume and environment they remained the slaves of their unnatural conventions. They even felt impelled to impose the artificiality of their culture on the free growth of nature, subjecting trees and hedges, shrubbery and flower beds to the regularity of geometrical design and the added artistic and mechanical devices of fountains, cascades, grottoes, statues, and every sort of plastic decoration. An age that had made the cult of pleasure its final goal was in the end haunted by its own restlessness and had become unable to enjoy the fruits of its cravings. An undertone of sadness vibrates in all the manifestations of this overripe culture of European aristocracy.

h) Religious Currents. The spiritual unrest of the Baroque age expressed itself in manifold ways, but it was most intensely alive in the circles that carried forward the impulses of the Catholic Restoration and among the leaders of a spiritual revival in the Protestant sects. These religious movements were reflected in a new ascendancy of mystical theory and practice, in the foundation of new religious orders, in the philosophical renascence, in the religious life and customs of the people, and in the symbolic language of plastic art, literature, and music.

The major source of the mystical and religious components of Baroque culture was Spain, where St. Teresa of Ávila (1515–1582) had carried out the reform of the Carmelite Order, founding seventeen convents and fifteen monasteries. In her autobiographical *Libro de su Vida* as well as in her other works she gives evidence of an extraordinary understanding of human psychology and a remarkable combination of mystical contemplation, eminent will power, and good practical sense. Her collaborator in the work of monastic reform was St. John of the Cross (1542–1591), a mystical writer and poet of great fervor, spiritual depth, and unusual literary talents, who brought the mystical revival in Spain to its full bloom and who influenced most of the German and French mystical authors of the following centuries.

The rebirth of scholastic philosophy (cf. p. 141 sqq.), that had been effected in the Universities of Salamanca and Coimbra in the course of the sixteenth century, soon spread to the Catholic institutions of higher learning in southern Germany and Austria. The works of the Portuguese Jesuits as well as the *Disputations on Metaphysics* of the Spanish Jesuit Suarez (1548–1617) were adopted as standard texts in German Catholic and Protestant universities and colleges. Christopher Scheibler, professor in the University of Giessen, wrote a work on Metaphysics (*Opus Metaphysicum,* 1617) which became known as the "Protestant Suarez." This happened at a time when the Jesuit Mariana's work *On the King* (1605, 1611), obviously advocating tyrannicide, was causing a stormy controversy between Jesuits and Protestants.

Swinging back and forth between extremes, Baroque mentality produced strange and one-sided religious attitudes in both Catholic and Protestant countries and individuals: Jansenism* and Quietism** in France, and

---

* Jansenism is a rigoristic ethico-religious system, developed by Cornelius Jansen (1585–1638), bishop of Ypres. He approached Luther's and Calvin's views in his pessimistic evaluation of human nature, his denial of free will, and his doctrine of absolute predestination.

** Quietism, as taught in the later Middle Ages by the "Brethren and Sisters of the Free

Pietism (cf. p. 364 sqq.) in Holland and Germany. In these movements an antirational sentiment is conspicuous, an emotional reaction against the rationalistic trends of the age.

The most popular preachers of the seventeenth century were those who appealed to religious feeling and imagination. But it must be said that the people at large were relatively little affected by the hysterical exaggerations of certain types of Baroque mentality. On the contrary, the lower classes had preserved their gay naïveté, their sense of humor, and their unvarnished vitality. They were unbroken in their moral and emotional life and, as in Luther's time, responsive to the one who had learned to think their thoughts and to speak their language.

Among the famous Catholic preachers in German lands was Procopius of Templin (c. 1607–1680), a Capuchin monk,* the author of three volumes of spiritual songs, comparable in their mild serenity to the better known hymns of Paul Gerhardt (cf. p. 298 sq.). Most effective as a pulpit orator and popular writer was Abraham a Santa Clara (Johann Ulrich Megerle, before he entered the Augustinian Order), 1644–1709,** the son of an innkeeper in the province of Baden. His fiery and soul-stirring sermons, perfect specimens of the art of rhetoric, represent in their pointed, antithetical style and rich imagery Baroque prose at its very best. His powerful word fanned the heroic spirit of the Austrian people in their determined resistance against the Turks and consoled them in the tribulations of the year of the plague (1679). In 1677 Emperor Leopold I made the Augustinian monk chaplain of the imperial court.

Widely read and thoroughly enjoyed by the common people were the didactic and devotional works of Martin of Cochem (1634–1712), a Capuchin monk of the Moselle region, who was equally famous as author and preacher and whose *Life of Christ* (1677) served as a textual pattern for several Passion plays.

i) Arts and Crafts. The style of the Renaissance had been given a cool reception in the northern countries of Europe and especially in Germany. Here the great masters on the whole continued the late Gothic tradition, although, with the exception of Grünewald (cf. p. 198 sq.), they welcomed the technical innovations and some of the formal values of the classical revival and embodied them in their creations.

It was this preponderance of the medieval tradition in German art that made it a particularly favorable medium for the stylistic tendencies of the

---

Spirit" and in the seventeenth century by Mme. de Guyon and, in a more moderate form, Archbishop Fénelon of Cambrai (1651–1715), demanded the complete annihilation of all active faculties of the mind ("mystical death") for the sake of absolute surrender to the will of God.

* The Capuchins, a branch of the Franciscan Order (cf. p. 134 sq.), were organized in 1525 to restore the original purity of the Franciscan ideal. In their external appearance they are distinguished from the Franciscans by their beard and a large cowl (capuche: *Kapuze*).

** Schiller (cf. p. 422) used Abraham a Santa Clara and his figurative language in the famous *Kapuzinerpredigt* of the first part of the Wallenstein trilogy (*Wallenstein's Camp*).

Baroque age, which in its very essence was a composite of Gothic and Renaissance, of spiritual fervor and beautiful natural form. It is nevertheless undeniable that artistically as much as intellectually the new Baroque style originated in Italy and Spain, the countries that had taken the lead in the Catholic reform movement. The extension of the Counter Reformation into southern Germany and Austria was soon followed by the adoption of the new art forms. As far as France is concerned, the heritage of antiquity and Renaissance was strong enough to preserve the classical artistic tradition essentially unimpaired even under the veneer of Baroque and Rococo. The style of the eras of Louis XIV, Louis XV, and Louis XVI are variations of an identical theme: they are a direct outgrowth and expression of courtly absolutism and political as well as cultural imperialism.

Hardouin-Mansard and Le Vau, the two architects of Louis XIV, the builders of the castle and palace chapel of Versailles, and Lenôtre, the creator of the royal gardens, set the standard of artistic taste for all France. Bernini's Baroque plan for the façade of the Louvre was rejected by the king in favor of the classical designs of Claude Perrault, in which grace and dignity combined to produce an effect of monumental simplicity.

The first powerful manifestation of Baroque sentiment in art may be found in the mature works of Michelangelo, in which the law of classical proportion and harmony gives way to a forceful and dynamic expressionism. From Michelangelo's design for the renovation of St. Peter's Cathedral in Rome to Bernini's (1598–1680) semicircular colonnades on St. Peter's Square a steadily growing mastery of the problems of space and architectonic masses may be observed. The architects of this period and their employers, the absolutistic princes, were beginning to plan and build entire cities as grandiose works of art, feeling themselves as sovereign masters of the realm of nature with its unlimited possibilities. In dictatorial fashion they applied to any given situation or problem a rule and order of their own making. Thus the typical Baroque city shows the same systematic uniformity as the absolutistic State, the princely army, and civic administration. Rome, the Eternal City, with its vast perspectives, its system of radiating streets whose lines converge in the focal *Piazza del Popolo,* provided the incomparable exemplar that was imitated and approximated in such German cities as Würzburg, Mannheim, and Karlsruhe. In the latter city the fanlike arrangement of streets serves only to emphasize the central and dominating structure of the princely castle. From his palace the prince overlooks the entire city, while in a graduated order the houses of nobles, court officials, merchants, and craftsmen are grouped in well-measured and increasing distances from the focal point. Since the times of Graeco-Roman antiquity city planning had not been practiced on such a large scale and with similar ingenuity and consistency.

In individual buildings the new consciousness of space expressed itself in multiple spatial combinations, the refracted light emanating from various hidden sources, resulting in a phantastic transfiguration of reality. As

Tabernacle in the Monastery at Andechs on the Ammer Lake

distinguished from the planned city the individual building shuns symmetrical design, providing instead for constant change and a confusing variety of directions. All clear limitations and solid boundaries are obliterated by the play of unexpected and irrational impulses. Architecture, sculpture, and painting fuse in a festive phantasmagoria of light and color. Whereas the Gothic master builders endeavored to dematerialize even those things that were most deeply steeped in matter, the Baroque architect and sculptor materializes even the most immaterial objects, fashioning plastic rays of light and tangible clouds. The result was a kind of exaggerated realism, feverish, convulsive, and overdescriptive. Angels are represented as healthy, naked, and precocious children and coquettish girls, and heaven becomes a glorified extension of the earth. Asceticism deteriorates into an enjoyment of pain or into sensual ecstasy or vice versa, revealing an almost pathological confusion of emotions.

The peculiar characteristics of the Baroque style may in part be explained by the universally felt urge for religious propaganda, for which art provided a symbolic language. In a world in which the Church had been forced to share its rule over men's minds with secular powers, the ancient spiritual message had to be convincingly and strikingly reaffirmed by every available means. By addressing men's senses and imagination the Church tried to reach man's intellect. In Protestant northern Germany the subtle and sublime language of music served as the exclusive artistic medium, while in the Catholic South all the arts in unison engaged the entire sensuous and intellectual organism of the human being. As in the age of the Reformation, the masses were once more stirred and moved by Christian impulses. In movement and countermovement, in attack and defense, in continuous agitation and struggle, the Baroque style acquired its distinctive features.

This new style was gratefully adopted, developed, and propagated by the Jesuits (cf. p. 254 sqq.), who formed the vanguard of the Catholic Restoration. This fact gave rise to the misnomer "Jesuit-Style," which term in its generalization by no means exhausts the rich possibilities of Baroque art. Nevertheless, the religious experiences of the age and certain changes in the liturgical and devotional practices of the Church found their expression in architectural form and were especially noticeable in the numerous Jesuit churches that covered city and countryside. Additional choir and nave space was to enable large congregations to follow the popular sermons and to have an unobstructed view of the pulpit, the great altar, and the liturgical ceremonies. The mysterious semidarkness of the medieval cathedral gave way to a brightly lit and loudly decorated interior. In the larger churches a second story in the form of an aisle gallery and enclosed box seats for the nobility and the court were added. While every Gothic church dominated all the surrounding buildings of the city, town, or village, the Baroque church is frequently co-ordinated with private or public buildings. In the Benedictine monastic settlement of Melk on the Danube the structural unit of the church is hardly distinguishable from the rest of the buildings.

Façade and interior show great vitality of architectural and sculptural design, plantlike tropical richness and plastic massiveness, and a tendency to create an effect of disconcerting unrest by a maze of opposing lines and broken or unfinished forms.

The first Baroque and Rococo churches and secular buildings on German soil were the work of Italian and French architects: the Church of St. Cajetan (*Theatinerkirche,* 1663–1675) in Munich was built by Agostino Barello, a native of Bologna, while the *"Residenztheater,"* the Amalienburg, and the interior of the royal palace (*"Residenz"*) in the same city are samples of the gay and delicate taste of François de Cuvilliés, a Walloon who came to Munich in 1724 and was most successful in introducing the elegance of French Rococo into Germany. But the Italian and French masters were soon superseded and surpassed by their German pupils, who became the creators of German Baroque as a national style.

In analogy to the Gothic style three major phases in the development of German Baroque may be distinguished: Early Baroque (*c.* 1580–1630), High Baroque (*c.* 1670–1720), and Late Baroque or Rococo (*c.* 1720–1770). The Thirty Years' War and its cultural consequences caused a temporary period of stagnation (*c.* 1630–1670). Architecture as the leading and socially most significant art proved equally creative in the ecclesiastical and secular spheres. Among the works of secular architecture the princely residences, palaces, pleasure castles, and parks rank foremost. The most fruitful regions are Austria, Bohemia (Prague), Bavaria, Franconia, Silesia, and Saxony (Dresden). The outstanding master builders are Fischer von Erlach (St. Charles Church, Vienna); Lucas von Hildebrandt (Belvedere Castle, Vienna); Daniel Pöppelmann (Zwinger, Dresden); Georg Bähr (*Frauenkirche,* Dresden); Jakob Prandauer (Monasteries Melk and St. Florian, Austria); Johann, Christoph, and Ignaz Dientzenhofer (Cathedral of Fulda and numerous buildings in Prague); Joseph Effner (Nymphenburg and Schleissheim Castles near Munich); Dominicus Zimmermann (churches Steinhausen, Wies in Bavaria); Michael Fischer (churches Zwiefalten, Ottobeuren in Swabia); Balthasar Neumann (Würzburg Castle; churches Vierzehnheiligen, Neresheim in Franconia and Swabia); and Andreas Schlüter. The last named master, a native of Danzig, is the creator of the Berlin Castle and the equestrian statue of the Great Elector, the only representative master of the much more austere and almost classical Baroque style of the Protestant North. The leading Baroque sculptors this side of the Alps are Raphael Donner in Austria and Andreas Schlüter in Germany. The brothers Kosmas Damian and Egid Quirin Asam of Munich (Church of St. John Nepomuk) are masters of the fully grown Rococo, unsurpassed in the fragile lightness and picturesque melodiousness of their figural compositions, their altarpieces, and their stucco decoration.*

---

* According to their birth dates the great Baroque architects belong in the following two generations of the seventeenth century: (1) Fischer von Erlach, Christoph and Johann Dientzen-

Presse- und Informationsamt der Bundesregierung, Bonn

Zwinger, Dresden, by Daniel Pöppelmann

Baroque painting achieved its greatest fame in Italy (Caravaggio, Tintoretto, Tiepolo), Spain (El Greco, Velasquez, Murillo, Zurbarán), Flanders (Rubens, van Dyck), Holland (Rembrandt), and England (Hogarth, Gainsborough). Most of the German masters were of second and third rank, but with their al fresco murals they provided a suitable background for the great works of the architects and sculptors. In their painted ceilings they create an imaginary heaven and the illusion of infinite space, a feast of dazzling light, silvery clouds, and radiant atmosphere, wherein angels and saints move with perfect ease. The prince-bishop of Würzburg had the central staircase and Emperor's Hall of Balthasar Neumann's magnificent castle decorated with paintings from the brush of Tiepolo, the great master of Venice.

The art of portrait painting, satisfying the thirst for fame and glory of princes and nobles, bishops and abbots, flourished no less than in the period of the Renaissance with its cult of individualism. The Baroque painters portray the cavaliers in heroic poses and the ladies as glamorous goddesses of love. Eighteenth-century Rococo developed the art of pastel painting (crayon painting) as a new and delicate pictorial technique, of which the earlier works of Anton Raphael Mengs (1728–1779), the court painter of King Augustus III of Saxony-Poland, are excellent examples. The arts of etching and engraving are best represented by the genrelike and at the same time more realistic works of Daniel Chodowiecki (1726–1801), who acquired fame with his illustrations of some of the masterpieces of German eighteenth-century literature (Klopstock, Gellert, Lessing, Goethe, Schiller, etc.).

The high quality of German craftsmanship held its own throughout the Age of Baroque and Rococo. The goldsmiths provided the sacristies and altars of the churches with precious chalices, monstrances, and variegated ornamental decorations. The arts of weaving and embroidery reached new heights in the making of tapestries, carpets, and liturgical vestments. The artistic locksmiths and blacksmiths created beautifully shaped table utensils and elaborately wrought and fancifully decorated iron gates. The refined taste as well as the frail iridescence of the Rococo shines forth from the graceful products of the porcelain factories of Dresden and Meissen, later on also of Berlin, Frankenthal, Ludwigsburg, Nymphenburg, and Vienna.*

---

hofer, Pöppelmann, Schlüter, Bähr, Hildebrandt, Prandauer were born in the fifties and sixties; (2) Zimmermann, the Asams, Joseph Effner, Balthasar Neumann, Michael Fischer, and Ignaz Dientzenhofer were born in the eighties and nineties. Many of the great monuments of German and Austrian Baroque architecture were destroyed during World War II.

* Porcelain clay for the manufacture of pottery was first used by the Chinese (seventh century A.D.). In Europe this ancient technique was rediscovered by Johann Friedrich Böttger (Meissen) at the beginning of the eighteenth century. The porcelain factory of Meissen was founded in 1710. The related process of the manufacture of faïence (from the Italian city Faënza) is of even earlier origin (Egypt, Babylon, Persia). It was cultivated by the Mohammedans in the Orient and by the Moors in Spain (c. 1100–1500). In Italy faïence is known as Majolica. The first German faïence factories were those of Hanau (1661) and Frankfurt (1666).

j) Literature. The major theme of drama and novel in the age of Baroque is the freedom of the human will to choose good or evil, heaven or hell. The struggle of the hero with the apparent arbitrariness of life and the inscrutable decrees of "Fortuna" (Roman goddess of Fate) has as its object and final goal the purification and mastery of the passions by the exercise of reason and free will.

Although some of the literary trends and creations of the early Baroque had to be discussed in connection with the social and cultural conditions of the period of the Thirty Years' War (cf. p. 284 sqq.), their significance can be more adequately appreciated if the spirit of the age of Baroque is used as a frame of reference. This is especially true of such authors as Jacob Böhme, Andreas Gryphius, Martin Opitz, Grimmelshausen, and others.

Two definite tendencies or branches are easily distinguished in the creations of Baroque literature: (1) a group of authors whose works bear the marks of courtly representation and didactic rationalization, and (2) the works of those writers who wish to express not the experiences of an entire class but personal and intimate feelings of merely private concern. The members of the first group are the creators of the truly representative works of Baroque literature, while the authors who belong to the second group fulfill the no less important historical function of preparing the way for the literature of the age of sentimentality (cf. p. 392 sq.) and enlightenment (cf. p. 368 sq.). What both groups have in common is a certain lack of moderation and proportion and the overstraining of either reason, emotion, or will.

The spiritual dynamism of the age is most poignantly alive in those dramatic works that were written by members of the Jesuit and Benedictine Orders. The authors were professors of Catholic colleges and universities, and their works were among the most effective instruments of religious propaganda in the period of the Catholic Restoration. The stage assumed the function of a great moral and educative agency by means of which the spectators were to experience the wished-for synthesis between earth and heaven, nature and supernature. The intended moral effect was contrition, repentance, and ultimate conversion. While the Protestant school drama used both the German and Latin tongues, the religious drama of the Catholics and particularly the Jesuits cultivated a neo-classical Latin style of great elegance and lucidity.

The sources and patterns from which the leading Jesuit dramatists derived inspiration were morality plays of the type of *Everyman,* which flourished especially in the Low Countries; the Humanistic school theater with its revival of the classical Roman comedy of Plautus (*c.* 250–184 B.C.) and Terence (*c.* 190–159 B.C.); and the biblical folk plays which were frequently produced in public squares.

The most talented Jesuit playwright of the early Baroque is the Swabian, Jacob Bidermann, whose *Cenodoxus* or *Doctor of Paris,* written when the author was twenty-four years of age, deals with the Faustian theme of the life, death, and judgment of a self-styled "superman." It is recorded that after the first performances several high-ranking courtiers were so deeply moved that they changed their entire mode of living, and that the actor who played the title role became a member of the Jesuit Order. The Catholic religious drama reached its perfection in the works of the Tyrolese Jesuit, Nicholas Avancini (1611–1686) and the Benedictine writer Simon Rettenbacher (1634–1706) of the monastery of Kremsmünster in Upper Austria.

The unreal, superrational, and allegorical character of these plays necessitated revolutionary changes and innovations in the art of stagecraft, for which again the Jesuits provided guidance and inspiration. The Baroque stage of the religious orders presents an utter contrast to the homely and often uncouth performances of the wandering troupes, whose members had to be satisfied with the most primitive equipment and who had no social standing. Nothing, on the other hand, was too costly and extravagant for the princely or monastic stage. Special consideration was given to elaborate costuming and stage setting. Artists and technicians of great reputation put their talents at the disposal of their ecclesiastical and secular employers. Ever new problems presented themselves, whose solution required the intuition and dexterity of artistic genius. Complicated mechanical devices and machinery had to create the illusion of pouring rains, flying clouds, howling storms. The scene had to be set for the convenience of the incalculable whims of the gods and goddesses of the classical pantheon as well as for the visions of saints and the apparitions of angels, demons, monsters, and phantoms. Up to the middle of the seventeenth century change of scenery had been effected by movable painted prisms ("Telari-Stage"), which enclosed a well-defined and limited static space. The Baroque period introduced the wings with painted perspective, thereby giving the scene additional depth and allowing for ever changing prospects and extended horizons. The most ingenious theater architects, stage designers, and stage decorators were three members of the Italian family Galli da Bibbiena (Fernando, 1657–1743; Giuseppe, 1696–1757; Antonio, 1700–1774). They exercised a noteworthy influence on the space concepts of Baroque architecture.

The ideal goal of Baroque drama and stagecraft was in a way an anticipation of Richard Wagner's (cf. p. 494 sqq.) theatrical *Gesamtkunstwerk* (the total or universal work of art), in which all the different arts unite and fuse. The physical magnitude and the processional and representational character of the performances proved favorable for the development of the open-air theater, in which a fitting background and setting was provided by the highly formal and decorative garden architecture or by triumphal arches, halls and temples of honor which were constructed for some particular occasion. The art of the drama tended to merge with parade, procession, ballet, festival play, Oratorio, and Opera.

Baroque drama as cultivated outside the religious orders, and the works of such authors as Andreas Gryphius (cf. p. 299) which had grown out of the religious premises of the Protestant Reformation, were either farcical slapstick comedy or dramatizations of grand historical and political events (*Haupt- und Staatsaktionen*). The comedies were frequently built around the dominant figure of the clown (*Hanswurst, Pickelhäring*) and were without literary significance. The *Haupt- und Staatsaktion* was a bombastic and bloodcurdling affair, with a heroic or phantastic plot, and from the linguistic point of view a medley of German, French, Italian, and Latin.

Comedy and *Staatsaktion* were combined in the offerings of the touring companies or troupes, especially the "English Comedians" who, between 1585 and 1660, produced more or less crude versions of Elizabethan and Shakespearean drama at German courts and in German cities. Their stage was of the simplest kind: a wooden framework, draped with curtains or rugs. The English language gradually gave way to German, and German touring companies eventually replaced the foreign troupes. Despite their often primitive taste the members of these companies were professional actors and therefore capable of improving the artistic quality of theatrical performances and of enlarging the scope of the dramatic repertoire. Johannes Velten (1640–1692), a German actor of excellent literary taste, worked unceasingly for the advancement of the German stage and was the first to enrich the offerings of his troupe by the inclusion of the works of the classical French authors.

Typical of the Baroque *novel* are the works of Lohenstein (1635–1683), Zesen (1619–1689), and Anton Ulrich, duke of Brunswick (1663–1714). They have in common the antithetical structure and the rhetorical artificiality of style and composition. For Lohenstein (*Arminius,* etc.) the ideal hero is somewhat like a map or mirror of the universe; he is an instrument in the hands of an incomprehensible universal intellect, not an unknowing or passive tool, to be sure, but an intelligent agent himself, who perseveres in temporal tribulations and achieves moral triumph in the ultimate mastery of the complexities of life. Zesen's *Adriatic Rosemund* has an educational, didactic, and nationalistic tendency, and his *Assenat* is a Baroque version of the biblical story of Joseph in Egypt. The latter takes the form of the political "Utopia" when it attempts a moral justification of royal despotism: Joseph succeeds in his scheme of a planned economy by reducing the Egyptian population to the status of serfdom. Ulrich von Braunschweig's (Brunswick) *Roman Octavia* depicts life as a "school of patience," in which the good are eventually rewarded, the wicked punished. The heroines are models of moral perseverance and representatives of perfect courtly decorum. The varying aspects of historic evolution reveal the essentially identical nature of man and the natural and divine law. The Baroque striving for universality is realized by making the novel a mosaic of epistles, orations, narratives, and lyrics. The ideology of the age of "Enlightenment" (cf. p. 368 sq.) is foreshadowed by a belief in a universal moral law, residing in human nature beyond and above all dogmatic distinctions.

France was the first country to revolt against the high-sounding verbosity and grandiloquence of Baroque literature. Molière's (1622–1673) comedies had ridiculed the stiltedness of the culture of his age, and Boileau (1636–1711) had demanded clarity, naturalness, and simplicity as requisites of a beautiful literary style. French literature had already adopted these very principles and had achieved a somewhat too faultless and academic classical perfection in the works of Corneille (1606–1684) and Racine (1639–1699). In Germany the first opposition to the exaggerations of Baroque literature likewise dates back to the seventeenth century. The taste of the middle class began to rebel against courtly bombast and demanded honesty and intelligibility of literary expression. And the opposition that came from mystico-religious quarters wanted to see the "language of the heart" reflected in the clarity, simplicity, and truthfulness of literary style. Enlightenment, Pietism, and Rococo were united in their antagonism to Baroque ostentation and pompous extravagance, although their opposition sprang from different sources. But all the anti-Baroque forces seemed crystallized in the works of Christian Gellert (1715–1769), who was the favorite author and the exponent of all three tendencies that characterized the period between Baroque and "Storm and Stress" (*Sturm und Drang,* cf. p. 394 sq.): rationalism, sentimentalism, and the smooth elegance of the Rococo. For Frederick the Great Gellert was "the most sensible" of the German men of letters, and Goethe, despite a more critical appraisal, saw in this poet's mediocre talents the bases of moral culture in Germany. In Gellert's fables and hymns we find moralism and introspection, common sense and the rational veneration of a deistically conceived Godhead, while in his novels virtue and vice are arrayed against each other in a forced and primitive chiaroscuro technique.

The authors of both Rococo and Enlightenment were animated by the comforting conviction of living in the best and most reasonable of all possible worlds. This is especially true of the "Anacreontics," * a group of poets who created for themselves an idyllic and hollow fools' paradise, wherein they could enthusiastically give vent to their epicurean dreams of wine, women, and song. Although their pale epicureanism remained confined to the printed page, they enriched German lyric poetry by new emotional accents. Ewald von Kleist (1715–1759), the most talented of their number, became the lyrical panegyrist of the Frederician army, marking the transition from the lighthearted Rococo to the heroic pathos of the "Storm and Stress" poets.

German literary Rococo reaches its peak in the later works of Christoph Martin Wieland (1733–1813), in which the pietistic sentimentalism of his youth gave way to the mildly skeptical and partly ironical mentality of the Rococo, in which a graceful and tolerant art of living is embodied in the form of a new and refined humanism. The high cultural acumen that is achieved by Wieland is evidenced by the broadness and flexibility of his

* The name refers to the Greek lyric poet Anacreon (sixth century B.C.).

literary taste and by the gift of empathy that enabled him to appreciate such widely divergent modes of artistic expression as those represented by Shakespeare (many of whose works he translated), the young Goethe, and Heinrich von Kleist (cf. p. 483 sqq.).*

k) Music and Opera. The churches, abbeys, and castles of the age of Baroque and Rococo, with their flowing façades, majestic porches, halls, and staircases, the soft lyricism of their interior decoration, signify the submersion of plastic architectural form in the spirit of music. The musical art forms therefore are not merely an important part of Baroque style but they seem to express its very essence. Some of the finest specimens of Rococo architecture are royal palaces, such as the famous "Gloriette," a hall of columns of fragile beauty in the park of Schönbrunn near Vienna, or the arcades and pavilions of Pöppelmann's "Zwinger" in Dresden, part of which housed one of the most famous art collections of Europe; they look like Mozartian Minuets in stone, like frozen music.

German church music in the seventeenth century received its chief inspiration from Italy, where two major schools may be distinguished: the Romans and the Venetians. The Romans, following the style of Palestrina (cf. p. 282), are more austere; the Venetians, most gloriously represented by Giovanni Gabrieli (1557–1612), are more worldly and richer in their vocal and instrumental color schemes. It was the Venetian school that exerted a direct influence on the German composers of the age of Baroque and Rococo.

Heinrich Schütz (1585–1672), Georg Friedrich Händel (1685–1759), and Johann Sebastian Bach (1685–1750) are the great German masters of the Baroque period. Schütz, a native of Thuringia, studied in Venice under Giovanni Gabrieli and subsequently received an appointment at the court of the elector of Saxony in Dresden. Most of his works are of distinctly religious character. He combined the polyphonic tradition of the sixteenth century with the new style (*nuove musiche, stile nuovo*) of the harmonically accompanied monody, and developed the standard forms for the biblical oratorio and "Passion." In his "Passions" and "Spiritual Concerts" he is the direct precursor of J. S. Bach. In his opera *Daphne,* for which Martin Opitz (cf. p. 299) wrote a German version of Rinuccini's Italian libretto, he introduced the recitative** vocal style.

Likewise a native of Thuringia was the great Johann Sebastian Bach, to whom, according to Schumann (cf. p. 493), "music owes almost as great a debt as a religion owes to its founder." He is the towering genius of the

---

* Of Wieland's works the drama *Lady Johanna Gray* and his prose translation of Shakespeare breathe the spirit of Enlightenment. His educational novel *Der goldene Spiegel* (*The Golden Mirror*) praises the representative of enlightened despotism. The novels *Agathon* and *Abderiten* construe a world of ideal classical culture, opposing exaggerated spiritualism and sensism. The narrative in verse, *Oberon,* is a masterpiece of the literary Rococo.

** The recitative style in music is based exclusively on the spoken word of the text, relinquishing all independent melodic and rhythmical paraphrases. It forms an integral part of the "representative style" (*stile rappresentativo*) of the early opera.

great musical heritage of German Protestantism. In him the style of musical
Baroque reaches its greatest spiritual depth, while at the same time he marks
the height and consummation of a development of musical form that extends over a period of three centuries, leading from the late Gothic, Renaissance, and early Baroque polyphony to modern homophony (harmony).
Bach is the only composer who embraces and unites in his works these two
distinct musical styles.

Bach, the father of twenty children, several of whom achieved fame as
composers and musicians, passed the greater part of his uneventful life as
an organist and cantor in the petty towns of Thuringia and in the neighboring city of Leipzig. After having completed his studies he was appointed
as court organist and concertmaster in Weimar in 1714 and three years later
as conductor (*Kapellmeister*) to the court of Prince Leopold of Anhalt-
Cöthen at Cöthen. In 1723 he became cantor at the Thomas School in
Leipzig and director of music in the two main churches of that city. In the
beginning he entertained friendly relations with the literary and academic
circles in Leipzig, among others with Johann Christoph Gottsched (cf. p.
378 sq.), who exercised a kind of literary dictatorship in Germany, but later
on he withdrew more and more from social intercourse. In 1736 Bach was
appointed as honorary court composer to the elector of Saxony, and in 1747
he accepted an invitation to visit the court of Frederick the Great, where
his son Emanuel was employed as a cymbalist. The constant strain on his
sight from early youth brought about his total blindness one year before
his death (1750).

Bach's musical compositions reveal a complete mastery of technical means,
logical structure, monumental form, and the sublimity of religious experience. The vocal arrangements of church chorals, in which the solo
arias function as lyrical interpretations of the musical core, grew out of the
sphere of organ music.* In the "Passions" of John and Matthew, the two
hundred church cantatas, the Magnificats, oratorios, and masses we have
examples of Bach's perfected personal style. In the *High Mass in B minor,*
written for the Catholic court of Saxony, the subjective elements of Bach's
spirituality blend admirably with the severe objectivity of the Gregorian
Chorale.

The composer's instrumental works include the numerous preludes and
fugues for organ and clavier, the sonatas, suites, concertos, and overtures for
various instruments and full orchestra. In the Cöthen period he composed
instrumental chamber music, while in the Leipzig period he produced his
greatest church music. In his fugues Bach developed the art of harmonic

---

* Piano and organ music were closely allied musical arts in the sixteenth and early seventeenth century. The credit for having created a genuine style of piano music belongs to the
English composers of the Baroque age (William Byrd, Orlando Gibbons, etc.). The early forms
of the pianoforte ("clavier," *Hammerklavier,* invented in the eighteenth century) were the
clavichord and the harpsichord, the former of soft, the latter of hard and metallic tonal
quality.

counterpoint* to its final perfection, achieving a complete synthesis of melodious and harmonious elements.

Georg Friedrich Händel, born in Halle in the province of Saxony in the same year as Bach, was a composer of much more cosmopolitan taste. Three years he spent in Italy and, after a short engagement in Hanover, he journeyed to London, where he stayed as director of the opera until his death (1759). He lies buried in Westminster Abbey.

Having familiarized himself at an early age with the musical styles of Italy, France, and England, Händel was ideally prepared to become a creative innovator in the universally cherished musical forms of oratorio and opera, English influence prevailing in the former and Italian influence in the latter. The dramatic intensity and dynamic rhythm of his works make Händel the foremost representative of a festive, majestic, and fully seasoned Baroque style. After the venture of the London opera had ended in failure, Händel gave his attention almost exclusively to the oratorio. In his instrumental compositions he continued and perfected the tradition that had been established by such Italian masters as Corelli (1653–1773) and Vivaldi (c. 1680–1743). His works include forty operas, thirty oratorios and Passions; Te Deums, cantatas, arias, Concerti Grossi, and numerous pieces of chamber music.

The most original contribution that the seventeenth century made to the development of musical styles was the creation of the new forms of *opera* and *music drama.* The immediate ancestor of the opera was the Italian and German *madrigal,* the most favored form of musical entertainment in the age of the Renaissance. In the madrigal several harmonically interrelated voices followed the lead of the upper voice in the interpretation of a poetic text, thus preparing the way for the recitative solo arias of the new operatic style.

The first great master of the European opera was Claudio Monteverdi (1567–1643), whose Opera *Ariadne,* first produced at the court of Mantua in 1608, moved the audience to tears. In the new *stile rappresentativo e recitativo* declamation and acting were harmoniously combined. As early as 1594 Jacobo Peri's (1561–1633) *Daphne,* with text by Rinuccini, had been performed in private before a group of Florentine connoisseurs. The first public opera house was opened in Venice in 1637. Ten years earlier Rinuccini's *Daphne* in Opitz's German version and with Schütz's music had been produced for the first time in Germany, and about the middle of the seventeenth century the art of the opera had conquered all the German court theaters.

For some time, however, the opera on German soil retained all the

---

* Counterpoint (Latin, *contrapunctus: punctus contra punctum:* "note against note") denotes the art of combining independent melodies in accordance with definite laws of musical composition. We distinguish a preharmonic and a postharmonic phase in the historical development of counterpoint. The preharmonic period reaches from the early medieval chant to the musical style of Palestrina. The postharmonic period begins at the end of the sixteenth century; its unsurpassed master is Bach and its ideal musical form is the fugue.

earmarks of the land of its birth: text, music, and singers were mostly Italian. In Vienna, Dresden, Munich, and elsewhere the courts cultivated the Italian type of opera and employed Italian composers, conductors, stage directors, and performers. Even in Hamburg, where the most serious attempt was made to create an indigenous operatic taste, many of the operas that appeared on the stage were German only in name but Italian in spirit and atmosphere.

Although Frederick the Great stated that he would "rather listen to a neighing horse than allow a German prima donna to sing at the Royal Opera," the Italian taste in music was gradually waning in the course of the eighteenth century. One of the reasons for this change was the growing melodramatic superficiality of the Venetian and Neapolitan styles. The serious-minded music lovers in Germany demanded depth, simplicity, and true feeling in place of ornamental flourishes, decorative trimmings, and sentimental lamentations.

Under the influence of the renewed interest in classical antiquity the Frankish composer, Christoph Willibald Gluck (1714–1787), convinced of the shallowness of Italian opera, became the creator of a new music drama that took its inspiration from Greek tragedy, subordinating the musical idiom to the propensities of a classically ennobled literary style and dramatic plot, and enriching the art of musical characterization by the reintroduction of chorus, dance, and orchestral accompaniment. The texts of Gluck's collaborator, Raniero di Calzabigi, show a keen realization of the German composer's revolutionary ideas, with which Gluck was able to turn the tide and break the stranglehold that Italy had gained on German music. The composer himself commented on his musical principles in the words with which he dedicated his opera *Alceste* (1767) to the duke of Toscana, the future Emperor Leopold II: "It has been my intention to confine music to its real task, i.e., to serve poetry for the sake of verbal expression and literary interpretation, without interrupting or weakening the plot by the addition of futile and unnecessary embellishment. It has been my further intention to do away with all those excesses, against which for some time common sense and good taste have revolted. I have considered it my special task to try to achieve a beautiful simplicity and to avoid the mistake of parading clever technical tricks at the expense of clarity."

The spirit of the Rococo and the neo-classical tendencies blend perfectly in the works of Joseph Haydn (1732–1809) and Wolfgang Amadeus Mozart (1756–1791). Together with Beethoven (cf. p. 426 sqq.) they are considered as the leaders of the new musical classicism of the Viennese school. Although Haydn's operas, masses, and other works of vocal music rank high, he is above all the great master of instrumental composition, especially of symphony and chamber music (string quartets), unequaled in the joyful and childlike optimism that permeates all of his works, revealing symbolically the placid beauty of the Austrian landscape and expressing the simple piety of the Austrian folk spirit. Haydn's oratorios are influenced by the choral style of Händel, adding to it the new elements of the rediscovery and musical illustration of nature.

Haydn and Mozart were the first and foremost creators of a popular musical style, breaking down the artificial barriers that separated the different classes of the German population and finding a way not only to the heart and soul of the people at large but demonstrating at the same time the possibility of a homogeneous and indigenous German culture.

In Mozart the delicate style of the Rococo experienced its final transfiguration. A child prodigy of extraordinary gifts but of unassuming modesty, Mozart achieved an early maturity of musical form, a sparkling gaiety, crystalline clarity, and sublime intelligibility, issuing from a great sensitivity and soft melancholy of mind and a profound realization of the tragic texture of life.

On his journeys to France, England, Italy, and the Netherlands Mozart was greeted with unending applause. His indebtedness to the Italian musical tradition, documented particularly in the Italian texts of his operas, did not prevent him from feeling deeply his obligations to the country and civilization of his birth. "I ask God every day," he told his father in a letter from Paris, "that He grant me to work for the greater honor of . . . the entire German nation."

In his works Mozart makes use of all the technical devices that his predecessors, above all Bach, Händel, Gluck, and Haydn, had developed and that were at his disposal. The thematic structure of Haydn's compositions became more expressive in Mozart's richer instrumentation. In the field of the opera he started out from the neo-Neapolitan *Opera Seria* but soon developed his own distinctive style in such operatic gems as *The Marriage of Figaro, Don Giovanni,* and *Cosi fan Tutte (All Act Alike).* His *Magic Flute (Zauberflöte)* became the paragon and adored model of the Romantic fairy opera (cf. p. 494 sq.).

The larger number of Mozart's more than six hundred works belong to the categories of the symphony (41), the sonata (53), and various types of chamber music. Several of his church compositions (masses, cantatas, vespers, litanies, etc.) and many of his arias and "Lieder" have achieved immortal fame. Mozart's swan song and a kind of funeral chant of the Rococo is the beautiful *Requiem* that he composed in 1791, in memory of the countess of Walsegg.

The Age of Rationalism. The modern world had taken its start from the individualism of Renaissance and Reformation. In Italy the ideal of the *uomo universale* (the universal or total man) had been conceived. In Germany Martin Luther had tried to establish a new church and society whose norms were not to be imposed from without but were to grow from the inwardness of the individual soul. In the following centuries the sovereign individual extended his dominion over the several provinces of life and civilization, conquering them one by one and step by step:

State, society, politics, economics, the arts, philosophy, morality, and religion.

a) *Philosophy and the New Scientific Methods.* In a seemingly disenchanted world, however, man began to discover new miracles. The great scientific geniuses of the seventeenth century found a new world in the study of nature: a world that appeared as self-sufficient, self-conserving, deprived of purposes and ends; a world that could be experimentally measured and rationally comprehended and explained. It appeared entirely possible to interpret all the phenomena of life in rational terms: religion and morals, State and society, art and science.

The new science itself was almost exclusively interested in observation, description, and experimentation, paying little attention to causal or genetic relations. It was engaged in reducing all qualitative distinctions to quantitative, extended, and therefore measurable entities. The many and perplexing phenomena of an atomistically split universe were rallied by the piercing intellect of Descartes (1596–1650), who forged a new theory of cognition and established a new unity of knowledge on the "infallible" authority of the science of mathematics. It was in 1619, the second year of the great war, that Descartes, then a soldier in the army of General Tilly, in his quarters in Neuburg on the Danube believed he had discovered the criterion of indubitable certitude in that self-consciousness of the thinking and doubting ego, which became for him the cornerstone of his philosophical system (*cogito, dubito — ergo sum:* "I think, I doubt — therefore I am"). Mathematically clear and distinct ideas and principles became for him the criteria of all truth.

However, the integral rationalism of Descartes was unable to bridge the gulf that separated mind and body, spirit and matter, "thought" and "extension." This unreconciled dualism remained a stumbling block and an open challenge for all the followers of Descartes to this day. Nevertheless, the Cartesian system presented itself as a tool for the rationalization of life in its entirety. Cartesian reasoning aided in the great discoveries in mathematics, physics, chemistry, biology, geology, and many related fields. Descartes himself was the creator of analytical geometry, whereby geometrical data may be translated into algebraic symbols and vice versa, and both Isaac Newton (1642–1727) and Gottfried Wilhelm Leibniz (1646–1716) discovered independently the differential calculus.

Baruch (Benedict) de Spinoza (1632–1677) developed his system of philosophical pantheism* *"more geometrico,"* making use of the method and terminology of Euclidean geometry. The world emanates with mathematical necessity from the one divine substance which man recognizes in only two of its infinitely many attributes: extension and consciousness, body and mind. The more the human mind becomes conscious of the divine origin and necessary constitution of the universe, the stronger is its control

---

* Pantheism denotes the identity of God and the universe, both being considered as parts or expressions of one and the same substance.

over emotions and passions and the greater its happiness. Although Spinoza did not share Descartes's and Newton's belief in a personal Creator and was excommunicated as a heretic by the synagogue of his native city of Amsterdam and denounced as an atheist by many of his contemporaries, his heart and mind were filled with religious reverence, with what he called the "intellectual love of God" (*amor intellectualis Dei*).

Rationalism and its Cartesian premises were carried to their extreme yet logical conclusions by the French philosophers of the age of "Enlightenment" (cf. p. 368 sq.), who prepared the way for the coming revolution. By their denial of God, the immortality of the soul, and free will, they resolved Descartes's metaphysical dualism into an all-embracing materialism and atheism. Julien de Lamettrie (1709–1751) defined man as a machine whose proper functioning is regulated by a reason which is itself the product of material and mechanical forces. The theorists of the French Revolution of 1789 transferred the method of scientific experimentation to a thoroughly planned and rationalized political and social economy. By a strange and paradoxical reversal of emphasis the freedom of the sovereign individual issued in the rule of the masses and the rise of collectivism.

While philosophical rationalism advanced triumphantly on the European continent, the British philosophers perfected the experimental method, based on sense experience and observation. Francis Bacon (1561–1626), the English lord chancellor, extolled critical judgment, gained by practical experience above mere book learning, and denied the existence of innate ideas. He expressed the conviction of most of his contemporaries when he coined the phrase: "Knowledge is power. We have as much power as we have knowledge." Thomas Hobbes (1588–1679), who for several years had been Bacon's secretary, became the philosophical spokesman of the absolutistic age when he described the State as the ferocious "Leviathan," devouring those who will not submit to its rule without questioning. The State, as the embodiment and supreme arbiter of all law, establishes, determines, and interprets all religious and moral values. John Locke (1632–1704), George Berkeley (1684–1753), and David Hume (1711–1776) carried the empirical* premises of their predecessors to their extreme conclusions: Locke denying the existence of substances, Berkeley denying the existence of an objective reality, and Hume espousing a complete skepticism.**

b) *Philosophy and Natural Religion* (*Deism*). The scientific spirit of the age of rationalism gradually developed a new religion of its own making, a scientific or natural religion, which took hold of pulpits, lecture halls, and the printed page. Its faithful adherents were convinced that the age of natural science had ushered in a golden age of supreme perfection, that it was to raise man to a higher level of existence, that it would bring forth a

---

* Empiricism derives all knowledge from experience. Only that is real which can be experienced. If intellectual experience is denied and only sense experience admitted, empiricism becomes sensism. Positivism, naturalism, and agnosticism are derivations of empiricism.

** Skepticism implies the denial of the existence or knowability of truth. Religious skepticism is often called agnosticism.

race that was more prudent, more contented, and infinitely happier. Descartes himself had visualized in his *Discourse on Method* that henceforth humankind would painlessly reap the fruits of the earth, that the evils and frailties of sickness and old age would disappear with the discovery of their causes, and that nature itself, once it was properly known, exploited, and dominated by man, would provide every aid that was needed for the salvation of mankind.

In the realm of religion, revelation and every supernatural, mystical, and miraculous element was eliminated, and religious dogma was subjected to the "natural light of reason" that was the common property of all men. What remained after this cleansing process was a so-called "innate" conviction of the existence of God, and a likewise "innate" consciousness of the moral law, the freedom of will, the immortality of the soul, and the dignity of human nature.

Luther's friend Melanchthon (cf. p. 331 sq.) had been the first one to outline the principles of a rationalistic theology, while Erasmus of Rotterdam (cf. p. 249 sq.) had set the first example of a rationalistic interpretation and criticism of the Scriptures. Spinoza in the seventeenth, and Kant (cf. p. 371 sqq.) in the eighteenth century continued and concluded the rationalization of religious beliefs, the latter making religion the servant of a self-sufficient (autonomous) morality.

The new religion of the rationalistic age was called "Deism." It retained the belief in a transcendent God as the "author" of nature. But while the Deists emphasized God's transcendence (His existence above the world, as its "Author"), they denied God's immanence (His existence within the world as its Sustainer). Once created, they claimed, the world is then left to follow its own intrinsic laws, without further interference by the extramundane God.

One of the earliest proponents of the system of natural religion was Lord Herbert of Cherbury (1581-1648), who mentioned the following five principles as bases of a rational theology: (1) there is a supreme being; (2) we owe reverence to this supreme being; (3) this reverence finds its expression in virtue and piety; (4) our trespasses must be atoned for by repentance; (5) God rewards and punishes us in accordance with His goodness and justice. Whatever else beyond these five principles is contained in any religious creed, is the result of clerical fraud or poetic fancy.

John Locke (1632-1704) advocates religious toleration and freedom of worship but wants to see atheists and Catholics deprived of these benefits, the former because they cannot swear any oath of allegiance, the latter because they themselves are intolerant. Locke admits the demonstrability of the existence of God and the possibility of God's extraordinary interference with the course of natural events. According to this philosopher the human mind is entirely passive, an "empty slate" (*tabula rasa*), upon which observations and experiences are inscribed. The term "empty slate," used in reference to the human mind, was first employed by Thomas Aquinas (cf. p. 145 sq.), who had linked it with the important concept of the "active intellect," denoting that mental spontaneity that reacts to external stimuli and draws universal ideas from particular observations (faculty of abstraction).

c) Rationalism in Germany. Among the first German scholars who adopted the rationalistic tenets of the French and English writers was the jurist and historiographer Samuel von Pufendorf (1632–1694). He was influenced by Thomas Hobbes and the Dutch jurist Hugo Grotius (1583–1645), who in his work "On the Law of War and Peace" (*De iure belli et pacis*) had laid the foundations of modern international law. Grotius based his concept of the "natural law" on the nature of man and that law and order which we observe in the universe. Pufendorf, who taught in the Universities of Heidelberg and Lund (Sweden), published his famous work on natural and international law (*De iure gentium et naturae*) in 1672. He considered human nature as the basis of all law, and human reason as its supreme authority. In his treatise on *The Christian Religion and its Relationship to Civic Life* (1687) he defended the absolute sovereignty of the State and called it a duty of all monarchs to provide for the happiness of their subjects, if necessary even against their will and by the use of force. The book won the admiration of the Great Elector (cf. p. 310 sq.) and gained for its author the titles of Privy Councilor and Royal Prussian Historiographer.

In the first half of the seventeenth century the great advances in mathematical studies were documented in such epochal works as John Kepler's *New Stereometry* (*Nova Stereometria,* 1615) and Cavalieri's *Geometry of Indivisibles* (*Geometria Indivisibilium,* 1635), both men introducing the notion of infinity into geometry. Transcending the limitations and the one-sided dogmatism of most of the rationalist doctrinaires, the universal genius of Gottfried Wilhelm Leibniz (1646–1716) rethought and reinterpreted the knowledge of his age in the terms of the past, the present, and the anticipated future. His synthetic mind was ever alert in discovering possibilities of unifying that which seemed to be irreparably divided and of reconciling apparently insolvable antinomies. Thus he endeavored to combine the scholastic-Aristotelian philosophy of the past with the mechanism and empiricism of his own scientific age. Against the rationalists he defended the integrity of the Christian concept of the Deity that both transcended the world and yet was essentially represented in its every part (Theism). He dreamed of a reunion of the separated religious denominations, and in his *Theodicy* (1710)* expounded in a novel way the principles of natural and supernatural theology. He tried to justify the dogma of the Trinity, the real presence of Christ in the consecrated Host (Sacrament of the Altar), and the doctrine of eternal damnation. The idea of a "perennial

---

* The term *Theodicy,* coined by Leibniz, denotes the philosophical and scientific attempt to justify the existence of God and to reconcile the divine attributes of infinite goodness, wisdom, and omnipotence with the actuality of physical and moral evil.

philosophy" (*philosophia perennis*), an expression first used by Augustinus Steuchus, librarian of the Vatican in Rome, in a book of the same title (1540), was resumed by Leibniz: he outlined the principles of a perennial philosophy that was to embrace the elements of truth contained in all the major philosophical systems of the past and present.

In his *Monadology* (1714) Leibniz developed some of the metaphysical concepts as contained in the nature philosophy of Giordano Bruno (cf. p. 275) and the Neo-Platonists of the early centuries of the Christian era. He described the world as a harmonically ordered system of "monads" — infinitely small, indivisible, and spiritual units, representing and reflecting the universe in varying and rising degrees of consciousness. God, the aboriginal monad (*Urmonade*), is also the one which possesses supreme and universal consciousness, the one which has preordained the substances and activities of all the other monads in a system or cosmos of "pre-established harmony." God Himself therefore is mirrored in the various gradations of being: in mineral, plant, animal, man, and the pure spirits. In such a magnificently ordered world physical and moral evil can only serve to contribute to the greater harmony of the whole by providing contrast motifs and complementary colors. As Leibniz considers the perfection of the universe more from an aesthetic than a moral or metaphysical point of view, he is bound to arrive at the optimistic conclusion that a world in which such harmony, unity, and integrity is achieved must be the best of all possible worlds.

With his insistence on the spiritual character of the individual monads Leibniz broke the chain of purely mechanical causation and reintroduced the Aristotelian and scholastic notion of purposes and ends (final causes). His deep insight into the nature of an organically developed individuality and personality made him the intellectual ancestor of German Idealism (cf. Chap. 9) and Romanticism (cf. Chap. 14), as represented philosophically by Herder, Goethe, Schiller, Kant, Fichte, and Hegel.

In the encyclopedic catholicity of his interests Leibniz was a typical Baroque philosopher. He is, however, remembered not only as a philosopher but as a great scientist and jurist as well. He made important discoveries in the fields of mathematics and physics and lasting contributions to the disciplines of history, political economy, international law, and linguistics. One of his most cherished projects aimed at the foundation of an international academy of sciences, and he finally succeeded in persuading Frederick III, the elector of Brandenburg-Prussia, to establish the Berlin Academy. Leibniz became its first president in 1700. He felt confident that science would eventually bring about an era of universal peace among the nations of the earth, and he greeted with enthusiasm the project of a league of nations that was presented to the Peace Congress of Utrecht by Abbé Saint-Pierre at the end of the Spanish War of Succession (1714).

Leibniz' correspondence extended to the most distant parts of the globe. He exchanged letters with the leading scholars in many countries, even with the Jesuit missionaries in faraway China. His acquaintance with leading statesmen and members of the nobility led to his appointment as German ambassador to the French court in 1672. As historiographer of the dukes of Brunswick Leibniz visited Vienna, Venice, Rome, Naples, Florence, Bologna, and Modena.

Among the several languages he mastered the philosopher gave preference to French, in the admiration of which he concurred with most of his contemporaries. Nevertheless he occasionally advocates the cultivation and improvement of the German language and regrets that the neglect of the national linguistic tradition has outweighed the benefits which otherwise could have accrued from the influence of French style and speech. Leibniz' own works, most of them written in French or Latin, give evidence of the almost universal scope of his interests and his knowledge, but they lack formal coherence and seem more like a monumental collection of ingenious essays than a carefully arranged system of ideas. The authentic edition of all his works, prepared by the Berlin Academy of Sciences, is nearing completion.

The so-called "popular" philosophers of German Rationalism were not greatly interested in the depth of Leibniz' metaphysical speculation. What appealed to them were his optimistic views concerning this "best of all possible worlds," because this optimism seemed to substantiate their own belief in the self-sufficiency of the universe and the unlimited perfectibility of man. To Christian von Wolff (1679–1754) belongs the merit, if merit it be, to have diluted and popularized the ideas of the great philosopher so as to make them intelligible to the average reader. From 1707 on Wolff lectured on mathematics, natural science, and philosophy in the University of Halle. He was expelled by order of King Frederick William I of Prussia when the Pietists (cf. p. 364 sqq.) objected to his rationalistic views. Frederick the Great, after his accession to the throne, called him back and made him chancellor of the university. For more than a quarter of a century Wolff's philosophy dominated the philosophical faculties of the German universities, and a whole generation of thinkers acknowledged in him their teacher. For Wolff there were no mysteries in heaven and on earth: everything became perfectly clear, simple, and natural once it was exposed to the tranquil searchlight of reason.

Nature, virtue, and reason were the three main themes of Wolff's speculation. He emphasized the equality of human nature and demanded that the precepts of the moral law be equally applied to all classes. He claimed that even peasants were able to read his treatises on logic. As the "genius of mediocrity" he appealed to members of all strata of society and counted among his pupils representatives of all professions.

The fame of having become the father of the German movement of "Enlightenment" (*Aufklärung,* cf. p. 368 sq.) Wolff shares with his colleague in the University of Halle, the jurist Christian Thomasius (1655–1728). From Leipzig, where he had started his academic career and where he had met with the opposition of Lutheran theologians, he moved to Halle and became one of the most popular teachers of the recently founded local university (1694). His high esteem for the German language as a medium of scientific and literary expression he demonstrated by delivering the first university lectures in German since the days of Paracelsus (cf. p. 273). He showed himself interested in the practical application of knowledge and demanded a thoroughgoing reorganization and vitalization of pedagogy. The cause of toleration and freedom of conscience was dear to his heart, and he fought with great vigor against antiquated and inhuman concepts and procedures in criminal law, especially against the still flourishing trials for witchcraft. Individual and social ethics Thomasius referred to the supreme tribunal of "common sense," and the quintessence of morality to him is the art "to lead a happy, contented, and gallant life by means of reason and virtue."

d) Rationalism in Education. The practical trend of Rationalism was reflected in the curriculums of the schools and universities. The time-honored "humanistic" education, based on formal discipline and proficiency in the liberal arts, was considered as obsolete and foreign to life. The rationalistic teacher was to prepare the student for the practical requirements of life, providing the tools for the acquisition of technical skill by means of vocational training. The "progressive" educators of the seventeenth century demanded that the student be confronted with actual problems and situations in State and society, in art and nature, and that rules and disciplines be enlivened by practical applications, by experiment and demonstration. "Realism" became the catchword of the new philosophies of education. One of the leading "reformers" in this field was Christian Weise (1642–1708), poet, teacher, and later on principal of the *"Gymnasium"** in Zittau (Saxony). He tried to educate his charges, most of them sons of noble families, in the spirit of the new pedagogy and to indoctrinate them with the new ideas.

In August Hermann Francke's (cf. p. 365) *Paedagogium* in Halle the chief emphasis in the curriculum was placed on natural science, mathematics, geography, and history, although, in accordance with Francke's pietistic convictions, all these subjects had their core and living source in religious instruction. The students were taught specific trades and on frequent visits to workshops they learned by observation as well as by practical application. A "Teachers' Seminary" (*Seminarium Praeceptorum*) in Halle was dedicated to the task of teacher training. By introducing his new methods of instruction into his orphanage and his school for poor children, Francke influenced the future development of the public school system in Germany. Public instruction on the grammar and high school level had for some time been in the hands of the Piarist Order, founded in 1597 by St. Joseph

---

* The *Gymnasium* is the earliest type of the German high school and may best be described as an equivalent of a liberal arts college that includes the lower high school grades (nine grades in all). It is distinguished from the later types of the *Realschule* and *Realgymnasium* by its strictly "humanistic" curriculum, embracing the liberal arts and the classical languages.

of Calasanza, a Spanish priest, and of the Congregation of the "Institute of Mary" (*Englische Fräulein*), founded by Mary Ward (1585-1645), an English nun. The members of these two religious orders conducted separate schools for boys and girls.

The opposition to this new progressive "realism" in education was strongest in the universities, which in many instances had become purely antiquarian in their interests and pursuits. In the course of the seventeenth century their vitality had suffered to such a degree that Leibniz proposed to let them die a natural death. Their scholarship was not merely out of tune with contemporary life and its pressing problems, but their blind allegiance to defunct authorities made them oblivious to the progress of science and rendered them incapable of independent research. About the turn of the century a gradual infiltration of the new ideas becomes noticeable. The University of Halle must be considered as the first German institution of higher learning in which the spirit of the modern age triumphantly celebrated its conquest of the past. It was at Halle that the principle of the freedom of teaching was solemnly proclaimed in 1711, when its *Rector* (president), Nicholas Gundling, in a speech delivered in honor of the first king of Prussia, praised the independence of scientific research. He called the university "the vestibule of liberty" and demanded that it lead its students fearlessly to truth and wisdom. He insisted that only free minds and free men would be capable of assuming such leadership as was needed in a university, and that by virtue of the demands of the natural law no man had the right to infringe upon another's freedom of conscience and conviction: "All compulsion in these matters is evil. . . . Teach, exhort, pray! If they listen, it is well; if they don't listen, learn to bear it. Truth rises before us: let him who can, ascend; let him who dares, take hold of her; and we will applaud" (*Veritas adhuc: qui potest ascendat; qui audet, rapiat et aplaudemus*).

e) *Methods of Adult Education.* In their endeavor to spread the new ideas and to raise the general standard of culture by means of increased knowledge and literacy, the leaders of the rationalistic movement addressed themselves to the general reading public in the new "moral weeklies," which made their first appearance early in the eighteenth century in England and were soon adopted and imitated in Germany. The weekly periodical was an offshoot of the pamphlets and newssheets which originated at the end of the fifteenth century. The first natural agents for the distribution of written and printed news were the postmasters, and in the beginning (*c.* 1500) it was the prevailing custom to add a special newssheet to one's letters. Basel, Strasbourg, Cologne, and Augsburg were among the earliest circulation centers of printed news pamphlets. In many instances the postmasters themselves were the compilers and editors of the news, but frequently princes and wealthy merchants had their own news correspondents who were stationed at the important centers of political and commercial activity.

The first regular weekly journal dates from the year 1609 and was edited in Strasbourg, while the first daily newspaper was published in Leipzig in 1660. The first home of the didactic and moralizing weeklies, however, is England. There the new type of family periodical appeared, designed to raise the intellectual and moral standards of the middle class and to influence individual and social life by means of criticism, satire, and moral instruction and edification. The most popular of the English moral weeklies were Sir Richard Steele's and Joseph Addison's *Tatler* (1707–1711), *Spectator* (1711–1712), and *Guardian* (1713). The most skillful of their German imitators were Johann Jacob Bodmer (*Discourses of Painters*, 1721–1723) and Johann C. Gottsched (*Vernünftige Tadlerinnen*, 1725–1727). More than five hundred different moral weeklies were published in Germany between 1713 and 1800. They represented an effective and novel form of adult education and were more influential than either book or sermon in the formation of public opinion and a general philosophy of life.

f) Social Divisions and Social Conventions. Although the Age of Absolutism and Rationalism had exalted the ruling prince beyond the pale of ordinary mortals, the social divisions among the different classes of subjects endured practically unabated. Peasants, burghers, and nobles, merchants and craftsmen, the learned and the unlettered were living their lives in accordance with definite social patterns, and the members of the upper classes attempted to meet the growing pressure of the less privileged by the erection of artificial barriers of etiquette and convention. The strict observation of all proprieties as to rank and title was the essential prerequisite of well-mannered social intercourse, and any infraction or neglect of one of the rules that referred to questions of precedence in rank was considered an unpardonable social crime.

The self-respecting carpenter, cobbler, tailor, baker, and confectioner, for all his strongly marked class consciousness, would proudly display on the signboard of his store or shop the coat of arms of the ruling princely house, if he was fortunate enough to count the court among his clients. He usually paid dearly for the privilege of calling himself *Königlicher Hofbäcker, Hofkonditor, Hofschneider* (royal court baker, court confectioner, court tailor). These titles often remained with the families and the business establishments of their bearers right down to the fall of the German monarchies in 1918.

Social rank and the powers and luxuries that it implied were considered as the most worthy goals of human endeavor, worthy enough indeed to justify the most abject kind of adulation and the sacrifice of honesty and character. It was the supreme ambition of the wealthy merchant to obtain a patent of nobility and thus climb one step higher on the social ladder. But even if this dream of a lifetime did not come true, he at least imitated the life of the nobility by the erection of palacelike and luxuriously furnished dwellings, by surrounding himself with numerous servants, and by an almost uninterrupted chain of social events, musical and theatrical entertainments, ballets, balls, and other festivities.

Although the absolutistic State had deprived the members of the nobility themselves of their ancient political prerogatives and privileges, they had been compensated by an even greater social prestige and by a definite consolidation of their economic and financial status. The pitiful position of the peasants made the tillers of the soil the prey of greedy nobles, and many of the huge lordly estates, especially in the German East, owe their origin to the exploitation and expropriation of a helpless peasantry.

g) *The Education of the "Cavalier."* The typical nobleman, however, felt truly at home only in the service of the court. As official members of the princely household the nobles occupied the positions of masters of ceremony, equerries (*Stallmeister*), chamberlains (*Kammerdiener*), chancellors, councilors (*Räte*), ambassadors, and army officers. The training of the future courtier or "cavalier" was entrusted to special "Knightly Academies" (*Ritterakademien*): boarding schools for young noblemen, the earliest of which were founded about the middle of the seventeenth century. The sons of Catholic nobles were frequently educated in the schools of the Jesuits.

Among the subjects to be mastered by the young nobleman a thorough knowledge of French and Latin seemed to be indispensable; the former on account of its cultural and literary values, the latter because it was the language of scholars and diplomats. The study of German and other modern languages was considered as desirable but received less emphasis. Poetry was esteemed as a potent means of adulation: to express one's homage and admiration in verse could hardly fail to impress the prince and gain his favorable response.

A person of noble rank was expected to be familiar with the latest developments in natural science and mathematics, with military science, and especially with the arts of fortification and shipbuilding. The study of history was recommended as "one of the most precious adornments of a titled person and, next to political science and common law, the most gallant part of his erudition."* Geography and the related disciplines of chronology, genealogy, and heraldry were highly praised because "without them it is impossible to understand history, to interpret intelligently the news, and to discuss rationally the problems of the modern state."** Most important, however, was a thorough familiarity with the science of politics and a complete mastery of the rules of political prudence.

Physical education and some training in the fine arts were to make the courtier alert and wide awake, socially fit in body and mind, adding to his appearance and behavior an external gloss and polish of physical and intellectual culture. The education of the young German nobleman was given its final touch by extended travel experience in foreign countries, preferably in Holland, England, France, and Italy.

Pietism. Medieval philosophy and theology had united rational and

---

* Dietrich Hermann Kemmerich: *Newly Opened Academy of Sciences,* etc. (1711).
** *Ibid.*

preterrational elements in a system of thought that harmoniously joined together scholasticism and mysticism (cf. p. 141 sqq.). But Luther and Melanchthon, in order to safeguard the edifice of their church, had eventually to eliminate all mystical religious impulses, and thus rationalism finally prevailed in theology as in other fields. In the centuries that followed the Reformation a growing number of individuals, unable to find an outlet for their thwarted emotional life in the rigid forms of orthodox dogmatism, began to segregate and separate themselves from the official churches and to form small groups, sects, and conventicles, in which they tried to satisfy their spiritual yearnings. In the seventeenth century, these timid beginnings converged in the movement which has been named Pietism.

In 1650 the former Jesuit priest Jean Labadie (1610–1674) had joined the Reformed Church in the Netherlands and had gathered a large following with his demand for a religious rebirth under the direct guidance and inspiration of the Holy Spirit. Influenced by Labadie's ideas, Philip Jacob Spener (1635–1705), a native Alsatian, drew up an ecclesiastical reform program (*Pia desideria,* 1675) which formed the basis of the pietistic revival movement. In the prayer meetings which he conducted in private homes and in churches (*Collegia Pietatis*) he preached a practical Christianity, a religion that was to penetrate into the innermost essence of human nature, a faith which was to document itself in works of mercy and charity. Following Spener's example, August Hermann Francke (1663–1727) opened his "*Collegia Biblica*" in Leipzig in 1686; they met with such enthusiastic response on the part of the students of the local university and the population of the city that the orthodox theologians, thoroughly alarmed, began to realize the threatening danger and succeeded in having the meetings prohibited by the civil authorities.

These disturbances in Leipzig, followed by similar ones in Hamburg, were the signal for the release of all the antiorthodox resentment that had been brewing among the laity of the Protestant churches. In this second and decisive stage of its development Pietism grew into a popular movement of large dimensions. The revolt of the laity, centering in the middle class (the *Third Estate*), issued in the first major onslaught against the absolute supremacy of the State and its ally, the Church. Religious "storm and stress" mingled with the manifestations of social and political dissatisfaction, and the revolt against the complacency of hidebound clericalism and secular despotism spread with amazing speed to various parts of Germany. Thus Pietism had reached its third stage. Enthusiastic sects and secret societies made their appearance, ancient and seemingly forgotten doctrines were revived, and all the many voices were passionately united in their outcry for the arrival of the Millennium.

On the surface Pietism showed itself violently opposed to Rationalism. It stressed personal experience, subjective feeling, the values of the inner life. But both Pietism and Rationalism were convinced that the nature of the Divinity could be comprehended empirically: the Pietist claimed that

God could be physically experienced in feeling and imagination; the Rationalist maintained that God could be known conceptually and intellectually. The one drew the Godhead into the individual heart; to the other the Deity became almost evanescent in the realm of impersonal abstraction. Pietists and Rationalists replaced a harmonious balance between emotion, will, and intellect by an exaggerated emphasis upon one of these faculties to the exclusion of the others. Pietism and Rationalism have in common the opposition to the orthodox churches and all forms of State religion; they both accentuate the ethical implications of religious doctrine, and they both believe in the testimony of the "inner light," to which the Rationalists refer as the "natural light of reason."

The ideal goal of the religious cravings of the Pietists was the rebirth of the human soul in Christ. To achieve this end they elaborated a richly graded scale of sensory and imaginative experiences, starting with the fearful sensation of sinful entanglements in a corrupt world, then gradually proceeding to a state of penitence and utter humiliation, and finally culminating in the hoped-for bliss of "conversion." Such an experience called for outward confessional manifestations, and thus the Pietists discovered in human emotions a creative force that softened the arid intellectualism of the age and made German thought and culture more sensitive to the beat of the human heart.

The deep religious feeling of the Pietists created for itself new forms of stylistic and linguistic expression which came to their fruition in the poetry of Klopstock (cf. p. 393 sq.). The elemental passion of the poets of the period of "Storm and Stress" was anticipated by Gottfried Arnold, whose *Unparteiische Kirchen- und Ketzerhistorie* (unpartisan history of churches and heretics) is mentioned with high praise in Goethe's *Dichtung und Wahrheit* (*Poetry and Truth*). It was the first work that applied the psychological method to Church history.

Arnold experienced his "revival" under Spener's guidance, and under Spener's influence he began to oppose the theology of his time. The complex world of his thought, the oscillating ways of his life, and the amazing intellectual range of his works mirror the most significant tendencies of the age. Religious "storm and stress" animates his vehement attacks against the conventional codes and rules of the compact majority in State and Church. He turns away from the disheartening actualities of the present and visualizes in sentimental yearning the fulfillment of his ideals in the times of the Apostles and the Fathers of the early Church. As a scholar, he had received a comprehensive scholastic and humanistic training, and the humanistic concepts of historical evolution are clearly noticeable in his historical works. He resigned as a member of the faculty of the University of Giessen because of the "insipid gossip, the ludicrous arrogance, hypocrisy, and false gravity of the universities."

Like the other Pietists, Arnold believed himself an instrument of the Godhead and wanted to see his poetry printed and published for the sake of the education and edification of others. According to him, genuine poetry has to serve the ultimate goal of life and it has to derive its inspiration from the eternal source of life. Spiritual revival he considered an absolute pre-requisite for the poet. Again the humanistic conception of science as a *"magistra vitae"* (guide of life), the humanistic conception of poetry as an "agreeable instruction" suggests a close relationship between Arnold's and the Humanist's point of view. In its striving for a unified and integrated Christian humanism Arnold's "pietism" is clearly distinguished from Luther's piety, which insisted on the actuality and the full preservation of the abysmal dualism between God and the world.

The social incentives of the pietistic movement were realized in Francke's schools and orphanages in Halle and in Count Ludwig von Zinzendorf's (1700–1760) foundation of the "Union of Moravian Brethren" (*Brüder-gemeinde*) at Herrnhut in Saxony. The original members of Zinzendorf's religious community were descendants of those Hussites (cf. p. 176 sq.) who had fought against the imperial armies to preserve their religious and national independence. At the beginning of the sixteenth century their sect numbered well over 100,000 followers. Several persecutions, however, as well as a relaxation of their original asceticism led to their gradual dis-integration. Many of them migrated to Prussia and Poland, but those who remained became, later on, the nucleus of Zinzendorf's Herrnhut foundation.

The beginnings of German immigration in the United States of America are closely linked with the pietistic movement and its policy of establishing foreign missions overseas. The first German colony in North America (Pennsylvania) was founded by groups of Mennonites (cf. p. 242) from southern Germany under the leadership of Daniel Pastorius (1651–1719), who landed in Philadelphia in 1683. Pastorius was one of Spener's disciples, and the settlers whom he had brought to the New World were the first to raise their voices in protest against the abuses of slavery. Members of Zinzendorf's community journeyed as missionaries to St. Thomas in the West Indies, while others joined their coreligionists in Pennsylvania. Zinzendorf himself paid several visits to their flourishing settlements.

The cultural fruits of Pietism are manifold but are most evident in reli-gious poetry, in the sentimental and autobiographical novel, in the art of letter writing, and in music. With its urge for soul-searching self-analysis, for a heavily charged emotionalism and personalism, Pietism represented a potent element in the formation of the new concepts of personality that inspired the classical writers and thinkers of Germany in the eighteenth and nineteenth centuries. Even the limitations imposed upon the members of the pietistic sects by a certain narrow provincialism and a puritanical denunciation of all worldly concerns could not prevent their movement in the long run from acting as a humanizing force, working for a more irenic and tolerant religious attitude, and from thus meeting halfway the prevalent currents of the age of enlightenment. Many of the leaders of German thought and culture in the following two centuries grew up in the shadow and shelter of this pietistic heritage, acknowledging their debt to a form of spirituality that illumined with its kindly light the years of their intellectual and moral formation (Lavater, Goethe, Jacobi, Schleiermacher, Novalis, Gerhart Hauptmann, etc.).

Enlightenment ("Aufklärung"). From the later Middle Ages and the Reformation to the period of princely absolutism and enlightened despotism the ancient authority of the Christian Church had steadily declined. The culture of the Rococo revealed the shaky foundations of a society whose members were still clinging to certain external forms of the past but had lost contact with all the vital meaning of the spiritual tradition of Western civilization. From the end of the seventeenth to the end of the eighteenth century the social and cultural life of Europe was presenting a splendid façade that carefully covered the symptoms of decay, but at the same time revealed a glittering unrest and a lack of stability and self-assurance that bespoke an uneasy conscience and a growing anxiety as to the final outcome of a dissipated and wasteful existence. When the life of European aristocracy had dissolved into an endless series of love affairs, scandals, festivities, and games, the time seemed to have arrived for the healthier members of the social organism to call for retribution and to restore poise and balance by a process of revolution and rejuvenation.

The production of Pierre Beaumarchais' (1732–1799) *Marriage of Figaro,* an excoriating satire on the decadent nobility, at the Théâtre Français in Paris in 1784, was an event that symbolized the approaching end of *"la folle journée"* (the mad journey).

a) The Origins of Enlightenment. The first and most effective broadside attack against the established authorities of the past came from the "republic of letters," the representative thinkers of the eighteenth century. The symptoms of cultural decline were not confined to any one country and, accordingly, the voices of social criticism were simultaneously heard in every part of Europe. But France, which for a long time had politically and culturally dominated the European scene, and where the disintegration of the monarchy and nobility was most marked, became the center of the revolutionary criticism of the *"philosophes."* The thirty-five volumes of the *Encyclopédie ou dictionnaire raisonné des sciences, des arts et des métiers* (*Encyclopedia,* or *Rational Dictionary of the Sciences, Arts, and Trades,* 1751–1780) became the great collective manifestation of revolutionary thought, wherein the criteria of modern individualism, rationalism, and mechanism were systematically applied to the fields of religion, philosophy, literature, science, and sociology. The editors were Denis Diderot (1713–1784) and Jean D'Alembert (1717–1783), and among the contributors were such illustrious thinkers as Voltaire, Turgot, and Montesquieu. The corruptness of the supposedly Christian civilization of Europe was here for the first time contrasted with the assumed superiority of the "noble savage" and the humane wisdom of Oriental thought. The leader in the attack against official Christianity, against intolerance and bigotry, was François Marie Arouet, better known by his pen name of Voltaire (1694–1778), who in the ninety volumes of his collected works subjected every department of human endeavor to his scathing criticism and who, with his "Essay on the Customs and the Spirit of the Nations," created a new type of critical historiography and cultural history (*Kulturgeschichte*). As the final goal of the human race he visualized an age of enlightened humanism, based on social responsibility and a natural and rational religion.

b) German Enlightenment. In Germany the new ideas met with warm response, but their radicalism was tempered by a certain reverence for traditional values and a more or less academic adherence to the principles of the French thinkers. For Kant (cf. p. 371 sqq.) enlightenment meant "emancipation from an immaturity that man had brought upon himself through his own fault." That immaturity he defined as "the incapability of using one's reason without external guidance. . . . You must be courageous enough," he said, "to make use of your own faculty of reasoning: that is the true motto of enlightenment."

The city of Berlin, where Frederick the Great had encouraged the propagation of the ideas of the French Encyclopedists, became the center and bulwark of German Enlightenment. The most distinguished representative of enlightened thought was Friedrich Nicolai (1733–1811), a Berlin book dealer, whose ideal of a philosopher was Christian Wolff (cf. p. 360), and who in his novels, satires, travel books, and philosophical essays exhibited a narrow, shallow, and intolerant rationalism. Though he was in contact with practically all the illustrious thinkers of the age, he antagonized most of them by his malicious and destructive criticism. In Schiller's and Goethe's epigrams (*Xenien*) of the year 1797 Nicolai is ridiculed as an empty-headed and coarse fellow, and in Goethe's *Faust* he appears as "Proctophantasmist" amidst the spirits, witches, and devils of the "Walpurgisnacht," among a motley crowd of creatures whom his enlightened zeal had all too sweepingly explained away.

Among Nicolai's collaborators, later on known as the "Nicolaites," the most capable was the Jewish popular philosopher Moses Mendelssohn (1729–1786), Lessing's (cf. p. 380 sqq.) friend, a representative of enlightened Deism (cf. p. 356 sq.), a man of the highest intellectual and moral caliber, an untiring worker for the advancement of the human race, and an eloquent advocate of religious toleration. In his aesthetic views he influenced Schiller and Kant, and his speculation on the sensitive faculty contributed to the increasing psychological knowledge of the age. The leading character in Lessing's drama *Nathan the Wise* bears the features of Moses Mendelssohn.

Many of the views of the enlightened German thinkers were transmitted to the reading public through several newly founded periodicals, taking the place of the "moral weeklies" (cf. p. 363), which had fallen into growing disrepute. Nicolai himself edited the "Library of Belles Lettres and the Liberal Arts" (*Bibliothek der schönen Wissenschaften und der freiei*

Künste, 1757), the "Letters Concerning the Most Recent Literature" (*Briefe, die neueste Literatur betreffend,* 1759), and the "General German Library" (*Allgemeine deutsche Bibliothek,* 1766). These periodicals, to which Nicolai, Mendelssohn, Lessing, and other authors contributed, tried to review critically the more recent publications in Germany and to spread general information regarding literary affairs. The most influential and long lived of the three journals was the *Allgemeine deutsche Bibliothek,* whose publication ceased in 1806, and which during these four decades molded to a large extent the standards of literary taste and critical judgment.

c) Secret Societies. The principles of enlightened thought were adopted and promoted by a number of secret societies, the most important of which was the institution of Freemasonry, founded at the beginning of the eighteenth century. The first masonic "Grand Lodge" was constituted in England in 1717. The *Book of Constitution* of the year 1723 stated as the purpose of the society the construction of the Grand Temple of Humanity, the education of an enlightened and united mankind that had freed itself from superstition and from the restrictions imposed by religious, political, and social dogmas, parties, and authorities. The individual members were to strive for personal ennoblement and the harmonious integration of their characters, on the basis of humanitarianism and religious toleration. Strict secrecy surrounded the complex organization of the society, whose elaborate symbolic rituals were in part derived from the medieval masonic guilds. The initiation proceeded by degrees from the stage of apprentice to that of journeyman and master.

The masonic movement rapidly gained a large following in all European countries. It was introduced in France and Ireland in 1725, in Scotland, Spain, Portugal, Italy, and North America during the following decade. The leaders of the American and French revolutions, Washington and Franklin as well as Mirabeau and Robespierre, were freemasons.

The first German Grand Lodge was established in Hamburg in 1737. German Freemasonry retained the belief in God and immortality and appropriated the spirit of German classical literature and philosophy, while in the Romanic countries the lodges adopted the atheistic and materialistic outlook of the Revolution of 1789. The antiecclesiastical character of Free-masonry was especially pronounced in Spain, Portugal, France, and Italy. In the latter country the lodge played a leading part in the nineteenth century in bringing about the destruction of the secular power of the papacy, the annexation of the Papal States by Italy, the secularization of education, and the national unification of the country. The Catholic Church has placed membership in the lodge under the penalty of excommunication (Decree of Clement XII of 1738 and canon 2335 of Canon Law, 1918), and the Fascist and National-Socialist governments of Italy and Germany suppressed the masonic lodges in their countries as incompatible with the interests of the national State.

In the eighteenth century most of the political and intellectual leaders of

Germany were admitted to membership in the lodge (Frederick the Great, Nicolai, Klopstock, Wieland, Herder, Goethe, Fichte, Mozart, Haydn, etc.), and in the nineteenth century members of the Hohenzollern dynasty and most representatives of Prussian officialdom were freemasons. Lessing, in his *Discourses for Freemasons* (*Gespräche für Freimaurer*), praised the ideals of Freemasonry as being in harmony with the spirit of enlightenment and true Humanism.

An interesting offshoot of Freemasonry was the "Order of Illuminati" (the Enlightened Ones), founded by Adam Weishaupt (1748–1830), formerly professor of Canon Law in the University of Ingolstadt in Bavaria. Aims, ideals, and organization resembled closely those of the masonic lodges, but the antiauthoritarian tendency was more conspicuous. The Order was suppressed in Bavaria in 1784 but experienced a short-lived revival at the end of the nineteenth century (1896–1933).

d) Critical Philosophy: Kant. The eighteenth century had produced a number of popular philosophers who, like Christian Wolff (cf. p. 360), had made philosophy accessible to the average man and woman, while at the same time depriving it of much of its former earnestness and depth. The limitations of the philosophical foundations of the age of enlightenment were realized by no one more keenly than by Immanuel Kant (1724–1804) who, himself deeply rooted in rationalistic thought, nevertheless succeeded in overcoming the narrowness of its dogmatism.

A native of Königsberg in East Prussia, Kant had attended the local university and accepted the main tenets of the widely acclaimed rationalistic systems of Leibniz and Wolff. He had made his own the scientific and mechanical explanation of nature as presented by Isaac Newton and had heartily approved of Descartes's saying: "Give me matter, and I shall construct a world." Kant's ideas on the origin of the planetary system from chaotic gaseous nebulae, as he laid them down in his "General Natural History and Theory of the Heavens" (1755), were later on resumed by the French astronomer and mathematician, Pierre Laplace (1748–1827), and formulated in the "Kant-Laplace Theory." But Kant was convinced that it was impossible to apply the mechanical explanation of nature to organic life, and he was unwilling to relinquish certain religious premises that had been implanted in his mind by the pietistic influences of his youth and that had been restated in Rousseau's (cf. p. 376) striking phrase: "Gravitation effects in the corporeal world what love creates in the world of the spirit."

Faced by the alternative of an all-embracing rationalism which left no avenue open to spiritual realities, and an integral empiricism which had ended in Hume's skeptical denial of the possibility of objective knowledge, Kant felt the necessity of transcending the limited viewpoint of either of these extreme positions and of combining their partial truths in a new philosophical synthesis.

It was the influence of Hume's philosophy that awoke Kant from his "dogmatic slumber" by shaking his naïve confidence in the absolute reliability of human reason. From now on, the all-important question in his mind concerned the possibility and validity of human knowledge.

Holding a chair as professor of logic and metaphysics at the University of Königsberg in East Prussia since the year 1770, Kant published his masterpiece, *The Critique of Pure Reason,* in 1781. The author himself likened the significance of this work to the revolutionary discovery of Copernicus: as Copernicus had demonstrated the illusory nature of the seeming revolution of the firmament around the earth, so Kant attempted to prove that human thought was not formed and determined by extramental objects but that the objects in the extramental world depended in their meaning and rational significance on the organization of the human mind. Things as they are in themselves (*"das Ding an sich"*) are inaccessible to human reason. They are only knowable as they appear to us (as *"phenomena"*), not as they actually exist outside the human mind (as *"noumena"*). Objective experience is molded into sensitive intuitions by the *a priori* (innate) forms of sensibility, space and time. The understanding *(Verstand)* in turn molds these intuitions into objects of knowledge, by means of the main categories of quality, quantity, relation, and modality. Thus the synthetic action of the understanding imparts meaning and coherence to the otherwise unrelated and unconnected series of our perceptions. Extension and duration being mere modifications of time and space, are purely subjective, and a "science of being" (ontology, metaphysics) becomes an absolute impossibility.

It was, however, just such metaphysical speculation that had been used by the rationalist philosophers (Descartes, Spinoza, Leibniz, etc.) as well as by the scholastics (cf. p. 141 sqq.) to prove the existence of God, the immortality of the soul, and the freedom of will. And Kant, too, had expressly stated that the primary concern of his speculation was the vindication of the religious claims of the past. It was his intention "to dethrone knowledge in order to make room for faith." How did Kant achieve his aim, and how was he able to combine the pretended subjectivity of all human knowledge with the validity of absolute and necessary norms and laws?

The answer is given in the *Metaphysics of Morals* (1785) and *The Critique of Practical Reason* (1788). In these two works Kant withdraws faith and religion from the sphere of pure reason and places them under the absolute dominion of the "moral law." Both Luther and Leibniz had been in search of objective norms, which were not to be imposed authoritatively from without but were to issue from the innermost essence of the individual. For Kant the realm of human freedom becomes the ground where individual independence (autonomy) and objective necessity meet. For him nothing is as indubitable as "the starry firmament above me and the moral law within me."

The "moral law" confronts man in the form of the "categorical imperative," which exhorts him to act in such a way that the principles of his actions may at any time be applicable to all mankind; to choose such maxims as may be made the bases of a universal law and rule. According to Kant, the freedom of will, the immortality of the soul, and the existence of God are truths that are inherent in the constitution and inclination of the moral nature of man. They cannot be demonstrated by pure reason, but they can and must be "postulated" by "practical reason" if human life is not to be voided of any and all meaning.

If the innate and imperative character of the moral law is admitted, man must also have the power to live up to its demands, i.e., he must have free will. But life on this earth is much too short to allow for the perfect fulfillment of the demands of the categorical imperative: therefore practical reason postulates the immortality of the soul. Furthermore, every human being longs for lasting happiness, and yet even the most perfect obedience to the moral law does not yield that result: there must be a power therefore that fulfills man's desire for eternal happiness, and this power we call God. Finally, the moral law demands justice and retribution, and we know from experience that this demand is frequently not satisfied in this earthly life. Practical reason, therefore, postulates the dispensation of perfect justice by the omniscient and omnipotent God in a life beyond.

In his emphasis on the power of human will as well as in the aesthetic speculation of his *Critique of Judgment* (1790) Kant had given a fuller and truer description of human nature than was current in the age of enlightenment. He had recognized the relative significance of the faculties of thinking, feeling, and willing as against the prevailing one-sided intellectualism. In his religious speculation, on the other hand, he agrees with the other spokesmen of the age in defining a good and noble life as the supreme form of worship. His "autonomous" ethics demands that the moral law be obeyed for its own sake, regardless of eternal reward or punishment and without the aid of dogmas, prayers, and cultic observances. While the philosopher thus upholds with the enlightened thinkers the emancipation of man from the authorities of the past, he does not share their optimistic view of human nature. In the treatise *Religion within the Boundaries of Pure Reason* (1793) he develops an ethical rigorism which insists that the inherent evil in human nature be overcome by a stern sense of duty and by the firm exercise of will power. He goes so far as to maintain that natural inclination and the moral law are contradictory, and that therefore a human action can only be termed moral if it is performed in opposition to the urges of our sensitive nature. Schiller (cf. p. 417 sqq.) who in other respects adopted Kant's moral philosophy, satirized his ethical rigorism in a pointed epigram,* while at the same time trying to overcome it by a process of

---

* *Scruple of Conscience*
  Willingly serve I my friends; but, alas, I do it with pleasure;
  Therefore I often am vexed, that no true virtue I have.
  Solution
  As there is no other means, thou hadst better begin to despise them;
  And with aversion, then, do that which duty commands.
  (Tr. by E. A. Bowring; Belford Clarke & Co., New York.)

education which culminated in the harmonization of natural inclination and the moral law.

Kant saw the meaning of history in the growing realization of moral freedom, eventually leading to the establishment of eternal peace among the nations of the earth (*On Eternal Peace,* 1795). In his personal life the philosopher embodied the very principles of his teaching and thinking, and his sincerity, simplicity, modesty, and moral earnestness made him one of the most admired and influential intellectual leaders of modern times.

e) Enlightened Theology. The movement of enlightenment in Germany tended toward antireligious radicalism only in a few instances. The majority of its representatives were neither atheists nor agnostics. One of the most revolutionary manifestoes of theological criticism was the so-called *Wolfenbüttel-Fragmente,* originally composed by the Hamburg orientalist and theologian, Samuel Reimarus (1694–1768), and later on published by Lessing (cf. p. 380 sqq.) without mentioning the name of the author (1774–1778). These "Fragments" represented part of Reimarus' more comprehensive "Apology for Reasonable Worshippers of God," wherein he attempted to prove the fraudulous character of the New Testament, claiming that the real teaching of Christ was in complete harmony with an enlightened and rational theology. Lessing in an explanatory note made several reservations as to his own critical point of view and insisted that it was the main purpose of his edition to stir up a theological controversy and to demonstrate Christianity as a living spiritual force: "The letter is not the spirit, and the Bible is not identical with religion. . . . There was religion before there was a Bible. Christianity existed before the Apostles and Evangelists wrote. Our religion is not true because the Apostles and Evangelists taught it: they rather taught it because it is true. . . . All the written documents cannot impart to it an inner truth if it has none."

Lessing's own views on the nature of Christianity are contained in an essay entitled "The Education of the Human Race" that was published in 1780, one year before his death. Here the great world religions — Paganism, Judaism, and Christianity — represent successive grades in an educational curriculum, arranged by God, the great schoolmaster. In each grade the presentation of the subject matter is adapted to the mental capacity of the learners. In the childhood stage of mankind (Paganism and Judaism) God had to reveal His will and guide His charges by means of visible and tangible signs, by promises of reward and punishment, while in the stage of adolescence He used the symbolism of the Christian dogmas to lead man's thoughts and endeavors to a higher spiritual plane. But the stage of maturity will be reached in the not-too-distant future, when men will no longer look out for rewards and no longer stand in need of punitive restrictions and coercive dogmas but will practice virtue for its own sake: "The time of a new and eternal Gospel will certainly arrive. Continue on your inconspicuous path, eternal providence!"

These views of Lessing's as much as those of Kant's may serve to illustrate how far the leading minds of the eighteenth century were removed from the comfortable complacency of the popular spokesmen of enlightenment, for whom their own age represented the apex of all that was true, good, and beautiful.

The friends of enlightened thought gradually gained hold of the highest positions in Protestant church administration and began to dominate the theological faculties in the Protestant universities. Being theological rationalists, most of them were opposed to Luther's doctrine of "salvation by faith alone" (*sola fide*), for which they substituted their own idea of "salvation by reason alone" (*sola ratione*). Others followed Luther in drawing a strict dividing line between faith and reason, eliminating every element of rationality from the religious sphere (*Fideism*).

In the Catholic territories of Germany the princes were the most powerful friends and protectors of enlightened thought. Empress Maria Theresa (cf. p. 313 sq.) as well as her son, Emperor Joseph II (cf. p. 320), promoted the ideas of enlightenment as a means of strengthening the foundations of the absolutistic State and of extending its supremacy over the Church. Pope Pius VI, on a special journey to Vienna, fruitlessly attempted to dissuade the emperor from carrying his ecclesiastical reform measures too far. All episcopal seminaries and monastic schools were closed by imperial decree, all contemplative religious orders were suspended and their property confiscated. The proceeds from the sale of the monastic estates were used for the establishment of new parishes and for the support of orphanages, hospitals, and poorhouses. The number of Church holidays was reduced and pilgrimages and processions were prohibited. The liturgy and the divine services were simplified and stripped of all external display.

The ideas of the enlightened age penetrated into Catholic schools and seminaries, into monasteries, convents, and parish houses. Nicholas of Hontheim, auxiliary bishop of Treves (1701–1790), published under the pen name of Justinus Febronius a widely read book on the papacy (*De statu ecclesiae,* 1763) in which he advocated the Conciliar Theory of the later Middle Ages (cf. p. 173 sq.), demanding that the papacy be divested of its absolute teaching and governing power over the clergy and laity.

The idea of a general secularization of ecclesiastical possessions was first conceived in Prussia in 1795. The plan was heartily seconded in the following year by the provincial administrations of Wurtemberg and Baden and received the approval of Emperor Francis II in 1797. The methods of procedure were discussed by the German princes with Talleyrand (1754–1838), formerly bishop of Autun, and at that time one of the chief councilors of Napoleon. The secularization was legally confirmed in the "Principal Decree of the Imperial Deputation" of 1803 (cf. p. 325). This decree of secularization cost the Catholic Church in Germany 1719 square miles of landed property with a population of three and one-half million and an annual revenue of about twenty-two million taler (approximately 66 million Reichsmarks or 17 million dollars).

The spirit of enlightenment was clearly in evidence in the increasing religious toleration between Catholics and Protestants and in several renewed attempts at effecting a reconciliation and reunion of the separated Christian denominations. In Prussia these irenic and ecumenic tendencies resulted in the unification of the Lutheran and Reformed churches in 1817, the year of the third centenary of the Lutheran Reformation. Other German lands imitated Prussia's example in the following decade.

After the death of Frederick the Great the Prussian government relinquished its benevolent protectorship of religious enlightenment. A decree of Frederick William II of the year 1788 threatened punitive action against the unorthodox Protestant clergy, and a royal order in Council of 1791 contained the following: "I can and shall never tolerate that the common people be drawn away from the old and true Christian religion by false doctrines or that writings which try to further such ends be printed in my country."

f) State and Society: Rousseau. The age of enlightenment designated the sovereignty of the people as the supreme norm of the State and its individual members. According to Rousseau (1712–1778), the body politic constitutes a distinct moral person that comes into existence by "the total alienation" of individual rights to the whole community. This is the political and social philosophy that Rousseau advocated in *The Social Contract* (1762), maintaining that lawful government derives its authority from the consent of the governed.

The idea of the sovereignty of the people had been advanced long before Rousseau: Aristotle had defined a citizen as one who shares in governing and in being governed (Pol. I, 12, and II, 2). He had taught that all citizens have in principle a claim to civil power, but that the exceptional individual ought to be made king by the choice of the freemen who constitute the State. Augustine and Thomas Aquinas had defined society as "a multitude, united by juridical consent (*iuris consensu*) and a community of interest" (*Summa Theologica*, 2–2, q. 42, a. 2), and the latter had placed the legislative power in the people or their vice-regent (*Summa Theologica*, 1–2, q. 90, a. 3). The Dominican and Jesuit scholars from the middle of the sixteenth century to Suarez (cf. p. 304 sq.) in the seventeenth century had taught that civil sovereignty is received from God by the people, who in turn entrust it to their rulers by constitutional consent.

Rousseau acknowledged his indebtedness to John Locke (cf. p. 356 sq.) who a century earlier, in his *Second Treatise on Civil Government,* had taught that civil society is juridically established by a covenant of the people, that the law of nature obligates them to observe this contract, and that sovereignty is limited in its power by this social covenant. The innovation in Rousseau's theory of the sovereignty of the people consists in his abandonment of the immutable bases of the natural law, so that the social contract is apt to become an arbitrary rule of the collective sentiment of shifting majorities. Theoretically and logically speaking, Rousseau's "social contract" would have to be renewed by each successive generation.

g) Enlightenment in Education. Convinced of its absolute intellectual superiority over the "dark" centuries of the past, the age of enlightenment attempted to inculcate its ideas into homes and schools. It is because of these didactic tendencies that the eighteenth century has been called "the pedagogical century." The doctrines of enlightenment were taught in the lecture halls of the universities, preached in the pulpits, and proclaimed on the stage. In 1784 Schiller (cf. p. 417 sqq.) delivered his famous lecture, "On the Stage, Considered as a Moral (didactic) Institution," in which he assigned to the theater the educational task of spreading the light of wisdom throughout the State: "Clearer ideas, truer principles, purer emotions emanate from here and flow through the veins of the people; the fog of barbarism, of dark superstition disappears, and night gives way to the victorious power of light." A manual dealing with every phase of social intercourse was published by Baron Adolf von Knigge (1752–1796), containing "precepts concerning human behavior so as to live happily and socially contented in this world, and to impart a like happiness to one's fellow men."

Education became one of the major concerns of enlightened State government. In Brandenburg-Prussia a general school directorate was created by Frederick the Great's minister of education, and in Austria Maria Theresa placed the entire school system under the supervision of a governmental committee. The reorganization of the public schools, however, was not begun until the end of the eighteenth century, although as early as 1717 King Frederick William I of Prussia had issued an edict that imposed on all parents the obligation of sending their children to school. Frederick the Great, his son and successor, considered the schools chiefly as means for the development of political efficiency and economic abundance, disregarding humanistic and truly pedagogical motives.

New educational impulses were awakened by Rousseau and two of his German-speaking disciples, Johann Basedow (1723–1790) and Johann Heinrich Pestalozzi (1746–1827), the former of German, the latter of Swiss nationality. With their deeper understanding of human nature and their broader conception of human life they softened the rigid educational philosophy of the enlightened doctrinaires and sympathized with the pedagogical ideals of the Pietists (cf. p. 364 sqq.). By introducing emotional incentives into education they tried to break away from the purely rationalistic and intellectualistic pedagogy that had prevailed under the influence of Cartesian philosophy and that had found its clearest formulation in the educational theories of Johann Herbart (1776–1841). But in trying to avoid the psychological mistakes of the rationalist educators, these German followers of Rousseau did not always escape the pitfalls of their master's sentimentalism and his all-too-optimistic faith in the intrinsic goodness of human nature "in the raw."

With the support of Prince Leopold Frederick of Anhalt-Dessau, Basedow founded his *Philanthropinum* in Dessau in 1774, a "humanitarian school for teachers and learners," from which corporal punishment was banished and in which the zeal of the student was to be stimulated by the cultivation of his creative self-activity and his social instincts. The formal discipline of the Latin schools was severely criticized as an "unheard-of waste of time." Knowledge was to be acquired not by memorization and drill but by a direct appeal to the nature of the child and by arousing his interest in playful co-operation with the educational aims of the teacher.

Rousseau's contempt of the abstract and theoretical knowledge of contemporary civilization and his glorification of the primitive state of nature was shared by Pestalozzi, the Swiss educator, who was instrumental in introducing the principles of the new pedagogy into the public schools. He was convinced that personal example, not subject matter, was the decisive factor in education. Instruction was to begin with visible demonstration, to proceed from there to the formation of concepts and ideal patterns, always taking account of the relative capacities of the growing child. The goal of all education is for Pestalozzi the harmonious development of the human faculties, the training of "head, heart, and hand" in constant interplay with the vital forces of life. Such a genuinely humane education was to provide the unshakable basis for any kind of vocational training.

To demonstrate the practicability of his theories Pestalozzi established a model institution on his small estate in the Swiss canton of Aargau, where he gave shelter and instruction to fifty beggar children. "For years," he wrote, "I have been sharing the life of fifty beggar-children, in poverty sharing my bread with them, living like a beggar myself, so that I might learn how to teach beggars to live like human beings." In 1799 he opened a second school for children of the poor in Stans, and in 1800 he found employment as a public school teacher at Burgdorf in the canton of Bern, where a few years later he founded a teacher's college that attracted the attention of the leading pedagogues of many countries.

h) Literature and Literary Criticism. For the enlightened mind the purpose of all art in general and of literature in particular was moral instruction, resulting in moral enjoyment, edification, and improvement. However, literary criticism in Germany advanced beyond these limited objectives as soon as it was forced to deal with literary works whose scope transcended the traditional scheme of literary rules.

Johann Christoph Gottsched (1700–1776), professor of poesy and philosophy in Leipzig, ruled for many years as the unopposed leader of the literary representatives of German enlightenment. It was only in his old age that he had to release his dictatorial grip on the world of letters and that his well-meant critical and literary endeavors became the object of scorn and ridicule.

Following the precepts of Horace's (65–8 b.c.) and Boileau's (1636–1711) poetics Gottsched made imitation of nature the criterion of poetic expression. As a disciple of Christian Wolff (cf. p. 360) he considered poetry and art as moral and educational agencies. In the tragedy of the ancients as well as in the neo-classical drama of the epoch of Louis XIV he admired most of all the smoothness and regularity of literary style and artistic form, disregarding altogether the underlying imaginative and emotional elements. Clarity, regularity, and naturalness he considered as the essential requisites of a good piece of literature. Thus, with his widely read *Attempt at a Critical Poesy for the Germans* (1730), published approximately one hundred years after Opitz' poetics (cf. p. 299), he gave evidence that literary criticism in the age of enlightenment was as far removed from the appreciation of the true nature of poetry as it had been in the preceding period of rationalism.

Perusing Gottsched's directions for the composition of a poem or a dramatic plot, it would seem that such a task is beset with few difficulties: "At the outset you must select an instructive moral lesson. . . . Next you must conceive the general outline of certain events in which an action occurs that most distinctly demonstrates the chosen lesson." This having been accomplished, there remains only the simple question: do you wish to turn your idea into a fable, a comedy, a tragedy, or an epic? If a fable, you must give your characters the names of animals; if a comedy, your persons must be burghers; but if a tragedy, you must employ persons of birth, rank, and appearance; and if an epic, "the persons must be the most impressive in the world, such as kings, heroes, and great statesmen, and everything must have a majestic, strange, and wonderful sound." Gottsched's model tragedy, *The Dying Cato* (1732), eclectically pieced together from French and English literary reminiscences, is a practical demonstration of what he considered great dramatic art, and the author encouraged his friends and admiring disciples to proceed along similar lines. Here as in his French models the "three unities" of time, place, and action, as demanded by Boileau, served to combine a swift-moving plot with a streamlined form.

Gottsched's limitations, which were largely those of his age, should not obscure his laudable and successful efforts to purify and ennoble the German language and to improve the repertoire of the German stage. He was as much opposed to the hollow bombast of the *Haupt- und Staatsaktionen* as to the coarseness of the popular *Hanswurstiaden,* and the public burning of a *Hanswurst* dummy on Caroline Neuber's stage in Leipzig was an act of symbolic significance in the history of German drama and the German stage. Caroline Neuber (1697–1760) was an actress and directress of discriminating literary taste who performed with her own troupe in Leipzig, Brunswick, Hamburg, Frankfurt on the Main, Vienna, and St. Petersburg (Leningrad). Though in the end she turned against Gottsched, she was one of his most devoted pupils during the years of his greatest influence.

The rule of Gottsched was finally broken and the artificially repressed forces of feeling and imagination restored in their own rights by the critical works of Bodmer and Breitinger, by the advanced literary theories of Lessing, and by the new aesthetic speculation of Baumgarten, Sulzer, and Kant. The Swiss scholars, Jacob Bodmer (1698–1783) and Johann

Breitinger (1701–1776), like Gottsched were interested in the unification and purification of the German language. But by their retrieval of the irrational and emotional impulses of literary creation they freed German literature from the bondage of sterile intellectualism and pointed forward to the movements of "Storm and Stress" and Romanticism. They called the attention of their contemporaries to the great writers of England and especially to John Milton (1608–1674), who in his *Paradise Lost* had created the great religious epic of Puritan idealism. They rediscovered the buried treasures of medieval German literature, above all the works of the *Minnesänger* (cf. p. 155 sq.) and the *Nibelungenlied* (cf. p. 154). And they had the good fortune of seeing their dreams of a German literary revival come true during their own lifetime.

What Bodmer and Breitinger had demanded and hoped for was fulfilled by the critical and creative genius of Gotthold Ephraim Lessing (1729–1781), in whom the movement of German enlightenment found its greatest literary exponent and its conqueror. His penetrating speculation proceeded from the rationalism of Leibniz (cf. p. 358 sqq.) and Mendelssohn (cf. p. 369) to the moralism of Kant (cf. p. 371 sqq.) and anticipated the humanism of Goethe and Schiller (cf. pp. 404–426). As a poet and dramatist he combined Gottsched's clarity of observation and composition with a rich knowledge of life and human nature, as transmitted to him by personal experience and literary exploration. In his critical wisdom and artistic form the major elements of the classical age of German literature are already in evidence. Although the themes and problems of his works were imposed upon him by his age, his queries were phrased with a pointed personal accent and the answers betrayed a courageous independence of thought and an inexhaustible treasury of information.

Lessing was fully aware that, being a child of a rationalistic age, his critical intellect often encroached upon his creative poetic faculties, and in the severe self-analysis that is contained in the final chapter of his *Hamburg Dramaturgy,* he said of himself: "I am neither an actor nor a poet. . . . I do not feel within me the lifespring . . . that by its own force flows richly, freshly, and purely. I have to force everything to the surface as with the aid of a pressure-pump. I would be very poor, cold, and purblind indeed, had I not learned in modesty to borrow from foreign treasures, to warm myself on foreign hearths, to strengthen my vision by making use of the lenses of art."

For Lessing God is identical with the rational order of the universe, and religion is the free affirmation and acceptance of this order. The meaning of individual and social life is realized in the progress from a blind obedience to urges and instincts, to actions that are informed and determined by the law of reason. Supreme reason and perfect morality converge. While Lessing shares most of these convictions with other representatives of the age of enlightenment, he parts company with them when he moves the final goal of human striving from the finite to the infinite: "Not the truth which any one possesses or supposes to possess, but the sincere endeavor that he has made to arrive at truth, makes the worth of a man. For not by the possession but by the investigation of truth are his powers expanded, wherein alone his ever-growing perfection consists. Possession makes us complacent, indolent, and proud. If God held all truth shut in His right hand, and in His left hand nothing but the ever-restless quest of truth, though with the condition of my erring for ever and ever, and if He should say to me: 'Choose!' — I should bow humbly to His left hand, and say: 'Father, give! Pure truth is for Thee alone!' "

Lessing, the son of a Lutheran pastor, was born in Upper Lusatia and, following the wish of his parents, devoted himself to theological studies at the University of Leipzig. Becoming more and more interested in other disciplines, he turned first to the study of medicine and subsequently to philology and philosophy. From Leipzig, Germany's "little Paris," where he had freely associated with the actors and actresses of Caroline Neuber's troupe, he went to Berlin, the city upon which Frederick the Great had impressed the stamp of his personality, the cultural center of German enlightenment. Together with Moses Mendelssohn and Friedrich Nicolai he edited the *Letters Concerning the Most Recent Literature* (1759–1765). Leading for several years the life of a free-lance writer, he accepted a position as secretary to General von Tauentzien, the governor of Breslau (Silesia) in 1760. In 1767 he received an appointment as dramaturgist and theater critic at the newly founded National Theatre in Hamburg. Although the failure of this ambitious enterprise in the following year left Lessing again without a position, the fruit of his activity as a theater critic, the *Hamburg Dramaturgy,* remains the noblest document of the struggle for the creation of a national stage as the symbol of a growing national consciousness. Lessing's wife, Eva König, whom he married after having been appointed ducal librarian in Wolfenbüttel (Brunswick) in 1769, died in the following year. Lessing himself ended his life in poverty in 1781. He had to be buried at public expense.

In the seventeenth of the *Letters Concerning the Most Recent Literature* Lessing, whom Macaulay has called "the foremost critic of Europe," launched his decisive attack on Gottsched. He blamed Germany's literary dictator for having fostered a type of literature that was foreign to the German temper and mentality. Gottsched, in his blind admiration of the neo-classical drama of France, had lost sight of the genuine classical qualities as they were embodied in ancient Greek tragedy. The misinterpretation of Aristotle's *Poetics* and the slavish observation of the "three unities" had led Gottsched and his followers to a misconception of the nature of tragedy and dramatic art in general. Lessing insisted that "the grand, the terrible, the melancholy appeals more to us [Germans] than the gallant, the delicate, the amorous. . . . He [Gottsched] ought to have followed out this line of thought, and it would have led him straightway to the English stage." Particularly in Shakespeare Lessing found all the depth and grandeur of the ancients and, in addition, a supreme clarity and rationality that made his tragedies superior to those of Corneille and Racine: "Corneille is nearer the ancients in the outward mechanism, Shakespeare in the vital essence of the drama."

It was in accordance with these convictions that Lessing in the *Hamburg Dramaturgy* (1767) demanded that the action of a play ought to grow out of the structural necessities of the individual characters and that these characters themselves ought to follow their intrinsic laws of self-realization. Corneille's tragic heroes call forth admiration, but the real tragic hero evokes fear and compassion in the heart of the spectator. Only in this way does the truly great tragedy succeed in bringing about the Aristotelian "Catharsis," effecting the purification of human emotions and passions. Of the "three unities" the unity of action is the only one that must be strictly observed, while those of time and place are of minor significance.

When Lessing thus advocated the emancipation of German literature from French influence, he was prompted by the twofold aim of making literature a sensitive instrument of vital contemporary thought, and of giving voice to the hitherto suppressed or subdued forces of the German national temper. There was no element of chauvinism in Lessing's deep love of his native country, its tradition and its culture, and he found it perfectly natural to reconcile his cosmopolitanism with his patriotism.

Lessing's *Laocoön* (1766), having as its object the re-establishment of the intrinsic laws and the specific boundaries of poetry and the plastic arts, is a work of chiefly historical significance. The proposed solutions of a highly complex problem suffer from an oversimplification, caused by the defective knowledge of the art of antiquity that was a characteristic mark of art criticism in Lessing's time. Sculptures of the type of the famous Laocoön group,* now known to be works of the decadent Hellenistic period of Greek art (*c.* 50 B.C.), were considered by Lessing and his contemporaries as prototypes of classical Greek style. Unaware of the fact that Greek statuary at the time of its origin was customarily painted with loud and lively colors, the admirers of antiquity in the eighteenth century praised its plainness as a special virtue and a true symbol of the idealization of human form and feeling.

Lessing bases his critical investigation on a comparison between the agony of Laocoön and his two sons as depicted by the ancient sculptors of Rhodos and by the poet Vergil (70–19 B.C.) in his epic *Aeneid*. He arrives at the conclusion that it is in the nature of the plastic arts to depict its objects *simultaneously in space,* while the art of poetry depicts a *sequence of events in time.* The plastic arts therefore must endeavor to select "the most fruit-

---

* The Laocoön group represents a Trojan priest with his two sons in the deadly embrace of two serpents which have been sent by the goddess Pallas Athene to avenge the disclosure of the presence of the "Trojan horse," in which were hidden the Greek warriors who were to open the city gates of Troy to the besieging armies outside the city walls. The Laocoön group was discovered in the palace of Emperor Titus in Rome in 1506 and is now in the Vatican Museum.

ful moment" to characterize a situation, whereas the poet can afford to evolve an action in successive stages, from its inception to its end. Thus Vergil could describe vividly and minutely the prolonged agony of the Trojan priest without violating the laws of poetry, while the Greek sculptors had to tone down Laocoön's wild outcry to a mere groan of pain. But in exercising this restraint and in choosing "the most fruitful moment" the plastic artists have been able to achieve an identical effect in their own proper medium of expression.

Lessing's dramatic works are ingenious applications and exemplifications of his artistic theories. *Minna von Barnhelm* (1763), Germany's first and foremost classical comedy, reflects the ethical and political climate of the age of Frederick the Great and the Seven Years' War (cf. p. 314). In Goethe's judgment it is a work of typically North German character, "the first dramatic creation of vital significance and specifically modern content." The plot is woven around the concept of soldierly virtue, the conflicts arising from the struggle between love and honor, feminine cunning and masculine stubbornness. It is comedy in that highest sense in which tragedy looms as an ever present possibility, and the solution follows from the inherent nobility and gentle wisdom of the leading characters. The logical structure of the play and the final victory of reason over emotions and passions are in line with the enlightened philosophy of its author.

Five years after the completion of *Minna von Barnhelm* Lessing presented Germany with her first classical tragedy. *Emilia Galotti* (1772), a modern version of the story of the Roman heroine Virginia,* is a fearless indictment of the moral corruption of the princely representatives of absolutism, marking the incipient revolt of the middle class against petty tyranny and social inequality. The integrity of the human soul is rated as of higher value than life itself. Carefully observing the conventional unities of time, place, and action, the play is a technical masterpiece of artistic economy and stylistic precision. It illustrates effectively the practicability of the author's theoretical views as expressed in the *Hamburg Dramaturgy*.

A poetic sequel to Lessing's edition of Reimarus' *Fragments* (cf. p. 374), and the greatest literary manifestation of the religious ideology of German enlightenment, is the drama *Nathan the Wise* (1779). In pleading the cause of religious toleration in the dialectic form of the drama, Lessing wrote the final chapter of his heated controversy with Pastor Goeze of Hamburg who had suspected him of being the author of the *Fragments* and had repeatedly attacked him for his supposed antireligious radicalism. When the threat of censorship made it impossible for Lessing to continue the controversy in the accustomed form of the literary tract and pamphlet, he returned to "his old pulpit," the stage, and wrote the story of Nathan, the Jewish sage.

The thesis of the play is most clearly expressed in the Parable of the

---

* Virginia, according to the legend, was killed by her father, the Roman tribune Virginius (*c.* 450 B.C.), to save her from being dishonored.

Three Rings which Lessing had found in Boccaccio's *Decameron* but which was first recorded in the medieval *Gesta Romanorum* (*Deeds of the Romans*), compiled by the monk Helinand at the end of the twelfth century. The fable tells of a ring, endowed with the magic power of rendering its bearer "pleasing to God and men." The ring is in the possession of a family whose members have passed it on from generation to generation, the father in each case willing it before his death to his favorite son, and thereby making his heir the master of the house. In the course of time it happens that the genuineness of the ring is called in question by three brothers whose father, loving each of his sons with an impartial affection, has committed the pious fraud of bequeathing to two of them perfect duplicates of the original ring. The judge to whom the brothers submit their case arrives at the conclusion that by their envy and discord they have proven that none of them could possibly have inherited the original ring with its inherent magic power. But while the ring itself may have been lost, its power may still be made effective if each of the three sons will endeavor to redeem its promises by a life of noble thoughts and deeds, by love for God and men. In other words, it is Lessing's conviction that Judaism (Nathan), Mohammedanism (Sultan Saladin), and Christianity (the Knight Templar) can best prove the validity of their respective claims to the possession of truth by the justice and charity that informs the lives of those who profess these different creeds. True faith, Lessing implies, manifests itself in good and noble conduct.

The religious philosophy that underlies Lessing's polemic treatment of the claims of the world religions is that of Deism (cf. p. 356 sq.). "Nathan's opposition to every kind of positive religion has always been my own," says the author of this play. Dogmas and revelations appear to him as crutches and atavisms of a less enlightened age, impeding true toleration and the realization of a truly humane morality and culture.

Lessing's critical and poetic efforts were at one and the same time revolutionary and conservative. He was progressive in his admiration and appreciation of Shakespeare, whose metrical form he adopted in the five-feet iambics of his "Nathan," thereby establishing a metrical norm for German classical drama. But he remained faithful to the great literary tradition of the ancients in his adherence to the formal principles of Aristotle whom he reinterpreted for his contemporaries and successors. The rules and laws of poetry and drama, in which he believed and which he defended, were never to infringe upon the creative freedom of the poet and artist: they were merely to act as tools and means to the end of poetic perfection. In his own work he demonstrated convincingly that the artistic genius is not the slave of rules but their master.

i) *Historiography*. It had been Machiavelli's (see p. 247 sq.) contention that the course of political and social history was determined by the prudent use of power and organization. If that was true, then politics was an art that could be learned and could gradually be developed into a science.

It was from Machiavelli that the great historians of the seventeenth and eighteenth centuries accepted the principle of what is called "pragmatic" historiography. It becomes the task of the historian to describe and explain psychologically the purposive actions of individuals in different ages in order to enlarge the scope of political experience and to provide guiding rules for the calculation and formation of future events. In this way the past history of the human race appears as a summation of rationally integrated occurrences and its future almost as a mathematical problem. The development of a strictly scientific method was to make it possible to proceed from one securely established truth to the next, all of them testifying and contributing to the optimistic belief in the solidarity and infinite perfectibility of mankind.

In contrast to the medieval concept of universal history the *Kulturgeschichte* and *Universalhistorie* of the eighteenth century pictured as the meaning and final goal of the history of mankind not the realization of the Augustinian "City of God," but the *"église philosophique"* (philosophical church) of enlightened minds, of an "educated" mankind. This kind of reasoning underlies the great historical works of Montesquieu (*De l'esprit des lois*, 1748), Voltaire (*Essai sur l'histoire générale*, 1754-1758), Hume (*History of England*, 1754-1763), Gibbon (*History of the Decline and Fall of the Roman Empire*, 1782-1788), Frederick the Great (*On Customs, Habits, Industry, and the Progress of the Human Mind in Arts and Sciences*, 1750), and Friedrich Schiller (*History of the Revolt of the Netherlands*, 1788; *History of the Thirty Years' War*, 1790-1792). All these writers considered their task from a scientific as well as artistic point of view and were eager to discover such "laws" as might enable them to predict and predetermine the future course of European history. They were all rationalists and pragmatists, no longer satisfied, however, with becoming the teachers of politicians but animated by the higher ambition of becoming the teachers of mankind. Like the rationalistic philosophers and poets they disregarded or underestimated the significance of the forces of imagination, emotion, and passion in human life and human history. They conceived of the human race as a homogeneous mass of individuals, considering the social, political, and national divisions as so many artificial and unnecessary barriers to universal understanding and mutual enlightenment. Their high esteem for the art and civilization of antiquity caused them to invent the unhistorical tripartition of history — Antiquity, Middle Ages, Renaissance — which afterward became a widely accepted scheme, and in which the intermediate "middle" age was described as a defection from the lofty heights of ancient culture, as a dark era of barbarism and superstition.

The inadequacy of the rationalistic and pragmatic approach to historical phenomena was first realized by Herder (1744-1803, cf. p. 396 sq.), who like Kant and Lessing was himself a child of the age of enlightenment and like them rose far above its limited perspective. He agreed with the pragmatic historians that the history of mankind was marked by a steady progress from the childhood stage of the Oriental civilizations to the adolescence and maturity of Greece and Rome, and the senility of the "dark ages." He, too, pleaded the cause of the education of mankind to true humanity, harmony, and happiness. But at the same time he recognized the relative significance and uniqueness of each historic epoch in its own rights, thereby debunking the myth of universal and infinite progress. With his emphasis on the "folk spirit" (*Volksgeist*) that causes the organic un-folding of aboriginal character traits in different ethnic groups of peoples, he anticipated the nationalistic ideologies of the nineteenth and twentieth centuries and furnished the spiritual weapons for the struggle for "national self-determination." For him every social, corporative, or national unit is more than a summation of its individual members: it is an organism of its own, following an inborn law of genetic and generic evolution. In this way the mechanical theory of State and society had to give way to the organic idea of cultural folk communities (*Kulturgemeinschaften*).

For Herder the unity and harmony of the human race was continuously realized in the concrete and manifold individual and social entities of human history. In his historical masterpiece that bears the title *Ideas on the Philosophy of the History of Mankind* (1784-1791) he demanded that no preconceived standard of measurement should be applied to any past epoch, event, or individuality, but that every such phenomenon be judged accord-ing to its own internal structure and the specific conditions and laws of its growth. Giving due consideration to the natural and spiritual forces of cultural formation, to climate and soil as much as to the several faculties of the human body and soul and to their symbolic manifestation in legend, song, and dance, in mythology, folklore, and religion, he led away from the generalizations of his age and became the intellectual ancestor of the historical spirit of the nineteenth century.

In the narrower circle of the provincial social conditions of his native Westphalia, Justus Möser (1720-1794), historiographer, statesman, and sociologist, followed a similar train of thought and arrived at similar con-clusions. In England Edmund Burke (1729-1797), leader of the Whigs in the House of Commons and author of the *Reflections on the Revolution in France* (1790), like Möser combined the political and social philosophy of enlightenment with the ideals of a new humanism. Möser considered a healthy and contented peasantry as the safest foundation of a prosperous State, and Burke, though a severe critic of the spirit and methods of the French Revolution, fought gallantly for the ideals of justice, liberty, and humanity. He was opposed to the exploitation of East India, to the burden of taxation imposed on the American colonies, to England's anti-Catholic legislation, and to the policy of oppression in Ireland. He reaffirmed the right of resistance against unlawful authority, but blamed the French revolutionists for having violated the duty of loyalty to the law of nature and the values embodied in sound tradition.

Both Möser and Burke weighed concrete realities and the complexity of human nature against the simplifications of abstract theories, trying to re-establish true liberty and human dignity on the solid rock of the natural law. Both men exercised a decisive influence on the political philosophy of the German Romanticists (cf. p. 470 sqq.) and presented the most valid arguments to the leaders of the counterrevolution and political restoration that followed the defeat of Napoleon. It was Friedrich Gentz (1764-1832), later on Prince Metternich's (cf. p. 461 sq.) right-hand man and one of the chief exponents of the political restoration movement, who in his earlier years had translated and annotated Burke's *Reflections* (1793), thereby popularizing in Germany one of the great classics of political literature and philosophy. Equally strong at the beginning of the nineteenth century was the influence of the political theories of Joseph de Maistre (1754-1821), the French statesman and philosopher, who vigorously and intelligently defended Church and State, the traditional authorities, against the ideas of 1789. But, at the same time, he recognized in the French Revolution a work of Providence and an inevitable result of historical constellations. What distinguished all these men from the representatives of a strictly rationalistic and pragmatic historiography was their closeness to life and their realization of the organic and genetic continuity of historic evolution.

j) The Natural Sciences. The methods of experimentation, measurement, and factual observation, as inaugurated by Galilei (cf. p. 275) and Bacon (cf. p. 356), led to several phenomenal discoveries in the natural sciences in the latter part of the eighteenth century. Enlightenment and natural sciences were linked by many bonds of common interest and agreed essentially in their philosophical premises. France and England, the leading political powers, and to a lesser degree Italy, assumed leadership also in scientific research, while in Germany the scientific endeavors of individuals and institutions were in the main dilettantic rather than systematic. The French *Académie des Sciences* (1666) and *Ecole Polytechnique* (1794), and the English *Royal Academy* (1682) had become the centers of scientific research. In Germany, too, a number of scientific academies were founded, but none of them could compare with their sister institutions abroad. While the English scientists remained always conscious of the limitations of the experimental method, French science in the age of enlightenment suffered from its implicit trust in the materialistic and mechanistic presuppositions of the prevalent philosophy. In Germany a more or less clear realization of the insufficiency of a mechanistic conception of nature led at the turn of the century to the rise of "nature philosophy" (cf. p. 501). This "nature philosophy," born of the protest of the spirit against the claims of materialism, bore rich though somewhat strange fruit in the speculation of the Romanticists (cf. p. 470 sqq.), but in turn acted as a powerful stimulus for the great scientific discoveries of the nineteenth century.

As far as the individual sciences are concerned, the German-speaking countries produced in the eighteenth century a large number of brilliant scientists in various fields. Leonhard Euler (1707-1783), the great mathematician and native of German Switzerland, who taught at the Academies of Berlin and St. Petersburg, and several members of the scholarly Bernoulli family of Basel (Switzerland) provided the theoretical bases for Laplace's astronomical speculation. Friedrich Wilhelm Herschel (1738–1822), a German musicologist and astronomer, constructed several giant telescopes and became widely known for his discovery of the planet Uranus. At about the same time the Italian Lagrange (1736–1813) and the Frenchman Arago (1786–1853) had made their important contributions to optics and astronomical physics.

The Italians Galvani (1738–1798) and Volta (1745–1827), the Frenchman Ampère (1775–1836), the Englishmen Davy (1778–1829) and Faraday (1791–1867), and the Dane Oerstedt (1777–1851) discovered the electrical currents and became the founders of the sciences of electrodynamics, electrochemistry, and electromagnetism. As early as 1663 the German physician Otto von Guericke (1602–1686) had constructed an electrical machine and observed the phenomena of electrical repulsion, conductivity, and induction. The same scholar invented the water barometer that proved the dependence of the weather on atmospheric pressure, and the air pump which utilized the new knowledge of the materiality and dilatation of the air. In 1654 Guericke had demonstrated the phenomenon of atmospheric pressure before the Diet of Regensburg, using two hollow hemispheres, one yard in diameter, which, after the air had been pumped out, could not be pulled apart by twenty-four horses.

The analyses of water and air, based on the experiments of the Englishmen Priestley (1733–1804) and Cavendish (1731–1810) and the Swedish apothecary Scheele (1742–1786), led to the discovery of oxygen and other gases and acids, opening up new possibilities for chemical research. In the first decade of the nineteenth century the chemistry of gases was systematically developed by the French chemist and physicist Gay-Lussac (1778–1850).

Medical science made rapid progress, especially in the field of surgery, after the widespread opposition to anatomical dissection had finally been overcome. Even in the middle of the seventeenth century the knowledge of the anatomy of the human body was in such a primitive stage that the court physicians of one of the margraves of Baden had to carry on lengthy disputes in their endeavor to determine the location of their distinguished patient's heart. The dissection of a pig was finally decided upon to arrive at a solution of the problem by way of analogy.

The earliest work on human anatomy, and for a long time the only one of its kind that was based on results obtained by the dissection of human corpses, was written by Andreas Vesalius of Padua (1514–1564), who thereby undermined the hitherto unquestioned authority of Galenus. It was not until two centuries later, in the age of enlightenment, that Vesalius' fellow countryman, Morgagni (1682–1771), established pathological anatomy as an independent science, laying the foundations for organographic diagnostics and scientific surgery. Gerard van Swieten (1700–1772), the court physician of Empress Maria Theresa, a pupil of Hermann Boerhaave (1668–1738) of the University of Leyden (Holland) where he conducted the first modern clinic, became the founder of the older Viennese school of medical and clinical science. In 1784 Emperor Joseph II established in the same city the *"Josephinum,"* an academy for military surgery, and the General Hospital with maternity ward and foundling house, a model institution that for a long time remained without parallel in Europe.

In the beginning of the eighteenth century pathological physiology was almost in as rudimentary a stage as pathological anatomy. The so-called "ontological" school of physiology explained disease by assuming the presence of independent organisms in the human body. This misconception was first successfully attacked and disproven by the English physician John Hunter (1728–1793), the founder of experimental pathology.

The mechanistic ideas of the French rationalists affected profoundly the physiological views of the eighteenth century. Human metabolism was compared with a hydraulic machine, the organs of respiration with a pair of bellows, the entrails with sieves. Medical science in its entirety was frequently conceived of as a mechanico-mathematical discipline. The many crudities of this physiological materialism found their counterpart in an increasing interest in mysterious and occult forces that were to afford an outlet for suppressed emotional and spiritual urges.

Kant was convinced of the therapeutic force and function of reason, and he wrote an essay in which he tried to demonstrate the "power of the human mind to gain mastery over one's pathological states by a mere firm resolution." But many of his contemporaries substituted for reason and mind a mysterious "live-force" which they endowed with the faculty of working all kinds of miracles. Galvani's experiments with frog legs and the explanation of the irritability and sensitivity of muscles and nerves as presented by the German scientist and poet Albrecht von Haller (1708–1777), gave rise to fantastic speculations as to the possibility of reviving the dead by irritation of the muscular and nervous systems. The German physician Franz Anton Mesmer (1734–1815), the discoverer of animal magnetism, believed in the presence of magnetic fluids and currents in all physical organisms, which might be used for therapeutic purposes. "Mesmerism" was adopted in certain quarters as a philosophy of life which was designed to elucidate the interrelations that exist between the different parts and beings of the universe, between macrocosm and microcosm. From Vienna, where the authorities looked with disfavor upon Mesmer's growing clientele, he went to Paris, where his miraculous cures attracted the attention of the sensation loving aristocracy on the eve of the French Revolution.

Likewise a strange combination of scientist and theosophist was the Swedish philosopher Emanuel Swedenborg (1688–1772), the founder of the "Church of the New Jerusalem," whose doctrines were ridiculed in Kant's *Dreams of a Visionary* (1766). He speculated on the interrelation of body and soul and the prophetic significance of dreams and, at the same time, worked out a coherent mechanico-rationalistic system of nature philosophy. He claimed to have received direct revelations of supernatural truths by means of his constant intercourse with the spirit world. Sweden-borg was the founder of the science of crystallography, and Mesmer was the first European physician of rank who taught and applied the methods of what became later known as hypnotic suggestion, psychotherapy, psycho-pathology, parapsychology, and psychoanalysis.

From his own autobiography and from Goethe's sympathetic description in the ninth book of *Poetry and Truth* we gain an intimate knowledge of the charming personality of Johann Jung-Stilling (1740–1817), a writer of pietistic leanings, a political economist and physician by profession. He, too, claimed direct intercourse with the spirits of the departed and was at home in the mystico-theosophical dreamlands of Paracelsus (cf. p. 273) and Jacob Böhme (cf. p. 270).

The Saxon physician Friedrich Hahnemann (1755–1843), likewise opposed to the current materialism of medical science, became the founder of homoeopathy, characterized by the attempt at effecting cures by the applica-tion of medicaments which produce in the human body symptoms similar to those of the disease: treating constipation with laxatives and acidosis with alcalizing agents. Vaccination against malignant pustules and smallpox, first practiced by the English country doctor, Edward Jenner (1749–1773), was a direct application of the therapeutic principles of homoeopathy.

Hahnemann's *Organon of Practical Medicine* (1810) became the classical handbook of all homoeopathists. His influence extended to England and North America, and some of his disciples opened the first homoeopathic institute in Philadelphia, forming the nucleus of the foundation of the Hahnemann College (1848) with its several hospitals and policlinics. In Washington, D. C., a public monument was erected in Hahnemann's honor.

Abraham Werner (1749–1817), the "father of geology," who taught at the internationally famous mining academy at Freiberg in Saxony, was the chief defender of the theory of "Neptunism," trying to relate all geological formations and changes to oceanic influences. His views exercised a certain fascination on Goethe's scientific theories as well as on the Romantic nature philosophy of Novalis (cf. p. 476), H. Steffens (1773–1845), and Franz von Baader (1765–1841). The "Neptunist" theory was refuted by the English geologist James Hutton (1726–1797), whose "Plutonism" explained geological transformations as the results of volcanic influences.

In the field of biology William Harvey's (1578–1657) hitherto accepted theory of organic evolution or preformation, maintaining the generation of plants and animals from original constitutional dispositions of species, was opposed in the eighteenth century by Friedrich Wolff's (1733–1794) theory of postformation or epigenesis which taught the spontaneous generation of new organisms from unorganized matter. Both theories were combined in the early twentieth century in Hans Driesch's (1867–1941) concept of "epigenetic evolution," according to which an organism is the result of the activation of constitutional dispositions, under the influence of biological factors and environmental conditions.

Chapter 12

GERMAN CLASSICAL IDEALISM

Germany and the Classical Heritage. The "European tradition" had its intellectual roots as much in the culture of antiquity as in the more recent forces of Christianity which superseded the former but never entirely abrogated this ancient legacy. The German tradition, on the other hand, showed itself opposed at several junctures to the smooth formalism and placid equilibrium of classical antiquity, asserting the irrational and mystical impulses of its own psychological and racial heritage. The first real synthesis of Graeco-Roman, Christian, and Germanic culture was embodied in the Carolingian Renaissance (cf. p. 51 sqq.), while the second European classical revival in the fifteenth and sixteenth centuries met with little response on the part of Germany. The religious dynamism of the Lutheran Reformation clashed with the worldly spirit of the Italian Renaissance, and the academic classicism of seventeenth-century France, though feebly imitated in Germany, evoked there at the same time the anticlassical movements of Pietism (cf. p. 364 sqq.), Sentimentalism, and "Storm and Stress." It was not until the latter part of the eighteenth century that the spiritual unrest of the German mind succeeded in achieving a classical harmony and perfection of its own stamp, a cultural and intellectual pattern that resulted from such an ideal blend of form and content as hitherto had only been realized by the singular artistic genius of Dürer (cf. p. 197) and Holbein (cf. p. 197 sq.). But this German classicism was so much a creation of the Germanic race that to this day it appears to prominent literary critics of France and England as unclassical to such an extent that they prefer to call it "Romanticism," grouping it together with the European romantic movement of the early nineteenth century.

The Revolution of Feeling. The classical writers and thinkers of Germany without exception experienced in their youth the influence of Rousseau (cf. p. 376), the European apostle of a new emotionalism, who became the leader of a whole generation in their revolt against the despotism of reason. To Descartes's *"exister c'est penser"* (to exist means to think) Rousseau opposed the slogan *"exister c'est sentir"* (to exist means to feel), calling attention to the neglected powers of will and heart and thereby challenging the complacency of an artificially organized society. For the individualism of rational human beings he substituted an individualism of sensitive hearts and souls. By making the feeling ego the final authority in life and culture he completed the victory of modern subjectivism, rehabilitating the inwardness of sentiment and fancy in the plastic and literary arts and rediscovering the landscape as a mirror of the human soul.

With Rousseau the German classicists started out by affirming strongly the right of nature to assert itself, but they ultimately supplemented and sublimated his message by the demand that nature be perfected by means of human reason and moral action. With Rousseau they shared the conviction that modern civilization had destroyed the fullness and oneness of human nature, but while Rousseau expected the restoration of its original integrity from a return to a primitive state of life, his German disciples pointed forward to the superior culture and the true humanity of a future day and age, to be ushered in by great personalities in whom the faculties of reason, will, and emotions would be reconciled.

Both Herder and Schiller advanced in their constructive criticism beyond Rousseau's one-sided anticultural pessimism, by their contention that civilization, by virtue of its own inherent vitality, could heal the wounds that it had struck. It was their belief that only a sham civilization could harm the integrity of human nature, but that a genuine and fully grown civilization would necessarily lead human nature to its true perfection. And Goethe more than anyone else exemplified in his life as much as in his works the fact that modern man, on his passage through ever rising planes of cultural education, through self-realization and intellectual discipline, could in the end attain to the reborn naïveté of pristine nature. Thus a "beautiful soul" for Goethe and Schiller was a human personality in which the faculties of intellect, will, and emotions were brought to complete harmony.

a) Sentimentalism ("Empfindsamkeit"). The growing importance of the middle classes in the eighteenth century brought about certain changes in the general intellectual, moral, and literary standards and ideals of the age. German culture and literature were no longer dominated by theological or dynastic social and communal interests but became more and more saturated with the individual experiences and concerns of average human beings. A happy and contented human life on this earth became the ideal goal of individual and social striving. This preoccupation with individual life sharpened the eye for the intimate psychological observation and description of human existence and the development of human characters.

Keen introspection, psychological reflection, and self-analysis are clearly manifested in the poetry and fiction of the first half of the eighteenth century and particularly in the sentimental novel, which was imported to Germany from England. Lawrence Sterne's (1713–1768) *Tristram Shandy* and *A Sentimental Journey through France and Italy by Mr. Yorick* were translated into German and infested the German sentimental and romantic novel with their emotional exuberance and somewhat scurrilous humor. James Thomson's (1700–1748) *Seasons,* with its detailed description of nature, found an echo in Haydn's oratorio (1801) of the same title, and

Samuel Richardson's (1689–1761) sentimental novels moved Christian Gellert (cf. p. 349) so deeply that he "was drowned with weeping," that he "sobbed with infinite joy" and considered Richardson a magician who commanded "all that is touching and overwhelming, enrapturing and intoxicating." Rapture and intoxication his English and German readers found in Edward Young's (1683–1765) gloomy *Night Thoughts on Life, Death, and Immortality* (1742–1745) and in James Macpherson's (1736–1796) romantic *Poems of Ossian* (1760–1764) which the Scottish poet falsely advertised as translations of the songs of a Gaelic bard of the third century A.D. Young's nature poetry and Macpherson's sentimental melancholy assumed a new and more vigorous life in Klopstock's odes and Goethe's *Sorrows of Young Werther* (cf. p. 409 sq.).

The sentimentalism that pervades these literary documents, bordering at times on exhibitionism, represented a violent reaction against the conventional and authoritarian culture of Rococo and princely absolutism and has its center in the self-assertion of the individual and his experiences. Letters, diaries, and memoirs became the favorite literary vehicles of personal confession and self-portrayal. All at once the German language lost its stilted artificiality, assuming color and expressive vigor. The science of physiognomics became for Johann Kaspar Lavater (1741–1801) the key that unlocked the sacred shrine of human personality, its riches, its mysteries, its unlimited potentialities. The feeling of universal friendship and brotherhood wove sentimental ties between all members of the human race, between man and nature, between nature and God, and nature itself became the intimate confidant of all sentimental souls: the gentle element that soothes and liberates, that heals and makes man whole and holy again. Thought, speculation, and practical demonstration were all dissolved in the waves of feeling, mystical affection and devotion, and awe-inspired exaltation.

b) Friedrich Gottlob Klopstock (1724–1803). Though an "apprentice of the Greeks" in the metrical form of his lyric poetry, Klopstock was a typical poet of the Germanic North, as far as the spirit and content of his works is concerned. His "expressionistic" style was the medium of his emotion and passion and showed little of the neo-classical "noble simplicity and quiet grandeur." However, in the midst of the sweet and sentimental trivialities of the anacreontic and pietistic poets his work represents another milestone on the road to classical German literature, and with his solemn conviction of the religious, social, and national significance of poetry, he restored to the realm of German letters dignity of form and sublimity of subject matter.

When the first three cantos of his *Messiah* were published in 1748, Klopstock was joyously acclaimed and adopted as Germany's first and foremost poet in modern times. Although the author of this religious poem was influenced in the choice of his theme by Milton's (1608–1674) religious epics, the twenty cantos of the completed work resemble in composition and style more the musical form of the oratorio than the epical narrative of its

English model. The poem is greatest in its lyric and dramatic passages and lacks the plasticity, concreteness, and individuality of objective and descriptive literary forms. In conformity with the Lutheran dogmatic premises of the work the human nature of Christ is completely submerged in the divine attributes of the Redeemer. What interests the author primarily is not so much Christ's passion and death, viewed as historic occurrences, but rather the psychological effects of the work of redemption on human souls, on angels, and on demons.

The characteristic features of the *Messiah* reappear in Klopstock's Odes and in his dramatic attempts. The positive and negative qualities of his poetry are well defined in Friedrich Schiller's critical appraisal: "His sphere is always the realm of ideas, and he makes everything lead up to the infinite. One might say that he deprives everything that he touches of its body in order to turn it into spirit, whereas other poets clothe everything spiritual with a body." God and immortality are the central themes of most of Klopstock's works, and they are all permeated with the conviction of the infinite value of the immortal human soul. Everything earthly and material is seen and evaluated from the point of view of eternity, and his devotion to nature is an eloquent testimony to the omnipresence and omnipotence of the divine spirit, manifesting itself in the circling stars of the skies, in the rhythmic cycles of the seasons, and in the elemental forces of nature. It is Klopstock's historic accomplishment to have freed the German language from the bondage of a sterile rhetorical intellectualism and to have made it a pliant medium for the direct lyrical expression of the impulses and experiences of the individual human soul.

c) Hamann and the "Storm and Stress" Movement. The modern individualistic trend that had found its first powerful manifestation in the Italian Renaissance and in the German Reformation was carried to extreme conclusions by the generation that succeeded that of Lessing and Klopstock. While the sixteenth and seventeenth centuries had still recognized a universal and divinely sanctioned law and order for mankind, the age of Enlightenment had set up humanity or its individual representatives as ends in themselves, so that ultimately man could be proclaimed as the measure of all things. The history of human civilization appeared as a dialectic struggle between individual and superindividual norms, the great epochs of history resulting from the harmonization of individual and social claims, and the epochs of decline revealing their maladjustment and open antagonism. No longer did the individual recognize himself as an integral part of a universal order, but he conceived of himself as an autonomous being whose innate law and individual nature set him apart, in sharp contrast to his age and social environment. In France the revolt of the individual and his victory was decided in the political arena; in Germany the scene of action was the realm of letters, and the victorious forces that were destined to assume the intellectual leadership of their nation were recruited from the awakening middle classes.

In 1760 a small pamphlet was published, bearing the somewhat obscure title *Socratic Memoirs*. Its author was Johann Georg Hamann (1730–1788), the "Magus of the North," who in sibylline language and in glowing colors painted the image of the sage of Antiquity as the true prototype of a great human personality. What were the essential features of this new and ideal type of man, of this new Socrates in whom the age of enlightenment had already seen the precursor of its own aspirations? For Hamann the new Socrates was a genuine product of creative nature, a genius who was impelled by the irresistible dictates of the "daimon" in his own breast, a being predestined from eternity to tragic conflict, to suffering, and death. In his exemplary greatness this new man resembled the heroes of Greek tragedy whose valor was derived from the mysterious depths of their divine origin and from the unconscious forces of nature. With this new concept of human personality Hamann dealt the deathblow to the arrogant humanitarianism and the complacency of the enlightened *"philosophes."* He gained the attention and enthusiastic following of the younger generation, out of whose ranks were to emerge the classical representatives of German culture and literature in the late eighteenth and early nineteenth centuries.

The literary revolution crystallized in the poems and dramas of the "Storm and Stress" (*Sturm und Drang*) movement, which derived its name from the title of one of Maximilian Klinger's (1752–1831) plays. With all "Storm and Stress" poets Rousseau's antirationalism and anticultural pessimism became a kind of obsession. But if Rousseau with his call "Back to Nature!" had indicted a corrupt social system and, in "Emile" and the "Nouvelle Heloïse," had tried to vindicate human emotions and passions, the writers who gathered around Herder and Goethe in Strasbourg mistook anarchy for freedom and arbitrariness for naturalness. Their aesthetic revolution was therefore essentially destructive, aimed, as it were, at all rule and authority and glorifying sensuality, voluptuousness, and the rule of instincts untrammeled. Their total lack of intellectual and moral bearings makes them crave for movement for the sake of movement. The hero of Klinger's "Sturm und Drang," about to join the American Revolution as a volunteer, gives vent to the restlessness and rootlessness of this "lost generation," when he exclaims: "Nowhere rest, nowhere repose . . . glutted by impulse and power . . . I am going to take part in this campaign. . . . There I can expand my soul, and if they do me the favor to shoot me down — all the better." For Wilhelm Heinse's (1749–1803) *Ardinghello,* passion, lust, and crime are necessary and legitimate forms of human life. The only true virtue is power, and weakness is the only real crime.

It would be difficult indeed to read any meaning into this squandering of youthful enthusiasm and poetic talent, if it were not for the fact that it was the historical function of the "Storm and Stress" poets to break up and fertilize the soil which was to nourish the genius of Herder, Goethe, and Schiller. In all the misspent energy and ill-directed idealism of this generation there was the spark of the undying vitality of youth and at the same time a spontaneity and radicalism that were needed as much for destruction as for regeneration.

"What is genius?" asks Lavater in his *Physiognomic Fragments* (1775–1778), and he answers: "Where there are efficiency, power, action, thought, feeling which can be neither learned nor taught by men — there is genius. Genius is what is essentially unlearned, unborrowed, unlearnable, untransferable, what is unique, inimitable, and divine. . . . Genius flashes; genius creates . . . ; it is inimitability, momentaneity, revelation. . . ." Taking this definition as a standard of measurement, none but Herder, Goethe, and Schiller lived up to its requisites.

The "Storm and Stress" poets' cult of Shakespeare was almost a case of mistaken identity: Shakespeare was of course not the "uncultivated genius," who disregarded artistic rules and aesthetic laws, but he was the great master who used them as tools and servile organs of a thoroughly disciplined artistic mind.

d) Johann Gottfried Herder (1744–1803). Out of Rousseau's glorification of the forces of primitive nature and out of Hamann's understanding of human personality and creative genius, Herder was able to evolve his own concept of the organic growth of human civilization, from its dark and unconscious beginnings to its mature intellectual documentation in distinct national cultures. As Hamann's most faithful disciple Herder made his own the definition of poetry as "the mother-tongue of the human race." Language appeared to him as a sublime symbol of the human mind, a genuine expression of the spirit of nations, races, and cultures that achieved its purest manifestation in the works of poetry and literature. Together with language and literature, however, he conceived of art, religion, philosophy, law, and custom as direct objectivations and realizations of the lives, instincts, environments, and living conditions of the peoples and nations of the past and present. The "inner form" that worked as an immanent, active principle in poetry and art was born of the spirit of the age; it tolerated no longer the imitation of obsolete styles of the past but demanded original creation born of the experiences of the living generations. In this way he visualized Homer, Luther, Shakespeare, and other great leaders and innovators in the realms of arts, letters, and human thought not only as autonomous personalities but at the same time as true representatives and mouthpieces of the spirit of their age, their people, and their material and spiritual environments. The fundamental unity of the genius and his maternal native soil, race, and cultural heritage was discovered, emphatically asserted by Herder, and transmitted to his great contemporaries of the

---

* Herder was born in Mohrungen (East Prussia), came under Kant's influence at the University of Königsberg (1762) where he studied medicine, theology, philosophy, and philology. From 1764–1769 he was employed as teacher and preacher at the Protestant cathedral school in Riga. In Strasbourg (1770) he associated with Goethe, who later on was influential in bringing about Herder's appointment as general superintendent (of the Church) in Weimar. His last years were embittered by his controversies with Kant and his estrangement from Goethe.

classical age and to the nineteenth century. His disciples and heirs could no longer consider poetry, literature, and art as a pleasant or inspiring pastime: he taught them to understand their endeavors and the finished products of their creative minds as the fruits of the innermost essence of individual and social forces in a given historical situation. Thus literary history was destined to become part and parcel of the history of the human mind and soul, and Rousseau's anticultural pessimism was sublimated and overcome by a joyous acknowledgment of the ever changing plenitude and diversity of intellectual forms and patterns. The immeasurably enlarged vision was enabled to travel far back into the German and European past, to extend its view into an anticipated future, and to survey the panorama of world literature from the static center of a new national consciousness.

It was thus a rare combination of great gifts — those of the philosopher, critic, and poet — that made it possible for Herder to perceive and correct the shortcomings of both Enlightenment and "Storm and Stress," to become the mentor of the young Goethe and the teacher of the writers and thinkers of the classical and romantic periods.

Among Herder's critical and poetic works the following deserve special mention as documents of the perspicacity and universality of his mind: in the *Travel-Journal* (*Reisejournal,* 1769) we discover the fruit of his early preoccupation with the problems of aesthetics, poetry, and pedagogy. He points to a new and true Humanism of the future, speculates on the basic requisites of a liberal constitution for the state of Livonia, and dreams of a renascence of Russo-Slavic civilization. In his *Fragments Concerning the More Recent German Literature* (1767) he continues and supplements the critical analyses of Lessing's *Literaturbriefe* (cf. p. 381). He dwells especially on the significance of poetic rhythm, meter, and style, and describes the evolution of literary expression from its primitive and timid origins in inarticulate sound to an intellectual maturity that subjects emotionalism and metaphorical imagery to order and rational law: a change and cyclical movement that recurs in each national organism and that regularly is marked by the gradual displacement of poetry by prose, leading eventually to abstract intellectualism and sterile rationalism. In comparing cultural and literary growth with the evolution of biological species, passing through the successive stages of primitivity, maturity, and death, only to make room for new beginnings, Herder anticipated Hegel's (cf. p. 502 sq.) "dialectical philosophy" of history as well as Spengler's (1880–1936)* theory of "cultural cycles."

The "Letters for the Promotion of Humanity" (*Briefe zur Beförderung der Humanität,* 1793–1797) contain Herder's condemnation of the vice of national pride which he considered "the greatest of all follies." "Education for humanity" is to bring about the harmonization of the natural, the moral, and the divine, culminating in the final reconciliation of Antiquity

---

* Cf. Oswald Spengler: *The Decline of the West* (New York: Alfred Knopf, 1939), trans. from the German: *Der Untergang des Abendlandes* (München, 1917; 1932).

and Christianity. In collaboration with Goethe and the historian and states-man Justus Möser (1720–1794) Herder published the essays "On German Arts and Customs" (*Von deutscher Art und Kunst,* 1773), to which he contributed his profound studies on Ossian and Shakespeare. He calls at-tention to the buried treasures of folk poetry and designates the comprehen-sion and interpretation of actual life as the essential function of literature.

To demonstrate the validity of his theories in a practical way Herder displayed in his collection of folk songs and ballads (*Stimmen der Völker,* 1778–1779) the poetic products of the creative *"Volksgeist"* of many nations and races. His poetic intuition faithfully preserves the spirit of the originals, in word, rhythm, and melody, and he shows himself as one of the great masters in the art of translation. It was perhaps his great versatility and flexibility as much as his strongly developed historical sense that deprived his own poetic creations of originality and lasting significance. He lives on as an inspired and inspiring seer, teacher, and pioneer, a leader into a promised land in which others might reap what he had sown.

Neo-Classicism and the New Humanism. Herder appears in his full and imposing stature when viewed as the standard-bearer in the momentous struggle that was being waged in Germany's classical age against meaningless conventions and the barrenness of an icy intellectualism. What he expected from the rebirth of a richer and truer view of life, and from a more complete realization of man's potentialities and innate aspirations, he sum-marized in the *Letters for the Promotion of Humanity* in these words: "Humanity: if we would give this idea its full vigor ... if we would inscribe it into our own hearts and those of our fellow-men as an unavoidable, general, and primary obligation — all our social, political, and religious prejudices might perhaps not entirely disappear, but they would at least be softened, restrained, and rendered innocuous."

a) *Greece and Rome.* For Herder's friends and contemporaries the ideal pattern of this exalted type of humanity seemed to be embodied in the world of Graeco-Roman antiquity. The New Humanism in the North, in France as well as in Germany, paid little attention at first to the heritage of ancient Greece. It was rather the ancient republic of Rome that beckoned with the splendid achievements of its art, literature, and intellectual culture. Englishmen were among the first to carry on systematic archaeological re-search on ancient Roman soil, and from England the new classicistic style of architecture penetrated into northern Germany. The shift of interest from Rome to Greece was chiefly due to the Platonic and Neo-Platonic program of studies in the monastic colleges of Cambridge and Oxford, where Plotinus, the head of the Neo-Platonic schools (203–269), was again read and appreciated in the seventeenth century. It was above all Lord Shaftesbury (1671–1713), the English moral philosopher, who eagerly ab-sorbed these Platonic teachings, reviving in his ethico-aesthetic treatises the Greek ideal of the harmony of the good, the true, and the beautiful. Shaftesbury's ideas, in turn, were adopted and further developed in the philosophical and aesthetic speculation of Herder, Goethe, Schiller, and some of the leaders of the German Romantic School (cf. p. 470 sqq.).

b) *"Noble Simplicity and Quiet Grandeur."* Johann Joachim Winckelmann (1717–1768), on the other hand, was attracted like Lessing to the art and literature of ancient Greece by a real inner affinity. Vexed and irritated by the vainglorious showmanship of the courtly culture of the Rococo and filled with compassion for the peoples and nations that smarted in the servitude of more or less enlightened despots, Winckelmann like Lessing escaped into the more humane climate of Greek democracy and found a haven of intellectual and moral repose in the purer and simpler forms of Greek art and literature. True enough, it was an idealized and partly unhistorical Greece to which both these writers paid homage but it was nevertheless also the Greece of the Homeric epics, of Attic tragedy and prose, of Xenophon, Plato, and Aristotle.

Greek art as Winckelmann knew and interpreted it, the art of "noble simplicity and quiet grandeur" (*edle Einfalt und stille Grösse*), became for him and his age the measure and standard of all artistic creation. "Back to Hellas!" became the battle cry of artists and poets, scholars and educators, burghers and nobles.

In Rome, Florence, Naples, and in the recently excavated cities of Herculaneum and Pompeii, Winckelmann inhaled the spirit of the ancient world. In the Roman copies of the masterpieces of Greek sculpture he admired the unity of form and content, the smoothness and gentle grace of lines and contours, the freedom and ease of the plastic form. Like Lessing he remained unaware of the fact that Greek art and life were not all smoothness, harmony, and ideal beauty, that under a smooth surface loomed tragedy and intense suffering as ever present realities, that the serenity of Apollo was constantly challenged by the dark irrationality of Dionysos, the god of the blind urge, of orgiastic intoxication and demonic lust.

Winckelmann's epochal *History of the Art of Antiquity* (1764), the result of his archaeological studies, contained his classicistic principles of aesthetic contemplation. The influence of the classical Greek writers was reflected in a measured and lucid prose which made the book accessible to many non-German readers.

c) *Neo-Classicism, the French Revolution, and the Style of the Napoleonic Empire.* Despite Winckelmann's conviction that only by imitating the Greeks could German artists and writers achieve real greatness, it was not the spirit of Hellas but the spirit of ancient Rome that appealed more universally to the sober taste and temper of the middle classes.

The struggle between the dying Rococo and the new classicism, beginning in France and Germany in the sixth decade of the eighteenth century, ended with the victory of the unimaginative and somewhat pedantic reincarnation of Roman civic republicanism in the ideology of Robespierre and the French Revolution. Cicero (106–43 B.C.), the great Roman orator, statesman, and philosopher, became the idol of the revolutionary leaders, who admired his legalistic mind and his ethical rigorism. He appeared to them as an ideal combination of a "popular philosopher" and an orator of overpowering eloquence. They quoted freely from him and other Roman authors and derided Danton for not complying with this fashion.

Napoleon, too, commanded all the devices of classical rhetoric and was fully conscious of the dynamic power of the spoken word. To Nietzsche (cf. p. 695 sq.) he appeared as "a statue of Antiquity in the midst of a Christian society." The artists who depicted Napoleon's features were struck by their resemblance to those of Emperor Augustus. The remaining feudal and dynastic political formations of medieval Europe were swept away by the French emperor, to be replaced by a political order of his own making, by a system that showed the characteristic marks of classical symmetry, simplicity, and rationality. By bringing about the "alliance of philosophy with the sword" he strove to resume the task of the Roman Caesars, to give peace to the world by establishing a unified dictatorial rule over the nations of Europe. He tried to revive Roman imperialism in a Christian garb, visited the tomb of Charlemagne at Aix-la-Chapelle, and crowned himself emperor in the presence of the pope. The structure and administration of his centralized empire was fashioned in accordance with the Roman model, and he made Roman law the basis of jurisdiction and Roman political ethics the basis of education. Artists and men of letters worked in the service of the Empire and were entrusted with the task of embellishing and glorifying its universal mission. The new "Punic War"* against the English "nation of shopkeepers" was to restore the absolute hegemony of the New Rome and to make the Mediterranean a "French Lake."

Thus the New Classicism, the style of the "Empire," carried forward by Napoleon's legions, went on its sweeping march of conquest throughout the territories and nations of the Western hemisphere. It found its outward expression in the increasing number of architectural monuments and newly planned cities that arose in the immense area that was flanked by St. Petersburg (Leningrad) in the East, Washington in the West, and Montevideo in the South. The simple lines and symmetrical designs of this cosmopolitan architecture followed the artistic example of ancient Rome and its modern replica, Paris, the imperial metropolis on the Seine.

d) *Neo-Classical Art in Germany.* The disintegration of the Holy Roman Empire and the political misfortunes of Austria and Prussia retarded and partly thwarted the development of the plastic arts in the German-speaking countries. The neo-classical style on German soil acquired significance as a component part of the great achievements of classical idealism in literature and philosophy but remained chiefly eclectic, imitative, and academic in architecture, sculpture, and painting. As the style of the political and social forces of conservation, tradition, and reaction it extended far into the

---

* Rome waged three "Punic Wars" with Carthage (264–146 B.C.) to secure military and economic supremacy over the dominating sea power of her political rival (Punic-Carthaginian Wars). Carthage was finally conquered and destroyed (149–146).

nineteenth century and disappeared only in the period of the revolutionary movements that paved the way for constitutional reforms and the political unification of Germany.

The public buildings and monuments which mark the period from the death of Frederick the Great to the revolution of 1848 (cf. p. 527 sq.) show a regularity and frugal rigidity of design that make them appear as foreign importations rather than as the manifestation of indigenous forces. Their cool and sober intellectualism found little response among the people at large who were much more attached to the still surviving art forms of a colorful popular Baroque or a soulful Romanticism. The representative style of the French *"Empire"* found its rather timid echo in the German *"Biedermeier,"* a manner of living and a style of interior decoration in which the stately neo-classical mannerisms were reduced to the intimacy of a bourgeois culture, whose neatness and narrowness reflected the mentality and social conditions of the German middle classes between 1815 and 1848 (the *"Vormärz,"* cf. p. 461 sqq.).

The most significant architectural monuments of German Neo-Classicism are found in Berlin, Munich, and Karlsruhe. In Berlin the Silesian architect, Karl Langhans (1733–1808), created the famous *"Brandenburger Tor"* (1789–1793), the symbolic gateway to the metropolis of the soldier-kings of Prussia.

The greatest master of the "Prussian style" in architecture was Karl Friedrich Schinkel (1781–1841), whose prolific building activity drew inspiration from the distant and disparate sources of Greek and Gothic architecture. As the son of a historically minded age he felt free to choose among the various stylistic possibilities of the past, but lacked the singleness of purpose and creative spontaneity that are required for the achievement of artistic unity and true originality. To him "Old Berlin" owes its characteristic architectural physiognomy, and his strongly developed sense of orderliness, balance, and clarity of design made him anticipate some of the principles of modern "functional" architecture. The "Old Museum" of Berlin (1822–1828) was the first building of its kind on the European continent (the British Museum was constructed according to the classicistic designs of Sir Robert Smirke between 1823 and 1855), and the Berlin *"Schauspielhaus"* (1818–1821) served as a model for most of the municipal and national playhouses of the nineteenth century. In his more than eighty buildings Schinkel utilized most of the historic styles of architecture with which he had become acquainted on his extensive travels. As a loyal servant of the royal dynasty of Prussia, Schinkel designed the spiked helmet (*Pickelhaube*) that became one of the best known symbols of Prussian militarism and was adopted by both the police force and the army (1842).

The sculptors of the "Prussian style" were Gottfried Schadow (1764–1850) and his pupil Christian Rauch (1777–1857), both of them neo-classicists, but both inclined to translate the classical repose of ancient statuary into the more characteristic and individualistic language of their own political and social environment. Among many other works each of the two sculptors created statues in commemoration of Frederick the Great. The base of Rauch's equestrian monument of the Prussian king in Berlin is largely occupied by the figures of Prussian generals, while to Kant and Lessing an overly modest space is allotted underneath the tail of Frederick's horse.

King Louis I of Bavaria (1825–1848) was one of the few German princes of the neo-classical period who continued the noble tradition of princely patronage of the arts, despite the adverse conditions of the times. Under his rule the neo-classical style experienced a belated flowering in southern Germany. By his consistent and vigorous cultivation of artistic and literary taste he made his court and the royal capital of Munich the cultural center of Germany. He commissioned Leo von Klenze (1784–1864) with the construction of numerous monumental buildings in neo-classical style ("Glyptothek" and "Propyläen" in Munich; the "Walhalla" near Regensburg; the "Befreiungshalle," commemorating the Wars of Liberation, near Kelheim).

Karlsruhe, the capital of the margraves of Baden, was transformed into a mathematically construed model city of dignified classicistic taste by Friedrich Weinbrenner (1766–1826), who superimposed on the Baroque ground plan the characteristic elements of the new style, and adorned the city gates, palaces, and many private residences with Doric and Corinthian ornamentation.*

Neo-classical German painting showed considerably less vitality and ingenuity than its sister arts. A quaint mixture of Antiquity and Rococo, of imitative-naturalistic and phantastic-theatralic elements characterizes most of the paintings produced in the age of Goethe and Schiller. Angelica Kauffmann (1741–1807), of Swiss nationality, created a large number of sentimental and genrelike works, allegorical and mythological subjects, gods and goddesses, Vestal virgins and sybils, heroically posing figural compositions and sober, commonplace portraits. Wilhelm Tischbein (1751–1829) is best known for his somewhat spectacular painting of Goethe in the classical setting of the Roman Campagna. Winckelmann's favorite was the court painter of the king of Saxony in Dresden, Anton Raphael Mengs (1728–1779), whom he placed even above his idol Raphael. Today Mengs appears to us as a faithful and diligent pupil of the great masters of the Italian Renaissance, a talented draftsman, but one whose paintings lack coloristic luster and spiritual depth. In the landscapes of Asmus Carstens (1754–1798), however, nature awakes from a trancelike sleep and begins to stir and move underneath the transparent classical veil. It is the spirit of Romanticism that gradually illuminates and transfigures the cool aloofness of the classical scene.

e) *The Science of Antiquity* ("Altertumswissenschaft"). The archaeological as well as linguistic interest in Antiquity was born of the neo-classical and neo-humanistic tendencies of the eighteenth century. The

---

* Many of the monuments of neo-classical German architecture were destroyed during World War II.

scientific exploration of the ancient civilizations of Greece and Rome (*Altertumskunde, Altertumswissenschaft*) grew out of the pioneer work of German philologists and included eventually every aspect of the life and culture of Antiquity. The actual founder of the new science was Friedrich August Wolf (1759–1824), professor of classical philology in Halle and Berlin, a pupil of Christian Gottlob Heyne (1729–1812) in Göttingen, who had taught him to evaluate classical literature and culture from the aesthetic and artistic point of view. Henceforth the study of the ancient writers was no longer primarily concerned with the imitation of classical figures of speech but was to serve the refinement of taste and the perfection of human character. Another one of Heyne's famous pupils was Wilhelm von Humboldt (1767–1835), a friend of Schiller and Goethe, who later on, as Prussian minister of education, was to introduce the ideas of the New Humanism into the Prussian schools (cf. p. 439 sqq.).

f) The New Humanism. The original philosophical and spiritual forces of the classical age, that are inseparably linked with the names of Goethe and Schiller as its greatest exponents, were Rationalism and Protestantism. It was the Protestant heritage that saved the classical literature and philosophy of Germany from the atomism, materialism, and skepticism with which the period of Enlightenment was befraught in France and England, and it was this Protestant religious and metaphysical component that gave to German "Idealism" its characteristic flavor.

This German Idealism crystallized in its dual poetico-philosophical aspect in the sister cities of Weimar and Jena, located in the idyllic province of Thuringia, in the very heart of Germany. Two small provincial towns, the one a minute princely residence, the other the seat of a university, harbored at the end of the eighteenth century an amazing number of great and unusual personalities, each of whom aided in his own individual way in shaping the German and European culture of the nineteenth century.

It was the great educational and spiritual goal of the New Humanism to lend to the idea of modern individualism a richer and deeper personal note, to visualize the humanizing process in the history of civilization as a victory of spirit over matter, of culture over nature. The cult of the great personality as the teacher and leader of men became the major concern and the central idea of the German intelligentsia, who thus gave to modern subjectivism its most refined and sublime expression. It was their conviction that only in a universal and total view of human life could individuality and subjectivity find their fullest realization. By expanding and extending his inner life into the cosmic reality of his surrounding world man would learn to see wholeness in every part and particle of the universe, he would impart meaning to his own existence and would understand the symbolic language of nature and art by making it part of his own being.

In this give-and-take between the subjective and objective realities, between the ego and the wealth of forms in the outer world, the New Humanist experienced his supreme happiness. His confidence in the self-reliant autonomy of a fully developed human personality revealed the un-shakable trust and certitude of a religious creed. Human guilt, error, and blindness were atoned for by the redeeming force of "pure humanity" *(reine Menschlichkeit)*. Human greatness was seen as the result of the moral and aesthetic conquest of the subhuman strata of life, and such a mastery of life was the precious reward of the self-discipline and unrelenting moral effort of the poet, the artist, the philosopher. Once more the Greeks provided the ideal pattern of the wished-for "harmony and totality" of life, the Greeks in whose *"Kalokagathia"* (*Kalos-*"beautiful"; *agathos-*"good") this classical harmony had found its verbal and factual expression.

Art was considered by the New Humanists as the most effective of all educative forces, the only one that was capable of truly reforming and reintegrating human life, and beauty was considered as the most trustworthy guide to goodness and truth. Kant's uncompromising dualism of nature and spirit, of sense faculty and reason, appears reconciled in Schiller's idea of the aesthetic education of man, leading to the harmonious development of all human faculties and potentialities. According to Schiller man shares his sensitive nature with the irrational animals, he shares his moral destiny with the spiritual powers, but he is unique in that he alone can embrace and resolve in his own being the opposing forces of matter and mind, of sense and reason, of nature and spirit. It is art that points the way to that ideal realm where true freedom is found in the tranquillity of the "beautiful soul."

In this fervent desire of the New Humanism to attain to moral and spiritual freedom in an ideal subjective and objective world, fashioned by art and resplendent with beauty, the "Religion of Humanity" (*Humanitäts-religion*) reveals its deepest significance: the New Humanism appears as another attempt of modern man to build a unified system of values, an integrated philosophy of life on the bases of modern individualism. The will to autonomy and self-responsibility, now stirring actively in the con-sciousness of the wide-awake middle classes, found its confirmation in an intellectual aristocracy, a "republic of letters" which was to replace the aristocracy of birth, rank, and title.

Goethe and Schiller. The two men in whom the literary and cultural trends of the post-Reformation centuries converge and climax seem to represent in their mentality and outlook not only two poles of German life but two specific types and possibilities of human existence as such. Coming from different social environments and passing through a different set of experiences, they seemed at first incapable of understanding each other. But when they at last realized that each stood in need of those complementary forces in the other which could serve to integrate their personalities and their works, the friendship they formed transcended in its implications and consequences the sphere of their individual destiny and became an event of the greatest national and inter-European significance. During the years of their mutual intellectual intercourse they both experienced the fruition of their lives and achieved the fullest realization of their literary endeavors.

If we venture to call Goethe a realist and Schiller an idealist, we do well to remain conscious of the limitations which are of necessity attached to such labels. Although the richness and complexity of a great human personality defies in the last analysis the rigidity of such a classification, it may aid nevertheless in circumscribing the ways in which reality is seen, approached, and mastered by individuals of an essentially different physical and intellectual structure. In the case of Goethe and Schiller it is legitimate to say that the one (Goethe) experienced reality unreflectingly with his entire sensuous organism, proceeding from the observation of the individual and concrete to generalizations and the formation of ideal types and concepts. Schiller, on the other hand, lived and moved in a world of ideal essences which, as intellectual experiences, were more real to him in their generality and universality than their feeble images in the world of sense experience.

a) Goethe's Personality. Goethe appeared on the German scene in the historically fateful hour when German civilization was about to throw off the yoke of an all-embracing rationalism. It was his privilege and his destiny to complete this liberation by virtue of a unique combination of the emotional and rational faculties, of elemental passion and tranquil rationality. He was deeply convinced that all life was mysteriously rooted in immeasurable depths and that it was the sacred duty of the human mind to render visible and reveal this secret meaning of life. He felt justified in calling himself the liberator of the Germans "because by the paradigm of my life they have learned that men must live from within, that the artist must work from within. For, no matter what he contrives or how he may act, he will always tend to realize fully his own individuality." In the realization of his own personal destiny, therefore, Goethe followed like Socrates the voice of his "daimon" and recognized in his work the incarnation of universal laws of being. Thus poetry and truth, life and work grew into an inseparable unity and harmony.

He was dissatisfied with the mechanical explanation of nature and mind as offered by the proponents of Cartesian mathematics, rationalist psychology, and descriptive natural science: he was looking for the "spiritual bond" that imparted structural and organic unity to isolated and seemingly disconnected phenomena. In his penetrating analysis of organic and inorganic nature Goethe inaugurated the systematic speculations of the nature philosophers of the nineteenth century and provided an important link between Aristotelian vitalism and the neo-vitalistic science of organic life in our own time.

Goethe appeared to his contemporaries as nature's favorite child, richly endowed with splendid gifts of body and mind, a perfect exemplar of the human species. Napoleon, not given to euphemistic exaggerations in his judgment of men, exclaimed upon meeting Goethe: *"Voilà un homme!"*

Goethe felt himself lovingly and reverently bound to all creatures and to all the mysterious forces of the universe. In silent admiration and awe he stood before the unknown and the unknowable. Like Kant he acknowledged the great ethical command of duty and was ever willing to obey it in the realization of his own self and in the service of the ideals of humanity. With other representatives of Germany's classical age he shared the belief in the common concerns of a united mankind, in a common human fatherland that was not limited by national boundaries. He confesses that as a true cosmopolitan he takes his stand above the nations, experiencing the good and ill fortunes of neighboring peoples as his own. Science and art, he feels, belong to the world, and before them the boundaries of nationality disappear. Only mildly interested in the political struggles of the day and rather indifferent to German national ambitions, he admires in Napoleon the genius of the great ruler and the greatness of a life of unbending heroism.

Goethe aptly characterized his works as "fragments of one great confession." This is especially true of his lyric poems which as autobiographical documents of his intimate feelings and experiences reflect every phase of an amazingly abundant and variegated life. Though surpassed in the epic and dramatic fields by the genius of Homer, Dante, and Shakespeare, he remains the foremost lyricist of the world and is unequaled in the universality of his creative work. He gave German literature the stamp of classical perfection and has gained for it a distinguished place among the literatures of the world. At the same time, he opened up for the German people the treasury of world literature and, in form and content, in style and diction, in poetry and prose, gathered its most precious gems and transplanted them to German soil.

b) Schiller's Personality. In Goethe's judgment the most remarkable of Schiller's qualities was an innate nobility of mind and soul which influenced everything and everyone that entered into the magnetic field of his personality. "Every one of Christ's appearances and utterances tends to make visible the sublime. He invariably rises and raises beyond vulgarity. In Schiller there was alive this same Christlike tendency. He touched nothing vulgar without ennobling it," Goethe wrote concerning his friend. If Goethe possessed or achieved a high degree of harmony within himself and between his own ego and the transsubjective world, Schiller fought a heroic battle against hostile forces within and without. His uncompromising devotion to a world of ideal values and his relentless struggle for the realization of ethical and aesthetic absolutes made his life tense, high pitched, and very lonely, a life that was cut short not only by the frailty of his physical constitution but by the all-consuming force of the spiritual fire that burned within his soul.

In no lesser degree than Goethe, Schiller attained in the end to classical perfection of form, and to mildness, equanimity, and moral greatness of character, but the different stages of his life's way were strewn with thorns and his victories were paid for with sacrifice and suffering. "His face resembled the countenance of the Crucified," wrote Goethe after their first meeting, and years later he said: "Everything in him was grand and majestic, but his eyes were gentle."

Schiller experienced life and world dualistically and dialectically as a struggle between the opposing forces of sensuality and spirituality, necessity and freedom, natural inclination and moral obligation. He was convinced that the breach could be healed and harmony ultimately restored by the moral and aesthetic education of mankind and by the recognition of universal and communal principles and institutions as they are manifested in the social and cultural organisms of family, folk, and fatherland. As moral freedom was the central concept of his life and work, he visualized the ideal human society of the future as resulting from the intellectual and moral greatness of a true leader whose leadership received its sanction from the eternal law of the universe and the inalienable rights of self-determining individuals. He was more interested in a national liberty that rested on these God-given human rights than in the demands of a listless nationalism which derived its justification from common biological and racial characteristics. Thus he was without question a "national poet," but at the same time a poet and thinker whose love and enthusiasm belonged to the entire human family and whose devotion to the weal of mankind made him a pre-eminent educator of his own people.

Great dramatist and moralist that he was, Schiller considered it as the supreme task of the tragic poet to arouse and purify man's moral conscience. He attempted the impossible, however, when he tried to introduce the Greek idea of an inexorable fate into the world of eighteenth-century Humanism and to save and preserve man's freedom and dignity in the face of the inscrutable and impersonal decrees of the ancient "Powers." His ambition to reconcile the ancient fate tragedy of Sophocles (496–405 B.C.) with the modern character tragedy (*The Bride of Messina,* cf. p. 425 sq.) remained unfulfilled, and the author was forced into the recognition that tragic guilt in post-Renaissance drama does not derive from the inflexible decrees of Fate but from the psychological inescapability of human life and personality as such.

c) Goethe's Life and Works. Three major phases in Goethe's development may easily be distinguished: the "storm and stress" of his youth, the classical maturity of his manhood, and the wisdom of his old age when everything transitory had become for him a symbol of the eternal and all human striving an approximation to a lasting peace and rest in God (*"Und alles Drängen, alles Ringen ist ewige Ruh' in Gott dem Herrn"*).

Johann Wolfgang Goethe (1749–1832) was a native of the city of Frankfurt on the Main, the scion of a well-to-do patrician family, whose early education was conducive to creating a well-balanced human character and in whom theoretical and practical knowledge and the faculties of intellect, will, and imagination could grow and unfold harmoniously.

At the age of sixteen Goethe entered the University of Leipzig to take up the study of law, in accordance with his father's wish. But his fertile mind was anxious to branch out into other fields, and while submerging joyfully in the glittering atmosphere of the frivolous Rococo society of "Little Paris," he derived lasting benefit from his acquaintance with Adam Friedrich Oeser, the director of the Leipzig Academy of Arts, who encouraged his interest in drawing and introduced him to the aesthetic writings of Winckelmann and Lessing. Goethe's literary style in this period as revealed in his earliest lyrics (*Annette,* 1767) is that of the Rococo (cf. p. 349 sq.) and the Anacreontics (cf. p. 349).

Goethe's stay in Leipzig was cut short by a physical breakdown, caused by a hemorrhage of the lungs, and the young poet had to return to Frankfurt to convalesce in the sheltered atmosphere of his parental home. It was during these months of sickness and gradual recovery that he submitted temporarily to the religious influence of pietistic sentimentalism, embodied for him in a most appealing form in the life and personality of Susanna von Klettenberg, who was one of his mother's friends. *The Confessions of a Beautiful Soul,* filling the sixth book of the novel *Wilhelm Meister's Apprenticeship* (cf. p. 412), represent Goethe's grateful acknowledgment of this early influence, and commemorate the mild and irenic piety of a pure and noble human heart.

In the spring of 1770 Goethe went to Strasbourg to continue his studies, and it was here that he experienced the influence of Herder and the self-styled geniuses of the "Storm and Stress" movement (cf. p. 349 sq.). Herder proved an inspiring and trustworthy guide in pointing out to Goethe the riches of the literary landscape, in revealing to his eagerly absorbing mind the secrets of Homer, Shakespeare, Rousseau, and Ossian, of Hebrew and folk poetry, opening his eyes to the breadth and depth of the realms of the spirit, and arousing in him the titanic force of his slumbering creative genius. Standing in awe before the rhythmical musicality of the rising contours of the Cathedral of Strasbourg, Goethe experienced a close kinship between his own youthful enthusiasm and the prayerful jubilation of the Gothic master builders (*Von deutscher Baukunst,* 1773).

The *Sesenheim Lieder* are radiant with the shimmer and fragrant beauty of young Goethe's love for Friederike Brion, the daughter of the pastor in a neighboring town, while *Goetz* and *Urfaust* speak of Goethe's tragic guilt in sacrificing Friederike's love and happiness to his own "titanic" need for freedom and self-realization.

After another brief stay in Frankfurt Goethe went to Wetzlar, the seat of the *Reichskammergericht* (Imperial Supreme Law Court), to practice law (1772). In the autumn of the same year he was back in Frankfurt. His love for Charlotte Buff, the fiancée of one of his friends, had prompted him to save himself by flight and thus to escape the remorse of another tragic entanglement. The episode itself provided the main theme for the autobiographical novel *The Sorrows of Young Werther* (1774).

The drama *Goetz von Berlichingen* (1773) was the first work by Goethe in which a new content was embodied in a new form and style. As such it became the great model of the "Storm and Stress" poets. But while his imitators admired the freshness and immediacy of Goethe's language and the unconventionality of his dramatic technique, they forgot that with him these devices were only means to convey more forcefully his own personal message. This message was presented in the form of a folk drama, based on the autobiography of the gallant Frankish knight (1480–1562) who in the age of religious revolt and social revolution had made himself the spokesman and leader of the rebellious peasants. Against Emperor Maximilian's "Land Peace" and the jurisdiction of the imperial court, Goetz maintained the law of individual self-help, nevertheless considering himself a loyal imperial knight to the end. To Goethe and his companions Goetz appeared as a symbol of German greatness, a model of personal courage, integrity, and moral conviction in a period of social decay and a purely conventional morality. The struggle between Goetz and his opponents reflects the passionate attack of Goethe's own generation upon the forces of stagnation and rationalistic petrifaction. The technical scheme of the three Aristotelian unities gave way to the dynamic spontaneity of Shakespearean composition, and the vitality of untamed nature broke down the artificiality of every rule that had its *raison d'être* not in the structural laws of character and language.

In the fate of Goetz, Goethe had first realized the tragic destiny of the great leader, the genius, and superman whose titanic will necessarily predestines him to tragic frustration and defeat in the petty world of spatio-temporal limitations. In fragmentary form and free rhythmical verse Goethe subsequently sketches the daimonic force that impels, informs, and devours the lives of Mohammed, Caesar, Socrates, Prometheus, and Faust.

In the original version of *Faust* (*Urfaust*, 1773–1775) titanic passion breaks into the peaceful atmosphere of an idyllic bourgeois world, with destruction and tragedy resulting from the impact. But Goethe's superman himself, in deed and misdeed, in craving, lust, and despair follows merely the dictate of his "daimon," the unbending law of nature itself, and he remains strong even in death and perdition. In Gretchen's songs and prayers, in the solemn invocation of the Earth Spirit, and in the responding chants Goethe reveals himself for the first time as the great master of lyric poetry.

With *The Sorrows of Young Werther* Goethe completes the literary cycle of the works of his youth. This sentimental novel is no less a document of passion than *Goetz* or *Urfaust,* but Werther's passion is "a sickness unto death" for which no remedy can be found in the world of action: from the outset it is condemned to devour itself in silent suffering and utter solitude. The superman of action has been replaced by the superman of emotion, of a feeling whose intensity is heightened and deepened by the gentle rhythm of nature in which it is embedded, carrying it in a predestined course from the crisp awakening of spring to autumnal melancholy and the icy loneliness of winter, from tender hope to passionate yearning and inescapable self-destruction.

For Goethe the completion of *Werther* was an act of liberation: he had freed himself from the sickness to which Werther had succumbed. Thus Werther had to die so that Goethe might be able to live a fuller and sounder life. The novel itself almost immediately became a best seller, and even Napoleon was not immune to the contagion of the "Werther-fever": he confessed that Goethe's novel accompanied him on all his campaigns.

The beginning of the second major period in Goethe's life and the classical stage in his creative work is outwardly marked by his arrival in the principality and town of Weimar in 1775. He had accepted the invitation extended to him by Charles Augustus, the reigning duke who, as hereditary prince of his duchy, had visited Goethe in Frankfurt and had been charmed by his genial and fascinating personality. In Weimar Goethe soon became the center of courtly society and the intimate friend and counselor of the duke. In this idyllic environment and in the midst of the intellectual elite that gathered together in the shade of the magnanimous princely patronage of arts and letters, Goethe spent with few and brief interruptions the remainder of his life, holding at one time or other the titles and positions of privy councilor, chamber president, minister of finance, prime minister, and director of the court theater.

It was during the first decade of his life in Weimar that Goethe was bound by ties of love and friendship to Charlotte von Stein, the wife of one of the court officials, whose wonderfully balanced character, in its rare unison of the graces of body and mind, corresponded more fully to Goethe's ideal of a "beautiful soul." His "storm and stress" subsided under the ennobling influence of a companionship which in its accord of hearts and intellects rose beyond the sphere of personal relationship into the realm of social responsibilities.

But Goethe's mind was still in the process of growth. His friendship with Charlotte von Stein gave him a presentiment of that classical harmony that was as yet unrealized in his work. His journey to Italy (1786–1788), undertaken as an attempted escape from his manifold social and official duties, symbolizes his actual entrance into the world of his longing, the realm of classical harmony and immaculate formal beauty. The pure and clear contours of the southern landscape, the "noble simplicity and quiet grandeur" of classical art effected in Goethe a poetic and moral renascence: "Together with the artistic sense," he wrote, "it is the moral sense which here experiences a great rejuvenation." As the "Faustian" wanderer from the North he stood in silent admiration before the tranquil beauty of the South, before the art treasures of Rome, Naples, and Sicily, taking the greatest of delight in this temporary refuge and restful haven.

The sojourn in Italy (*Italian Journey,* published 1815–1829) yielded immediately a rich literary harvest: *Egmont* (1787), *Iphigenia* (1787), *Tasso* (1789), and the *Faust-Fragment* (1790) are the dramatic creations that embody the ideal of classical form. In *Egmont* Goethe wanted to portray a historical character who leads his people in their struggle for freedom. Count Egmont (1522–1568), the stadholder of Flanders and Artois, places himself at the head of the Dutch rebellion against the Spanish army of occupation and is executed at the behest of the duke of Alva. As was the case in *Goetz,* the political tendency of the play is democratic and anti-authoritarian. Classical in its stylistic form, the rhythmically moving language in Egmont is musically expressive. The operatic finale and the general lyrical character of the work may have inspired Beethoven's Egmont compositions.

Iphigenia was begun in 1779 (in prose) and completed in Rome in 1787 (in blank verse). Its theme was suggested by Euripides' (*c.* 480–407 B.C.) two dramas (*Iphigenia in Aulis* and *Iphigenia on Tauris*). In Goethe's *Iphigenia* the external motivations of the action as depicted by the Greek playwright are translated into inner, spiritual forces, appeasing and defeating the powers of retribution that haunt Orestes and Iphigenia, the children of Agamemnon, by the irresistible persuasion of love and "pure humanity."

The classical verses of *Tasso* (begun in 1780 and completed in 1789) breathe the "fragrance of the gentle sadness of the departure from Rome." In the portrait of the great poet of the Italian Renaissance Goethe pictures part of his own self. As Torquato Tasso enjoys fame and princely favor at the court of Alfonso, duke of Ferrara, so Goethe was privileged to live and work at the court of Weimar and was favored by the friendship and liberality of Charles Augustus. And Tasso's relation to the princess reflects and immortalizes Goethe's own debt of gratitude to Charlotte von Stein. Goethe's often conflicting duties as a poet and minister of State are mirrored in the antagonism between Tasso, the impractical man of thought and poetic contemplation, and Antonio, the statesman, the realistic man of action. The problem of Tasso is the problem of Goethe, their common goal being the reconciliation between the ideal and the real, between contemplation and action.

The sojourn in Rome with its pagan enjoyment of nature and the free reign of the life of the senses leaves its imprint also on Goethe's mature lyric poetry, especially the *Roman Elegies* (1789) and *Venetian Epigrams* (1790). The former is dedicated to Christiane Vulpius, the daughter of an official of the court library in Weimar, whose light and happy temper and natural simplicity offered Goethe a much needed sensuous complement of his own weighty life and character, and who lived with him as his common-law wife from 1788 until 1806, when the union was legalized.

The unconventionality of his relations to Christiane Vulpius contributed to Goethe's gradual estrangement from the courtly society of Weimar and to his increasing loneliness after his return from Italy. In 1791 he took over the direction of the newly founded court theater and in the following year took part in the campaign against the French revolutionary armies (cf. p. 324). His antagonism to the spirit of the French Revolution was at the same time a determined struggle for the preservation of the world of his own ideals, a world in which personal values maintained their prerogatives as against the claims of a collectivized society. This courageous and uncompromising self-assertion is expressed in poetic form in the crystalline clarity of the classical meters of *Hermann and Dorothea* (1797), an epic poem that sets a genrelike idyl of German middle class life and culture against the dark and bloody background of the French Revolution.

In the meantime Goethe's life and work had received new content and purpose through the friendship with Schiller. In his remarkable letter of August 23, 1794, the younger poet had interpreted Goethe's character and poetic significance with such unusual insight and striking accuracy that Goethe could in all sincerity confess: "You have given me a second youth, you have restored my poetic talents." The epistolary exchange of thoughts between the two princes of German letters lasted until 1799, when Schiller moved from Jena to Weimar to be in even closer contact with his admired friend.

Together the two friends composed a series of epigrams known as *Xenia** (1797), filling the second volume of Schiller's *Almanac of the Muses* (1796–1800), in which they castigated the mediocre literary taste of their contemporaries and ridiculed a number of popular favorites in the realm of letters.

As early as 1785 Goethe had completed the original version of his novel *Wilhelm Meister* (*Wilhelm Meister's theatralische Sendung*). The final version, *Wilhelm Meister's Apprenticeship* (*Lehrjahre*) appeared in 1795–1796 and was soon universally acclaimed as the unexcelled model of a truly poetic and artistic masterpiece. It is a typically German novel in that scenery, situations, and social environment center in the development of a human character (*Entwicklungsroman, Bildungsroman*). The original version tells of the preparation of a sensitive and talented youth for his artistic lifework, using the world of the theater as a social and poetic background. The *Lehrjahre,* on the other hand, paint a broader picture of the personal and social influences that mold Wilhelm Meister's character and to whose guidance and direction he submits, after having overcome such antisocial and undisciplined forces as arise within himself and in the world around him. These forces are personified in the romantic and mysterious figures of Mignon and the Harper, manifestations of that "daimonic" element by which Goethe as much as Wilhelm were both attracted and repelled, ever conscious of its fascination and its danger.

Schiller's death in 1805 was an irreparable loss to Goethe. He tried to forget his grief by turning with redoubled zeal to his earlier preoccupation with the natural sciences. In 1784 he had discovered the intermaxillary bone in the human skull which confirmed for him his theory of biological evolution by establishing a definite relationship and analogy between the lower

---

* *XENIA* (Greek = hospitable gifts) are epigrams whose classical pattern was established by the Roman poet Martial (*c.* 40–102).

and higher animal organisms. The *Metamorphosis of Plants*, published in 1789, demonstrated the leaf as the original organ of all plants, and in his *Theory of Colors* (*Farbenlehre*, 1810) he turned against Newton's ideas concerning the dispersion of light. His scientific research extended to the fields of botany, morphology, mineralogy, and meteorology. In several hymnic essays he expressed his unshakable belief in an omnipresent divine power that informs and animates nature in all its parts and that has designed for every being the law and reason for its existence.

In the years 1807–1808 the first part of *Faust* was completed and published in its final form. Then followed the cycle of the masterpieces of the third major period of his life, including the novel *Elective Affinities* (*Wahlverwandtschaften*, 1809), the autobiographical memoirs of *Poetry and Truth* (*Dichtung und Wahrheit*, 1811–1814), the series of stories and episodes entitled *Wilhelm Meister's Travels* (*Wanderjahre*, 1821–1829), the poem entitled *Trilogy of Passion* (*Marienbad Elegy*, 1823), and the second part of *Faust*, completed in 1831.

Elective Affinities, the first major work of Goethe's old age, uses four main characters to illustrate the parallelism of the moral and natural laws and their immutability in their respective spheres. Elective affinities exert their force of attraction no less in human nature than in chemical elements. The inviolability of the moral law as exemplified in the marriage bond becomes tragically evident in the destruction of two human beings who sacrifice the demands of duty to the urges of passion. For the first time Goethe designates rational self-control, self-limitation, and resignation as the social obligations of an enlightened morality.

In *Truth and Poetry* Goethe gives a poetically colored account of his life from early childhood days to his twenty-sixth year. The work is filled with cultural and literary reminiscences and reveals the author's affectionate attachment to home and family, to all the natural and human forces that had sheltered his youth and shaped his character.

The fruit of Goethe's study of Oriental poetry was the *Westöstlicher Divan* (1814–1819), a collection of original and paraphrased lyrics in an Oriental setting, inspired by his love for Marianne Willemer, who herself contributed some of the poems. In some of the most accomplished verses of the "Divan" (*"Ist es möglich, Stern der Sterne. . . ."*) Goethe followed Dante's example in glorifying love as the symbolic manifestation of that supreme law that moves the stars and sustains the universe.

The most precious jewel, however, of the lyric poetry of Goethe's old age is the *Marienbad Elegy* (1823), in whose majestic stanzas Goethe's renunciation of the last great passion of his life is reflected, the renunciation of his love for Ulrike von Levetzow, a girl who was seventeen years of age when he first met her in Marienbad and in whose blossoming youth the sensuous beauty and rapture of life had beckoned to him once more. The three parts of this *Trilogy of Passion* (*Trilogie der Leidenschaft*) mirror the threefold struggle of passion versus wisdom, ending with a resignation that vibrates with the undertones of a narrowly avoided tragic despair. Once more, as in the stormy days of *Goetz* and *Werther* Goethe freed himself from the impending danger of destruction by entrusting his woe to the magic medium of poetic sublimation: *"Und wenn der Mensch in seiner Qual verstummt, gab mir ein Gott zu sagen was ich leide"* (And where man grows silent in his despair, a God has granted me the poetic gift of expressing my suffering).

d) Goethe's "Faust." "The main business is finished," Goethe wrote in his diary in 1831, the year before his death. At long last he had completed and sealed the manuscript of *Faust,* and therewith he considered his poetic activity closed and consummated. He had begun this great mosaic of his life as a young man, shortly after his return from Leipzig. The *Urfaust* bore the marks of his "storm and stress"; some of the most sublime passages of the first and second part owed their completion and artistic perfection to the influence of Schiller's constructive criticism; the rest embodied the wisdom and mature art of Goethe's old age.

Thus the *Faust* drama in its entirety recapitulates and summarizes the author's life and reflects the major phases of his poetic development. *Faust,* then, is the great master's most complete and authentic biography. But it is much more than that: aside from being Germany's greatest poetic document and one of the rare accomplishments of human genius, the drama represents and illustrates six decades of the literary and cultural history of Germany. And yet, with all its timely documentary values, it spans and covers a much wider area: it is typically German in that it creates timeless symbols of specific Germanic characteristics, and it is profoundly human in that it succeeds in reaching altitudes that permit a survey and interpretation of life and reality in their universal and eternal aspects.

When Goethe wrote the first verses of *Faust* Prussia was still ruled by Frederick the Great and France by Louis XV. When he sealed the manuscript shortly before his death Europe was shaken by the aftereffects of the July Revolution in France (1830): Louis Philippe, the "Bourgeois King," ruled in France, and Metternich (cf. p. 461 sq.) controlled the destinies of Europe from the capital of Austria. When Goethe conceived the Gretchen tragedy of the *Urfaust* the structure of the Holy Roman Empire was still outwardly intact. When he published the *Faust-Fragment* Europe began to feel the reverberations of the French Revolution of 1789. When he wrote the classical scenes of the second part the new political order of nineteenth-century liberalism (cf. p. 523 sqq.) began to dawn, Germany was preparing for constitutional government and eventual political unification, the ideas of a system of world trade and world economy were beginning to gain ground, and there was talk of the building of railroads and the construction of the great canal systems of Suez and Panama. All these enormous changes in the outlook of men and in their modes of living are in one way or another traceable in Goethe's *Faust,* so that we may be able to find in its sequence of ideas an expression of the shifting and contrasting problematics of the eighteenth and nineteenth centuries.

The first part of *Faust* differs from the *Urfaust* in that Goethe here no longer dwells on the violent and tragic encounter between a titanic human will and the orderly world of a well-tempered middle class morality, but the emphasis is shifted to the struggle between Faust and Mephistopheles as representing two essential forces and possibilities of human nature. The addition of the "Prologue in Heaven" raises the drama to a perspective which permits a universal view of Faust's destiny within the huge framework of humanity, its aspirations and its aims. The tragedy assumes more and more the character of a morality play.

Faust, dissatisfied with the wealth of human knowledge which he has made his own, penetrates into the spheres of the veiled unknown, with the aid of Mephistopheles, pledging his immortal soul to the devil if ever his intellectual curiosity, his lust for life, his "longing infinite" can be satisfied. The rejuvenated Faust emerges from the fullest enjoyment of sensuous reality with the bitter sensation of remorse, and the "two souls within his breast," his sensual and spiritual desires, remain more disunited than ever: he is farther removed than ever from satiety and complacency.

In the second part of the play Mephistopheles introduces Faust into the arena of social and political action. Faust has learned to confine his desires to the attainable, but within that sphere of measurable and concrete realities he wishes to perform great human and social deeds. He passes through the stages of Goethe's own path of life: at the emperor's court he renders invaluable service to State and society, busying himself with problems of government, finance, and war. At the emperor's request he undertakes his descent to the "Mothers," pictured as personifications of a realm of Platonic ideas, as the aboriginal and eternally creative prototypes of all things. In his encounter with Helen of Troy Faust comes face to face with the absolute perfection of classical beauty, and Helen's catastrophic evanescence makes him realize that he is not prepared as yet to embrace the ideal and rest in its contemplation. But his unfulfilled longing urges him on to the entrance of Hades, Helen's abode. He is granted the rare favor of listening to the mighty heartbeat of the earth, the great mother of life, whose vital forces pass into his own being. The most intimate contact with nature discloses to him the secret of the perfect appreciation of beauty.

The ultimate union of Helen and Faust symbolizes the synthesis of South and North, of Greeks and "Goths," of classicism and romanticism. The off-spring of this union is the child Euphorion,* in whom romantic passion appears enshrined in classical form.

Faust's social and humanitarian efforts are cut short and his vision is destroyed by the blinding breath of the gray figure of "Care" and by Death,

---

* In creating this allegorical figure Goethe had in mind the personality and poetry of Lord Byron.

the great affirmant of the corruptibility of man's physical nature. The satisfaction in the enjoyment of the beautiful present moment that Faust in the hundredth year of his earthly life has not yet experienced, he anticipates as he sinks into his grave. Angelic hosts, battling for his soul, carry his incorruptible self to the feet of the *"Mater Gloriosa"* before whose throne the blessed spirit of Gretchen intercedes for the salvation of her one-time seducer.

According to Goethe the key to Faust's salvation is found in the angels' chant:

> Whoe'er aspires unweariedly
> Is not beyond redeeming.
> And if he feels the Grace of Love
> That from On High is given,
> The Blessed Hosts, that wait above,
> Shall welcome him to Heaven!
>
> (Bayard Taylor's translation)*

The meaning of these verses is amplified by the following pronouncement of the author of *Faust* as recorded by Goethe's secretary J. P. Eckermann, in his *Conversations with Goethe* (1836, 1848): "In Faust himself we find an ever higher and purer activity to the very end, and, coming from above, the succor of Eternal Love. This is fully in agreement with our religious concepts, according to which we are saved not by our own efforts alone but by the supporting divine grace."

In the fifth act of the second part of *Faust* the hero's destiny is no longer determined by the terms attached to the original blood pact with Mephistopheles but by the metaphysically more important wager between God and Satan, which is the major theme of the "Prologue in Heaven." Faust who like Parzival (cf. p. 153) went through earthly life as a "knight errant" has paid the toll and fulfilled the law of his undeviating quest of truth, goodness, and beauty and is thus granted the bliss of eternal rest *"in Gott dem Herrn."*

In the image of Faust's ripening wisdom and in the challenging circumstances which obstructed his plans and efforts Goethe divined the fate of Western mankind in the nineteenth century. He realized the inevitability of the onrushing machine age which would irreverently call in question those personal and spiritual values that imparted meaning and dignity to his own life and which he recognized as a precious heritage and bequest of the past. "The approaching machine age tortures and frightens me: it draws near like a thunderstorm, slowly, slowly; but it continues in its direction, and it

---

* Wer immer strebend sich bemüht,
  Den können wir erlösen.
  Und hat an ihm die Liebe gar
  Von oben Teil genommen,
  Begegnet ihm die selige Schar
  Mit herzlichem Willkommen.

will come and strike" (*Wilhelm Meister's Travels*). He foresaw the coming of a civilization that would enfranchise the masses and dis-enfranchise the human person, that would develop new methods of production and generate technological advances and material prosperity. And while he welcomed and blessed the spirit of invention and progress, he was nevertheless keenly aware of the price that was to be exacted. He was aware of the dangers that threatened from a preponderance of a purely practical and utilitarian philosophy of life, and he observed clearly the relative insignificance of material progress as compared with the permanency of man's moral nature and problems: "There will be new inventions, but nothing new can possibly be conceived as far as the moral nature of man is concerned."

It had been Faust's intention to utilize technology for the creation of land and opportunities for a free and industrious people, but in carrying out his plans he had to rely on questionable helpers whose aid stained his lofty idealism with the blemish of insufficiency and guilt. The harmony of moral and material development had been Goethe's ideal goal, but he knew full well that the hour was near when the incongruity of material and moral forces would become strikingly evident in the historic evolution of Western civilization.

e) Schiller's Life and Work. The major phases in the development of Goethe and Schiller are identical: from the "storm and stress" of his youth Schiller turned to the classical form of his mature works and in his philo-sophical writings gave ample proof of that seasoned wisdom which permeates the literary documents of Goethe's old age.

Friedrich Schiller's short life (1759–1805) was as dynamically moving in tempo and rhythm as might be expected when we weigh the magnitude of his work against the scarcely three decades that were granted to him for its execution. He was born at Marbach on the river Neckar, the son of an army surgeon of Charles Eugene, duke of Wurtemberg. His father later on became a captain and overseer of the princely gardens of Solitude Castle near Stuttgart.

Young Schiller attended the Latin school at Ludwigsburg, where his extraordinary gifts attracted the attention of Charles Eugene, who decreed that Friedrich continue his studies at the newly founded military academy (the *"Karlsschule"*). His major fields of interest at that time were theology and medicine, and he was finally permitted by the authorities to substitute the latter for the course in jurisprudence which had been prescribed for him much against his will.

Schiller's craving for free and independent thought and its literary expression was stifled by the rigid discipline and strict censorship in the *"Karlsschule."* The spirit of revolt that was brewing within him was fanned to a feverish pitch by his acquaintance with those writers who had declared war on outmoded conventions and the soulless regimentation of the human mind. The works of Shakespeare, Rousseau, Lessing, Klopstock,

Wieland, and the "Storm and Stress" poets could be acquired and read by the students of the military academy only as bootleg literature, but the enthusiasm that was aroused by these authors was all the greater.

Schiller was eighteen years of age when he wrote *The Robbers* (1777), his first tragedy, bearing the motto *"in tyrannos"* (against the tyrants) and giving vent to his thirst for freedom and his hatred of despotism. The drama was published in 1781 and was produced for the first time on the stage of the National Theatre in Mannheim in the following year. Schiller had secretly attended the performance and witnessed the enthusiastic reception that was given to his play. In the meantime the author had completed his doctoral dissertation *On the Interrelation between the Animal Nature and the Spiritual Nature of Man,* had taken his degree and received an appointment as staff surgeon. Returning from a second secret journey to Mannheim, Schiller was arrested and forbidden by his princely employer "to write any more comedies." Unable to bear any longer the enslavement of his creative mind, he broke the chains of his "Stuttgart Siberia" and fled to Mannheim.

Though the problem of the *Robbers* was suggested by the unfortunate experiences of Schiller's youth and by his growing dissatisfaction with the existing social order, the general tendency remains essentially unchanged in all his future dramas: he strives to depict the world and its inhabitants, not as they actually are but as they ought to be. In the bitter accusations of the *Robbers* he expresses rhetorically his indignation over the moral failings of his "emasculated century" and his hunger for human greatness and moral regeneration. Of the two hostile brothers, Karl and Franz, the former is a victim and symbol of degraded and enslaved humanity, while the latter is the representative of the corruption and demoralization of the upper strata of society. Although the chiaroscuro technique of this drama, with its almost primitive contrasts of good and evil, results in an oversimplification of the leading characters, Schiller's revolutionary thesis is powerfully brought home.

The expected financial aid from Baron von Dalberg, the director of the Mannheim Theatre, was not forthcoming and Schiller's second drama (*Fiesco*) was unfavorably criticized and rejected by the authorities. The homeless and penniless poet found temporary refuge on the small estate of Frau von Wolzogen in Bauerbach near Meiningen, where he completed his third drama, *Love and Intrigue* (*Louise Millerin*). Dalberg finally was persuaded to accept this drama as well as a revised version of *Fiesco* and to appoint Schiller for one year as official dramatic author for the Mannheim National Theatre.

Fiesco (1782) was Schiller's first historical tragedy, dealing with the unsuccessful revolt of an ambitious nobleman against the republic of Genoa. *Love and Intrigue* (*Kabale und Liebe,* 1783), a vivid portrayal of the tragic plight of the middle classes and their desperate struggle against their aristocratic oppressors, derives its color and persuasive force from Schiller's personal ire and resentment. Ferdinand, the son of the all-powerful minister of state Walter, and Louise, the daughter of the town musician Miller, are made the innocent victims of social prejudice and of the damnable intrigues of a dehumanizing system of political corruption.

Love and Intrigue is artistically the most convincing of Schiller's early works, combining the passionate feeling of the "Storm and Stress" poets with the coolly calculating dramatic composition of Lessing's *Emilia Galotti*. As a stage play it proved even more successful than the *Robbers*.

When Charles Augustus, duke of Weimar, paid a visit to the Hessian court at Darmstadt, Schiller was permitted to read to him the first act of his forthcoming drama *Don Carlos* and the duke expressed his approval by bestowing upon the playwright the title of a Councilor of the State of Weimar. Nevertheless, Schiller's external circumstances were very much unsettled. He was suffering from ill health and was brought to the brink of destitution and despair by lack of funds. More than ever before he was in need of friendship and human understanding as well as of material aid. He therefore accepted gratefully the generous invitation of one of his admirers, the youthful jurist Gottfried Körner of Leipzig. In a thoroughly congenial environment he spent two happy and productive years (1785–1787) in Körner's household, first in Leipzig and, after Körner's marriage, in Dresden. The joyful exuberance of this idyllic interlude in Schiller's life is reflected in his *Hymn to Joy* (*Lied an die Freude*), some of whose moving stanzas were embodied in the choral finale of Beethoven's Ninth Symphony.

On Körner's country estate at Loschwitz, near Dresden, Schiller completed his drama *Don Carlos* (1787), the crowning achievement of the dramatic endeavors of his youth and the first of the mature creations of his manhood. Originally it had been Schiller's intention to make Don Carlos, the son of King Philip II of Spain (1555–1598), the hero of a domestic tragedy in the royal family, but four years of intensive preoccupation with the subject matter had shifted the focus of his interest from the personal and psychological to the universally human aspects of the problem. Thus the completed work became Schiller's first great historico-philosophical tragedy. Carlos' idealistic friend, the marquis of Posa, became the central character, the real hero, whose tragic death is not only a moral lesson to the unstable and self-centered dauphin but a voluntary sacrifice to the ideals of freedom of thought and conscience, a sacrificial offering that is no less inspired by the loyal devotion of true friendship than by an even more steadfast devotion to the cause of humanity. As the loose dramatic composition of the earlier works is stylized and tightened by the adoption of the five-foot iambic verse, so the subjective and chiefly negative polemics of Schiller's "storm and stress" gives way to a positive and constructive idealism of classical temper and balance.

A very similar development is noticeable in Schiller's early lyric poetry which culminates in the philosophical poem entitled *The Artists* (*Die Künstler*, 1789). In this poem the author praises art as the unique prerogative of man, deriving the exalted dignity of the artist from his mission and obligation to lead mankind to the heights of intellectual and moral culture.

In 1787 Schiller had moved from Dresden to Weimar. Goethe was still in Italy, but the poet made other valuable contacts with leading representatives of Weimar society. On a journey to the neighboring province of Thuringia he made the acquaintance of Charlotte von Lengefeld, who became his wife in 1790. In the house of the von Lengefelds in Rudolstadt Schiller and Goethe met for the first time. Although no more intimate relationship resulted from this casual contact, for the time being, Goethe was instrumental in securing for Schiller a (poorly paid) position as professor of history at the University of Jena.

In connection with the writing of *Don Carlos* Schiller had felt the necessity of taking up the systematic study of history. The immediate result of these studies was the *History of the Revolt of the United Netherlands* (1788). In 1789 he began his academic activity in Jena with an inaugural lecture on the nature and purpose of universal history (*Universalgeschichte*). In the winter of 1791 Schiller suffered the first serious attack of the lingering disease which gradually undermined his physical strength and made him realize that only his great will power could lengthen the span of his life sufficiently to permit him to complete his poetic mission. His remaining years were an almost continuous struggle against creeping consumption, brought upon him partly by the privations of his youth.

Schiller knew that in order to become Goethe's equal in the realm of letters, and worthy of the great man's friendship, he had to clarify and purify his art so as to achieve a classical perfection and unity of form and content. The study of history served him as a means for the understanding of the meaning of life, the nature of man, and the destiny of mankind. His *History of the Thirty Years' War* (1790–1792) follows the general direction of his dramatic and lyric production, moving away from the subjective and imaginative interpretation of experiences and events toward an objective and sympathetic evaluation of cultural and historical evolution. But the more deeply he delved into the events of the past the clearer it became to him that the knowledge of history was in itself insufficient for a true understanding of its meaning. Therefore, he concluded, a more adequate discipline was needed to clarify those fundamental concepts and principles that could in turn be used as starting points and motivating forces for moral action. Thus he felt the urge to supplement and integrate the study of history by the study of philosophy. He approached both history and philosophy from a practical or pragmatic point of view, looking in both disciplines for a broader and firmer basis of his art and a metaphysical justification of his own poetic existence.

Most of Schiller's philosophical works are the fruit of his preoccupation with Kant and particularly with the *Critique of Practical Reason* and the *Critique of Judgment* (cf. p. 372 sq.). The "Discipline of Morals" that he postulates culminates in the idea of human self-determination and moral freedom. Its basis is the harmonization of that which is and that which ought to be, of natural inclination and moral law and obligation. This harmonization will be the result of a struggle for moral perfection, a struggle that is brought to a happy conclusion in the placid tranquillity of the "beautiful soul." These thoughts in all their manifold ramifications are luminously expounded in the treatise *On Grace and Dignity* (1793). In the *Letters Concerning the Aesthetic Education of Mankind* (1794) he emphasizes once more the moral and cultural significance of art and beauty. The *Letters* were suggested by the noble experiment and dismal failure of the French Revolution, the first practical attempt in modern times to construct a State in accordance with the demands of reason. Why, asks Schiller, was this gigantic undertaking bound to fail? He answers that modern mankind was not sufficiently educated or prepared to risk the dangerous leap from unreason to reason. And how could some future attempt be undertaken with a better chance of success? The commonwealth of reason cannot be established, says Schiller, until all individual members of this ideal State of the future have become reasonable. However, "there is no other way of transforming a sensual into a rational human being but by making him first into an aesthetic being." Aesthetic education only can bring about the reconciliation of nature and reason, sensuality and morality, blind instinct and the sense of duty. It is the privilege of art to lead man through the realm of beauty gradually into the most sublime regions of human civilization.

The most personal of Schiller's philosophical works is the essay *On Naïve and Sentimental Poetry* (1795-1796), in which he attempted a justification of his own art and modern art in general and which provided the succeeding generation of romantic writers with important principles of literary criticism and aesthetic judgment. For Schiller it was a question of artistic self-vindication: he had to prove to his contemporaries and to his own satisfaction that his own and Goethe's poetry represented two equally valid types of literary expression and could thus exist side by side, each in its own right. All poetry, says Schiller, affects us by reflecting the harmony of life and nature. But there is an essential difference in the ways in which ancient and modern poetry achieve this end: the ancient poet was a child of nature, living in intimate relationship with his surrounding world and transposing this harmonious outlook into this poetic works. The modern poet, on the other hand, has lost this original naïveté, in his own nature as well as in his relationship to the outer world. He has intellectually risen above the state of nature and has thus become conscious of conflicts and contrasts that can only be resolved by a supreme effort of his creative genius. While the "naïve" (ancient) poet experiences the objects of reality in their concreteness and simplicity, the "sentimental" (modern) poet experiences and loves the ideas that are manifested in the world of objects. The ancients and those few who, like Shakespeare and Goethe, are their kin in modern times, are like unto nature in their view and rendition of life; the moderns, on the other hand, must strive to regain the lost harmony of nature and a second naïveté by the roundabout and thorny way of reasoned reflection and the resolve of their will.

The time had finally arrived for that unique and blessed friendship that for one decade united idealism and realism in one common effort: the friendship between Schiller and Goethe. The second meeting, so momentous in its consequences, occurred in Jena in 1794, on the occasion of a scientific convention. Five years later, in 1799, Schiller moved from Jena to Weimar in order to be nearer to Goethe and in closer touch with the court theater of Weimar which henceforth was to provide the forum for the products of his dramatic genius.

The influence of Goethe on Schiller's production bore its first fruit, however, in the field of lyric poetry. Always richly and heavily laden with thought, Schiller's lyrics now began to clothe their profound intellectual content with a classical form that was enhanced by the sheen of a new radiance and lucidity. A series of poems that dealt with various phases and aspects of human and social culture was concluded with the masterful *Song of the Bell* (*Das Lied von der Glocke,* 1800), which in reality is a song of domestic and public life, symbolically interwoven with the successive stages of the casting and the social functions of a church bell.

At last, twelve years after he had completed his *Don Carlos,* years filled with unceasing intellectual activity and recurrent mental anguish and physical suffering, Schiller resumed his dramatic production, that mode of literary expression in which he had no rivals and in which his sovereignty remained unchallenged.

Beginning with the *Wallenstein* trilogy in 1799, his classical dramas followed each other in rapid succession. Schiller himself considered the three parts of *Wallenstein* (*Wallenstein's Camp,* a prelude in one act; *The Piccolomini,* a play in five acts; *Wallenstein's Death,* a tragedy in five acts) as a kind of test case to demonstrate to what extent he was able to conform his own style and outlook to that of Goethe. In Goethe's judgment Schiller's *Wallenstein* was "so great that there is no second work that could be compared with it." In the fate of Wallenstein, the great imperial general of the Thirty Years' War (cf. p. 284 sqq.), Schiller wanted to portray "a great and mighty destiny which exalts man while it crushes him." The work is richer in objective description and realistic observation than any other of Schiller's dramas. It is, however, not only the first great example of a modern realistic drama, it is also the first modern historical tragedy that can hold its own when measured by the genius of Shakespeare. Wallenstein, standing at the height of his fame and power, falls victim to the "daimonic" forces of his nature and drags himself and others into the dark abyss of anarchy and annihilation. It was Schiller's intention to illustrate how the precious gift of freedom may cut both ways, because true freedom must rise above chance and arbitrary will and whim, conforming its decisions to the eternal order of a morally meaningful universe.

Presse- und Informationsamt der Bundesregierung, Bonn

Goethe-Schiller Monument, Weimar,
by Ernst Rietschel

In *Mary Stuart* (1800) Schiller dramatizes the tragic tale of Mary, Queen of the Scots, and her hopeless struggle against her implacable adversary, Queen Elizabeth of England. Madame de Staël (1766–1817), in her book *De l'Allemagne* describes Schiller's *Mary Stuart* as the most touching and the most ingeniously planned and executed among all German tragedies. And, truly, in its architectonic grouping of characters and its symmetrical composition it is quite unique and almost in a category by itself.

The Maid of Orleans (1801) Schiller calls a "romantic tragedy," to indicate that his treatment of the subject matter transcends the realistic frame of historical events. The heroine of this play is Joan of Arc (1412–1431), the French peasant girl of Domremy, who at the age of seventeen joined the royal armies of France, leading them in the liberation of Orléans and in their decisive victory over the English. Captured by the enemy, she was tried by an ecclesiastical court and burned at the stake. Vindicated in 1456, she soon became the symbol of French patriotism and was canonized by the Church in 1920.

In Shakespeare's *Henry VI* Joan of Arc, seen through the eyes of English nationalism, appears as a damnable witch whose black magic caused the defeat of the English. In Voltaire's *Pucelle d'Orléans* (1775) the Maid becomes the object of unsavory satire. For Schiller, on the other hand, she is a divinely inspired prophetess, "a noble image of humanity," whose pure features have been defiled by prejudice and cynicism. Conscious of her divine mission and endowed with supernatural power, Joan succumbs to tragic guilt when she opens her heart to human love. However, she atones for a moment of forgetfulness by her final victory and heroic death.

The patriotic fervor of this play contrasted sharply with Goethe's cosmopolitanism and with Schiller's own former convictions as espoused in *Don Carlos*. It was Schiller's first contribution to an awakening national consciousness, a poetic prelude to the beginning struggle for national liberation and unification. An indication of Schiller's fondness for the poetically transfigured *Maid of Orleans* is his words: "You are a creature of my heart; you will be immortal."

After the completion of his "romantic tragedy" with its loose and colorful texture, Schiller felt the desire to write a heroic drama "in Greek manner," a work that would revive the spirit and style of Greek tragedy and would thus offer the author an opportunity to match his own talents with those of the ancients. Form and fable of the *Bride of Messina* (1803) follow closely the Greek models, and Schiller introduces into modern drama that "analytical technique" which was perfected in some of Ibsen's social plays but which had its ancient paradigm in Sophocles' *King Oedipus*. The analytical dramatist delves into the prehistory of the events to unveil step by step the motivations of the ensuing tragic conflicts.

The Bride of Messina bears the subtitle *The Hostile Brothers* and is a "tragedy with choruses." The scene is laid in Messina on the island of Sicily, and the underlying idea is expressed in the two concluding lines: "Life is not the highest of goods, but guilt is the greatest of evils." The inexorable and impersonal "Fate" that arbitrarily rules over gods as well as men takes here the form of a curse, pronounced by the ancestor of a princely family and revived in the mortal hatred of two brothers, a hatred that is fanned by their ardent love for the same girl, who in the end turns out to be their own sister. While adopting in externals the ancient Idea of Fate, Schiller almost imperceptibly introduces certain psychological motivations that make the action more convincing and compatible with human nature as viewed from Christian and modern premises. The tragic guilt of the leading characters has its ultimate source not in the decrees of Fate but in the propensities and moral failings of the individuals. While in Greek tragedy the chorus functioned as an "ideal person," objectively reflecting the "voice of the people" or the abstract principles of universal reason, Schiller's two choruses are decidedly partisan, participating in the action as "real persons" and at the same time as collective magnifications of the mutually exclusive claims and interests of the two brothers.

Schiller's last completed drama was destined to become also his most popular one. The plot of *Wilhelm Tell* (1804) was based on Aegidius von Tschudi's (1502–1572) partly historical, partly legendary account (*Helvetian Chronicle*) of the liberation of the cantons of Schwyz, Uri, and Unterwalden from Austrian supremacy, constituting the beginning of Swiss independence (1291, cf. p. 169 sq.). Never having been able to acquire a firsthand knowledge of the country and people of Switzerland, Schiller had to rely on his fertile imagination and on the study of travel books and scientific descriptions of the Alpine regions, to reproduce local color and to achieve ethnological as well as psychological accuracy.

In making Tell the soul and moving force of the Swiss rebellion, Schiller succeeded in anchoring the national struggle for liberation in the personal struggle of a free man for his inalienable human rights, and by welding three separate actions into one he gave added strength and *élan* to the underlying idea. Thus from the beginning of his dramatic production to the end Schiller remained true to himself, uncompromising in upholding the ideal of freedom and a sworn enemy of all ethical relativism. In *Wilhelm Tell* he created a national festival play that stimulated and sanctioned the national aspirations of the German people.

When death came Schiller was in his forty-sixth year. His physical strength was exhausted but his mind was in the prime of health and vigor. Twenty-two years after his death his earthly remains were exhumed and transferred to the princely tomb at Weimar, where Goethe too is buried.

Musical Classicism: Ludwig van Beethoven (1770–1827). What Goethe and Schiller had accomplished in the media of language and literature was independently achieved by Beethoven in the world of musical sound. Like the literary giants of Germany's classical age, its lonely musical genius, though linked with his great predecessors by intellectual and historical kinship, created his own artistic form, to enshrine in its symbolism the timeless values of his human experience.

The fiery pathos of Beethoven's instrumental music was his exclusive and unique possession, the new and personal organ with which he expressed the creative power of the human spirit and communicated his response to the fundamental questions of human existence. So great was the vitality and unity of content and form in his works, so disquieting and extraordinary the denouement of tragic conflicts and tensions, that the classical temper of Goethe recoiled from such an immediacy of elemental passion. Beethoven's genius, like that of Goethe, embraced world and mankind, but in contrast to Goethe he was always tragically alone with himself and with his art, disdaining and disregarding social conventions and attachments in both his life and his work. Human suffering and human guilt weighed more heavily upon him than on Goethe, and only in his music was he able to triumph over the vicissitudes and contingencies of life. By virtue of his strong and pure artistic will, he forced the complex mass of his emotions into unity and achieved a brilliance of form of whose purifying force he was himself fully aware when he said: "Those who learn to understand my music will free themselves of all the misery with which all the others are burdened." And in a letter of the year 1802, addressed to his brothers, he gives an indication of the deepest motivations of his work as a composer: "Godhead," he writes, "Thou lookest down upon my innermost being, Thou knowest it, and Thou knowest that love of human kind and the will to do good to others abide therein."

Beethoven was born in the city of Bonn on the Rhine, where his grandfather had migrated from Louvain (Löwen) in Belgium and had held the position of *"Hofkapellmeister"* at the court of the princely elector of Cologne. His father, a drink addict, was employed as a tenor singer in the princely chapel and was Ludwig's first music teacher. At the age of thirteen the boy was appointed as second court organist and shortly afterward joined the princely orchestra as a violist. The elector himself paid the expenses for Beethoven's trip to Vienna, making it possible for the young musician to continue his studies under the venerable master Haydn (cf. p. 354 sq.).

The death of his father in 1792 caused Beethoven to prolong his stay in Vienna indefinitely. Aided by excellent recommendations, he was admitted to the circles of the Austrian nobility, and in 1795 he introduced and soon endeared himself to the public as an accomplished pianist and a composer of rank. A few years later he began to feel the effects of a defect in his organ of hearing, a disease which was gradually aggravated and ended in complete deafness. Beethoven, becoming more and more retiring, solitary, and unsociable, retreated into his own self and began to live exclusively in the hidden world of his inner sense of hearing and feeling. But it was during these years of utter loneliness and seclusion that his vision and creative powers were most active, producing some of the most sublime miracles in the realm of musical sound.

In the development of Beethoven's musical style three major periods may be distinguished. In the first group of compositions he shows his indebtedness to the musical forms and the social ideals of the Rococo. The second stage reveals Beethoven as the great master of a new and highly personal musical classicism. In the works of his third and final period the composer encompasses a spiritual realm of a height, breadth, and depth that spans and bridges the chasm between time and eternity.

To the works of Beethoven's youth (1795–1802, op. 1–50) belong his first three piano sonatas, dedicated to Haydn; the First Symphony (1800, op. 21); the first string quartets; and a number of other instrumental and vocal works. The compositions of the classical stage (1803–1815, op. 53–100) include, among others, the Third Symphony (*Eroica,* 1804, op. 55, originally dedicated to Napoleon Bonaparte); the Sixth Symphony (*Pastoral,* 1808, op. 68) with its fascinating musical interpretation of nature ("psychical" program music); the Seventh Symphony (1812, op. 92) with its full scale of emotional and dramatic values, reaching from gentle and dreamlike lyricism to somber mourning and exultant jubilation; and the light and vivacious Eighth Symphony (1812, op. 93), marking a happy equilibrium in the midst of a titanic struggle. To this classical phase of Beethoven's development belong also *Fidelio* (1805), his only opera, his first great *Mass (in C),* and numerous pieces for orchestra, among them the musical compositions to Goethe's *Egmont.* Among the major works of the third period stand out the *Missa Solemnis (Solemn High Mass in D,* 1824), composed on the occasion of the consecration of Archduke Rudolph as bishop of Olmütz, the foremost of Beethoven's ecclesiastical compositions and the most convincing documentation of a sincere piety that had its roots in the Catholicism of his Rhenish homeland. His grandiose Ninth Symphony (1824, op. 125), combining the symphonic form with that of Cantata and Oratorio and thereby creating a novel mode of musical expression, was composed when Beethoven had already lost his sense of hearing. The last movement, ingeniously interwoven with the words of Schiller's *Hymn to Joy,* contains the sum total of Beethoven's life. Its theme is the striving of a human heart that yearns for the blessed pastures of purest joy and lasting happiness but, still caught in the grip of life's anguish and sorrow, attains its victory in a gallant and defiant acceptance and affirmation of the challenge of destiny: "However Life be, it is always good" (Goethe).